CSR, Sustainability, Ethics & Governance

Series Editors

Samuel O. Idowu, London, United Kingdom
René Schmidpeter, Cologne Business School, Germany

More information about this series at
http://www.springer.com/series/11565

Karen Wendt

Editor

Responsible Investment Banking

Risk Management Frameworks,
Sustainable Financial Innovation
and Softlaw Standards

 Springer

Editor
Karen Wendt
Responsible Investmentbanking
Groebenzell
Germany

ISSN 2196-7075 ISSN 2196-7083 (electronic)
CSR, Sustainability, Ethics & Governance
ISBN 978-3-319-10310-5 ISBN 978-3-319-10311-2 (eBook)
DOI 10.1007/978-3-319-10311-2

Library of Congress Control Number: 2014952679

Springer Cham Heidelberg New York Dordrecht London

Springer International Publishing AG Switzerland is part of Springer Science+Business Media (www.springer.com)

Foreword

Corporate social responsibility (CSR) in its general sense expects all modern corporate entities to help society to solve all its social, economic and environmental problems regardless of whether or not they were instrumental in creating these problems in the first place. This we believe is a reasonable expectation which no one now argues with, even those who are still sceptical about the desirability of CSR. Behaving responsibly has never been more desirable in our world than it is today for many reasons. First, we live in a global economy where any little mishap in one particular nation state may result in serious consequences in all the 196 countries that presently make up our world, and the recent financial crisis is the evidence for saying that. Second, globalisation has meant that trade and culture of the world's nations are now well integrated with free flow of goods, services, capital and people between these nations, and this makes it even more important for a high degree of responsibility to be demonstrated by corporate entities. However, there are still many issues which have still not been properly addressed and still set back progress in the field of corporate social responsibility in many parts of the world, and this we believe is unsustainable.

The following issues still require actions and concerted efforts by governments, international organisations, corporate entities, NGOs, the civil society, standard setters and so on to enable CSR to be fully embedded globally into business activities.

The main challenges to be addressed are:

- Human rights abuses
- Pollution
- Unsustainable use of non-renewable resources
- Poor infrastructure
- Bribery and corrupt practices
- Poor labour and working conditions

- Poverty
- Discrimination
- Access to health care and fight against diseases
- Climate change

Fifty years ago, these were problems people talked about but did little or nothing to find solutions. It has now become apparent that these are issues that will continue to stand in the way of progress in the field of CSR and global development if they are not addressed properly.

Banks and other financial institutions were directly implicated in the serious global financial downturn that besieged our world in 2007. Does this make companies in the implicated industries socially irresponsible? We certainly don't believe that this is the case. All it means is that there are still some excesses and reckless practices prevalent in the way business is created and conducted regardless of whether or not CSR is in place and that CSR has not yet been fully integrated into the entire value chain and core activities of the financial services industry. Unsustainable business practices and models need curbing, and failing to do this might result in an even more serious and damaging financial crises than the one which we witnessed nearly 7 years ago and with the impacts still lingering. Our world economy will not sustain a reoccurrence of this. Banks and other financial institutions have a fiduciary obligation towards their customers regardless of whether these customers are depositors, investors or borrowers. Customers have impliedly put their faith and trust in these financial institutions and rely on them to act at all times in their best interests, and a very high degree of responsibility is therefore required. Simultaneously, financial institutions have fiduciary duties towards society. This is exemplified by the United Nations Guiding Principles on Human Rights. Financial institutions have to respect human rights in business and proactively ensure that they are not involved in silent complicity with other market players in human rights breaches.

The Equator Principles which has been revised twice and now in their third edition, we believe, need widening to encompass lending in general terms. Minimum standards for due diligence are not only desirable for assessing lending for projects but for all lending and borrowing decisions. We believe that as things stand in this area, there is a too narrow focus. Likewise, risk management is not enough. We need a positive vision for banking and orientation towards positive impacts and shared values.

Our world would shut down without banks and financial institutions, we cannot function without them, but irresponsible excesses and unsustainable bonus culture will undermine trust in banking and financial institutions and as such do more harm than good to citizens in the global village if sustainability is not at the core of what these institutions do. In purview, sustainability needs to define strategies and actions of financial institutions. The chapters in this book have competently amplified that a different banking approach is possible, and they have explored why issues relating to the triple bottom line—social, environmental and economic dimensions—must be embedded into corporate strategies. The book is a welcome addition to the corporate and academic world, and we recommend it unreservedly to all citizens of the world regardless of their industry of operations.

Finally, we congratulate Karen Wendt for assembling these world-class thoughts by world-class authors on these issues of global importance at this critical point of the twenty-first century.

London, UK   Samuel O. Idowu
Cologne, Germany   René Schmidpeter

Introduction for Responsible Investment Banking Book

Mainstreaming sustainable finance into business decision-making is becoming an increasingly attractive prospect for finance institutions worldwide. Accessing new markets for financial mechanisms, creating positive returns for more sustainable products and services and meeting a rising demand for capital financing for environmental solutions to climate change threats are but a few of the opportunities that are being seized by finance institutions as they reduce their exposure to economic instability and invite more sustainable returns on their investments.

As recently highlighted in the UNEP's *Global Environmental Outlook 5 For Business* Report, the finance sector is well positioned to positively influence the behaviour of businesses from all sectors of the economy. It is estimated that as much as US$1 trillion per year for the next few decades will be required to address a range of environmental impacts, providing the finance sector with an unprecedented opportunity to finance a low-carbon, resource-efficient and sustainable pathway to a green economy.

Moreover, by ensuring that financial services and transactions are conducted in accordance with the principles of sustainable development, finance institutions will also be enhancing transparency on client companies' environmental and social impacts, and protecting themselves from legal liabilities and reputational damage.

This was a resounding message at UNEP Finance Initiative's (FI) 2013 Global Roundtable in Beijing, where over 400 participants, including policymakers, regulators and representatives from academia, civil society and the scientific community, discussed what it takes to realign the financial system. To illustrate the value of cooperative approaches, a few examples are outlined below.

Regulators: Creating Enabling Environments

For financial institutions to mainstream sustainability in their operations, and thus influence the behaviour of the private sector at large, an enabling regulatory environment is essential. Sustainable finance frameworks are emerging internationally, demonstrating joint leadership between policymakers, regulators and the financial sector to integrate sustainability considerations in financial thinking, with the overall goal of placing economic growth on a more sustainable path.

Examples of this include the Green Protocols in Colombia and Brazil, Nigeria's Sustainable Banking Principles, Kenya's Sustainable Finance Initiative, China's Green Credit Policy and Indonesia's Green Banking Policy.

Stock Exchanges: Acting as Catalysts for Positive Change

Acknowledging the important role stock exchanges could play in improving corporate disclosure of environmental impacts and risks, the Sustainable Stock Exchange Initiative has been set up by UNEP FI and others to encourage a peer-to-peer learning platform for exploring how stock exchanges, in collaboration with investors, regulators and companies, can encourage sustainable business practices.

Industry Associations: Levelling the Playing Field for the Industry

Representing the interests of the financial sector at national and regional levels, industry associations are also perfectly situated to make the case for sustainability, by sensitizing their members to the link between environmental and social risks and opportunities and a healthy business. Using their convening and leveraging powers, they can play a key role in mainstreaming sustainability across the financial sector at the national, regional and global level.

They can also help to ensure that the private sector is better prepared to embark on sustainable business practices, with the introduction of new policies and the creation of new products in support of the transition to a green economy.

Scientific Community: Providing Data for Informed Decision-Making

A recent survey conducted among UNEP FI members revealed that financial institutions are seeking better access to climate information to inform risk management practices within their industry. It is hoped that a better transfer of climate information from the scientific to the financial community will play a key role in accelerating the implementation of adaptation measures by the private sector more broadly.

Civil Society Organizations: Acting as the Radar for Societal Concerns and Expectations

The complex functioning of the financial sector, and the financial crisis, has led to an increasing disconnect between the finance sector and population at large. By reconsidering the 'raison d'être' of finance, by both the financial institutions and society, the link between the two can be reshaped and reinforced. A confident and robust sustainability approach must include a continuous and honest stakeholder engagement process between all societal stakeholder groups.

The finance industry: Improving Understanding, Sharing Knowledge and Taking Action

Industry-led efforts to factor in Environment, Social and Governance issues into decision-making are probably most indicative of the fast-evolving field that is sustainable finance. Often, even in the absence of robust regulatory environments, finance institutions have tried to better understand what sustainability means for them and how it can act as a means of mitigating risks and identifying opportunities.

Voluntary commitments to sustainability through global partnerships, such as UNEP FI, or industry specific ones, such as the Principles for Sustainable Insurance, Principles for Responsible Investment or Equator Principles, are illustrative of this phenomenon. The need to understand, embed, account for and report environment-related issues led to the formation of partnerships, such as the Natural Capital Declaration and the development of guidance for financial institutions on greenhouse gas emissions related to lending and investment services and operations.

Another area where collaborative partnerships have had increasing traction over the past years is finance and human rights. Arriving at a clear and commonly accepted understanding of what is expected from finance institutions in terms of human rights is still a work in progress. However, the many examples in this book indicate that the topic is now on the agenda of industry, policymakers and the wider global community.

The financial crisis and the escalating natural resource and climate-related crises reveal that profits are not sustainable if the business approach disregards environment, communities and society at large, and that the system as a whole depends on making sure that these considerations are at the root of basic financial transactions.

The contributions in this book testify to the willingness and capability of the finance sector, and thought leaders in business and academia, to put sustainability at the core of business strategy design and execution. UNEP supports the convening of academia and business to help create pathways to the creation of sustainable models of investment and finance, resilient business and banking, and believes that *Responsible Investment Banking and Asset Management* provides a sound basis for further discussion on creating sustainable markets and, in the long run, sustainable societies.

About UNEP FI:

Founded in 1992 and based in Geneva, Switzerland, the United Nations Environment Programme Finance Initiative (UNEP FI) was established as a unique partnership between UNEP and the global financial sector, to recognize the links between financial institutions and environmental, social and governance (ESG) challenges and to identify, disseminate and help implement best practices of integrating sustainability in financial institutions' operations. UNEP FI's members recognize sustainability as part of a collective responsibility, and support approaches to anticipate and prevent potential negative impacts on the environment and society.

Achim Steiner
UN Under-Secretary-General and
UNEP Executive Director

Contents

About the Authors

Alexey Akulov After graduation from university Mr. Akulov worked for Center of environmental audit and management at the Department of natural resources and environmental protection of Tomsk region. In 2007–2013 Mr. Akulov worked for the international environmental consultancy firm ERM at its Moscow branch finally as Head of transaction services practice. In 2013 Mr. Akulov joined Vnesheconombank and took a position of the Head of sustainable finance unit. His key responsibilities include development and implementation of responsible finance practices into the bank's credit and investment operations in line with the internationally recognised sustainability standards and approaches.

Elena Amirkhanova is a London based Partner and the Global Head of Sustainable Finance Services at ERM. Elena helps developers secure finance and supports lenders from around the world. Her previous roles at ERM include managing the ERM Eurasia Impact Assessment and Planning Practice out of the Moscow office, working with clients in the Mining, Oil & Gas and Infrastructure industry and providing advice on potential impacts and risks associated with new developments. Elena has been responsible for overseeing more than 60 environmental and social projects for Financial Institutions and wide range of multinational and national companies, including companies working in the Former Soviet Union, Africa and Asia.

Prior to joining ERM, Elena worked for UNEP, UNDP and Trans-Siberian Gold Management in Russia and for the US Fish and Wildlife Service in Washington, DC.

Liselotte Arni joined UBS in 1997 and heads the Environmental and Social Risk function since 2003. She advises senior management on advancement and implementation of UBS's Environmental and Human Rights Policy, has firm-wide responsibility for coordinating UBS's Environmental & Human Rights programme and develops and implements principles and independent risk control frameworks for environmental and social (including human rights) risks within UBS Group.

She represents UBS in the UN Environment Program Finance Initiative (UNEP FI) and is a member of the advisory boards of University of Zurich Competence Center for Human Rights (UZHR) and of Swiss Center of Expertise in Human Rights (SCHR). She helped shaping the Thun Group of Banks discussion paper (together with peers and colleagues) on implications of the UN Guiding Principles on Business and Human Rights for the financial industry.

Cem B. Avci has conducted research on soil and groundwater pollution assessment and remedial design through analytical and numerical methods. His expertise includes aquifer parameter assessment and site investigation methods for soil and groundwater quality assessment. Professor Avci has participated in a number of impact assessment and quantification research in field of oil and gas, energy and infrastructure projects conducted in Turkey.

Professor Avci has over 20 years of experience in the consulting field of environmental related projects. His expertise includes environmental and social impact assessment studies, environmental due diligence studies, waste management and contaminated land remediation, soil and groundwater quality investigations. Dr. Avci worked several years in the United States on Superfund Projects where he was involved in site investigation and remediation projects.

Christine Berry is currently a Researcher at the New Economics Foundation. She was previously Head of Policy and Research at ShareAction (formerly FairPensions), where she authored the research on which her chapter is based. She is also a Trustee of the Finance Innovation Lab. She is writing in a personal capacity.

Curan Bonham is responsible for impact evaluation of the portfolio of investments managed by the funds of Conservation International's Ecosystem Finance and Markets Division. He has led monitoring and evaluation projects in more than a dozen countries, particularly focused on the nexus between agriculture, conservation and finance. A forester by training, Curan is a member of the Global Impact Investing Network's Land Conservation Standards Working Group, American Evaluation Association and the Society of American Foresters. He has published numerous papers and peer-reviewed articles on protected areas management, impact investing and conservation finance.

Bridget Boulle
Work:
2012–current: Program Manager at the Climate Bonds Initiative, London
2011: SRI Analyst at Henderson Global Investors, London
2008–2010: Senior Researcher, Pension Investment Research Consultants (PIRC), London
2007: Consultant at Kaiser Associates Economic Development Consultants, Cape Town

Denis Childs began his career at the Société Générale Group in 1978.

In 1981 he moved to Société Générale Corporate & Investment Banking to develop Export Credit Department that became a leader of the industry.

In 1993 he created the bank's worldwide Commodity and Trade Finance business line and integrated mining, oil and gas and power project finance that were also recognised as leaders in the industry.

End of 2008 he started a new challenge both heading the emerging and sustainable development department of the CIB and heading a Group project aiming at integrating E&S as a financial subject in all activities of the bank (CIB, French and international retail, . . .) and developing 'Positive Impact Finance'.

Denis Childs holds a Master's in Law and an MBA in banking from Paris I and IV Universities.

Eric Cochard is Head of Sustainable Development at Crédit Agricole CIB since 2007. A civil engineer graduate of Saint Etienne School of Mines (1978) with an engineering doctorate on the mining economy (CERNA 1983), he joined the Crédit Lyonnais Industrial Research Department. He spent 10 years in project financing. It was during this time that the Equator Principles were drawn up. He has been Head of Sustainable Development at Crédit Agricole CIB since 2007, coordinating the publication of sector policies for Crédit Agricole CIB and is involved in a number of think tanks dedicated to responsible financing. As part of Crédit Agricole CIB's support of the Finance and Sustainable Development Chair at Paris-Dauphine, he is a member of the Steering Committee of the Research Initiative that was created in 2013 to address the issue of quantifying the CO_2 emissions attributable to the financial sector.

John Martin Conley is William Rand Kenan Jr. Professor of Law at the University of North Carolina at Chapel Hill. He received his undergraduate degree in classics from Harvard and his J.D. and Ph.D. (anthropology) degrees from Duke. He has written several books and numerous articles on topics such as the anthropological and linguistic study of the American legal system (with William O'Barr), the culture of business and finance, scientific evidence and the law of intellectual property as applied to emerging technologies. His recent research projects have focused on the cultural and linguistic aspects of the corporate social responsibility movement (with Cynthia Williams), corporate boards (with Lissa Broome and Kimberly Krawiec) and the emerging discipline of genetic medicine. He is also a counsel to the North Carolina law firm of Robinson, Bradshaw and Hinson, where he specialises in intellectual property.

Debbie Cousins is an environmental and social specialist with 20 years of experience in the areas of environmental and social impact assessment (ESIA), environmental and social due diligence and auditing, environmental health and safety risk management frameworks and the development and implementation of Corporate Social Responsibility policy, management systems and best practices. She is currently working as the Senior Environment and Social Advisor within the European Bank for Reconstruction and Development (EBRD)'s Environment and Sustainability Department. Debbie is a Chartered Environmentalist and is the Financial sector representative on the Professional Standards Committee at the Institute of Environmental Management and Assessment.

Alexander James Cox is a Partner and Head of ERM's Central Europe Risk practice providing strategic, operational, tactical risk advisory and management consultancy services across multiple sectors and company life cycles. Key focus is on enterprise risk management, environmental, social, health and safety risks and the development of linkages across the risk disciplines back to enterprise risk management and in-house insurance programmes. Alexander has also worked in two Investment Banks as developing and implementing Operational Risk frameworks, assessment methodologies and risk reporting processes.

Sonal Pandya Dalal has focused on integrating ecosystem services (ES) values into corporate sustainability strategies for the past 15 years. Serving as the Director of Conservation International's Business and Sustainability Council, she serves as a trusted adviser and technical expert to corporate partners to build support for bold sustainability goals, innovations and investments that make business a positive force for nature conservation and human well-being. Ms. Pandya Dalal is currently working as a Core Team member with a consortia led by WBCSD and IUCN to build the Natural Capital Protocol, transforming the way business operates through understanding and incorporating the impacts and dependencies of natural capital.

Alok Dayal is the Senior Director—Credit and Environment Risk at IDFC Ltd. He is an Engineer and an MBA by qualification. He has over 19 years of experience in the infrastructure financing business. As a project financier he has been involved in appraising and financing numerous energy (generation and distribution), transportation and real estate projects. Along with his credit risk function he is also currently heading the environment risk group at IDFC Ltd. In this role he has been closely associated with IDFC's initiatives in the areas of sustainable finance and responsible investing and in enhancing IDFC's internal environment and social risk assessment processes. He played a key role in IDFC's journey to become the first Indian Institution to sign up to the Equator Principles. He is currently engaged in leading the many initiatives with regard to formulating processes and frameworks within IDFC Ltd in its evolution as an Equator Principles institution.

Alicia De la Cruz-Novey has over 18 years' of experience in the conservation field, with both the social and biological sciences. She has focused specifically on the implementation and evaluation of programs and projects related to stakeholder engagement, community participation, community consultation, protected areas, public perceptions, monitoring of biodiversity and ecotourism. She has expertise in social due diligence, project monitoring for lenders and promoters, auditing environmental and social management systems, social research methods, survey design and quantitative and qualitative techniques for data collection. Alicia has worked in the field with indigenous groups, local communities and NGOs, and has been involved in projects in various sectors including the oil and gas industries, tourism, and the agricultural and governmental sector. She is also experienced in analyzing the compliance of projects with the Equator Principles and the International Finance Corporation (IFC) Performance Standards on Social and Environmental Sustainability.

Patricia M. Dinneen has focused on Emerging Markets for most of her 36-year career. She joined EMPEA in February 2014 as a Senior Adviser and was appointed Chair of the EMPEA Impact Investing Council in 2013, to help professionalise and scale the impact investing industry. Previously she served as Managing Director at Siguler Guff & Company, a global private equity investment firm with over US$10 billion in assets under management. During her 9+ years at Siguler Guff, Dr. Dinneen built and managed the BRIC private equity business, focusing on Brazil, Russia, India, China and select frontier markets. She has also held positions at Cambridge Associates, British Telecommunications, Hughes Communications, RAND Corporation and the U.S. White House. Dr. Dinneen holds degrees from the University of Pennsylvania (B.A.), London School of Economics (M.Sc.) and MIT (Ph.D.). She is involved in multiple philanthropic and impact investing activities.

Gavin Duke is an Investment Manager with Aloe Private Equity. He has led numerous high impact and sustainable investments and exits in UK, China and India. Based in the London office, he focuses on screening new investment opportunities and portfolio management. Prior to joining Aloe, Gavin spent two years with an early stage VC investor specialising in renewable energy, following a six-year term as a Chemical Engineer for two blue chip multinationals. Gavin has an MBA from Imperial College and a Masters in Chemical Engineering from the University of Manchester.

Gisela Maria Freisinger has issued the biography "Hubert Burda der Medienfürst", New York, the "Insiderlexikon" and works as an author for the German journal "manager magazin". Her focus is on gender topics and she also writes portraits. She is the facilitator and moderator of the series "culture meets business" ("Kultur trifft Kommerz").

Steve Gibbons is a co-founder of Ergon and is a specialist in international legal standards. He has over 20 years experience in devising and delivering consultancy, research, advice and training on a range of labour and human rights issues. He is a UK-qualified lawyer.

He has consulted to major international institutions, multinational companies, not-for-profit organisations and trade unions, including the ILO, World Bank Group, EBRD, the European Commission, London 2012, the ETI, the UK Department for International Development and OSCE. Steve has a particular expertise in facilitating stakeholder dialogue and also devising and managing grievance and dispute resolution mechanisms in line with the UN Guiding Principles, including the procedure for the London 2012 Olympic Games. He is a co-founder of the UK's leading innovative online training company for lawyers CPDCast® and a regular conference speaker.

Arun Gore as the President and CEO of Gray Ghost Ventures is responsible for portfolio management and day-to-day operations of the management company Gray Ghost Management & Operations. He also serves as a board member of a number of the Portfolio Companies. Arun understands the markets, challenges and opportunities associated with investing in early-stage businesses and brings an informed perspective and practical experience to the leadership of the Manager.

Arun brings an extensive background in mobile telecommunications, international supply chain and financial consulting. His 35+ years of experience in the United States, Asia, Africa and the Middle East, which includes serving as a member of the executive team at T-Mobile USA as the Chief Financial Officer of Cook Inlet T-Mobile, has been valuable in underwriting international investment opportunities and working with the entrepreneurs of portfolio companies.

Since 2006 Arun has been actively engaged in promoting and supporting impact investments for Gary Ghost. In 2008, he moved to Atlanta to take over the management of the impact investment funds and, subsequently, the management of the entire Gray Ghost operations.

Dr. Isil Gultekin is a Principal Environmental Consultant and Environmental and Social Impact Assessment (ESIA) Practice Leader at ELC Group Consulting and Engineering Inc. (Royal HaskoningDHV Turkey). Her areas of expertise include undertaking ESIA studies in line with international standards (such as Equator Principles, IFC, EBRD), gap analysis of national Environmental Impact Assessment (EIA) studies with respect to international standards, Environmental and Social Due Diligence (ESDD) studies and Environmental, Health and Safety regulatory reviews. She has undertaken ESIA/ESDD studies for a variety of projects in the fields of infrastructure, ports, oil and gas, healthcare, mining, wind and hydro power.

Jonathon Hanks is a founding Partner of Incite (www.incite.co.za), a global advisory network based in South Africa that help its clients build competitiveness by delivering social value, with a primary focus on emerging markets. Incite provides strategic advisory and reporting services to many of South Africa's leading companies. Jonathon is a member of advisory groups to the International Integrated Reporting Council (IIRC) and the South African Integrated Reporting Committee (IRC). He recently chaired an international multi-stakeholder negotiating process that developed a global standard on social responsibility (ISO 26000). He was instrumental in bringing the international Carbon Disclosure Project (www.cdproject.net) to South Africa, in partnership with the National Business Initiative. He lectures on executive programmes for the University of Cape Town, Wits and the University of Cambridge Programme for Sustainability Leadership. In addition to his corporate advisory work, he consults to organisations such as the GRI, ILO, ISO, UNEP, UNCTAD and the UNGC.

Rolf D. Häßler holds a university degree in economics. He has more than 20 years of professional experience in business consulting and research with a focus on environmental and sustainable management and reporting, issues management and Socially Responsible Investment (SRI). His professional activities included work for imug Consulting, scoris and the Sustainable Business Institute at the European Business School. From 2004 to 2007 he has been responsible at Munich Re's Environmental Management Unit for communication on environmental and sustainability matters, SRI as well as Munich Re's participation in the UNEP FI Climate Change Working Group. From 2007 to 2014 he has been Director and Head of Corporate Communications at oekom research. Since January 2015 he is managing partner of the NKI -Institut für nachhaltige Kapitalanlage GmbH in Munich.

Christian Hertrich

University of Stuttgart—Ph.D. (Dr.rer.pol), Finance, First
2010–2013
Research focus: Portfolio optimization, financial econometrics, derivatives
First-class honours with Distinction
University of Cambridge—Master, Finance
2009–2010
Focus: Equity derivatives, investment management, econometrics, fixed-income analysis

ESB Business School Reutlingen
B.Sc., European Business Administration 2001–2003
Focus: Corporate finance, accounting, international finance
Comillas Pontifical University
B.Sc., International Business Management (E-4)1999–2001

L. Reed Huppman is co-director of ENVIRON's International Finance practice with 30 years' experience in applied sustainability consulting, particularly related to major international project development and finance, including corporate and project environmental and social policies and management systems. He has managed and contributed to numerous interdisciplinary studies, including environmental and social impact assessments, due diligence audits for financial transactions, public consultation and capacity building and training in sustainable finance. He is an IFC-certified trainer on the Performance Standards on Social and Environmental Sustainability, and has delivered training to a number of Equator Principle financial institutions, investment funds, private equity firms and extractive industry clients. Reed has worked for the World Bank in the former Soviet Republics for 4 years and was seconded for 2 years to the IFC.

Samuel O. Idowu is a Senior Lecturer in Accounting at London Metropolitan University, UK, and a Professor of CSR and Sustainability at Nanjing University of Finance and Economics, China. He is a freeman of the City of London, UK, and a Liveryman of the Worshipful Company of Chartered Secretaries and Administrators. He researches in the fields of Corporate Social Responsibility (CSR), Corporate Governance and Accounting. He has led several edited books in CSR and is the editor-in-chief of Springer's reference books like the CSR Encyclopedia and Series Editor of CSR, Sustainability, Ethics and Governance with Springer.

Olivier Jaeggi Prior to founding ECOFACT in 1998, Olivier Jaeggi worked in credit risk control at UBS, where he was in charge of managing environmental risks. He graduated in environmental engineering from the Swiss Federal Institute of Technology (ETH) Zurich, and has completed executive education programmes at Harvard Business School and at the University of Oxford. He is a member of PRMIA's subject matter expert advisory group on reputational risk and, since 2012, has contributed to the annual sustainability report produced by the MIT Sloan Management Review in collaboration with the Boston Consulting Group. He is also a regular contributor to the sustainability blog of the MIT Sloan Management Review.

Barnim G. Jeschke

Educational background: studies of business administration at Berlin, Kiel, New York (MBA); doctorate studies at Berlin and University of Maryland (Ph.D.).

Professional background: management consultant; International Marketing Director for corporations in Switzerland and Monaco; venture capitalist at Dusseldorf and Munich; start-up entrepreneur and business developer; professor of Sustainable Management at FOM Munich; currently heading the Project management of BER Airport Berlin-Brandenburg – likely the most complex building project in Europe.

Till Hendrik Jung graduated in political and social sciences from the Institut d'Etudes Politiques in Paris and the Free University of Berlin, where he wrote his master's thesis on CSR strategies of companies.

In 2004, he joined the independent Munich-based rating agency oekom research. As an analyst he was responsible for the corporate research in sectors including automobile and machinery. Since 2010, he is Director International Relations, and since May 2011 he is Director Business Development at oekom research and mainly responsible for client relations and business development. He is member of the PRI Fixed Income Working Group.

Christine Kaufmann has been a professor for international and constitutional law at the University of Zurich, Switzerland, since 2002. In 2012 she was elected vice dean of the law school.

After completing her doctoral thesis on the Right to Food Christine Kaufmann served first in the legal department and then as Director of Human Resources at the Swiss Central Bank from 1991 to 2000. From 2000 to 2001 she was a visiting scholar at the University of Michigan Law School and worked on her habilitation project on the topic of Globalisation and Core Labour Rights. From 2001 to 2002 she served as Director of Legal Research at the World Trade Institute (WTI) at the University of Bern, where until 2012 she was the Co-Director of the NCCR Research Project Trade Regulation and is still a Member of the Board. From 2004 to 2012 Christine Kaufmann was a member of the Bar Association Examination Panel of the Canton (State) of Zurich.

In 2009, she initiated the foundation of the Centre for Human Rights Studies at the University of Zurich, which she now chairs. In 2013 she was appointed co-president of the newly set up Federal Advisory Committee of the National Contact Point for the OECD Guidelines for Multinational Enterprises together with State Secretary, Marie-Gabrielle Ineichen-Fleisch.

Yann Kermode holds a master's degree in environmental management and has over 16 years practitioner experience of managing environmental and social risks in the financial industry. As deputy head of UBS's environmental and social risk function, Yann supports the development and implementation of principles and independent risk control frameworks for environmental and social risks within the UBS Group. Yann represents UBS in the Human Rights Working Group of the UN Environment Program Finance Initiative and the Financed Emissions Initiative of the GHG Protocol. Together with other bank representatives, he recently helped shape the Thun Group of Banks discussion paper on implications for the financial industry of the UN Guiding Principles on Business and Human Rights.

Sean Kidney co-founder and CEO Climate Bonds Initiative.

The Climate Bonds Initiative is an investor-focused NGO based in London. It works internationally to mobilise debt capital markets to fund a rapid, global transition to a low-carbon and climate resilient economy.

The Initiative advises banks, investors, governments and NGOs about structuring programmes to maximise the leverage of public sector resources. That includes green investment banks, green securitization and 'sustainable financial solutions' for large-scale energy efficiency schemes.

Projects include developing proposals for the European Commission's DG Climate on Europe's role in mobilising private sector capital for climate solutions, helping organise the Green Bonds workstream for the UN Secretary-General's Climate Summit, and working with the Chinese Government's State Council on how to grow green bonds in China.

The Climate Bonds Initiative also runs an International Standards and Certification Scheme for climate bonds; investor groups representing US$22 trillion of assets sit on its board.

Nanno Kleiterp was appointed as CEO and Chairman of the Management Board in 2008. Before that, he was responsible for FMO's risk-bearing profile as Chief Investment Officer from 2000. From 1987 to 2000, he held a number of positions within FMO, including Manager Small- and Medium-sized Enterprises, Regional Manager Latin America and Chief Finance Officer. Prior to FMO, he gained extensive experience in private sector development while working in Nicaragua, Mexico and Peru.

Heidrun Kopp, M.B.A., M.A. After studies in Vienna, London and the USA in the banking sector, especially for the region of Central and Eastern Europe, she started working for Raiffeisen International. Since 2008, the focus of her work is on CSR and Sustainability. The integration of CSR into the core business and the importance of sustainability ratings were presented in numerous expert panels, lectures and publications to the public. She has special personal commitment to the improvement of basic financial knowledge, especially in adolescents with and without a migration background.

Nina Kruschwitz has worked for MIT Sloan Management Review since the foundation of the sustainability and innovation research initiative, conducted in collaboration with the Boston Consulting Group, in 2009. She has been co-author author of numerous reports, articles, blogs and interviews on the topic of sustainability. Prior to joining MIT SMR, she was the managing editor of the Fifth Discipline Fieldbook Project, and co-author of 'The Necessary Revolution: How Individuals and Organizations Are Working Together to Create a Sustainable World (Doubleday, 2008)' with Peter Senge et al.

Suellen Lambert Lazarus is a Washington DC-based independent consultant advising clients in international finance, private sector development, investment structuring, independent evaluation and sustainability. Her work includes assisting financial institutions with development and implementation of environmental and social policy, strategy and training. In 2010–2011, she led the Strategic Review for the Equator Principles (EP) Association to produce a multi-year strategic vision. From 2006 to 2009, Ms. Lazarus was Senior Adviser at ABN AMRO Bank and represented ABN Amro on the EP Steering Committee. Ms. Lazarus worked at the World Bank and International Finance Corporation (IFC) for 23 years including as director of IFC's Syndications Department where she was instrumental in the development and launch of the EPs and as Special Assistant to the Executive Vice President of IFC.

Christian Leitz As Secretary to the UBS Corporate Responsibility Committee (CRC), one of the five Board of Directors committees, Christian assists the Committee's Chair in putting together the agenda for the Committee and prepares the accompanying documentation. The CRC supports the firm's Board in fulfilling its duty to safeguard and advance the Group's reputation for responsible corporate conduct and to assess developments in stakeholder expectations and their possible consequences for UBS.

Christian coordinates UBS's corporate responsibility reporting and has particular responsibilities in the area of NGO (non-governmental organisation) communications and analysis. He is also head of the UBS Historical Archives and the firm's corporate historian, acting as a centre of competence for all questions pertaining to historical issues at the firm.

Haiying Lin is an Assistant Professor at the School of Environment, Enterprise and Development (SEED), University of Waterloo, Canada. Her interests include corporate sustainability strategy, strategic alliances for complex environmental issues, alliances for innovation, cross-sector partnership, voluntary environmental programmes, stakeholder involvement in environmental governance, global corporate responsibility and corporate sustainability in the emerging economies.

Raul Manjarin heads ECOFACT's environmental and social risk assessment team. Prior to joining the company in 2007, he worked as Finance and Administration Coordinator for Doctors Without Borders in Kyrgyzstan and as a Credit Officer at Banco ProCredit in Nicaragua. He holds a Master's Degree in Economics from the University of Neuchâtel and a Master's Degree in International Relations from the Graduate Institute of International Studies in Geneva.

Owen McIntyre is a Senior Lecturer and Director of Research at the Faculty of Law, University College Cork. His principal area of interest is Environmental Law, with a particular research focus on International Water Law. He serves on the editorial boards of a number of Irish and international journals and is widely published in his specialist areas. Current international appointments include:

– Chair of the IUCN World Commission on Environmental Law's Specialist Group on Water and Wetlands.

– Honorary Lecturer at the UNESCO Centre for Water Law, Policy & Science, University of Dundee.

– Panel Member of the Project Complaints Mechanism of the European Bank for Reconstruction and Development (EBRD).

– Member of the Scientific Committee of the European Environment Agency. In April 2013, the Irish Minister for Agriculture, Food and the Marine appointed Dr. McIntyre to the statutory Aquaculture Licences Appeals Board.

Ariel Meyerstein United States Council for International Business New York, New York

Vice President, Labor Affairs, Corporate Responsibility and Governance April 2014–present, where he leads USCIB's policy work and international engagement on labour and employment issues and corporate responsibility at multi-stakeholder processes, including the International Labor Organization and OECD. He worked for various law firms Chadbourne & Parke, LLP New York, New York, as Litigation Associate March 2013–April 2014, and Debevoise & Plimpton, LLP New York, New York, March 2011–March 2013.

He holds a Ph.D., Jurisprudence & Social Policy Program, from University of California, Berkeley (2011). The topic of research for his Dissertation was: 'On the Effectiveness of Global Private Regulation: Implementation of the Equator Principles by Multinational Banks'. He was awarded the Umeå School of Business Award at 2011 UN Principles for Responsible Investment/Sustainable Investment Research Platform Conference.

Herman Mulder is a member of the board of the Dutch National Contact Point (NCP) of the OECD Guidelines for Multinational Enterprises. Mulder is a former senior executive vice president at ABN AMRO, and is now an independent board member with a focus on sustainable development issues.

Gloria Nelund Chairman and Chief Executive Officer, TriLinc Global

Gloria spent 30 years on Wall Street as one of the most successful and visible executives in the international investment management industry. After retiring from Deutsche Bank as CEO of their US$50 billion North America Private Wealth Management division, she co-founded TriLinc Global, a private investment company dedicated to creating impact investment products that will attract significant private capital to help solve some of the world's most critical issues.

Gloria has significant expertise in the creation, management and distribution of investment products for institutional, high net worth and retail investors and, throughout her career, has been a pioneer in the development of socially responsible and impact investment products.

In addition to her activities with TriLinc, Gloria is Chairman and Independent Trustee for RS Investments, a mutual fund complex with more than US$20 billion in assets under management. She is also a lifelong supporter of development-oriented philanthropic causes. Gloria currently sits on the board of multiple not-for-profit organisations and actively supports entrepreneurship research and education. She is an active speaker and guest lecturer on Impact Investing and Ethical Leadership at conferences and several top business schools, including Columbia, Wheaton, Kellogg, MIT, and Georgetown.

Dustin Neuneyer works part-time as Head of Continental Europe for PRI Principles for Responsible Investment. He is responsible for engaging with and supporting European signatories in their RI and ESG practice and implementation, and fostering the development of the PRI European Network. Dustin also works as independent consultant on finance sector and sustainability, business strategies, risk management and implementation. He has more than 13 years of experience in sustainable finance, responsible investment and banking and ESG integration gained through his positions as Director at corporate and investment bank WestLB and Senior Advisor to think tank and lobby NGO Germanwatch. Dustin developed and implemented first of its kind ESG approaches on business activities related to coal-fired power generation and on offshore oil drilling and production including the Arctic as well as on stakeholder dialogues.

Alexandra Niessen-Ruenzi is the Chair of Corporate Governance at the University of Mannheim since 2010. Alexandra Niessen-Ruenzi is a Professor of Finance at the University of Mannheim (Germany) since 2009. She studied business administration at the University of Cologne (Germany) and holds a Ph.D. in finance. Before joining Mannheim University, she was a visiting scholar at Northwestern University and the University of Texas at Austin. Professor Niessen-Ruenzi mainly works in the area of corporate finance and asset management. Her papers on gender differences in the mutual fund industry won several prizes, including best paper awards at the Academy of Management, German Finance Association and Society for the Advancement of Behavioural Economics.

Niamh O'Sullivan Before starting her Ph.D. in 2005 in the accounting section of The University of Amsterdam Business School (UvA ABS), Niamh spent four and a half years with the United Nations Environment Programme Finance Initiative (UNEP FI) in Geneva, Switzerland. Here, she acted as project manager for the UNEP FI African Task Force (ATF) and the UNEP FI-GRI (Global Reporting Initiative) Financial Services Sector Supplement Working Group. Niamh's Ph.D. research adopted a qualitative approach and focused on the institutionalisation and social accountability dynamics surrounding the Equator Principles (EP) between 2003 and 2008. In 2010, Niamh defended his Ph.D. and was awarded Cum Laude and also won the 2010 Emerald/EFMD Outstanding Doctoral Research Award in the Interdisciplinary Accounting Research Category. Niamh currently works as an Associate Analyst with Sustainalytics in Amsterdam.

Henrik Ohlsen born in 1979 is Managing Director of the German Association for Environmental Managemement and Sustainability in Financial Institutions (VfU). As such, he works on building the business case to stimulate banks, insurance firms and investors to better integrate sustainability and climate change factors into their business-processes.

Henrik's approach to sustainability is from an sustainability reporting and controlling point of view and therefore he focuses on advancing sustainability KPIs.

In his previous capacities in a local administration and a consulting firm, Henrik worked in the field of environmental management. Henrik graduated in 2008 from the University of Augsburg with a Master's degree in Political Science (Major), international law (minor) and psychology (minor).

Sebastian Philipps works as Corporate Partnerships Specialist for the Asian Development Bank (ADB) in Bangkok. He is responsible for the business engagement strategy under the Core Environment Program and supports the development of new concepts for sustainable investments in natural capital.

Prior to his ADB assignment, Sebastian was with the Collaborating Centre on Sustainable Consumption and Production (CSCP), a former UNEP Centre. In his five years with the Centre he acted as international project manager and researcher, and also developed the business area Sustainable Finance.

Sebastian Philipps has worked on sustainability, finance, transport, and energy topics in China, Thailand, Cambodia, the United Kingdom, and Germany. He is an economist and China scholar by training and also holds a degree in business administration.

Dariusz Prasek, Director, Project Appraisal Environment and Sustainability Department European Bank for Reconstruction and Development

Dr. Prasek currently holds the position of Director of Project Appraisal at the Environment and Sustainability Department in the European Bank for Reconstruction and Development. He is responsible for coordinating environmental and social due diligence on a variety of Bank operations. Dr. Prasek joined the Bank in 1992 and has been responsible for the environmental and social appraisal and risk management of Bank operations across different sectors. Before joining the Bank, he was an advisor for the United Nations Conference on Environment and Development (Earth Summit). Dr. Prasek holds a Ph.D. in environmental engineering from the Warsaw University of Technology. From 1987 to 1991, he was assistant professor at the University's Institute of Environmental Engineering. Dr. Prasek has published articles in the fields of solid waste management, environmental management and environmental aspects of project financing.

Christina Raab leads the consultancy unit at the organization MADE-BY where she works towards integrating sustainability into the business models and value chains of the apparel and textile industry. Prior to this engagement she headed the team for sustainable infrastructure, products and services at the Collaborating Centre on Sustainable Consumption and Production (CSCP). In this role she was responsible for the development of sustainability strategies for various private and public sectors and for sustainable finance from a consumer and business perspective. Previously Christina Raab worked for several years in the area of environmental management at an international consultancy firm and at the United Nations Industrial Development Organization (UNIDO). She holds a PhD in materials chemistry from the University of Technology in Vienna and the University of California in Santa Barbara.

Vineet Rai with more than 19 years of experience in leading innovative interventions in the development finance sector, is the Founder and Managing Director of Aavishkaar and Co-founder and Chairman of the Intellecap Group of companies. Vineet's interests include early-stage venture capital, micro enterprises, microfinance investments, Incubations and social investment advisory. Vineet chairs the Board of Villgro, an Incubating and Funding Platform, and Intellegrow, an Intellecap subsidiary providing venture debt services to Impact enterprises.

A frequent speaker at national and global forums, Vineet has received numerous awards including the G 20—SME Innovation in Finance Award in 2010, the UNDP-IBLF World Business Award in 2005 and Lemelson Venture Fund Award in 2007 on behalf of Aavishkaar. He has also received the Ashoka Fellowship and Honorary Membership of XLRI Alumni Association. Driving on Indian roads is one of his passions and he tries to cover 50,000 km every year.

Marcus Regueira holds an MBA from Wharton and 25 years of experience in investment banking and Private Equity in Brazil and the United States. He is a Founding Partner at FIR Capital, a Brazilian Private Equity firm, and Co-Founder and Managing Director of FIRST—Brazil Impact Investing Fund. A Board Member of the Brazilian Private Equity and Venture Capital Association (ABVCAP), Marcus was its President from 2006 to 2008 and is Advisory Council Member of the Emerging Markets Private Equity Association (EMPEA). He is a Board Member at C.E.S.A.R., an award-winning centre of applied innovation; he is also a Co-Founder and Board Member of Instituto Hartmann Regueira, an institute for strategy and best management practices in impactful investing.

Jim Roth is a leading expert in the global mass-market insurance sector, and a pioneer of commercial microinsurance. Formerly Vice President of The Microinsurance Centre, Jim was also ILO Chief Technical Adviser on microinsurance in India, and has acted as a consultant to multinational insurance companies such as AIG and Allianz and banks such as KFW and ADB. He sourced and led one of LeapFrog's largest investments, into Shriram CCL, a distributor of low-cost financial services including insurance, savings and investment products for the emerging Indian consumer.

Yasemin X. Saltuk is an Executive Director for J.P. Morgan's Social Finance team, focused on client advisory and thought leadership. She works with both issuer and investor clients of the firm on their impact investment strategies and publishes data and analysis for investors in the market. She authored Impact Investments: An Emerging Asset Class (2010), which is widely recognised as the seminal work introducing impact investments to mainstream investors. Her research has produced the largest data set for the market and her publications are referenced and utilised by practitioners and academics alike.

Henry Schäfer is holder of the Chair of General Management and Corporate Finance at the University of Stuttgart. Prof. Schäfer is one of the leading German research capacities in SRI and CSR. He has published several text books in finance and is consulting several major well-known global firms. Since 2007 he is founding partner of EccoWorks GmbH, an advisory firm for the integration of sustainability issues in investments and business development strategies.

René Schmidpeter holds the Dr. Juergen Meyer Endowed Chair of International Business Ethics and CSR at the Cologne Business School. For more than 15 years he has worked and done research in the field of sustainability and corporate social responsibility. He is Section Editor of the CSR Encyclopedia and Series Editor of CSR, Sustainability, Ethics and Governance with Springer.

Heffa Schuecking is the founder and director of the German environment and human rights organisation urgewald, which focuses on the impacts of German companies and banks abroad. She has two decades of experience campaigning on financial institutions and is considered to be one of the most effective environmental advocates in Germany.

In 1994, Heffa was the first German to win the prestigious Goldman Environmental Prize, often referred to as the 'Green Nobel'. And in 1995, she was designated 'Woman of the Year' by Mona Lisa, Germany's most influential women's TV show. She has designed many inspirational and successful advocacy campaigns and was awarded the annual Utopia Prize in the category 'Exemplary Individuals' in 2010. In the same year, her organisation received the Solbach-Freise Award for Civil Courage. Urgewald plays a leading role in the international NGO network 'BankTrack', which monitors the activities of commercial banks worldwide and seeks to establish binding environmental and social policies for the financial sector.

Monika Schulz-Strelow In 2006 Monika Schulz-Strelow founded FidAR—Women to the boards initiative which is a non-partisan initiative, campaigning for an increase of female board members in Germany. With FidAR she developed a ranking that shows the number of women working in the supervisory boards in each of the 160 German quoted companies—the so-called WoB-Index (Women on Board Index). Currently FidAR is working on the 'Public WoB-Index' to identify the number of women on supervisory boards in Germany's public companies.

With her company b.international group, she helps national and international investors to enter the markets in Berlin, Germany and Austria. Throughout her affiliation with BAO BERLIN International Ltd., where she spent 9 years on the board, she intensified international relations for Berlin business community and built business networks in Europe and became a door opener to the European Commission.

Alexander Seidler who joined UBS in 2000, has a Group wide oversight function for decisions related to environmental and social risks. This role covers client and supplier onboardings and transaction decisions for the Investment Bank, Wealth Management and Asset Management. Alex holds a Master in International Relations from the University of Geneva and a Ph.D. in Finance and Banking from the University of Zurich exploring the Socially Responsible Investment behaviour of Swiss pension funds.

Katharina Serafimova is Head of Finance Sector Engagement at WWF Switzerland. She works on international projects to improve the environmental performance of financial institutions. Key topics are the role of the finance sector regarding decarbonization, sustainable commodities and bio-diversity. Katharina is an environmental specialist graduated from ETH Zürich. She also holds a master's in business communication. Previously, she has worked as Head of Corporate Sustainability at a Swiss private bank. Before, she managed the Biogenic Resources team of Ernst Basler + Partner, a Swiss engineering, planning and consulting company. She worked with key industries, such as power production and construction, to deal with increasing demand of biogenic resources, such as wood or agricultural commodities.

Renana Shvartzvald graduated from the Adi Lautman Interdisciplinary Program for Outstanding Students at Tel Aviv University. Her diverse studies included many aspects of environmental and social sustainability such as business practices, public policy and exact sciences. Renana received her Master's degree in environmental policy, summa cum laude, from the Porter School of Environmental Studies at TAU in collaboration with the Freie Universität Berlin.

Renana is currently a member of Vital Capital's investment team, where she is responsible for social and environmental impact analysis and policy.

Agustin Silvani is the Managing Director of Carbon Finance at Conservation International (CI). To date, CI has been one of the most active investors in land-based climate projects having deployed over US$30 MM in 20 reforestation, afforestation and REDD+ projects around the globe. More recently, the Carbon Fund has worked to "green" key agricultural supply chains through the development of public–private partnerships in tropical forest countries. As part of CI's Ecosystem Finance and Markets unit, Agustin is tasked with creating and executing innovative financial mechanisms to encourage sustainable development and has led the development of "green" bonds and natural capital funds in conjunction with JPMorgan Chase, the World Bank and BNP Paribas, among others. Before CI, Agustin worked in capital markets and project finance, including 6 years spent on the commodities desk of a UK trading group.

Achim Steiner Acting on the nomination of Secretary-General Kofi Annan, the UN General Assembly in 2006 unanimously elected Achim Steiner as the Executive Director of UNEP for a 4-year term. He became the fifth Executive Director in UNEP's history. At its 83rd plenary meeting in 2010, the UN General Assembly, on the proposal of the Secretary-General Ban Ki-moon, re-elected Mr. Achim Steiner as Executive Director of the United Nations Environment Programme for another 4-year term.

Joan Trant is the Director of Marketing and Impact and a key member of the TriLinc Global Executive Management team with responsibility for the planning, development and implementation of the Company's marketing strategies, marketing communications and public relations activities, and for leading the Company's impact efforts, including supporting the continued development of the impact investing industry. Prior to joining TriLinc Global, Joan launched and was Executive Director of the International Association of Microfinance Investors (IAMFI). IAMFI's Limited Partner members' microfinance commitments/investments totaled US$780 million, and General Partner members managed an aggregate portfolio of US$1.84 billion. IAMFI led the microfinance investment industry with proprietary research, contributions to third-party publications, educational and networking meetings, tailored member services and consensus-building for investor best practices.

Elizabeth van Zyl is a Partner of Citrus Partners LLP with over 18 years experience providing social and environmental expert advice to natural resources, transportation, industrial, construction, energy, transaction, stakeholder engagement and policy projects.

Elizabeth delivers due diligence and compliance-focused fast-track assignments for both private clients and International Financial Institutions (IFIs), reviewing social and environmental performance of companies and of projects against international standards, including IFC Performance Standards, EBRD Performance Requirements and Equator Principles III, and establishing operational corrective action plans to deal with operational and compliance risks.

Elizabeth specifically provides advisory support on social risks associated with labour and working conditions, code of conduct, grievance management, community safety, health and security, involuntary resettlement and land acquisition and stakeholder engagement and community relations.

Thomas Vellacott, B.A., M.B.A., M.Phil., F.R.S.A. (43) is CEO of WWF Switzerland, the conservation organisation. WWF Switzerland has 260,000 supporters and forms part of WWF's global network. WWF's mission is to stop the degradation of the planet's natural environment and to build a future in which humans live in harmony with nature.

Thomas holds degrees in Arabic and Islamic Studies from Durham, in International Relations from Cambridge and in Business Administration from IMD. Previously, he worked in private banking for Citibank and as an engagement manager for McKinsey & Co. Prior to taking on the role of CEO in 2012, Thomas spent 9 years heading up WWF Switzerland's programme division and was responsible for the organisation's national and international conservation projects. Thomas has been a member of WWF since he was 8 years old.

Shally Venugopal currently runs the Internet start-up MYOLO, a resource to apply for personal finance, insurance and government services. Shally previously led WRI's Climate Finance and the Private Sector project—a project that works with policymakers and private sector financiers to increase the finance and investment flows to climate change-related projects in developing countries. Her past work at WRI focused on the financial implications of climate change from the perspective of the corporate and investor community, working with partners like Standard & Poor's, IFC and HSBC. Before joining WRI, Shally worked in Morgan Stanley's Microfinance Institutions Group, where she was responsible for client and capital markets' coverage of South and Central Asian Microfinance Institutions and in Morgan Stanley's Public Finance Division, covering US domestic public sector infrastructure clients. Her prior experience includes working at the Penn Institute for Urban Research, L.E.K. Consulting and Bearfoot Investments.

Shally, a native Singaporean, graduated with a B.S. in Economics from the Wharton School at the University of Pennsylvania, with concentration in Finance and Mathematics.

Raimund Vogelsberger has a background in Environmental Engineering and Technology Risk Assessment, with over 30 years of international environmental consulting experience. His areas of expertise include environmental and social compliance assessment, due diligence of power and infrastructure projects on behalf of Equator Principle Financing Institutions and development and implementation of environmental and social management systems in alignment with IFC and EP requirements.

Mr. Vogelsberger joined ERM Germany in 2003 as Partner in Charge of the M&A Transaction Services Practices and currently is responsible for Impact Assessment and Sustainable Project Finance Services across the Central and Eastern Europe/Turkey Region.

Margaret Wachenfeld is the Director of Research and Legal Affairs at the Institute for Human Rights and Business where she leads the think tank's research programme. Just prior, she spent 6 years as a Senior Policy Adviser on children's rights at UNICEF. Earlier, Ms. Wachenfeld was principal external advisor on human rights for the International Finance Corporation (IFC, World Bank Group). She also advised European Bank for Reconstruction and Development (EBRD) and European Investment Bank (EIB) on human rights and environmental issues. Margaret was a staff lawyer at IFC where she worked on the environmental and social dimensions of IFC's investments first in the Legal Department then later in the Environment and Social Development Department. Earlier, Margaret was a senior associate with the law firm of White & Case. She started her career as counsel at the Danish Institute for Human Rights.

Dr. Olaf Weber is an associate professor in sustainable finance at the School for Environment, Enterprise and Developments (SEED), University of Waterloo, Canada and is the director of the master's program in Sustainability Management. Currently he is working on projects on integrating reputation risk indicators into credit risk assessment procedures, on the relation between the sustainability performance and the financial performance of banks, on sustainability reporting of Chinese companies and on measuring the impact of microfinance, social banking and impact investing.

Karen Wendt Founder of Responsible Investmentbanking, has been head of the Equator Principles Team of a top tier global bank, where she introduced the Equator Principles, an environmental and social risk management framework. Karen started her career at Deutsche Bank after achieving her Bachelors Degree from the University of Regensburg and working for the European Commission. She holds an MBA from the University of Liverpool. Karen Wendt has been one of the initiators of the Equator Principles and has been a Member of the Steering Committee of the Equator Principles Financial Institutions Association since its inception. She has undertaken research on investment banking culture, the role of alignment of interests and values and the impact of leadership behaviour on trust and value identity. She has more than 20 years experience in investment banking. In addition she is editor of scientific books on the subject of responsible investment banking and positive impact investment and finance.

Cynthia Williams, B.A. (Neurobiology), University of California at Berkeley; J.D., New York University. Practised law for 5 years at Cravath, Swaine & Moore, New York, N.Y. Prof. Williams taught at the University of Illinois College of Law until 2013, when she joined the faculty of Osgoode Hall Law School in Toronto, Canada. Her Harvard Law Review article, 'The Securities and Exchange Commission and Corporate Social Transparency', 112 HARV. L. REV. 1197 (1999), was an early argument for required social, environmental and governance information. Her 2007 article, 'Putting the "S" Back in CSR: a Multi-Level Theory of Corporate Social Responsibility' (with Ruth Aguilera, Deborah Rupp and Jyoti Ganapathi), 32:3 Academy of Management Review 836 (2007), was awarded best paper prize by Sir Adrian Cadbury at the University of Birmingham International Conference on Corporate Governance (2005). Professor Williams helped found and is on the board of the Network for Sustainable Financial Markets, a global think tank of academics and financial market participants.

Manuel Woersdoerfer is Postdoctoral Research Fellow, Cluster of Excellence 'The Formation of Normative Orders', at Goethe-University Frankfurt, Frankfurt am Main/Germany. He holds a Ph.D., in Business Ethics/History of Economic Thought (GPA: magna cum laude). His Thesis discusses The Normative and Economic-Ethical Foundations of Ordoliberalism. He holds also a Master of Arts, Philosophy and Economics (GPA: 1.3) 2004–2007 from University of Bayreuth, Bayreuth/Germany.
He has been a Visiting Researcher, Osgoode Hall Law School, York University/Canada July–Nov 2013, a Visiting Researcher, Institute of Foreign Philosophy, Beijing University/China Nov–Dec 2012, and Visiting Researcher, Centre for Ethics, University of Toronto, Toronto/Canada Jan–May 2012.

Damien Wynne had headed various business firms prior to starting to work as a coach in self-development. He was industrial refrigeration and air conditioning director of a refrigeration company, off-licence owner of investment real estate company Budapest/Hungary before founding the Light Grids Self Development School.

Editor's Contribution

Karen Wendt

1 Leading thoughts on Responsible Investment Banking and Presentation of Authors

1.1 A New Business Model Is on the Cards

"The business of business is business", Milton Friedman replied, when asked what economics contribute to the welfare of society (Milton Friedman 1970). In his view, business contribute much to the welfare of society by producing goods and services, supporting economic growth and providing employment. But questions of finite planetary resources, climate change vulnerability, loss or reduction in biodiverse natural habitats, decrease in ecosystems services, drilling in the arctic, poor labour conditions in many markets, questions over human rights, accompanied by social unrest connected to infrastructure projects, and speculation in natural resources and soft commodities and the question of access to drinking water have brought new meaning to responsibility for business and the financial industry in particular.

The major resource in investment and banking besides efficient IT systems and competent staff is trust. Trust is the fuel banks more than any other type of company run on—and if the source runs dry, the vital role of this otherwise invisible source of fuel becomes very apparent. Banks can be described as organisational beings advising society: "Give me your money, I will care for it and keep and invest it for you. You can have it back anytime, anywhere with interest and compound interest. You even do not need to move it physically with you". The question is, does society still believe it's true?

The effect of lost trust became evident following Lehman Brothers' bankruptcy. Banks were wary of lending to each other (since they could not assess the liquidity

K. Wendt (✉)
Responsible Investment Banking, Groebenzell, Germany
e-mail: info@responsible-investmentbanking.com

© Springer International Publishing Switzerland 2015
K. Wendt (ed.), *Responsible Investment Banking*, CSR, Sustainability, Ethics & Governance, DOI 10.1007/978-3-319-10311-2_1

1

of their counterparties), and clients became nervous about their savings. Despite all the bailout funds, emergency parachutes and political declarations that savings are guaranteed by governments and states, what remains today is a huge loss in trust. The consequential damage of the Lehman case was more than 100 banks filing bankruptcy, and the indirect effects of the creation of bailout programmes, state guarantees and solvency crisis of states have not yet been counted.

Big banks such as Citibank and Merrill Lynch had to digest major subprime losses. This has not just been the failure of risk management systems, but market failure on a range of issues and, finally, the failure of the homo oeconomicus model. The melody of the shareholders value model on global markets came to an abrupt end. Shareholders value—the main song—we've heard over the past years is a concept that aims to address the principal-agent problem. The theory posits that information asymmetry between the agent (the management of a company) and the principles—the shareholders—needs to be reduced, because shareholders do not know where the money is invested by the company. Their ultimate litmus test is financial performance. Is the financial performance in line with shareholder value expectations? Does the company provide more value increase than the shareholder could achieve elsewhere?

Milton Friedman, father of this idea, wrote that any business executives who pursued a goal other than making money were "unwitting puppets of the intellectual forces that have been undermining the basis of a free society these past decades". They were guilty of "analytical looseness and lack of rigor", and he stipulated that a corporate executive who devotes any money for any general social interest would "be spending someone else's money... Insofar as his actions in accord with his 'social responsibility' reduce returns to stockholders, he is spending their money". It may be that environmental and social issues have been argued over and categorised under the business case for sustainability in order to address Friedman's concerns. The business case for sustainability tries to show how the business model is enhanced by taking environmental and social considerations on board and helps making companies more resilient.

The financial crisis has now proved that markets are not always information efficient, that market failure may be a by-product of lost trust that has manifested itself during crisis by malfunction of the interbank market and lending running dry. In addition, it has shown that the principal-agent problem does not exist solely between shareholders and management but has other layers in banking—first, clients as fund providers do have the same principal-agent problem and may have quite different needs and expectations than shareholders about what should be done with the money they provide to their banks for custody. Serving these two very different principals at the same time can be like riding a horse from opposite sides. It is often argued that this should not be a fundamental conflict, because banks have the possibility to operate with Chinese walls, much the same as other institutions. But this has not hold true in a crisis. Not only have there been spillover effects from the mortgage subprime crisis affecting all kinds of business but likewise overarching topics such as rainforest destruction, human rights and soft commodity speculation cannot be solved by the application of Chinese walls. Today, some years after Lehman, let's examine recent events. A number of CEOs of big institutions have been forced to resign taking responsibility for Libor, Euribor and other kinds of manipulation, because of lack of duty of care, lack of best practice due diligence (for instance, for embargo checks) or insufficient risk management. An increasing number of bank clients are filing grievances with their institutions and campaigning to migrate their deposits to more responsible and sustainable banks. The outmigration of funds could become the next big thing, if banks cannot demonstrate the responsible use of funds.

Likewise, banks are now punished for not having executed the required strategic foresight on eco-social aspects. For example, civil society is requiring World Bank finally to implement human rights into their due diligence framework. The "From Mainstreet to Wall Street" study published by Bank Track details the illegal destruction of rain forest, and in the "migrate your bank account" campaigns, civil society asks customers to move their accounts to more sustainable and responsible banks that do not support or engage in food (soft commodity) speculation, for instance. As this book is being written, EU negotiators struck a deal to outline new regulations that would cap trading of the commodity derivatives blamed for driving up food prices. Under the new rules, speculation on financial products linked to what people eat, such as wheat, corn, soybean and sugar, would be limited. In the view of the European Commission, the rules on agricultural derivatives would "contribute to orderly pricing and prevent market abuse, thus curbing speculation on commodities and the disastrous impacts it can have on the world's poorest populations". At the same time, some commercial banks stress that research from Oxfam and Foodwatch on food speculation may have been loose. The debate remains controversial, and some institutions are exiting soft commodity speculation.

1.2 The Need for Strategic Foresight and the Ushering of the Anthropocene

Despite the struggle, post-Lehmann with nonperforming loans, increased regulation, declining trust, liquidity crunch, market failure and recent scandals, there is simultaneously a compelling need for strategic foresight in investment, asset management and international investment banking. At the same time, banks are asked to increase transparency and accountability, in a business so far driven by confidentiality. Creation of profit per se will not support the current banking model forever.

There are tough challenges ahead for society, and banks and the entire financial industry can play a fundamental role in helping to solve them, such as achieving the target of limiting global warming to maximum 2 %, minimising climate adaptation risk for society and in finance, respecting human rights in business throughout the entire value chain and—last but not least—helping redefine value chains and focusing on positive impact creation for communities and the climate through investment and finance and thus be of service to society and environment while ushering in the new era of mankind. Living in what geologist call the Anthropocene, an era in which the population of the global village is forecasted to increase from 2.5 to 9.5 billion within just 100 years (from base year 1950 to 2050) combined with climate change, may emerge as the most compelling challenge. This provokes new ways of living and raises important questions such as access to fresh water for everyone, access to nutrition, food and other ecosystems services while at the same time as using no more of the planet's resources than are available.

Since banks finance the economy, they can take a stance and help focus on positive impact investment and finance to address the challenges. We are already using ecosystems resources faster than they regenerate. According to World Wildlife Fund (WWF), we use finite resources as if we had one-and-a-half planets to hand, meaning we would need two planets by 2030 and three by 2050 to cover our needs of water, food and electricity if we do leave the living and business mode unaltered. *The Economist* recently ran the cover story, *"Welcome to the anthropocene—geology's new age"*, *an age* characterised by increasing population, growing urbanisation, many more demanding and achieving higher standards of living—plus climate change. John Beddington, previously the chief scientific adviser to the UK government, called this combination "the perfect storm". If we were aliens looking in from outside on planet Earth and asking whether this was a place we would invest in, we would see the following pattern: companies making huge profits, so this looks good, but at the same time using many more resources than the planet has to offer. Would you invest in planet Earth?

Climate change continues to be a pressing issue. The developed world needs to take dramatic steps to adjust its means of production and consumption. The mismanagement of public goods such as water, emissions, fisheries and other ecosystems services cannot be allowed to continue. Current value chain management fuels climate change, increases climate adaptation risks and even threatens humanity, writes Heffa Schücking from urgewald in this book in her contribution "Sustainability on planet bank". She depicts the flaws and current inconsistencies between aspirational statements made by financial institutions and reality in finance and investment on the ground. In 2010, nearly 200 nations agreed that global warming must be limited to 2° Celsius to avoid worst case climate change scenarios such as a drop in water availability by 50 % by 2060 in many regions if we continue with current emission trends (according to the turn down the heat report issued by the World Bank). This scenario could lead to large-scale displacement of populations, an increase in epidemic disease, rising sea levels and extreme heat waves, potentially exceeding the assimilation capacity of many societies and natural systems. The reconstruction costs after the 2013 typhoon Haiyan hit the Philippines are estimated to total US $15 billion, according to *The Economist*. The damage attributable to 2005 Hurricane Katrina alone has amounted to more than US $0.1 trillion in 2012. The numbers challenge the insurance models of insurance companies worldwide and provide evidence that climate-friendly markets are needed and conventional value chain management overhauled.

"Are the worlds' financial markets carrying a carbon bubble?" The 2012 Carbon Tracker Initiative's Report asked, and in 2013, the Carbon Tracker followed suit with its report on "wasted capital and stranded assets". Climate change has developed into a risk to nature and humanity and likewise presents a huge risk to the financial community and insurance markets but continues to be overlooked.

While the reaction of policymakers to the challenge appears to be slow, given the short time window left to change course, public banks are moving away from coal finance, while analysts from the largest commercial banks such as Citi, Deutsche Bank, HSBC and Goldman Sachs question the business rationale for further investment in coal.

Finally, there may be the need to add different perspectives to investment and banking that allow for the recreation of trust to fuel long-term success in the investment and banking business. This requires that clients and society will consider financial institutions again as their fiduciaries and agents which requires alignment of interests between the clients of financial institutions, the institutions themselves and the will to create opportunities to transform crisis.

Value chains of production and consumption will have to change and innovative means put forward that the public and private sectors can collectively pursue to foster climate-friendly solutions, products and, above all, climate-friendly markets. Today, accessing finance for climate-friendly projects can be challenging due to the limited track record of these markets and their current emergent state, resulting in limited awareness and discomfort in these markets by the private sector. This book will examine emerging solutions and proposals for addressing these risks including innovative *public–private financial instruments and climate bonds. Amassing experience with these new instruments and with new value chains will help to create a body of knowledge and a track record to make mainstream solutions currently still in the fledgling stages.

While we are discussing the business case for sustainability, reality has already provided us with the sustainability case for business. Business needs a sustainable planet in order to be able to operate long term. A sustainable planet will be dependent on certain characteristics that will also help to stabilise markets: a reduction in social tension over projects, soft commodities and public goods, respect for human rights, labour and wages people can live off, extinguishing harmful child labour and forced labour, functioning ecosystems, climate change resilience and the ability to create eco-efficient solutions.

The Doughty Centre for Corporate Responsibility has identified sustainable development as one of the emerging business benefits. Advantages ultimately derived for business by sustainable development can be defined as meeting the needs of the present without compromising the ability of future generations to meet their own needs. The Doughty Centre illustrates the case of Unilever with its dramatic new strategy: to double its business while reducing its environmental impacts. A convincing example in the financial field is the strategy of the Dutch Development Finance Institution FMO with its *"double the impact, half the footprint"* initiative. Doubling the impact means doubling the positive impact, as the investment, asset management and finance industry can really make a difference in engendering capital flows to projects, companies, regions and societies that maximise positive impacts for the population with minimum resource usage and sound business practices respecting human rights, international labour law and eco-efficiency. Creating and maximising positive impacts through investment and finance, as envisioned in FMO's *Double the impact half the footprint initiative*, can take investors and financiers a long way in international finance and foreign direct investment in a strategic anticipatory manner. It will always need to be combined with sound environmental and social due diligence and risk management practices and good governance to make it work, but at least the focus shifts from risk management to positive impact creation. Creating and maximising positive impacts through investment and finance, applying sound environmental and social risk management practices, developing the required strategic foresight skills and applying sound governance practices are what this book will discuss.

1.3 *Encouraging Signs of Shift in Focus Towards People Orientation*

There are already encouraging signs that the market view is shifting. According to recent information, EBRD is scraping coal finance, US EXIM halting US financing coal abroad, BNP Paribas, Credit Agricole, Barclays, Nordea, Commerzbank, DZ Bank, DekaBank and BayernLB, and LBBW all abandoning speculation of soft commodities based on pressure from investors and non-governmental organisations (NGOs) but likewise due to unfavourable capital requirements for operating trading books. At the same time, international guidelines such as OECD Guidelines for Multinational Enterprises (and the financial sector) are gaining momentum and providing sharper teeth. Voluntary initiatives on human rights such as the Thun Group emerge. Models for measuring the positive handprint in green house gas (GHG) savings instead of only the negative GHG financed emissions footprint come into awareness and are described here by Sebastian Philipps, Hendrik Ohlsen and Christina Raab in "the positive handprint". Development of products based on preservation of ecosystems services allows the climate to emerge. The role investment banks and private investment can play in fostering ecosystems conservation and sustaining innovation is depicted by Conservation International providing a bunch of examples, schemes and products. Katharina Serafimova and Thomas Vellacott from WWF posit in "prepared for the future" that banks play a pivotal role in addressing global issues like creating a low carbon economy and actively create business opportunities based on the current environmental and social challenges. Dustin Neumeyer posits in this book in his contribution, "Why not? Sustainable finance as a question of mindset. A plea for a confident sustainable business strategy", that sustainability in finance, including fundamental changes to business as usual and touching on alleged taboos, can and should be much more easily and effectively achievable than is generally accepted. The question of mindset is closely intertwined with the question of culture, a component which goes much deeper than any regulation and permeates the DNA of investment and banking organisations. At least it is encouraging that regulators and in some countries parliament take a closer look into building blocks of organisational identity and value congruence that then shape organisational culture and the antecedents of products, procedures and performance.

Human rights are also on every agenda. We witnessed an astonishing and successful complaints procedures against Norges Bank Investment Management (NBIM), trustee of the Norwegian pension fund by the Norwegian National Contact Point (NCP). Despite NBIM being one of the first signatories to the UN Principles for Responsible Investment was accused for investing in Korean steel company POSCO in spite of human rights violations. On 27 May 2013, the Norwegian NCP published its final statement, concluding that NBIM violated the OECD Guidelines by (1) refusing to cooperate with the NCP and (2) by lacking a strategy to identify and address human rights impacts.

This ruling has been a wake-up call for the financial industry. A number of authors take up the ball on human rights, and we will discuss those issues more detail in the Human Rights section.

A Broader View on Social Issues Is Taken by the ISO 26000 Standard John Hanks guides us through the ISO 26 000 standard, explaining the reason for its creation, guiding us through all stages from inception, development and expansion explaining its opportunities and weaknesses while reviewing its global role in promoting social responsibility.

1.4 The World Is Becoming Multipolar

At the same time, we see another megatrend. The world is becoming multipolar. CEO of FMO Nanno Kleiterp writes in this book: Economic activity and political power are shifting from the West to the East and the South, creating a multipolar world. The world where the rich countries dictate which values are the norm and put conditions on trade and aid is over. Equality and reciprocity will be key in relations between nations. For example, Turkey and Mexico may soon become high-income OECD countries, while currently low-income countries such as Nigeria and Vietnam are expected to be in the G20 by 2050. We have added a regional perspective therefore to Responsible Investment Banking and asset management. Alok Dayal and Ashok Emani share a regional perspective on "Adopting EP (Equator Principles) in India: challenges and recommendations for future EP outreach". The contribution nicely dovetails with a number of other contributions dealing with the Equator Principles. There is an entire section on Equator Principles, I herewith refer the reader to. Alexey Akulov explains in his contribution "Implementing ESG (Environmental, Social Governance) in the financial sector in Russia: The journey towards better sustainability" implementation progress made in Russia. Risk Management and governance are repeated themes here, and its proliferation to other regions of the world is key in order to amass and share experience and create a global level playing field on good governance in the financial industry. In Turkey emerging practice in the field of environmental and social risk management is presented by Prof. Dr. Cem B Avcı and Dr. Işıl Gültekin in their contribution on "environmental and social risk management in emerging economies: An analysis of Turkish financial institution practices". Being one of the fastest growing economies in the world and sitting at the interface between Europe and Asia, Turkey has a key ambassador role in mingling concepts from the west and the east.

Stakeholder engagement is another emerging topic, and it can help a lot in making difficult projects socially acceptable. Alicia de la Cruz provides us of an example of stakeholder engagement in Peru in her contribution "stakeholder engagement model: Making ecotourism work in Peru's protected areas" and thus adds experience gained in South America to this book. Prof. Olav Weber and Dr. Haiying Lin present the progress in China with regard to accountability and responsibility in "CSR reporting and its implication for socially responsible investment in China".

1.4.1   New Value Chains and Products Focusing on Positive Impacts

The private sector around the world is now able to step up, playing a key role in wealth creation but also in redefining value chains and creating friendly markets for climate, ecosystems services and social needs through the creation of new products. The need for integration of sustainability and productivity increases will further the creation of different value chains, and private companies will need to excel in having access to the very first producers in these value chains and control the sustainability of their value chains to enable survival in the long term. We should see more development cooperation funds improving sustainability and effectiveness deep within the value chain and likewise increased engagement and investment by private equity players redefining value chains and creating long-standing positive impacts that will outlive the tenor of the investment. The investment industry will either follow suit or will run the risk of being crowded out by more sustainable investors and financers.

The council of the Emerging Markets Private Equity Association (EMPEA) writes in this book: "Recognizing the growing importance of impact investing, EMPEA established an Impact Investment council in 2013 to play a leading role in professionalizing and scaling the industry, focusing specifically on market-based solutions for major global social and environmental challenges. In the past 10 years, the asset class (emerging market private equity) has generated attractive returns outperforming benchmarks for public securities investments, such as the S&P 500".

They present examples for the rationale of newly defined value chains and demonstrate how these equity investments or ventures have produced new positive impacts. Société Generale, represented by Denis Childs, shares a new emerging approach of positive impact finance, an endeavour the bank has embarked on with other French banks, industrial companies, the insurance sector, civil society and the government to create and finance sustainable innovation.

Emerging trends such as positive impact investment and finance and the creation of new, climate-friendly, eco-efficient markets and new value chains by some market players will either inspire the huge multinational banks at global scale to redefine their business models and help structure and finance new products that encourage new value chains or other financial players will pick up the ball and create the financial models of the future, which, for conventional banks, may mean, they slip down the food chain over time if they do not follow suit.

1.5 Multinational Banks Being Pulled into the Role of a Co-regulator in Many Regards

Multinational banks have increasingly fallen into the role of a co-regulator even if they do not intend to do so. One reason is their leverage.

The policies and standards of core good governance values adopted, increasingly represent quasi-legal requirements and, in some countries, soft law standards such as the Equator Principles, even shape legal requirements. This organic movement towards the emergence of a universally accepted governance standard, applicable to both private and public sector at a global level, outperforming the strategic speed of policymakers in adopting and creating such a global standard, has been described in recent literature as "global administrative law". "As regards convergence, the concept of global administrative law addresses the rapidly changing realities of transnational regulation, which increasingly involves industry self-regulation, hybrid forms of private–private and public–private regulations, network governance by state officials and governance by intergovernmental organisations with direct and indirect regulatory power", according to Owen Mcintyre in "development banking ESG policies and the normativisation of good governance standards".

1.6 Using the Power of Transformation

Because multinational banks and investors have been very effective in creating global administrative law, it is assumed they can be just as effective in going beyond GDP and create positive impacts through investment and finance. This will entail redefining value chains and creating climate-friendly and eco-efficient markets that respect human rights. Contributions that demonstrate the leverage of the multinational institutions come from Dariusz Prasek, who describes how EBRD is maximising its influence and impacts on both clients and financial institutions in

"EBRD environmental and social governance standards and their impact on the market".

Debbie Cousins, also from EBRD, describes in "implementing environmental and social risk management on the ground—interfaces between clients, investment banks, multilaterals, consultants and contractors" how ESG is implemented on the lending level within the companies financed and what challenges it brings about.

The list of challenges and opportunities continues at length and so do emerging new concepts of socially and environmentally friendly investment and finance. There is much ahead, and strategic foresight and thought leadership, stakeholder engagement and cooperation will be necessary, to master and turn challenges into opportunities for good sustainable business.

There have been many recent scandals relating to investment, investment banking and asset management. But this does not mean that the industry has become worse. The reason many more scandals are now discovered is probably because the regulatory authorities, investors, stakeholders and even clients now take a closer look post-crisis. In particular, NGOs are scrutinising the net and, over the past years, have published information on human rights violations, rainforest destruction, disconnects between aspirational statements and commitments made by banks and investors. While it appears that the investment and investment banking community is under siege and trust vanished, this creates the chance for investors and investment banks to turn this around, grow their business resilience and create a robust strategic model of sustainable finance, investment and asset management. It is the intent to witness the emergence of those solution creation approaches here, document them as good practice and engender more thought leadership, discussion and more mainstreaming of those approaches.

1.7 Adding Use of Funds to the Investment Triangulum: Investment Can Be Fun Rather than Unpleasant Necessity

It may likewise be a positive consequence of the banking crisis that we are now seeing more active stakeholders, aware regulatory bodies and the emergence of a new theme for financing and investment. Rather than letting the investment and finance community float on in the magic triangulum of risk, liquidity and return, a new component needs to be added: the component of usage of funds. Future investment banking, fund flow and asset management will need to turn more rectangular, considering, risk, return, liquidity and use of funds. This is no less and no more than society and fund givers (including private banking clients) regaining power and taking responsibility for the use of their funds. We can regard it as a useful redefinition of the principal-agent problem, which has been around for some time in the investment industry. The time of "give me your money, live and enjoy, we will take care of the details" is over. The simultaneous focus on shareholders and clients, both adopting the principal role currently, creates dilemmas in banking, as the interests for those two groups greatly diverge, particularly to the extent shareholders are unwilling to include environmental and social considerations—part of the use of funds component—in the equation. To the extent that clients and fund givers require sustainable use of their funds including consideration of environment and social components, there is no "alignment of interest" between clients, fund managers and shareholders and perhaps even not a robust interpretation of fiduciary duties.

It may be an illusion simply to see the shareholders as principles; banks also take the role of agent in their dealings with their customers. Long term, the financial industry will need to satisfy their customers. Financial Institutions losing their customer base may have less access to funds, liquidity and profit potential. Customers are struggling with the same information asymmetry as shareholders. Most of them however will not only expect their institution to maximise profit but likewise to be of service to society in solving global challenges. Evidence for this is provided by the genesis of the Equator Principles, which have been created in response to loss of customer funds and a grudging public. Bridging divergent views between shareholders and clients leads to the need for creating alignment of interest along the whole value chain and in first place between customers and shareholders.

The use of a funds component in contrast to liquidity, risk and return, however, does not explicitly form part of the capital asset pricing model (CAPM) and value-at-risk calculations mostly used, but it is a real component influencing the value of a company—and even of a whole industry. In "More fun at lower risk", Prof. Henry Schäfer and Christian Hertrich suggest that SRI assets should form part of the investment strategies of each and every fund. Choosing SRI assets can be regarded as a way of adding the use of funds component to the investment triangulum at least for a part of the portfolio.

The good news is that portfolios adding SRI assets outperform traditional investment allocation strategies according to research undertaken by them in their contribution "More fun with lower risk—New Opportunities for PRI-Related Asset Management of German Pension Insurance Funds". They demonstrate "that Social Responsible (SRI) portfolios outperform in all contemplated investment scenarios, independently of the underlying investment strategy" and therefore should form part of the investment strategies of any fund. Choosing SRI assets can be regarded as a way of increasing fun with investment as performance increase and likewise the benefit for the planet, making investment more enjoyable. A new generation of investors may have more fun in creating and buying positive impact funds and do something good with money even in low or no interest scenarios rather than looking solely at stock exchange charts and buy and sell in milliseconds leaving a lot of nervousness with investors. The more SRI products will be created, the better the strategy may work, as it will become mainstream rather than marginalised. The question to be answered will be how much SRI will be effectively available on the market without diluting the SRI criteria. This leads us directly to the necessity of stakeholder engagement and cooperation with large companies in investment and banking and the creation of new engagement and sustainable entrepreneurship platforms to allow a pipeline for positive impact investment and finance large enough to make money investment enjoyable for clients both in terms of performance as of good consciousness.

1.8 Information-Efficient Markets Put Up for Question

Interesting phenomena in this regard are micro-structures in the market. Whereas conventional portfolio managers work with market volatility and share price movements in comparison to the movement of indices, in order to define risk, sustainable portfolio managers use exclusion criteria according to their environmental, social and governance (ESG) due diligence. Based on their ESG due diligence, they sell or buy certain stocks. Traditional portfolio managers using the CAPM approach label investment and disinvestment on exclusion factors as a form of "noise trading". The sustainable portfolio managers are noise in their system, and it will be interesting to see what happens when sustainable portfolio management gets mainstream and noise traders become the rule rather than the exception. How much noise trading will the market digest? Will sustainable portfolios create a new market segment? How much responsible investment opportunities will be available on the market? Will such a market segment be sourced by enough liquidity? Will we see a clear segregation of trading markets while at the same time we see a combination model in asset management, where asset managers are complementing their portfolios with SRI investments?

A first and direct effect of different approaches between sustainable portfolio managers and conventional portfolio managers is that the exclusion list portfolio managers use may have the opposite effect than intended. While sustainable portfolio managers sell shares on certain exclusion criteria for ESG reasons, this may create a direct effect for conventional fund managers: they buy the shares because, according to the CAPM, the shares seem undervalued, so conventional traders will see them as under priced. This leads to the interesting question of whether share prices accurately reflect the company value. Sustainability managers selling shares heavily invested in coal—do they just correctly interpret the carbon bubble? If so, will their behaviour in the short-term create windfall benefits for conventional portfolio managers, because "noise traders" enable conventional portfolio managers to buy carbon-loaded shares at a discount?

Whether or not information-efficient markets exist, as assumed by the Capital Asset Pricing Model, has been brought into question by research undertaken by Tri Vi Dang. In Information Acquisition, Noise Trading, and Speculation in Double Auction Markets, he concludes that:

"There is a large set of parameter values where in any equilibrium with positive volume of trade the traders play mixed strategies and ex ante identically informed, rational traders evolve endogenously to noise traders, speculators, and defensive traders. Because of defensive trading the allocation is inefficient, i.e. not all gains from trade are realized.

Because of endogenous noise trading the price is not fully revealing of the traders aggregate information".

1.9 The Death of Distance, Business Context Factors and a New Paradigm: The Rectangle of Investment and Finance

With the penetration of the Internet across the globe, information is one mouse-click away. Misconduct, discrepancies between commitments and actions quickly become apparent, with a skilled information-filtering community behind it, requiring any company, but in particular investment banks and investors, strategically to rethink their business models as they are under immediate and permanent scrutiny from stakeholders, some of them powerful enough to influence the profitability of their investments and also their reputation and model of operation.

These external groups, combined with changing political and regulatory frameworks, can provide banks and investors with a very different matrix of context factors to their investments and lending within a very short time period. One could argue that this could lead investment banks to even more short-termism to get rid of the risks that context factors may pose, but this could be short-sighted rather than foresight, because with increased short-termism, the cross-selling opportunities and customer retention and loyalty vanish. In addition short-termism and risk avoidance by short turn over periods do not make a financial institution or investor immune to reputation damage. This is in particular true since many manipulation cases (of interest rates or currencies) have demonstrated reputation damage is as relevant for short-term business as for long-term business. Short-termism cannot help avoid reputation risk, whereas robust governance combined with a culture embracing values that are shared with society can.

In advisory and underwriting as well as in liquidity management and rate fixing, negative impacts can still be traced back to institution in an age where information travels around the world on a mouse-click and confidentiality is no insurance against revelation in the global village. While it can always be argued that not using environmental and social foresight in short-term business is rational, where the risk is passed on quickly or immediately, such a strategy does not make an institution immune from reputation risk, whereas consistent application of best practice environmental and social considerations and governance does.

The degree of interconnectedness and cross-links between context factors will provide more complex decision situations, and it will be important to understand the key context factors that can make or break a deal or even an entire institution.

However that logic may not be applicable to unregulated parts of the shadow banking system that may not care a lot about reputation. They target a different group of customers than investment funds and multinational banks that have to unify investment banking and commercial banking under one roof top.

Coincidently with the death of distance, the role of fiduciary agreements and fiduciary duties of investors is currently redefined and now focusing more on investors' responsibility towards society and their fundamental ethical norms, as the case of Norges Bank Investment Management (NBIM) proves. This has the potential to be a game changer in the discussion of the principal-agent problem, as fiduciary duties force investment banking and investment funds to take into account client interests and environment and human rights irrespective of shareholder value. Prof. Barnim Jeschke provides a model here for identifying and calculating the risks and impacts that context factors pose to investment and finance in monetary terms in his contribution "managing assets in a complex environment: an innovative approach to sustainable decision-making".

The investment triangulum can now be enriched by the use of funds component and communicated to clients. The financial industry has fiduciary duties when investing client money. This entails the due application of environmental and social governance when investing clients' money. Fiduciary duties are particularly important for custodians such as pension funds. In the book, Christine Berry leads us through the ESG requirements custodians need to apply to fully cover their fiduciary duties on financial, social and environmental performance in her contribution "fiduciary duty and responsible investment: An overview".

1.9.1 The Genesis of the Equator Principles and Their Impact on the Market

As already mentioned, clients can migrate their funds to more responsible institutions if they do not agree with the use of funds by their institution and can remind banks by voting with their feet that they play the role of a principal, too. The concept of the all-powerful customer is nothing new. According to Peter Drucker "there is only one valid definition of business purpose—to create a customer". Financial institutions therefore are well advised to put their customer first and listen to their requirements. At the same time, clients need to be vocal on what they consider acceptable in terms of environmental and social performance. In a time, where interbank market-based lending covers only a small part of liquidity used in lending and customer deposits are a major source of funding, clients need to use their responsibility towards society when investing their money, and banks need to align their interests to the responsible customer.

A well-known example of outmigration of funds because of unsustainable international finance and the effects it can have on financial institutions was the "Cut your Card" campaign against a major US financial institution back in 2002, which resulted in boxes of cut-up credit cards being sent to the chairman of the bank. Civil society and Rainforest Action Network (RAN) had been criticising the bank for destroying the rainforest. In 2003, RAN began a television campaign showing clips of destruction, overlaid with the question, "do you know where your money is currently?" Celebrities cutting up their credit cards requested the audience to do the same. It was a very effective campaign and an important inflection point.

In 2003, other banks had reached similar tipping point with civil society campaigns. A groundling public disagreeing as to where banks were investing their customer's money and clients worrying about their money was the catalyst that forced banks to create the first framework on managing environmental and social risk in project finance and beyond—the Equator Principles. The EPs are still the most effective and internationally accepted voluntary framework for managing environmental and social risk in project lending and the basis on which most instruments for management of nontechnical risks have been created in international lending. Herman Mulder, one of the architects of the Equator Principles, shares his journey to sustainability and the inflection points he encountered along his way in banking in his contribution "tipping points: Learning from pain".

Reed Hoppman takes us through the development phases of ESG standards and the rise of the Equator Principles, in his interview "Implementing International Good Practice Standards: pragmatism versus philosophy".

In the interview with Elena Amirkhanova and Rai Vogelsberger, the newly adjusted IFC Performance Standards underlying the Equator Principles are discussed with a focus on the cross-cutting issues in "ERM on IFC Performance Standards". The IFC, International Finance Corporation, is a subsidiary of the World Bank dealing with the private sector. The IFC Performance Standards have been created in 2006 together with the environmental and social policy and are updated from time to time.

Many of the contributions to *Responsible Investment Banking* deal with the Equator Principles, and most of the contributions dealing with risk management or co-regulation also touch on them. Several authors focus on the further development of the EPs and their role as a reference framework and as a best practice example that voluntary commitments and frameworks do work, if designed appropriately.

Suellen Lazarus, responsible for the strategic review of the Equator Principles, shares the strategic route the Equator Principles have undertaken in "the Equator Principles: Retaining the gold standard. A strategic vision at 10 years".

Manuel Wörsdörfer provides a critical review on them, proposing further changes to enhance their impact in "10 years Equator Principles: A critical appraisal".

Ariel Meyerstein shows in his research "Are the Equator Principles greenwash or game changers? Effectiveness, transparency and future challenges?", the impact the Equator Principles have had on project finance and the development opportunities they do provide for the financial industry. Whereas project finance and project-related corporate loans do form only a small portion of investment banking, they carry considerable environmental and social risk. In addition, the aggregate global volume in project finance would rank No. 15 in gross domestic product (GDP) if project finance was a state.

However, a shortcoming of the Equator Principles that is often emphasised is their reach. This applies to their scope as well as to their predominantly Western membership. The contribution from Credit Agricole, represented by Eric Cochard, "Translating standards into successful implementation: sector policies and Equator

Principles", demonstrates that financial institutions are going beyond the reach of Project Finance. Credit Agricole has used the Equator Principles as a cornerstone to develop wider ESG policies that cover their whole range of financing activities in controversial or risky sectors, and not just the project-related section. In addition, the scope and reach of the Equator Principles have recently been enlarged by extending their scope and by attracting institutions from different areas of the world, like India and Russia.

1.9.2   Investors: The New Drivers of Sustainable Development and the Principles for Responsible Investment

One thing being a prerequisite in changing paradigm and therefore in changing markets is leverage. Many financial institutions and investors as well as companies use CSR, but it is not at the core of their business activities and many do not put it at the core of their strategies. This may become increasingly dangerous, because it is at the edge of becoming a key success factors. While the term CSR is a "burned" term for many and put in equivalence with green wash or good communication, the triple bottom line, governance, transparency and reporting are attracting more focus from potential institutional investors. This book wants to show that CSR has to be redefined and re-organised in order to help risk management, people orientation and growth opportunities. Examples follow here in the book on responsible investment banking.

Investors increasingly ask for transparency and evidence of integration of environmental and social performance combined with good governance (ESG) into the entire value chain of company operations. In 2013, a group of financial investors responsible for a portfolio of US $3.3 trillion urged 1,900 companies from 44 countries to join the United Nations Global Compact and to comply with the 10 principles. United Nations Global Compact, or UNGC, is a United Nations initiative to encourage businesses worldwide to adopt sustainable and socially responsible policies and to report on their implementation. The Global Compact is a principle-based framework for businesses, stating ten principles in the areas of human rights, labour, the environment and anti-corruption.

Investors are now urged to taking up the topics of climate change biodiversity, ecosystems services and access to drinking water with the newly adjusted OECD Guidelines for Multinational Companies.

The Carbon Disclosure Project, for instance, has a membership of more than 700 members, with funds under custody of more than US $87 trillion. They require companies to engage for the climate, ecosystems services and biodiversity. They may yet be the most potent new player on the sustainability block, with the power and leverage to change the game.

They can count on the support of sustainability rating agencies providing sustainability ratings. They often play the role of an enforcement agent by scrutinising sustainability aspirations of companies and financial institutions comparing them to reality on the ground.

They have created a lot more transparency in the field of sustainability and scrutinise to what extent commitments made by companies and financial institutions, for instance, under Soft Law Standards, the Equator Principles or the Principles for Responsible Investment are integrated into the entire value chain.

More than 1,200 institutional investors, asset managers and financial institutions have committed themselves by recognising the Principles for Responsible Investment (PRI) to integrate sustainability criteria into their investment. Together they manage more than US$30 trillion, representing a share of around 45 % of global investments. A success story, then? Rolf Häßler and Till Hendrik Jung from reputable research companies give an overview of the aims and development of the PRI, introduce the contents of the six principles and highlight the opportunities and risks of signing the PRI for investors and asset managers. The updating of the PRI requires—according to the authors—a dual strategy: outreach and enlarging the membership on one hand and, at the same time, going deeper, focusing on improving the quality of implementation of the PRI by the signatories

Gavin Duke, Investment Manager of Aloe Private Equity, writes here: "conventional wisdom states that ESG is a necessary cost centre that reduces reputation risk, whereas this chapter introduces ESG as a framework for profit creation and strategic direction". His contribution illustrates how ESG due diligence can add value to investors throughout the investment process, from selection to exit, for example, in an IPO (independent public offering) get a better sales price. His chapter "Sustainable Private Equity investments and ESG Due Diligence Frameworks" showcases how detailed ESG adds value to portfolio companies throughout the investment process from selection and structuring, to portfolio management and exit.

1.10 Consequences for Trust and the Role of Culture

There still is a massive discrepancy between the expectations from society, regulators and sustainability rating agencies towards banks on one hand and internal top-line requirements on the other hand. This does have consequences for the analysis of banking culture—since culture deals with external adaptation to market environment and internal integration. Edgar Schein has defined culture as the result of a group's accumulated learning. It is a pattern of shared basic assumptions and value orientations that a team, group or organisation has invented and learnt in order to master the dilemma of external adaptation to its market environment and internal integration to enable daily functioning and alignment, which has worked well enough to be considered valid and be passed on to new members as the correct way to think and feel in relation to this dilemma.

The role of banking culture has been thoroughly scrutinised in the recent past by regulators and governments. Responsible Investment Banking draws on current research on banking culture with a contribution from Cynthia Williams and John Conley "The Social Reform of Banking".

Williams and Conley map out the current culture of banking, paint a compelling picture of current shortcomings and problems and offer good practice examples and solutions. Their stance is that the current culture and its context factors do not support sustainable business development. Their research draws on recent reports collected by governments following the recent scandals in investment banking. They continue by proposing reforms in banking culture not only through regulation but also by instilling commitment over compliance and voluntary cooperation through international soft law as a co-regulation factor. Using the Equator Principles as an example, they demonstrate how voluntary frameworks do contribute to cultural change in banking.

Experiencing post-crisis seems to imply that banking culture is a strong element in enhancing or decreasing trust inside and outside of the institution. Likewise it seems to be a strong element even in fast-growing emerging economies. Heidrun Kopp describes the intercultural elements of banking in the fast-growing Eastern European countries and the impact of culture and intercultural communication on the take up of sustainability in her contribution "Corporate Social Responsibility in modern Central and Eastern Europe".

1.11   Homo Oeconomicus: An Illusion?

The homo oeconomicus model has been questioned recently by modern neuro-physiologists and neuro-economists. For example Akerlof and Shiller posit that the concept of the rational homo oeconomicus is outdated and that non-economic motives such as avoidance of conflict and fairness do influence the behaviour of market players even beyond the avoidance of the so-called nontechnical risks (how environmental and social considerations are often labelled). A good example again may be the banking crisis kicked off by the Lehman insolvency, illustrating how much psychology is driving decisions in the market and providing evidence of the crucial role of trust. Trust has various layers as Mark Kramer has described in Trust in Organisations. Trust can be a rational choice to avoid transaction costs and as such very often is used in form of deterrence based trust (if you fail to service my trust, I will not trust you any longer). At the same time, trust can be competence based or identity based. Definitely the higher elements of trust like competence and identity-based trust have vanished in investment and banking as many market players will not identify with the model of banking and investment, with the players in the industry and the industry as such any longer and a positive commonly shared vision with society is missing. A new engagement with society and the huge challenges will be required to re-establish identity-based trust, which can only emerge when investment and banking align interest with the interests of a prospering society. Likewise competence-based trust may have vanished post-Lehman, and a more transparent approach including much more elements of stakeholder engagement will be required to re-establish the perception of competence in investment and banking again including a new culture and banking DNA. One element in re-establishing trust could be a new positive vision of investment and banking focusing on positive impacts in cooperation with society, shifting the focus from risk management to people orientation.

1.12   The Acknowledgement of Human Rights as a Fundamental Inalienable Right Rather than a Social Risk Issue in Investment and Banking

Human rights are an important cross-cutting issue in investment and banking as they touch on a number of issues business normally comes across in daily operations. The contributors focus on it not only from a risk management perspective but mainly from a people perspective. Human rights are not alone about the impact investments and projects have on communities, but also on the labour market, and living wages. Steve Gibbons brings his expertise in the topic of international labour law laid down in the International Labour Law Organization's standards (ILO standards) and the UN Guiding Principles of Business and Human Rights to this book in his contribution "Hard labour: workplace standards and the financial sector". The contribution deals with the four core labour standards: no harmful child labour, no forced labour, freedom of association, non-discrimination and gender equality as well as with the new instruments of Human Rights Impact Assessments. The topic of human rights is likewise in the focus of the EU. As we issue the book, the EU is discussing directions and rules for reporting nontechnical risks, as environmental and social issues are often known in their draft non-financial disclosure directive. However, it is not enough to observe human rights if they pose a risk to finance.

Prof. Christine Kaufmann, who has advised the Thun Group of Banks, writes here in her contribution "Respecting Human Rights in Investment Banking—A Change in Paradigm" that human rights have to be respected for their own sake. In this people-oriented focus, "human rights are not only considered if their breach poses a risk to investors and banks but for their own sake—as the inalienable right of every human being".

The UN Guiding Principles on Business and Human Rights have initiated that shift in focus from risk management to inalienable right. The British government supports the shift in focus. It plans, as part of its action plan for implementing the UN Guiding Principles for Human Rights in Business to require companies to report on their implementation of a human rights policy, requesting them to "be transparent about policies, activities and impacts and report on human rights issues and risks as appropriate as part of their annual reports".

Investment banks, fund managers and equity investors would be well advised to take the issue into account and make human rights due diligence part of their investment equation.

In strengthening the "S" in ESG: What new developments in human rights and business bring to the table for investors", Margaret Wachenfeld writes "Investor initiatives such as the UN-supported Principles for Responsible Investment and the International Corporate Governance Network are evidence of the growing consideration of a broader range of non-financial factors in investment choices. However, the "s" (social) factor has tended to lag behind the increasingly systematic and formalised approaches to environmental and corporate governance issues, partly due to a perceived lack of clarity and standards". The UN Guiding Principles now provide a new internationally accepted framework to address human rights. Investors and financial institutions now possess a shared, consistent framework to benchmark and evaluate company performance and hold companies accountable.

UBS, the driving force behind the Thun Group of Banks, shares its experience of integrating human rights due diligence in the core activities of a bank. In "UBS and the integration of human rights due diligence under the United Nations (UN) Protect, Respect and Remedy Framework for Business and Human Rights", Liselotte Arni, Christian Leitz, Alexander Seidler and Yan Kermodi from UBS describe the implementation process of the statement by the Thun Group of Banks within UBS.

1.13 From Shareholder Value to Stakeholder Value

In contrast to the principal-agent theory that defines only the shareholders as principals, the stakeholder theory developed first by Edward Freeman in 1984 includes all interest groups affected by the operations of a company. He writes on his website early 2014:

> "Every business creates, and sometimes destroys, value for customers, suppliers, employees, communities and financiers. The idea that business is about maximising profits for shareholders doesn't work very well, as the recent global financial crisis has taught us. The twenty-first century is one of "Managing for Stakeholders". The job of executives is to create as much value as possible for stakeholders without resorting to trade-offs. Great companies endure because they manage to get stakeholder interests aligned in the same direction."

Stakeholders are not only those interested groups that are affected but also those who affect the business operations of a company themselves, such as regulators, trade unions, governments and non-governmental organisations (NGOs) often referred to here as civil society. At the International Bankers Forum in Frankfurt on 28 February 2013, Rainer Neske, member of the Board of Deutsche Bank, declared: "There is a massive discrepancy between the expectations towards banks and the public perception of banks. We need to leave our towers, go out and conduct stakeholder dialogue at eye level".

1.14   Stakeholder Engagement and Shared Values

Albert Einstein's once noted that his definition of "insanity is doing the same thing over and over again and expecting different results". Continuing with old models such as disclosure to stakeholders and using the communications department to manage communications may not be enough to engender new trust and find new solutions to old problems in investment and banking. Missing out on the opportunities of stakeholder engagement and the concept of shared values would leave the investment banks in old paradigms.

Missing out on stakeholder engagement in banking is like running a bank without an investor relations department; many advisors on stakeholder engagement agree like Heike Leitschuh and Susanne Bergius. Stakeholder engagement is not just the disclosure of actions to stakeholders nor just an instrument to be used to de-escalate conflict after it has occurred. It should be a permanent, outcome-oriented engagement process that makes full use of the strategic elements to allow for a new, broader-style risk analysis and better decision quality that develop robust and resilient stakeholder relations, which can be used to identify weak signals for emerging risks and opportunities and be incorporated as a core tool to recreate trust.

A good stakeholder dialogue ultimately aims to overcome confrontation and disclosure states and enable consultation, followed by cooperation and finally partnership. A number of contributions deal with stakeholder engagement. Elizabeth van Zyl describes the benefits of stakeholder engagement from a project risk management perspective and Alicia de la Cruz from a benefit creation perspective. Both contributions demonstrate its value and illustrate how stakeholder engagement can be a game changer for a company, as well as informing strategic decision-making.

The concept of aligning stakeholder interest with company interests as far as possible has also been reinvigorated by a publication by Porter, the guru on strategic positioning, and Kramer, the leading expert in researching trust in organisations in the *Harvard Business Review* in 2011, combining the concept of stakeholder engagement with going beyond financing gross domestic product and enabling reconnect company success with social progress. They write:

> "The capitalist system is under siege. In recent years business increasingly has been viewed as a major cause of social, environmental, and economic problems. Companies are widely perceived to be prospering at the expense of the broader community.... This diminished trust in business leads political leaders to set policies that undermine competitiveness and sap economic growth. Business is caught in a vicious circle. A big part of the problem lies with companies themselves, which remain trapped in an outdated approach to value creation that has emerged over the past few decades. They continue to view value creation narrowly, optimizing short-term financial performance in a bubble while missing the most important customer needs and ignoring the broader influences that determine their longer-term success. How else could companies overlook the well-being of their customers, the depletion of natural resources vital to their businesses, the viability of key suppliers, or the economic distress of the communities in which they produce and sell? How else could companies think that simply shifting activities to locations with ever lower wages was a

sustainable 'solution' to competitive challenges? The presumed trade-offs between economic efficiency and social progress have been institutionalised in decades of policy
choices. Companies must take the lead in bringing business and society back together.
The recognition is there among sophisticated business and thought leaders, and promising
elements of a new model are emerging. Yet we still lack an overall framework for guiding
these efforts, and most companies remain stuck in a "social responsibility" mind-set in
which societal issues are at the periphery, not the core. The solution lies in the principle of
shared value, which involves creating economic value in a way that also creates value for
society by addressing its needs and challenges. Businesses must reconnect company
success with social progress".

Integrated reporting will help concentrate the minds of leaders on shared values
as integrated reporting opens the door to an integrated rating that blends financial
environmental and social performance. Going one step beyond shared values leads
us to the concept of positive impact investing and finance. As such the concept of
stakeholder engagement, shared values and positive impacts has been integrated as
emergent themes into this book.

A supporting factor will be the proliferation of new value chains which will help
to provide enough supply for SRI investment. It appears that the current appetite of
institutional investors for SRI investment may be even bigger than the market
supply.

1.14.1   From Shared Values to Positive Impacts

Global megatrends will force society, business and banking to extend value creation
beyond financial goals in order to take environmental and social solutions on board.
This applies, in particular, to the domain of population growth, climate change,
climate adaptation, fresh water and ecosystems services, as well as human rights
fair labour, and access to food, agricultural services, health and education. In all
these areas, the financial system is called to duty, as political solutions by
policymakers come into play too slowly and too timidly. The individual versatility
of financial institutions and their clients, as well as the more mobile venture capital
and equity funds, will be key determinants of economic success blended with
environmental and social progress and will also determine our future. They will
influence the extent and the circumstances under which economic success will be
feasible in the global village with underdeveloped governance structures and weak
governance context in many countries and markets. Catalysts for a new value chain
definition emerge from politics (P), environment (E), society (S), technology
(T) and organisational learning (O) which are often referred to as the PESTO
context factors of the future.

Positive impact investment and finance goes one step beyond shared values.
Shared values mean asking a company to concentrate on the quadrant that maxi-
mises economic, environmental and social value by investing capital and is about
leveraging core activities and partnerships for the joint benefit of the people in the
countries where the company operate. It is comparable to the concept of blended
value (where financial, environmental and social performance are calculated and

blended in one indicator). The underlying meaning is companies create business and societal value when they take a broader and longer-term view of their business activities.

Positive impact investment and finance likewise places the focus on supply chains but adds the element of extension and transformation of supply chains and PESTO factors and includes elements that do not show up directly in the social reporting of investment and banking and do not fit under the current standards and schemes. It draws on cross-functional and cross-sectoral cooperation and the creation of shared knowledge and new shared value chains. Positive impact finance and investment place the focus on positive impact creation for society into the centre of strategy, product development, technological innovation and supply chain transformation. A number of products currently emerge on this field, some of them still small, many of them with the potential of becoming mainstream.

Shally Venugopal presents in her contribution "Mobilising private sector climate investment: Public–private financial innovations" a number of these instruments focusing on a climate-friendly economy. Proposed solutions entail public support mechanisms for private capital investment, equity and de-risking instruments, climate bonds or other thematic bonds, asset-backed securities to refinance green or sustainable credits, social pay for performance bonds, development impact bonds or, tradable put and call options for emissions, waste or other by-products. Examples of each of the structures are given in her contribution to this book.

Another instrument is social bonds. In the case of Social Impact Bonds, bonds are created through a public commitment to pay a group of private sector investors for social success or positive social impact outcomes as measured by defined key performance indicators. The public sector will pay the private investor only when the social performance meets or exceeds the KPI under a pay for performance scheme. The model was first implemented in the UK to reduce prison recidivism.

Similar pay for performance models exists for ecosystems services as the contribution of Conservation International demonstrates. In "An investigation on ecosystem services, the role of investment banks and investment products to foster conservation" written by Dalal, Sonal Pandya, Bonham, Curan, and Silvani, Agustin for Conservation International. The authors provide examples where banks and investors accept pay for performance bonds or structures, however still on a low scale. The challenge ahead is to make mainstream such concepts so that they can unleash a considerable impact on the market.

Climate Bonds are another rising star, which are rapid by creating a new market. The Climate Bond Initiative estimates that the number of outstanding climate-themed bonds doubled between 2012 and 2013 from US $174 billion to US $364 billion. The sector currently is largely fuelled by public sector issuance such as The Ministry of Railways in China, Development Banks and the World Bank. However, Climate Bonds do transform existing supply chains for capital and allow big institutional investors access to climate funding. The appetite of investors appears huge. Zurich Insurance recently announced its intention to invest US $1 billion in green bonds. The concept, mainly used by public issuers, can be exported to the private sector.

The International Energy Agency (IEA) estimates that, on current trajectories, the world is, in the words of IA Chief Economist Fatih Birol, "barrelling" towards 6–7 °C warming, and that this would have "catastrophic" impacts.

The IEA also estimates that, worldwide, US $1 trillion of investment in energy, transport and building sectors are required each year—above business as usual—to reduce energy-related carbon emissions in line with a 2 °C global warming scenario.[1]

Climate Scientists now recognizes that 2 °C warming is very likely, leading to significant adaptation pressures. According to the UN Environment Programme, adaptation and the sustainable management of natural resources such as forests, fisheries, agriculture and water will require an average additional annual investment of US $1.3 trillion out to 2050.

In order to meet the IEA's US $1 trillion target, the challenge is not to creating new capital, but by shifting a portion of existing investment into low-carbon development.

Public sector balance sheets are severely constrained and are likely to remain so. The bulk of the money is going to have to come from the private sector, in particular from the US $83 trillion of assets under management by institutional investors.[2] If structured correctly, the good news is that the US $1 trillion required is investment not cost. Investment in high capital expenditure projects can deliver stable returns over a long period using a thematic bond market.

A thematic market is a labelled bond market where use of proceeds are specifically devoted to a particular purpose, in this case addressing climate change and environmental problems.

Many investors—for example those representing USD23 trillion of assets under management that signed 2013 declarations[3] about the urgent need to address climate change—express interest in green bonds, subject to their meeting existing risk and yield requirements. That interest in *equivalence* has been the key driver in sustained issuance and oversubscriptions of thematic green bonds in 2013 and 2014.

From 2007 to 2012, the market grew slowly with only a small spike in 2010 but in mid to late 2012 three French provinces, Ile-de-France, Provence-Alpes-Côte d'Azur and Nord-Pas de Calais, issued green bonds that were heavily oversubscribed—this increased the market interested in thematic bonds. In 2013 the IFC issued a US $1 billion (benchmark size) green bond in February and shortly after the EIB issued a 650 million Euros Climate Awareness Bond, which it then tapped again to make it a 900 million Euros. The size of these bonds were a turning point in the market (up to that point, few bonds reached US $200 million) and stimulated interest from both banks and investors.

---

[1] International Energy Agency, ETP World Energy Outlook (2012).

[2] OECD (2014).

[3] http://globalinvestorcoalition.org/

In 13 January 2014, major banks issued "Climate Bond Principles" to guide the development of the Climate Bonds market. This is a big development. With even more banks expected to sign up to the principles, they are likely to have a major impact, and it can be expected that we will see a fast-moving market. Bridget Boulle and Sean Kidney from Climate Bonds Initiative share their first-hand experience in developing this standard in their contribution "The opportunity for bonds to address the climate finance challenge". They write "2013 saw a niche, thematic 'green bond' market become a new asset class and a talking point amongst mainstream and SRI investors alike. The development of this thematic asset class has the potential to marginally, but significantly, reduce friction and transaction costs for investors looking for a means of addressing climate change, helping to reduce the cost of capital and speed flows of that capital". Positive impact investment and finance has the potential to align customer interests, with shareholders' and stakeholder interests alike and therefore is a cornerstone in creating a new banking and investment paradigm. The aligned interest of investors, clients, financial institutions and their shareholders concentrating on a universally shared objective is instrumental in overcoming the classical trade-offs and dilemmas faced by banks and investors.

New standards like the Climate Bond Principles are emerging, because the existing products need to be overhauled or complemented and the according standards do not fit those new products. We may see more of those new standards in the future, for instance, for social bonds or positive impact finance.

1.15   ESG Implementation

Sustainability in banking and investment stands and falls with governance, reporting and external assurance. Despite all new concepts, institutional investors and multinational banks are large flagships in contrast to many smaller and more versatile equity investment companies. Alex Cox demonstrates in his contribution "Fit-for-purpose and effective Environment, Social and Governance (ESG) management: ESG implementation challenges, concepts, methods and tips for improvement" that ESG is a strategic leadership tool. The chapter explores the investment bank structure and the optimum approaches to integrate ESG into the risk management process. The chapter also discusses key elements of building the business case for why ESG is important and for closer oversight and integration into the "business-as-usual" process. ESG has the capacity of transforming culture and leadership in investment and banking and raises awareness beyond number crunching. Thereby it helps produce positive outcomes. This requires that financial institutions and institutional investors make a leadership statement, integrate ESG in the key performance indicators that steer the enterprise and consistently implement a supporting organisational structure and weakness identification procedures in their Environmental and Social Risk Management Systems throughout the value chain and throughout the product lines.

In their contribution "The case for Environmental and Social Risk Management in investment banking", Olivier Jaeggi, Nina Kruschwitz and Raul Manjarin argue that a great body of literature looks into responsible investment; however, considerably less attention is paid to lending and to the direct relationships between banks and their corporate clients. Some of these clients are associated with controversial business practices, sectors, projects, and/or countries that, in turn, are associated with detrimental environmental and social impacts. In the context of their article, they focus on environmental and social (E&S) risks. E&S risks are risks that occur when investment banks engage with such clients. They discuss five factors that put pressure on banks to address E&S risks more systematically as E&S issues harbour considerable potential for damage in the here and now and that investment banks take a risk if they underestimate them.

The internal perspective on systems and governance is complemented by the external stakeholder perspective. Niamh O' Sullivan undertakes a deep review of the application of the Global Reporting Initiative (GRI) Financial Sector supplement by financial institutions. She discusses the progress and achievements but also the shortcomings in reporting in a benchmark study against GRI criteria in her contribution: "The Global Reporting Initiative (GRI) Guidelines and External Assurance of Investment Bank Sustainability Reports: Effective tools for consistent implementation of ESG Frameworks?" The role of the Global Reporting Initiative Financial Services Sector Supplement is explained, and the benefits of external assurance of financial sector sustainability reports are depicted as is the evolution of investment bank social accountability. Specific attention is paid to the perceived effectiveness of the GRI Guidelines and external assurance mechanisms.

1.16 Diversity and Gender Issues in the Financial Sector

Last but not least, diversity in investment and finance remains an issue. Would Lehman Brothers have failed if they had been Lehman Sisters? Monika Schulz Strelow addresses the under-representation of women on boards and the effect this has on business. As founder of the Women on Boards Indicator WOB, she has made measurable and easily accessible to fund managers the problem of under-representation. Some fund managers already take performance indicators such as the WOB into consideration in their investment strategy and require minimum representation quotas. The question of women on boards is part of a broader diversity discussion. It does not have its root in the question on women quota alone but on what is required to ensure supervisory boards of companies represent society and its diverse shareholders and how this translates into representation of those diverse groups on company boards. The WOB targets the heart of the question how do we create a sustainable society.

Alexandra Niessen-Ruenzi's contribution on "Sex Matters: Gender differences in the financial industry" challenges the assumption that men do better with money.

In her data, she could not find any gender-specific differences in fund performance. This means that although there seems to be a strong view that women can't be trusted to deliver as good an investment performance as men when it comes to money management, there is no reason not to trust women in asset management. The liquidity provided to female-managed funds is about a third lower than to male-managed funds, but this has nothing to do with the women's qualifications or performance. So there should be no reason why capital flow to a fund depends on male or female fund management, but reality shows it does. The prejudice about women's capabilities in investment and banking needs to be revisited and corrected. To make this happen, the problem needs to be made explicit, and more women need to apply for fund management roles to mainstream female fund management.

Once again, the "measure it and it will change" rule that applies in investment and banking all over the place needs to be implemented in the diversity and gender approach to foster sustainable investment, banking and fund management.

1.17   Leadership and Its Role in Transforming Culture in Investment and Banking

Even the best models of governance will not be able to create commitment to environmental and social considerations in investment and banking, if the leadership commitment is missing. Leadership commitment is expressed by leadership statements, a responsible investment and banking strategy, responsible behaviour in dilemma situations and likewise by taking ESG into the list of key performance indicators by which the institution is steered. Social identity theory tells us that the attitude and perceived behaviour of leaders have a self-amplifying power and instil the desire in followers to be and act like the leader. The most important and all-permeating factor for instilling voluntary cooperation in creating responsibility in investment and banking will be leadership and—influence the other side of the leadership coin—culture. Leaders that cannot transform the culture of their institutions may find themselves as victims of the existing corporate culture down the road. Leadership and culture can instil voluntary cooperation of employees or—create a climate of fear and over-competitiveness, a winning-at-all-cost attitude, fostering a unipolar approach that only focuses on financial returns, no matter what. The positive leverage of culture on the business models of investment and banking however can be huge, as the creation of the Equator Principles Movement in investment banking has demonstrated. This is also acknowledged by those criticising the current twists in banking culture like Williams/Conley. They stress the Equator Principles have transformed the risk culture in the project finance part of investment banking and have supported the creation of new organisational learning and voluntary cooperation, creating a self-amplifying power beyond the scope of Equator Principles. Williams/Conley stress in their contribution to this book that culture is an important factor in strengthening or undermining banking regulation.

Good governance as well as new paradigms of responsibility and positive impacts creation need to be instilled with the support of leadership and will transform into a new culture when taken up by followers and integrated in balanced scorecards. This requires leadership taking a stance.

1.18   The Aim of Responsible Investment Banking

This book intends to aid the creation of a new vision of investment and banking, one which is focused on creation of positive impacts, integration of sustainability into the entire value chain in investment and banking and the creation of shared values by contributing new ideas and concepts to the discussion of *responsibility in investment banking and asset management* and mingle them with already existing experience on environmental and social risk management and governance. Not all the areas of investment banking and capital trade have been covered, because, in certain areas, the vision and the tools for responsible behaviour have not yet been fully developed, tested and applied. But plenty of areas are covered like existing and tested concepts of ESG risk management in lending, responsible asset management and equity investments. Those concepts are complemented by new ideas like green bonds, ESG integrated know-your-customer checks, social impact investing shared values and positive impact finance. Transparency and reporting are enriched with the concept of external assurance. Key aspects in responsible investment and banking are human rights, international labour law, climate, eco-systems services and biodiversity, stakeholder dialogue, culture, gender and ways to reduce footprint while increasing positive impacts. These issues are discussed in dedicated chapters to facilitate a deep and rich exchange of perspectives.

Many contributions shift the focus from risk management to people and a new vision of positive impacts. I have made sure that the collection also offers good practice product and process solutions

The book aims to provide positive vision for investment and banking and its role in making people's lives better rather than worse. At the same time, it offers a balanced overview of what concepts, solutions and products are currently available. It demonstrates the industry's best efforts and explains best practice approaches, frameworks, systems, tools, industry standards and international soft law together with some emerging concepts. Share prices rise and fall with positive visions of the future and therefore the creation of a positive impact investment and finance vision for mankind needs to be established and pursued and can become the new mantra in investment and finance.

The book takes a forward-looking approach in order to focus on solutions and proactive strategies within the financial industry. The next step to consider will be integrated reporting and integrated ratings of companies to create a market for sustainable entrepreneurs, rather than having a sustainability rating plus a financial rating. Separate ratings are the wrong message to the market, as there is the expectation that financial, environmental and social performance will influence each other and a blended rating will finally help prove the business case for sustainability and demonstrate that responsible companies perform better. The Dow Jones Sustainability Index has been a first step into the right direction here. Currently, the financial ratings and the sustainability ratings are performed by different types of rating agencies. There is, therefore, a continuing disconnect between the two types of rating. It would be helpful also to foster responsibility in investment and banking to establish a triple bottom line approach incorporating all three performance components into one rating and advance integrated reporting. Integrated reporting will not only help to point investors towards the companies that are performing well on the three pillars of finance, environment and society, but robust environmental and social performance will also have a positive financial impact on share prices.

Finally, *Responsible Investment Banking* also benefits from various viewpoints of authors who share their experience dedication, passion and dilemmas. This book intends to enrich the discussion on responsibility in investment and banking, create new insights and help shift the focus to positive impact finance and investment.

1.18.1   Addressing Some Fundamental Issues

Before reading this book, it's worth clarifying certain issues that often become confused when we talk about responsibility. Corporate social responsibility, responsibility, the social licence to operate and legitimacy are not the same thing. So it's important to define what we mean by responsibility. The term CSR occurs often throughout this book. Wherever possible, we have used the term ESG— environmental and social governance—to stress the importance of governance aspects.

To guide discussion, three key questions are put forward, to which any institution, in any industry, should be able to provide valid and reliable answers if it wants to stay in the market and avoid slipping down the food chain: *"What do we produce and offer?" "How do we produce it and offer it?"* And *"why do we produce and offer it?"* We can easily use these three questions to take us through the spheres of shared values in banking and asset management and also to address the motives: *"Why are we doing what we are doing?"* And *"should we do something differently?"*

This connects directly with the questions of leadership and culture, and how investment and banking can contribute to a better world with less social tension and influence the creation of materially positive impacts for society overcoming scarcity. Paradigms and basic assumptions commonly shared within the investment and banking sector—and their limitations—equally will be discussed and solutions sketched out. However, readers will have to make their own appraisal on sustainability in investment and banking, and hopefully, contribute to this fascinating discussion.

2 Defining CSR, Responsibility and Responsible Investment Banking

2.1 CSR: A Dazzling Concept

There is no firm definition of corporate social responsibility. In the same decade as Milton Friedman made his famous statement "*the business of business is business*", Dow Votaw hypothesised in "*Genius becomes rare*" in "*The Corporate Dilemma*" published with S.P. Sethi:

> "The Term (CSR) is a brilliant one. It means something, but not always the same thing to everybody. To some it conveys the idea of legal responsibility or liability, to others it means social responsible behavior in an ethical sense, to still others the meaning transmitted is that of "responsible for" in a causal mode; many simply equate it with a charitable contribution; some take it to mean socially conscious. Many who embrace it most fervently see it as a synonym for "legitimacy" in the context of belonging or being proper or valid, some see it as a sort of fiduciary duty imposing higher standards of behavior on businessmen than on citizens at large".

For corporations, the question of CSR is increasing exponentially in relation to their perception of legitimacy. Legitimacy is commonly understood as a "generalized perception or assumption that the actions of an entity are desirable, proper, or appropriate within some socially constructed system of norms, values, beliefs, and definitions" (Suchman 1995).

While CSR still does not share a unified definition, it has developed an important element that is shared throughout the book in every contribution, regardless of whether the focus is on standards, frameworks, best practice, fiduciary duties, international soft law, co-regulation or hard regulation: CSR means considering holistically people, planet and profit—often referred to as triple bottom line—and not just financial performance per se. Attention to and performance according to the triple bottom line approach can be regarded as the minimum common denominator for addressing CSR issues in business. The triple bottom line is in the process of becoming a mainstream element not only in addressing risks and reputation but also in mainstreaming management tools. Therefore, this book applies robust performance on the triple bottom line as the accepted definition of CSR.

For a wider understanding of the different concepts of Corporate Social Responsibility, the following four key concepts are useful references: one from Caroll,[4] the

---

[4] **[Carroll, 1979, 2008, 500]**: "The social responsibility of business encompasses the economic, legal, ethical and discretionary expectations that a society has of organizations at a given point in time."

EU,[5] Mallenbaker [6] and the World Business Council for Sustainable Development.[7] I herewith refer the reader to those sources for a deeper understanding of the CSR concept.

2.2 The Concept of Responsibility

Applying the triple bottom line is a star, but it still does not provide us with a useful definition of responsibility. Further elements need to be added to the core CSR/Triple Bottom Line approach to create responsibility, and they are governance and corporate citizenship with stakeholder engagement, transparency, reporting and disclosure and transmitted also by culture and leadership.

2.2.1 Governance

The Triple Bottom Line approach often remains silent on the elements that enable and ensure implementation throughout the company in a consistent manner. In order to turn the triple bottom line approach operational and consistently applied, management tools and measurement tools are needed, such as a company Environmental and Social Risk Management System, with an organisational structure, a product approval process that includes environmental and social considerations and, for banking, a know-your-customer check—to name a few. This element of implementation is referred to as **governance**. Without governance, it is not possible to get to grips with ensuring *implementation* of CSR and the triple bottom line approach. Governance will ensure appropriate monitoring, which can lead to the creation of a learning organisation by further developing the systems on a permanent basis, in line with new discoveries, challenges and emerging themes.

2.2.2 Culture and Leadership

Many authors in this book have added governance to the triple bottom line approach. Governance tells the management of a company, the financing

---

[5] **EU Definition of CSR:** "A concept whereby companies integrate social and environmental concerns in their business operations and in their interaction with their stakeholders on a voluntary basis."

[6] **Mallenbaker Definition:** "CSR is about how companies manage the business processes to produce an overall positive impact on society."

[7] **The World Business Council for Sustainable Development (WBCSD):** "Corporate Social Responsibility is the continuing commitment by business to behave ethically and contribute to economic development while improving the quality of life of the workforce and their families as well as of the local community and society at large."

institutions and the wider public how leadership, organisational structures and programmes, processes and policies interrelate and support the implementation of the triple bottom line approach. While governance is helpful in facilitating compliance, it doesn't always ensure the integration of environmental and social topics into the risk culture of banking. Absorption into the DNA of investment banking is needed to create commitment above and beyond compliance with the triple bottom line. Banking culture has the potential to engender this shift from compliance to commitment. Systems and process alone cannot transmit the message of responsibility sufficiently. Institutions are not just chains of command and control along an organisational chart or a hierarchy. They are likewise a network of people, and therefore leadership and culture serve as the transmitters of messages that cannot be transported alongside the command and control scheme, as command and control cannot instil voluntary cooperation or motivation.

2.2.3 Corporate Citizenship: Stakeholder Engagement, Transparency and Reporting

As the financial industry does not operate in a vacuum but has to deal with multiple systems, markets, regulatory bodies, customer and country orientations, it needs to operate in alignment with stakeholders and society. The ultimate objective of banking, from its historic roots, is financial intermediation and the financing of economies.

Banking cannot, therefore, be regarded as remote from society. Banking represents society and its aspirations, be they growth, exploitation of resources or resource efficiency and a green economy. This alignment with society and communities is often referred to as corporate citizenship. It usually encompasses stakeholder engagement, transparency, reporting and disclosure. Stakeholder engagement is the key pillar at the core of each responsibility strategy. A number of contributions here demonstrate the benefits it offers to companies, the financial sector, communities and society. Stakeholder engagement should not be confused with disclosure required by national law or annual reporting. It is a much more proactive and interactive approach and establishes a permanent dialogue in a structured manner in order to create mutual trust, including procedures and plans, as well as taking notice of vulnerable groups and be inclusive of them.

It enables interest-based negotiations, as opposed to position-based negotiations. Stakeholder engagement goes beyond conflict resolution, crisis management and includes cooperation, in some cases collaboration and allows stakeholders to influence business strategies. Stakeholder engagement aims at achieving good citizenship relations and to engender mutual trust. I leave it to the authors to explain these variations further. Reporting and Transparency are additional elements to corporate citizenship and address the element of stakeholder disclosure. Figure 1

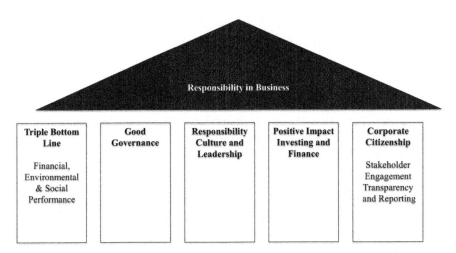

Fig. 1 Depicting responsibility

provides an overview of how corporate responsibility can be depicted. Responsibility merges the elements of the triple bottom line approach, good governance and citizenship demonstrated through best practice stakeholder engagement and disclosure.

2.3 Investment Banking and Asset Management Defined

Investment banking can be defined in various ways. In general, investment banking is a specific division of banking related to the creation of capital for other companies and specialises in securities market activities including underwriting, trading, asset management, advisory activities and corporate restructuring such as mergers and acquisitions. Commercial banking relates to deposit-taking and lending.

Investment banking as well deals with off-balance sheet structures in lending and with securities business. Investment banks underwrite new debt and equity securities for all types of corporations. In a wider sense, investment banking includes specialist know-how for large and complex financial transactions requiring that kind of special expertise. Using customer deposits for this kind of lending and not just interbank loans has become mainstream.

Investment banks likewise act as an intermediary between a securities issuer and the investing public, often accompanied by taking on an underwriting role. They facilitate mergers and other corporate reorganisations and act as a broker and/or financial adviser for institutional clients. The investment banking model also includes trading on capital markets, research and private equity investments. An investment bank, likewise, trades and invests on its own account.[8]

Some banks include wealth management within the investment banking arm. Wealth management is a practice that, in its broadest sense, describes the combination of personal investment management, financial advisory and planning disciplines directly for the benefit of high-net-worth clients.[9]

In order to acknowledge the flow of capital and the critical role of managed funds, I am also including the other side of the coin of capital creation: the management and investment of the exiting flow of funds. This domain has gained increased importance on the sustainability agenda, as the managed pension funds, the funds moved by institutional investors worldwide and the asset and fund management industry has a huge impact on responsible behaviour and environmental and social performance of companies worldwide. Issues such as human rights, climate, triple bottom line and governance apply equally to investment of funds and capital creation.

3 Pillars of Responsible Investment Banking and Asset Management

Responsible Investment Banking and Asset Management is depicted in Fig. 2. In this book responsibility in investment and banking means the application of the triple bottom line, transparent reporting and disclosure according to accepted international standards as defined by the Global Reporting Initiative (GRI) and best practice stakeholder dialogue by using international recognised soft law standards as benchmarks, plus applying governance frameworks and tools throughout the value chain in the sphere of influence of investment banking as defined above. This is complemented by a socially and environmentally aware culture and leadership and acknowledgement of fiduciary duties. An informed understanding of impacts and risks that investment banking and asset management pose to society helps to identify, address and manage them. By adding the focus of creation of positive impacts for communities and society as a whole in this book, the way is paved for a more proactive approach to Responsible Investment Banking. Banks and investors have a duty of care towards society to avoid human right breaches, for instance, and likewise have to act as fiduciary for their clients, many of them not

---

[8] See Financial Times Lexicon, Internet http://lexicon.ft.com/Term?term=investment-bank, accessed on January 5, 2014.

[9] http://lexicon.ft.com/Term?term=wealth-management

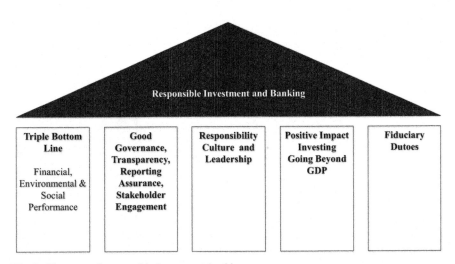

Fig. 2 Elements of responsible investment banking

wanting money to go into business that breaches human rights or destroys the public goods like water, air or soil.

4 Responsibility and Its Relation to Legitimacy and the Social Licence to Operate

An institution's decision of whether to behave in a sustainable manner and the success of its strategy ultimately will be validated by society.

While there are good reasons to apply responsibility for its own purpose, the impacts that investment banking has on society are reflected by the support investment banking and asset management is given by society. Actions ultimately are validated by society. This is normally expressed in perceived legitimacy or the social licence to operate. The social licence to operate is a parameter used to assess and manage the reputation of a company or bank. Discussions on the social licence to operate often draw on Thomson and Boutilier's (2011) "pyramid model", which considers four potential levels of support by society:

According to Thomson and Boutilier (2011), a social licence to operate (SLO) is a community's perceptions of the acceptability of a company and its local operations. Based on extensive interviews with resettled villagers about the ups and downs of their relationships with a Bolivian mine over a 15-year period, Thomson and Boutilier identified four levels of the SLO. They claim that the level of SLO granted to a company is inversely related to the level of socio-political risk a company faces. A lower SLO indicates a higher risk.

Fig. 3 Depicting the Social
Licence to Operate
(according to Thomson/
Boutilier)

Level of the Social Licence to Operate

Psychological identification:
Trust Boundary

Approval : Credibility Boundary

Acceptance

Rejection: Legitimacy Baundary

The lowest level of SLO is having the social licence withheld or withdrawn. This implies that the project, company or bank is in danger of restricted access to essential resources (e.g. financing, legal licences, raw material, labour, markets, public infrastructure). Losing a social licence represents extremely high socio-political risk.

The next higher level of SLO is acceptance. In Fig. 3 this layer covers the greatest area in order to indicate that it is the common level of social licence granted. If the company establishes its credibility, the social licence rises to the level of approval. Over time, if trust is established, the social licence could rise to the level of psychological identification, where the level of socio-political risk is very low.

While performed on an investment level by Boutilier and Thompson, the model has acquired acceptance on a wider base over the past 2 years.

Looking at Fig. 3, it is apparent that transparency and walking the talk and sticking to commitments present themselves as useful elements in climbing up the legitimacy latter from Acceptance to Approval. The obvious question is "*why should banks strive to achieve approval, isn't acceptance just good enough?*" Since the scandal-plagued summer of 2012, where, in rapid succession, came public charges that traders at up to sixteen of the too-big-to-fail global banks had engaged for at least 5 years in global manipulation of the London interbank offered rate, or Libor, the clear answer is no.

Acceptance allows banks walk along the legitimacy boundary and any unforeseen event pushes them down towards rejection. Examples from the recent banking crisis demonstrate that investment banking has to regain trust and even legitimacy. Investment banking practices examined through analyses of the banking crisis in 2007 reveal unsustainable products and behaviours. In 2012, the British Parliament ordered an independent review on the culture and practices of investment banking. In the Salz Report *Changing Banking for Good* [10] published in 2013,

---

[10] http://www.parliament.uk/documents/banking-commission/Banking-final-report-vol-ii.pdf

inter alia the culture, governance, products, practices and the struggle for survival in banking are scrutinised and proposals for improvement made.

Even by 2011, an Oliver Wyman Report presented at the world economic forum in Davos came to the conclusion that since the banking crisis, for all the rhetoric about a new financial order, and all the improvements made or planned, many of the old risks remain, and this is of major concern. The report inter alia names short-termism and the unwillingness of shareholders to accept lower returns on equity as major risks.

In the Netherlands, the banking authority AFM considered self-regulation of the Product Approval and Review process through the Dutch Banking Code insufficient and in 2010 advocated legal rules (AFM 2010). The industry currently appears to be walking between the boundaries of legitimacy and credibility. This may be a result of marginalising responsibility in investment banking in some areas rather than mainstreaming it. In other words, in order to regain credibility and trust, it is necessary to mainstream responsibility in investment banking further and expand on existing concepts. Figure 3 shows that stakeholder engagement is a prerequisite to achieve identification with a company. This element should be strengthened by investment banks.

Regarding investment and banking, readers will draw their own conclusion about the financial industry over time. Does investment banking enjoy widespread approval or just acceptance? Is the industry walking within the legitimacy boundary or has it regained credibility?

The discourse and the perspectives of the authors may be valuable in answering these questions.

5   How to Read This Book: Four Lenses and a Tool Kit

You can read this book from various perspectives:

- Through the lenses of a stakeholder wanting to create best practice engagement and to maximise impacts while asking for transparent reporting or assurance and inclusion
- Through the lenses of politics, regulation, creation of international soft law and normativisation of good governance standards, addressing likewise issue like diversity, gender and cultural influences
- Through the lens of a sustainable innovation strategy, concentrating on the upside potential of responsibility, allowing more profit with lower risk, increasing positive impacts with lower footprints, optimising risk management and value creation for society and business at the same time increasing resilience and placing successfully new environmentally and socially responsible products, the market is thirsty for, thus taking investment and banking towards sustainable innovation

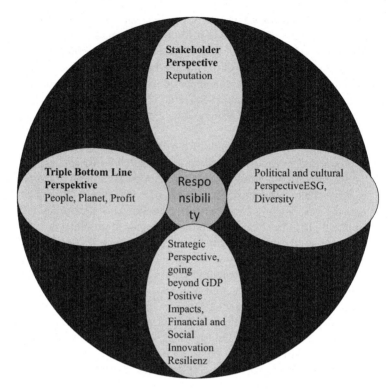

Fig. 4 Focus and Approaches in responsible investment banking and Asset Management

- Through the classical lenses of corporate social responsibility and the triple bottom line approach

The strategic perspective may create more prosperity with lower risk for clients, stakeholders and shareholders and is currently represented here with a number of grassroots initiatives. While the stakeholder lens primarily looks in from the outside, the political, cultural and resilience perspective combines market adaptation and internal integration of market requirements and is inclusive on stakeholders and society, whereas the CSR perspective deals with the creation of a robust triple bottom line approach and fundamentally takes an internal perspective concentrating on risk management systems. However, most of the contributions cut across all four areas, as context and operational factors are not independent, rather closely linked, exerting mutual influence.

Figure 4 illustrates the various lenses, which form part of responsible business conduct. In other words, all the areas need to be covered to achieve responsibility in investment banking.

Responsible Investment Banking offers a number of management tools to understand and implement multidimensional requirements designed to ensure responsible business conduct in a proactive, solution-oriented approach in consideration of important context factors. The tool kit development very much goes hand in hand

Fig. 5 Overview on
Implementation Tools

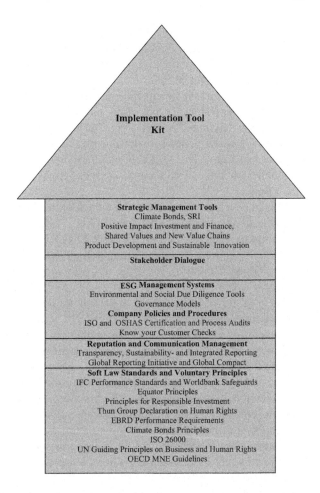

with the historic development of CSR standards, principles and Best Practice creation. A short overview is given in order to allow the reader to sort and categorise, what is described in more detail in the various contributions to this book.

The past 15 years have seen a proliferation of Environmental and Social Soft Law Standards, Guidelines and Risk Management Frameworks and tools as demonstrated by Fig. 5.

The IFC Performance Standards launched in 2006 encourage sound environmental practices and focus on key areas of concern such as labour, resource efficiency, communities, land-take and involuntary resettlement, biodiversity, indigenous people and cultural heritage. The EBRD Performance Requirements apply a similar approach. The Equator Principles Framework is based on the IFC Standards.

The UN Principles for Responsible Investment constitute a standard to be applied in asset management. They consist of a set of principles developed by a group of institutional investors reflecting the recognition that environment, social and governance issues do affect performance of investments.

Guidelines applicable to any sector, not just the financial industry, consist of ISO 26000, the UN Guiding Principles for Business and Human Rights and the OECD Guidelines for Multinational Companies (MNE Guidelines). They apply to the investment and financial industry as well. These overarching standards not particularly designed for investment and banking but for all kinds of business. ISO 26000 provides guidance for all types of organisations on social responsibility principles, and the UN Guiding Principles for Business and Human Rights introduce the protect and respect remedy framework for human rights for all kinds of companies and organisations. The OECD Guidelines for Multinational Companies (MNE Guidelines) address a full range of ESG issues but apply in OECD Member states only.

Recent developments include the launch of the Climate Bond Principles and the Thun Group Declaration on Human Rights.

Company Policies, Procedures and ESG Risk Management Systems implement ESG requirements on the ground on the basis of standards and guidelines.

The Global Reporting Initiative helps to shape and benchmark sustainability reports.

There is no one-size-fits-all approach to stakeholder engagement since the context may require different concepts. IFC Performance Standards provide a framework for sound stakeholder engagement with communities on a project level.

The newest tools in the Responsible Investment Banking and asset management box are the strategic investment and asset management perspective represented by green bonds, positive impact investment or finance and the shared values approach.

I intentionally have not created a chronological journey through the book as I want to emphasise that all these concepts exist in parallel, are connected and develop as a context system. A rigid structure would have not allowed the reader to glimpse the connectivity and emerging grassroots approach and take on board other factors such as culture and gender. Please regard the tool box as an orientation rather than a rigid scheme.

Many of the factors here are interconnected as culture permeates most of the issues and international co-regulation influences risk management and eco-social issues and vice versa. While in most cases the book provides a holistic view on issues such as climate change or human rights, the different factors allow the reader to disintegrate the topics and drill down on a certain aspect in a certain context.

Conclusion

One point shines through most of the contributions and that is that investment and banking need new paradigms and that responsibility in investment banking and asset management is not in its final state, but rather a learning journey in a very dynamic environment that will evolve further. Looking for permanent improvements, new ways of doing things and transforming responsibility into a more proactive approach focusing on positive impacts rather than

(continued)

applying reactive strategies to apparent recent inconsistencies will be important to push the envelope to more sustainable business practices and gain more buy-in. This needs to be supported by a new culture.

Edgar Schein has defined culture as the result of a group's accumulated learning in order to master the dilemma of external adaptation to its market environment and internal integration to enable daily functioning and alignment. The basic assumptions are not normally put up for test. Basic assumptions and resulting group values create artefacts such as strategies, communication style and cultural language, products and leadership styles of "how we do things around here" and influence sustainable innovation capacity, strategic speed, time to market and adoption of new products and value chains.

Investment and Banking has reached a crossroad, where the industry needs to find ways to align interests between its shareholders, clients and stakeholders and shift focus from risk management to people orientation. Ecosystems services are rather a social than an environmental topic. Water scarcity and creation of flows of refugees as a consequence of net loss in ecosystems services may serve as an example. This underscores the new people orientation focus that investment, banking and asset management need to embrace. The industry needs a new strategic vision: aligning interests and collective concentration and collaboration towards positive impacts and shared values. This will infuse fun as a new element of investment and finance. It is more fun to invest in positive impacts and in SRI with lower risk. Stories and visions do move markets and share prices. The most romantic idea is capable of making money at the stock exchange, when the story is compelling. So how about positive impact investment and finance being the next new big thing? These new models have the potential to go mainstream and overcome traditional trade-offs seen in the past decades.

A number of contributions revisit old models with a view to propose change and solutions. Unipolar shareholder and bonus orientation will not take the industry further. The industry has arrived at an inflection point. A different investment and banking paradigm is possible. And this spirit creates a self-amplifying power. The financial industry is not separate from society; it represents society and is able to align to the needs of society creating positive impacts and increased wealth for society while reducing its footprint on climate and ecosystems.

References

AFM. (2010, October 18). *Wetgevingsbrief van de AFM aan het ministerie van Financiën.* Amsterdam: Netherlands.

Boutilier, R. G., & Thompson, I. (2011). *Modelling the social licence to operate Internet.* Retrieved from http://socialicense.com/publications/Modelling%20and%20Measuring%20the%20SLO.pdf

Friedman, M. (1970, September 13). The social responsibility of business is to increase its profits. *New York Times.*

Suchman, M. C. (1995). Managing legitimacy: Strategic and institutional approaches. *The Academy of Management Review, 20*(3), 571–610. http://www.jstor.org/stable/258788

Fit-for-Purpose and Effective Environment, Social and Governance (ESG) Management: ESG Implementation Challenges, Concepts, Methods and Tips for Improvement

Alexander Cox

Abstract This chapter explores the investment bank structure and the optimum approaches to integrate ESG into the credit risk process. The chapter also discusses key elements of building the business case for both why ESG is important and the need for closer oversight and integration into the "business-as-usual" process. It also explores how leadership, governance and culture can, or rather should be, created and maintained such that the successes of ESG integration once complete are not diminished through time. The chapter is written in the first person, drawing from the author's risk management experience over the past decade, without reference to specific institutions to allow more open expression of core issues and challenges, providing valuable tips and techniques to achieve successful change programmes.

1 Introduction

The important point to note about the observations and discussion items here is that they cover a variety of methods, tools, touch and leverage points to optimise and maximise your chance to better understand the system you are trying to influence and positively effect. Every system has the same challenges because people are all different, which creates the greatest challenge of all: asking people to behave and act consistently, not just because they are told to, but because they believe in that system. In the time that I have spent in risk management and consulting for risk projects, the greatest difficulty is not creating a smart solution to a particular process, not the 100 % checklist that covers everything, nor the fullest most comprehensive set of key performance indicators. It is simply the question whether

A. Cox (✉)
ERM Central Europe, Neu-Isenburg, Germany
e-mail: Alexander.cox@erm.com

© Springer International Publishing Switzerland 2015   43
K. Wendt (ed.), *Responsible Investment Banking*, CSR, Sustainability, Ethics & Governance, DOI 10.1007/978-3-319-10311-2_2

the day the project concludes will the objectives of the process last and stand the test of time? In reality, nothing does, but the legacy of any great process or system is that it becomes part of the DNA of the organisation such that it can self-evolve and become greater than the sum of the contributions that created it. This is only achieved with the right people.

A great friend of mine who has held a variety of leadership positions always told me:

> You may think the greatest asset you have are the buildings you own or the client accounts you run, but at the end of the day, when the lights of your firm go out, your company stops; it's your people, and don't forget that!.

She was so right across so many levels. Looking back at all my projects, their success has hinged on the enthusiasm, values of the leader and their ability for access and credibility at the highest level of senior management.

The following sections will hold this theme of people and their importance. It is human nature to focus immediately on the process to improve and write a great document to prove it. This is needed of course, but hopefully this chapter will explain that process improvement is only 50 % of the battle, and the remaining half is building the culture and people around it to make it sustainably grow, evolve and add value to your organisation.

2   Core Challenges for ESG Management Improvement Programmes

I hate to be negative, normally assuming a position of realistic optimism, but on this occasion I will start with the former and end with the later. The following is a list of core challenges that an ESG manager will face at some time during the programme or during final operation:

- Weak senior management or lack of commitment
- Lack of segregation between front office and ESG credit risk advise
- Seen as a burden not a value add
- Involved too late in the process
- Not seeing all the deals
- Not enough resource to proactively develop the process and improve
- Not enough time to provide thorough advise and at the right time
- Lack of demonstrable competency in ESG topics at the investment and credit committees
- Higher focus on pre-investment rather than credit monitoring
- Less ESG focus on equity investments although higher risk
- Difficulties in ensuring fund managers maintain the capabilities to maintain the mandate for indirect investments

- Covenant wording and triggers difficult to implement
- And, of course, many others

To meet these challenges head on, the following success factors, concepts and techniques will provide a good chance to overcome these.

2.1 Useful Risk Management Concepts and Principles

2.1.1 Risk Management Principles and Three Lines of Defence

Discussing and creating a new or enhanced ESG process in a bank, it's useful to be familiar with the concept, "three lines of defence model". In its simplest terms, it is a way to describe how risk is managed and the assurance needed to test that the adequacy of controls is achieved in an organisation. The table below simplifies the meaning and highlights what each group is trying to achieve.

Three lines of defence model applied to an ESG function

	First line of defence	Second line of defence	Third line of defence
Which groups are involved?	**Risk takers** *anybody at any level that can impact the success of the bank*	**Advisors** *e.g. legal credit risk and ESG function*	**Independent Auditors** *Audit internal/external*
What is the role of those groups?	**They do business** *while actively managing and* **owning** *risks*	**Advise on ESG risk management** *giving guidance to the 1st line and support/ monitor the implementation of ESG risk management*	**Assure** *that first line is performing and not exposing the bank inappropriately,* **and** *the second line is providing the right advise/monitoring for the first line to succeed*
Typically committee with final authority	Investment committees Investment operating committees	Board operating risk committee Credit (approval) committee Operational risk committee Compliance and legal committee New business committee (new products)	Audit committee Board audit and risk committee Board meeting
Measure of success	**Performance** *Outcome focused, measured by KPIs i.e. no reputational damage in the market from ESG impacts*	**Fit for purpose** *Processes and systems designed and implemented correctly*	**Level of comfort of the board** *No surprises*

The importance of the third line cannot be understated as so often I've seen the second line of defence conducting its own annual review of its own systems, which will never truly achieve the independence required. Even cross audits[1] are questionable as the auditors are peers and colleagues of the auditees. This can cause bias and "softening" of the findings encountered, which defeats the value of the review. The challenges often faced by the third line, or internal audit, is the lack of in-house competency to understand the specifics of the topic and assess materiality. For the larger banks, auditors with a background in credit risk and some ESG experience are normally acceptable, but for the smaller institutions, this is practically impossible, and therefore third-party assurance should be sought.

A useful reference is sections 96–108 of the Prudential Regulatory Authority's approach to banking supervision that outlines core requirements of risk management. The messages within those sections are pertinent to any risk topic that is material enough to require oversight. An extract is shown below to illustrate:

> The Prudential Regulation Authority's approach to banking supervision April 2013
>
> 108. To the extent warranted by the nature, scale and complexity of the business, the PRA expects these (risk) functions to be independent of a firm's revenue-generating functions, and to possess sufficient authority to offer robust challenge to the business. This requires these functions to be adequately resourced, to have a good understanding of the business, and to be headed by individuals at senior level who are willing and able to voice concerns effectively.

The section highlights the importance of a strong individual leader and segregation of duties and the ability to offer robust challenge to the business. These messages, among others, within these sections need to be considered in structuring the new system at both credit risk level and ESG levels.

2.1.2   Keeping the Implementation Balanced

Finding the right balance between hard controls in the system and the "softer" value-based methods is key. All too often companies are overburdened with processes and check list, and people become disillusioned with micra and forget about the macro reason for the systems being. This causes the business to perceive that the ESG function adds less value, and invariably as time goes on budgets are cut and controls are slimmed. This then moves the approach from rule-based towards principle-based management, which again has its challenges, i.e. greater dependence on the individuals' values and judgement. After time, this leads to a lack of consistency and quality across the organisation, and the pendulum swings back again towards rule based, unfortunately, normally following some large issues

---

[1] Cross audits are the method of assurance or review using other risk practitioners or auditors from another region or business unit within the same organisation.

in the press. A fit-for-purpose and balanced approach needs to be sought at the outset. A structured approach to defining new "ESG management system" is to follow the broad steps of the "Integral Model,"[2] developed by Peter Fink for the Health and Safety sector, where lessons can be learnt in the financial sector. The core elements of the integral model are shown in the following diagram:

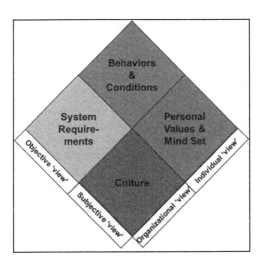

The Safety Culture Diamond

The broad definitions are outlined in the table below for reference

Integral model element	Broad definition
Behaviours and conditions (decisions)	Desired outcome of system: people doing the right thing at the right time, every time
System requirements	Behaviours are influenced by the tangible and factual parts of the system, e.g. processes, tools, documents
Personal values and mindset	Behaviours are influenced by the individual's personal attitudes, experiences and expectations
Culture	Behaviours are influenced by the company culture which underlines the system and the personal values of the individuals

---

[2] Safety Culture and Safety Management Systems: Why Management Systems Alone Can't Guarantee Model Employee Behavior, Jul 17th, 2010.

All the quadrants (red and blue) are linked and influence each other and, as such, in consideration of developing a full system, must all be considered and developed for the system to work. Section develops this further in the context of leadership and governance.

2.1.3 Keeping the Implementation Fit for Purpose

If there is one key phrase that has served me well as a risk manager and management consultant, it is "fit for purpose". This simple phrase creates a feeling that it will be "business aligned", "value adding" and "efficient cost" without giving any further details. It also means that, as a process designer, you should always design the tools and methods reflecting on the inherent risk of the activity and develop controls accordingly. In one organisation, I have seen a risk team completely change in a year because they had made the mistake of designing the "best on paper" system a bank could want. But it was so complete that it became burdensome and irrelevant to parts of the business where risks were negligible and did not meet required turnaround times on the key deals. It was simply over-engineered, and material messages were not rising to the top. They had not balanced intellectual completeness and purity for operational practicality and materiality, i.e. it wasn't **fit for purpose**.

2.2 Key Methods and Techniques for Change

2.2.1 Identify Stakeholders

Every organisation has their challenges and strengths, but the important aspect is that the ESG function and credit teams need to focus on the material objective and issues. They need to provide great service, value adding products and relationships to the borrowers while, at the same time, underwriting the best credit for the bank within the bank's risk appetite. To meet this objective successfully, understanding the roles of the stakeholders, the core credit process itself, and providing material fit-for-purpose solutions and advice go a long way.

For the purposes of this chapter, I won't go into the variety and types of front office departments because many institutions often have different names for similar activities, and these change regularly, often depending on how the profit and loss (P&L) account roll-up. However, support functions are generally standard across the industry and is important to understand and know these groups within the institutions you work for both as stakeholders to seek support and to leverage their mandates to achieve your goals. Examples are listed below:

Group	Stand-alone P&Ls: (first line)	Supporting functions (second line)	Assurance functions (third line)
Typical stakeholders	Private banking (including wealth management), retail banking, wholesale banking, capital markets (trading and sales, corporate finance, project finance, investment banking), asset management, trust business, private equity (proprietary trading), corporate treasury (general and money markets)	Credit risk, credit monitoring, market risk, liquidity risk (or asset and liability management), operational risk (including business continuity management), legal, compliance (anti-money laundering, regulation management, client take-on activities, etc.), IT (including risk IT and information security), HR and company secretary	Internal audit (internal and external)

The importance of identifying the stakeholders and their roles is key to the successful integration of any new ESG process. Rules and regulations that they are custodian of may give the additional reason and strengthening your mandate for change. For example, rules within the operational risk arena such as the segregation of duties and independence of risk assessment from the front office provide a red line when setting up any changes to the credit risk and investment process. These regulations are widely discussed since the financial crisis exists in almost all developed regulatory regimes and would be a strong supplement, if not a key reason, to any business case for change.

2.2.2 Build a Compelling Business Case

There are numerous books, websites, publications, consultancies and even TV shows presenting a wide spectrum of ways to develop a commercially viable business case. All sources have something to offer depending on the audience, so when creating your approach be cognisant that certain value drivers are important for some stakeholders may be the exact opposite for others. For any system, particularly for an ESG management system, to truly live in an organisation, they must have a compelling reason to exist and the right personalities to drive it. In this light, the table below provides an overview of some value drivers mapped to each type of stakeholder identified previously. Also, and in order to ensure that the developer of such a programme is prepared for the invariable challenges in creating change, I have mapped key perceived challenges or "push-backs" to help preparation.

Group	Stand-along P&Ls (first line of defence)	Supporting functions (second line of defence)				Board and assurance functions (third line of defence)	
	Front office (origination and deal teams)	Risk management	Legal	Compliance	Corporate affairs/ marketing	Internal audit	Board
Principal stakeholders							
Personal value drivers (key examples)	Creates better quality credit Achieves access to additional "green" money	Creates better quality credit Feel additional worth from positively impacting the environment/ society Potentially reduced capital charges	Increased governance checks reduce overall legal exposure (equity investments)	Additional client take-on checks will reduce risk Another reason to further requirement-based controls	When properly implemented provides confidence behind public disclosures on ESG (e.g. equator principles) Brand value	Feel additional worth from positively impacting the environment/ society	Increased brand value Create market differentiator
Personal Challenges (key examples)	Cost for due diligence is higher Loss of "nimbleness" in the market due to additional paperwork No expertise nor resource to support	Lack of competence to cover this topic	None identified	Another requirement to review stressing resources	None identified	Lack of competence to cover this topic	Low perceived commercial value

The examples above should be used as a starting point before developing the objectives of the programme and garnering stakeholders' views on this topic. The important point is that every material stakeholder must be regarded and their perspective and opinions taken into consideration. Any ESG implementation programme must as minimum have tried to include them in the implementation and final solution and where this is not possible, feedback to the stakeholders the reasons why. Only in this way will the buy-in and understanding across the organisation be maintained.

The only final comment to add when developing a thorough business case is that where possible quantify the up- and downsides. Firstly, bankers like numbers, and when you have well-thought out assumptions, reliable data and clear messaging, these can be the single winning ticket to making this happen.

There are some thorough publications exploring the value of ESG to an investment. Goldman Sachs in 2009 issued a study showing the correlation between positive ESG performance and the reduction of delays to operating the assets (see Exhibit 25: Strong correlation between ESG scores and timely delivery of projects; page 22) (http://www.borsaitaliana.it/bitApp/view.bit?lang=it&target=StudiDownloadFree&filename=pdf%2F78052.pdf).

Find relevant studies in the market, demonstrate case studies where it went wrong, and build your case for change with financial metrics and qualitative analysis.

2.2.3 Objective Setting for ESG Management System

Objective setting is the starting point for any a new process and key to provide direction. In many cases, they can be as simple as "being compliant to equator principles", but in others, it can be more profound. I worked with one client, and their stated aim was to improve the carbon footprint of all their investments during the lifetime of the asset. This also included the obligation to maintain this improvement programme after sell-down with the new owners of the debt, an honourable but challenging undertaking. These developed and agreed objectives provide the reference point in the event of project decision points (e.g. which assets to include) as well as the level of resources required to deliver such a plan.

Another core aspect of process of change is to gather momentum through collective buy-in during the development and execution of the process, easy to say, hard to deliver. The heart of achieving this is firstly maintaining objectivity, remaining at all times commercially focused, being firm on the steps and aspects that matter the most (i.e. not arguing for the sake of arguing). Thus, in heading through the change process, gathering stakeholders into the design stage is key to ensure that ownership and responsibility and buy-in develop. Most people do not want to pollute, and most do not want to impact communities nor endanger animals.

This value can gain some initial interest and buy-in, but regrettably more is needed to maintain the interest. The value driver of simply writing better debt for the bank has been the best headline to keep the process going.

In the event that even this fails to lift interest and energy, each stakeholder needs to be made aware they are accountable and responsible for their step, and understanding the risks to the bank and managing them effectively is non-negotiable. Avoiding a nasty individual "surprise" can be a very strong back-up to push through your ideas and succeed in keeping everyone focused and energised. Planning the proverbial list of "carrots" and lining up the "sticks" closely behind makes most things in life, as well change programmes in banks, run smoother.

2.2.4   Create Your Own Structure

Often when I ask the question to clients and colleagues, "what do you think good should look like?", the answer often includes the name of a standard or of an institution that has developed a reputation for good performance. In reality, a standard firstly blinds you to doing better and secondly what fits for one company may not for another. There are a number of very clear challenges when looking to design, develop and implement an ESG system discussed in this section.

A variety of international standards and guidance have been discussed elsewhere in this book, and I will not go through the merits of each standard. The pros and cons are extensively discussed, and any Internet search will provide numerous opinions. What I will say, though, is that it is important to have a document to hang your hat on. Meaning that having a benchmark and a goal allows the users to identify with the topic, make it recognisable among other institutions that choose to implement an ESG Framework (market differentiator) and allow a point of reference to continue to improve. I live by the principle in both my operating and consulting lives that we should not design a system only to meet a requirement, but develop the right system that by the virtue of it being effective, holistic and meaningful meets the core requirements of the regulation. As in reality regulations are and should be the minimum requirement of expected behaviour and most certainly not the maximum to obtain the tick of compliance!

For any would-be leader of change, the following macro level steps are a good list to begin the planning. Objectives surrounding each area will help to focus comments, challenges and discussion. The following four areas of change are core to maintaining a structured approach and are in order of priority: governance, people, processes and technology.

The following summary table outlines some core aspects for review

Step	Aspects for consideration	Typical duration for development (can be run in parallel)
Governance	• Ownership • Appetite • Committee structure and mandate • Approval of budgets • Incentivisation for success • Development and approval of a policy • Drive assurance • Etc.	3–6 months
Enabling people	• Hiring of a functional leader • Training of key responsible staff • Training of key stakeholder in the process • Development of all procedures and guidance required for the processes and technologies to meet the objectives of the policy • Etc.	6 months to 2 years
Defining processes	Development of all processes that meet the objectives set out for the process, some of these process include: • First review of deal for ESG categorisation • Input into scope of technical due diligence studies • Definition of conditions precedent to match the deal appetite and risk appetite • Develop conditions subsequent to maintain the performance of the loan to ESG issues • Develop external looking flagging mechanisms to monitor independently borrower performance • Etc.	1–3 years
Information solutions and technology	Using IT to materially create efficiencies to support the above processes	2 years

No change programme can be finished and self-maintaining through the completion of a quick 3-month project. Success hinges on commitment, effective prioritisation of material elements and permanent inclusion of "fit-for-purpose" solutions that match the size of the entity and deal flows. Any leader of the process should chalk down approximately 2–3 years to reach a successfully operating model that meets the initial objectives. Realising this and setting those expectations early save pain later down the line!

2.2.5   Credit Process Alignment

Developing any process in an organisation needs to be aligned to the core processes of the organisation. This has two benefits: first, it's efficient and there is less pain for all involved, and second, there is a common reference point to start to map new processes in a systematic way. It is incredible that when interviewing credit risk and ESG professionals, the core process steps have not been standardised nor clarified for a common understanding, often even at the credit risk level. The steps certainly exist, but the naming convention and consistency across products and P&Ls do not.

The table below outlines a typical credit process for a normal credit transaction often associated with the need for ESG analysis with example ESG actions mapped to each step, for illustration purposes.

Credit Step	• Example ESG Actions
Origination	• Inclusion of ESG requirements on website and in marketing material
First Screen	• High level screening that ESG criteria are satisfied, Ensure scope of DD will identify key ESG aspects
Financial Review	• ESG due diligence and development of ESG covenants and reporting requirements
Pre-Approval Review	• ESG Statement of risk level and compliance with ESG Policy
Final Approval	• Internal sign off of compliance with ESG Policy
Signature	• Signature of client compliance with ESG Requirements
Conditions Subsequent (CS)	• Handover of CS requriements and development of internal mechanisms to operationalise the monitoring effectively
Portfolio Management	• Ongoing monitoring of compliance with ESG Policy –Watch List / Media • Tracking / Breach of Covenants / Action Plan Review
Exit Strategy	• ESG Requirement to ensure ESG benefits are continued

These cores of the credit process need to be the blueprint for all new processes for debt and equity investments where ESG topics need to be materially assessed. To leverage these core steps, the credit risk and ESG functions need to understand the differences in process, timing and ultimate inherent risk of each asset when investing in debt or equity products or through direct or indirect investment (i.e. intermediaries). These four dimensions (debt, equity, direct, indirect) each need to be reviewed and considered in developing the full suite of controls to be implemented.

It is worth noting that the value of the asset is not often correlated directly with the risks posed to the bank, particularly when relating to reputation risk. For example, indirect investment in equity is often the last area to be focused on, but can pose the greatest threat to the bank's reputation if left relatively uncontrolled from an ESG perspective.

Once the core credit processes have been mapped out and the ESG process developed, then a useful method to further clarify multiple stakeholders' roles in the process is to create "swim lane" process maps. A screenshot from one previously developed is shown below for a part of the first screen process. These steps are then created for each of the credit steps showing how and when the ESG team will be involved in the overall process.

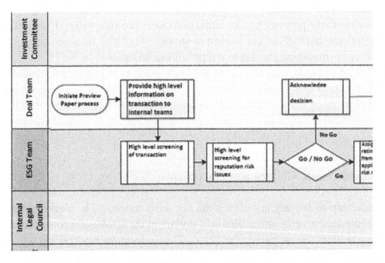

Develop or, as a minimum, finalise these swim lanes with your stakeholders to build again the buy-in and to create a common understanding of the ESG role.

2.2.6 Management of Conflicts of Interest

Segregation of duties is one of the key challenges facing any ESG functions as they often need to provide front office with their analysis of ESG issues and provide the credit risk function an independent review and approval of any deal. An impossible task within this set-up.

For reference, under the SYSC 5.1 regulations from the FSA in the UK, a useful definition of segregation of duties is as follows:

A firm should normally ensure that no single individual has unrestricted authority to do all of the following:

1. Initiate a transaction.
2. Bind the firm.

3. Make payments.
4. Account for it.

This structural set-up is often easy to demonstrate on paper but is less convincing when conditions 1 and 2 above are compromised when those involved in the credit application for ESG are often requested also to approve the contents during the credit approval process. Once this occurs, points 3 and 4 are automatically executed as all necessary documentation, and approvals are complete. Thus indirectly there is no true segregation of roles in the credit approval process for ESG.

The four conditions above are relatively simple to meet for large organisations because they have the resources to fund the segregation through different competency groups, but, for smaller institutions, teams are already stretched and overloaded and to maintain the independence becomes a core challenge. So often in reviewing these processes in organisations over the past years, I've noticed that ESG functions themselves are having to straddle the lines between supporting the front office in analysing the deals and providing an opinion to the credit risk teams on quality of the deal with respect to the bank's wider risk appetite. This is a clear conflict, and how this is resolved, if at all, is most often down to how seriously an organisation takes the ESG analysis and the trust they have in the objectiveness, skills and empowerment of the individuals managing the conflict themselves.

2.2.7   Leadership, Culture and Governance

The leadership of any organisation is the key to its success. The markets understand this, and companies can lose millions of dollars in the stroke of a few minutes when company leaders are negatively affected. This individual's perceived value to the organisation is not based on the time he spends in the office, nor the number of deals he writes, but is simply linked to the individual's drive, strategy and the culture he instils in his organisation that makes it work. He creates the foundations and DNA template for the organisation that influences all employees as they join and remain at the company. This common bond and underlying instinct makes the company move forward autonomously, aligning the tasks, actions and decisions to this individual's vision and strategy. This DNA provides the core values of the organisation, which are then translated and implemented as one travels through the levels of the organisation. This is experienced tangibly at the credit risk level, through numerous touch points in an organisation. A selection of methods for illustration purposes is shown in the table below. These methods have been mapped to the "line of defence" as discussed previously.

Examples of impacts of leadership attitude to the ESG topic on the three lines of defence

Cultural drivers	First line of defence (e.g. risk takers)	Second line of defence (e.g. advisors)	Third line of defence (e.g. assurers)
Objective	Excluded sectors for equity/debt products as they are judged to be "not green"	Adequate and fair budgets to deliver proactively ESG activities Performance monitoring: deals rejected on ESG issues	Frequent ESG performance and advisory reviews and improvements
Subjective	Annual balanced score card (BSC) review includes comments from ESG function on behaviour	Annual BSC of ESG team includes comments from credit risk on ESG's commercial focus in dealing with ESG aspects	Tracking the amount of feedback (e.g. number of requested clarifications, challenges, ad hoc reviews, etc.) from the board and senior management on the ESG management information produced
Individual	Rewarded financially for tangibly improving the ESG performance of a deal	Providing guaranteed training budget to maintain best practice awareness	Annual ESG training for auditors and board members
Company wide	Risk appetite for "high risk" deals with ESG aspects made available in transparent company policy	Embedding of ESG function into all relevant credit risk processes including membership in relevant credit committees	Frequent communications around the ESG topic celebrating successes

The table above can be sketched out with all the desired touch points on the ground of a system, and series of actions, activities projects and trainings can be focused to address deficiencies.

The concept of splitting the "ESG system" into four core aspects of objective, subjective, individual and company (or group) is discussed in the previous section with the concept of the "Integral Model". This model as mentioned is a useful means to ensure that we, as risk managers, consider the issues holistically. So often as humans we focus on the tangible (e.g. processes, documents and checklists), and we often leave out the softer aspects of values and culture. This remains in focus when considering the "blue and red" sides of the "Integral Model". This colourful and meaningful topic is discussed in the next section.

The governance of any company, business line, site or entity is key to its success. There is much written about corporate governance and appropriate structures to ensure this. A useful source of information as a starter is from the Professional Risk Managers' International Association (www.prmia.org) where they have published several years ago the PRMIA Principles of Good Governance. This publication provides a useful checklist as a starting point for any gap analysis or improvement programme around the governance topic. ESG governance itself can also be developed with this list by adapting it to the relevant credit risk, investment process and overall board oversight process, for example. For clarity, the publication states the following useful definitions:

Governance The framework of authority for an organisation within which its institutional objectives are pursued and within which risk management operates.

Also, this guidance outlines ten core elements to sound governance in an organisation as listed below:

- Key competencies
- Resources and processes
- Ongoing education and development
- Compensation architecture
- Independence of key parties
- Risk appetite
- External validation
- Clear accountability
- Disclosure and transparency
- Trust, honesty and fairness of key people

Use the list as trigger words to test your core governance ESG processes to find weaknesses and focus efforts to closing the gaps. This area is one of the most important, so if this is structurally wrong, it will be near impossible to succeed.

Conclusion

In all banks and investment institutions, there are differences in the cultures, leadership and above all processes, but the core elements outlined here provide some starting points for development or perhaps an aide-memoire for further evolution of existing systems that need tweaking.

To aid any would-be ESG management system developer, risk manager or leader, the following "must-haves" may be useful:

- Assign strong senior leadership.
- Enthusiastic, commercially focused ESG leader with access and credibility at the highest level of senior management.
- Understand all stakeholders and their value drivers.
- Set key objectives for each of the areas of governance, people, process and technology.
- Developed processes and methods must be fit for purpose.
- Swim lane process maps to engage wider stakeholders.
- Governance mechanisms maintained without question especially membership on credit committee.
- Ensure independent voice on the board.
- Segregation of front office with credit risk.
- Full alignment to the core credit process.
- Incentivise the right behaviours and penalise non-compliance.
- Annual review of performance and continuous improvement commissioned by the board.

Challenges and Advantages of IFC Performance Standards: ERM Experience

Elena Amirkhanova and Raimund Vogelsberger

Abstract This chapter discusses an interview with two partners from Environmental Resource Management (ERM) about important environmental and social issues in the IFC's recently revised Performance Standards. These include climate change, biodiversity and ecosystems, stakeholder engagement, gender and business and human rights. They represent issues, where earlier requirements have been made more explicit, as well as emerging themes that have been introduced. This chapter addresses how these issues are reflected as cross-cutting themes rather than as stand-alone topics. This chapter also discusses conceptual and political dilemmas and challenges related to some of these themes, as well as practical aspects such as implementation and integration into decision-making and management systems.

Can you explain some of the history behind the IFC Performance Standards? Why they have become such a success story and what IFC is doing to keep them relevant? The IFC as a member of the World Bank Group initially relied on the World Bank guidelines for evaluating project-specific pollution prevention and control measures and used Pollution Prevention and Abatement Handbook issued in 1988. In 1998, IFC Board of Directors formally approved some of the World Bank Safeguard Policies on environmental and social issues. Almost ten years later they were replaced by the eight IFC Performance Standards. In addition to the Standards, the IFC Environment Health and Safety Guidelines were published in 2007.

In our opinion, the Standards have become so successful because of a number of reasons. First, IFC was one of the earliest lending institutions to develop a set of standards that can be used across different industries and sectors worldwide. Second, Equator Principles which have been adopted by 80 International Financial Institutions around the world refer to IFC Performance Standards for more specific requirements. Third, the Standards can be applied even when there is no intention to apply for project finance, as they are internationally recognised as essentially the "benchmark" for environmental and social aspects of a project development. Finally, IFC puts a lot of effort into keeping the Standards up to date. For example,

E. Amirkhanova (✉) • R. Vogelsberger
ERM Global Sustainable Finance Head, ERM 2nd Floor, Exchequer Court St Mary Axe, 32, London EC3A 8AA, UK
e-mail: Elena.Amirkhanova@erm.com; Raimund.Vogelsberger@erm.com

© Springer International Publishing Switzerland 2015
K. Wendt (ed.), *Responsible Investment Banking*, CSR, Sustainability, Ethics & Governance, DOI 10.1007/978-3-319-10311-2_3

it revised the Performance Standards and published the new version in 2012 and is in the process of reviewing the EHS Guidelines, to be published in 2016; the process of review and update of course includes substantial comment and input from the public.

Are there any areas where the 2012 overhaul of the Performance Standards has left room for interpretation or improvement? Can any gaps be filled by emerging best practice? The nature of the IFC Performance Standards assumes a degree of flexibility and interpretation. The idea behind the Standards is ongoing improvement of the projects through their lifetime, rather than just a "static" compliance. Although the IFC Performance Standards are called "standards", in reality they are rather *guidance* for project development than a set of very prescriptive requirements. Standards are aimed to be used around the world in different sectors and regions, thus, they are *asking questions* rather than giving exact answers. As such, there is always a degree of flexibility on a project by project basis, in particular with regard to the extent that is required to assess certain risks, e.g. project-associated facilities, involvement of third parties, human rights, cumulative impacts and others.

In our experience, addressing these issues in practice relies on development of more specific approaches that can vary from country to country. For example, greater attention to human rights in recent years has been driving the development of human rights due diligence tools, methodologies and specific indicators to measure performance, etc. Just a few years ago, not many people had heard of human rights due diligence, but now this is clearly an emerging best practice.

Has environmental, social and governance risk identification and management according to 2012 IFC Performance Standards become more convenient or more complex, is it more mainstream now or more effective? IFC has clarified a lot of aspects, for example, in relation to stakeholder engagement, supply chain, security arrangements, to make them clearer and easier to implement and to address the demands of the changing world. At the same time, the Standards became more complex as there are a number of the so-called "cross-cutting issues", which require an integrated approach and deep knowledge of interrelations between different subject areas and topics. So we definitely see more clarity on one hand and more complexity on the other.

You mention these cross-cutting issues now in the 2012 IFC Performance Standards. Can you explain which issues they cover? A number of topics (such as climate change, gender, human rights and water) impact more than one specific field or area and are generally affected by a series of interlinked factors (that is why they are called "cross-cutting"). These issues cannot be addressed in isolation and require an integrated approach and actions.

That is why IFC's approach to cross-cutting issues is to integrate them into the existing Performance Standards and to address them across multiple Standards, rather than developing stand-alone one on each topic.

In our experience, this multi-topic and multi-standard approach is appropriate and reflects the reality. For example, if we look at water, there are clearly the natural/ecological factors to be considered as well as the social and economic aspects of how these resources are utilised—or not. The application of a single Performance Standard alone would not do justice to the multifaceted aspects of this issue.

Let's talk about one of the most relevant cross-cutting issues: human rights. Can you give us a view on how the work of Prof Ruggie has influenced the 2012 IFC Performance Standards? Human rights is one of the most critical and fundamental issues, it is something that people will literally fight for. Although they were not called as such, we have seen in our work that these issues have been emerging for many years.

The greatest achievement of Prof John Ruggie and the UN Protect, Respect and Remedy Framework is that it recognises the relevance and importance of human rights in a business context and provides clarity on what it means for business and financial institutions.

According to IFC in the course of the 2012 Performance Standards update, the IFC analysed different approaches to strengthen the human rights requirements, reviewed the Performance Standards against various documents including the Ruggie Framework and reflected some elements in the Performance Standards and Guidance Notes interlinked with human rights.

The 2012 IFC Performance Standards introduce human rights considerations and human rights language. IFC also requires clients to identify and address relevant business issues via social and environmental due diligence which can incorporate human rights due diligence. Furthermore, all the other cross-cutting issues are closely interlinked with human rights.

In addition to the IFC Performance Standards, the Guidance Note 1 refers to the International Bill of Rights and suggests that a project developers should address the "respect" and "remedy" aspects of the Ruggie Framework by implementing a management system that assesses and mitigates human rights risks and by introducing a grievance mechanism to allow the affected public (and employees) to freely address their concerns. It also uses the same logic as the Ruggie Framework and requires clients to "start from the top" and to establish an umbrella policy for their project organisation that should cover all the social and environmental issues and drive performance.

Based on individual circumstances, clients may need to consider these and other requirements and tools.

How big is the impact of the human rights cross-cutting issues on the financing and investment markets? Can you identify already some regional differences in terms of uptake, level of due diligence and implementation? What are the main challenges? It's still early days in the application of these requirements, but we can definitely say that human rights considerations form now an integral part of any social impact assessment developed to meet IFC Standards.

Also, human rights due diligence is becoming more common, and in some cases, financial institutions do decide to step away from projects because of the identified risks. The challenge is that it is not clearly specified when and how human rights due diligence should be conducted. Given that this specific due diligence is still new to the project developers and lenders, and due to implementation uncertainties, there is some resistance with regard to its execution. What we also see is that lenders play an important role and influence (positively!) on how developers are approaching this issue.

This is a very fair question about regional differences. Due to different political situations, legislative regimes and governance procedures (e.g. the extent of use of government security forces varies in Europe, Latin America and Africa), such issues as employee rights, safety, resettlement, women rights or rights of indigenous people can be viewed differently within the framework of local legislation as well as regional, cultural and historical context.

Another challenge is the practical difficulty in identifying and reporting human rights issues, as the process may often require additional data gathering or even legal investigation that is not always possible for an outside party or within the available scope or timeframe of the overall due diligence. Furthermore, both developers and lenders in some cases still feel "uncomfortable" to use "human rights" language.

In what cases is a human rights impact assessment as per IFC Performance Standards required? Is there any emerging best practice? Although there is no direct requirement to conduct a specific human rights impact assessment, the IFC does require businesses to take responsibility to respect human rights. So in reality, human rights form an integral part of many lenders' social impact assessments as this is a cross-cutting issue relevant to all aspects of the operation: from provision of potable water to workers to the rights of migrant workers, from prevention of negative impacts to local communities and restoration of livelihoods of displaced people, to mitigation of wider impacts on water and land in a long-term perspective. The key here is to make sure that all the impacts and risks have been identified and assessed from a human rights perspective and reflected accordingly using an appropriate terminology.

There is an emerging best practice in this regard. For example, the International Business Leaders Forum and IFC, together with the UN Global Compact, developed a Guide to Human Rights Assessment and Management in 2010.

There are also some specific tools developed in different countries. The Human Rights Impact Assessment for Security Measures was issued by the Canadian Human Rights Commission in 2011, which provides guidance for Canadian organisations with responsibilities for national security to help them create and maintain security measures that respect human rights.

Also, we are seeing that many large oil and gas and mining corporations are developing internal procedures and key performance indicators to identify human rights related impacts and risks and assess performance on local levels.

Another cross-cutting issue is gender. Can you explain to us the main issues that need to be addressed? When is a gender assessment required? Gender is one of the most sensitive issues to address. It is multidimensional and is closely linked to different impacts on women and men due to social norms or legal barriers.

Gender-related issues can include different project risks and impacts as well as opportunities for men and women, legal inequality, discrimination and others. As an example resettlement and livelihood losses often affect men and women differently—in some regions rights of women to hold or own a property are not recognised. Another example is different values—cultural heritage can be valued differently by men and women.

Gender aspects are normally included in the impact assessment or due diligence, but the degree of their consideration would vary depending on the region, particular area and nature of the project. Given the complexity of the issue, it is sometimes challenging to identify and assess all the various gender-related impacts; we have to be creative in our approach. For example, consultation process should include both men and women, and to achieve this in some countries we organise separate meetings or focus groups for women and run by women because in mixed meetings men will likely dominate.

Could you give us an example of a complex project with issues related to resettlement or indigenous people, and how you managed to solve them? One of the examples is a project run by ERM Peru for a Copper Corporation. The project is located in a rural area of Peru. Mine development plan requires resettlement which is being performed by a Peruvian company. Developer is considering international project finance and has asked ERM to review the resettlement against the Equator Principles—and respectively IFC Performance Standards. ERM performed a gap analysis to check whether the local Peruvian contractor completed the resettlement in line with both Peruvian laws and IFC Standards. ERM also liaised with the community to review their involvement and the degree to which the implementation was in fact consistent with agreed plans. With this information, ERM created an action plan that the developer is now implementing. ERM returns to the project periodically to verify whether the recommendations have been met. Another recent example is a development of an Environmental and Social Impact Assessment (ESIA) for Mongolian company. In order to develop coal mine and build essential infrastructure to become Mongolia's most advanced coking coal operations the Company applied for international financing from the European Bank for Reconstruction and Development (EBRD) and other international financial institutions. The proposed mine and railway are in Mongolian Gobi Desert where nomadic herders still live; it is also a migratory path for several endangered species. The project had an ambitious schedule which relied upon the ESIA being completed in time to take the environmental and social topics off the "critical path" prior to financing.

ERM mobilised a large in-country field team of Mongolian specialists supported by experienced ERM staff from across the world to carry out all the various ESIA activities, including impact assessment, public consultation, resettlement planning, monitoring and evaluation and corporate advice on best practice in resettlement for nomadic people. ERM team worked closely with the client to provide "real-time" inputs into the planning and decision-making process. Resettlement was a key impact of the project which required careful management. "Resettlement" from IFC perspective was not limited to physical displacement of people's homes or businesses, but also included impacts on livelihoods such as farmland or pastures used for a railway. These impacts were managed through a combination of early engagement with herders as well as strategic approach to public consultation and disclosure. By mobilising the right team and focusing on the client's needs, ERM managed to deliver the ESIA ahead of schedule and to a quality that was judged by EBRD as the "world class". Some of the successful elements of project management such as hosting a "mitigation workshop" have now been integrated as a best practice within ERM's internal impact assessment and planning procedures.

Many problems with the cross-cutting issues arise when governments get involved, such as resettlement of people and use of indigenous resources, meeting energy demand with large hydro dams. What are the most complicated issues you have experienced in this respect and how did you manage to solve them? We face a number of common challenges working on projects when governments are involved: first of all, difficulty in identifying who is responsible and accountable for meeting the lenders' requirements as completely different parties involved at different stages of project implementation; second, very limited flexibility in terms of project design especially if it had been developed and approved by a government; and third, communication and interaction between stakeholders might present a particular challenge. Of course, in many cases, we have to also pay attention to different political factors or lobbying interests of certain groups.

Another challenge is linked to the requirement of IFC to take into account not only a project itself, but the entire associated infrastructure that will be linked to and will depend on project. It is often difficult to assess impacts related to "associated facilities", for example in many cases neither us nor our clients—usually private companies—can get access to the relevant information.

The key factor to success is to identify the potential risks and gaps as early as possible, identify (or even nominate!) responsible parties and to initiate a negotiation process when it is not yet too late. We have multiple examples when pressure from lenders played a crucial role in improving some elements of projects, for example, changing design of a mine to meet up-to-date health and safety standards or implementing offsets and creating a nature protected area as a biodiversity compensation measure in the course of a road construction. Although these measures might be seen as spending extra time and money, but effectively they create a better outcome longer term.

Another complex, cross-cutting issue is ecosystems services. While "ecosystem" itself is an environmental issue, "ecosystems services" is considered a social issue: How can the two go together? You are right that ecosystem services is a complex issue. In reality, it has social and environmental components as it is based around products or socio-economic benefits people obtain from ecosystems and natural processes.

The ecosystem services approach was designed to look at the holistic and more sustainable management of natural resources and to ensure that they are available in the long term, for example, that the habitats these ecosystems support remain viable for future generations.

The objectives behind the ecosystem services concept is to ensure more integrated approach to the identification, assessment and mitigation of environmental and social risks that go together hand in hand.

A good example is water, which provides a wide range of essential ecosystem services people heavily depend on. Such issues as water quality, access to water and water pollution not only affect people's quality of life, but all the other organisms from microbes to plants and animals. In 2009, one of the global surveys revealed that public concerns over water were ranked ahead of climate change, depletion of natural resources, air pollution and biodiversity destruction. In addition, in July 2010, the UN General Assembly recognised access to safe drinking water and sanitation as a human right.

An ecosystem services approach is aimed to look at surface and groundwater as an interlinked system; it needs to understand the sources and end points of water use and their link to ecological function and human well-being. Lastly it needs to look at all of these issues in the context of other activities (mining, farming, etc.) in the area. In order to address the above an integrated water management programme should be designed covering water use, discharge, pollution, storm water and flooding as well as impacts on regional and local water resources, cumulative impacts and the relationship between surface and groundwater systems.

In a nutshell, what are the trickiest issues when dealing with biodiversity and ecosystems services? Ecosystem services and biodiversity-related issues are well known to scientists and policymakers, but they are rather new for financial institutions and developers. Biodiversity is traditionally viewed from a holistic rather than practical perspective, and it is not widely known why it is important for companies and how it can affect sustainability of their business in the future.

The concept of ecosystem services links both holistic and practical points of view together. However benefits that people and businesses derive from ecosystems are well understood, but how to manage impacts and risks related to ecosystem services is not clear and requires additional explanation. Using an example of water – unsustainable use of water may cause shortage of resources not only for local populations but for local companies as well. Environmental protests may result in project delays and millions in direct and indirect costs. Building this understanding requires time and effort from consultants, lenders and all the interested parties.

An impact mitigation hierarchy used by IFC—namely, to avoid, minimise, mitigate and manage—is still new for many developers. It requires a shift in thinking and a change in mindset from the use of natural resources at any cost to thorough consideration of all the alternatives and even refusal to implement the project.

IFC Standards suggest a number of practical measures. These include "no net loss" of biodiversity when project-related impacts on biodiversity are balanced by measures taken, exclusion of certain land areas from development for further conservation, establishment of biological corridors to minimise habitat fragmentation, restoration of habitats during and/or after operations, and some others.

Practical implementation of these measures requires high-quality professional advice and should be underpinned by studies, and in many—and probably even most—cases there is no single solution that can address all the issues. Another challenge is to make sure that these measures are identified and included in the design at early stages of the project development. This requires consultation with affected stakeholders and joint efforts of governments, financial institutions and companies. In any case, if these measures are built in design soon enough, then they are not that costly, and implementation is more manageable.

The last, but not least, important cross-cutting issue is climate change. IFC has been accused of doing too little as a standard-setter to effectively address climate change and is said to be blind on the subject. What measures do the new IFC Performance Standards offer and how do they combat climate change? Climate change is a tricky issue, not only for IFC but for other lending institutions, policymakers and advisors because the external context has evolved rapidly in this area.

In 2008, the World Bank issued its policy paper "Development and Climate Change: Strategic Framework for the World Bank Group". This document has set the stage for IFC Performance Standards to support low-carbon economic development and to address climate change impacts, impacts on ecosystem services through implementation of risk-appropriate climate adaptation measures.

The Performance Standards address climate change in a number of direct and indirect ways including environmental and social assessments, more clear commitments and reporting. Given that climate change is a very complex cross-cutting issue it is reflected in all the Standards.

More specifically IFC amended the requirements on resource efficiency, ecosystem services approach, community impacts, water protection and others. For example IFC Standards look at community health and safety communities in the light of climate change and refer to natural hazards, climate-related risks for workers, exposure to diseases, impacts on natural waterways, etc.

Another example is that the scope of direct GHG emissions expanded to include not only purchased electricity but also steam, heating and cooling and requires an assessment of options for low-carbon technologies.

IFC Performance Standards can provide a good guidance, but implementation is a challenge.

For example, project-specific climate change risks are still not well understood by developers, such as risks to workers' health, safety and working conditions. Another challenge is that many developers still do not believe that climate change may affect their operations, delay projects or increase costs.

The updated Equator Principles III have adopted the new (2012) IFC Performance Standards. How does that multiply the impact of those standards? Are there any alternatives to the IFC Standards in emerging markets? The Equator Principles do multiply the impact of IFC Performance Standards in a number of ways.

All the financial institutions that adopt the Equator Principles ultimately take the responsibility to ensure that the borrowers apply IFC Performance Standards to their projects. As of December 2014 there are 80 Equator Principles Financial Institutions, the so-called Equator Banks. This significantly increases use of the IFC Standards by potential borrowers. Equator Banks together provide a huge portion of international project financing; interestingly, there is a leverage effect too because many project deals involve a consortium of lenders—and so even if there is just one Equator Bank in a consortium, the project will have to meet Equator Principles and hence IFC Standards. Some developers apply IFC Standards even when they are not looking for project finance, but want to be in line with international good practice to manage risks more effectively.

Initially, Equator Principles were applied to project finance only, later their scope was expanded to include advisory services. Some Equator Banks used the Principles for a limited number of projects, while others voluntarily applied them to other forms of financing and wider range of financial products. Third version of Equator Principles (EP III) formally added bridge loans and project-related corporate loans to the mix, and many Equator Banks expect that this will increase a number of projects requiring EP review. However, it is still early days as EP III formally became effective only in January 2014.

Although IFC Performance Standards are sometimes challenging to implement, they are very widely used in emerging markets. For most projects located in the EU, North America, Australia, Japan and other higher-income countries it is assumed that national legislation is sufficiently robust to address the key environmental and social topics as well as ensure public participation. The IFC Standards are mainly intended for those countries where regulations are not as stringent (or not uniformly enforced) and where there is a higher risk that project-affected people may not have sufficient legal rights or practical means to voice their opinions. Thus, for projects in emerging markets, IFC Performance Standards remain the "standard benchmark" from an environmental and social perspective. Depending on a project location and lenders additional standards can be applied too. In our experience, these standards are often based on IFC Standards, however there are some specifics, for example if EBRD or European Investment Bank (EIB) are involved their lending policies require compliance with Directives of the European Union—and these can be quite stringent.

Currently, there are a lot of discussions about consistency of different standards and their application. Some people feel that another layer of complexity is added as standards seem to have a different scope: IFC applies its standards across all financial products; Equator Banks apply EP III to project finance, project-related corporate loans, bridge loans and advisory services etc. EIB, EBRD and other lenders have their own standards and requirements to their application. What needs to be done to achieve better consistency in standards, their application and scope? In our work we use multiple international standards developed by different financial institutions. The first impression might be confusing as there are standards developed by IFC, EBRD, EIB, Asian Development Bank (ADB), various export credit agencies (ECAs) and others. However detailed comparison shows that they are generally in line with each other. There are still some challenges when a company is dealing with multiple financial institutions, but overall principles and logic are very similar as all of them are regularly updated and reflect the same global trends in international financing.

Could you give us an example of a project where multiple requirements were successfully used? ERM performed an Equator Principle environmental and social assessment of the Tangguh Liquid Natural Gas (LNG) project in the Bintuni Bay area of Papua Province, Indonesia, some 3,200 km from Jakarta. This is a tropical area, biologically rich, physically dynamic and sparsely populated by indigenous communities. We were commissioned to carry out our assessment on behalf of a consortium of international commercial banks, the Asian Development Bank and the Japanese Bank for International Cooperation (JBIC), as well as several ECAs. The objectives included technical support and advice to the project lenders and working with the Tangguh LNG project team to ensure an environmental and social alignment with international standards. As a basis of our evaluation we compiled the "most stringent" requirements based on the Equator Principles/IFC Performance Standards, JBIC and ADB Guidelines, and the World Bank Safeguard Policies. In this way we could give comfort to all the lending consortium members that their respective standards (at a minimum) were reflected within the assessment.

If you had to draw a conclusion on the 2012 IFC Performance Standards, what would it be? The 2012 IFC Performance Standards represent an important step in updating our approach to deal with "classic" environmental and social topics while incorporating the new ones such as cross-cutting issues. After the revised Standards were formally issued by IFC the typical echo from some industry representatives was that the Standards are too stringent, while from the NGO side— that they did not go far enough; on balance IFC probably reached an appropriate middle ground.

In summary, there are so many interlinked and complex issues that have implications in wider geographical, environmental, social and economic context and in long-term perspective, but must then be considered for specific projects in certain locations. At the risk of repeating a widely used phrase, the key conclusion for successful application of the Standards would nevertheless be: "Think globally, act locally".

EBRD Environmental and Social Governance Standards and Their Impact on the Market

Dariusz Prasek

Abstract The European Bank for Reconstruction and Development (EBRD) aims to achieve impact by integrating sustainability into its investment strategies, departmental scorecards, due diligence standards, portfolio supervision systems and technical assistance. This forms an important part of the value that the EBRD brings to its clients and countries of operations, as well as delivering high-level environmental and social quality assurance. All EBRD-financed projects must meet rigorous environmental and social standards in accordance with the bank's Environmental and Social Policy and are subject to detailed due diligence and monitoring. In this way, the EBRD provides assurance to its management, shareholders and stakeholders that the bank's projects will contribute to sustainable development and avoid or minimise environmental and social risks. The EBRD seeks outcomes that not only protect and benefit society and the environment but which also address the business case for sustainability by helping clients reduce risk, improve efficiency and achieve business growth. This chapter explains the practical approach with which the bank implements its sustainability mandate.

1 Introduction

The European Bank for Reconstruction and Development (EBRD) invests in changing people's lives in 34 countries from central Europe to central Asia and the southern and eastern Mediterranean (the SEMED region). Working primarily with the private sector, the bank invests in projects, engages in policy dialogue and provides technical advice that fosters innovation and builds sustainable and open market economies. Established in 1991 in response to the widespread collapse of communism in central and eastern Europe, one of the challenges immediately apparent to the EBRD was a chronic environmental legacy caused by years of ecologically destructive practices. At that time, growing international attention

D. Prasek (✉)
Environment and Sustainability Department, European Bank for Reconstruction and Development (EBRD), London, UK
e-mail: prasekd@ebrd.com

© Springer International Publishing Switzerland 2015   71
K. Wendt (ed.), *Responsible Investment Banking*, CSR, Sustainability, Ethics & Governance, DOI 10.1007/978-3-319-10311-2_4

centred on worldwide environmental problems and the concept of sustainable development. As a result, the founding agreement of the EBRD included an explicit commitment to environmental and sustainable development in all of its activities.

Since its founding days, the EBRD has striven to ensure that all of its projects meet rigorous environmental and social standards in accordance with the bank's Environmental and Social Policy and are subject to detailed due diligence and monitoring. In this way, the EBRD provides assurance to its shareholders, management and other stakeholders, including the public and civil society, that the bank's projects will contribute to sustainable development and avoid or minimise environmental and social risks. The bank aims to achieve impact by integrating sustainability into its investment strategies, departmental scorecards, due diligence standards, portfolio supervision systems and technical assistance. This forms an important part of the value that the bank brings to its clients and countries of operations, as well as delivering a high level of environmental and social quality assurance. The bank further places a strong emphasis on engagement with stakeholders and is an active participant in international sustainability initiatives and policy development and further operates a robust independent complaint mechanism. The EBRD seeks outcomes that not only protect and benefit society and the environment but which also address the business case for sustainability as a contributor to business growth. Helping clients to manage environmental and social risk, improve energy efficiency and increase female participation in the workforce or involving communities in project development is fully aligned with the EBRD's central mandate and purpose. This chapter explains a practical approach with which the bank implements its sustainability mandate and further presents a number of case studies to demonstrate the bank's successes in integrating sustainability into projects.

2   Assurance Through the EBRD's Environmental and Social Policy

The EBRD's Environmental and Social Policy (E&S Policy) requires that all projects are assessed, structured and monitored to ensure that they are environmentally and socially sustainable, respect the rights of affected workers and communities and are designed and operated in compliance with applicable regulatory requirements and good international and industry good practice. The E&S Policy is composed of ten specific Performance Requirements and works in conjunction with other bank policies, particularly the Public Information Policy and the Project Complaint Mechanism, to provide a high level of assurance, transparency and accountability.

The EBRD's Environmental and Sustainability Department is responsible for the appraisal, clearance and monitoring of the bank's projects from an environmental and social perspective in terms of the E&S Policy. Prospective projects are screened at an early stage into one of the four categories, depending on the potential environmental and social impacts and risks associated with the project and the level and type of environmental and social due diligence that is required before final project approval:

- Category A projects are associated with potentially significant and diverse environmental and social impacts and risks requiring detailed impact assessments and management plans.
- Category B projects are associated with environmental and social impacts that are site specific and that can be addressed through readily available management and mitigation techniques.
- Category C projects have minimal environmental or social impacts.
- FI projects are those where the EBRD is investing in a financial intermediary, such as a bank, microfinance institution or private equity fund.

The environmental and social impact assessments and due diligence undertaken for projects, which generally involves independent consultants and specialists, seek to understand and assess potential environmental and social impacts and risks, identify appropriate mitigation measures and structure the projects to meet the bank's E&S Policy. New greenfield projects should be designed to meet the policy from the outset, while existing projects that may be subject to expansion, for example, will be required to meet the policy within an agreed time frame. A key aspect of the appraisal and due diligence process is identifying the potential for environmental and social benefits and improvements so as to further integrate sustainability into the project design. To ensure that these measures and improvements are implemented and that the E&S Policy is met, the EBRD may agree an Environmental and Social Action Plan (ESAP) for a project. This ESAP forms part of the loan agreement, and each action is subject to a particular time frame.

As per the bank's Public Information Policy, environmental and social project information is disclosed through appropriate channels including on the EBRD's website. This allows stakeholders to raise any questions or voice any concerns about a project, which are taken into consideration during project appraisal. At various stages during project appraisal and due diligence, environmental and social issues, and any recommended terms and conditions, are reviewed by the relevant EBRD investment committee prior to the final approval of the transaction.

Following approval, environmental and social issues are then monitored during the implementation phase of the project through regular client reports to the bank on a project's environmental and social performance, including progress against a project ESAP and, where appropriate, by means of site visits by EBRD staff and independent consultants. The bank provides enhanced supervision and assistance for projects that do not fully meet the bank's requirements. A lack of environmental and social reporting is one of the factors that can trigger enhanced monitoring by the EBRD, resulting in more frequent site visits or help with capacity-building initiatives.

The EBRD further monitors compliance with its obligations under the E&S Policy through its Project Complaint Mechanism (PCM). Launched in 2010 to replace the Independent Recourse Mechanism (IRM), the PCM affords individuals, groups and organisations that may be adversely affected by an EBRD-financed project an opportunity to make a complaint to the bank. The PCM is overseen by the Office of the Chief Compliance Officer (OCCO) and is independent from the EBRD's banking operations and the Environment and Sustainability Department.

The approach to project appraisal and environmental and social due diligence described above applies to all of the EBRD's investment operations, including the bank's investments in the small- and medium-sized enterprises (SME) sector, via relevant framework facilities for transactions of 10 million euros or less.

The E&S Policy, the Public Information Policy and the Project Complaint Mechanism were updated in 2014 after an extensive review process which involved consultation with various stakeholders.

3 Making an Impact

The bank aims to achieve impact by integrating sustainability into its projects. It achieves this through specific investment strategies, departmental scorecards which promote the integration of sustainability in the bank's investments, the bank's environmental and social and associated policies, through project monitoring and through technical assistance. Key focus areas of the bank include addressing climate change and improving energy efficiency, promoting gender equality and empowerment, investments in water and sanitation, improving road safety and occupational health and safety and promoting sustainability through financial intermediaries.

3.1 Climate Change and Energy Efficiency

The EBRD addresses climate change and energy efficiency through its Sustainable Energy Initiative (SEI). The SEI aims to scale up sustainable energy investments, improve the business environment for sustainable energy investments and develop effective measures to address key barriers to market development. In 2014 EBRD invested over 3 billion euros though the Sustainable Energy Initiative (SEI), which account for 34% of total investments. The Bank's cumulative investments under the SEI passed 15 billion euros, supporting over 850 projects worth more than 80 billion euros.

The EBRD region, which has historically had high emissions and a poor energy efficiency record, continues to offer the possibility of significant absolute reductions to greenhouse gas (GHG) emissions through the upgrade or refurbishment of existing facilities. A loan to PKN Orlen, Poland's leading oil refining and retail group, will finance substantial environmental and energy efficiency improvements at the company's Plock refinery complex. The loan will not only bring about a significant reduction in emissions such as sulphur dioxide and nitrogen oxides but will also enable the company to reduce its annual CO_2 emissions by more than 140,000 tonnes and help accelerate Poland's compliance with the European Union's Industrial Emissions Directive. The company will also implement an integrated and externally certified carbon and energy management system across all of its operations, which will allow for the continuous monitoring of energy and emission intensities, key performance indicators, as well as regular public disclosure of its performance.

Another area where the EBRD has been active in the reduction of GHG emissions is through associated petroleum gas (APG) flaring reduction projects. Globally, APG flaring wastes some 140 billion cubic metres of gas per year, roughly equivalent to one-third of the annual gas consumption in the European Union, and contributes to more than 400 million tonnes per year of CO_2 emissions. The EBRD has financed two important gas flaring reduction projects in Russia for Monolit and Irkutsk Oil. Monolit is an example of how an integrated approach can be employed to address the environmental problems of gas flaring and deliver several valuable products. At Monolit, APG is treated with innovative technology for gas processing and gas-to-liquid conversion to produce dry gas, LPG and gasoline, which are used on site and sold to other nearby oil operations, thus minimising the need for grid infrastructure. The project will result in ~95 % of APG being utilised rather than being flared. Irkutsk Oil is developing a similar concept in phases, whereby the residual APG is also reinjected into the oil fields.

3.2 Gender Equality and Empowerment

The bank's Strategic Gender Initiative (SGI), approved by the EBRD Board of Directors in April 2013, promotes gender equality and the empowerment of women in the bank's investment and technical cooperation projects. The SGI builds on the efforts made since the Gender Action Plan was launched in 2009 and emphasises the corporate commitment and values that the EBRD places on gender equality as an integral part of promoting sound business management and advancing sustainable growth in its countries of operations. The bank, through the SGI, has developed a structured approach to gender equality in order to mainstream it throughout its activities focusing on the provision of access to finance, access to services and access to employment and skills.

The EBRD has sought to improve access to credit for women entrepreneurs by supporting its client banks in increasing their portfolio of micro-, small- and medium-sized enterprises owned and/or managed by women. The Yapi Kredi Bank SME Asset-Guaranteed Bond is one of the first and most recent examples of successful efforts to promote women entrepreneurship in Turkey. The bank's investment will be used to expand YKB's SME lending operations to finance SMEs operating in agribusiness in the priority regions and SMEs that are managed or owned by women.

The bank has also launched several pilot projects in the Municipal and Environment Infrastructure (MEI) sector in order to promote gender equality and achieve a more equitable benefit distribution of the bank's investments in the sector. In the Kyrgyz Republic, a technical cooperation assignment is helping the city of Bishkek to develop systems and tools that ensure equal access for men and women to all its municipal services, including water and wastewater systems, urban transport and solid waste. All feasibility studies for MEI investments now include a component for a gender analysis.

The bank's recent involvement in the privatisation of the Turkish ferry company Istanbul Deniz Otobusleri (IDO) resulted in a significant increase in the number of female employees at the company, which was driven through a bank technical cooperation project to improve gender equality and worker diversity.

3.3 Water and Sanitation

In 2014 the EBRD financed 41 projects in the MEI sector, representing a total EBRD commitment of 717 million euros. Such investments are expected to benefit a total of 5 million people in the EBRD region by providing them with improved water services, district heating, solid waste facilities and other municipal infrastructure. The bank has recently provided financing and technical assistance for various wastewater and water supply upgrade projects in Romania, Georgia and Armenia, which not only improved wastewater collection and treatment as well as sanitary and community health conditions but also led to consequential reductions in effluent discharges to surface water bodies, resulting in cleaner rivers and lakes and more sustainable ecosystems. The EBRD is furthermore involved in providing financing and technical assistance for greenfield wastewater and drinking water projects in the SEMED region.

3.4 Road Safety

Road safety in the EBRD's countries of operation is a major problem with some 50,000 fatalities and 500,000 casualties every year. The socio-economic cost of road accidents is also a very real factor for the victims and their families. According to international studies, seven out of ten people seriously injured in road accidents fall into long-term poverty due to loss of income and loss of income earning potential. The EBRD takes this problem seriously and is trying to improve road safety investments in road infrastructure that meet international good practice standards. Road safety considerations are an important and integral component of the project preparation and due diligence process for all bank-financed transport projects. In Ukraine, the EBRD is participating in the financing of the most recent rehabilitation of the M06 Highway section between Kiev and Chop. The key rationale and objectives of the rehabilitation project included improving road safety along this section particularly for communities living near to and utilising the highway for access. Key improvements include speed restrictions, crossing and turning areas and sidewalks. In Serbia, the EBRD Republic of Serbia Rehabilitation and Safety Project will finance the rehabilitation of 2,500 km of roads, with explicit road safety improvement targets and plans to identify a private sector partner to fund a targeted road safety awareness campaign.

The EBRD also participates in road safety policy dialogue and other international initiatives such as collaboration with the UN, other MDBs and organisations such as the Commission for Global Road Safety. In addition, the bank operates road safety technical cooperation programmes, which can deliver targeted support, such as training, where it is needed on projects.

3.5   Occupation Health and Safety

Occupational health and safety can be a particularly important challenge for companies and their investors. The EBRD's countries of operation's economies include a significant share of heavy industries, which are often associated with high risks to workers. In addition, health and safety awareness in companies and among the workforce can often be weak, and the quality of enforcement by the regulatory authorities can be variable. Occupational health and safety forms an important element in the E&S Policy and is a key feature of the work that the bank conducts during both project due diligence and project implementation and monitoring. The bank has strengthened its emphasis and resources in recent years and has established technical cooperation programmes to deliver training and other forms of technical assistance to selected clients and industry sectors.

In 2006 the EBRD signed a loan with Natron Hayat, an integrated pulp and paper factory in central Bosnia and Herzegovina. The purpose of the loan was for the restart of the pulp production line, purchase new equipment and overall modernisation and renovation of the facilities. The modernisation project introduced a number of environmental improvements both in the production process and end-of-the-pipe environmental technology. A visit by the EBRD identified higher than expected rates of workplace injuries and worker illness, and the bank, together with Natron Hayat, identified improvements that could be made to the safety culture of the workforce. Drawing on the results of a baseline health and safety audit, a plan was developed to allow the company to adopt an internationally recognised health and safety management system. Training programmes were developed and delivered for specific groups including supervisors and senior management to improve their understanding of how to motivate and lead workers to act more safely.

3.6   Financial Intermediaries

The EBRD works closely with financial intermediaries (FIs) to promote environmental and social risk management and sustainability in the financial sector. The key environmental and social sustainability objectives of the bank's investment in FIs are:

- The provision of specialised facilities for sustainable energy financing.
- A growing emphasis on inclusive finance, particularly in relation to women-owned SMEs.
- Ensuring that all FIs adopt environmental and social risk management practices based on the E&S Policy.

Energy efficiency lending to FIs through the Sustainable Energy Financing Facilities (SEFF) model continues to grow. By the end of 2012, the EBRD had provided loans to 75 partner FIs that had on-lent to sub-borrowers supporting more than 41,900 sustainable energy projects and produced projected lifetime energy savings of more than 140,000,000 MWh and projected emission reductions of 55,000,000 tonnes CO_2 equivalent.

EBRD's commitment to gender quality and empowerments is also supported through loans to FIs. In 2012, the EBRD signed a credit line with Turkey's Garanti Bank entirely dedicated to female owners or managers of SMEs. This credit line, which will form part of Garanti Bank's existing Women Entrepreneurs Support Package, will make it easier for female entrepreneurs to access the financing they need.

FI clients of the bank are required to develop and implement Environmental and Social Management Systems (ESMS) to ensure that the activities and projects they finance meet certain environmental and social standards. In parallel, the EBRD places considerable emphasis on capacity building in order to assist FIs to understand and meet these standards. The bank has recently developed a free-of-charge online environmental and social training programme specifically for FIs.

4   Engagement with Civil Society

Sustainable development is more likely to be achieved with the involvement of the whole of society, and the bank seeks to promote this inclusive approach. The bank's open communication with civil society enhances the bank's effectiveness and impact across its countries of operations. Civil society includes non-governmental organisations (NGOs), policy and research organisations, community-based organisations, women's groups, business development organisations and other socio-economic and labour market participants. Civil society organisations (CSOs) are both influential audiences and partners of the EBRD in our countries of operations. These organisations provide a valuable contribution to the development of the bank's policies and strategies and the implementation of projects, particularly on complex, large-scale operations. Furthermore, civil society plays a key role in promoting public dialogue about decisions that affect the lives of local people and the environment, as well as holding governments and policy-makers publicly accountable.

5 Project Evaluation

Project evaluation at the EBRD is a bank-wide effort. The evaluation department has a primary responsibility for evaluation policy and procedures and for monitoring and delivering the bank's overall evaluation programme. It validates and reviews self-evaluations prepared by the management, assesses the adequacy of the self-evaluation process and conducts independent evaluations of bank operations, programmes, strategies and policies. Its analysis is used to assess performance and identify insights and lessons from experience that the institution can then use to improve the effectiveness of future operations. The evaluation of bank projects, whether by EBRD management or by evaluation department, encompasses several individual performance indicators leading to an overall performance rating. One of the indicators is environmental and social performance, which includes health and safety, labour and other relevant social issues. Evaluation also assesses the extent of environmental and social change over the course of the project and attributable to it. Projects are usually assessed 1–2 years after final disbursement of finance by the EBRD, with assessments made against project objectives, the requirements of the bank's Environmental and Social Policy, and the relevant country and sector strategies. In recent years, 89 % of projects that have been subject to independent evaluation have been rated 'satisfactory or better' in terms of their environmental and social performance. Positive environmental change has been achieved in 86 % of cases.

Conclusion

The EBRD will continue to integrate sustainability into its projects and operations and endeavour to ensure that environmental and social project risks are avoided or minimised. The review of the bank's Environmental and Social Policy will ensure that the consideration of environmental and social issues and sustainability remain at the forefront of the bank's activities, particularly as the bank increases its presence in the SEMED region. Key aspects of the bank's sustainability objectives such as promoting gender equality and empowerment and energy efficiency are expected to feature more prominently in the bank's projects together with the bank's ongoing support of sustainable business activities in the SME sector through financial intermediaries.

Implementing Environmental and Social Risk Management on the Ground: Interfaces Between Clients, Investment Banks, Multi-laterals, Consultants and Contractors: A Case Study from the EBRD

Debbie Cousins

Abstract Assessing and understanding the potential environmental and social (ESG) risks is an essential step in the preparation and development for a project seeking investment. Understanding the due diligence process, the scope of issues to be covered and how interfaces or relationships between key parties can potentially affect the risk profile of the project and timeline for financial approval is explored in this chapter. Including ESG requirements as a key component of the investment works best when incorporated early in the project cycle and should ensure that the project meets national requirements and standards. However, the introduction of International Lenders may broaden the ESG risk analysis and therefore require the project to be recalibrated to meet an additional set of standards, requirements or principles. This can be a challenge for all parties involved. This chapter considers some of the lessons learnt from the environmental and social appraisal processes and from the monitoring of project development and implementation in practice, or 'on the ground' of large-scale infrastructure projects. It explores some complexities of interfaces and how they address project ESG risks and highlights areas where there may be some capacity building needs.

1 Introduction

Project environmental and social (ESG) risks encompass a wide range of issues including environmental pollution/contamination, occupational health and safety, community safety, involuntary resettlement, labour and stakeholder engagement.

D. Cousins (✉)
Environment and Sustainability Department, European Bank for Reconstruction and Development, London, UK
e-mail: cousinsd@ebrd.com

© Springer International Publishing Switzerland 2015
K. Wendt (ed.), *Responsible Investment Banking*, CSR, Sustainability, Ethics & Governance, DOI 10.1007/978-3-319-10311-2_5

Processes routinely used during due diligence to assess these risks include impact assessments, audits and analysis, reviews of management system arrangements and ongoing stakeholder dialogue and feedback. Regulatory Frameworks provide the background for determining most of the risk issues that should be addressed in the preparation and implementation of a project. However, lender standards seek to achieve best management and operational practices, which sometimes go beyond national law and can pose challenges in the environmental and social due diligence (ESDD), construction, operation and decommissioning performance of a project. There are numerous factors that influence the successful management of ESG risks during due diligence and project implementation.

This chapter explores the ESDD process from the European Bank for Reconstruction and Development's (EBRD) perspective, drawing from a wealth of experience gained on large infrastructure projects with different levels of complexity, risk and magnitude of impacts. As part of assessing the risk profile of a project, the ESDD will consider such factors as the nature of the project and its scale, the specific location and potential receptors, existing facilities and historical activities on site, form of the Bank's finance and security package, potential reputational risks of the sector and individual project and the environmental and social benefits of the project.

Despite the differences that exist due to the diverse characteristics of projects, there are some overarching themes that occur as interface challenges across all these projects.

2 Interfaces

Each project has numerous interfaces on environmental, health, safety (EHS) and social issues. The main stakeholders involved in the ESDD process that commonly interact on these issues will usually include:

- The client team (finance, procurement, Human Resources and EHS)
- Client consultants and advisors
- Banks and their independent consultants and advisors
- Regulators
- Contractors (design, engineering, procurement and construction)
- Project affected people (PAP)
- Civil society organisations.

Communication and engagement between these parties is essential in ensuring that information on risks and issues is shared and addressed. This chapter will make reference to a number of these key parties, or interfaces, to describe their role and influence in affecting environmental and social risks and impacts.

Mismanaging these interfaces can have long-term impacts on the project financing timetable, project implementation in terms of risk management and monitoring and project preparation timescales and also have significant financial costs. Figure 1 provides examples of the wider potential impacts of the interface mismanagement.

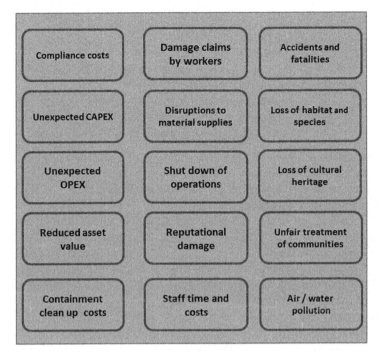

Fig. 1 Potential impacts of the mismanagement of interfaces

To better understand the interface challenges, it is helpful to understand the due diligence process and issues that may need to be addressed (see Sect. 4). To provide context to the ESDD process, the next section provides some details on the EBRD ESG requirements (see Sect. 3).

3   EBRD Policy Requirements

The EBRD provides loans, equity and guarantees for direct investments for a wide variety of projects in sectors including power and energy, natural resources, transport, municipal infrastructure and manufacturing industry. The Bank's Environmental and Social Policy (ESP) 2008 (EBRD 2008) requires that all projects are assessed, structured and monitored to ensure that they are environmentally and socially sustainable, respect the rights of affected workers and communities and are designed and operated in compliance with applicable regulatory requirements and international good practice. The approach to ESG due diligence reflects the nature and potential impacts associated with a particular project. Prospective projects are screened by EBRD at an early stage and categorised, depending on the level and the type of due diligence, information disclosure and stakeholder engagement that is required before the final Board approval of the project. For direct investment projects:

- Category A projects are those with potentially significant and diverse environmental and social impacts, requiring detailed Environmental and Social Impacts Assessments (ESIAs).
- Category B projects are those with impacts that are site specific and can be addressed through readily identifiable management and mitigation measures.
- Category C projects are those having minimal or no adverse impacts.

Projects cannot always be immediately categorised so EBRD sometimes needs to undertake Initial Environmental and Social Examinations to determine the appropriate category and scope of the due diligence required.

All potential projects seeking financing from the Bank require some level of due diligence process, no matter what stage it is in its development, to determine the risks and impacts associated with the investment. Any gaps between proposed risk control measures and the Bank's Performance Requirements (PRs) are captured via remedial measures defined within an Environmental and Social Action Plan (ESAP). This is included in the loan agreement against which the investment proposal will be benchmarked and monitored.

EBRD also has a Public Information Policy (PIP) (EBRD, Public Information Policy, July 2011) which is founded on a number of principles including the following: transparency, accountability and governance, a willingness to listen and receptive to comment from all stakeholders. The Bank's PIP specifies the 'minimum' requirement for certain project information to be disclosed. These timescales allow stakeholders time to submit comments to the Bank and its Board of Directors for consideration before the Board discussion of a project.

Information on environmental and social issues and proposed mitigation measures are included via Project Summary Documents (PSD) (see www.ebrd.com/pages/project/psd.shtml). These are required to be posted on the EBRD website at least 30 calendar days prior to consideration of the project by the Board of Directors for private sector projects, and at least 60 calendar days before Board discussion for public sector projects. In addition, for higher risk 'Category A' projects, clients are required to disclose ESG information as outlined in Fig. 2 in the public domain. ESIAs need to be publicly available for at least 60 days for private sector projects and 120 days prior to Board consideration for public sector projects. The 120-day disclosure period reflects the US Environmental Impact Assessment (EIA) disclosure requirements for public sector projects. EBRD also requires that ESIA document remain in the public domain for the duration of the Banks financing of the project.

The timing of the information disclosure required by the PIP is important in the ESDD process and in organising the preparation of projects before Board submission. If PIP requirements are not met then a policy derogation will need to be requested with reasons to support why the information disclosure requirements could not be achieved. An annual report on the implementation of the PIP is posted on the EBRD website which includes a summary of any PIP derogations and the

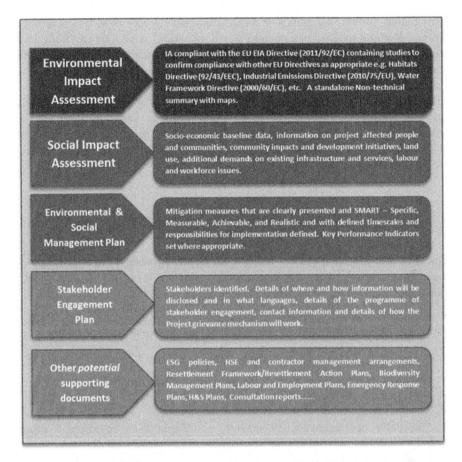

Environmental Impact Assessment
IA compliant with the EU EIA Directive (2011/92/EC) containing studies to confirm compliance with other EU Directives as appropriate e.g. Habitats Directive (92/43/EEC), Industrial Emissions Directive (2010/75/EU), Water Framework Directive (2000/60/EC), etc. A standalone Non-technical summary with maps.

Social Impact Assessment
Socio-economic baseline data, information on project affected people and communities, community impacts and development initiatives, land use, additional demands on existing infrastructure and services, labour and workforce issues.

Environmental & Social Management Plan
Mitigation measures that are clearly presented and SMART – Specific, Measurable, Achievable, and Realistic and with defined timescales and responsibilities for implementation defined. Key Performance Indicators set where appropriate.

Stakeholder Engagement Plan
Stakeholders identified. Details of where and how information will be disclosed and in what languages, details of the programme of stakeholder engagement, contact information and details of how the Project grievance mechanism will work.

Other *potential* supporting documents
ESG policies, HSE and contractor management arrangements, Resettlement Framework/Resettlement Action Plans, Biodiversity Management Plans, Labour and Employment Plans, Emergency Response Plans, H&S Plans, Consultation reports......

Fig. 2 Category A projects—documentation required to meet EBRD PRs

disclosure periods of ESIAs associated with projects that have been reviewed by the EBRD Board that year (www.ebrd.com/downloads/policies/pip/pip-implementa tion.pdf).

3.1 EBRD and Other Lender ESG Standards

The information required to support lending decisions and the level of ESDD scrutiny varies according to the lending parties involved. 'Lender standards' such as EBRD PRs (EBRD, Environmental and Social Policy, 2008), EU standards, IFC Performance Standards (IFC 2012), Equator Principles (EQ 2013) and OECD Common Approaches (OECD 2012) are increasingly aligned, as much has been done to move towards greater consistency of standards in multi-lender situations.

This enables project categorisation and due diligence processes to be streamlined. From a lender's perspective, environmental and social issues are often the most visible aspects of the Banks involvement in a project. Gaps with lender requirements identified during due diligence can provide an early indication of potential problems ahead. Early pre-emptive action to address gaps is usually easier and cheaper in the long run. Frequently, National EIAs have to be 'topped up' with the additional information in order to meet lenders' standards. Therefore, early engagement between the lender group and the client to confirm the lenders' standards that will apply is an important first step in the due diligence during project preparation by the client.

4   Due Diligence Process: Assessing the ESG Risks

ESG risks are project specific. Complex infrastructure projects are usually associated with higher risk issues requiring closer scrutiny and review of interfaces. High-risk issues vary widely, but include:

- Multiple emissions at or near regulatory limits
- Large-scale construction with large-scale temporary or migrant workforce
- A poor safety performance
- Significant retrenchment
- Extensive contaminated land or risk for land or water contamination
- Unsustainable demand on water resource
- Involuntary resettlement or economic displacement
- Potentially significant adverse impacts on vulnerable or endangered species and/or habitats in Natura 2000 sites
- Impacts to a monument of cultural importance due to increased traffic access
- Adverse NGO attention with local community grievances

Other important factors that are part of the risk profile assessment and increase the interface challenge, affecting ESDD timelines, include:

1. EIA exemptions
2. Extended permitting processes
3. Lack of stakeholder engagement on siting decisions
4. Limited capacity and enforcement of national regulatory requirements, as they can impact on the quality of regulatory controls that are defined within decision documents and permits, used to manage the ESG project risks
5. Lack of cohesion or inconsistencies with national development plans or strategic assessments
6. Government-led resettlement

Usually, in large-scale projects, initial due diligence takes the form of a 'gap analysis' of the prepared project documentation against the Banks PRs and includes a site visit to assess the potential EHS and social risks. This is often the first time that the client and the lender ESG group liaise in any detail on the ESG project risks. Requests for relevant ESG project documentation needed routinely include EIAs, Social Impact Assessments (SIAs), risk assessments, details of Environmental and Social Management System (ESMS) arrangements, feasibility studies, engineering reports and designs, soil investigations, information on air and water quality modelling, health and safety performance data, monitoring, expropriation plans and information on stakeholder engagement for the project. Experience indicates that well-organised and complete information provision has a direct impact on the timely identification of potential gaps with lender standards and the completion of due diligence.

Equally important as project documentation is early discussions and time spent with the client EHS representatives to review and assess the management capacity within the organisation and its contractors, and how ESG risk management is organised and monitored on the ground. These discussions will cover such issues as:

- The role of the EHS manager (if they have one)
- Senior management involvement in ESG issues
- The status of the company's (and contractors) environmental, health and safety standards, human resources systems and controls
- EHS performance and monitoring
- Level of engagement with local communities and how concerns or complaints are managed
- Potential supply chain issues including the role of contractors and subcontractors in managing ESG risks while carrying out project activities
- Monitoring and reporting arrangements

At this initial stage of the ESDD, lender standards (EBRD PRs) and requests are often perceived as being too stringent by the client. These views may be because of a lack of in-house capacity or embedded attitudes that question the process. Sometimes it stems from a different attitude to ESG risk and differing levels of risk appetites resulting in conflicting views between client and lender. Common statements made are: 'What is the problem—we comply with national law?', 'we already meet FIDIC requirements—what else do lenders need?', 'we have a safety rule book and our safety record is good—we know how to manage our risks', and 'we have already had public hearings, why do we need more stakeholder meetings?'.

Appointed consultants may often find themselves acting as an interface, educating their clients in what the lenders' requirements are and what international standards are relevant and in the steps of the ESDD process.

Feedback from previous EBRD clients has shown a number of common concerns that were raised by internal stakeholders once the project appraisal or ESDD has started. These include:

- Scope of due diligence: was much broader than was anticipated—EBRD requirements are not just about environmental controls but extend to labour, health and safety, social and stakeholder engagement. Experienced consultants were needed

- Required documentation: the information and documents requested went beyond what was required by regulatory requirements and included requests for evidence of decisions made historically (e.g. siting of an alignment, the alternatives considered and the stakeholder engagement related to these planning processes) and for mitigation proposals not covered in national law (e.g. compensation for informal land users)
- Area of influence (PR1): it was unclear for some time what this was and what project-related issues would fall within this (see Sect. 4.1)
- Social impacts/land acquisition and compensation (PR1 and 5): legal requirements are being met and currently do not require an SIA. It was unclear how to address Lender standards and provide compensation for economic displacement and informal land users or address differing opinions on the application of exclusion zones that are not covered under national laws (see Sect. 4.2)
- Stakeholder engagement (PR10): the clients considered provision of EIA information was sufficient, and it was unnecessary to translate documents, engage more extensively with the local community and target various stakeholder groups, particularly for Category A projects, as the EIA process includes a public consultation process (see Sect. 4.5).
- Health and safety (PR2 and 4): legal requirements are met with no fatalities and maybe only minor injuries recorded. No issues had been raised as a result of any inspections by the Safety or Labour Authorities and there was a safety team in place, so clients were uncertain as to what more is needed (see Sect. 4.3).
- Pollution prevention (PR3): current operations have been compliant with national regulatory requirements with no fines, so questioned the need for additional site investigations
- Biodiversity (PR6): competent Authorities were satisfied with the level of assessment, so questioned why there was a need for more extensive baseline data collection over a full year and involvement of additional specialists (see Sect. 4.4)
- Cultural Heritage (PR8): the relevant Ministry has not requested any further information on potential archaeological sites, so clients questioned the need to engage with other experts and the local community on cultural heritage

A number of these issues are explored below.

4.1   Area of Influence (PR1)

The project definition and a shared understanding of the final project ('ESG story of the project') need to be discussed by all parties early, so that the scope of the project impacts and its area of influence can be agreed. ESG risks associated with area of influence issues are frequently poorly addressed and are raised as gaps during due diligence.

Examples of area of influence components can include:

- Client-controlled activities, assets and facilities directly owned or managed by the client that relate to the project activities that may not be located within the site boundaries such as power transmission corridors providing power for the project, access roads to the project site and construction camps located a few miles from the site where workers temporarily reside.
- Supporting/enabling activities, assets and facilities under the control of the client and necessary for the completion of the project such as construction contractors, outsourced environmental services, such as waste collection and disposal contractors, or the operation of a dedicated wastewater treatment facility.
- Associated facilities or businesses that are not funded by loan as part of the project but depend exclusively on the project and whose goods and services are essential for the successful operation of the project such as a mine that supplies ore only to a single processing plant or an approach road for a bridge project.
- Facilities, operations and services owned or managed by the client that are part of the security package for the loan which may be assets that are physically or commercially separate from the project, such as assets owned by a parent company which may have E&S risks that could affect the value of the assets.
- Areas and communities potentially impacted by cumulative impacts from further planned development of the project or other sources of similar impacts in the geographical area, any existing project or condition and other project-related developments that can realistically be expected at the time due diligence is undertaken. This would include projects being constructed in Phases, where impacts from other projects are expected to contribute to potential negative impacts. These could typically be the increased loss of critical impacts, deterioration of environmental quality standards and public health conditions which could lead to raised opposition to the project by local stakeholders.
- Areas and communities potentially affected by impacts from unplanned but predictable developments caused by the project. These may occur later or at a different location on large infrastructure projects, as the economic situation of an area can be altered, thus changing employment patterns or increasing demand for existing resources. Examples include a new road leading to increased hunting in previously inaccessible areas, triggering further construction along the road route or leading to increased STDs due to an influx of construction workers.

Interface challenges usually arise because impacts from area of influence issues have not been adequately addressed in ESIAs or feasibility studies. Also, sometimes, there has been insufficient engagement with third parties to assess their contribution to the cumulative environmental and social impacts of the project, so EBRD is concerned about the potential risks that may occur as a result. To avoid adjustments to the project, early planning and scoping of projects through consultation are recommended. This will allow risks and impacts linked to a project's area of influence to be incorporated into the project preparation process, avoiding delays and enabling appropriate mitigation measures to be agreed for potential impacts that are identified.

4.2   Consideration of Social Impacts (PR1 and PR5)

Projects need to consider the impacts of their activities on neighbours and the local community. Both the positive aspects (providing employment opportunities, additional services, access to improved infrastructure) and the negative impacts (disturbance, influx of workers, noise, dust, land acquisition) and access problems (access to transport, utilities, homes, grazing lands, etc.) should be identified. Risks need to be understood from an early stage so that they can be actively managed to maintain a 'social licence to operate' and enable timely engagement with project stakeholders to allow the development of relationships at key interfaces. In practice, however, the coverage of social issues is often lacking in project assessments and documentation because SIAs are not typically required under national law.

An SIA is a document that describes the project context and baseline situation, analyses social risks and opportunities, addresses the concerns and opportunities for project affected people and provides an insight into the local political, economic and social dynamics that may affect a project. For an SIA to be a valuable exercise, it should not stop at describing and analysing, but adopt a mitigation hierarchy (Fig. 3) and should also offer practical steps on how to avoid, minimise or mitigate or compensate negative impacts and how to build on project positive social aspects. Understanding how the broad range of project stakeholders contributes to the success of the project is also important.

Too often, poorly executed SIAs focus to a large extent on secondary data collection with little relevance to direct project impacts. Project impacts on vulnerable groups, impacts on livelihoods, labour and human rights, security and safety

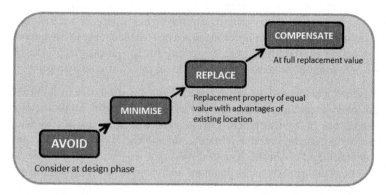

Fig. 3 Social/resettlement mitigation hierarchy

considerations due to increased traffic and influx of workers (mobile men with money) are just a small sample of social issues that are often poorly addressed, if at all, in infrastructure project assessments. Depending on the nature of the project and the local context, social impacts can be versatile and thus require varied responses.

Involuntary resettlement and livelihood restoration on large infrastructure projects are usually addressed under a legal framework for expropriation, on the basis that owners of properties are to be compensated for their losses to a level that they are expected to be able to acquire new properties and resettle and/or re-establish their businesses in other locations. EBRD similarly seeks compensation for lost assets at 'full replacement value' to be applied and restoration of livelihoods and additionally requires that living conditions are improved amongst displaced people at resettlement sites. However, this is often not a straightforward process and people generally need additional assistance to be able to restore their standards of living and further improve them. These processes are supported by EBRD requirements for engagement with the affected people and development of appropriate plans setting out the required actions to appropriately manage resettlement and/or livelihood restoration. To ensure that all displaced people are properly assisted in line with lender standards, it is essential to view resettlement/livelihood restoration planning practices wherever possible in advance of expropriation processes. However, it is recognised that resettlement and livelihood restoration can be complicated by issues related to land tenure and registration of properties, informal construction (in both urban and rural settings), the existence of Roma slum settlements, the circumstances of refugees and internally displaced persons and the operation of informal businesses.

For some projects, vulnerable groups such as Roma, the homeless and waste pickers were not immediately viewed as a significant project risk. Furthermore, links with representatives from project-affected groups or institutions such as social welfare and housing departments were not explored to try to establish who and how many people were likely to be directly affected by the project and to what extent.

The most difficult cases have involved people who do not possess legal title to the lands they occupy and who are therefore typically not entitled to any compensation according to national laws. The difficulties in collecting information and finding solutions for these vulnerable groups can be further compounded as often the lack of personal or registration documents is commonplace. Documentation, however, is required for the provision of social assistance or benefits, and acquiring documentation is a prerequisite for sustainable project outcomes. Without such information it is not always possible to fully determine the potential risks and suitability of the project response to these risks at an early stage, particularly in relation to the livelihood restoration measures or resettlement needs of vulnerable project-affected people.

Early links with institutions and project-affected people can help Clients to build cooperative relationships and enable resettlement and livelihood restoration needs or community impacts to be jointly addressed. SIAs should draw from these relationships to define project-specific measures and demonstrate how the mitigation hierarchy will be applied. Well-managed interfaces with accurate and timely sharing of information can help with the implementation of tailored, practical and culturally appropriate solutions to project-specific social impacts and risks. This often requires interaction over an extended period of time between key stakeholders, who have the shared commitment that no one should be worse off as a result of the project.

4.3   Health and Safety (PR2 and PR4)

Lender standards specify the need for working conditions to be in compliance with national labour laws, health and safety regulations and international good practice (EBRD PR2). These requirements apply to all permanent and temporary workers on site, whether they are employed directly or by construction contractors, subcontractors or labour agencies. Equally important is the need to minimise risks to the health and safety of the local community due to the project (EBRD PR4). So due diligence seeks to ensure that operational controls and monitoring and reporting systems are adequate to verify that health and safety risks are being managed to a tolerable level. It also looks at interface arrangements, whether between contractors working on site, delivery of supplies or links with emergency services to assess the strengths and weaknesses of the shared approach to Health and Safety management.

Frequent examples of hazards and associated risks found on site include:

- Moving vehicles: risk of crushing and impact injuries
- Access and egress routes: risk of injury from falls, slips and trips
- Inadequate lighting: risk of contact with obstacles, slips and trips
- Noise: risk of damage to hearing (tinnitus and occupational deafness)
- Machinery and work equipment: exposure to moving parts and the risk of being drawn in and crushed or electrocution
- Hazardous materials including dust—risk of allergic reaction, respirator reaction, lung diseases and explosion
- Lack of warning signs for specific hazardous areas.

As a minimum, there is a need to identify and control potential workplace hazards to minimise the risk to workers, enforce safe systems of work and the use of safety equipment, provide training to workers on hazards to their health and the precautions that are required, document and analyse work-related accidents, injuries and illness and develop emergency response plans to prevent, mitigate and recover from emergency situations. How these are managed and communicated to various parties working on site is an important factor in demonstrating if key interfaces are able to effectively manage the project risks at each project phase and identify the potential weak links needing additional operational controls. Sadly there have been fatalities on projects and it is vital that lessons are learnt to avoid reoccurrence (Fig. 4).

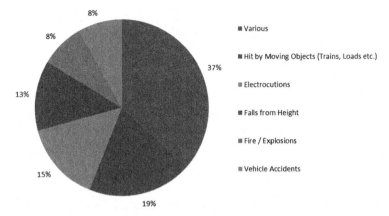

Fig. 4 Causes of fatalities on EBRD Projects (2012)

Compliance with EU Occupational Health and Safety (OHS) standards is a benchmark for EBRD, and information on the effectiveness of controls is vitally important. Files of risk assessments on a shelf are worthless if there are no measures being implemented on site to avoid, prevent and mitigate hazards and risks. Not recognising the risk, lack of safe systems of work, lack of adequate information, instruction, training or supervision and incorrect selection of equipment or control measures are just a few factors that are indications of a poor safety culture that would need to be improved to meet expected standards. Incidents are not just down to workers violating safety rules, so incident reporting and investigation processes, including how client and workers interact, are an important component of the risk management processes that need to be assessed. A client's health and safety performance record, including summary findings of any recent labour or safety inspection, fines imposed, cases outstanding, as well as examples of safe practices and controls (such as measures to ensure that working hours are not excessive and are recorded and regulated in accordance with national law) are other indicators that are reviewed as part of due diligence.

Regular risk assessments of the workplace to prevent accidents and diseases occurring are necessary together with project-specific Health and Safety plans defining the health and safety management systems detailing the responsible staff on site. Too often, template or generic plans are provided that lack details on site-specific issues that need to be managed, particularly emergency response arrangements. This is of particular concern when there may be lack of consultation and coordination when there are numerous contractors working on site. They can sometimes all be working to their own procedures and controls with limited consideration of how they need to link and work together. The need for engagement between parties is particularly relevant for emergency planning and response where roles and responsibilities need to be clearly understood and conveyed. To address this, some projects define shared HSE arrangements formally in documented plans or procedures, usually as part of the responsibility of the lead or principal contractor. This is then supported by monitoring, reporting and change management processes to verify that the arrangements are working effectively.

Concerns regarding contractor management arrangements also extend to health and safety standards of worker accommodation (which needs to meet national requirements as a minimum) and how relationships between the workforce and the local community will be managed. EBRD will seek compliance with international good practice for accommodation (currently defined within IFC/EBRD Workers' accommodation processes and standards 2009) and details of how the project intends to manage and mitigate for the influx of a large number of workers, usually men, to avoid conflicts within the contractor compound and with neighbouring communities (code of conduct, community development programmes, sourcing of supplies locally, etc.).

Community health and safety issues (PR4) sometimes lack the depth of assessment expected, as challenges relating to the potential impacts can range from:

- The fire and life safety of a building
- Pressure on existing health services due to the influx of workers. At the worst case that can mean increased loss of life due to the capability of local medical facilities unable to cope with major incidents associated with a project (no burns unit)
- Conduct of and conflict with workers
- Impacts to local infrastructure
- Access and security issues
- To increased number of vehicles, equipment and activities within the local vicinity.

The interface between the project and local communities regarding measures to ensure public safety is very important. Any information needs to be relevant to the audience, timely and communicated.

It is no surprise, therefore, that HSE interface arrangements between the client and its contractors and subcontractors are high on the list of concerns that EBRD considers during their review and monitoring of projects (see Sect. 6.3). From the outset it is important that there is a shared understanding of the risks, control measures and emergency response arrangements for the site and mechanisms to communicate, monitor and improve health and safety performance on site and in the wider community.

4.4   Impacts on Biodiversity (PR6)

Any project's potential impacts on biodiversity and living natural resources need to be identified and characterised through the environmental and social appraisal process and be sufficiently comprehensive and conclusive to satisfy local law and lender's requirements (EBRD PR6). Assessments of biodiversity resources should be sufficient to characterise baseline conditions and potential impacts commensurate with the risk. This must be consistent with a precautionary approach and the biodiversity mitigation hierarchy to avoid, minimise, mitigate and/or offset significant residual impacts. A project should be designed so that it achieves no net loss or a net gain of biodiversity.

For EBRD in particular, biodiversity assessments (equivalent to an 'appropriate assessment' under Article 6(3) of the EU Habitats Directive) have become a particular area of focus during due diligence. In EU member states and candidate states, these assessments need to be completed to ensure that projects will not adversely affect the conservation values for which an area is subject to protection, and this in turn protects the overall coherence of the (designated and/or proposed) Natura 2000 network. The same approach is also used (conduct assessments sufficient to avoid significant adverse effects on conservation values of concern) for protected areas in non-EU countries, and in areas of particular biodiversity value in all countries regardless of their protection status. Recent experience at EBRD has highlighted that assessments should be as complete as possible prior to project approval. If additional data are needed to reduce uncertainty or to refine mitigation, they should be collected prior to disbursement of funds that could lead to irreversible impacts. This can have a direct effect on the project financing timetable, so it is important that provisions are made at an early stage to ensure that adequate baseline data is available for the project.

The following issues have been raised on projects in respect of habitat protection and conservation assessments:

- A thorough survey for species of flora of conservation significance needs to be conducted, in the appropriate season, in areas to be cleared for construction works.
- The client needs to retain qualified and experienced experts to assist in conducting the appraisals, and teams need to include local experts with knowledge of data sources, age and relevance.
- Where appropriate, bio-monitoring needs to extend over all four seasons to provide recent adequate data on flora and fauna and their life cycles and habitats.
- Biodiversity and habitat data may be closely held by NGOs, state institutes, agencies, etc., and must be assessed to ensure it represents recent/current conditions and is suitable for its intended purpose. Wherever possible, project data should be made available for public use.
- Habitat loss must be assessed along with direct and indirect impacts on organisms and populations.
- Mitigation measures including the compensation measures to offset habitat loss need to be clearly defined.
- Risks and impacts must be fully understood and addressed using the 'precautionary principle' prior to any action being taken that could cause irreversible or unacceptable impacts.

Decision documents or permits will include specific requirements that need to be addressed; these will include controls that need to be implemented in the field by on-site workers. EBRD may also define additional mitigation measures within an ESAP that would need to be applied. Therefore, measures needed to operationalise the necessary mitigation to protect biodiversity should be included in project planning, construction management plans, management systems, contract documentation, noise management plans, etc., so that any constraints are incorporated (e.g. nesting periods, hunting bans, designs for animal crossings, fencing of areas). Responsibilities need to be clearly assigned for the oversight of the implementation of the mitigation measures. Ideally interactions between interfaces concerned with biodiversity protection will work together to enable agreed precautionary principles to be applied in practice.

There is almost always a need for post-approval monitoring for projects that could cause adverse effects on biodiversity. Monitoring is often required in order to verify the efficacy of required mitigation to refine mitigation when there is uncertainty as to its ability to prevent or control impacts, or to fill data gaps, with information that is needed to fully define designs or mitigation measures. The purpose of post-approval monitoring must be fully understood, as well as how the monitoring data will be used and shared. Regardless of the purpose of monitoring, any new data is to be fully evaluated and appropriate decisions made regarding project designs and operation, with material changes reported to lenders and if appropriate information shared with the public.

To achieve compliance with the biodiversity requirements of EBRD requires good planning and adequate resourcing. Timely contributions from stakeholders are important not only in the scoping and assessment of impacts on biodiversity but also in the continued monitoring of the project.

4.5 Stakeholder Engagement (PR10)

It is very important that clients manage information, communication and expectations between the numerous project interfaces/stakeholders to ensure controls to address ESG risks are known and managed to avoid difficulties in project implementation. Stakeholders vary between projects and more can emerge as a project progresses, but well-managed interfaces between the project and stakeholder groups (Fig. 5) can help in the support of the project.

Stakeholder identification and engagement is primarily the responsibility of the client and should begin as early as possible, so that links and engagement with stakeholders can be planned. The nature of engagement activities carried out and the results of these are usually seen by lenders as a good insight into the client's general capabilities and approach to ESG risk management. Unhappy communities or individuals can certainly be a significant risk to any project, no matter what the size is. Protests can result in roads being blocked, damage to assets and delays to the project or court action. People will react on the basis of what they perceive to be impacts, so adequate information needs to be in the public domain on a timely basis to advise them of the project or activities, the potential impacts and what kind of

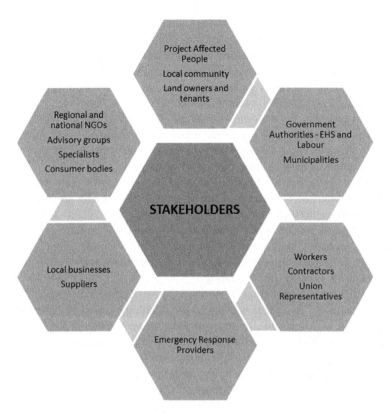

Fig. 5 Examples of typical stakeholder groups

mitigation is planned. Stakeholder engagement needs to be managed well and needs to be balanced, so that the project impacts, risks and mitigation measures and benefits are easily understood and that expectations are managed. For example, if a local community believes that everyone will get a job from a new activity and then this does not occur, there may be difficulties in project implementation.

Frequently, there is often a focus on engagement with statutory stakeholders and information provision rather than meaningful stakeholder consultation and engagement by many clients until EBRD becomes involved. The typical disclosure of an EIA and public hearing often only allows a few people to voice their opinions (often mostly negative). Meaningful consultation means that a variety of voices are heard, including from those people who may benefit from the project, as well as quieter voices who would not speak up in a public meeting. There can be an initial reluctance to undertake measures to directly engage with project-affected people, however.

EBRD requires that information be disclosed and that the project-affected persons, in particular, be given an opportunity to give their opinion on the impacts and risk control measures of the proposed project. It is important that all parties are able to demonstrate that stakeholders have been 'fairly' treated; the engagement has been culturally appropriate and 'meaningful'. This may mean that in order to create dialogue between the community and company different approaches to engagement are needed. For example, this could mean organising the location of meetings at a time and a place that is more comfortable and accessible for particular target groups. This could include evening meetings to allow outreach to people who work during the day, small forums held during the day at a school with childcare facilities so that women feel more secure and can participate or individual face-to-face meetings with small fishing communities at a café if the fishermen would feel uncomfortable in a larger public meeting situation.

Generally, there is often insufficient focus on diversity of opinion, taking into account that men and women or elderly people and young people may have different views, priorities and opinions on the impact and risks of a project. When planning stakeholder dialogue, the needs of different stakeholder groups must be taken into account, for example, by providing female contact points for raising grievances or women-only meetings in certain cultures where they would not be able to attend a general public meeting.

Many elements of stakeholder engagement are carried out as part of normal business operations, but there is often no overarching plan coordinating this. Due diligence can highlight the limited interface between internal departments and contractors on ESG issues and communication with external stakeholders. Typically there is a need for additional information to be provided in a stakeholder engagement plan (SEP) on such issues as the project location and areas that are subject to impact; what project information will be disclosed and in what languages; where information will be made available (web, offices, community buildings); who the identified stakeholders are; a timetable of events such as details of meetings, dates project and ESIA information will be disclosed; how people can submit comments; contact information for the client and its contractors working on the project; and also the provision of a grievance mechanism. For Projects with ESIAs it is important that there is a clear programme for the ESIA disclosure and details of how the project plans to respond to any ESG issues that are raised. The details of the stakeholder outreach and definition of responsible parties for its implementation included in the SEP enable EBRD to have assurance that risks are managed. SEP should be succinct descriptions of the above information and separate from the detailed project information. They should not be complex or highly technical.

Early identification of project stakeholders and strategies for their engagement is important at every stage of a project development. Roles and responsibilities need to be clearly defined as interaction with stakeholders on Project ESG issues will be at numerous points. In particular, clients need to ensure that contractors are committed to the communication plans and application of the project grievance mechanism, as the commencement of construction works usually coincides with increased interest in the management of ESG impacts.

Well-planned and implemented stakeholder engagement can significantly contribute to ensuring that projects are on time and on budget, and timely information exchange between project interfaces can also contribute to the clients' licence to operate. Good stakeholder engagement can enable design or proposed management changes to a project to be addressed early to avoid retrospective measures being applied which can often be more costly and difficult.

5 The Importance of the ESAP and Monitoring Its Implementation

The ESAP is the final output from the gap analysis site visits, discussions with the client, review of stakeholder concerns and other findings identified during the due diligence process. Any gaps between proposed risk control measures and the lender standards are captured via remedial measures defined within an ESAP. Usually presented in a tabular format these plans define the action needed, time framework for its implementation and the responsible party (Fig. 6). For Category A projects EBRD requires that the ESAP is a publicly available document, disclosed before the Board consideration of the project, enabling stakeholders to review its content. The finalised version against which the project will be monitored is appended to the loan documentation.

Historically, ESAPs have had a heavy emphasis on environmental requirements as a priority, with limited coverage of health and safety, labour or resettlement issues. However, increasingly the coverage of ESAPs and supporting plans (such as road safety management plans, resettlement action plans or retrenchment plans) is broadening to more fully reflect the full scope of the EBRD PRs.

It is extremely important that the client fully understands the environmental and social commitments defined within the ESAP, well in advance of finalising loan agreements and signing. At times, the negotiation of the ESAP can fall to the clients' finance team, who accepts the ESAP requirements, but does not truly understand the implication of the commitments that will form part of the loan documentation. It is later that the reality of the commitment becomes apparent. Now the client is faced with the challenge of interpreting the ESAP requirements

Action	EHSS Risk/ Liability/ Benefits	Legislative Requirement /Best Practice / EBRD PR	Investment Needs/ Resources	Responsible Party	Timetable Action to be Completed by End of Year	KPI Target and Evaluation Criteria For Successful Implementation
Environmental and Safety Management requirements to be implemented through all staged of the project and included in contractual requirements of the contractor	Identified within ESIA but include: pollution prevention, OHS risks, community objections, EHS risks in supply chain	PR 1	Client and contractor resources and budgets	Client ESMP framework HSE Director	Contracts end of 2013	ESMP in place. Contracts include HSE provisions.

Fig. 6 Typical ESAP format

and responding to EBRD concerns to provide more evidence of its implementation, holding up the request for disbursement.

Early due diligence and disclosure of project information can often contribute to an easier ESAP preparation process. Large round-table discussions attended by numerous people should be avoided when seeking final resolution on issues, but experience shows that this is not always possible in practice. ESAPs that are publicly disclosed during the ESIA consultation period are not fixed at that point, as they are subject to amendment up until the finalisation and signing of the loan documentation. This allows stakeholder feedback on proposed mitigation measures to be taken into account.

Agreement on the ESAP can be a drawn out negotiation process between the client and their technical advisors and a separate team of lender advisors, plus representatives from lenders, contractors and lawyers, with each party scrutinising the wording and commitment of each ESAP action. Finding the middle ground can be achieved with good preparation and planning, particularly if due diligence is started early. With good information sharing, effective relationships will be established, and key decision makers will be well briefed in advance of the final negotiation of the ESAP. All parties need to take a solution-based approach, avoid reopening issues and be prepared to negotiate realistic measures to address potential risks that have been identified through the due diligence process.

The need to achieve financial close by an agreed deadline usually focuses on the efforts of those involved in the negotiation of the final ESAP so that ESG issues do not hold up the overall deal. This can mean that a final version of ESAP involves some intensive multiparty discussions, concessions and policy derogations in some instances. However, wherever possible last-minute discussions to finalise an ESAP should be avoided.

ESAPs can be amended during the project implementation phase, with the agreement of EBRD. This can be necessary when mitigation measures are found to be inadequate or the risk profile of a project change; for example, additional measures relating to excavations were added to the ESAP following an increased number of incidents during excavation works where excavations collapsed on people or the public fell into unprotected trenches.

5.1 Monitoring (ESP 2008 and PRs)

The EBRD considers it essential that the environmental and social performance of the projects' compliance with its environmental and social covenants is monitored for as long as the Bank maintains a financial interest in the project. Monitoring ensures that the applicable standards and the implementation of the ESAP are being substantially met. It also tracks ongoing environmental and social impacts associated with the Project and provides a measure and feedback on the effectiveness of mitigation measures. As a minimum, clients are required to provide annual ESG monitoring reports to the EBRD. However, high-risk infrastructure projects may also be subject to on-site inspections by independent parties, with the frequency of site visits varying. As the monitoring capacity of regulatory authorities (whether they be health and safety, environment or labour) is often limited due to lack of resources, it is essential that clients establish their own effective monitoring programme. They need to ensure that they have the internal capacity on site to cover routine assessments of the current ESG risks related to the project, particularly during on-site works.

By undertaking lender monitoring visits it is possible to verify ESAP requirements have been implemented. It allows the appraisal of the EHS culture, levels of motivation on site and a review of on-site risks. Frequently ESAPs require the development of systems or procedures, which are duly provided by the client or its contractors; however, it is only through viewing work in progress that the level of implementation of the controls can be fully established. Where necessary, EBRD may require that additional mitigation measures or controls are applied to improve the management of ESG risks.

During monitoring site visits EBRD has routinely seen problems with:

- Weak management commitment to EHS
- ESAP not integrated into Client/Contractor management systems
- Spoil management requiring additional rehabilitation and remediation works
- Insufficient erosion control
- Lack of biodiversity protection measures
- Lack of enforcement of confined space operational controls
- Poor organisation and housekeeping
- Problems with emissions control, particularly with older facilities
- OHS generally: management systems lacking, no near-miss tracking or root cause analysis, 'blame the victim' attitudes, lack of PPE
- Construction safety: working at height, electrical and mechanical safety
- Traffic management: on-site and fleet management
- Waste management: both on-site and local waste management infrastructure
- Slow progress in implementing mitigation measures for project affected vulnerable groups.

On-site monitoring visits only enable a small sample of ESG risks to be reviewed. They are also scheduled, so they can take place when risky activities are deliberately not being carried out. However, the visits provide a new pair of eyes on site and can enable emerging risks to be identified that may not have been apparent at the time of the due diligence process and so were not included in the ESAP. This is often relevant for the many construction projects that are subject to a monitoring site visit, when the risk profile may have changed due to the changing activities on site and improved controls are then identified.

The ESG interface between clients and lenders established during due diligence can be just as important during the monitoring and implementation phase where the need to find solutions for ESG risks can become immediate. This is most evident in the event of an incident, where under loan conditions the client is responsible for reporting accidents and incidents to the EBRD when it is considered to have a significant adverse effect on the environment or on public or occupational health and safety. This usually means those incidents that are required to be reported to a government authority, such as: if there has been a fatality or hospitalisation of one or more workers, or an incident or accident that involves the loss of more than five persons not directly or indirectly employed by the project, including accidents involving vehicles or pedestrians. Sadly, EBRD does receive reports of fatalities and upon request has shared guidance and good practices from other projects to try and prevent re-occurrence.

Clients will benefit from establishing ESG monitoring programmes at an early stage. Projects with good reporting records tend to assign clear responsibilities for data collection and ask that routine data is provided by contractors. This is supported by regular monitoring of on-site practices and tracking of the resolution of non-compliances that are identified, so that a full picture of the ESG performance of the project site(s) can be provided.

6 Key Interfaces: Some of the Challenges and Lessons Learnt During Due Diligence and Monitoring of Lender Financed Projects

The client, consultants and contractors (the three Cs) all play a vital role in the successful and timely completion of due diligence and in achieving compliance with lender standards during the implementation of a project. The following section provides a few examples of common issues that frequently arise amongst these key roles.

6.1 The Client

Time is a commodity that clients often do not have, particularly during the preparation of the ESG documentation required for financing. It can be a frustration that advisors are under or over scoping issues due to their lack of experience or knowledge of EBRD PRs and other lender standards. Equally, a lack of understanding by clients of what needs to be done and how long it may take for ESG documentation and studies to be prepared results in poorly defined terms of reference for consultants, occasionally with near impossible timescales for completion (supplementary ESIA, Human Rights assessments and additional baseline survey collection are not activities that can be completed overnight). EBRD can help by defining scopes of work and clarifying area of influence issues early with clients, but often they are not requested to do so.

When Lenders enter at the start of the ESG due diligence, there will usually be general agreement relatively quickly with the client on the lender standards (EBRD

PRs, EU standards, IFC Performance Standards or Equator Principles) and their approach to complete the necessary review of documentation and disclosure of information. However, clients can get into a 'spin' due to broad nature of the lender standards, the perceived inconsistency of approach in the implementation of the lenders requirements, area of influence issues, and what information needs to be provided to what stakeholders and by when. These concerns should be discussed, clarified and addressed to enable the project to be fully structured to meet the lender standards and establish effective working relationships to avoid delays and mis-understandings that may affect the financing timetable. On a number of projects, EBRD has facilitated workshops and provided training to clients and their contractors on the EBRD PRs and their application to address such issues.

Clients also remark that it is not easy working with large lender groups particularly on large complex projects, when many people are trying to input into the decision-making process. An Independent Environmental and Social Consultant (IESC) working with a lead 'environment' bank has proved to be an effective solution to managing the various interfaces on the lender side in some cases.

Early agreement of the scope of the project, a due diligence plan and strong project management with well-planned but open communication all help to manage the numerous interfaces and demands placed on clients during the due diligence process.

6.2 Consultants

Lowest price is often the main criteria in the selection of ESG consultants, but the lowest price option at the start may not always equate with the lowest cost option at the end of the ESIA preparation or due diligence process, particularly on large infrastructure projects. Clients should be aware that inexperienced consultants can and do cause delays to projects; in some cases new consultants are needed to plug gaps or even redo previous studies. It can cause huge frustration to both clients and lenders when lengthy reports or ESAPs are prepared that lack focus on the material issues of the project or fail to address lender requirements. Client consultants' selection criteria should include team members with practical experience of lender standards, which can always be verified via requests for references from lenders.

International financing often means considering a wider scope of ESG issues and it very quickly becomes evident which consultants are new to lender standards. Consultants should know where there are 'differing' requirements between lenders standards and national laws and provide solutions as to how the project can address these. Local consultants often have the knowledge of local legislation and local context, but can lack experience in the practical application of addressing gaps with lender standards (this is particularly relevant for social issues and stakeholder engagement).

Equally, over-reliance on international consultants should be avoided. Sadly, international consultants can sometimes fail to incorporate the value of the contribution that local partners can provide to the ESIA and due diligence process with the cultural awareness and local insight that they bring. What is needed is a balanced team able to prepare a project to meet national and international standards with a solutions orientated approach.

Consultant teams should incorporate specialists who can competently consider environmental and social issues, occupational and community health and safety, involuntary resettlement, labour and stakeholder engagement practice to fully address EBRD requirements.

The Lender IESC can on complex projects prove to be a valuable interface to negotiate a timely resolution on issues during the due diligence phase as well as add value during project implementation and monitoring. A good IESC will seek to navigate a resolution when faced with differing opinions on the level of compliance with lender standards. During monitoring an experienced lender IESC can provide potential solutions to an issue with the client, drawing from other project examples. They should not act as a tax inspector scrutinising every single piece of data but look at the systems and controls, focusing on a range of risks. They are the eyes and ears of the Lenders on the ground, but also need to provide a solutions orientated approach when issues of non-compliance with lender standards are identified.

6.3   Contractors

ESAP requirements need to be applied by all workers on site. Contractors play a significant role in the success of a project and the effective management of EHS risks. Ideally, EHS provisions and ESAP requirements will be included in the 'Particular EHS Conditions of Contract' for construction works and also set out in the tender specifications for any contract. Sometimes a client may not have made such provisions within existing contracts and there can be a reluctance to issue Contract amendments to cover EHS Conditions, because of the potential associated financial implications. However, in practice the ESAP requirements will need to be applied during the implementation of the project.

Clients are not always in a position to control the project ESG risks, so they need to ensure that their contractors do. Contracted workers must be competent and have the correct resources and equipment to undertake the work to the appropriate standard. Clients need to ensure that their contractors have controls in place to manage ESG risks through procedures, systems and plans before works commence. Such controls include environmental, health and safety plans, risk assessments, emergency response arrangements, training (site induction) and adequate provision of PPE for all workers working on site. Many EPC contractors have established EHS management systems and procedures that are frequently used on projects throughout the world, but do not always cover the broad needs of the EBRD PRs and are not tailored to address the project-specific risks.

Reviews of recent EPC documentation for infrastructure projects have shown social requirements on issues such as stakeholder engagement, worker accommodation standards and worker grievances are limited or missing.

It is equally important to ensure that there is sufficient communication between the client and contractors where there are overlapping jurisdictions, so that all participants are clear on their roles and responsibilities when managing certain risks. There should be agreement on controls and supervision arrangements for EHS issues, no 'hiding' of non-compliances and opportunities to share good practice. Regular reassessment of the risks of the workplace needs to be established so operational controls are amended with each new project phase and project EHS risks are recalibrated and shared. This is particularly relevant for such issues as traffic management measures on site (site entrances, one-way systems, speed limits, designated safe areas for vehicles to unload), but also would apply to maintaining the site boundary, a code of conduct for worker behaviour and managing responses to project-related community grievances.

Conclusions and Recommendations

Organisations and projects vary greatly in their complexity, their potential ESG risks and their barriers to implementation. This chapter highlights some of the interface issues that arise frequently during the ESG due diligence and monitoring of Lender financed large infrastructure projects. Effective management of the interfaces on a project is essential to achieve the common aim that all project stakeholders share, 'no injuries to workers, no damage to the environment and no harm to communities', which are reflected in the EBRD PRs when successfully applied.

The following table summarises recommendations to help improve ESG risk management on the ground based on the issues discussed in this chapter.

(continued)

Recommendations for how management of ESG interfaces can limit financial and HSE risks and impacts.

Project Preparation

- Environmental and social issues are often the most visible aspects of the Lenders involvement in a project. Lenders seek to understand the potential ESG financial and reputational implications of projects through due diligence. So early project categorsation and confirmation of any area of influence is important.
- Project impact assessments need to consider both the potential positive and negative risks and impacts, with better coverage of:
- social issues including labour;
- potential workplace and community hazards;
- stakeholder engagement
- application of precautionary approaches and the mitigation hierarchy.

Project Implementation

- Clients should ensure that consultants and contractors are competent; have a shared understanding of the specific E&S risks of the project; understand where there are interface arrangements that need to be managed and have the appropriate resources to undertake the work to the appropriate standard.
- Clients monitoring systems should provide a robust measure of ESG performance against Lender standards, which not only includes institutional arrangements, emissions control, regulatory compliance, health and safety management but also social performance and the level of public consultation and participation.
- Monitoring results should review the effectiveness of agreed mitigation measures and how the ESAP is being implemented via integration into existing Client and Contractor management and monitoring systems.

Lenders could benefit from:

- Supporting more practical training, sharing of case studies and building of 'local' capacity, particularly in social and stakeholder engagement requirements.
- Facilitating capacity building is required to support the implementation of Lender standards on the ground.

Clients may benefit from:

- Agreeing a due diligence plan with Lenders and confirm area of influence issues and communication protocols
- Specifying Lender E&S standards in procurement and contract requirements

Consultants may benefit from:

- Better utilization of local consultants for social and stakeholder engagement
- Establishing cross functional teams that integrate international and local experience
- Capacity building in the practical application of Lender standards and international good practice

Contractors may benefit from:

- Incorporating Lender Standards/ good practice requirements into Project EHS Management systems, site EHS Plans, EHS monitoring and reporting processes
- Establishing and documenting site specific EHS interface arrangements with the Client and other contractors on site in early phases of project implementation.

Lender participation on a project can require clients to improve working conditions, environmental performance and the bottom line (through optimising the management of water, energy, emissions and waste). Lender standards also support measures to give people and wider society a voice, requiring broader stakeholder engagement with the workforce and amongst project-affected people, particularly the vulnerable, who may otherwise have been excluded. Furthermore, management of ESG interfaces as required by lenders can be effective in addressing ESG risks and impacts.

In practice, there is no 'one-size-fits all' approach to environmental and social risk management, but lessons learnt can be shared and small changes made to reduce risks. However, where possible ESG standards need to be defined and taken into account at the earliest possible stage in the project planning cycle, so that the Projects ESG risks are known and keep pace with the development plans for the project. Clients and their contractors should understand why they need to take certain actions and that they are not a burden but a protection measure or an opportunity. Sometimes it requires a change of attitude, but often the success of a project can be directly linked to managing interfaces and building relationships that support the sharing of good practice when managing ESG issues.

References

EBRD. (2008). *Environmental and social policy*

EBRD PIP. (2011). *EBRD, Public information policy*, July 2011.

EBRD IFC. (2009) *Workers' accommodation: Processes and standards*, September 2009. IFC and EBRD.

EQ. (2013). *Equator principles III—2013*. http://equator-principles.com/index.php/ep3

IFC. (2012). *IFC performance standards and guidance notes*—2012 edition. http://www.ifc.org/wps/wcm/connect/Topics_Ext_Content/IFC_External_Corporate_Site/IFC+Sustainability/Sustainability+Framework/Sustainability+Framework+-+2012/Performance+Standards+and+Guidance+Notes+2012/

OECD. (2012). *Common approaches for officially supported export credits and environmental and social due diligence (the "Common Approaches")*. http://search.oecd.org/officialdocuments/displaydocumentpdf/?cote=TAD/ECG%282012%295&doclanguage=en

Translating Standards into Successful Implementation: Sector Policies and Equator Principles

Eric Cochard

Abstract The Equator Principles have become a market standard in the area of project finance within the space of a few years and now form the basis of environmental and social risk management systems among financial institutions of all sizes and nationality. This in itself is a great achievement that needs to be preserved. The third version of these principles, launched on their 10th anniversary, broadens the scope of application to certain corporate financing activities directly linked to a project. Even with this development, which concerns financing methods where it seems reasonable to carry out such due diligence procedures, the Equator Principles still only cover a small share of the activity of the commercial banks that have adopted them. Some financial institutions have thus decided to establish broader coverage of their activity using sector CSR policies that specifically set out the environmental and social analysis criteria to be considered when reviewing projects in specific economic sectors. Despite examples of cooperation between banks to establish agreement of the stakes involved and to define best practices, there has not been a coherent response from the financial sector. The implementation of shared policies seems a long way off, and even the definition of guidelines seems complex due to different sensitivities of the financial institutions, which generally reflect the social acceptability of their activities within the societies in which the banks operate. While difficult, cooperation between financial institutions in the area of sector policies is vital if these policies are to truly contribute to more sustainable development of the economy.

On June 4, 2003, ten major international commercial banks (ABN AMRO, Barclays, Citigroup, Crédit Lyonnais, Crédit Suisse, HypoVereinsbank, Rabobank, the Royal Bank of Scotland, WestLb and Westpac) adopted the Equator Principles, a charter to ensure that the projects they finance are socially responsible and respect the environment.

E. Cochard (✉)
Head of Sustainable Development, Crédit Agricole CIB, 9 quai du Président Paul Doumer, 92920 Paris La Défense Cedex, France
e-mail: eric.cochard@ca-cib.com

© Springer International Publishing Switzerland 2015   109
K. Wendt (ed.), *Responsible Investment Banking*, CSR, Sustainability, Ethics & Governance, DOI 10.1007/978-3-319-10311-2_6

Ten years later, what might have remained a voluntary initiative for many has become a market standard in the area of project finance and a symbol of responsible behaviour in the banking sector. Nearly 80 financial institutions have signed up to the initiative. However, it has become a victim of its own success, struggling to evolve from its original framework, as a result of which some Equator Principle Financial Institutions (EPFI) have begun to develop CSR sector policies.

1 Sector Policies Versus the Equator Principles

1.1 The Contribution of the Equator Principles

The Equator Principles involve a voluntary commitment by the signatories to ensure that financial institutions conduct due diligence procedures and that clients-borrowers analyse and manage the impact of their projects in accordance with the World Bank environmental and social standards and notably the International Finance Corporation's Performance Standards. The latter cover themes such as forced population displacement, respect for biodiversity and human rights. In concrete terms, the EPFIs undertake to conduct due diligence on the projects they finance with a view to the social and environmental impacts of the projects and to ensure that the borrower analyses the potential impact of their project and draws up action plans to reduce these impacts as much as possible and offset those that cannot be avoided.

Having rapidly become a market standard, these Principles have helped to improve the environmental quality of projects being financed, notably the quality of impact studies and action plans (preservation of biodiversity, management of waste and hazardous materials, etc.) and the quality of consultation and assistance for populations affected, which are key aspects of the World Bank standards.

They also play a protective role because they have a restrictive impact on commercial banks. In fact, by obliging them to formalise their analysis procedures and to take into account environmental and social aspects of the projects being financed, they have enabled better control by the banks of their credit and reputational risk. The benefits produced have led to a rapid expansion of their use in the financial community.

From ten banks in June 2003, there were around 80 signatories on the eve of the charter's 10th anniversary, essentially comprising European, Japanese and North American banks but increasingly including emerging country banks from South America, Africa, the Middle East and Asia. While some have criticised the "free-rider" behaviour of a few institutions with a minor presence in the project finance sector, the importance of developing these standards for the financial sector needs to be stressed. The Equator Principles today form the basis of the CSR systems of many of the world's big and small financial institutions, serving as a common language that is now irreplaceable.

The 10th anniversary of the Equator Principles saw the official launch of EP III, which extends the scope of application to certain other financing methods, when there is a noted link between the financing and the construction or expansion of an industrial asset, an essential condition for the identification of environmental and social impacts and therefore for the material possibility of conducting the due diligence procedures provided for in the Equator Principles.

1.2 Why Sector CSR Policies?

Although there has been some confusion in the past, the Equator Principles are necessarily limited in their scope of application. This is an important factor. The principles were designed for a very specific method of financing, i.e. project financing as defined by the Basel Committee on Banking Supervision, the repayment of which depends solely on the revenues generated by the project. While this is a symbolic banking activity, it represents a relatively low share of banks' overall activity.

After several years of talks to adapt the Equator Principles according to the specific features of new products included in the scope without distorting them, EP III shows clear progress. But even after extending the scope to include new financing methods such as certain types of buyer credit loans, the Principles still cover only a small percentage of the overall activity of EPFIs. The implementation thresholds (amount of loan notably) may be gradually lowered over time, but this does not fundamentally alter this observation.

Most of banks' other activities could probably never be subjected to the due diligence required under the Equator Principles. This is because they do not meet two necessary conditions. On the one hand, the Equator Principles as they exist today are applied on the assumption that the use of the funds is precisely known and is linked to the construction or expansion of an industrial asset or infrastructure (existence of an impact study and a plan for the management of residual impacts). And on the other, the financial institution and the client must have the necessary leverage (e.g. when the bank is financing equipment used in the construction of a larger project, does the client have access to the impact studies of the entire project and can it influence its characteristics?).

While project financing is traditionally subject to significant due diligence and to tailored legal documentation due to the risks involved for the bank (reimbursement is solely based on the project's cash flow, without guarantee from the developer), the same requirements are not usually applicable to other methods of financing, and their social acceptability may be doubtful. Imagine, for example, an individual client accepting a property loan from a bank on the condition that a maximum temperature level within the property is respected, or a car loan on the condition of certain eco-driving commitments. And where is early reimbursement of the loan demanded if these conditions are not met? What seems natural for project financing within the framework of the Equator Principles is not obviously applicable in other cases.

This does not mean to say that financial institutions should ignore the impact of their financing and investment activities. Etymologically, to be responsible means to act in return or to answer for one's actions. CSR therefore incorporates the notion that the company (bank or client) reports on the direct or induced consequences of its activity, including environmental and social impacts.

For this reason, several commercial banks are seeking to introduce social and environmental criteria into their financing policies and to publish these criteria within sector CSR policies.

1.3   Developing Sector Policies

The CSR criteria used to assess transactions essentially reflect the societal objectives that the bank feels are most relevant and generally concern respect for human rights, the prevention of global warming and the preservation of biodiversity.

Incorporating the principles adopted by the UN Human Rights Council in 2011,[1] the OECD's key principles for multinational companies stress the obligation to "seek ways to prevent or mitigate adverse human rights impacts that are directly linked to their business operations, products or services by a business relationship, even if they do not contribute to those impacts". This obligation is based on the performance of reasonable due diligence.

Where climate change is concerned, a scientific consensus exists, within the framework of the IPCC, on the presence of global warming, its anthropological origins and the levels at which we need to limit greenhouse gas emissions to keep the consequences of climate change within acceptable levels. One direct result of this is that companies will have to adopt more carbon-efficient development models, and the notion of energy efficiency will become key in many economic sectors.

A scientific consensus also exists on the importance of biological diversity for humanity and on its impoverishment due to certain human activities. The obligation to offset negative impacts where they cannot be avoided or reduced may in the future concern many countries and economic sectors.[2] Initially financial in nature, offsetting increasingly involves compensation "in kind", with the emergence of the concept of a net impact,[3] and is set to concern a growing number of clients.

Financial institutions are not looking to take over from national authorities and international bodies in defining the objectives and regulatory framework surrounding such global societal objectives. Neither can they define the investment policies of their clients, which design, build and operate the projects they finance. One of the

---

[1] After 6 years of research involving governments, businesses, civic bodies and investors under the direction of Professor John Ruggie, the United Nations Human Rights Council adopted in 2011 principles based on three pillars, "protect, respect and remedy", reaffirming the duty of states to protect, the responsibility of companies to respect and the need for access by victims to recourse, legal or otherwise, in order to repair abuses committed.

[2] For certain infrastructure projects, this obligation has been inscribed in French law since 1976.

[3] In France, the Caisse des Dépôts et Consignation created the CDC Biodiversité fund to propose 'natural assets' to industrials needing to offset their impacts.

fundamental roles of a commercial bank is to assist its clients and in this way help to finance the real economy.

As part of their CSR policy, however, financial institutions cannot ignore major issues of public concern. In fact, since each financial institution determines its own financing and investment policies, through the financing it grants, it can contribute to the achievement of societal objectives. From a risk perspective, they are also concerned by the consequences of these objectives on their clients.

Taking account of societal objectives does not involve moral judgement by those in charge of banks' accounts, as may sometimes be the case for certain stakeholders that question the financial sector. What the banks seek is to draw as far as possible on existing or emerging consensus in the area of good practice. A comparison of the anticipated benefits and costs (economic, environmental and social) of the financed activities and investment is central to sector CSR policy.

In concrete terms, looking at the sensitive defence sector, an international consensus has emerged on the banning of anti-personnel mines and cluster munitions thanks to the Ottawa and Oslo treaties. The sensitive nature of negotiations on light arms is also reflected by the existence of international talks on the subject. Financial institutions that have published policies for this sector have generally adopted strict positions concerning the financing of the two former categories and conduct very close management of the financing of the latter. Crédit Agricole's policy rules out financing of the former, while for the latter, authorisation must come from the head office compliance team in cases where the importing country shows a particularly high level of risk associated with human rights and areas of conflict.

1.4 Complementary or Competing?

While sector CSR policies generally cover all forms of financing (unlike the Equator Principles), their scope is smaller as they refer to particular economic sectors.

Both the Equator Principles and sector CSR policies contribute to banks' management of credit and reputational risk related to the environmental and social impacts of the activities they finance. Banks that develop sector policies are therefore generally looking to harmonise as much as possible their requirements with regard to the two approaches, while acknowledging that the leverage for action differs. The general idea is that the bank does not end up financing a project under one method which it would not finance under another, even if the nature of the potential due diligence depends largely on the financing method used.

Sector policies offer a more specific approach to aspects that are still inadequately covered by the IFC standards underpinning the Equator Principles (such as greenhouse gas emissions), or which do not feature at all in the standards (e.g. related to nuclear energy, shale gas or armaments). Banks must therefore propose analysis as well as exclusion criteria, which may prove particularly difficult

Table 1.1 Equator Principles vs. CSR sector policies

	Equator principles	CSR sector policies
Type of commitment	Due diligence process common to several financial institutions	List of criteria used by a financial institution to assess transactions/clients
Financial projects covered	Project finance, Advisory + some Project-Related Corporate Loans and Bridge Loans (EP III)	All transactions/clients
Sectors covered	All sectors	Sector specific
Frame of reference	International Finance Corporation/World Bank	Diverse and sector specific
Key factors of success for implementation	Involvement/training of business lines. Proper monitoring/control	Same
Cooperation among financial institutions	Significant (around 80 FIs committed around the world)	Limited

since a consensus on what constitutes best practice has not yet been clearly established internationally.

Two difficult examples that we have encountered concern coal-fired thermal plants and the shale gas sector. We supported discussions between several financial institutions on these two subjects within the framework of two market bodies, the French Observatoire de la Responsabilité Sociétale des Entreprises (ORSE) (French observatory of corporate societal responsibility) and the international Climate Principles. This culminated, in both cases, in the preparation of guidelines for these sectors which we then made available to the entire financial community.

Although sector CSR policies may seem like an additional level of complexity in analysing projects, an approach that is as coherent as possible with the Equator Principles is generally sought, and, in the final analysis, these two risk management tools seem to complement each other more than compete with each other (see Table 1.1).

1.5 Key Success Factors for Implementation

One of the keys to the success of the Equator Principles is the fact that they were developed collectively by CSR and project finance professionals. The resulting cross analyses during preparation meant that balanced, realistic requirements could be established.

For instance, each bank that signed the Equator Principles defined its own implementation procedures, which vary somewhat as a result. We cannot say that one model is better than another. In order to be efficient, the method of implementation must be appropriate to the establishment's culture and should not involve new procedures being artificially pinned on to existing ones by someone without any real knowledge of the business.

The model developed by Crédit Agricole CIB involved first-level implementation by the operating business lines themselves. This obviously required considerable training of front officers, with technical support available for the most difficult cases. From our 10 years of experience, we have seen the positive effect of gradually developing the sales employees' capacity to anticipate and therefore manage the environmental complexity of many large infrastructure projects worldwide. Although this concern does not date from June 2003, the formalisation of due diligence procedures has triggered a genuine virtuous circle.

Before decentralising due diligence procedures, appropriate control systems must be in place. A natural first-level control is the risk department, which examines the sales employees' analysis of all aspects of the project. At Crédit Agricole CIB, this was completed by the creation of a committee for assessing transactions that show environmental or social risk (CERES), which is chaired by the head of compliance. This committee plays a crucial role, issuing recommendations before taking decisions on any operation it believes requires close monitoring of environmental and social aspects.

The key success factors for sector policies are the same. We used the same implementation model, with one governance text adapted for each business line and setting out the procedures to be followed regarding the Equator Principles, the sector policies and a sensitivity analysis for environmental and social risks.

It also seems important that the sector policies are written in close collaboration with the risk department and business line concerned. This will ensure good assimilation of the texts and thus easier implementation. We therefore went as far as having the texts formally validated by the same committee that validates the business line strategies. This means that any upstream discussions can be settled and the sales strategy and CSR policy of each economic sector concerned can be aligned as best as possible.

These advances, whether in the Equator Principles or in new sector policies, will not come without internal debate. Such debate is warranted and will ensure that issues are understood, discussed and validated. The implementation of CSR procedures will in many cases involve considerable change management and an inevitable learning curve (denial and protest followed by increasingly proactive implementation). The sector policies are not likely to differ in this regard. This is necessarily time consuming, but it will mean greater knowledge of sectors and clients and therefore, in the end, greater proximity with the latter.

2 Sector Policies in Practice

2.1 Which Sectors to Choose?

Two standard questions that arise for all financial institutions about to prepare sector policies are as follows: Where to start? What sectors need to be treated as a priority?

It would seem natural to begin by selecting the sectors that are most important for the financial institution, but this is not as evident as might seem. We have often noted that the first policies published are more of a reflection of the sector's level of sensitivity than of their relative importance to the bank's activity.

Taking the questions raised by society into account is perfectly legitimate. Sector policies play a role in the management of reputational risk, so the questions asked by our stakeholders merit the attention of the financial institutions. As such, policies concerning the defence sector are among the most frequent of the published policies. It is often the case that they were prepared following a campaign to raise awareness of the terrible effects for local populations of anti-personnel mines and cluster munitions, before such arms were prohibited by the international community through the Ottawa and Oslo treaties.

But responding to these questions alone is not enough. A significant investment of time is necessary to achieve a satisfactory result. Selecting a few sectors to begin with means ruling out certain other sectors, at least for a certain length of time. How does a financial institution justify ignoring sectors in which it has a significant presence and concentrating on sectors associated with a media campaign but of only marginal importance for the institution? For this reason, certain banks look at the relative importance of their potential impact. This type of approach is likely to prevail in the future because it corresponds precisely to the notion of responsibility.

Such an approach often requires complex preliminary research. As an illustration, Crédit Agricole CIB drew up a map of the greenhouse gas emissions associated with the economic activities financed by it to determine the bank's priority sectors in the area of climate change. This work, conducted based on the P9XCA[4] greenhouse gas emissions calculation methodology developed at the Paris Dauphine University, showed that two industrial macro sectors, energy and transport, accounted for more than 80 % of the emissions caused by the bank. For this reason, after treating the energy sector, the bank opted to develop a set of policies for the transport sector in 2013, even though on the whole this is not a highly controversial activity for the bank.

---

[4] Cf. Antoine Rose. Greenhouse gas emissions calculation methodology developed as part of the Finance and Sustainable Development Chair. Report of the Chair to appear.

2.2 How Technical Should They Be?

Another important question is how technical the published texts should be. Experience shows that the preparatory work of these policies can rapidly give rise to debate of a highly technical nature. Including all aspects of such debate in the final result may lead to a text that is difficult to understand beyond a small circle of experts and thus which is also difficult to apply. That said, overly simplified policies would raise the risk of excessive short cuts that could give rise to arbitrary decisions concerned more with the potential impact on public opinion than with the real environmental and social impact.

There is no certainty that an ideal solution can be found. What is needed is a balance between both extremes, based on which financial institutions can respond differently depending on the circumstances. The trend nevertheless is for a relatively long text, using straightforward vocabulary, covering each topic as accurately as possible.

The policies concerning the nuclear energy sector are a very good example. The few banks that have published a policy on this sector have tended to opt for fairly technical texts about the analysis criteria (mentioning specific agreements signed by states and specific types of audits, e.g. by the IAEA). Similarly, the policies for coal-fired thermal plants all tend to refer to the technology or energy efficiency of the installations being financed. The Climate Principles published interesting guidelines on the subject, establishing a link between technology, energy efficiency and greenhouse gas emissions. The banks that followed these guidelines selected one of these more-or-less quantitative indicators, giving results that were nevertheless similar.

2.3 The Matter of Exclusions and Corporates

Unlike the Equator Principles, sector policies often include explicit exclusions. But the fundamental intention is the same since this usually involves excluding situations rather than sectors.

For example, activities that have a negative impact on areas considered "critical" by the Equator Principles (e.g. Ramsar and UNESCO sites) are often excluded. While exclusions are not explicitly mentioned in the Equator Principles, they occur through the strict application of the IFC Performance Standards underlying the principles, which prevent certain situations occurring. Similarly, certain situations are prevented due, for example, to the criteria concerning respect for fundamental labour rights, or the consultation of affected populations, and agreement being necessary in the case of native peoples.

The biggest difference is undoubtedly the a priori exclusion in certain policies of activities in situations where responsible management of environmental or social factors looks difficult, if not impossible, to achieve. This is notably the case in

Crédit Agricole CIB's policies for offshore oil drilling in the Arctic, open-pit bituminous sands projects, subcritical coal plants (excluding small plants in certain countries), hydroelectric plants at which the size of the reservoir is disproportionate to the energy produced and artisanal mining.

One particular difficulty concerns the application of exclusions in the case of groups operating multiple activities. It is up to each financial institution, therefore, to define a threshold above which it excludes a group involved in activities that do not comply with its policies. The ORSE proposes a threshold of 20 %.

2.4   Involvement of Stakeholders

Clients and professional associations may be consulted on a case-by-case basis during the process of drafting sector policies to ensure that all complexities related to technical issues are correctly factored in.

Financial institutions also draw heavily on the technical expertise of both internal and external independent consultants. The main environmental or social issues of the different sectors are integral to the knowledge that institutions must acquire on the activity sectors they finance.

The views of the main environmental NGOs are also sought when preparing the policies. However, active participation by NGOs in the review process is not frequent given their often strong views. Thus, certain NGOs call for the exclusion of entire economic sectors. And the sum of these exclusions may prove to be somewhat unrealistic.

For example, in the energy sector, certain NGOs call on financial institutions to refrain from financing nuclear power plants, coal-fired thermal plants, shale gas operations or most hydroelectric projects, regardless of the stated energy policy of the public authority concerned. As such, participation by NGOs in the definition of sector policies can create considerable difficulty.

2.5   Taking the Example of Crédit Agricole CIB's Energy Policy

The energy sector, and notably the electricity generation sector, is of particular importance due both to the central role it plays in economic development and the level of greenhouse gas emissions currently produced by it (notably CO_2 emissions during the combustion of fossil fuels). In northern countries, the main issue is often the rate of transition to a less carbonated economy, notably through the development of renewable energies or energies that generate low carbon levels (nuclear energy), while for southern countries, the main issue is that carbon restrictions are often seen as a hindrance to their development.

Crédit Agricole CIB decided to establish a policy for this sector that would include specific principles and rules for climate change as well as the other societal issues identified. For the purpose of coherence, it was decided to prepare a policy for each of the main sector components, the oil and gas industry, shale gas, coal-fired thermal energy, nuclear energy and hydraulic energy, and to publish these texts on the same date so as to highlight the fact that they form a coherent whole. The idea is not to choose between the different subsectors but rather to define clear and precise rules to be used for each sector when individually analysing financing and investment projects. A policy for the mining and metals sector was also added.

All of the main principles presented above have been respected: use as much as possible of existing and developing consensus, referencing of best practices and exclusion of situations that are considered unacceptable. We worked to identify the main societal challenges and best practices in each sector.

Public and professional international organisations (the World Bank, the International Energy Agency, the International Atomic Energy Agency, the Extractive Industries Transparency Initiative, the International Petroleum Industry Environmental Conservation Association, the International Council on Metals and Mining, etc.) were the main source of reference in defining these best practices. We also took account of the recommendations of working groups on the financial sector (such as Climate Principles and ORSE Guidelines) and carefully read the texts published by our colleagues.

An important feature of our process was the in-depth discussions we held internally. We systematically teamed up in working groups that included sustainable development specialists, specialised advisors from the sectors concerned, the risk department and the main business lines concerned. This inclusive process gave rise to instructive and often highly technical debate, which frequently required more time than we had anticipated, but what is essential is that we set out the basis for real comprehension of the challenges involved and ultimately for strong support for the policies.

This support is crucial to the efficient implementation of the policies. These are not rules that are set arbitrarily by a sustainable development department but are well thought-out criteria that reflect the complexity of the industries involved and take account, as far as possible, of the challenges identified, whether economic, environmental or social. The texts were systematically approved by the bank's Strategy and Portfolio Committee, chaired by the general management, ensuring comprehensive alignment of both the strategy and the policies.

2.6 What Lever for Implementation?

The question of how much leverage a bank has for implementing voluntary principles or policies is closely linked to the matter of the potential competitive disadvantage in relation to its rivals, an issue that systematically came up during our internal discussions and which was raised also when we participated in the launch of the Equator Principles.

In the case of the Equator Principles, the matter was settled fairly rapidly because these principles are applied across the project finance market. This is undoubtedly due to the relatively closed environment that these banks operate in and the fact that the principles were initially adopted by ten large banks of different nationalities, representing a significant share of the market.

The situation seems more complex in the area of sector policies. As these are designed to cover all forms of intervention by financial institutions, the number of players potentially being impacted is much larger. A handful of banks would not have a significant impact on the markets concerned. Efforts should therefore be combined to foster a single approach to the challenges involved and best practices. Financial institutions would benefit from cooperation to develop common guidelines for establishing sector policies as it would facilitate their implementation and impact, helping to secure a greater contribution to the sustainable development of the sectors covered.

That said, the publication of policies by a few pioneer financial institutions would not be without an impact as it would necessarily create a precedent and serve as a reference for other financial players. Even where the form may differ, the fundamental idea tends to converge, at least where analysis criteria are concerned.

2.7   What Is the Situation at Present?

Only a few establishments have published CSR sector policies, and the areas covered vary greatly. We are still a long way from a market standard similar to the Equator Principles that were established 10 years ago.

Is it possible to achieve greater cooperation over and above the guidelines published within the framework of the Climate Principles and the ORSE? While this seems desirable, there are various obstacles that should not be ignored. Cooperation of this nature would go well beyond the definition of a due diligence process applicable to a particular situation that covers only a small part of the investment conducted worldwide and of commercial banks' activity (as is the case of the Equator Principles). Coal-fired thermal energy, nuclear energy and shale gas are all socially acceptable activities to varying degrees depending on the country, and this is naturally evident in the appetite of banks operating in this area, whose primary role is to finance the economy of these territories. The definition of shared rules for a large number of financial players worldwide with necessarily different sensitivities is therefore a complex exercise.

Could the Equator Principles or another existing initiative play a role as catalyst for the distribution of these best practices? At any rate, these initiatives provide an established network that it would be a shame not to use. However, it would be dangerous if they were to become merely a discussion forum from which each player would choose what interests them. We must be careful to preserve the value added by initiatives like the Equator Principles, which today are synonymous with precise and compulsory due diligence procedures. Changes that would damage this clarity would be questionable. The challenge ahead therefore is to use these initiatives as best as possible to ensure progress in the way we incorporate environmental and social considerations into the banking world without distorting them.

Conclusion

This could be done successfully if certain conditions were respected. Technical work (such as the acquisition of expertise) would have to be prioritised over simple discussions. Significant work to explain what is expected would also be necessary, with a clear distinction being made between compulsory processes and ancillary work. But it is particularly important that any potential broadening to ancillary work would be accompanied by coherency and transparency in the implementation of the Equator Principles themselves by all members.

The introduction of reporting by the members to the association in Equator Principles III is unquestionably a significant step in this direction. But this will clearly not be enough unless it is accompanied by transparency of implementation at the level of each institution. Among the potential scenarios, we could, for example, introduce a mechanism for external auditing of statistics and procedures, similar to what certain European banks, including Crédit Agricole CIB, have already been practising for several years.

Cooperation between financial institutions in the area of sector policies therefore seems difficult to achieve, and we should not underestimate the problems it would raise. But it is nevertheless desirable if we want these policies to truly contribute to more sustainable development of the economy.

This is obviously a question for financial institutions and notably those that have developed and applied the Equator Principles.

The Equator Principles: Retaining the Gold Standard – A Strategic Vision at 10 Years

Suellen Lambert Lazarus

Abstract Launched in 2003, the Equator Principles (EP) signaled a major shift by international banks in their approach and responsibility for environmental and social outcomes in the projects to which they were lending. Ten European, US and Australian banks originally adopted the EPs. Within the first year, this had grown to 25 financial institutions from 14 countries, including a Japanese bank and an export credit agency. Ten years later, there are 80 Equator Principles Financial Institutions (EPFIs) from countries as diverse as Mauritius, Mexico and Morocco. In 2006, the EP were revised to reflect changes in IFC's Performance Standards and needed modifications based on implementation experience. The update process took less than six months, expanded the scope of the EPs and introduced reporting requirements. In 2010, the EP Association embarked on another revision process (EP III), which took more than two-and-a-half years to complete. What changed to make the process so much slower? Were the EP Association's aspirations for this revision higher, were the issues more complex, did the broad geographic scope of the EP membership make consensus more difficult or had the management of EP Association become less efficient? The management system of the EP Association with its rotating chair, 14-member steering committee and ten working groups is both a strength and a weakness. With its flat structure and lack of dedicated professional resources, the EP Association now has to work longer and harder to develop solutions, reach consensus and make decisions. This extended process provides some insight into the complexity of managing a voluntary global standard with a broad range of constituencies. Among the trade-offs that had to be navigated were the desire to introduce more robust and consistent reporting requirements while recognising that some countries have a culture of corporate privacy; and addressing climate change and promoting lower carbon outcomes while accommodating those countries actively developing carbon-intensive industries such as tar sands, hydraulic fracturing and coal reserves. EP III reflects breakthroughs including the expansion of the scope of the EPs to include Project-Related Corporate Loans and strengthened reporting requirements. The release of EP III at the Association's 10-year anniversary provides the opportunity to reflect on what the EPs have achieved and where challenges remain.

S. Lambert Lazarus (✉)
Consultant of the Strategic Review of Equator Principles, Washington, DC, USA
e-mail: suellen@lambertlazarus.com

© Springer International Publishing Switzerland 2015   123
K. Wendt (ed.), *Responsible Investment Banking*, CSR, Sustainability, Ethics & Governance, DOI 10.1007/978-3-319-10311-2_7

Ten years to the date after its initial launch, the Equator Principles (EP) Association adopted the third iteration of the EPs, known as EP III. Adoption of EP III on June 4, 2013, was the culmination of almost three years of work beginning with the Strategic Review process begun in October 2010.

The update had been a long, slow process and took far more time than the EP Association expected. Was it a success? The EPs are a framework for financial institutions to apply in assessing environmental and social risk in their project finance business. Since their launch in 2003, there are now 80 Equator Principles Financial Institutions (EPFIs) on 6 continents in countries ranging from Bahrain to Uruguay and from Canada to South Africa. The purpose of this chapter is to take stock of the EPs at 10 years. In so doing, we will explore whether the EPs have achieved their objectives, what impact the EPs have had on the financial sector, and what are the prospects and challenges for the future. As part of this process, we will also examine the issues that were identified in the Strategic Review and determine how they were fulfilled or not fulfilled in the EP III revision process. The review was designed to produce a 5-year strategic vision 'to ensure that the EPs continued to be viewed as the "gold standard" in environmental and social risk management for Project Finance within the financial sector'.[1] Is there a strategic vision to guide the EPs through the next 10 years and will they remain the gold standard?

1   The Need

We need to first lay the groundwork for why the EPs were originally drafted and adopted by a small group of leading financial institutions. When the discussion on what became the Equator Principles began in October 2002, the leading project finance banks had a large pipeline of major projects in the planning stages, many in developing countries and with vast impacts. Projects included such industries as mining, oil and gas pipelines, petrochemicals facilities, hydropower generation and pulp and paper manufacturing. Some of these projects were in remote locations in frontier markets. They impacted indigenous peoples, endangered species, fragile ecosystems and protected habitats; others crossed international borders and involved governments with weak regulatory regimes or histories of human rights abuses. They all presented complex environmental and social issues, and, for the most part, the banks had little capacity to analyse or manage these risks. Non-governmental organisations (NGOs) were actively campaigning against some of the most high-profile projects. Shareholder resolutions were introduced at annual shareholders meetings of some of the banks to block environmentally sensitive projects.

---

[1] About the Equator Principles Strategic Review—2010/2011, http://equator-principles.com/index.php/strategic-review-2010–2011

At the time, the banks lacked a framework to analyse projects for environmental and social risk in emerging markets. They also lacked the internal expertise to evaluate these risks, and it is unlikely that they knew the right questions to ask to identify the risks. In developed countries, banks could generally rely on domestic laws, regulations, permits and oversight. The projects in developing countries challenged the risk management capabilities of the banks, but, at the same time, their most important clients were sponsoring these projects. It was hard to say no to them and not risk losing their business to competitors. Turning down a project did not mean that it would not get done or that its environmental and social performance would be improved. It just meant that another institution would lead the financing and earn the associated fees.

As some of the major banks considered how to address environmental and social issues in emerging market projects, they worried about competition with one another on these issues. Clients could shop among banks for the environmental standard that was most efficient for their project or, more likely, for the bank that paid the least attention to these issues. Nonetheless, the banks recognised that they were facing real environmental and social risk in these projects that could translate both to financial loss and reputation damage. But no one bank could tackle this issue alone. They felt it was essential to 'level the playing field' and have one standard that they all agreed upon rather than each bank developing its own approach. Thus, the EPs were launched in 2003.

Drafted by 4 banks[2] and adopted by ten banks[3] just 7 months later, the EPs provide procedural steps for the banks to apply when evaluating projects and standards against which to benchmark projects. The procedural steps require the identification of environmental and social risks and impacts and then involve an assessment process. The drafters of the EPs utilised the International Finance Corporation's (IFC's) Safeguard Policies, which were redrafted in 2006 and became the IFC Performance Standards and subsequently incorporated into the EPs, as the basis for project assessment. These standards cover cross-cutting environmental and social issues and define the responsibilities of the borrower for preventing and mitigating harm to people and the environment in project development and operation. The EPs also incorporate the World Bank Group's Environmental, Health and Safety (EHS) Guidelines, which provide industry-specific performance levels considered 'good practice' in environmental protection and safeguarding worker and community health and safety. It is important to note, however, that under the EPs, projects in high-income Organisation for Economic Co-operation and Development (OECD) countries, as classified by the World Bank,[4] do not use the IFC Performance Standards and

---

[2] ABN AMRO, Barclays, Citigroup and WestLB.

[3] The 10 original adopting banks were ABN AMRO (Netherlands), Barclays (UK), Citigroup (US), Crédit Lyonnais (France), Credit Suisse Group (Switzerland), HVB Group (Germany), Rabobank (Netherlands), Royal Bank of Scotland (UK), WestLB (Germany) and Westpac Banking Corporation (Australia).

[4] See World Bank Database, http://www.data.worldbank.org/income-level/OEC.

the EHS Guidelines, but instead rely on relevant host country environmental and social laws and regulations.

With the adoption of the EPs, banks were empowered to access environmental and social risk in projects and discuss these issues in an informed way with their clients, could have some confidence that their competitors were approaching these issues in a similar way and were able to respond to critics. Some might argue that they did not necessarily get it right, but the banks were now able to deal with these issues systematically and thoughtfully.

Have the EPs been a success and accomplished the objectives of the adopting banks? The Preamble of EP III describes this objective as:

> We, the Equator Principles Financial Institutions (EPFIs), have adopted the Equator Principles in order to ensure that the Projects we finance and advise on are developed in a manner that is socially responsible and reflects sound environmental management practices.[5]

The press release of the initial adopting banks[6] also reveals some of their ambitions for the EPs:

> We are pleased that the banking sector is increasingly recognising the importance of environmental and social issues in conducting its business with its clients. The Equator Principles will set a common baseline particularly relevant for one of the most vulnerable areas: project financing in emerging markets.
>
> Herman Mulder, Co-head of Group Risk Management, ABN AMRO

> The adoption of the Equator Principles signifies a major step forward by the financial sector to establish a standardized, common framework to address the environmental and social issues that arise from development projects. We are extremely proud to be part of this voluntary, private-sector initiative and we are confident that we will see more and more banks active in project finance adopt these principles in the coming months.
>
> Charles Prince, Chairman and Chief Executive Officer, Citigroup Global Corporate and Investment Bank

> Crédit Lyonnais is pleased to be associated with the Equator Principles initiative as a means of promoting environmentally and socially responsible conduct amongst the participants in this important market.
>
> Alain Papiasse, Deputy Chief Executive, Head of Crédit Lyonnais Investment and Corporate Banking

> The Equator Principles with their guidelines in the area of social and environmental responsibility are an important step towards a more vigorous advancement of sustainability in global project financing. They will help to ensure that ecological and social standards are observed and will promote transparency in business dealings.
>
> Kai Henkel, Head of Global Project Finance, HVB

These ambitions can be summarised as:

---

[5] The Equator Principles (June 2013), Preamble (2).

[6] Press Release: 'Leading Banks Announce Adoption of Equator Principles' (4 June 2003), http://www.equator-principles.com.

- Getting other banks to focus on environmental and social issues in their business.
- Creating a common framework among financial institutions for projects in emerging markets.
- Keeping the standard voluntary and private sector focused.
- Beginning the process of advancing sustainability in project finance (i.e. this is the first of many steps).

2 Market Penetration

The key objective for the EPs was levelling the playing field for financial institutions engaged in project finance to eliminate competition on environmental and social risk management practices. For the EPs to be successful, they needed to be adopted by the key players in project finance to achieve a high degree of market penetration. Very quickly, the EPFIs were well on their way to achieving this objective. Of the ten initial adopters of the EPs, most of these banks were leaders in global project finance.[7] According to the press release at the time of adoption, these banks were estimated to account for 30 % of the project finance market:

> Together, these banks underwrote approximately $14.5 billion of project loans in 2002, representing approximately 30 % of the project loan syndication market globally in 2002, according to Dealogic.[8]

Eight of the ten original banks were from Western Europe, one was a US bank and one was Australian. Five of these banks (Citigroup, RBS, HVB, WestLB and ABN AMRO) were among the top ten global project finance banks in 2003.[9] By the end of 2003, six more major banks had joined the EPs including the first Japanese bank, two Canadian banks and three more leading European banks.[10] In 2004, the first export credit agency (ECA) (EKN, Finland) adopted the EPs, thus extending their reach to a government-owned institution working in the private sector. And, also in that year, the EPs were adopted by the first emerging market and South American bank (Unibanco, Brazil). At its 1-year anniversary, there were 25 EPFIs from 14 countries. In 2005, the first African bank (Nedbank, South Africa) adopted the EPs.

By July 2006, when the EPs were revised to incorporate the revised IFC Performance Standards and to make other changes, there were 40 EPFIs. At its fifth anniversary in 2008, there were 60 EPFIs including new adopting banks from Argentina, Chile, Uruguay and Oman. Together they announced:

---

[7] See footnote 3 above.

[8] Press Release: 'Leading Banks Announce Adoption of the Equator Principles' (4 June 2003), http://www.equator-principles.com.

[9] Dealogic, 2003 mid-year ranking.

[10] The six additional banks were CIBC (Canada), HSBC (UK), ING (Netherlands), Mizuho (Japan), Royal Bank of Canada (Canada) and Standard Chartered (UK).

The EPs have become the global standard for project finance and have transformed the funding of major projects globally. In 2007, of the US$74.6 billion total debt tracked in emerging markets, US$52.9 billion was subject to the EPs, representing about 71 percent of total project finance debt in emerging market economies. The EPs are now considered the financial industry 'gold standard' for sustainable project finance.[11]

By 2014, there were 80 EPFIs. Members include Industrial Bank Co, the first and only Chinese EPFI (2008), two Mexican banks (2012), a Peruvian bank (2013) and IDFC, the first Indian bank (2013) to adopt. The addition of these banks was an important achievement in extending the reach of the EPs, and much of it had to do with the outreach efforts of the EP Association. IFC also played a role in outreach efforts.

But the global financial crisis that began in late 2008 set into motion a series of changes in the financial industry that are still being felt today and which had a major impact on the project finance market (see Graph below). From steady market growth from 2003 to 2008, peaking at US$250 billion in 2008, the global project finance market contracted to US$140 billion in 2009.[12] The crisis altered the European and US bank markets. A look at what has happened to four of the original EPFIs reveals some of that change:

- ABN AMRO was broken up in October 2007 with its international business sold to RBS (UK) and its Dutch business to Fortis (Netherlands). After Fortis's collapse in 2008, the Dutch government acquired the domestic operations of ABN AMRO.
- RBS was acquired by the British government in October 2008. As part of its restructuring, in November 2013, the management announced that it would be focusing on UK business.[13]
- HVB is now part of the UniCredit Group, headquartered in Italy.
- WestLB was downsized and became Portigon Financial Services, a financial service provider, in June 2012. It no longer lends and is no longer an EP member.

With constrained capital and a reduced risk appetite, project finance portfolios of the European and US banks were rapidly reduced. The project finance market still has not recovered to precrisis levels and stood at US$198 billion in 2012. At the peak of the market in 2008, Europe, the Middle East and Africa had a 55 % share of the project finance market. In 2012, that share was down to 34 %. Meanwhile, the Asian market was growing. With its tremendous demand for infrastructure and strong liquidity of local financial institutions, Asian banks quickly ramped up lending for Asian projects. Asia's share of the project finance market grew from 17 % in 2008 to 45 % by 2012.[14]

---

[11] Press Release: 'Equator Principles Celebrate 5 Years of Positive Environmental Impact and Improved Business Practices' (8 May 2008), http://www.equator-principles.com.

[12] Sources: 2003–2009 data: Project Finance International; 2010–2012 data: Thomson Reuters.

[13] 'RBS Places Troublesome Assets Worth £38bn in Internal "Bad Bank," The Guardian (1 November 2013).

[14] Ibid.

Since 2009, there has been less mention of the EPs' scope of coverage of the project finance market. Among the major project finance banks in 2012 were State Bank of India, Korea Development Bank, Axis Bank (India), ICICI Bank (India), China Development Bank and OCBC (Singapore), none of which are EPFIs.[15] EPFIs continue to dominate the list of lead arrangers, but the influence of non-Equator banks has grown.

Without major inroads in EP adoption by leading Indian and Chinese banks, there is the risk that the playing field will not continue to be levelled. Thus, a major challenge for the EPs comes from China and India where banks do not apply the EPs and can compete for projects in Asia, Africa and Latin America by having lower environmental and social standards.

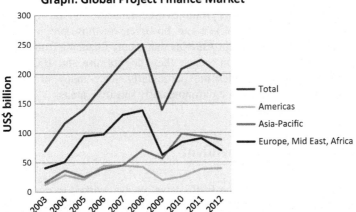

Graph: Global Project Finance Market*

*Sources: 2003–2009 Project Finance International
2010–2012 Thomson Reuters

3 Convergence Around a Common Standard

While the share of coverage of the project finance market by the EPs may have slipped, a notable success is that the EPs have driven the application of a common environmental and social risk management framework in emerging markets. Increasingly, the IFC Performance Standards are used as the benchmark in project finance not just among EPFIs, but also with multilateral development banks (MDBs), bilateral development agencies and ECAs. In 2008, the European Bank for Reconstruction and Development (EBRD) redrafted its Environmental and Social Policy and incorporated the Performance Requirements that draw largely

---

[15] Sources: Thomson Reuters, Project Finance Review, Full Year 2012; Dealogic Full Year League Tables 2012.

from the IFC Performance Standards.[16] In 2012, the OECD revised the Recommendation of the Council on Common Approaches for Officially Supported Export Credits and Environmental and Social Due Diligence (The Common Approaches) incorporating the IFC Performance Standards as the reference standard for project finance projects.[17]

In July 2012, the World Bank launched a 2-year process to review and update its Safeguard Policies in part with the objective of bringing their policies more closely in line with the IFC Performance Standards.[18] This consultation process has been extended and will continue into 2015.

Convergence around an agreed environmental and social standard by MDBs, ECAs, bilateral development agencies and EPFIs contributes to a virtuous circle in promoting better environmental and social outcomes for projects in emerging markets. Borrowers can plan projects knowing the standard they are expected to meet to obtain financing, and this promotes other lenders, who may not be EPFIs, to use this standard as well. There is a gap, however, for those projects in emerging markets in Africa, Asia and Latin America that secure financing from most Chinese and Indian financial institutions since they do not use the IFC Performance Standards. This gap is troublesome particularly since many of these projects involve extractive industries in environmentally sensitive areas.

4 Voluntary and Independent

Driven by liability concerns, the EPFIs have always worked to make it clear that they were each adopting the EPs independently. Hence the disclaimer in EP III:

> The Equator Principles is a baseline and framework for developing individual, internal environmental and social policies, procedures and practices. The Equator Principles do not create any rights in, or liability to, any person, public or private. Financial institutions adopt and implement the Equator Principles voluntarily and independently, without reliance on or recourse to the IFC, the World Bank Group, the Equator Principles Association, or other EPFIs.[19]

Accordingly, when a financial institution adopts the EPs, they do not become a signatory to the EPs or a member of an official EP club with oversight responsibilities, although it does appear like that to the outside world. The EP Association is an unincorporated association of EPFIs with the responsibility only for 'management,

---

[16] EBRD, Environmental and Social Policy (May 2008) (15).

[17] Working Party on Export Credits and Credit Guarantees, 'Recommendation of the Council on Common Approaches for Officially Supported Export Credits and Environmental and Social Due Diligence (The "Common Approaches")' (28 June 2012) (9).

[18] http://www.worldbank.org/safeguards

[19] The Equator Principles (June 2013) (11).

administration and development' of the EPs,[20] and it was not officially formed until July 2010.

Each financial institution independently agrees to adopt, implement and comply with the EP requirements and has the autonomy to implement and comply with the EPs as they see fit ('voluntarily and independently'). When a financial institution adopts the EPs, they agree that they fulfil, or will fulfil, several requirements, including:

- Being active in project finance
- Paying the annual fee
- Implementing environmental and social risk management policies and procedures to comply with the EPs
- Not lending to projects where the borrower will not or is unable to comply with the EPs.[21]

As competitors and to avoid liability risk, it is not feasible for the EPFIs to have oversight responsibility for one another. Instead, a bank self-certifies that it meets the adoption requirements and that it has or will implement the EPs. Independent verification by a third party of implementation procedures should be a longer-term objective of the EP Association and is discussed more below. At a minimum to build trust, accountability requires that new entrants provide comprehensive reporting on their implementation. EP III has made good progress in the area of reporting as discussed below.

Independence has had an impact on how the EPFIs have organised themselves. It was not until July 2010, 7 years after the EPs were first launched, that the EPs formed the EP Association and adopted Governance Rules. Gaining agreement to form such an association and the legal opinions surrounding it was a long and slow process. A rotating chair, a Steering Committee of core banks providing management and strategy for the EPs, and Working Groups focusing on priority issues continue as the loose management structure of the EP Association. In April 2008, an EP secretariat was hired to provide administrative support to handle matters related to adoption by new entrants, finances and communications.

The reliance on independence whether in the area of individual bank adoption or implementation or in how the EPs organise themselves, while strategically appropriate at the time of the launch, has over time worked to the detriment of the EPs. Without an official structure, for many years, the EPs did not have adequate control over their message. Their critics, such as BankTrack, a network of civil society organisations that track the operations of financial institutions, were reporting and identifying flaws in EP implementation from the earliest days of the EPs. On the first anniversary of the EPs, BankTrack issued, 'Principles, Profits or Just PR',[22]

---

[20] The Equator Principles Association Governance Rules (June 2010) (2).

[21] *Ibid* (7–10).

[22] BankTrack, 'Principles, Profits or Just PR—Equator Principles Anniversary Report' (June 2004).

and at the second anniversary, they issued, 'Unproven Equator Principles'.[23] This was the start in a long series of critical reports on the EPs. While the EP Association, through their working group for stakeholder relationships, often met with civil society organisations to discuss implementation and respond to criticism, BankTrack reports garnered broad publicity and may have hurt the EP brand. Lack of its own EP annual report or of any collective reporting or even of good quality and accessible individual EPFI reporting meant that others were telling the EP story, and often critically and incorrectly.

The impact and success of the EPs are dependent on both external and internal factors. Externally, changes in the financial market post-crisis mean that there are new prominent players in the project finance market, particularly major banks in India and China, which are not EPFIs. At the same time, the influence of Western European and US banks in the project finance market is reduced. While the EP Association has done some effective outreach work, this needs to be strengthened with additional resources to make more substantial inroads in India and China and bring more of these banks under the EP tent.

Notably, the growing convergence among multilateral and bilateral financial institutions, ECAs and EPFIs around the IFC Performance Standards has served to provide a common framework for projects in emerging markets. The broad range and diversity of EPFIs has inspired this convergence process and is a major success of the EPs. For the most part, it is accepted practice for international financial institutions to require project developers to meet these standards. This alone has raised the platform for sustainability in project finance.

5 Prospects and Challenges for the Future

The Strategic Review was designed to provide a long-term path for the EPs to remain on the cutting edge. The recommendations included both near- and medium-term measures for the EP Association to undertake, some to be incorporated into EP III and others relating to general leadership and governance. The recommendations also encompassed some steps that were longer-term and would take more time to implement.

The Strategic Review concluded that:

> The Equator Principles Association needs to advance as an organization and create a sustainable platform for its success and continued development, and to assert its leadership role in environmental and social risk management in the financial industry. It must excel at delivering its core mission... of ensuring that the projects that its members finance are developed in a socially responsible manner and using sound environmental management practices. At the same time, it must expand its membership to encompass new entrants in the project finance market, broaden its scope to accommodate the greater ambitions of its members, and address evolving environmental and social risk management needs (Lazarus and Feldbaum 2011a).

---

[23] BankTrack, 'Unproven Principles—The Equator Principles at Year Two' (June 2005).

A discussion of some of the specific findings, recommendations and implementation status of these recommendations follows.

5.1 Exercising Leadership

The EP Association is respected in the financial industry and looked to for leadership on environmental and social risk management. As an industry leader ('gold standard'), which they wish to remain, the EP Association has a responsibility to promote high standards of environmental and social risk management and sustainability in the financial industry. Despite the limited mandate of the EPs to project finance business, this leadership role extends well beyond project finance to the broader financial industry. With the first press conference announcing the launch of the EPs, the EPFIs marked themselves as leaders in the sustainability field. With the quick growth in membership, they were embraced by the industry. EPFIs are sought out to speak at conferences, to run training sessions and to be interviewed in the media about sustainability issues. For reasons relating to the more limited mandate of the EPs to project finance, but also due to lack of resources, this leadership role has not been systematically supported by the EP Association. It is also true that what each EPFI knows best is their own financial institution, and, therefore, this is what they talk about rather than talking about the EPs.

But because of the stature of the EP Association within the financial community, they have convening power and a platform. The Strategic Review recommended that they use this platform to promote discussion of improving environmental and social risk management in the financial sector. Some of the EPFIs have done this through their work on the Climate Principles, the Carbon Principles and, more recently, on the Cross Sector Biodiversity Initiative (CSBI), which is designed 'to develop and share good practices and practical tools to apply the new IFC Performance Standard 6 on Biodiversity Conservation'.[24] But, there is still much more that can be done to provide leadership on sustainability from creating an EP forum to discuss emerging issues to working together with other organisations that have complimentary objectives such as the Global Reporting Initiative (GRI) and the Principles for Responsible Investment (PRI). All of this, of course, requires more resources.

Within the EP Association, leadership is needed to ensure that the EPs evolve with growing understanding on environmental and social impacts, assessment methodology, mitigation techniques and community engagement practices. Leadership is needed to ensure that membership standards are high and implementation requirements are met.

---

[24] http://www.equator-principles.com.

5.2 The Need for Adequate Resources

The Strategic Review emphasised the importance of additional resources for the EP Association:

> As other voluntary organisations have learned, to ensure the long-term viability of their initiative, it is essential to put in place a lasting structure that can facilitate achievement of objectives and protect its brand. Much of the frustration with the pace of accomplishment of the EPs can be sourced back to the reliance on the spare time of EPFI members to implement its agenda. The EPs have the lowest fee structure and smallest level of staffing of any comparable voluntary organization that we could identify. This low budget approach served the organisation well up to a point, and considering the resources devoted to the EPs; its achievements to date are extraordinary. But, the organization is now beyond the point that this model is working (Lazarus and Feldbaum 2011b).

In 2008, the EPFIs outsourced responsibility of EP administrative matters to a secretariat. The secretariat's role has increased from one part-time staff to now requiring a second administrator. Other than this, the EP Association lacks a dedicated staff and office. The management of the organisation is handled by EPFIs who, in addition to their other responsibilities within their financial institutions, volunteer their time as EP chair, Steering Committee members and leaders and members of Working Groups.

The annual dues for EPFIs have increased from about US$2,000 equivalent to today's level of US$5,000 equivalent per year, giving the EP Association an annual budget of about US$400,000. This budget, while improved, remains low by comparison to similar organisations and can only cover the secretariat, the website and some annual meeting costs. This lack of resources means that new initiatives take longer to implement.

Now that EP III has been adopted, the EP Association needs to focus on such priorities as developing an audit system for EP reporting, revising the Governance Rules, including re-examining EP adoption criteria, implementing a more active outreach effort to financial institutions in China and India and developing an EP forum, among other things. These initiatives would be achieved far sooner if the EP Association had the funding to hire additional resources. To sustain momentum, more dedicated professional resources are essential.

5.3 Transparency and Reporting

The Strategic Review strongly focused on the need for better information disclosure by the EPs on implementation and on project level reporting. Inadequate disclosure means that it is difficult to determine whether an EPFI is fulfilling its responsibilities under the EPs. While the EPFIs recognise that disclosure is essential to promote accountability and trust for an independently implemented voluntary standard, with a few exceptions, the degree of disclosure by EPFIs has been limited and inconsistent. Despite recognising the need for disclosure, the issue is complicated because standards of disclosure differ among members with, for example, institutions in Japan having a tradition of limited transparency. There is also concern that more disclosure brings more NGO scrutiny or that more disclosure might expose inconsistent treatment of projects among EPFIs. Instead, this is one of many good reasons to improve disclosure.

It was not until EP II, in June 2006, that reporting requirements were introduced and then they were exceedingly slim.

> Principle 10: Each EPFI adopting the Equator Principles commits to report publicly at least annually about its Equator Principles implementation processes and experience, taking into account appropriate confidentiality considerations.[25]

A footnote to this principle indicated that reporting should at a minimum include the number of transactions screened by each EPFI, the categorisation of transactions and information on implementation. A Guidance Note on Equator Principles Implementation Reporting, issued in December 2007, is most notable for its disclaimer:

> The document is not to be viewed as a required reporting framework, but rather a guidance document to assist Equator Principles Financial Institutions in the development of their EP implementation and reporting methodologies, if needed.[26]

Not surprisingly, the quality of reporting has varied substantially from those EPFIs that provide the bare minimum data in a not very accessible format to those that detail their implementation measures; provide considerable information on the projects that they had reviewed in the past year, including disclosing project names; and chronicle the challenges that they have confronted. Each report is in a different format and the relevant information is often buried deep in a bank's annual corporate social responsibility (CSR) report. This disparity in reporting and the lack of accessibility undermine confidence in implementation, which is the opposite purpose that good reporting should serve.

The EP Association made improvements in EPFI reporting requirements in EP III. Annex B of EP III specifies minimum project reporting requirements that include disclosure, by project category, of sector, region and country designation and whether an independent review was undertaken. Implementation reporting now includes detailing the responsibilities, staffing and reporting lines for those reviewing projects for EP compliance and how the EPs have been incorporated into credit procedures and risk management policies of the institution. More detailed implementation reporting is also specified for new EP adopters. EP III also provides for identification of names of projects financed under the EPs. These names are disclosed not by the EPFIs, but through the EP secretariat for subsequent publication on the EP website. While this has not been stated, the assumption is that this annual listing of EP projects will not include the names of the EPFIs providing the financing for these transactions, which is an unfortunate lack of transparency.

---

[25] The Equator Principles (July 2006) (6).

[26] Guidance Note on Equator Principles Implementation Reporting (December 2007).

New adopters, in the first year after adoption, according to the EP Governance Rules, remain exempt from reporting details on their project finance transactions.[27] To speed up implementation for new adopters, this exemption should be eliminated.

Progress was also made in EP III on client reporting with the requirement that clients disclose their environmental and social impact assessments online. This requirement is waived for clients that do not have a website, which is an unnecessary exemption. To promote communication with stakeholders, clients should be expected to have a website.

As recommended in the Strategic Review, next on the agenda is for the EP Association to develop an assurance standard for third-party auditing of EPFI reporting. Independent auditing of CSR reports has become commonplace, particularly in Europe. An audit process for EPFI reporting would provide a means of independent verification without concerns of oversight of one EPFI over another. It would increase confidence in reporting and also raise the quality of reporting. To be most effective, there should be an agreed standard developed by the EP Association for all EPFI audits.

6 The Duck Test

Because of the limit of the EPs to project finance, one EPFI's project finance deal may be another EPFI's corporate loan. Thus, one bank applies the EPs to the transaction and the same transaction is exempted from the EPs by another institution. The Strategic Review recommended eliminating this inconsistency through the extension of the EPs to corporate loans where the majority of proceeds of the loan were used to fund a single asset. In other words, the application of 'the duck test' was suggested: if it looks like a duck, swims like a duck and quacks like a duck, then it probably is a duck. If it looks like a project finance deal and if it has the characteristics of a project finance deal, then regardless of what it is labelled, it should be treated as a project finance deal and the EPs applied to it.

EP III did address this issue by expanding the scope of the EPs to include Project-Related Corporate Loans where 'the majority of the loan is related to a single Project over which the client has Effective Operational Control'.[28] This is good progress and will help reduce inconsistent treatment of projects among EPFIs. Whereas the EPs extend to project finance loans with a minimum capital cost of US$10 million, the limit for Project-Related Corporate Loans is higher with a minimum loan amount of US$100 million and a minimum individual EPFI exposure of US$50 million. These higher limits should be monitored carefully to ensure that the EPs are now capturing Project-Related Corporate Loans with major environmental and social risk.

---

[27] The Equator Principles Association Governance Rules, Section 6(b) (June 2010) (10).

[28] The Equator Principles (June 2013) (3).

7 Membership Has Responsibilities

What are the core requirements of being an EPFI? In addition to paying dues and reporting, it is developing the management system and policies and procedures to implement the EPs throughout the organisation, training staff and ensuring that projects are assessed, implemented and monitored according to EP requirements. As discussed above, entry criteria to become an EPFI are not performance based and not verified. The Strategic Review recommended development of a simple audit process to determine if new applicants have the implementation capacity in place to become an EPFI. For banks in frontier markets, it might be appropriate to have training resources available to assist new applicants meet these core requirements and grant funding might be available to support this objective.

EPFIs that do not meet their EP obligations undermine the effectiveness and reputation of the EPs. Removal from the official list of EPFIs, or delisting, now occurs only when an EPFI fails to meet its annual reporting requirement or fails to pay its annual dues. But some EPFIs rarely, if ever, participate in EP meetings and some may have demonstrated little evidence of applying the EPs. They may not be doing any project finance lending, but then they fail to meet the EP requirement of being active in project finance. Thresholds for continued inclusion of an EPFI based on performance measures need to be specified. After a grace period for correction, there should be delisting.

8 Climate Change and Human Rights

The EPFIs have grappled with increasingly complex environmental issues in projects over the past few years, many of which involved carbon-intensive industries including coal-fired thermal power plants, mining of tar sands and natural gas hydraulic fracturing. Most EPFIs felt it was important that the 2012 redraft of the IFC Performance Standards provided more guidance on climate change, and they encouraged IFC to focus on this issue.[29] EP III provides a general recognition of the importance of limiting climate change impacts in the preamble.[30] But perhaps the banks wished IFC to focus on this issue because it was a difficult one for the EPFIs and it was easier to have IFC take the lead.

While the EPFIs hoped that the revised IFC Performance Standards would go further, they do provide for an alternatives analysis for projects with projected high greenhouse gas (GHG) emissions and for the client to '*implement* [emphasis added]

---

[29] EP Steering Committee letter to IFC Executive Vice President, Lars Thunell (8 February 2011), http://www.equator-principles.com.

[30] The Equator Principles (June 2013) (2).

technically and financially feasible and cost-effective options to reduce... emissions during the design and operation of the project'.[31]

In EP III, an annex was included to provide guidance on climate change, the alternatives analysis, and reporting on GHG emissions.[32] But in this annex, the language relating to the analysis has been changed in a way that creates confusion rather than clarifies the meaning. Here 'the alternatives analysis requires the *evaluation* [emphasis added] of technically and financially feasible and cost-effective options to reduce ... GHG emissions'. The client is expected to document these options. The word 'implement' as specified in the IFC Performance Standard is assiduously avoided. But, the annex also states, 'This does not modify or reduce the requirements set out in the applicable standards (e.g. IFC Performance Standard 3)'.[33] Thus, it is unclear whether the client is expected to implement the alternatives analysis or not. The one thing that is clear is that this was a difficult area for the EPFIs.

EP III also introduces carbon emissions reporting by clients. Projects producing emissions over 100,000 tonnes annually are required to publicly report their emissions. At emission levels of 25,000 tonnes, clients are 'encouraged' to report.[34] However, in the IFC Performance Standards, reporting is expecting at emission levels over 25,000 tonnes, although it is unspecified whether this reporting is public or to IFC. The disparity between the EPs and the Performance Standards is unfortunate and confusing.

Impressively, EP III also introduced the responsibility of the EPFIs to respect human rights and to undertake human rights due diligence in accordance with the United Nations (UN) Guiding Principles on Business and Human Rights.[35] This responsibility is mentioned throughout EP III and may be more explicit than in the IFC Performance Standards.

9   Making It Easier

Managing an organisation with participants across the globe with different capacities, interests and expectations is challenging, but doing it effectively and efficiently is the key to maintaining and building on the EP Association's success. Several measures can be taken to facilitate the effectiveness of the organisation.

---

[31] IFC Performance Standard 3 (1 January 2013) (2).

[32] The Equator Principles, Annex A (June 2013) (12).

[33] *Ibid.*

[34] *Ibid.*

[35] 'Guiding Principles on Business and Human Rights: Implementing the United Nations "Protect, Respect and Remedy" Framework' (16 June 2011) http://www.ohchr.org

9.1 Not Everyone Needs to Decide

With the large Steering Committee, currently at 14 members, and consensus-based, inclusive decision-making, it is hard work to be an EP chair. If the chair exercises too much authority, the Steering Committee members may object, but with multiple and often opposing positions on issues, decisions need to be made to achieve progress. Someone needs to decide and impasses need to be overcome, and there are times when efficiency trumps consensus and less democracy results in better outcomes than more democracy. The position of chair demands considerable time and energy and, not surprisingly, it is not eagerly sought out. At times and on some issues, it would be appropriate to allow the chair to have more autonomy perhaps with the help of an executive committee. Future chairs would benefit from being able to exercise leadership and having more authority on select issues.

9.2 Tools and Chat Rooms

The EP Association has offered some implementation seminars and workshops on specific topics such as documentation, grievance mechanisms and biodiversity offsets. Many EPFIs also participate in annual community of learning events provided by IFC and in regional discussion groups. But, it is fair to say that quality and consistency of implementation continues to vary among EPFIs. As there are more EPFIs spread across the globe, ensuring consistency in implementation is more challenging. The EP Association needs tools to assist members in improving all aspects of EP implementation from categorisation to project monitoring. While avoiding confidentiality issues, online resources for EPFIs including training modules and chat rooms would facilitate a better exchange of information and better outcomes across continents.

9.3 Protect the Brand

The EP Association needs to define itself rather than being defined by its critics. To achieve this, communication is essential. With their new website and the work of the communications working group, the EPs have done a better job of communicating and issuing press releases. They would benefit from an annual report that tells their story each year on what has been achieved and what they are working on along with a big media launch of the report.

9.4 Tiered Membership

As noted in the Strategic Review, 'Minimum membership criteria reflect a single-tier membership category and do not distinguish diverse membership capacities and ambitions' (Lazarus and Feldbaum 2011c). Accommodating EPFIs with vastly different experience and capacity under one standard is a very broad range to accommodate. It also means that less can be achieved by keeping all EPFIs at the same level. While the EP Association umbrella should be big enough to actively engage both newcomers and established players, it could be done more effectively through tiered membership.

However, tiered membership was not incorporated into EP III and has not been endorsed by some EPFIs. While they value independence in implementation, they also want all EPFIs to be the seen as implementing the EPs in the same way. But, they do not. Even among the original adopting EPFIs, some banks have done a better job of implementing the EPs than others. At some, the EPs are consistently implemented throughout their global networks, whereas other banks still struggle with this. Ten years out, some of the banks should be doing better on implementation than they are. Yet, these EPFIs all wish to be seen as leaders. Keeping a single-tier structure allows this perception to remain. But this is holding the others back. Tiered membership would establish a baseline level of EP performance while providing a consistent framework for those institutions with greater ambitions and levels of performance to be identified. Higher tiers of membership could be associated with increased disclosure or with application of the EPs to a broader product range or both, but within clearly specified boundaries for performance. Tiered membership would give new entrants something to aspire to. And most importantly, tiered membership would promote a higher level of environmental and social performance in project finance and that will help fulfil the overarching objective of the EPs.

10 The Future Is Now

Through the broad application of the IFC Performance Standards and the growing numbers of EPFIs across the globe, the EP Association has made considerable progress in achieving its objective of levelling the playing field in project finance. EP III signifies a major evolution of the EPs in setting a high standard for project finance with more transparency, improved stakeholder engagement and consultation methods and more focus on climate change, human rights and biodiversity, among other important changes.

Thus, the EP Association has effectively laid the groundwork for the EPs to remain the 'gold standard' of environmental and social risk management for project finance in the financial sector. Now, the devil is in the details. Its leadership role needs to be embraced, resources fortified, implementation improved, audit standards developed, membership criteria strengthened and verified and outreach efforts enhanced. The EP Association, with limited resources, an unwieldy management structure and considerable patience, has achieved a great deal. There are high expectations for the EP Association to achieve even more. With leadership, resources and an improved structure, they will be well positioned to retain the gold standard.

References

Lazarus, S., & Feldbaum, A. (2011a, February). *Equator principles strategic review*. Final Report, Executive Summary (i)

Lazarus, S., & Feldbaum, A. (2011b, February). *Equator principles strategic review*. Final Report, Executive Summary (5).

Lazarus, S., & Feldbaum, A. (2011c, February). *Equator principles strategic review*. Final Report, Executive Summary (9).

Development Banking ESG Policies and the Normativisation of Good Governance Standards

Development Banks as Agents of Global Administrative Law

Owen McIntyre

Abstract As investment banks, both multilateral development banks (MDBs) and private sector actors, adopt comprehensive environmental, social and governance policies and standards to circumscribe the projects and activities they finance, these policies and standards reflect and contribute to the formation of a range of widely accepted standards of good governance that are increasingly understood as formal legal or quasi-legal requirements. Such policies and standards promote a number of core 'good governance' values, including transparency of decision-making, broad public participation in decision-making and policy formulation, delivery of reasoned decisions, reviewability of decisions, accountability of decision-makers and respect for proportionality in decision-making and respect for human rights, which are prevalent in national systems of administrative law and increasingly applied, mandatorily or voluntarily, to a range of actors including private sector lenders. The ESG policies and standards initially adopted by MDBs, which often incorporate and informally enforce values set down in national and international law on environmental protection and human rights, are now reflected in the Equator Principles adopted by 80 private sector lenders in 35 countries. This tendency towards the emergence of a set of universally accepted good governance standards, applicable to both public and private actors at global, regional, national and local levels of administration, has been described as the phenomenon of 'global administrative law'. The trend in investment banking towards the adoption and implementation of ESG policies and standards can therefore be explained in terms of global administrative law while, at the same time, the investment banking sector might be regarded as an exemplar of this gradual move towards the development of global standards of good governance practice.

O. McIntyre (✉)
Faculty of Law, University College Cork, Cork, Ireland
e-mail: o.mcintyre@ucc.ie

© Springer International Publishing Switzerland 2015
K. Wendt (ed.), *Responsible Investment Banking*, CSR, Sustainability, Ethics & Governance, DOI 10.1007/978-3-319-10311-2_8

1 Introduction

It is increasingly normal for international development banking institutions, including multilateral development banks (MDBs) and many private sector lenders, to adopt comprehensive environmental, social and governance (ESG) safeguard policies and standards to circumscribe the projects and activities they finance. This is particularly the case in the financing of major infrastructure projects in developing countries or economies in transition. It is increasingly apparent that these policies and standards both reflect and contribute to the formation of a broad range of widely accepted standards of good governance, increasingly presented as formal legal or quasi-legal requirements. Such policies and standards promote a number of core 'good governance' values, which are prevalent in almost all national systems of administrative law and are increasingly applied, mandatorily or voluntarily, to a broad range of international or transnational actors.

The ESG policies and standards initially adopted by MDBs, which often incorporate and informally enforce values set down in national and international law on environmental protection, social protection and human rights, are also now reflected in the Equator Principles (EPs), adopted by 80 private sector lenders in 35 countries covering over 70 % of international project finance debt in emerging markets. This organic movement towards the emergence of a set of universally accepted good governance standards, applying to both public and private actors at the global, regional, national and local levels of administration, has been described by observers of the 'global administrative law' phenomenon. Therefore, the trend in international development banking practice towards the adoption and implementation of ESG policies and standards can be explained in terms of global administrative law while, at the same time, the international development banking sector might be regarded as a key driver of this gradual move towards the evolution of global standards of good governance practice.

1.1 The Emergence of Development Banking ESG Safeguard Policies

Because major development projects can significantly impact the natural environment and the social wellbeing of local communities, MDBs have for many years been concerned to integrate environmental and social protection requirements into their lending practices. The essential role played by MDBs and other development agencies in the informal adoption and implementation of the legal standards, principles and procedures inherent to the overarching goal of sustainable development has been widely acknowledged (Handl 2001; Richardson 2002; Gowland Gaultieri 2001; Kohona 2004). As early as 1980, the Brandt Report called on MDBs to assist in environmental assessments to ensure that an ecological perspective would be incorporated into development planning (Independent Commission for International Development Issues 1980: 115; Shihata 1992: 2). More generally, in 1985, the Brundtland Commission advised that MDBs assist developing countries in making the transition to sustainable development (World Commission on Environment and Development 1987: 337).

The World Bank, unsurprisingly as the principal global development lender, was at the forefront of such efforts and led the way for the regional MDBs and other international financial institutions (IFIs). Since 1970, the Bank had prepared guidelines for staff to determine how to weigh environmental factors in any given project (Shihata 1992: 4), and these guidelines were substantially expanded and widely communicated in 1972 (World Bank 1972). In the early 1980s, international lenders began to engage in coordinated efforts in this regard, with the World Bank and a range of international financing agencies, including regional MDBs, the EEC, the OAS, UNEP and UNDP, signing the 1980 New York Declaration pledging their support for the creation of systematic environmental assessment and evaluation procedures for all development activities. In 1981, the Bank played a key role in deliberations leading to the adoption of the Cocoyoc Declaration, which included recommendations for incorporating environmental policy into the development process intended for the Bank and other multilateral funding agencies in the appraisal of projects they were considering for funding (Shihata 1992: 3–6). Whereas the Bank had previously published sectoral policy papers for areas containing sections relating to environmental safeguards, including rural development (1975), forestry (1978), agricultural land settlement (1978) and fisheries (1982), in May 1984, all such policy guidelines were consolidated, updated and issued as a formal operational manual statement—OMS No. 2.36, *Environmental Aspects of Bank Work*.

The World Bank's environmental policy was considerably strengthened by the issuance in October 1989 of Operational Directive (OD 4.00) on environmental issues, which was revised in 1991 and renamed as OD 4.01 on Environmental Assessment (Shihata 1992: 8–9). The Bank also developed policies on social protection, adopting Operational Directive 4.30 on Involuntary Resettlement in June 1990, requiring, inter alia, that 'involuntary resettlement should be avoided or minimised where feasible' and that a resettlement plan must be prepared to ensure that displaced persons are treated appropriately. Demonstrating a clear understanding of the close link between the potential environmental and social impacts of major projects, OD 4.30 attempts to integrate environmental and social safeguards, requiring that the resettlement plan consider the environmental aspects of projects, such as deforestation, overgrazing, soil erosion or pollution, in order to provide appropriate mitigation measures in the interests of the people displaced (Shihata 1992: 12–13).

The sophistication and coverage of the ESG policies and standards adopted by MBDs have continued to develop. Consider, for example, the case of the European Bank for Reconstruction and Development (EBRD), which adopted its first Environmental Policy in 1991 but is now subject to the 2008 Environmental and Social Policy (ESP). The scope of the Bank's safeguard policy has evolved over time to ensure greater protection regarding social impacts and, at the time of writing, the

2008 Environmental and Social Policy is undergoing a fundamental review expected to result in greater emphasis on compliance with international human rights values and requirements. Modelled on the format of the Performance Standards adopted by the International Finance Corporation (IFC), the private sector lending arm of the World Bank Group, the EBRD's 2008 ESP contains detailed procedural and substantive requirements for the avoidance or mitigation of harm liable to be caused by projects set out under 10 Performance Requirements (PRs), each relating to a particular type of environmental or social impact, type of lending or good governance practice. These include:

PR 1: Environmental and Social Appraisal and Management
PR 2: Labour and Working Conditions
PR 3: Pollution Prevention and Abatement
PR 4: Community Health, Safety and Security
PR 5: Land Acquisition, Involuntary Resettlement and Economic Displacement
PR 6: Biodiversity Conservation and Sustainable Management of Living Natural
    Resources
PR 7: Indigenous Peoples
PR 8: Cultural Heritage
PR 9: Financial Intermediaries
PR 10: Information Disclosure and Stakeholder Engagement

The EBRD's 2008 ESP is intended to ensure that the Bank promotes, through its lending activities, a broad range of ESG values and outcomes. For example, in setting out the Bank's commitment to such values, the Policy stipulates that the Bank will:

> 'focus upon priority environmental and social issues facing the region ... such as climate change mitigation and adaptation, desertification, biodiversity conservation, energy and resource efficiency, poverty alleviation, promotion of decent work, reducing social exclusion, access to basic services, gender equality, transparency, and social development'.

It also emphasises classic good governance values and practices, reaffirming that the Bank 'is strongly committed to the principles of corporate transparency, accountability and stakeholder engagement' and, further, that it 'will promote similar good practices amongst its clients'.

It is also apparent, however, that the Policy is very concerned with ensuring compliance with the environmental and social standards set out under various regimes existing under national, EU or international law, sometimes regardless of whether such rules are directly applicable to the Bank's client in any formal sense. For example, the 2008 ESP stresses that 'EBRD will seek to ensure... that the projects it finances ... are designed and operated in compliance with applicable regulatory requirements and good international practice'. It also declares that '[t]he Bank is committed to promoting European Union (EU) environmental standards', even though the majority of the states in which it operates are not EU Member States. The central relevance of international law for determining the standards of environmental and social protection afforded under the 2008 ESP is apparent from the express commitment that:

'The EBRD will actively seek, through its investments, to contribute to the effective implementation of relevant principles and rules of international law related to the environment, labour, corporate responsibility and public access to environmental information'.

It elaborates on the relevant standards of corporate responsibility to explain that internationally agreed instruments include the International Labour Organisation (ILO) Tripartite Declaration of Principles concerning Multinational Enterprises and Social Policy and the Organisation for Economic Cooperation and Development (OECD) Guidelines for Multinational Enterprises. Both instruments represent precisely the kind of nonbinding, voluntary guidelines commonly associated with the 'global administrative law' (GAL) phenomenon explained below. Regarding normative requirements of international law applicable within the jurisdiction where the client operates, the 2008 ESP guarantees that '[t]he EBRD will not knowingly finance projects that would contravene country obligations under relevant international treaties and agreements related to environmental protection, human rights, and sustainable development'. More specifically, it stipulates that the stakeholder interaction required under the Policy 'should be consistent with the spirit, purpose and ultimate goals' of the Aarhus Convention (UNECE 1998), the EU Environmental Impact Assessment Directive and, where relevant, the Espoo Convention (UNECE 1991), 'regardless of the status of ratification'. In detailing safeguards applicable under each Performance Requirement, the Policy refers to, and thereby incorporates, a wide range of binding international conventions and EU instruments, as well as many nonbinding or voluntary guidelines or governance regimes. For example, PR 2 on Labour and Working Conditions alludes to a plethora of ILO conventions and guidelines, while PR 6 on Biodiversity Management refers to a range of relevant international conventions and EU directives, as well as voluntary guidelines on biodiversity-inclusive EIA adopted by the Conference of the Parties (COP) of the 1992 Convention on Biological Diversity. It appears that the ESG safeguard policies of MDBs incorporate widely accepted international legal standards, regardless of their direct applicability to the client, thus requiring these institutions to act as informal agents for the promotion of compliance with or enforcement of such standards.

For lenders such as the EBRD or IFC that focus on private sector lending, these standards of environmental and social governance are imposed upon private corporate entities, against which most requirements of international law could never be formally applied. In addition, the Equator Principles (EPs) (Clayton 2009), the third iteration of which have just been introduced, provide a minimum due diligence framework for determining, assessing and managing environmental and social risk the participating private sector banking institutions are committed to implementing in their internal environmental and social policies, procedures and standards for financing projects. As regards the environmental and social safeguard standards applicable, the EPs distinguish between projects in 'Designated Countries', i.e. those 'deemed to have robust environmental and social governance, legislative systems and institutional capacity designed to protect their people and the natural environment', where 'compliance with relevant host country laws, regulations and permits that pertain to environmental and social issues' is required, and those in 'Non-Designated Countries', where there must be 'compliance with the then applicable IFC Performance Standards on Environmental and Social Sustainability ... and the World Bank Group Environmental, Health and Safety Guidelines'. The Equator Principles Association website recognises growing 'convergence around common environmental and social standards', as well as the 'development of other responsible environmental and social management practices in the financial sector and banking industry', such as the Carbon Principles. Tacitly acknowledging the seminal importance of the IFC's Performance Standards in such a process of convergence, the website notes that '[m]ultilateral development banks, including the European Bank for Reconstruction and Development, and export credit agencies, through the OECD Common Approaches, are increasingly drawing on the same standards as the EPs'.

2 The Role of Independent Accountability Mechanisms

The recent establishment by all MDBs of independent accountability mechanisms (IAMs) tasked with ensuring compliance with their ESG policies has greatly enhanced the role of MDBs as informal agents for ensuring compliance with emerging norms of environmental and social protection. Whereas many such norms have been routinely ignored by governmental authorities and those directly responsible for causing environmental or social harm, IAMs provide a potentially effective mechanism for the enforcement of MDB safeguard policies and thus international standards, at the 'coalface' of project implementation. This simple fact has achieved much in terms of engendering a compliance culture within MDBs, governmental agencies and corporations involved in major infrastructural and industrial development and a culture of citizens' expectations in terms of the justiciability of ESG standards (McInerney-Lankford 2010; MacKay 2010; Levinson 2010; Di Leva 2010).

Once again, the World Bank led the way in 1993 by establishing the Inspection Panel following calls for greater accountability within the World Bank in the 1992 Wapenhans Report (World Bank 1992) and harsh criticism over the Sardar Sarovar Dam Project in India (Oleschak-Pillai 2010: 409). The Inspection Panel has competence to receive and investigate complaints from people claiming to have suffered material adverse effects due to a failure by the Bank to follow its operational policies and procedures in the design, appraisal or implementation of a project and to make specific recommendations to the Board based on its findings. The various IAMs since established by all MDBs play a number of roles, including compliance review, problem-solving or an advisory function (Nanwani 2008: 204–208). The Project Complaint Mechanism (PCM) established by the EBRD, for example, enjoys both a compliance review and a problem-solving role.

As regards the 'convergence around common environmental and social standards' alluded to above, the wider community of MDBs and other accountability mechanisms has for some years been engaged in institutionalised cooperation, coordination and the sharing of experience through an IAMs Annual Meeting hosted each year by one of the MDBs, as well as a members-only on-line Web portal. More cofinancing of projects by two or more institutions has made necessary greater cooperation among IAMs and is now reflected in IAMs' operating procedures. For example, EBRD PCM Rule of Procedure 16 provides:

'Once the PCM registers a Complaint, if the Project at issue in the Complaint is subject to parallel co-financing by other institutions, the PCM Officer will notify the accountability mechanism(s) of the parallel co-financing institution(s) of the Registration of the Complaint and will communicate and cooperate with the accountability mechanisms of such institutions(s) so as to avoid duplication of efforts and/or disruption or disturbance to common parties. Where appropriate, the parallel co-financing institutions will consider establishing a written cooperation agreement addressing such issues as confidentiality and sharing of information'.

While each IAM must work to ensure compliance with the specific requirements of the particular ESG policies of the MDB by which it has been established, it is reasonable to assume that such cooperation, coordination and shared learning will encourage IAMs to adopt common approaches to the interpretation and enforcement of ESG standards and thus to their continuing development.

3   The Phenomenon of 'Global Administrative Law'

The emerging concept of Global Administrative Law (GAL) addresses the rapidly changing realities of transnational regulation, which increasingly involves, inter alia, various forms of industry self-regulation, hybrid forms of private–private and public–private regulation, network governance by state officials and governance by intergovernmental organisations with direct or indirect regulatory powers, and 'begins from the twin ideas that much global governance can be understood as administration, and that such administration is often organised and shaped by principles of an administrative law character' (Kingsbury et al. 2005: 2). It is proposed that these disparate regulatory regimes, some voluntary and some mandatory, and operating at various levels (sector-specific, national, regional and global):

'together form a variegated "global administrative space" that includes international institutions and transnational networks involving both governmental and non-governmental actors, as well as domestic administrative bodies that operate within international regimes or cause transboundary regulatory effects'. (Kingsbury et al. 2005: 3)

These authors include among examples of such regulatory regimes and networks business-NGO partnerships in the Fair Labor Association, OECD environmental policies to be followed by national export credit agencies, regulation of ozone-depleting substances under the Montreal Protocol, sustainable forest use criteria for certification of forest products developed by the Forest Stewardship Council, the Basle Committee of central bankers, the Clean Development Mechanism under the Kyoto Protocol and, significantly, World Bank standards for the conduct of environmental assessments. Benedict Kingsbury deliberates further on the idea of a 'global administrative space' and explains that it 'marks a departure from those orthodox understandings of international law in which the international is largely inter-governmental, and there is a reasonably sharp separation of the domestic and the international' and that it reflects the practice of global governance, whereby 'transnational networks of rule-generators, interpreters and appliers cause such strict barriers to break down'(Kingsbury 2009: 25). Remarking on the 'highly decentralised and not very systematic' nature of much of the administration of global governance, Kingsbury observes that '[s]ome entities are given roles in global regulatory governance which they may not wish for or be particularly designed or prepared for' (Kingsbury 2009: 25), bringing to mind the reluctant development of ESG safeguard policies by MDBs in the wake of controversial lending decisions in the 1980s and early 1990s.

Crucially, in respect of the normative content of GAL, and reflective of its key procedural governance aspects, the leading proponents of the GAL phenomenon observe that:

> 'These evolving regulatory structures are each confronted with demands for transparency, consultation, participation, reasoned decisions, and review mechanisms to promote accountability. These demands, and responses to them, are increasingly framed in terms that have an administrative law character. The growing commonality of these administrative law-type principles and practices is building a unity between otherwise disparate areas of governance'. (Kingsbury et al. 2005: 2)

The function of administrative law generally is to protect individuals by checking the unauthorised, excessive, arbitrary or unfair exercise of public power and, by so doing, to give direction to the practices of administrative bodies, particularly in terms of their responsiveness to broader public interests. Proponents of GAL argue that it can perform a similar function for global administrative structures and point out that many of the regulatory measures cited above have resulted from the efforts of global administrative bodies, often stimulated by external criticism, to improve internal accountability and bolster external legitimacy (Kingsbury et al. 2005: 4). One needs only to consider the establishment of ESG policies, and of accountability mechanisms to enforce such policies, by all major multilateral development banks, or the widespread inclusion of mechanisms for NGO participation and representation in the decision-making structures of regulatory bodies. In an attempt to provide a definition of the concept of GAL, the same leading proponents explain that it:

> 'encompasses the legal mechanisms, principles and practices, along with supporting social understandings, that promote or otherwise affect the *accountability* of global administrative bodies, in particular by ensuring these bodies meet adequate standards of transparency, consultation, participation, rationality, and legality, and by providing effective review of the rules and decisions these bodies make'. (Kingsbury et al. 2005: 5, original emphasis)

In addition, they accompany this definition with a broad understanding of the 'global administrative bodies' that generate GAL norms and to which such norms might apply, to include:

'intergovernmental institutions, informal inter-governmental networks, national governmental agencies acting pursuant to global norms, hybrid public-private bodies engaged in transnational administration, and purely private bodies performing public roles in transnational administration'. (Kingsbury et al. 2005: 5)

Much of the normative content of the ESG concept and in particular the procedural rights of individuals and communities normally contained therein, along with the policies, procedures and decisions of the disparate entities that seek to give effect to the values contained therein, can be viewed through the prism of GAL.

As regards the sources of GAL rules and principles, leading scholar Benedict Kingsbury emphasises that 'there is no single unifying rule of recognition covering all of GAL', while including the conventional sources of public international law, i.e. treaties, fundamental customary international law rules and general principles of law, but also certain principles associated with 'publicness' in law (Kingsbury 2009: 23). He suggests that '[p]rinciples relevant to publicness include the entity's adherence to legality, rationality, proportionality, rule of law, and some human rights', which are manifested in 'practices of judicial-type review of the acts of global governance entities, in requirements of reason-giving, and in practices concerning publicity and transparency' (Kingsbury 2009: 23). In an account of GAL, which is slightly more sceptical about the difficulty of identifying a universal set of administrative law principles, Harlow systematically identifies and describes four potential sources as a foundation for a global administrative law system:

'first, the largely procedural principles that have emerged in national administrative law systems, notably the principle of legality and due process principles; second, the set of rule of law values, promoted by proponents of free trade and economic liberalism; third, the good governance values, and more particularly transparency, participation and accountability, promoted by the World Bank and International Monetary Fund; and finally, human rights values'. (Harlow 2006: 187)

Harlow concludes from her examination of these sources that 'there is considerable overlap between principles found in these different sources' (Harlow 2006: 188). Kingsbury also includes among the sources of GAL the rules, standards and safeguards developed as a result of processes of the so-called private ordering, such as the various technical guidelines adopted by bodies such as the International Standards Organisation (ISO), though he cautions that such '"[p]rivate ordering" comes within this concept of law only through engagement with public institutions' (Kingsbury 2009: 23).

As regards the specific normative content of GAL, Kingsbury identifies certain '[g]eneral principles of public law [which] combine formal qualities with normative commitments in the enterprise of channelling, managing, shaping and constraining political power' (Kingsbury 2009: 32). In addition to certain 'more detailed elements, or requirements … particularly review, reason-giving, and publicity/ transparency', his indicative list of such general principles of public law includes:

1. *The Principle of Legality*—requiring that actors within a power system are constrained to act in accordance with the rules of the system
2. *The Principle of Rationality*—requiring the justification of decisions, including that decision-makers give reasons and produce a factual record for decisions
3. *The Principle of Proportionality*—requiring a relationship of proportionality between means and ends
4. *Rule of Law*—requiring particular deliberative and decisional procedures
5. *Human Rights*—requiring protection of human rights values which are intrinsic (or natural) to a modern public law system (Kingsbury 2009: 32–33)

He further identifies three broad categories of public global administrative activity to which the rules and principles of GAL might apply and which in turn generate practices which can give rise to such rules and principles. These include:

1. The institutional design, and legal constitution, of the global administrative body
2. The norms and decisions produced by that entity, including norms and decisions that have as their addressees, or otherwise materially affect:

   (a) Other such public entities
   (b) States and agencies of a particular state
   (c) Individuals and other private actors

3. Procedural norms for the conduct of those public entities in relation to their rules and decisions, including arrangements for review, transparency, reason-giving, participation requirements, legal accountability and liability (Kingsbury 2009: 34)

While it is clear that rules and principles of GAL are relevant to the institutional design and thus to the legitimate functioning of MDBs, including in particular the accountability mechanisms established by all MDBs that are so central to ensuring compliance with environmental and social safeguard policies, it is the second and third categories of administrative activity listed above that play a significant role in the development of the normative status and content of ESG standards. The environmental and social safeguard policies adopted by MDBs, and increasingly by private sector lenders, as well as the interpretative statements and quasi-judicial compliance decisions issued by MDBs' accountability mechanisms, lend much-needed support to and substantially inform the ESG concept while also illustrating the practical utility of the GAL concept as a means of understanding common normative approaches which converge from complex, chaotic and pluralistic origins.

While Harlow includes human rights values as a source of GAL norms, she does so 'only to the extent that these are procedural in character' (Harlow 2006: 188). In other words, she highlights that 'many international human rights texts contain due process rights of a type traditionally developed in and protected by classical administrative law systems' (Harlow 2006: 188). However, Kingsbury appears to suggest that the substantive normative content of human rights regimes might in some instances be relevant by suggesting that 'some human rights (perhaps of *bodily integrity*, privacy, personality) are likely to be protected by public law as an intrinsic matter (without textual authority)' (Kingsbury 2009: 33). The human right to bodily integrity is often closely linked to, and under many human rights texts derived from, the right to health and, indeed, further connected to mutually related standards of protection of the human environment. Therefore, Kingsbury's express reference to bodily integrity implies that substantive human rights values must be relevant to the identification of GAL norms and vice versa. While many economic social and cultural rights are largely concerned with informational, participative and other procedural elements, it is difficult to imagine that substantive human rights values would not be relevant to, and captured by, the general public law principles of proportionality and rationality.

Some people have serious misgivings about the GAL phenomenon and highlight the hazard it represents for democracy and traditional political processes, for developing economies, and for the coherence and predictability of applicable legal standards (Harlow 2006: 207–214). The key concern is that GAL tends to subvert the traditional democratic processes vital to the legitimacy of law, for example, by circumventing the requirement of state consent under international law, by means of which states have traditionally exercised sovereignty. The role of quasi-judicial bodies, in particular, raises concerns over the juridification of the political process and of 'government by judges' by virtue of a general empowerment of a transnational 'juristocracy' (Harlow 2006: 213). The undermining of sovereign democratic processes and the emergence of common and universal administrative standards presents a particular risk for developing economies, which may not have had a significant role in generating the practice upon which these standards are based. Harlow suggests that administrative law is largely a 'Western construct', which is protective of Western values and interests and may impact unfavourably on development economies, leading to a 'double colonisation' involving 'a complex process of "cross-fertilisation" or legal transplant, whereby principles from one administrative law system pass into another' (Harlow 2006: 207–209). She suggests that often '[g]ood governance in this all-embracing sense is, however, simply not obtainable ... and, at least for the foreseeable future, it may be necessary and even preferable for them to settle for less costly, "good enough governance"' (Harlow 2006: 211).

Because of the nonsystematic nature of the processes shaping GAL, the rules and standards invoked as inherent to the GAL concept may often lack clarity and certainty. As Kingsbury points out, the difficulty in identifying universal rules and principles stems from the fact that:

> '"[g]lobal administrative law" is not an established field of normativity and obligation in the same way as "international law". It has no great charters, no celebrated courts, no textual provisions in national constitutions giving it status in national law, no significant long-appreciated history'. (Kingsbury 2009: 29)

Similarly, Harlow notes that there is 'no shortage of candidates for a set of universal values' and alludes to the ideological battle raging in this regard between '[h]ard-line economic liberals', '[s]ofter economic theorists' and 'the movement for cosmopolitan law and social democracy' (Harlow 2006: 208). She highlights the considerable disparity of principle that exists '[e]ven within the systems in which modern administrative law [has] developed' and points out that '[a]t least four administrative law families have been identified within the EU alone' (Harlow 2006: 208). However, as argued below, the coherent nature of MDB environmental and social policies, which continue to evolve systematically through regular review processes involving consultation with their shareholders and with international civil society and institutionalised cooperation with the wider MDB community, as well as the carefully structured incorporation of accountability mechanisms within the Banks' governance structures, does much to address such concerns about legitimacy, normative clarity or Western bias, thus marking out MDB safeguard policies as an exemplar of the GAL phenomenon.

Therefore, rather than attempting to provide a comprehensive and coherent unifying theory of global governance arrangements, the GAL concept is merely an observed phenomenon that seeks to explain the growing commonality apparent among the administrative principles and practices which increasingly apply across otherwise disparate areas of governance. As Kingsbury explains:

> '[E]ndeavouring to take account of these phenomena, one approach understands global administrative law as the legal mechanisms, principles and practices, along with supporting social understandings, that promote or otherwise affect the accountability of global administrative bodies, in particular by ensuring that these bodies meet adequate standards of transparency, consultation, participation, rationality and legality, and by providing effective review of the rules and decisions these bodies make'. (Kingsbury 2009: 25)

Conclusion

The ESG safeguard policies adopted by MDBs and many private sector banking institutions involved in development lending, along with the establishment of robust independent accountability mechanisms, reflect a growing culture of good governance values that incorporate a range of standards of administrative behaviour, including the transparency of processes for the environmental and social appraisal of projects and of decision-making processes for their approval, public participation in such processes, the reviewability of decisions taken and the accountability of those involved. Lawyers increasingly refer to the emergence of the phenomenon of 'global administrative law', by which such good governance standards are normativised in binding policies—a phenomenon that neatly describes the role of MDB and other safeguard policies and their associated accountability mechanisms.

References

Clayton, N. (2009). The equator principles and social rights: Incomplete protection in a self-regulatory world. *Environmental Law Review, 11*, 173.

Di Leva, C. E. (2010). International environmental law, the World Bank, and international financial institutions. In D. Bradlow & D. B. Hunter (Eds.), *International financial institutions and international law* (p. 343). The Hague: Kluwer Law International.

Gowland Gaultieri, A. N. (2001). The environmental accountability of the World Bank to non-state actors. *British Yearbook of International Law, 72*, 213.

Handl, G. (2001). *Multilateral development banking: Environmental principles and concepts reflecting general international law and public policy*. The Hague: Kluwer Law International.

Harlow, C. (2006). Global administrative law: The quest for principles and values. *European Journal of International Law, 17*(1), 187.

Independent Commission for International Development Issues (Brandt Commission) (1980). North-South: A program for survival. http://files.globalmarshallplan.org/inhalt/psu_2.pdf.

Kingsbury, B. (2009). The concept of "law" in global administrative law. *European Journal of International Law, 20*(1), 23.

Kingsbury, B., Krisch, N., Steward, R.B., Weiner, J.B. (2005). Global governance as administration—National and transnational approaches to global administrative law. 68/3&4 Law and Contemporary Problems, *68*(3&4), 1.

Kohona, P. T. B. (2004). Implementing global standards—The emerging role of the non-state sector. *Environmental Policy and Law, 34*(6), 260.

Levinson, J. I. (2010). Worker rights and the international financial institutions. In D. Bradlow & D. B. Hunter (Eds.), *International financial institutions and international law* (p. 321). The Hague: Kluwer Law International.

MacKay, F. (2010). Indigenous peoples and international financial institutions. In D. Bradlow & D. B. Hunter (Eds.), *International financial institutions and international law* (p. 287). The Hague: Kluwer Law International.

McInerney-Lankford, S. (2010). International financial institutions and human rights: Select perspectives on legal obligations. In D. Bradlow & D. B. Hunter (Eds.), *International financial institutions and international law* (p. 239). The Hague: Kluwer Law International.

Nanwani, S. (2008). Holding multilateral development banks to account: Gateways and barriers. *International Community Law Review, 10*, 199.

Oleschak-Pillai, R. (2010). Accountability of international organisations: An analysis of the World Bank's inspection panel. In J. Wouters, E. Brems, S. Smis, & P. Smitt (Eds.), *Accountability for human rights violations by international organisations* (pp. 401–429). Antwerp: Intersentia.

Richardson, B. (2002). *Environmental regulation through financial organisations*. The Hague: Kluwer Law International.

Shihata, I. F. I. (1992). The World Bank and the environment: A legal perspective. *Maryland Journal of International Law and Trade, 16*, 1.

UNECE. (1991). *Convention on environmental impact assessment in a transboundary context (Espoo)*. Retrieved from http://www.unece.org/fileadmin/DAM/env/eia/documents/legaltexts/Espoo_Convention_authentic_ENG.pdf

UNECE. (1998). *Convention on access to information, public participation in decision-making and access to justice in environmental matters (Aarhus)*. Retrieved from http://www.unece.org/fileadmin/DAM/env/pp/documents/cep43e.pdf

World Bank. (1972). *Environmental, health and human ecological considerations in economic projects* (World Bank Staff Handbook). Washington, DC: World Bank.

World Bank. (1992). *Effective implementation: Key to development impact.* (Report of the World Bank's Portfolio Task Force; The Wapenhans Report). Washington, DC: World Bank.

World Commission on Environment and Development (Brundtland Commission) (1987). Our common future. http://www.un-documents.net/wced-ocf.htm

Environmental and Social Risk Management in Emerging Economies: An Analysis of Turkish Financial Institution Practices

Işıl Gültekin and Cem B. Avcı

Abstract Turkish Financial Institutions (FIs) have come to recently realise that nonfinancial factors can materially affect an institution's long-term performance. Environmental and social issues (i.e. pollution, resource depletion, wastes, biodiversity, land acquisition and resettlement, labour and working conditions, occupational/community health and safety, cultural heritage) have been recognised to pose risks to the Turkish FIs through their project finance operations. This awareness developed in parallel to the concept of sustainability being embraced by Turkey's corporate sector. Several large Turkish lending institutions have developed environmental and social (ES) management systems for evaluation of the projects considered for financing. Although the majority of these are based on international standards that include ES performance criteria of the International Finance Corporation (IFC), European Bank for Reconstruction and Development (EBRD) and European Investment Bank (EIB), they do not yet fully encompass the requirements of the international standards in the actual implementation process. The projects considered for financing are typically subject to the Turkish Environmental Impact Assessment (EIA) Regulations that set the commitments for the project owner for environmental protection based on the Turkish regulatory framework. Compared to the international standards, there are gaps in the Turkish EIA studies that include a lack of a structured impact assessment, insufficient baseline studies and limited community engagement programmes. These gaps may eventually pose legal risks to the project during development and operations and also to the lending institution in terms of financial and reputational risks. Although several institutions have developed ES management systems internally, experience shows that these systems initially focus on following the Turkish EIA process without fully assessing issues such as biodiversity, cultural heritage and social impact assessments including expropriation and resettlement issues. This chapter will provide an overview of ES procedures of large lending institutions in Turkey and discuss generic data gaps

I. Gültekin
ELC Group Consulting and Engineering Inc. (Royal HaskoningDHV Turkey), Istanbul, Turkey
e-mail: Isil.Gultekin@elc.rhdhv.com

C.B. Avcı (✉)
Boğaziçi University, Istanbul, Turkey
e-mail: avci@boun.edu.tr

© Springer International Publishing Switzerland 2015
K. Wendt (ed.), *Responsible Investment Banking*, CSR, Sustainability, Ethics & Governance, DOI 10.1007/978-3-319-10311-2_9

between Turkish EIA studies and international requirements as well as the evaluations of ES risk management systems in place. Discussions include main risks and opportunities in applying international standards in investment finance in Turkey as well as identifying future trends.

1 Introduction

Global economic growth has shifted from the developed world to the developing countries (such as Brazil, Russia, India, China, South Africa and Turkey) within the last decade. These emerging economies have experienced rapid population growth, mass urbanisation and industrialisation with all their potential dangers for the environment and social conditions. These markets have presented huge investment opportunities as well as environmental and social (ES) risks and challenges (Sullivan and Bilouri 2012). The emerging market institutions, including Financial Institutions (FIs), were reported to generally lag behind their developed market counterparts in implementing policies, governance structures and systems to manage ES risks (Brewer 2012; van Dijk et al. 2012). Among these countries, Turkey represents the largest emerging market in the process of accession to the European Union (EU), and until 2010, ES risk management was not a systematic part of Turkish FIs' operation system. Turkish FIs' assessment of ES risks in financing decisions was limited to two channels of financial capital supply: (1) local private equity funds whose limited partners/investors included international development finance institutions (DFIs) and (2) Turkish FIs channelling programmed loans from DFIs to local firms with ES conditionality (Ararat et al. 2011).

The multilateral financial sector has served as an important mechanism for addressing issues related to long-term environmental, economic and social degradation (Hachigian and McGill 2012; Gitman et al. 2009; Richardson 2005; Meyerstein 2011; Sarro 2012) in the financial capital supply decisions. The International Finance Corporation (IFC) Report 'Banking on Sustainability: Financing Environmental and Social Opportunities in Emerging Markets' (IFC 2007) shows evidence of the potential benefits of adopting sustainability including ES risk assessment as a business strategy. It also points out how dramatic shifts in FIs' awareness of these benefits have come to occur by reassessing their business practices and engaging in sustainability-oriented risk management. Institutional investors tasked with long-term project management are integrating more and more ES considerations into decision-making and ownership practices to assess investment opportunities and threats.

Turkish FIs have come to realise since 2010 that nonfinancial factors can materially affect an institution's long-term performance. Turkish FIs recognised that ES issues (i.e. pollution, resource depletion, wastes, biodiversity, land acquisition and resettlement, labour and working conditions, occupational/community health and safety, cultural heritage) posed risks to the Turkish FIs through their project finance operations. This awareness developed in parallel to the concept of sustainability being embraced by Turkey's corporate sector (Ararat et al. 2011;

Briefing 2010; PWC 2011). These nonfinancial factors including ES risks are presently being more incorporated into a disciplined, fundamental investment process in order to gain a more accurate assessment of enhanced investment returns. In relation to this, the integration of sustainability policy through addressing ES issues has recently become an integral part of project risk management approach undertaken within the Turkish banking sector. The present study provides an overview of the regulatory framework that drives the ES risks in Turkey and the strength and weaknesses of the risk management systems that a number of large Turkish FIs have adopted to mitigate ES risks. The main difficulties and opportunities in applying international standards in investment finance in Turkey are also discussed as well as potential future trends.

2 Regulatory Setting and Present ES Risks

2.1 Regulatory Setting and EIA Framework

The current Turkish regulatory setting has undergone a significant improvement since 2004 when the transition period for EU accession started. This improvement covered various aspects including environmental legislation. Turkey has adopted the EU 'Environmental Acquis' into its national environmental legislation, where new laws and regulations were introduced and the existing ones were revised to meet EU criteria. One of the most fundamental changes was the amendment of the Environmental Law (issued initially in 1983 based on the constitution—Official Gazette Date/Number: 11 August 1983/18132) in 2006 with the Law on Amendments to the Environmental Law (Official Gazette Date/Number: 13 May 2006/26167). Within the scope of this amending law, requirements related to inspection and penalties have been improved. As a result, regulations have gained strength with respect to their implementation. With the enhanced environmental legislative framework, approval of environmental permits for new investments or upgrading of existing investments has become one of the most important criteria for investment approval.

The most important environmental permit that is a prerequisite to implementing proposed investments is to meet the requirements of the Turkish Environmental Impact Assessment (EIA) Regulation. The projects considered for financing are typically subject to the EIA Regulation, which requires a positive EIA decision as part of the permitting process and also sets the commitments for the project owner for environmental protection based on the Turkish regulatory framework. The EIA Regulation requires that a study be conducted to assess the potential impacts of the project and develop the necessary mitigation measures to avoid and/or minimise these impacts. The EIA Regulation in Turkey was first introduced in 1993; underwent revisions in 1997, 2002, 2003, 2008 and 2013 (current EIA Regulation—Official Gazette Date/Number: 03 October 2013/28784); and became in line with the EU EIA Directive (which has been in force since 1985 and applies to a wide range of defined public and private projects).

Depending on the type of the project, its capacity or the location of the activity, the EIA Regulation classifies projects in two annexes (Annex I and Annex II) based on the potentially expected environmental impacts. Projects listed in Annex I are subject to a comprehensive EIA process, whereas projects listed in Annex II are subject to selection-elimination criteria. The projects listed in Annex I of the EIA regulation are initially required to submit an EIA Application File to the Ministry of Environment and Urban Planning (MEUP) in accordance with the specified format given in Annex III of the EIA regulation followed by holding a public consultation meeting. Subsequent to the public consultation meeting, a meeting to determine the scope and special format of the EIA Report is held by the MEUP commission and the EIA report is then expected to be submitted to MEUP within 1 year after the receipt of the special format. The projects listed in Annex II are required to prepare a Project Description Document in accordance with the specified format given in Annex IV of the EIA Regulation and submit it to the relevant Provincial Directorate of Environment and Urban Planning (PDEUP). Public consultation is not mandatory for Annex II projects.

In order to proceed with the investment, the projects listed in Annex I should obtain an 'EIA Positive' decision, whereas Annex II projects should obtain an 'EIA not Required' decision. In cases when 'EIA Required' decision is given for Annex II projects, the project should undergo a detailed EIA process and obtain an 'EIA Positive' decision. In accordance with the Turkish EIA Regulation, projects are not granted any incentive, approval, permit, construction and utilisation licence if they do not obtain an 'EIA Positive' or 'EIA not Required' decision; and projects that are initiated without obtaining the mentioned EIA decisions are suspended by either MEUP or PDEUP.

The data obtained from MEUP has showed that a total of 42,994 applications have been made since the enactment of the first EIA Regulation in 1993 until the end of 2012 (Turkish EIA Statistics: http://www.csb.gov.tr/db/ced/webicerik/webicerik557.pdf). The data has showed 2,797 EIA Positive decisions, 32 EIA Negative decisions, 39,649 EIA not Required decisions and 516 EIA Required decisions have been taken. The distribution of EIA Positive and EIA not Required decisions with respect to sectors are given in Table 1.

It should be noted that projects which have been included in the government's investment programme prior to 1993 have been exempted from the requirements of the EIA Regulation since the first EIA Regulation in Turkey was enacted in 1993. In the current EIA Regulation, this exemption, as depicted in provisional Article 2 of the EIA Regulation, covers projects that have been included in the public investment programme prior to 23 June 1997 whose planning phase is completed and bidding has started or which has started production or operation as of 29 May 2013.

2.2   ES Risks and Evaluation of EIA Procedures

Over the past 10 years, public awareness on environmental issues has increased in Turkey and nongovernmental organisations (NGOs), including environmentalists and professional organisations, such as the Chamber of Environmental Engineers

Table 1 Sectoral distribution of EIA decisions

Sector	EIA positive decisions percentage	EIA not required decisions percentage
Mining	26	51
Energy	22	6
Industry	13	12
Tourism/housing	7	7
Transportation/coastal	9	2
Agriculture/food	9	13
Waste/chemical	14	9

and Chamber of Architects or trade unions, have become more active in Turkey. The exemption rule of previously planned government investment programme projects from the EIA Regulation has also attracted the attention of these organisations. This was mainly due to the fact that these projects represent large-scale infrastructure projects that have potentially large adverse impacts on the environment. In addition, the quality and content of EIA Reports or Project Description Documents have also started being questioned by NGOs in recent years, particularly for energy investments. The NGOs and other pressure groups have filed several lawsuits against MEUP for the invalidation of EIA decisions granted to major projects. This has posed a threat for the development of the projects as construction permits are valid only with an approved EIA decision. Moreover, lawsuits have caused delays in the project implementation schedules even if the EIA decisions are not cancelled as a result of lawsuit process. These developments have translated into rising ES risks that Turkish FIs are facing as part of the project finance implementation.

The EIA procedures were reviewed in this study in order to identify potential ES risks from an FI perspective (Table 2). Evaluation of the Turkish EIA procedures was conducted considering the evaluation criteria developed by Wood (2002), which is based upon the various stages in the EIA process. These include the consideration of alternatives, project design, screening, scoping, report preparation, review, consultation and public participation, mitigation, decision-making and monitoring of project impacts.

3 Assessment of Turkish FIs' ES Risk Management System

3.1 Basis of ES Risk Management System

Considering the above mentioned risks, a number of large Turkish FIs instituted ES risk evaluation procedures and adopted ES policies and management systems. The aim was to manage the exposure to ES risks related to their loan processes that went beyond taking into account only the EIA approval decision of projects. In addition

Table 2 Evaluation of Turkish EIA procedures

Criterion	Criterion met	Comments	Potential risk
1. Is the EIA system based on clear and specific legal provision?	Yes	There is no requirement for an EIA for projects that have been included in the public investment programme before 1993 and/or 1997	Some projects (including large-scale infrastructure projects) which may have adverse impacts on the environment are not assessed and ES risks are not quantified
2. Must the relevant environmental impacts of all significant actions be assessed?	Partially	The assessment is not comprehensive and structured. Cumulative impacts are not covered. Ancillary facilities (i.e. transmission lines related to power plants) are not covered and considered as a separate project	The project may be impacted negatively or may be subject to cancellation due to these issues that are not fully assessed
3. Must evidence of the consideration, by the proponent, of the environmental impacts of reasonable alternative actions be demonstrated in the EIA process?	No	Alternatives are often not considered	Lack of alternative assessment may mean that the selected project may have greater ES impact than potential alternatives and is less defendable in public eye
4. Must screening of actions for environmental significance take place?	Partially	Lists of activities, thresholds and criteria often allow considerable discretion	Subjective screening may lead to important adverse impacts to be neglected during EIA process
5. Must scoping of the environmental impacts of actions take place and specific guidelines be produced?	Yes	The EIA assessment must include the scoping of impacts and specific set of commitments must be provided to be in line with the regulatory framework	
6. Must EIA reports meet prescribed content requirements and do checks to prevent the release of inadequate EIA reports exist?	Yes	The reports must be prepared based on the format provided in the EIA Regulation. Specific to Annex I projects, a special format is defined by the authority commission	
7. Must EIA reports be publicly reviewed and the proponent respond to the points raised?	Partially	Weak stakeholder engagement. No grievance mechanism is established	Lack of strong stakeholder programmes may lead to important ES factors being missed in the EIA process
8. Must the findings of the EIA report and the review	Partially	The statistics given in Table 1 indicates EIA	The commitments dictated within the EIA

(continued)

Table 2 (continued)

Criterion	Criterion met	Comments	Potential risk
be a central determinant of the decision on the action?		decisions are rarely taken against the project implementation. A large number of commitments are requested from the project owner to obtain a positive EIA decision	potentially prove to be inapplicable from a construction and operation point of view of the project. The project commitments are not strongly monitored by the MEUP at present
9. Must monitoring of action impacts be undertaken and is it linked to the earlier stages of the EIA process?	Partially	Monitoring of action impacts are required by the regulations. However, the periodic monitoring practice at present has room to develop	The project commitments are not strongly monitored by the MEUP at present. This results in regulatory noncompliance which allows for lawsuits against the EIA decision
10. Must the mitigation of action impacts be considered at the various stages of the EIA process?	Partially	Basic mitigation measures and mostly based on reference to the relevant regulations. Mitigation implementation practice is often unsatisfactory	The project commitments are not strongly monitored by the MEUP at present. This results in regulatory noncompliance which allows for lawsuits against the EIA decision
11. Must consultation and participation take place prior to, and following, EIA report publication?	Partially	Public consultation is mandatory only for Annex I projects and is limited to one public meeting during the scoping phase, where the project is to be implemented. When the EIA report is completed, it is open to public comments at the authorities for a defined period	Limited or no public consultation may adversely affect the Project and may result in no social licence to operate
12. Must the EIA system be monitored and, if necessary, be amended to incorporate feedback from experience?	Partially	Modifications to the EIA procedures take place on a need basis	
13. Are the financial costs and time requirements of the EIA system acceptable to those involved and are they believed to be outweighed by discernible environmental benefits?	No	The importance of a proper EIA as a risk tool is not fully understood by the project owners. The large majority believe that financial and time costs of EIA outweigh its benefits	The poor perception of EIA studies by the project owners lead to poor EIA study quality being undertaken by third parties due to price and time pressures allowed to perform the EIA

(continued)

Table 2 (continued)

Criterion	Criterion met	Comments	Potential risk
14. Does the EIA system apply to significant programmes, plans and policies, as well as to projects?	Partially	There is a draft Strategic Environmental Assessment (SEA) Regulation in Turkey which is not yet in force. Some selected model studies were undertaken as SEA practice for programmes, plans and policies to meet the requirements during EU accession, which is still ongoing	Previous investment programmes have not fully embraced the ES aspects from the view of SEA perspective, and only project-level EIA was undertaken to date, whose risks are described above

to the national factors that include legislative issues and changing expectations of the society, expectations of international FIs also played a role to integrate sustainability and consideration of ES risks by Turkish FIs more comprehensively above the national requirements.

The majority of the Turkish FIs' policies and management systems has been based on international standards that include ES performance criteria of International Finance Corporation (IFC), European Bank for Reconstruction and Development (EBRD) and European Investment Bank (EIB). The reason for choosing international standards that included ES performance criteria could be seen as an integration process with the international finance community in order to have the same platform for assessing ES risks. Major international FIs such as IFC, EBRD and EIB have developed their own environmental and social policies and performance standards required to be fulfilled by their clients to help ensure the sustainability of the projects that are financed. In addition, the Equator Principles (EPs) have been developed as a voluntary Risk Management Framework and adopted currently by 78 financial institutions, for determining, assessing and managing ES risks in projects, and is primarily intended to provide a minimum standard for due diligence to support responsible risk decision-making.

3.2   Structure of ES Risk Management System

Turkish banks are categorised into two classes, namely, (1) deposit banks either with public or private capital and (2) development and investment banks either with public, private or foreign capitals (Turkish Banking Association: http://www.tbb.org.tr). Review of ES procedures for a number of large banks from each category has indicated the following:

- Deposit banks with public and private capital have gone beyond the national requirements in cases when these banks sign protocols with international institutions such as the World Bank. Additional requirements include review of the EIA reports to check compliance with World Bank standards, preparation of action plans and undertaking new or additional public consultation as appropriate to the project.
- Development and investment banks with public and private capital have implemented internal procedures to assess ES risks. The requirements of ES policies and management systems within these FIs vary from implementation of risk assessment models to more comprehensive ES impact assessment systems. Some FIs use risk evaluation models for rating environmental risk under specific headings for all projects. In cases when the project risk is evaluated as moderate and/or high, the FI in coordination with its client develops a plan to reduce and/or monitor impacts, whereas projects with anticipated high risks does not go beyond the initial evaluation stage. On the other hand, some FIs implement more detailed ES risk management systems for projects above a specific investment cost and that consider international standards such as Equator Principles (which rely on IFC) to the extent possible and also apply exclusion lists and sectoral principles (i.e. oil and gas, energy, mining, infrastructure and transportation, waste management). These also include implementation of sector-specific risk evaluation models and, depending on the risk group identified as a result of evaluation, require specific actions to be undertaken by the project owners, which may include evaluation of project's ES impacts by an independent consultant, preparation and implementation of an Environmental and Social Management Plan (ESMP) and regular monitoring reports.

3.3   Evaluation of ES Risk Management System

Projects that are considered for financing by international FIs such as IFC, EBRD and EIB need to undergo a detailed ES risk and impact assessment process to cover various ES issues that include labour and working conditions; resource efficiency and pollution prevention; community health, safety and security; land acquisition and involuntary resettlement; biodiversity conversation; indigenous peoples; and cultural heritage. During the ES impact assessment process, a stakeholder engagement programme is required to be implemented to cover affected and interested stakeholders such as the nearby communities to the project area and the governmental and nongovernmental organisations at national, regional and local levels; and the stakeholder engagement is expected to continue throughout the lifetime of a project.

Although a number of Turkish FIs have internally developed ES management systems as indicated above, experience has shown that these systems initially focus on following the Turkish EIA process without fully assessing key issues that are integral in the way that EIAs are conducted. When compared to the international

Table 3 Key gaps in Turkish EIA studies

Issue	Gaps with respect to international standards	Risks
Scoping and impact assessment	• Scoping not conducted adequately • Impact assessment not structured and comprehensive • Lack of social impact assessment • Lack of cumulative impact assessment • Limited definition of project's area of influence • No discussion of alternatives • Some projects (including large-scale infrastructure projects) may be exempted from the EIA Regulation	• Lawsuits by public and other organisations requesting reassessment of impacts or cancellation of exemptions
Baseline data	• Baseline data collected through desktop studies to a great extent • Insufficient baseline studies to assess biodiversity • Lack of baseline studies to assess cultural heritage	• Significant damage to habitats, flora and fauna • Significant delays in the project schedule upon encountering archaeological finds during construction
Stakeholder engagement	• Minimal stakeholder engagement with only selected governmental authorities and the nearby settlements, or no stakeholder engagement with the wider public	• Potential public protests
Expropriation/ resettlement	• Government-led expropriation/ resettlement process which does not include all affected people covered by international standards	• Potential adverse impacts in livelihoods and life standards of affected people
Mitigation measures	• Pollution prevention and control techniques include basic mitigation measures and do not cover detailed measures	• Lack of specific mitigation measures, i.e. at sensitive areas, may lead to significant damages
Health and safety	• Lack of assessment of labour and working conditions and occupational health and safety issues • Lack of determining community health, safety and security impacts	• Potential accidents during construction and operation from poor management of occupational, health and safety issues • Grievances by nearby communities
Monitoring	• Limited monitoring during the construction and operation phases of a project	• Potential nonconformities overlooked which result in adverse ES impacts and in potential fines

standards, there are several gaps in the Turkish EIA studies that include but are not limited to a lack of a structured impact assessment, insufficient baseline studies and limited defined community engagement programme. Issues such as biodiversity, cultural heritage, expropriation and resettlement are in general covered in the EIA study to a limited extent. A review of key gaps in Turkish EIA studies with respect to international standards and potential implications is summarised in Table 3.

These issues may eventually pose legal risks to the project during development and operations and also to the lending institution in terms of financial and reputational risks. Although the ES risk management systems of the selected Turkish FIs have requirements above the Turkish EIA approval, these ES risk management systems do not require a full Environmental and Social Impact Assessment Study (ESIA) for projects which may mitigate the risks depicted in Table 3. The FIs may tend to only focus on the major risks depending on the type and location of the project and may ask relevant additional studies such as air quality modelling for power plant projects, ornithological studies and visual impact assessments for wind power plant projects, ecosystem assessment reports and fish passage installations for hydropower plant projects.

Independent ES due diligence may only be requested for projects with high risk, and the majority of the ES risk evaluations are conducted internally within FIs. The contents of Environmental and Social Management Plans (ESMP) that are requested for projects also differ within FIs. The monitoring of the projects is either conducted by FIs themselves or independent consultants; however, the effectiveness of these monitoring is also questionable as the period of monitoring is limited, i.e. once a year. In general, FIs in their loan agreements with their clients refer to the adherence to the Turkish EIA Regulations and other relevant Turkish environmental legislation as a must. In cases, when an ESMP is prepared, it is included as an attachment to the loan agreement and the clients are expected to meet the requirements of the ESMP.

4   Risks and Benefits of Applying International Standards for Turkish FIs

The improvement of ES risk management and efforts to follow international standards during project finance by Turkish FIs bring both risks and opportunities to the FIs and project owners. One of the main risks for implementing international standards is the creation of unfair competitiveness among Turkish FIs that implement risk management systems as ES risk management (including following international standards) are not implemented by all of the Turkish FIs. The FIs that expect more than the national requirements can be seen as creating undue difficulties in providing loans. This is mainly due to the lack of awareness in ES issues by the project owners as they consider that their project holds already an EIA approval that is sufficient to proceed with the investment according to the Turkish regulatory requirements. In addition, project owners do not prefer to (1) undertake additional stakeholder engagement and public disclosure above the requirements stated in the Turkish EIA Regulation and (2) agree to additional costs and time to upgrade the existing studies to international standards. Another important challenge from the project owner's perspective is that, although the projects hold national EIA approvals, the implementation of additional ES risk management procedures may reveal that some of the projects are not feasible (such as related to inadequacy of the ecological flow for a hydropower project or cumulative impacts which were not assessed clearly at the time of EIA process).

On the other hand, there are several benefits of applying ES risk management that include reduced financial risks and likelihood of ES risks arising from projects subsequent to the signing of loan agreements, improved ES risk management and improved performance of projects through understanding of ES issues and their implications, increased corporate value/enhanced reputation both for Turkish FIs and the project owners and improved relationships with the stakeholders. There is also an indirect positive impact that the additional requirements asked by the Turkish FIs creates awareness among some of the Turkish firms authorised to prepare EIA Reports resulting in better quality EIA reports and also among MEUP leading to more strict reviews during preparation of EIA reports. A number of large-scale projects are co-funded by international FIs together with Turkish FIs. These projects require EPs and IFC standards to be implemented together with the national EIA regulations. This had led to an increasing flow of knowledge in the implementation of robust ESIA studies between international investors, consultants and legal advisors which is improving the quality of the EIA practices in almost all projects being presently considered.

5 Status of Discussion in Literature and Key Stakeholder Groups

The topic of ES risk management and integration of international standards into the evaluation criteria during project finance within the Turkish FIs has not been widely discussed in literature. One article was identified that discusses the role of banks in the process of sustainable development and sustainable banking practices in Turkey (Oner-Kaya 2010). Other relevant research mainly focused directly on sustainability, corporate social responsibility and sustainable investments (Ararat et al. 2011; PWC 2011; Corporate Social Responsibility Association 2008; World Business Council for Sustainable Development 2010; TaslakRapor 2012). A limited number of Turkish FIs issue sustainability reports where their ES risk management approach is discussed.

Among business associations, the Banks Association of Turkey, a professional organisation that is a legal entity with the status of a public institution, has established a working group named as the Role of Financial Sector in Sustainable Growth, aiming to build up general approach related to the protection of the environment during loan processes and other services of banks. Eighteen banks are currently members of this working group. The United Nations Global Compact (UN Global Compact) which is a strategic policy initiative for businesses that are committed to aligning their operations and strategies with ten universally accepted principles in the areas of human rights, labour, environment and anticorruption launched a Local Network in Turkey in October 2002 which is one of Turkey's largest sustainability platform. Three Turkish banks are members of the United Nations Global Compact. In addition, two of these banks are members of the United Nations Environment Programme Finance Initiative (UNEP FI) which is a global partnership between UNEP and the financial sector, focusing on understanding the impacts of environmental and social considerations on financial performance. Another important association is the Business Council for Sustainable Development Turkey (BCSD Turkey), a non-profit association established in 2004 that is the representative of the World Business Council for Sustainable Development helping companies to understand the concept of Sustainable Development as well as to implement Sustainable Development into their daily business practices, thus creating a sustainable platform that enables interaction among business leaders, government, NGOs and civil society at a national and international level. Together with UNEP FI and UN Global Compact Turkey, BCSD Turkey has recently organised Sustainable Finance Forum with the involvement of Turkish and international FIs to discuss existing responsible finance practices in the country, reveal related gaps and challenges and suggest recommendations to increase the contribution of the financial sector to sustainable development in Turkey. The Regional Environmental Center Turkey (REC Turkey) is also one of the active independent international organisations working on different fields of sustainable development to provide support to environmental stakeholders on topics such as environmental policy, biodiversity, climate change, renewable energy, environmental information and water and waste management. REC Turkey issues publications on the mentioned topics and organises training to the private sector, national and local governments and nongovernmental organisations for capacity building.

6 Future Trends and Recommendations

The following trends are presently noted:

- There is an increasing awareness and increasing flow of knowledge among local EIA consultants, project owners and Turkish FIs related to the need for reviewing the adequacy of local EIA studies and upgrading these to an international ESIA study, as needed prior to finalising the project loan processes.
- MEUP has also been more aware of the needs for social impact assessments and cumulative impact study requirements because of the increased public awareness and international ESIA implementation. There is also a trend to increase the effectiveness of the monitoring requirements during construction and operational phases of the projects where EIA approval has been granted.
- The knowledge of local consultants performing EIAs is increasing as they are asked to provide more detailed EIA studies by project owners who seek financing from Turkish FIs that have ES risk management systems.

- There is an increasing trend within the government entities such as the State Planning Institution, Ministry of Energy, to take into account environmental aspects in their investment process.
- There is an increased awareness of the usefulness of the international systems within the overall banking community in mitigating risks.
- There is an increased awareness among project owners that ESIAs prepared based on IFC standards and EPs are minimising risks against court litigation and lead to more favourable project finance assessment by FIs.

These trends indicate that the ES management systems for the Turkish FIs will become more robust and will likely be embraced by the overall Turkish Banking Industry.

The following key recommendations are suggested to enhance the applicability of ES risk management systems:

- Capacity building within the consulting companies through seminars, workshops and trainings to enhance understanding and assessing ES risks based on international standards.
- Creating a wider awareness on the need to adequately assess ES risks, among project owners and the banking industry through seminars, workshops and trainings.
- Partnering with universities to implement short-term educational programmes aiming interested groups.

Conclusions

ES risks inherent in project finance operations can materially affect a financial institution's long-term performance. ES issues typically include pollution, resource depletion, wastes, biodiversity, land acquisition and resettlement, labour and working conditions, occupational/community health and safety, and cultural heritage. If not properly managed, the ES risks can adversely affect project operations and lead to legal complications and reputational impacts that threaten the overall success of the project. This, in return, poses a direct financial risk to the FI.

Turkish FIs have recognised that ES issues pose risks for project financing. As a result, ES risks are presently being more incorporated into the investment process in order to gain a more accurate assessment of enhanced investment returns. A number of large Turkish FIs instituted ES risk evaluation procedures and adopted ES policies and management systems, which are presently based on international standards that include ES performance criteria of IFC, EBRD and EIB. Experience has shown that these systems initially focus on following the Turkish EIA process without fully assessing key issues that are integral in the way that EIAs are conducted (i.e. through an ESIA study) and may ask additional studies (i.e. air quality modelling,

(continued)

ecosystem assessment reports) to evaluate specific issues as appropriate to the type and location of the project. However, when compared to international standards, there are several gaps in the Turkish EIA studies that include but are not limited to a lack of a structured impact assessment, insufficient baseline studies and limited defined community engagement programme that require careful consideration.

ES management systems of the Turkish FIs are likely to become more robust to minimise the gaps with respect to international standards within the present systems as well as being embraced by the overall Turkish Banking Industry. The reason for this trend is an increased awareness by the regulators, NGOs, public and project owners on the effectiveness of implementing robust ES risk management systems. This view is developing mainly from successful implementation of these principles to large-scale projects that are co-funded by international FIs together with Turkish FIs and effective information dissemination from these case studies to involved parties.

References

Ararat, M., Yurtoglu, B. B., Suel, E., & Tura, D. (2011). *IFC sustainable investment country reports, sustainable investments in Turkey 2010*. Final Report, IFC, Washington, DC.

Brewer, J. (2012). *Evolving markets: What's driving ESG in emerging economies?* EIRIS Emerging Markets Report, Turkey.

Briefing. (2010, August). *Istanbul stock exchange sustainability index (ISESI) project 2010-2011*. Briefing.

Corporate Social Responsibility Association. (2008, March). *Turkey corporate social responsibility baseline report*. Corporate Social Responsibility Association, Turkey.

Gitman, l., Chorn, B., & Fargo, B. (2009). *ESG in the mainstream: The role for companies and investors in environmental, social, and governance integration*. BSR.

Hachigian, H., & McGill, S. M. (2012). Reframing the governance challenge for sustainable investment. *Journal of Sustainable Finance and Investment, 2*(3–4), 166–178.

IFC. (2007). *Banking on sustainability: Financing environmental and social opportunities in emerging markets report*. Washington, DC: IFC.

Meyerstein, A. (2011). *On the effectiveness of global private regulation: The implementation of the equator principles by multinational banks. Dissertation for the degree of Doctorate in Philosophy in Jurisprudence and Social Policy*. Berkeley: University of California.

Oner-Kaya, E. (2010). The role of banks in process of sustainable development and sustainable banking practices in Turkey. *İşletmeAraştırmalarıDergisi, 2*(3), 75–94.

PWC. (2011). *Türk İş Dünyası'nda Sürdürülebilirlik Uygulamaları Değerlendirme Raporu*. PWC.

Richardson, B. J. (2005). The equator principles: The voluntary approach to environmentally sustainable finance. *European Environmental Law Review, 14*(11), 280–290.

Sarro, D. (2012). Do lenders make effective regulators? An assessment of the equator principles on project finance. *German Law Journal, 13*(12), 1525–1558.

Sullivan, R., & Bilouri, D. (2012). Responsible investment in emerging markets: Framing the discussion. *Journal of Corporate Citizenship, 48*, 5–9.

Taslak Rapor. (2012). *Rio'dan Rio'ya: Türkiye'de Sürdürülebilirlik Kalkınmanın Mevcut Durumu*. Taslak Rapor, Turkish Ministry of Development, Turkey.

van Dijk, A., Griek, L., & Jansen, C. (2012). *Bridging the gaps—Effectively addressing ESG risks in emerging markets*. Sustainalytics

Wood, C. (2002). *Environmental impact assessment: A comparative review* (2nd ed.). Harlow: Prentice Hall.

World Business Council for Sustainable Development. (2010, February). Vision 2050. The new agenda for business. World Business Council for Sustainable Development

More Fun at Lower Risk: New Opportunities for PRI-Related Asset Management of German Pension Insurance Funds

Christian Hertrich and Henry Schäfer

Abstract The main focus of our chapter is to assess the suitability of Social Responsible Investments (SRI) for the strategic asset allocation of German pension insurance funds. Our analysis considers prevailing regulation in Germany for asset allocation as well as alternative investment models that disregard the strict investment framework currently in place. Using the Vector Error Correction (VEC) methodology, a multivariate stochastic time series model, we estimate the data generating process of the underlying input variables of a representative asset portfolio. A bootstrap simulation on the estimated VEC models allows generating future return paths of the underlying portfolios. These return distributions will subsequently be used as input for the various asset allocation strategies we have chosen (both outright as well as derivative overlay structures). The empirical results of our research study are valuable: SRI-structured portfolios consistently perform better than conventional portfolios and derivative overlay structures enable pension fund managers to mitigate the downside risk exposure of their portfolio without impacting average fund performance.

1 Introduction

In the majority of European capital markets, institutional investors represent the most important investor type. Amongst them, pension funds play a preeminent part given the investment volume they usually manage in their fiduciary role.

As of today, 65.3 % of European Social Responsible Investment (SRI) assets are owned by pension funds, albeit 98.1 % (or 3,161 billion euros equivalent) of these investments are held by public pension funds and only 1.9 % (61 billion euros) by occupational pension schemes. There are, however, clear signs that corporate pension funds are intending to expand their SRI commitment within their investment portfolios.[1] Analysing, for example, the global composition of the

---

[1] See Eurosif (2010, p. 16).

C. Hertrich • H. Schäfer (✉)
University of Stuttgart, Stuttgart, Germany
e-mail: h.schaefer@bwi.uni-stuttgart.de

© Springer International Publishing Switzerland 2015
K. Wendt (ed.), *Responsible Investment Banking*, CSR, Sustainability, Ethics & Governance, DOI 10.1007/978-3-319-10311-2_10

253 signatories (asset owners only)[2] of the UN Principles for Responsible Investment (PRI) evidences that approximately 50 % are institutional investors categorised as 'non-corporate' pension funds, while 24 % of signatories are corporate pension schemes.[3] Using as reference 138 European asset owners that appear as signatories and applying the same percentages, there are to date a total of 102 institutional pension schemes in Europe committed to SRI, with 33 funds belonging to occupational pension schemes only. The distribution by country of these 138 asset owners is nevertheless skewed towards three countries: in the UK, there are 28 (20.3 %) asset owners registered as PRI signatories, 27 (19.6 %) in the Netherlands and 17 (12.3 %) in Denmark.[4]

It is important to keep in mind that SRI is not art for art's sake. Some investors try to impact the Corporate Social Responsibility (CSR) of a firm or a state. Others focus on the optimisation of the risk-return trade-off that SRI-structured portfolios might promise. To take into account environmental, social, governance or ethical issues in investing means to encompass different stakeholders' interests that should impact the issuers of securities or financial contracts towards CSR-related strategies and policies[5]:

'SRI seems to provide investors with a framework to include moral considerations whereas CSR is a framework to investigate how the investment targets act in ESG areas'.[6]

Harjoto and Jo (2011) argue that SRI is a way to evaluate a company's response to several stakeholders.[7]

European countries differ widely in the progress of how entities within the retirement provision system cope with the SRI approach. The differences stretch from country-specific regulations, different types of paying systems with defined contribution and the defined-benefit plans as benchmarks over to the different roles of public and company-related pension schemes. Often linked is the institutional character of a retirement provider, either as a trust type, for example, in the UK and the Netherlands, or the insurance type that can be found, for example, in Germany and Finland. Another crucial point is the divergence in asset preferences and asset management practices amongst such entities.[8]

For Germany, the German Forum for Responsible Investing (FNG) repeatedly unveils in its annual reports the continuous reluctance of German entities of the

---

[2] See PRI (2012).

[3] See PRI (2011, p. 56). Based on a representative survey amongst asset owners that are also PRI signatories.

[4] See PRI (2012). Here we have applied the percentages of the PRI (2011) report on the current numbers of PRI signatories, as the 2012 disclosure on the asset split by investor type is not available to date.

[5] See Hockerts and Moir (2004).

[6] Scholtens and Sievänen (2012, p. 3).

[7] See Harjoto and Jo (2011).

[8] See for an actual analysis of drivers and impediments of SRI in pension funds Sievänen et al. (2012).

occupational pension system to integrate SRI into their portfolios.[9] German pension funds and related entities are highly regulated and exhibit a high risk aversion that is, amongst others, best reflected in their asset allocation preferences towards fixed income bonds of reputable public issuers. Due to such an extraordinary institutional environment, many of the empirical works done by academics and practitioners in the field of SRI are focusing primarily on performance-related issues (the so-called 'under- or outperformance' question). Many pension fund managers nonetheless argue that purely performance-related issues are not their main focus for the daily asset management business. Instead, they are faced with challenges to avoid shortfall risks and complain the lack of empirical research on SRI for such risk-related topics. It appears that the need for more risk-related empirical evidence in the SRI context is for most of the German entities of the occupational pension system highly relevant.[10]

This chapter puts forward an excerpt of the main results of an up-to-date empirical work that has focused on the opportunities SRI-based asset allocation strategies offer to cope with investment risk. The work demonstrates that under the specific regulatory environment in Germany and considering the asset allocation preferences of German Pension Insurance Funds, a shortfall risk approach can provide a suitable recommendation on how to structure an SRI portfolio to best benefit the fund and its beneficiaries.[11] The chapter will first describe briefly the specific regulatory requirements of German Pension Insurance Funds as the most important type of the five-layer system of Germany's occupational pension system, followed by an explanation of how these investors approach SRI investing. Subsequently, there is a short summary of the methodology applied as well as the time series used and, finally, a summary of the main empirical results and conclusions.

Apart from contemplating portfolios that adhere to prevailing market practice in terms of asset allocation as well as regulatory constraints for occupational pension schemes in Germany, we will also simulate portfolio compositions of pension funds in the UK as well as the Netherlands. Both countries play a leading role in European SRI investing for pension funds and have already obtained sizeable and relevant occupational pension systems.[12]

---

[9] See FNG (2013) and similar findings in Sievänen et al. (2012).

[10] See Union Investment (2011). Union Investment managed a detailed survey in 2011 that revealed the need for further empirical evidence, in particular for pension funds, for SRI-related topics.

[11] The empirical analyses are carried out in detail in Hertrich (2013).

[12] Based on a total AuM base of European pension funds of 4,170 billion euros for 2009, Dutch and UK pension funds obtain a total market share of 62.8 %. The German pension fund market, on the other hand, only represents 4.2 % of the overall market. See Eurosif (2011, p. 14).

In terms of relevance of the pension fund system in relation to the GDP of the respective country, the Netherlands are the undisputed leader within all OECD countries with a figure of 129.8 % of GDP. The UK, with 73.0 % of GDP, is also above the weighted average of 67.1 % of GDP. In Germany the asset base of domestic pension funds reaches a mere 5.2 % of GDP. See OECD (2010, p. 8).

2 Pension Insurance Funds as an Important Part of the Five Available Occupational Pension Plan Alternatives

2.1 Occupational Pension Plan Alternatives in Germany

German corporations are increasingly offering their employees occupational pension plans. While at the end of 2001 only 31 % of companies had a pension plan in place, by the end of 2007, already 51 % of corporations did so. For large corporations (more than 1,000 employees) this rate was as high as 97 %.[13] With 12.3 million pension members, 15.1 % of Germany's total population is currently covered by an occupational pension plan.[14]

There are five occupational pension alternatives that can be offered by law to employees in Germany. These alternatives are defined in the BetrAVG, the *Law for the Improvement of the Company Pension Scheme*: the Direct Pension Commitment ('Direktzusage'), the Support Fund ('Unterstuetzungskasse'), the Direct Insurance ('Direktversicherung'), the Pension Insurance Fund ('Pensionskasse') and the Pension Fund ('Pensionsfond').[15]

These schemes differ primarily in terms of supervision by the German regulator, tax and legal treatment, pension contributions as well as benefit payments.[16] The pension plans can be further divided into an external and an internal system. The Direct Pension Commitment and the Support Fund represent the internal pension schemes of the BetrAVG, for which there is a direct legal relationship for pension benefits and contributions between employer and employee. In the external alternatives, i.e. the Pension Insurance Fund, the Direct Insurance and the Pension Fund, on the contrary, the employer interconnects an external, independent third party that is responsible for all pension-related aspects of the company. In this scenario, the employer has a direct claim for his/her pension benefits to the third party provider, while the employer remains subsidiarily liable only.[17]

Referencing data provided by Schwind (2011) on the relative size of occupational pension schemes, Pension Insurance Funds achieve the second largest market share in Germany with 23.6 % of total AuM (107 billion euros) in occupational pension plans invested, after Direct Pension Commitments with 54.0 % (245 billion euros). Pension Insurance Funds are therefore the largest external occupational

---

[13] See Bundesministerium fuer Arbeit und Soziales (2008, p. 32).

[14] See Bundesministerium fuer Arbeit und Soziales (2008, p. 11, p. 22 and p. 32). Large corporations are defined as companies with more than 1,000 employees. For the current population, we have used the 2010 figure of 81.5 million inhabitants as reported by Statistisches Bundesamt (2011).

[15] See Rohde and Kuesters (2007, p. 18) et seq.

[16] See Doetsch et al. (2010, p. 15).

[17] Sec. 1 Par. 1 No. 3 BetrAVG regulates the subsidiary role of the employer.

pension plan.[18] Moreover, the particular investment restrictions imposed by the legislator as well as regulator make their portfolio management highly challenging and offer an attractive area for research analysis. For these reasons, we will focus in the remainder of this study primarily on the Pension Insurance Fund.

2.2 Pension Insurance Fund (Pensionskasse)

The BetrAVG defines a Pension Insurance Fund as an independent pension institution that offers employees and their surviving dependent a legal claim for benefits originated from an occupational pension arrangement.[19] The VAG, on the other hand, states that a Pension Insurance Fund is a life insurance company, which offers its members insurance coverage for any potential shortfall an insured employee or his/her surviving dependents may suffer due to retirement, disability or death. Moreover, the Pension Insurance Fund shall execute its insurance business via a capital-funded system.[20]

As it is the case for the Direct Pension Commitment and the Support Fund pension schemes, the Pension Insurance Fund involves the company as the contribution payer, the employee as the insured counterparty of the contract as well as member of the pension fund and the pension fund itself as the insurance provider.[21] Employees have also the flexibility to contribute additional funds to their pension plans via deferred compensation payments or direct payments.[22]

Based on official statistics published by the German Federal Financial Supervisory Authority (BaFin), there are today 150 regulated Pension Insurance Funds in Germany.[23] Using underlying assets under management as reference, Pension Insurance Funds have a total asset base of 115.8 billion euros. Within the German insurance sector, Pension Insurance Funds obtain 9.7 % of market share, behind life insurers (62.5 % or 742.7 billion euros), health insurance companies (16.0 % or 189.6 billion euros) and accident insurance corporations (11.6 % or 138.0 billion euros).[24]

Using the number of pension members released by the Federal Ministry of Labour and Social Affairs, Pension Insurance Funds have benefited from the highest growth in terms of pension members between the end of 2002 and the

---

[18] See Schwind (2011, p. 476).

[19] See Sec. 1b Par. 3 BetrAVG.

[20] See Sec. 118a VAG. Retirement is hereby understood as the 'inability' to continue with the work obligations due to reaching retirement age.

[21] See Doetsch et al. (2010, p. 20).

[22] See Braun (2010, p. 32).

[23] See BaFin (2012a).

[24] See BaFin (2012b, p. 3).

end of 2007, more than doubling the number of contributors from 2.1 million members to 4.5 million (+114.9 %).[25]

The importance of Pension Insurance Funds is expected to change fundamentally in the coming years, as Germany's society is facing significant challenges (primarily an aging population and a concurrent decline of the working population) that will impact the role capital-funded occupational pension plans to play in the future. Capital-funded pension schemes, both occupational and individual private plans, are expected to counterbalance the forecasted funding gap of the state pension system. To date, nonetheless, the relevance of occupational pension schemes in Germany remains relatively low: despite the 51 % of market share amongst German employees, the pension benefits originated from occupational pension schemes represent only 5 % of total pension benefits[26] and 3 % of pension income.[27] In other European countries, on the contrary, the shift towards occupational and private pension plan solutions has already occurred. In the Netherlands, for example, occupational pension schemes already represent 40 % of pension benefits, while in the UK and in Switzerland the market share is 25 % and 32 %, correspondingly.[28]

2.3 Asset Allocation of Pension Insurance Funds in Practice

The legal and regulatory framework for the investment management of German Pension Insurance Funds is primarily defined in the Insurance Supervision Act (VAG), the Investment Ordinance (AnlV or 'Anlageverordnung')[29] and the various circular letters of the BaFin (in particular R 4/2011[30]).[31] The prime objective of these regulations is to ensure that pension promises by companies made to beneficiaries will be fulfilled when benefits are claimed in the future. For that purpose, the asset-liability management of Pension Insurance Funds requires monitoring and regulation. As stated by the BaFin, 'insurance undertakings must invest the guarantee assets and the other restricted assets in a way that ensures maximum security and profitability, while maintaining the insurance undertaking's liquidity at all times, maintaining an adequate diversification and spread'.[32]

Current legislation imposes asset allocation restrictions for Pension Insurance Funds that ultimately lead to a fixed income-dominated investment portfolio, as in

---

[25] See Bundesministerium fuer Arbeit und Soziales (2008, p. 110).

[26] See Frankfurter Allgemeine Zeitung (2005).

[27] See Statistisches Bundesamt (2007, p. 594).

[28] See Frankfurter Allgemeine Zeitung (2005).

[29] See BaFin (2011a).

[30] See BaFin (2011b).

[31] See Frere et al. (2009, p. 64).

[32] Bafin (2012c). Citation refers to Sec. 54 Par. 1 VAG.

theory it is possible to allocate up to 100 % into corporate bonds, government or supranational securities. For risk-seeking fund managers, however, a portfolio could not be invested more than 35 % in risky capital. In practice and with nearly constant shares in the long term, fixed income securities represent approximately 86 % of the total asset allocation of Pension Insurance Funds, whereas riskier equity assets are only 5 % of the asset pool.

Bonds issued by governments and supranational institutions are the most relevant asset category with 55.0 billion euros [47.5 % of the combined assets under management (AuM)] of investments, followed by corporate bonds with 45.3 billion euros (39.1 %). While pension funds in other European countries are considered to be important investors in the real estate sector due to the long-term investment horizon of the underlying assets and the steady cash flows, real estate investments asset allocation of Pension Insurance Funds has experienced only minor changes in the past 5 years amid the turmoil caused by both the credit crisis post the Lehman collapse in September 2008 and the impact of the European sovereign credit crisis on financial markets since its outbreak in autumn 2009.[33]

3 Relevance of SRIs in the German Occupational Pension Scheme System

Obtaining reliable data on the actual SRI involvement by German pension schemes remains a difficult task. As we have identified so far, pension funds in neighbouring European countries tend to have significant investments in SRI assets, and they also represent the largest group of UN PRI signatories. Germany, on the other hand, has only eight signatories (5.8 % of all European signatories, asset owners only) and is therefore considerably underrepresented, particularly taking into account its leading economic position in Europe. Moreover, there is only one public entity that is involved in pension fund management (the 'Bayerische Versorgungskammer'), whereas there is to date no single private-sector occupational pension scheme represented.[34]

In this context, Schäfer (2005) states that although occupational pension schemes are supposed to be the precursors of SRI investing in Germany, they have so far disappointed, primarily due to a limited product range for non-equity products and the restrictive investment rules set by the German regulator.[35] Nevertheless, recent events are indicating that the low involvement of German pension funds in the SRI space is potentially changing. A representative survey-based study

---

[33] We will assume for the remainder of our research study that the European sovereign debt crisis unfolded in autumn 2009 when the Greek fiscal crisis became public. See Featherstone (2011, p. 194) et seq.

[34] See PRI (2012).

[35] See Schäfer (2005, p. 560).

by the Bundesministerium fuer Umwelt, Naturschutz und Reaktorsicherheit together with Fortis Investments (2008) suggests, for example, that in the long-term ESG considerations in the strategic investment management of German occupational pension schemes will improve the risk-adjusted performance of the funds and promote overall sustainable development.[36]

As German Pension Insurance Funds offer in most cases defined contributions with capital guarantee, the priority of their asset management is shortfall risk management. Therefore, the integration of SRI styles into the conventional portfolio management of German Pension Insurance Funds should be expected to focus on the ability to cope with such a risk-related asset management approach. Existing empirical studies on the performance of SRI portfolios in comparison to conventional benchmarks ignore such relationship to date.

Prevailing literature on the willingness of occupational pension schemes to invest in SRI suggests institutional settings are essential.[37] The study of Sievänen et al. (2012) made a detailed investigation into pension funds' characteristics that could determine their attitude towards SRI.[38] For German Pension (Insurance) Funds, the study figured out that the regulatory environment is of highest importance, i.e. the more legal obligations to integrate SRI in a pension fund's portfolio exist, the higher the SRI market share will be. As legal obligations in Germany are the exception, an important incentive to invest in SRI is therefore lacking. Other general drivers of SRI are both the pension plan type and the pension fund size. Large pension funds (by number of staff and AuM) that offer defined-benefit contributions are publicly owned and of statutory nature seem to have a significant higher attitude towards SRI than their counterparts. Such a prototype of SRI-minded pension fund can nonetheless be hardly found in Germany, which sheds further light on the reluctance of German pension funds to invest in SRI.

4 Empirical Analysis

4.1 Methodology and Objectives

The main objective of our empirical analysis is to compare the risk-related performance of SRI to conventional assets under the prevailing investment framework for Pension Insurance Funds in Germany. The principal elements of our theoretical foundation are stochastic time series regression models (in particular the Vector Error Correction Model or VEC) and the bootstrap simulation technique, as both will enable us to generate future return paths for the underlying investment

---

[36] Bundesministerium fuer Umwelt, Naturschutz und Reaktorsicherheit, Fortis Investments (2008, p. 5).

[37] See, e.g. Bengtsson (2008b), Cox and Schneider (2010).

[38] See Sievänen et al. (2012).

portfolios. Rigid testing procedures both in the identification and the diagnostic checking phase of the regression model, combined with 'optimised regressions' for the VEC model itself, will ensure that the fitted model adequately captures the data generating process of the underlying time series data.

We will also define a number of investment allocation strategies that will allow portfolio managers not only to replicate prevailing outright strategies followed by Pension Insurance Funds but also to explore the structural flexibilities the German regulator BaFin allows these investors in terms of derivative overlay structures.

The aim of defining these investing approaches has been to outline allocation strategies that represent a wide range of possible investment opportunities for pension fund managers, depending on their respective risk appetite. The return distributions obtained from the bootstrap simulation will act as input for these allocation strategies. In the following we will present the results of simulating all investment strategies defined in this section.

Traditional mean-variance performance measures will not suffice to assess the suitability of the investment strategies under consideration. Due to the risk-averse portfolio allocation and investment style German Pension Insurance Funds have showed in the past and the capital preservation character of pension plans with defined contributions with capital guarantee, a new set of performance measures is required. We defined the risk measurements based on lower partial moments (LPMs), as they allow for return distributions that are non-normally distributed. These measures further offer an adequate downside risk assessment so that we could determine which investment strategies combined with which portfolio allocations yield more appropriate risk-return combinations. Once a regression model has been fitted that captures the data generating process of the underlying assets, we will run bootstrap simulations on the estimated model to simulate potential future return paths of the target portfolios. A large number of simulated data points per time period and a long-enough forecasting time horizon (3 years) will yield a return distribution that will be subsequently used as input variable for the strategic asset allocation strategies we have chosen for German Pension Insurance Funds.[39]

4.2 Simulated Investment Strategies

4.2.1 Outright Strategies

Main strategies simulated for all three portfolios are Buy-and-Hold and Constant-Mix (as the two outright methods). They will be enriched by hedging of the equity assets of the portfolio by using put and collar derivative overlays.

In the Buy-and-Hold outright strategy, the investor usually maintains the initial portfolio weights unchanged during the entire investment period of 1 year. At the

---

[39] For more technical details see Hertrich (2013).

end of this period, the initial weights are reinstated. During the year a rebalancing could only occur should one of the regulatory maximum caps for the asset classes is reached. In such an instance, the portfolio would be returned again to its initial weights. In the Constant-Mix scenario, the portfolio is rebalanced at the end of every month to its initial portfolio weights. This method thus leads to a lower probability of breaching the regulatory caps. Constant-Mix methods lead to an asset allocation in year 3 that is similar in its asset weights to the one at inception. It is therefore characterised as a very rigid investment methodology.

4.2.2   Derivative Overlays

A put option-based investment strategy involves acquiring an at-the-money (ATM)-strike, 1-year maturity put on the total value of the equity portfolio. At the end of each year, the options are cash-settled, and new options with the same structural characteristics are bought on the new nominal value of the equity portion of the fund. For the collar strategies, the investment manager purchases an ATM put option on the underlying equity assets and sells a call option with a 15 % premium. Both options will have a 1-year maturity. All collars are cash-settled at maturity, and new collars, with the same terms, are bought recurrently for another 1 year.

The Bond Call Option strategy implies the acquisition of an ATM call option on the entire nominal amount of the equity allocation (in our case 5 % at inception). The equity portion of the fund will subsequently be sold down to 0 %. Therefore, the entire equity exposure of the fund is replicated via the ATM call option. This option has a 1-year maturity and will be cash-settled at the end of the investment period. At the beginning of the following year, a new ATM call option on 5 % of the underlying equity is acquired.

The Yield Enhancement method consists of selling OTM call options on an existing equity portfolio. This is a common portfolio strategy to increase the overall yield of the fund. In our analysis, a 115-strike, 1-year maturity call option is sold at the beginning of each period on the nominal amount of the equity portfolio. For share price movements above the strike at maturity, the portfolio will forego upside, whereas for any value below the strike, the returns of the fund will be enhanced by the option premium received at inception.

4.3   Time Series Used

Each of the portfolios used in our empirical analysis will be composed of a certain number of indices, each of which will represent a particular asset class. For both the Standard Portfolio (SP) as well as the SRI Portfolio (SRI), there will be five asset classes included in total, following the most relevant asset classes that German Pension Insurance Funds have been invested in the past 5 years: (1) equities (5 % weight), (2) government bonds (45 %), (3) corporate bonds (40 %), (4) real estate investments (5 %) and (5) money market instruments (5 %). The Alternative Portfolio (AP), the third fund contemplated, will be similar to the SRI Portfolio with the main difference that 10 % of the assets under management are allocated to alternative investments.[40]

To enable an adequate and representative comparison amongst the different portfolios, it has been an essential requirement in the index selection process that the indices chosen follow a matching principle. This method implies that for each asset class in the respective portfolio, a comparable index is selected that shows a similar composition. In general, any of the underlying SRI indices (for equities, corporate bonds and government bonds) will have their respective counterpart in the Standard Portfolio (SP) as benchmark. A similar matching principle has been applied in various academic papers, in which SRI performance has been compared to non-SRI assets.[41]

This matching principle is thereby reflected in the comparison between standard and SRI indices. This approach guarantees that the respective asset classes in the two portfolios have similar industry and country allocation, and hence, any form of allocation tilt is avoided.

The matching principle also ensures that the SRI screening and selection methodology that underlie both the equity allocation (via the STOXX Europe Sustainability Index) and the corporate bond segments (via the ECPI Corporate Bond index) are the same, so that the final asset pool for corporate bonds is selected following a similar procedure than the one applied to the equity portfolio.[42]

4.4 Summary of Empirical Results

Comparing the results from our simulation studies across all portfolios and investment strategies will allow us to rank each strategy by its suitability within a certain performance or risk indicator. The focus of our comparison will thereby be to select strategies that reduce the downside risk exposure of the fund.

Table 1 summarises the relative assessment of the results obtained for the respective portfolio strategies. In terms of portfolio approach, our results provide

---

[40] In connection with this allocation into alternative investments, bonds investments, both corporate and government bonds, will decrease accordingly by 10 percentage points. The alternative asset allocation is thereby equally split between commodities and hedge fund assets.

[41] For comparison amongst investment funds, see Mallin et al. (1995), Gregory et al. (1997) for UK investment funds, Statman (2000) for US funds, Kreander et al. (2005) for European funds and Bauer et al. (2005) for an international mix. For pure SRI index performance studies, see Sauer (1997), Kurtz and diBartolomeo (1996) and Statman (2006).

[42] Both equities and corporate bond indices follow a best-in-class approach with a negative screening ex-AGTAFA. More details on the index methodologies can be found in STOXX (2012) for the Stoxx Europe Sustainability index and ECPI (2011) for the ECPI Corporate Bonds index.

Table 1 Relative comparison across portfolios and investment strategies

Average portfolio value				Maximum			
Best	Value	Worse	Value	Best	Value	Worse	Value
1. SRI: Bond Call Option-B&H	110.09	*1. SP: outright-CM*	*107.34*	1. AP: Bond Call Option-B&H	142.91	*1. SP: collar-CM*	*126.74*
2. AP: Yield Enhanc.-B&H	110.01	*2. SP: put-CM*	*107.38*	2. SRI: Bond Call Option-B&H	142.10	*2. SP: Yield Enhanc.-CM*	*127.76*
3. AP: Bond Call Option-B&H	109.93	*3. SP: Yield Enhanc.-CM*	*107.47*	3. AP: outright-B&H	141.14	3. AP: collar-CM	128.64
Minimum				Standard deviation returns (in %)			
Best	Value	Worse	Value	Best	Value	Worse	Value
1. SRI: collar-B&H	92.03	*1. SP: outright-CM*	*85.82*	1. AP: collar-CM	4.68	1. SRI: Bond Call Option-B&H	5.50
2. SRI: put-B&H	91.47	*2. SP: Yield Enhanc.-CM*	*86.39*	2. SP: collar-CM	4.73	*2. SP: outright-B&H*	*5.47*
3. SRI: collar-CM	91.23	*3. SP: Bond Call Option-B&H*	*87.61*	3. SRI: collar-CM	4.74	3. SRI: outright-B&H	5.46
Omega				Downside deviation (in %)			
Best	Value	Worse	Value	Best	Value	Worse	Value
1. AP: collar-B&H	200.29	*1. SP: outright-CM*	*27.70*	1. AP: collar-B&H	0.39	*1. SP: outright-CM*	*1.08*
2. SRI: collar-B&H	184.59	*2. SP: Yield Enhanc.-CM*	*34.91*	2. SRI: collar-B&H	0.40	*2. SP: Yield Enhanc.-CM*	*0.94*
3. AP: Yield Enhanc.-B&H	172.62	*3. SP: put-CM*	*39.33*	3. AP: Yield Enhanc.-B&H	0.44	*3. SP: Bond Call Option-CM*	*0.85*
Sortino ratio				Upside potential ratio			
Best	Value	Worse	Value	Best	Value	Worse	Value
1. AP: collar-B&H	23.45	*1. SP: outright-CM*	*6.44*	1. AP: collar-B&H	23.56	*1. SP: outright-CM*	*6.68*
2. SRI: collar-B&H	23.20	*2. SP: Yield Enhanc.-CM*	*7.51*	2. SRI: collar-B&H	23.33	*2. SP: Yield Enhanc.-CM*	*7.73*

(continued)

Table 1 (continued)

Average portfolio value				Maximum			
Best	Value	Worse	Value	Best	Value	Worse	Value
3. AP: Yield Enhanc.-B&H	21.35	*3. SP: put-CM*	*8.37*	3. AP: Yield Enhanc.-B&H	21.47	*3. SP: put-CM*	*8.59*

Source: Own representation. Abbreviations used: '*B&H*' Buy & Hold, '*CM*' Constant Mix, '*Yield Enhanc.*' Yield Enhancement, '*SP*' Standard Portfolio, '*SRI*' SRI Portfolio, '*AP*' Alternative Portfolio. Underline highlighting indicates an SRI strategy (both for the SRI Portfolio and the Alternative Portfolio) that manages to yield results in the top tier of the respective investment strategy. Italic highlighting indicates that the respective strategy of the Standard Portfolio generates a performance that belongs to the worse 3 portfolio returns in that category

empirical evidence that the SRI-structured portfolios (both the SRI Portfolio as well as the Alternative Portfolio) consistently outperform the Standard Portfolio, both for the outright scenarios and the various derivatives overlay structures contemplated. While the performance difference is on average not excessive, it is nonetheless constant and consistent. More importantly for the purpose of our study, SRI portfolios yield overall better downside risk figures than conventional portfolios, indicating a more conservative risk exposure in bearish market environments, therefore consequently minimising tail risk.

The overall conclusion in terms of downside risk is apparent: outright strategies using Constant-Mix methods emerge as the least appropriate investment strategies for Pension Insurance Funds. In more detail, within the downside risk measures we have determined, the worst performers are strategies from the Standard Portfolio (SP) using Constant-Mix methods as underlying strategy. In addition, outright strategies rank as the worst performers overall. With regard to minimum values obtained after our 3-year investment horizon, the outright strategy and the Yield Enhancement techniques within the Standard Portfolio yield the lowest values. When using average portfolio values as indicator of suitability of a respective investment strategy, again the Standard Portfolio produces the lowermost figures. We therefore conclude that based on the outcome of our simulation study, a combination of Standard Portfolio, Constant-Mix and outright methods represents the worse downside risks for German Pension Insurance Funds.

The most appropriate investment strategies for a risk-averse manager of a Pension Insurance Fund, on the contrary, are predominantly collar hedging derivative overlays, because they allow the portfolio manager to optimise the risk management on the risky equity portion of his/her investment portfolio.

The premium generated by the upper strike call subsidises the cost of implementing the structure and leads to a better downside risk profile than simply acquiring put options. Collar derivatives, combined with Buy-and-Hold methods in particular, enable a portfolio manager to get the best downside risk profile of all strategies simulated. Collars also generate the highest minimum values, consequently reducing the risk of a major one-off shortfall event, and yield the lowest portfolio volatility. For those managers focused on generating high-yielding investment portfolios, the Bond Call Option methodology, combined with the Buy-and-

Hold technique, will draw the best results. Table 1 replicates our best and worst performing portfolio strategies from different investment perspectives.

5 Alternative Investment Approaches: UK and Dutch Models

The focus now will be to ignore the restrictive regulatory environment under which Pension Insurance Funds operate in Germany and simulate strategies that have asset allocations geared towards a higher equity exposure as well as alternative investments.

The motivation for this exercise is to get a better understanding of how alternative pension portfolios may perform with the aim to draft a recommendation for policymakers on whether the current regulatory framework for Pension Insurance Funds in Germany may be appropriate or require amendments. In the following we replicate the average portfolio allocation for pension funds in the UK and the Netherlands, the two largest pension fund systems in Europe.

5.1   UK Pension Fund Model

Based on the historical asset allocation of UK pension funds over the past 5 years, we have run our simulations on an asset allocation of 55 % equities, 40 % bonds (with 60 % European government bonds and 40 % European corporate bonds split), 1 % real estate investments and 4 % alternative assets (50 % commodities, 50 % hedge fund assets). Replicating also the same investment strategies as we did for the German Pension Insurance Fund portfolio, we obtain the following results (Table 2).

Allowing the initial equity allocation for the simulation to start at $t = 0$ at 55 % yields remarkable results with regard to portfolio performance as well as downside risk measures. The outright strategy, for example, leads to the highest maximum portfolio value of all strategies considered in our research study (181.88 in year 3) so far, in comparison to our previous absolute maximum of 142.91 (+27.27 %) for the Alternative Portfolio (AP) applying the Bond Call Option strategies in the Buy-and-Hold approach. At the same time, however, the outright strategy of the UK model also leads to the lowest portfolio value recorded, with 70.81, and therefore more than 17.49 % below our previous minimum of 85.82 recorded for the outright strategy (Constant Mix) of the Standard Portfolio.

From a downside risk perspective, the collar derivative structure yields again the most risk-averse profile: (1) a minimum value of 89.28 and hence 18.47 percentage points above the minimum for the outright strategy; (2) a standard deviation for the portfolio returns of 5.21 %, which is 6.74 points lower than the volatility of the

Table 2 Comparison across investment strategies: UK pension fund model (after year 3)

	Aver. value	Max	Min	Std. dev. returns (%)	Omega	Downs. dev. (%)	Sortino ratio	Ups. pot. ratio
Outright	106.55	181.88	70.81	11.95	3.29	5.47	1.03	1.48
Hedging put	103.05	161.58	83.12	9.44	1.99	4.65	0.55	1.10
Hedging collar	105.55	126.01	89.28	5.21	11.43	1.50	3.52	3.86
Bond Call Opt.	108.91	177.13	80.47	10.28	8.43	2.76	2.90	3.29
Yield Enhanc.	109.09	141.78	76.19	9.20	9.01	3.12	2.66	2.99

Source: Own representation. Underline highlighted cells indicate the best-performing investment strategy within the respective category after an investment period of 3 years, whereas italic highlighted cells denote the worse performing approach in the corresponding group

Table 3 Comparison across investment strategies: Dutch pension fund model (after year 3)

	Aver. value	Max	Min	Std. dev. returns (%)	Omega	Downs. dev. (%)	Sortino ratio	Ups. pot. ratio
Outright	109.30	157.36	82.41	8.22	15.54	1.99	4.29	4.59
Hedging put	107.32	148.37	87.91	6.83	16.95	1.36	5.03	5.35
Hedging collar	108.67	127.50	91.21	4.67	108.99	0.50	16.27	16.42
Bond Call Opt.	110.74	159.78	85.43	7.84	39.29	1.13	8.76	8.99
Yield Enhanc.	110.66	136.48	85.54	6.61	44.32	1.14	8.72	8.92

Source: Own representation. Underline highlighted cells indicate the best-performing investment strategy within the respective category after an investment period of 3 years, whereas italic highlighted cells denote the worse performing approach in the corresponding group

outright portfolio with 11.95 %; and (3) the best downside risk indicators of all five major LPM-based risk measures contemplated in this scenario.

5.2 Dutch Pension Fund Model

The assumed asset allocation for the Dutch pension fund model is as follows: equities 30 %, bonds 60 % (85 % European government bonds, 15 % European corporate bonds), 5 % real estate and 5 % alternative investments (50 % commodities, 50 % hedge fund assets). These numbers are based on the average allocation for the time period 2007–2011.

Lowering the equity exposure to 30 % of the overall allocation in the Dutch model in comparison to the UK approach with a 55 % equity proportion has a significant impact on the risk profile of the portfolio values at the end of year 3. For the outright strategies the maximum achievable value decreases by -13.48 % from 181.88 to 157.36, the minimum value shifts by 11.60 points to 82.41 and the downside risk measures improve considerably as does the Upside Potential Ratio (by factor $3.1\times$ from 1.48 to 4.59).

Both hedging strategies, despite generating the lowest average portfolio values, yield nevertheless also the highest minima. The collar structure, in particular, offers the most conservative risk profile in terms of downside risk measures. Its Omega value, for example, is with 108.99 more than $7\times$ higher than the corresponding number for the outright strategy. Furthermore, the collar offers the highest upside potential with an Upside Potential Ratio of 16.42, $3.6\times$ the respective outright number. The Bond Call Option strategy, with an average portfolio value of 110.74 (versus 109.30 for the outright method), has an attractive downside profile (Sortino ratio of 8.76 in comparison to 4.29 for the outright approach) and an appealing upside participation (Upside Potential Ratio of 8.99 vs. 4.59 outright).

Conclusions

Social Responsible Investments (SRI) are playing an increasingly important role in European occupational pension systems. There are sufficiently compelling reasons for a pension fund to consider SRI as part of the overall portfolio allocation: an intrinsic motivation to invest in SRI, corporate governance aspects, reputational risks, external stakeholder pressure, fiduciary duty as well as regulatory requirements. While empirical studies exist that compare the performance of SRI assets to conventional asset classes, such analyses tend to be predominantly equities focused and not tailor-made to German occupational pension plans.

Within the five occupational pension plans available to corporations, in the German occupational pension system, the Pension Insurance Fund plays a predominant role in terms of size, members as well as growth rates. The restrictive investment flexibility of Pension Insurance Funds, in particular their considerable overweight in fixed income securities, has not been considered to date in any research study. This empirical study attempts to close this research gap by pursuing an empirical method that enables to simulate SRI strategies for equities, corporate bonds and government bond securities and compare their performance to conventional assets, all under the restrictive investment framework prevailing in Germany for Pension Insurance Funds.

From the viewpoint of capital guarantee of invested funds, all three portfolios (simulated for German Pension Insurance Funds) achieve their objectives (on average) in all strategies used. However, as the downside

(continued)

risk measures indicate, some investing approaches imply a larger risk of missing capital preservation at the end of the investment period, while other strategies enable the portfolio manager to better risk control the composition of his/her asset allocation.

The side-by-side comparison of portfolios invested exclusively in conventional asset classes versus SRI-structured portfolios offers unambiguous results. SRI portfolios outperform in all contemplated investment scenarios, independently of the underlying investing strategy. Furthermore, Alternative Portfolios that invest in all equities as well as bond assets in SRI-screened securities but have up to 10 % of the total assets under management allocated towards alternative investments (hedge fund assets and commodities) perform on average better than the corresponding SRI-only portfolio. This conclusion applies to average achieved returns as well as downside risk measures applied in our analysis. Our results suggest therefore Pension Insurance Funds should consider SRI assets as part of their strategic asset allocation consideration. Furthermore, our preliminary conclusions are aligned with those of similarly structured research studies that focus on a direct comparison of conventional assets versus SRI assets.

Overall, analysing the return distributions of the contemplated investment strategies reveals that outright strategies underperform more complex portfolio methods from a return perspective, from a volatility aspect as well as from a downside risk angle. Between the two outright strategies, Buy-and-Hold is the dominant methodology for all three portfolios simulated. Collar hedging strategies with 100/115 strikes, in particular combined with Buy-and-Hold techniques, on the other hand, achieve the best downside risk protection in all three portfolios, while also minimising the volatility of portfolio returns. They seem therefore suitable for the asset management of German Pension Insurance Funds. However, should the objective of the portfolio strategy be to obtain the highest absolute portfolio values, Bond Call Option methods yield maximum returns as well as the highest average portfolio values, independently of the portfolio chosen.

Our results also show that both the Dutch and the UK pension fund models change significantly the risk-return profile of portfolio value distributions (versus the standard models assumed for the German Pension Insurance Fund), particularly in terms of downside risk management. While this is justifiable and appropriate for pension fund systems that do not offer their beneficiaries capital guarantee on their contributions, such asset allocations pose a challenge for defined contributions with capital guarantee pension models.

Our results suggest Pension Insurance Funds should consider SRI assets as part of their strategic asset allocation consideration. Our preliminary conclusions are aligned with those of similarly structured research studies that focus on a direct comparison of conventional assets versus SRI assets.

References

BaFin (Bundesanstalt fuer Finanzdienstleistungsaufsicht). (2011a). *Anlageverordnung (AnlV)— Verordnung ueber die Anlage des gebundenen Vermoegens von Versicherungsunternehmen.* Accessed March 27, 2013, from http://www.bafin.de/cln_117/nn_722564/DE/Unternehmen/ VersichererPensionsfonds/Kapitalanlagen/kapitalanlagen __node.html?__nnn=true.

BaFin (Bundesanstalt fuer Finanzdienstleistungsaufsicht). (2011b). *Rundschreiben R4/2011 – Hinweise zur Anlage des gebundenen Vermoegens von Versicherungsunternehmen.* Accessed March 28, 2013, from http://www.bafin.de/cln_117/nn_722564/DE/Unternemen/ VersichererPensionsfonds/Kapitalanlagen/kapitalanlagen__node.html?__nnn=true.

BaFin (Bundesanstalt fuer Finanzdienstleistungsaufsicht). (2012c). *Investments.* Accessed June 19, 2013, from http://www.bafin.de/EN/Supervision/InsuranceUndertakingsPensionFunds/ Investments/investments_node.html.

BaFin (Bundesanstalt für Finanzdienstleistungsaufsicht). (2012a). *Liste der Pensionskassen mit Geschäftstätigkeit, homepage of the BaFin.* Accessed June 11, 2013, from http://www.bafin.de/ SharedDocs/Downloads/DE/Liste/Unternehmen/dl_li_vu_pensionskasse_mit_gesch.html? nn=2696686.

BaFin (Bundesanstalt für Finanzdienstleistungsaufsicht). (2012b). *Einzelangaben zu den Kapitalanlagen der Erstversicherungsunternehmen. Bestand in den einzelnen Versicher- ungssparten 4. Quartal 2011.* Accessed June 10, 2013, from http://www.bafin.de/ SharedDocs/Downloads/DE/Statistik/2011/dl_kapitalanlagen_4q_11_va.pdf?__ blob=publicationFile&v=2.

Bauer, R., Koedijk, K., & Otten, R. (2005). International evidence on ethical mutual fund performance and investment style. *Journal of Banking and Finance, 29,* 1751–1767.

Bengtsson, E. (2008). A history of Scandinavian socially responsible investing. *Journal of Business Ethics, 82,* 969–983.

Braun, M. (2010). Betriebliche Alterssicherung im Spannungsfeld von betrieblicher Altersversorgung und betrieblicher Altersvorsorge, Aachen (Dissertation admitted at the University of Bayreuth, 2009).

Bundesministerium fuer Arbeit und Soziales. (2008). *Situation und Entwicklung der betrieblichen Altersversorgung in Privatwirtschaft und öffentlichem Dienst 2001–2007. Survey conducted by TNS Infratest Sozialforschung.* Accessed August 04, 2013, from http://www.bmas.de/DE/ Service/Publikationen/Forschungsberichte/Forschungsberichte-Rente/forschungsbericht-f384. html.

Bundesministerium fuer Umwelt, Naturschutz und Reaktorsicherheit and Fortis Investments. (2008). *Occupational pensions and sustainable investments in Germany, Frankfurt.* Accessed August 15, 2013, from http://www.sd-m.de/files/Hesse_Occupational_pensions_and_SRI_in_ Germany.pdf.

Cox, P., & Schneider, M. (2010). Is corporate social performance a criterion in the overseas investment strategy of U.S. pension plans? An empirical examination. *Business and Society, 49,* 252–289.

Doetsch, P., Hagemann, T, Oecking, S., & Reichenbach, R. (2010). *Betriebliche Altersversorgung* (3rd ed.). Freiburg.

ECPI. (2011). *ECPI euro bond index family.* Accessed July 07, 2013, from http://www.ecpigroup. com/PDF_Indici/ECPI_Euro_Bond_INDEX_RULES.pdf

Eurosif (European Sustainable Investment Forum). (2010). *European SRI study 2010.* Accessed August 12, 2013, from http://www.eurosif.org/research/eurosif-sri-study/2010

Eurosif (European Sustainable Investment Forum). (2011). *Corporate pension funds & sustain- able investment study.* Accessed May, 04, 2013, from http://www.eurosif.org/research/corpo rate-pension-funds

Featherstone, K. (2011). The Greek sovereign debt crisis and EMU: A failing state in a skewed regime. *Journal of Common Market Studies, 49*(2), 193–217.

FNG. (2013). *Marktbericht Nachhaltige Geldanlagen 2013. Deutschland, Oesterreich und die Schweiz*. Accessed August 07, 2013, from http://www.forum-ng.org/images/stories/Publikationen/fng_marktbericht_2013_72dpi.pdf.

Frankfurter Allgemeine Zeitung. (2005). Deutschland rueckt ab vom Glauben an die staatliche Rente. In: Frankfurter Allgemeine Zeitung, 04-May-2005, no. 103, section ‚Wirtschaft', p. 24.

Frere, E., Reuse, S., & Schmitt, S. (2009). Asset liability management bei Pensionskassen—Einfluss aktueller Problemstellungen und Auswahl von geeigneten Assetklassen. *Finanz Betrieb, 2*, 62–73.

Gregory, A., Matatko, J., & Luther, R. (1997). Ethical unit trust financial performance: Small company effects and fund size effects. *Journal of Business Finance and Accounting, 24*(5), 705–725.

Harjoto, M. A., & Jo, H. (2011). Corporate governance and CSR nexus. *Journal of Business Ethics, 100*, 45–67.

Hertrich, C. (2013). Asset allocation considerations for pension insurance funds, Berlin (Dissertation admitted at the University of Stuttgart, 2013).

Hockerts, K., & Moir, L. (2004). Communicating corporate responsibility to investors: The changing role of the investor relations function. *Journal of Business Ethics, 52*, 85–98.

Kreander, N., Gray, R., Power, D., & Sinclair, C. (2005). Evaluating the performance of ethical and non-ethical funds: A matched pair analysis. *Journal of Business Finance and Accounting, 32*(7), 1465–1493.

Kurtz, L., & diBartolomeo, D. (1996). Socially screened portfolios: An attribution analysis of relative performance. *The Journal of Investing, 5*(3), 35–41.

Mallin, C., Saadouni, B., & Briston, R. (1995). The financial performance of ethical investment funds. *Journal of Business Finance and Accounting, 22*(4), 483–496.

OECD. (2010). *Pension markets in focus*. Accessed April 18, 2013, from http://www.oecd.org/dataoecd/46/46/45637367.pdf.

PRI (Principles for Responsible Investment). (2011). *5 years of SRI—report on progress 2011. An analysis of signatory progress and guidance on implementation*. Accessed May 20, 2013, from http://www.unpri.org/publications/2011_report_on_progress_low_res.pdf.

PRI (Principles for Responsible Investment). (2012). *Signatories to the principles for responsible investment*. Accessed June 25, 2013, from http://www.unpri.org/signatories/.

Rohde, W. G., & Kuesters, S. (2007). *Betriebliche Altersvorsorge* (2nd ed.). Berlin.

Sauer, D. (1997). The impact of social-responsibility screens on investment performance: Evidence from the domini 400 social index and domini equity mutual fund. *Review of Financial Economics, 6*(2), 137–149.

Schäfer, H. (2005). Wie nachhaltig ist die Geldanlage in Deutschland? In: *Zeitschrift fuer das gesamte Kreditwesen* (pp. 16–20).

Scholtens, B., & Sievänen, R. (2012). Drivers of socially responsible investing: A case study of four nordic countries. *Journal of Business Ethics, 115*(3), 605–616.

Schwind, J. (2011). Die Deckungsmittel der betrieblichen Alterversorgung 2009. *Betriebliche Altersversorgung, 5*, 476–477.

Sievänen, R., Rita, H., & Scholtens, B. (2012). The drivers of responsible investment: The case of European pension funds. *Journal of Business Ethics, 117*(1), 137–151. doi:10.1007/s10551-012-1514-0.

Statistisches Bundesamt. (2007). Einnahmen und Ausgaben von Rentner—und Pensionaershaushalten—Untersuchungen auf der Grundlage der Ergebnisse der Einkommens—und Verbrauchsstichprobe 2003, section Wirtschaft und Statistik, no. 6, Wiesbaden, 2007. Accessed February 06, 2013, from https://www.destatis.de/DE/Publikationen/WirtschaftStatistik/WirtschaftsrZeitbudget/EinnahmenAusgabenRentner.pdf.

Statistisches Bundesamt. (2011). *Bevoelkerungsvorausberechnung-Entwicklung der Bevoelkerung in Deutschland bis 2060*. Accessed March 14, 2013, from http://www.destatis.de/jetspeed/potal/cms/Sites/destatis/Internet/DE/Content/Statistiken/Bevoelkerung/

Vorausberechnung/Bevoelkerung/Tabellen/Content50/Bevoelkerungsvorausberechnung, templateId=renderPrint.psml.

Statman, M. (2000). Socially responsible mutual funds. *Financial Analysts Journal, 56*(3), 30–39.

Statman, M. (2006). Socially responsible indexes. *The Journal of Portfolio Management, 32*(3), 100–109.

STOXX. (2012). *STOXX equity index methodology guide.* Accessed July 10, 2013, from http://www.stoxx.com/download/indces/rulebooks/stoxx_indexguide.pdf.

Union Investment. (2011). *Institutionelle Anleger befuerworten nachhaltige Investments, news article published on the homepage of Union Investment on 03-Aug-2011.* Accessed September 29, 2013, from http://unternehmen.union-invesment.de/Newsletter/Pressemitteilungen/9da644ee77900c22cf8def5f05c36e26.0.0/PM_20110801_Nachhaltigkeitsstudie_2011.pdf.

Hard Labour: Workplace Standards and the Financial Sector

Steve Gibbons

Abstract A number of issues arise when considering the application of the principles contained within the Equator Principles and the IFC Performance Standards on labour to a range of transactional and advisory work of financial institutions. Many are difficult to assess, for example, freedom of association, non-discrimination and wages and the criticality of issues such as child labour and forced labour, so it is paramount that financial institutions better understand the scope of their potential actions and those of their clients in this area. It is also important to understand the terrain of engaged stakeholders, including trade unions and national government. This chapter will consider the following: standards to be applied; issues that arise, with examples of several; the tensions between the scope of Performance Standard 2 (PS 2) and national rules; practical steps that banks can take and the limits on banks' activities; and the role of impact assessment studies, social auditing and other forms of assessment reports. The chapter will also place the question firmly in the context of financial sector implementation of the UN Guiding Principles on Business and Human Rights.

1 Introduction

Labour issues have been core, in some sectors, to any sustainability, CSR or other corporate responsibility agenda for nearly two decades. This is particularly so for businesses with closely integrated supply chains producing highly visible products for consumers in low-cost sourcing countries. One only has to consider the challenges faced by international retailers and clothing and footwear brands and their responsibility, regarding the issues around low cost labour or otherwise, for labour rights abuses in countries from China to Bangladesh.

S. Gibbons (✉)
Labour and Human Rights, Ergon Associates, Charlotte, NC, USA

8 Coldbath Square, EC1R 5HL London, UK
e-mail: steve.gibbons@ergonassociates.net

© Springer International Publishing Switzerland 2015   193
K. Wendt (ed.), *Responsible Investment Banking*, CSR, Sustainability, Ethics &
Governance, DOI 10.1007/978-3-319-10311-2_11

When it comes to due diligence efforts of financial institutions, however, labour and human resources have traditionally been less visible. While environmental, land and indigenous people issues have for some time been notable concerns for financial institutions, with many banks employing environmental specialists, and some social specialists, labour is less obviously considered.

The introduction of IFC Performance Standard 2 in 2006 initiated a process that is gradually accelerating. In addition to the dynamics created by the application of PS2, the causes of this change are various. First, there is slowly increasing awareness: from financiers as to the potential risks, to the project, the reputation of the financing organisation and to the rights of workers, arising from poor labour practices, and from worker organisations and NGOs on the role and responsibility of banks or DFIs in relation to labour conditions in significant projects that they finance. Secondly, as the emerging human rights and business agenda become clearer, some 2 years after the adoption of the UN Guiding Principles on Business and Human Rights (UNGPs), it is obvious that labour issues can arise in almost any project, whereas other human rights issues such as indigenous people's rights, land rights, security, etc. are necessarily restricted by the nature of the project and the country in question. As such, for any bank purporting to take human rights seriously, the consideration of labour issues is an obvious and relatively manageable starting point.

The aim of this chapter is to set out some of the key issues relating to responsible banking and labour. As an overview, it cannot go into the necessary depth with complex labour issues in difficult projects, but outlines some of the key trends and challenges. It also sets out some of the approaches a financial organisation may consider to understand better, and subsequently mitigate, effectively labour risks in its portfolio.

2 Different but Not New

One of the key points about labour standards is that, when considering legislation and workplace implementation, we are not talking about some new form of regulation or about areas not previously covered by either expectation from stakeholders or legislation. Most States have had some form of labour law for decades. The International Labour Organisation (ILO), founded in 1919, was particularly active in the promulgation of international labour conventions in the decades following World War II and is still central in all issues related to international labour standards, as a source of international law, an expert body of knowledge and an implementer of technical cooperation. This is not to say that there is widespread respect for, or implementation of, labour standards, but it is important to bear in mind that there will be an existing framework of national legislation and practice for all projects to be financed by banks or DFI. There also may be additional regulation in the form of collective bargaining in many countries.

There are also instances where the way labour is recruited or managed has changed in recent decades and which challenges traditional forms of labour legislation. These include: use of migrant workers recruited through intermediaries;

recruitment of workers indirectly through labour brokers; extended and complex supply chains for the manufacturing of goods; the use of many contractors with their own workforce, most notably in construction structure and infrastructure; and the subcontracting of tasks previously carried out by direct employees—from cleaning to financial back-office tasks. In all of these circumstances, responsible finance can provide the initiative and pressure to ensure that labour rights are properly implemented to complement national legislation and enforcement.

A financial institution may encounter numerous different labour issues relating to a project, closely tied to the nature of that project. So, for example, the commodity trade finance of cocoa may give rise to questions about potential child labour at a field level in the supply chain—the use of harmful child labour in many source countries is widespread. A significant question then arises about the financial institution's control and leverage over the supply chain in general and over specific conditions that allow child labour in particular. In short, the labour issues appear very remote from the financial instrument. On the other hand, labour employed in the construction of a highway supported with project finance is more visible to the financier, and the kinds of labour issues will be much more focused on occupational safety and health, wages, trade union rights migrant workers and the like. There will also be the added complexity of dealing with different layers of contractors. Finally, while credit lines provided to other financial institutions may raise questions about the employment conditions within those institutions, the more likely labour issues will relate to the ultimate recipients of finance guaranteed by the credit line and the jobs affected as a result. Again, how much visibility of leverage over labour conditions in such circumstances does a financial institution have?

3 Understanding the Normative Framework: PS2 and Beyond

The principal standard applied by banks and DFIs to labour issues is IFC Performance Standard 2.[1] When the Performance Standards were adopted in 2006, it was the first time that labour issues had been applied to development finance. The subsequent adoption of the Performance Standards as an underpinning of the Equator Principles and the principles applied by the European Development Finance Institutions significantly extended the number of transactions in theory, requiring due diligence and monitoring on labour issues.[2]

Prior to the adoption of the first version of the Performance Standards in 2006, most financial institutions had few provisions or safeguards governing how their

---

[1] EBRD and a number of other intuitions apply separate but very similar standards.

[2] The role of the Performance Standards more generally when either directly applied or applied through the lens of the Equator Principles is considered in more detail elsewhere in this book, so it is assumed that the reader understands the routes by which they may apply.

clients managed labour in either direct or indirect workforces. The most that was in place was a general prohibition of the use of forced and child labour by IFC, by dint of its membership of the World Bank Group, and a more general assertion to comply with provisions of the four core labour standards by EBRD, as a result of a somewhat Delphic footnote to the then operational sustainability policy. The adoption of PS2 in 2006 changed all this and also put labour issues specifically on the map as a stand-alone component to be considered during financial sector due diligence.

Surprisingly, stakeholders, including international trade unions, generally have accepted, if not acclaimed, the content and process elements of PS2, with the ITUC stating that 'it is clear that IFC's PS2 has set a new standard concerning workers' rights protections for public providers of development finance'.[3]

PS2, unlike some private sector supply chain codes of conduct, seeks to blend international standards with national law. This is useful in setting effective bench-marks for clients. What is particularly innovative about PS2 compared to other international labour norms applicable to the private sector is the mix of standards based on management systems and those more directly based on defined normative standards. The latter are restricted to the core labour standards: child labour, forced labour, freedom or association and non-discrimination. The focus on process and management systems allows for both due diligence and monitoring to address impacts through actions and activities, rather than outcomes.

The requirements of IFC PS2 include that all clients should:

- Adopt a human resources policy appropriate to its size and workforce (para 8).
- Provide documented information to workers about their rights, working conditions and terms of employment—including hours, wages, overtime, etc. (para 9).
- Respect collective bargaining agreements. Where these agreements do not exist, or do not address particular terms and conditions, the client is required to provide 'reasonable' working conditions and terms and conditions (para 10).
- Identify migrant workers and ensure that they are engaged on substantially equivalent terms and conditions to nonmigrant workers carrying out similar work (para 11).
- Put in place, if accommodation is provided within the terms of PS2, the policies on the quality and management of the accommodation and provision of basic services. The services must be provided in a non-discriminatory way and should not inhibit freedom of movement or association (para 12).
- Comply with national law where national law recognises rights of freedom of association. Where national law substantially restricts this right, the client should not restrict workers from developing alternative mechanisms to express their grievances and protect their rights. The client should not influence or control these. In any event, the client should not discriminate against worker

---

[3] Labour Standards in World Bank Group Lending. Lessons Learned and Next Steps. International Trade Union Confederation, November 2011.

representatives or discourage workers from electing their representatives (para 13–14).

- Not discriminate on personal grounds (para 15–17).
- Prior to any collective dismissals, seek alternatives to retrenchment. In the event of retrenchment, the client should develop a plan to mitigate the adverse impacts of retrenchment, based on consultation with workers and their organisations. The client should also comply with all payments and ensure that all outstanding back pay and social security benefits and contributions are paid (para 18–19).
- Provide a grievance mechanism for workers to raise workplace concerns (para 20).
- Not employ child labour at all within the internationally defined criteria or young people under 18 in hazardous conditions (para 21).
- Not employ forced labour within the international definitions (para 22).
- Provide a safe working environment and comply with national and international health and safety standards (para 23).
- Ensure that contractors are reputable and also to take steps to ensure that contractors implement the provisions of PS2. They should also ensure that workers employed by contractors have access to a grievance mechanism (para 24–26).
- Where there is a high risk of child labour or forced labour in a primary supply chain, identify those risks and take appropriate steps. The client should then monitor the supply chain on an ongoing basis. Where there is a high risk to safety, the client should take steps to ensure that the primary suppliers within the supply chain are taking steps to prevent life-threatening situations (para 27–29).

3.1   Which Projects Create PS2 Questions?

Labour issues could potentially be present in any sector and in any country. So long as people are being employed in the project being financed, there will be potential labour issues. The IFC CAO suggests that 'since almost every IFC client is an employer, PS2 is relevant across the entire IFC portfolio'.[4]

This analysis is borne out by IFC's own 2009 analysis of Performance Standards engaged during the due diligence process based on the first 3 years of operation. In the analysis, PS2 issues were raised in 100 % of category A cases and 99 % of category B cases.[5]

While labour issues could, in theory, arise on any project, there is clear limitation on the number of occasions that financial organisations characterise labour risks or

---

[4] Compliance Advisor Ombudsman, 2013 Annual Report.

[5] IFC's Policy and Performance Standards on Social and Environmental Sustainability and Policy on Disclosure of Information: Report on the First Three Years of Application. July 29, 2009. IFC, Washington DC.

PS2 compliance issues as sufficiently serious to warrant specific due diligence or identified remedial measures or a labour action plan. What's more, based on our knowledge and interactions with financial institutions and consulting and audit firms, the number of labour audits, assessments, desk studies or other due diligence exercises carried out during any one year related to financial transactions is limited compared to those relating to supply chain social auditing programmes. The 2009 analysis referred to above suggested that 17 labour audits had taken place on IFC projects in 3 years. This should be taken in the context that, with the possible exception of some of the European Development Finance Institutions, IFC carries out many more labour audits and assessment.

So, it appears there are potential labour issues in most projects, but limited instances of detailed due diligence. This is understandable, based on a combination of the following:

- Lots of labour and HR issues are manageable and within the control of the client.
- Even if it is not easily manageable, clients will tend to suggest it is.
- There is limited understanding within financial institutions of when a labour issue becomes more serious.
- Some of the more difficult labour issues lie one step removed from the client's direct control; think supply chain and contractors.

3.2 What Issues Do We See?

To better understand the difficult labour risks, it may be helpful to outline some of the thematic labour issues that Ergon comes across in its consulting and advisory practice in labour and the financial sector. With all the associated caveats this entails, given the restrictions on confidentiality and disclosure around labour issues and the lack of public information. The thematic issues we see regularly include the following:

3.2.1 Migrant Workers

In some countries and industries, projects simply would not be completed without migrants; one only has to think of construction in the Gulf States. In others, migrant workers are brought in by contractors for either skills or cost reasons, and their presence gives rise to tensions with the local community. We see the two extremes here—the high-skill, high-pay 'expat' and the low-skill, low-pay 'migrant'. Those migrant workers will also potentially be in a vulnerable position with regard to the enjoyment of their rights, with risks of forced labour and poor working conditions.

3.2.2   Trade Union Rights

In some countries there are restrictive legislative provisions or practices which affect the ability of workers to join trade unions. The finance sector often finds this issue difficult to deal with, particularly as investment or banking staff will have strong loyalty to their client, who will often have entrenched views on such issues. Further, the experience and expectations of bankers often mean that their understanding or expectation of trade unions is loaded with political and cultural biases. What's more, the issue of trade unions and freedom of association is not a binary compliance issue as some questions like hours, safety and wages can be. It is a difficult issue which takes time and effort to properly understand and deal with.

3.2.3   Contractor Management

Many projects with significant finance involve at least some degree of construction. This is particularly so in project finance. The key factors here are the labour-intensive nature of such work and the fact that most labour will be engaged through a contractor. The added layer of controls and legal responsibilities, alongside the short-term nature of much employment through contractors—in India, for example, day labour is very common—makes implementing PS2 requirements and national labour law challenging. This is not to say that the pressure of the application of PS2 cannot make significant change come about. An Iraqi union leader reports that 'We still have a long way to go in Iraq to make labour laws just for all workers, but in the meantime the international instruments and support have been crucial for us, and we are pleased that we were able to use IFC's PS2 to correct the unfair treatment of many of the sub-contracted workers'.[6]

3.2.4   Child Labour and Exploitation in Mining Supply Chains

Many commodity supply chains, from cotton to cocoa, have reported instances of child labour at the field level. This is common knowledge both in the countries from where the product is sourced and internationally. The degree of leverage and responsibility of the financing organisation in relation to trade finance, credit lines or other instruments poses a challenge here. However, there are a number of transactions that have been flagged as being high category social risk arising from potential child labour in the supply chain, with a requirement for appropriate steps to be established and implemented. Collaborative and innovative solutions can go a long way.

---

[6] Behind the World Bank's Projects in Iraq. Peter Bakvis, Equal Times, 19 July 2013.

3.2.5 Payment of Wages

Issues with wages can arise from nonpayment of social security contributions, through late payment, to low wages which—although in line with national legislation—are below that which provides an adequate standard of living as a result of the very low level of the national minimum wage. While timely payment should be easy to resolve, endemically low wages are a difficult issue to address. However, banks have a very good understanding of their clients' cost base and commercial realities and need to consider the degree to which they wish to support projects that are unable to provide an adequate standard of living for those who rely on them for their livelihoods.

3.3 What Are They All Complaining About?

While the Compliance Advisor Ombudsman (CAO)[7] is not the only independent complaint or grievance mechanism for Development Finance Institutions (DFI), it is the one that has received a defined number of complaints over recent years and the one that demonstrates some interesting trends and outcomes.

With regard to the percentage of complaints related to labour issues, the latest Annual Report of the CAO reports that labour issues were identified in 29 % of all complaints.[8] The CAO reports that this represents a 'steady increase in complaints raising labour-related grievances'.

A sample of CAO complaints, as published on the Ombudsman's website and reported in the Annual Report, gives the following examples:

Allegations of poor working conditions and breaches of principles related to freedom of association in Indian plantation agriculture (Tata Tea and APPL).
Long-standing allegations about freedom of association in a Latin American airline (Avianca).
Freedom of association in a Turkish manufacturer (Standard profile).
Various worker health and working conditions issues in plantation agriculture in Central America (Nicaragua Sugar).
Poor wages and long working hours in relation to an equity investment in an English language school in Mexico. A second complaint came from a specific employee about his dismissal (Harmon Hall).

---

[7] The Office of the Compliance Advisor Ombudsman (CAO) is the independent accountability and recourse mechanism for the International Finance Corporation (IFC) and the Multilateral Investment Guarantee Agency (MIGA), the private sector lending and insurance arms of the World Bank Group. CAO addresses complaints from people affected by IFC and MIGA projects with the goal of improving social and environmental outcomes on the ground and fostering greater public accountability of IFC and MIGA. CAO reports directly to the World Bank Group President.

[8] CAO Annual Report 2013, p. 22.

Looking at the complaints raised before the CAO, one reading is that there is a surprisingly small number of complaints about labour issues in total, given the fact that labour is potentially an issue in every investment. It is more likely that labour will only become a serious enough issue to lead to a complaint being lodged when (a) there is sufficient collective interest and resource to support a complaint, for example, with the backing of the international or national trade union movement—which will tend to focus on high-profile freedom of association disputes—or (b) there is a sufficiently motivated individual with a workplace grievance. In both instances, the dispute will be elevated to the level of a complaint related to IFC on the grounds that the affected individuals are not getting what they want from the national system and also that they have sufficient understanding or knowledge of potential leverage from complaining to the CAO.

This does not provide us with any additional guidance on what might be practical risk areas of nonalignment with PS2 in the project, but rather what is likely to give rise to a public high-profile complaint, namely, significant trade union disputes and serious workplace grievance and conflict. This analysis is borne out by the recent complaint lodged with the CAO because of the events at the Lonmin mine in South Africa in 2012.

A final publicly available source on information related to, again, IFC finance and labour issues is the ITUC's report 'Labour Standards in World Bank Group Lending Lessons Learned and Next Steps: Assessing labour risks, some ideas and approaches'.[9] In this report, the ITUC outlines a number of case studies of projects that have been brought to IFC's attention. Four of the five case studies are already mentioned above in the context of the CAO, but the fifth involves allegations of child labour in relation the subcontracting of the sales of phone cards by a telecom company. Common to all the complaints, unsurprisingly given the authors of the report, are allegations related to restrictions on freedom of association and collective bargaining.

3.4   Which Challenges Face the Banks?

The key challenges for banks over labour issues are predominantly related to their capacity, understanding and resources to deal with labour issues. In 2009 the ILO carried out a series of semi-structured interviews with banks and DFIs and found the following[10]:

In most cases, implementation of social considerations still lags substantially behind environmental issues.

---

[9] Labour Standards in World Bank Group Lending: Lessons Learned and Next Steps. ITUC, November 2011.

[10] The promotion of respect for workers' rights in the banking sector: current practices and future prospects. ILO. Employment Sector, Employment Working Paper, No.26. 2009.

Banks varied in their capacity to integrate labour considerations into their lending and project management, with EPFIs rarely having any specialists with specific knowledge of labour issues.

Banks have difficulty obtaining specific and credible information concerning labour issues.

Banks need support and practical tools.

Banks need labour experts on the ground.

Even IFC, which has significantly more resources than any other organisation directed at environmental and social due diligence, could do better, according to the CAO. The 2013 Annual Report states that:

> The labour appraisals completed this year indicate that PS2 poses particular challenges that differ somewhat from those encountered in other environmental and social work. As a result, CAO questions whether IFC policies, procedures, and staffing structures provide a robust framework for the advancement of PS2 objectives with its clients. Given the relative newness of the labour standard, CAO has found IFC generally lacks deep experience with regard to labour issues and lacks appropriate frameworks for categorizing PS2 risk.

4 Labour Looks Different: The Problem with Impact Assessment

When we look at how labour issues are assessed either in a financial sector due diligence or through an environmental and social impact assessment process, the conception of how the project impacts on workers is important. More often than not, workers are ignored or, if they are taken into account, it is as something that impacts on affected communities, rather than something that is impacted upon. So, due diligence or ESIA will consider the degree to which an influx of workers will impact on existing community operation either through livelihood issues, sexual health or otherwise. Employment impact is often seen inevitably positive as jobs are created, and this is considered to be, without question, a positive thing.

This is not to say that job creation is negative—it is a very positive contribution to community and local development, but there should be more consideration of the quality of jobs and the nature of the work. The fact that the workers cannot be identified at the time of due diligence for many projects should be irrelevant, and there are ways and means to estimate impact on quality of jobs and also to assess the key risk issues for compliance with PS2.

5 Lessons for Financial Institutions

5.1 Understand Your Issues, Know Where Your Problems Might Be and What You Can Realistically Do About It

A key insight of the UNGPs was to stress the importance of due diligence on human rights issues. Financial organisations are normally good at due diligence. The challenge here is to apply the same kind of rigour and resource that are applied to financial and corporate due diligence, to performance on human rights issues. As Deanna Kemp and Frank Vanclay state:

> "In the domain of business, the notion of human rights due diligence is as much routine as it is revolutionary. It is routine in the sense that businesses customarily conduct due diligence to satisfy themselves that a proposed business action, transaction or acquisition has no hidden risks to the business. It is revolutionary in the sense that instead of only considering risks to the business, human rights due diligence requires the business to consider risks to people".[11]

5.2 On Difficult and Context-Laden Issues, Don't Take Your Client's Word for It

A little independent research and verification can go a long way. There is a significant amount of information in the public domain and specialist organisations and information sources from the ILO through the labour and human rights consultancies. In country, governments, trade unions, business organisations and experts often have crucial information about a particular issue or sector.

5.3 Workers and Communities Are Equally Affected

Too often workers are ignored in stakeholder engagement programmes. Workers will face the impact of any negative labour-related issues just as they will benefit from improved job prospects that can arise from new investment. In either case they have a valid point of view and are useful sources of information, not just on labour issues but on a whole range of responsibility questions. The issue is building capacity and expertise in interviewing workers so as not to compromise them or their employment relationship.

---

[11] Kemp and Vanclay; Human rights and impact assessment: clarifying the connections in Practice. Impact Assessment and Project Appraisal 2013, Vol 31, No. 2 p. 86.

5.4 Seek Expert Advice

This can be in the form of international expertise or local counsel. Labour auditors serve their purpose, but are often ill equipped to deal with the kinds of complex predictive issues that the financial sector face. As mentioned above, at a country-level government, the ILO, academics, business organisations and trade unions can provide a wealth of information.

5.4.1 How Does It Look from the Workers' and Managers' Point of View?

This is not suggesting that bankers become worker rights advocates, but considering what financial intervention can mean in human terms—both for employees and managers—is a useful exercise in determining your influence and leverage and where consequences are beyond your control. If you are financing a business plan that involves significant restructuring, then some workers will lose their jobs, implemented by their managers, who might also lose their jobs. This is a natural consequence and should mean that the financial institutions check in with its clients to understand how this will be managed and ensure that the relevant PS2 and national law standards are adhered to.

UBS and the Integration of Human Rights Due Diligence Under the United Nations (UN) Protect, Respect and Remedy Framework for Business and Human Rights

Liselotte Arni, Yann Kermode, Christian Leitz, and Alexander Seidler

Abstract UBS, headquartered in Switzerland, is one of the world's leading financial services companies, offering international wealth and asset management as well as investment banking services. UBS is fully committed to corporate responsibility. This commitment is incorporated in the principles and standards set out in the bank's Code of Business Conduct and Ethics. These apply to all aspects of UBS' business and the ways in which the firm engages with its stakeholders—from the products and services offered to its clients, its management of environmental and social risks, to the way UBS protects the well-being of its employees and society at large. As part of this, and in line with the firm's endorsement of the UN Global Compact, UBS adopted the 'UBS Statement on Human Rights' in 2006, setting out the firm's position on human rights issues with regard to its employees, suppliers and clients. This chapter explains how the UBS environmental and social risk framework developed over time with regard to incorporating aspects of human rights when vetting prospective corporate clients and executing their transactions. In particular, it illustrates how the UN 'Protect, Respect and Remedy' Framework for Business and Human Rights, together with discourse between committed universal banks convened as the Thun Group, contributed to the successful integration of human rights into UBS' due diligence process.

1 Introduction

In October 2013, UBS and other banks launched the Thun Group of Banks' discussion paper on banking and human rights. The paper was the result of discussions among a group of banks interested in sharing their experiences and ideas with regard to the implementation of the United Nation's (UN) Guiding

L. Arni • Y. Kermode • C. Leitz (✉) • A. Seidler
UBS AG, Zurich, Switzerland
e-mail: Liselotte.Arni@ubs.com; Yann-x.kermode@ubs.com; christian.leitz@ubs.com; alexander.seidler@ubs.com

© Springer International Publishing Switzerland 2015   205
K. Wendt (ed.), *Responsible Investment Banking*, CSR, Sustainability, Ethics &
Governance, DOI 10.1007/978-3-319-10311-2_12

Principles on Business and Human Rights. For UBS, the launch of the paper marked the culmination of more than a decade's work to understand what human rights means in a banking context and how to address related risks. This chapter provides insights on this development process.

2 Development of UBS' Corporate Responsibility Strategy

In a famous address to the World Economic Forum on 31 January 1999, UN Secretary-General Kofi Annan challenged business leaders to join an international initiative—the UN Global Compact—that would bring companies together with the UN 'to give a human face to globalisation'. For UBS, this was timely. The firm already had a long record of dealing with environmental issues and had recently started to bring all the firm's activities in areas of particular societal relevance under a single corporate responsibility umbrella. The UN Global Compact and its underlying principles in the areas of human rights, labour, the environment and (from 2004) anticorruption[1] brought strong institutional backing to these efforts.

In July 2000, UBS senior management therefore attended the first Global Compact Leadership Summit in New York, and UBS was among the original 43 companies (of which three were banks) that pledged to adhere to the Global Compact's Principles on human rights, labour standards and the environment. Determined to translate this commitment into concrete action, UBS then firmly established responsibility for the oversight of corporate responsibility at the highest level of the firm—the Corporate Responsibility Committee. Chaired by UBS' Chairman, the committee was mandated to monitor and provide direction on the firm's corporate responsibility commitments and activities. As such, in August 2001, the committee approved a comprehensive corporate responsibility strategy reflecting the Global Compact's principles.

Today, UBS' commitment to corporate responsibility is incorporated in the principles and standards set out in the bank's Code of Business Conduct and Ethics. These apply to all aspects of UBS' business and the ways in which the firm engages with its stakeholders—from the products and services offered to its clients, its management of environmental and social risks, to the way UBS protects the well-being of its employees and society at large.

---

[1] The United Nations Global Compact (2000) ten principles are derived from the Universal Declaration of Human Rights, the International Labour Organisation's Declaration on Fundamental Principles and Rights at Work, the Rio Declaration on Environment and Development and the United Nations Convention Against Corruption.

3   Development of the UBS Statement on Human Rights

In 2003, the Corporate Responsibility Committee (CRC) commissioned a review of UBS' human rights-related policies and practices. The review showed that in contrast with environmental issues, human rights appeared to play only a secondary role, and their consideration was largely based on individual initiatives in areas such as compliance, human resources or community affairs.

The review further showed that human rights were often perceived to involve a very complex set of social, political and economic issues that did not easily lend themselves to management systems and processes typically used in a business context. It also highlighted the limited availability of external guidance for addressing human rights issues in business. The UN had endeavoured to explore the human rights responsibilities of business, but after comprehensive and, in part, heated discussions, this attempt at establishing a norm on the topic (the so-called Norms on the Responsibilities of Transnational Corporations and Other Business Enterprises with Regard to Human Rights[2]) did not advance beyond a draft document. But the discussions had focused the minds of observers, notably companies, to consider more closely the extensive and complex area of human rights—if they had not already done so previously.

UBS was no exception. Building on the results of the review, intensive internal discussions were held to define common ground and understanding around a UBS position on human rights. Externally, UBS also held discussions with other banks, which eventually led to the publication of a human rights guidance tool for the financial sector by the UN Environment Programme Finance Initiative.[3] In December 2006, after being endorsed by all relevant business divisions, the Group Executive Board (GEB) approved the UBS Statement on Human Rights,[4] which then was publicly disclosed as part of the UBS Annual Report in March 2007.[5] In the statement, UBS for the first time publicly expressed the bank's commitment to respect human rights by recognising the responsibility of the private sector to respect human rights and support governments in their implementation. Also, UBS acknowledged the importance of human rights not only for its own operations but also in its interaction with suppliers and clients, which means its core business activities including retail and private banking, corporate and investment banking and asset management.

Building on the concept of sphere of influence advocated by the Global Compact, the UBS Statement emphasises varying degrees of influence it has on these stakeholder groups to address human rights. As an employer, UBS acknowledges that it can directly support compliance with human rights standards applicable to its employees through human resources policies and practices. In its interaction with

---

[2] United Nations (2003).

[3] UNEP FI (2011).

[4] UBS (2006).

[5] UBS (2007).

suppliers, leverage is limited, but human rights standards can be addressed by considering business practices of significant suppliers and by integrating relevant aspects into contractual relationships with them. With regard to clients, the statement highlights that the leverage UBS has to promote human rights standards may be even more restricted then for suppliers, but that it takes human rights into account when vetting prospective clients and also in executing transactions.

With this explicit reference to employees, suppliers and clients, the statement addressed the full scope of UBS' human rights impacts embracing the different activities and initiatives in a single document. At the same time, as a high-level document, it provided the appropriate fundament to progressively advance these activities and initiatives in the bank which back in 2006 were still characterised by different levels of maturity and implementation.

4   Integration of Human Rights into UBS' ESR Framework

4.1   Employees

For example, no significant adjustment was needed with regard to embedding human rights into UBS' employment practices as shown by a review of UBS' human resource policies and guidelines conducted by Group Human Resources in 2006. Existing policies and guidelines were mapped against the UN Global Compact and the Business Leaders Initiative on Human Rights (BLIHR) Matrix.[6] The review showed that UBS was well positioned regarding the safeguarding of the rights of its employees and that relevant human rights aspects such as rights to equal opportunity and non-discrimination, rights to security of persons or rights of workers were already supported by established internal human resource policies and guidelines.

4.2   Suppliers

In contrast, room for improvement still existed in the way how UBS addressed human rights in its supply chain. This supply chain was characterised by a very heterogeneous supplier base where human rights risks appeared less prevalent than in supply chains of, for example, manufacturing companies. Apart from client gifts and other goods carrying the UBS logo which had long been subject to sophisticated environmental and human rights assessments, such screens were not applied across the whole of UBS' supply chain. This changed in 2006 when the GEB mandated the issuance of a group-wide guideline for selecting and dealing with suppliers,

---

[6] United Nations (2004).

focusing on those suppliers where UBS has influence through direct contractual agreements.

A key challenge to this approach was that at that time no centralised sourcing organisation existed at UBS. As a consequence, different views existed among independent sourcing regions about the relevance and application of human rights and environmental standards. While proponents of the sourcing organisation largely supported the view that human rights should be interpreted regionally taking account of a different regional, cultural or ethnic context, group functions favoured the development of a single and global benchmark that would help to avoid an inconsistent application of human rights standards across the organisation. To address this initial dissent, a working group was established, consisting of representatives from all sourcing regions as well as environmental, legal and communications experts. The working group quickly came to the conclusion that only a global sourcing standard reflecting the universality of human rights as established and recognised by international law would serve as a practical way to promote and respect human rights standards across UBS' global supply chain and to address respective human rights risks for UBS.

Building on the internal expert knowledge that was developed for high-risk products such as branded goods and client gifts but also by leveraging expertise from other industries, the group developed a responsible supply chain management guideline that set clear standards and defined consistent decision-making processes throughout all divisions and regions. Early 2008, the guideline was launched together with an externally disclosed Responsible Supply Chain Standard[7] that used the UN Global Compact principles as central point of reference. While the standard established minimum standards with regard to human rights, environmental and anticorruption practices that should be included in contractual relationships with UBS' suppliers, the guideline provided sourcing staff with direction for identifying, assessing and monitoring human rights and environmental risks. Under the new framework, prior to any new or renewed contract, adequate supplier due diligence was required. Although the level of due diligence varied considerably in depth depending on the specific sourcing context, the guideline established that vetting should always be sufficient to provide assurance that suppliers comply with UBS' standards.

To support sourcing staff in the light of these new vetting requirements, UBS developed a set of tools that were integrated into the existing sourcing processes, including a standardised supplier self-certification questionnaire, independent third-party ratings of suppliers' past human rights and environmental performance, as well as product-specific purchasing standards that address potential human rights or environmental impacts in a product's value chain. Where performance gaps of suppliers were identified during the due diligence stage or after contracts have come into effect, remediation plans had to be established to improve supplier performance and mitigate risks for UBS. The combination of these due diligence

---

[7] UBS (2008).

measures helped establishing a robust and structured system that helped in minimising risks in UBS' supply chain and that was favourably rated by different sustainability rating agencies.

4.3   Clients

In 2006 gaps still existed in regard to how UBS addressed human rights in the due diligence of its clients. While environmental risks for many years were considered to be material to the extent that they could influence a client's earnings, assets or reputation, this did not necessarily hold for risks arising from business relationships with clients exposed to human rights issues. They were largely absent from risk control processes, although certain human rights-related issues were part of compliance-driven processes such as Know Your Customer and Anti-Money Laundering. This neglect can partly be attributed to the fact that from a credit or liability perspective, human rights risks were widely considered to be immaterial. However, growing discussions about the role and responsibilities of business in regard to human rights stirred by the debate around the 'Norms on the Responsibilities of Transnational Corporations and Other Business Enterprises with Regard to Human Rights' and the appointment of John Ruggie as the UN Special Representative for Business and Human Rights in 2005 were to lead to a paradigm shift in how banks looked at human rights risks. Increasingly the significance of human rights risks did not arise only from a compliance, credit or liability perspective but also from an ethical and reputational perspective.

In particular, public perception was growing that banks have considerable leverage over their clients' behaviour and as such should seek to influence client actions to promote good corporate conduct. UBS was increasingly challenged by advocacy investors and NGOs for providing finance to clients associated with human rights violations. For example, in 2008 the bank was criticised by NGOs and investors for providing finance to companies operating in Sudan.

To address these risks, UBS decided to enhance its access to information on human rights violations gained in the course of standard client and transactional due diligence. The pertinence of this approach was confirmed by John Ruggie in his 2008 report to the UN Human Rights Council, in which he proposed a three-pillar 'Protect, Respect and Remedy' Framework for business and human rights: instead of trying to define the boundaries of the corporate responsibility to respect by using the controversial concept of sphere of influence, John Ruggie argued that business should identify and assess its potential impact on right holders through the process of due diligence.[8]

Taking a risk-based approach, UBS decided to initially focus on clients operating in high-risk sectors and to develop specific industry sector guidelines that

---

[8] United Nations (2008), p. 19.

provided the business with assistance and guidance when engaging with clients active in sectors that typically associated with potentially negative human rights and environmental impacts. A first pilot guideline for the metals and mining sector was finalised in 2008. Additional guidelines for chemicals, oil and gas, utilities, infrastructure and forestry followed in 2009. The guidelines provided an overview of key environmental and human rights issues that may arise in the various life cycles of the sectors and summarise industry standards in dealing with them.

In 2009, the GEB and the CRC further strengthen the environmental and social risk framework by identifying controversial activities where UBS will not do business and by establishing an escalation path for transactions with corporate clients exposed to such areas. This list of controversial activities was derived from an internal and external assessment and consultation process and established 'do no harm' standards where impacts on the environment and human rights holders are considered highest and where internationally accepted standards are available. Crucially, these 'do no harm' standards meant that human rights were no longer assessed only in terms of their impact on UBS but also on how human rights holders themselves were impacted, a change of paradigm that was advocated by UN special advisor John Ruggie.

The resulting UBS position on controversial activities was disclosed beginning of 2011.[9] The position stipulates that UBS will not knowingly provide financial services to corporate clients nor will purchase goods or services from suppliers, where the use of proceeds, primary business activity or acquisition target involves certain environmental and social risks such as illegal logging, illegal use of fire for land clearance, child and forced labour or infringements of indigenous peoples' rights. In addition further areas of concern were defined covering issues such as mountaintop removal coal mining (MTR)[10] or the production of controversial weapons[11] where UBS would do business only under pre-established guidelines.

Another crucial step to strengthen UBS' due diligence was reached in 2011 with the integration of human rights and environmental data from a third-party provider into UBS' standard client onboarding system. This integration meant that any information associated with a potential client, including alleged breaches of environmental and human rights standards, was now made available in a single onboarding tool and that this information was presented to a great variety of internal users in a consistent and familiar way.

The strengthening of UBS' due diligence framework and processes is reflected in the significant increase of transactions and client onboarding cases referred to environmental and social risk units for enhanced assessments, as shown in Graph 1.

However, the journey did not end there. In June 2011, the UN Human Rights Council approved the so-called UN Guiding Principles on Business and Human

---

[9] UBS (2011a).

[10] UBS (2011b).

[11] UBS (2011c)

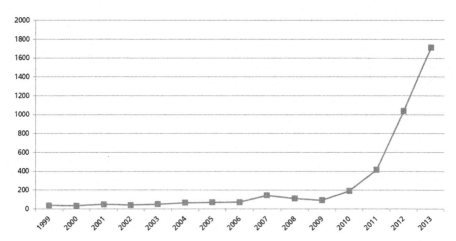

Graph 1 Environmental and social risk referrals to specialised units for enhanced due diligence (1999–2012)

Rights.[12] As John Ruggie said in March 2011, the Guiding Principles 'will mark the end of the beginning: by establishing a common global platform for action, on which cumulative progress can be built, step-by-step, without foreclosing any other promising longer-term developments'.[13]

5   The Thun Group of Banks on Banking and Human Rights

UBS and other banks—as indeed companies from across all industrial sectors—had followed the progress made on John Ruggie's mandate very carefully. Early on in this process, it had become clear that the efforts of the Ruggie team were very likely to lead to constructive answers to a challenging topic, but that banks would have to develop a banking-specific understanding of the Guiding Principles, as these were deliberately not focused on a particular business sector. At this point, some banks decided to jointly consider these developments and conclusions and, eventually, to share experiences and ideas regarding the implementation of the Guiding Principles.

Preliminary deliberations led to a first meeting of bank representatives, organised by UBS in May 2011—1 month before the aforementioned approval of the Guiding Principles—in its conference centre on the shores of Lake Thun in

[12] United Nations (2011b).

[13] United Nations (2011a), p. 5.

Switzerland. Assisted by expert input from the University of Zurich Competence Centre for Human Rights, discussions among the banks involved (i.e. the Thun Group of Banks as this informal group soon become known) continued over the next 2 years and ultimately led, in October 2013, to the launch of the so-called Thun Group discussion paper on banking and human rights.

Never intended as a norm of standard of compliance, the paper provides thoughts on what the topic of human rights might mean for banks in practice and initial guidance to banks keen to address human rights issues in their core business activities. Specifically, the discussion paper aims to support banks in mapping and analysing their potential adverse impacts in relation to human rights and also looks at related risks including reputational, legal, operational and financial risks.

The Thun Group discussion paper examines how different business lines within banks can implement human rights due diligence, including retail and private banking, corporate and investment banking and asset management. This distinction was deemed important because banks operate a host of complex processes with a highly diverse range of products and services for their clients, including a broad range of individual, institutional and corporate clients covering all industry sectors. Each business has its own risk profile and requires tailored risk management approaches. A crucial element of due diligence that does run across all business lines is the need, as advocated by the Guiding Principles, to take a broader view of potential impacts on rights holders, rather than focusing on banks' own commercial or reputational risks.

At the time of the launch of its discussion paper, the group expressed its hope that the document would support the integration of the Guiding Principles into the policies and practices of banking institutions as well as helping to encourage constructive dialogue with a wider group of stakeholders globally. For UBS, participating in the development of the Thun Group discussion paper has been a fruitful learning process. It contributed to the revision of the bank's Environmental and Human Rights Policy in early 2014[14] and helped in strengthening the case for considering human rights risks beyond the traditional fields of corporate and investment banking, onto the road less travelled of ESG (including human rights) integration in mainstream investment research and advisory.

Conclusion

The Thun Group process implies a clear understanding that it is sensible for banks to engage proactively in the ongoing debate around the Guiding Principles and their implications—and that the topic of human rights will increase in importance for banks.

This is of course true beyond the banking sector. While the UN Guiding Principles are nonbinding, they have nevertheless already prompted legal

(continued)

---

[14] UBS (2014).

developments. The European Union, the USA and other countries have introduced binding rules impacting on business responsibility in relation to human rights.

UBS has—as shown in this chapter—monitored and analysed developments pertaining to the topic of business and human rights for many years and has, at various points during this time, acted upon the conclusions of its analysis. UBS participation in the Thun Group of Banks is a natural progression in this process—as is a concomitant careful evaluation of the recommendations of the Thun Group's discussion paper as regards potential next steps for the firm. This reflects responsible business practice (by minimising related risks) and underlines UBS' desire to manage its impacts on society responsibly.

From a UBS point of view, a key lesson from the Thun Group discussions around the UN Guiding Principles was that these helped to strengthen the case for considering human rights risks across business lines. Notwithstanding, however, banks must make their own assessment and draw their own conclusions about further integration of human rights considerations into their policies and practices.

References

UBS (2006). UBS statement on human rights, available on page 30 of the 2008 CR Online Report. www.ubs.com/global/en/about_ubs/corporate_responsibility/commitment_strategy/reporting_assurance/reports.html

UBS (2007). Annual report, page 72. www.ubs.com/annualreport

UBS (2008). Responsible supply chain standard. www.ubs.com/global/en/about_ubs/corporate_responsibility/cr_in_operations/chain_management.htmlUBS

UBS (2011a). Position on controversial activities. www.ubs.com/global/en/about_ubs/corporate_responsibility/news_display_page_corporate_responsibility.html/en/2011/01/28/position_von_ubs_bei_beziehungen_zu_kunden_und.html

UBS (2011b). Position on mountaintop-removal coal mining. www.ubs.com/global/en/about_ubs/corporate_responsibility/news_display_page_corpo-rate_responsibility.html/en/2010/11/09/ubs_releases_statement_on_mountaintop_removal_coal.html

UBS (2011c). Position on controversial weapons (amended in February 2013). www.ubs.com/global/en/about_ubs/about_us/news/news.html/en/2013/01/07/20130107b.html

UBS (2014). UBS environmental and human rights policy. www.ubs.com/global/en/about_ubs/corporate_responsibility/commitment_strategy/policies_guidelines.html (exact address not yet published).

UNEP FI (2011). Human rights guidance tool for the finance sector. www.unepfi.org/humanrightstoolkit/index.php

United Nations (2003). Norms on the responsibilities of transnational corporations and other business enterprises with regard to human rights, E/CN.4/Sub.2/2003/12. www1.umn.edu/humanrts/links/NormsApril2003.html

United Nations (2004). A guide for integrating human rights into business management. www.integrating-humanrights.org/

United Nations (2008). Protect, respect and remedy: A framework for business and human rights. www.business-humanrights.org/SpecialRepPortal/Home/Protect-Respect-Remedy-Framework

United Nations (2011a). Guiding principles on business and human rights: Implementing the United Nations "Protect, respect and remedy framework", A/HRC/17/31. www.ohchr.org/EN/Issues/TransnationalCorporations/Pages/Reports.aspx

United Nations (2011b). The guiding principles on business and human rights. www.business-humanrights.org/UNGuidingPrinciplesPortal/TextUNGuidingPrinciples

United Nations Global Compact (2000). Ten principles. www.unglobalcompact.org/AboutTheGC/TheTenPrinciples/index.html

Strengthening the 'S' in ESG: What New Developments in Human Rights and Business Bring to the Table for Investors

Margaret Wachenfeld

Abstract Attention to environmental, social and governance (ESG) issues is moving along a trajectory from being a niche topic of specialised investors to a conventional consideration among an increasingly wide range of mainstream investors. The S (social) factor has always been the junior partner in the triumvirate, lagging behind the increasingly systematic and formalised approaches to environmental and corporate governance issues. This is partly due to a perceived lack of clarity and standards, a vagueness surrounding what falls into the S pot and a lack of the hard edges of national corporate governance or environmental regulations. S issues have often been seen instead as something nice to have in the annual report. However, with the infusion of human rights into the S agenda, the S is changing, taking on a more defined shape along with some hard edges that are prompting businesses, and increasingly investors, to wake up and pay attention.

1 Introduction

Attention to environmental, social and governance (ESG) issues is moving along a trajectory from being a niche topic of specialised investors to a conventional consideration among an increasingly wide range of mainstream investors.[1] The S (social) factor has always been the junior partner in the triumvirate, lagging behind the increasingly systematic and formalised approaches to environmental and cor-

---

[1] The Principles for Responsible Investment (PRI) (2011), *Report on Progress* 2011, welcome message from the Executive Director, notes that 'the tanker is turning' and that while mainstream capital markets still have a long way to go, 'new mainstream investment practices have clearly emerged in the last half-decade', p. 1, http://www.unpri.org/publications/?category=PRI% 20Reports%20on%20Progress

M. Wachenfeld (✉)
Institute for Human Rights and Business, Brussels, Belgium
e-mail: Margaret.wachenfeld@ihrb.org

© Springer International Publishing Switzerland 2015   217
K. Wendt (ed.), *Responsible Investment Banking*, CSR, Sustainability, Ethics &
Governance, DOI 10.1007/978-3-319-10311-2_13

porate governance issues.[2] This is partly due to a perceived lack of clarity and standards, a vagueness surrounding what falls into the S pot and a lack of the hard edges of national corporate governance or environmental regulations. S issues have often been seen instead as something nice to have in the annual report. However, with the infusion of human rights into the S agenda, the S is changing, taking on a more defined shape along with some hard edges that are prompting businesses, and increasingly investors, to wake up and pay attention.

Investor initiatives such as the UN-supported Principles for Responsible Investment (PRI),[3] the UN Environment Programme Finance Initiative (UNEP FI)[4] and the International Corporate Governance Network (ICGN)[5] are proof of the growing consideration of a broader range of non-financial factors in investment choices from an increasing number and type of investors. These initiatives, and the work of increasingly specialised professional service providers, offer innovative research and management approaches to advance the understanding and integration of ESG issues into investment decision-making. All three initiatives, as well as other individual investors, are taking on new workstreams on human rights issues[6] or incorporating human rights into their ESG work.

2   Why Should Business Pay Attention to Human Rights?

Human rights are not an entirely new concern for investors. Responsible investors, notably socially responsible investors and certain pension and faith-based investors, were important participants in earlier divestment movements driven by human

---

[2] For example, corporate governance issue continue to dominate PRI collaborative engagements. As reported in the PRI *Annual Report 2012*, 35 % of engagements covered corporate governance; 26 % were related to environmental issues; 24 % were about environmental, social and governance (ESG) issues; and only 15 % were on social issues. PRI *Annual Report 2012*, p. 5. This is a similar ratio to engagements reported in the 2010 report, *PRI Annual Report 2010*, p. 10. http://www.unpri.org/publications/?category=PRI%20Annual%20Reports

[3] The PRI was founded with 20 institutional investors in 2006; by 2013 membership has grown to almost 1200 spanning asset owners, investment managers and professional service providers.

[4] UNEP FI has over 200 finance sector members, including investors, and was established to understand the impacts of environmental and social considerations on financial performance, http://www.unepfi.org/index.html

[5] ICGN members are largely institutional investors who collectively represent funds under management of around US$18 trillion with a mission to raise standards of corporate governance worldwide, https://www.icgn.org/

[6] PRI is launching a new collaborative engagement on labour standards in agricultural supply chains and human rights in the extractive sector, http://www.unpri.org/areas-of-work/clearing house/coordinated-collaborative-engagements; UNEP FI has a workstream on human rights, http://www.unepfi.org/work_streams/human_rights/index.html; and ICGN has incorporated human rights issues into its ESG Integration Programme, https://www.icgn.org/education

rights concerns in apartheid South Africa, Myanmar and Sudan. They have communicated with companies for many years on supply chain and labour rights issues, expanding into a wider range of human rights issues ranging from water to ICT issues to human trafficking.[7] This chapter addresses why businesses, and more particularly investors, will want to pay increasing attention to human rights in a more systematic way.

First, unlike a number of other ESG issues, human rights are defined and supported by a wide range of legally binding international treaties.[8] They are an S issue that is not optional. The treaties are internationally binding for countries that have signed them and clear signposts of accepted international standards even for countries that have not. These standards have been repeated in national constitutions and national laws and interpreted and applied by courts at all levels, building an extensive web of international and national jurisprudence. Numerous internationally binding human rights standards have become legally binding on business through the intermediation of national laws and through references in contracts or an increasingly wider array of international standards that are legally or contractually binding. There is, therefore, a legal dimension to many human rights issues that is beginning to 'bite', through legal penalties, disqualifications, and litigation that is catching the attention of corporate counsel and other corporate directors.

Second, increasingly, both E and S issues are being expressed in human rights terms. 'Human rights' are becoming the umbrella for the expression of many sustainability issues.[9] Using human rights terminology highlights the link to impacts on people, moving issues out of a purely scientific or technocratic discourse. In addition, with human rights discourse come the linked concepts of accountability and social justice that are equally relevant to other sustainability topics.

Third, human rights have a resonance with global audiences that other social issues often do not have. There is a good reason that people pay attention to these issues from every corner of the globe—because human rights express many core ideas that people value deeply: protection of their children, education, basic notions of justice, access to clean water and freedom of speech. Governments, and

---

[7] For a brief overview of some of the issues investors have been involved in, see Institute for Human Rights and Business, 'Investing the Rights Way: A Guide for Investors on Business and Human Rights', 2013, Part Three, which reviews investor initiatives on a range of human rights issues, http://www.ihrb.org/publications/reports/investing-the-rights-way.html and E. Umlas 'Human Rights and SRI in North America: An Overview', 2009.

[8] There is the Universal Declaration of Human Rights, nine core international human rights treaties and a much wider range of additional human rights instruments, declarations, recommendations and guidance documents. http://www.ohchr.org/EN/ProfessionalInterest/Pages/Universal HumanRightsInstruments.aspx

[9] For example, at a recent meeting of OECD National Contact Points (NCP) for the OECD Guidelines on Multinational Enterprises, the NCPs noted that since the update of the OECD Guidelines in 2011 adding a chapter on human rights, virtually all of the complaints have cited the human rights chapter.

increasingly businesses, are denounced regularly for their violations of human rights. They are rarely, if ever, criticised for paying too much attention to human rights.

Fourth, human rights are increasingly being 'translated' for business into business-relevant standards, terminology and concepts. As with other ESG issues, there will remain a need for specialists, but there is an increasingly accessible and growing movement—the business and human rights movement—that is turning international human rights standards into standards for business. These standards exist along a continuum from binding to voluntary. The recently completed 6-year process of developing the UN Protect, Respect and Remedy Framework and the accompanying UN Guiding Principles on Business and Human Rights (the UN Guiding Principles) ended a decade-long debate at the international level around the human rights responsibilities of business that includes investors and other companies in the financial sector. The human rights chapters of other global standards, such as the OECD Guidelines on Multinational Enterprises[10] and ISO 26000,[11] are purposely aligned with the UN Guiding Principles. But there are a whole range of other existing and developing standards on human rights issues specifically for the private sector—sector specific, topic specific, context specific—that help businesses figure out how to respect human rights. Given the increasing attention to business and human rights issues, we can expect further initiatives.[12]

3 Why Should Investors Pay Attention to Human Rights?

Investors, as businesses themselves and as owners, are paying more attention to human rights. The reasons for doing so are the same for other relevant financial and non-financial issues: risk and opportunity.

Because human rights—and the risks of failing to respect them—are climbing up the business agenda, they can no longer be sloughed off as an issue of the 'lunatic fringe' or 'do-gooders' or seen as exclusively for large extractive companies operating in fragile states. They are becoming a mainstream consideration, driven by increasing recognition of risks to company operations—direct financial risks from penalties and judgements; operational interruptions from strikes, blockages and demonstrations; reputational risk and the management time consumed; and worker and consumer dissatisfaction and disaffection. Particularly when investing in emerging markets, risks cannot be understood in purely financial terms as the

---

[10] OECD Guidelines on Multinational Enterprises, 2011, see Chapter IV on human rights, http://mneguidelines.oecd.org/text/

[11] ISO 26000 Guidance on Social Responsibility, Sect. 6.3 on human rights, http://www.iso.org/iso/home/standards/iso26000.htm

[12] Just tracking the Business and Human Rights Resource Centre website for a few days is enough to give some understanding of the rapid development of the field. www.bhrrc.org

challenges are far more complex. Investment in emerging markets, for businesses and for investors, requires a deeper understanding of broader challenges in these societies in order to accurately gauge the level of risk.

Requirements—hard and soft—are important components shaping risk. Some areas of human rights have long been incorporated into national law in forms familiar to business—labour rights, non-discrimination, privacy, health and safety of workers and consumer protection law, to name a few. Governments are adopting legislation that references human rights or the human rights due diligence concepts of UN Guiding Principles, further ingraining the clear trend of human rights moving from a fringe issue on a trajectory to becoming a daily operational concern.[13] Although most sustainability reporting is produced on a voluntary basis, current and proposed legislation across several jurisdictions focuses on requiring more transparency from companies in connection with human rights-related performance and violations.[14] Human rights are also appearing in various guises in contracts—through reference to codes of conduct in supply chain contracts, to specific clauses on operating standards in joint venture agreements and to condition precedent requirements in mergers and acquisitions,[15] via references to the IFC Performance Standards and Equator Principles in project and corporate finance transaction documentation.

The UN Guiding Principles, although not a binding UN treaty and therefore not a legally binding requirement, are neither a 'law-free zone'.[16] They are seen as an authoritative global reference point that sets out global expectations on business behaviour with respect to human rights. The unanimous endorsement by the UN Human Rights Council in 2011 of the UN Guiding Principles[17] is widely seen as irreversibly validating the idea that companies share a basic responsibility to

---

[13] For example, the California Transparency in Supply Chains Act of 2010 applies to all retailers and manufacturers with annual global revenues of more than US$100 million that do business in California. It requires these businesses to disclose their efforts to eradicate slavery and human trafficking in their supply chains by publicly posting information on their websites.

[14] Directive of the European Parliament and of the Council amending Directive 2013/34/EU as regards disclosure of non-financial and diversity information by certain large undertakings and groups, http://ec.europa.eu/internal_market/accounting/non-financial_reporting/, and the Danish reporting initiative which has been updated to include a requirement to report on human rights. http://csrgov.dk/legislation

[15] Institute for Human Rights and Business and the Global Business Initiative on Human Rights, 'State of Play: The Corporate Responsibility to Respect Human Rights in Business Relationships', (2012), http://www.ihrb.org/publications/reports/state-of-play.html

[16] International Bar Association, Interview with Professor John Ruggie, Special Representative of the UN Secretary-General on business and human rights—transcript. http://www.ibanet.org/Article/Detail.aspx?ArticleUid=4b5233cb-f4b9-4fcd-9779-77e7e85e4d83

[17] Member States on the Human Rights Council at the time included, notably, China, Russia, Brazil, the United States, the United Kingdom and Saudi Arabia.

respect human rights alongside governments' obligations to protect human rights.[18] This means the argument whether business has human rights-related responsibilities should be over, with the focus now shifting to implementing those responsibilities. A recent article about a 2-year research project on barriers to responsible investment noted that:

> "normative frameworks were identified as important because investors are more likely to take specific social issues into account in their investment decisions and in their engagement when there is a clear consensus around what the expectations of companies are. The reason is that the risks to companies are greatest in situations where they violate or risk violating existing legislation or agreed societal norms (ie where their behaviour could be characterised as "unacceptable")."[19]

The UN Guiding Principles are just such a normative framework.

Fiduciary and reporting responsibilities of boards and company management require that companies manage and consider material risks and disclose such risks to the company and to its shareholders. As highlighted above, those risks increasingly include human rights risks. More investors 'accept that good fiduciaries should take them [human rights] into account in investment decision-making'.[20] Recent research has also shown that 'there is growing evidence that investors are starting to accept engagement as an essential feature of their responsible ownership duties',[21] indicating that investors are beginning to take a more proactive approach to managing these types of risks.

This leads to the final reason why human rights should be on the investor radar screen. While the focus in the press, among stakeholders and in boardrooms has

---

[18] The earlier, draft UN 'Norms on the Responsibilities of Transnational Corporations and Other Business Enterprises with Regard to Human Rights' of 2003 aimed to spell out business responsibilities, specifically, to set out, in a single, succinct statement, a comprehensive list of the human rights obligations of companies. While many civil society organisations welcomed the Norms, business generally opposed them, rejecting the notion that companies had direct legal obligations in relation to human rights. States, for the most part, came out on the same side as business.

[19] 'How institutional investors can tackle poverty and development', Posted by Rory Sullivan and Helena Viñes Fiestas on Aug 8, 2013, Ethical Corporation. http://www.ethicalcorp.com/print/36858?utm_source=http%3A%2F%2Fuk.ethicalcorp.com%2Ffc_ethicalcorporationlz%2 F&utm_medium=email&utm_campaign=1679%20Finance%20Clicks%20Aug%2013%20Content%20e2&utm_term=How%20institutional%20investors%20can%20tackle%20poverty%20and%20development& utm_content=45952

[20] NEI Investments, letter to UN Working Group on Human Rights and Transnational Corporations and Other Business Enterprises, 8 December 2011. http://www.google.be/url?sa=t&rct=j&q=&esrc=s&source=web&cd=1&ved=0CDAQFjAA&url=http%3A%2 F%2Fwww.ohchr.org%2FDocuments%2FIssues%2FTransCorporations%2FSubmissions%2FBusiness%2FNEIInvestments.pdf&ei=xTubUu-NFYShyQPq34GAAw&usg=AFQjCNFIKDuKWq5fOKgJsnPuMnhtz71gSA&bvm=bv.57155469,d.bGQ

[21] 'How institutional investors can tackle poverty and development',
Posted by Rory Sullivan and Helena Viñes Fiestas on Aug 8, 2013, Ethical Corporation, http://www.ethicalcorp.com/print/36858?utm_source=http%3A%2F%2Fuk.ethicalcorp.com%2Ffc_ethicalcorporationlz%2F&utm_medium=email&utm_campaign=1679%20Finance%20Clicks%20Aug%2013%20Content%20e2&utm_term=How%20institutional%20investors%20can%20tackle%20poverty%20and%20development&utm_content=45952 Sullivan article

primarily been on risks from a failure to respect human rights, no investor needs to be reminded that where there is risk there is opportunity, if the risks are well managed. The business case for positive relations with employees is an old story, as is the case for diversity in the workforce and the boardroom. Other human rights will take the same trajectory, demonstrating that treating people decently—workers, communities outside the factory gate or consumers—makes sense. Demonstrating responsibility at a time when confidence in the financial sector remains low makes even more sense.

4   What Is Expected of Investors?

The key message to investors regarding human rights is that 'the train has left the station' and it is time to get on board. The UN Guiding Principles apply to all businesses, large and small, in whatever sector the business operates. This means that the UN Guiding Principles apply not only to the businesses in which investors invest but also to the financial sector itself. The financial sector has started to take up the challenge of parsing through the implications of the responsibility to respect human rights, with work underway in the banking sector at UNEP FI and among the 'Thun Group' of banks, at the OECD in its work on analysing human rights in the financial sector and in other initiatives highlighted in this book.

Investors are expected to 'get their own house in order' as a good first step in understanding what the responsibility to respect human rights means. The good news is there is clearer guidance on what is expected of investors to help them on their journey. As noted above, the updated OECD Guidelines on Multinational Enterprises (the OECD Guidelines) contain a new human rights chapter that is aligned with the UN Guiding Principles. A unique feature of the OECD Guidelines is the National Contact Point (NCP) system that provides mediation between complainants (typically NGOs or trade unions) and companies when disputes arise with respect to implementation of the OECD Guidelines by an OECD-based company, whether they operate inside or outside the OECD. In a case in 2013 involving the Norwegian Bank Investment Management (NBIM), the Norwegian NCP issued a 'final statement' under its procedures, setting out a clearly articulated explanation of the application of the human rights due diligence requirements under the OECD Guidelines for investors, including when holding a minority position.[22] This is integrated into the discussion below.

Other European NCPs handling cases involving the financial sector and home to significant financial institutions, namely, the UK and Dutch NCPs, agreed that the human rights obligations of the OECD Guidelines apply to all investors, including minority shareholders. The issue is not whether minority shareholders have a responsibility to respect human rights, but rather how they are expected to exercise

---

[22] See: http://oecdwatch.org/cases/Case_262. The UN Office of the High Commissioner for Human Rights (OHCHR) issued a corroborating interpretation of the UN Guiding Principles on Business and Human Rights that comes to the same conclusion as the Norwegian NCP.

that responsibility. These NCP findings are part of the increasingly penetrating spotlight focused on the financial sector.

The journey typically starts with internal operations, such as deciding if an investor's human resources policies and procurement requirements reinforce or undermine human rights standards. These are important first steps for investors, but like other actors in the financial sector, investors have a much bigger impact on human rights through their investments. As owners, investors have a business relationship with all the companies in which they invest. That business relationship directly links them to the human rights impacts of their investee companies. That linkage carries responsibilities to respect human rights as elaborated briefly below. The interesting question therefore is what does the responsibility to respect human rights look like for investors and their investment selection and portfolio management? It looks realistic because both the UN process to develop the UN Guiding Principles and the OECD process to develop the OECD Guidelines were built on existing business approaches, together with years of consultation with business, business associations and investors.

For some investors, the journey will be familiar because the suggested approach is the same used by many investors to manage other ESG issues. For other investors that have been topic focused, looking at a few selective human rights issues, such as human rights and extractive operations, or labour rights in supply chains or investing in Myanmar, or using specific benchmarks such as the Access to Medicines Benchmark, the move to a systematic approach to human rights will mean expanding the focus, using a risk-based approach to identifying human rights risks based on the companies or funds to be invested in and their contexts rather than pre-selecting a topic(s) of focus. These targeted engagements have played and will continue to play an important role in highlighting the relevance of human rights issues to business and building clarity around expectations on human rights performance, but they are no longer the end of the story.

What the UN Guiding Principles signal, and the NCP case clarifies, is the shift away from a topic-focused approach that sometimes takes the least controversial or most media friendly route, towards an approach that is systematic and prompts companies to address all their key human rights impacts.[23] As the Norwegian NCP case states:

> companies should not simply choose to only address a small spectrum of human rights if they may have a significant impact on a range of other rights. Rather responsibilities are tied to impacts: enterprises should be prepared to address the impacts they have, not just those they find of interest.[24]

---

[23] See: The Norwegian National Contact Point for the OECD Guidelines for Multinational Enterprises, Final Statement, Complaint from Lok Shakti Abhiyan, Korean Transnational Corporations Watch, Fair Green and Global Alliance and Forum for Environment and Development v Posco (South Korea), ABP/APG (Netherlands) and NBIM (Norway), 27 May 2013, http://oecdwatch.org/cases/Case_262.

[24] See: The Norwegian National Contact Point for the OECD Guidelines for Multinational Enterprises, Final Statement, Complaint from Lok Shakti Abhiyan, Korean Transnational Corporations Watch, Fair Green and Global Alliance and Forum for Environment and Development v

This also applies to investors: given the wide range of human rights risks that may be represented in their prospective investments or existing portfolios, investors need to build their capacity to understand, assess and manage with their investee companies that full range of potential or actual human rights risks.

The suggested management of human rights issues follows the same pattern as managing other ESG issues. The UN Guiding Principles set out a series of familiar steps that investors can follow to set up or reinforce their existing management systems, briefly discussed below.[25] The first step begins with a necessary signal from management, acknowledging the investor's responsibility to respect human rights and signalling its approach. It should provide clear guidance to investment staff that human rights are a core part of investment criteria and to potential investee companies. It can take numerous forms: a core-values statement that includes references to human rights, investment policies that include guidance on human rights or a stand-alone human rights statement. More and more mainstream investors are issuing such statements.[26]

As important as policy statements are, they need to be backed up by a supporting due diligence process and management system to identify human rights risks among prospective investment targets that is integrated alongside other due diligence inquiries. The second major step is carrying out human rights due diligence which itself has a number of sub-steps, elaborated below[27]. It is no coincidence that the UN Guiding Principles use the due diligence term—a concept and terminology already familiar to business and investors. The due diligence steps outlined—assessing, integrating and acting on assessment findings, tracking and communicating—are familiar steps for due diligence processes and typical management system approaches.

Investors have a range of tools and services at their disposal to assess investments. ESG service providers are including human rights risk as a routine part of

---

Posco (South Korea), ABP/APG (Netherlands) and NBIM (Norway), 27 May 2013 http://oecdwatch.org/cases/Case_262. The UN Office of the High Commissioner for Human Rights issued a corroborating interpretation on the application of the UN Guiding Principles on Business and Human Rights to minority investors that comes to the same conclusion as the Norwegian NCP.

[25] UN Guiding Principle 15 provides: 'In order to meet their responsibility to respect human rights, business enterprises should have in place policies and processes appropriate to their size and circumstances, including: (a) A policy commitment to meet their responsibility to respect human rights; (b) A human rights due diligence process to identify, prevent, mitigate and account for how they address their impacts on human rights; (c) Processes to enable the remediation of any adverse human rights impacts they cause or to which they contribute'. http://www.ohchr.org/EN/Issues/Business/Pages/InternationalStandards.aspx

[26] See the list of companies with some form of human rights statement: http://www.business-humanrights.org/Documents/Policies

[27] The UN Guiding Principles 17–21 refer to a four-part human rights due diligence process: assessing human rights risks, acting on those risks and integrating that action into the company's risk management system, tracking how the risks have been dealt with (and making any necessary corrections) and then communicating with relevant stakeholders about the issues. http://www.ohchr.org/EN/Issues/Business/Pages/InternationalStandards.aspx

ESG information. Some investors chose to exercise norm-based exclusions in a number of different ways: on the basis of the company's past record and reputation on human rights, on particular human rights issues (e.g. child labour or forced labour) or operating in particular contexts (such as earlier in South Africa, Sudan, Myanmar, North Korea) and on the basis of sales of particular equipment (use for torture or defence). Others consider human rights issues alongside other ESG information without making the information an explicit in/out choice but rather as an issue for portfolio management.

Where investors have a large number of companies to screen or manage, a risk-based approach to human rights issues is appropriate, recognising that investors may not be able to screen or manage all investments for human rights issues. In these cases, due diligence should focus on two criteria. First, investors should focus on gathering information about potential or portfolio investments where there is a risk of severe human rights impacts. Focusing on the potentially worst situations first makes sense—such as where lives and livelihoods will be predictably at risk or where there may be gross violations of human rights (such as torture or widespread rape or systematic discrimination) or severe violations (such as forced labour or the worst forms of child labour).[28] The other criteria also make intuitive sense—focusing on sectors and countries and contexts where adverse human rights impacts are most likely. This type of information, which ESG analysts typically collect from a wide range of sources, is based on considerations such as (1) the operating context (e.g. countries, regions or particular operating environments that are high risk, such as conflict zones, fragile states, authoritarian regimes); (2) the particular operations, products or services involved (if there are typically human rights risks associated with them)[29]; and (3) other relevant considerations (which might include a company's poor track record on human rights performance).[30] This directs investors to concentrating on managing those investments that have the potential for the greatest human rights harm.

Prior to the investment, investors could use this type of information to decide not to invest because the human rights risk is too high, or they could seek to impose conditions or changes in the management systems of a portfolio company to better manage significant human rights concerns. Once in the portfolio, investors have a

---

[28] See, for example, *Red Flags – Liability Risks for Companies Operating in High Risk Zones –* which highlights liability risks for companies operating in high-risk zones, www.redflag.info

[29] See, for example, European Commission guides for three sectors (employment and recruitment, ICT and oil and gas) that highlight the very different kinds of human rights issues relevant to different sectors. http://ec.europa.eu/enterprise/policies/sustainable-business/corporate-social-responsibility/human-rights/

[30] The OECD Guidelines Commentary indicates that context and severity should be the considerations. OECD Guidelines for Multinational Enterprises, Chapter IV, Commentary, para. 40. The UN Guiding Principles themselves indicate that context and types of operations, products or services should be used in the prioritisation process. UN Guiding Principles, II (B) (16), Commentary.

number of tools to exercise their influence: shareholder proposals, engagement with management and the threat of divestment, for example. PRI investors and other investor platforms come together for collaborative engagements,[31] shareholder proposals on human rights are on the rise,[32] and public statements of disinvestment by the Norwegian pension fund are used by other investors to guide investment choices.

If investors have sufficient holdings to control or direct a company's actions, it should exercise its control to ensure the company puts in place appropriate management controls to prevent human rights abuse or, if abuses are flagged, to stop such actions, prevent further harm and remedy the harm. It should not cause harm which might be the case, for example, if imposing a shareholder resolution that requires the company to increase production in such a way that the only option is to impose working conditions that violate human rights standards or by directing the company to enter into high-risk operating contexts without taking any human rights advice or precautions to reduce the risk of being involved in human rights harms.

In the case where investors are minority shareholders in a company, and therefore not in a position to direct or control, they nonetheless remain directly linked to a company's human rights abuses through their share ownership and therefore retain a responsibility to respect human rights with respect to their investment. What is expected in these circumstances is that, as shareholders, investors exercise their leverage to try to persuade the company in their portfolio to take action to address human rights issues. In other words, minority shareholders are not expected to 'fix' the situation themselves but rather to use what leverage they have as owners to persuade the company to respect human rights. Although minority shareholders may need to exercise more creativity to obtain and exercise leverage than majority shareholders, leverage is not a mathematical calculation that automatically equates to the percentage of ownership. Leverage to persuade investee companies to take action can be increased using a range of contractual and non-contractual techniques and exercised alone or together with others, and over a period of time and through different settings.[33]

The last step in the human rights due diligence process is communication or the 'showing' part of 'knowing and showing' on managing human rights issues.[34]

---

[31] See PRI, collaborative engagements, http://www.unpri.org/areas-of-work/clearinghouse/

[32] Raz Godelnik, Shareholder Resolutions Receive Record Levels of Support in 2011, 17 August 2011 http://www.triplepundit.com/2011/08/shareholder-resolutions-2011/

[33] See: The Norwegian National Contact Point for the OECD Guidelines for Multinational Enterprises, Final Statement, Complaint from Lok Shakti Abhiyan, Korean Transnational Corporations Watch, Fair Green and Global Alliance and Forum for Environment and Development v Posco (South Korea), ABP/APG (Netherlands) and NBIM (Norway), 27 May 2013, http://oecdwatch.org/cases/Case_262.

[34] Professor John Ruggie, the UN Special Representative on Business and Human Rights, who led the development of the UN Protect, Respect and Remedy Framework and the UN Guiding Principles on Business and Human Rights, coined the phrase 'knowing and showing' to capture the essence of the human rights due diligence process.

Communication can play many important roles, particularly when investors join together to send clear messages to companies about the importance they attach to respect for human rights. Such a clear market signal, particularly when accompanied by definitive steps such as further investment or disinvestment as appropriate, puts an investor's 'money where their mouth is'.

The general lack of transparency in the investment industry is coming under the spotlight. The Norwegian NCP case against NBIM reviewed the sovereign wealth fund's management system in detail against the OECD Guidelines human rights requirements. The NCP case highlighted the increasing interest and expectations of more transparency about how investors are exercising their own responsibility to respect human rights. Investors have long pushed for transparency from the companies they invest in; the spotlight is now turning on investors. They may increasingly have mandatory reporting duties covering their approach to non-financial risks under reporting legislation. Investors who are PRI members are required to publicly report against standardised indicators from October 2013. Given the widespread attention to the NBIM case in the press,[35] the increasing number of cases citing the human rights chapter under the OECD Guidelines and the expanding focus on the financial sector and human rights generally, there is likely to be further focus on investors' human rights management systems.

Finally, what is particularly new in the UN Guiding Principles approach is the emphasis on righting any wrongs specifically by providing remedies for human rights harms done. Setting up operational level grievance mechanisms can be an effective means of enabling accessible, local and timely access at the company level to a process for resolving complaints for employees and communities affected by a company's actions. Such grievance mechanisms provide a channel for those directly affected to raise concerns and allow grievances to be addressed early and directly, potentially preventing the exacerbation of harms and the escalation of grievances.[36]

Where investors cause or contribute to a portfolio company's actions that result in negative human rights impacts, they should equally be active in working with the company to provide remedies for the existing harms and prevent future harms. In the more likely scenario where the investor is a minority shareholder, it is expected that the investor use its leverage to persuade its portfolio company to provide

---

[35] Richard Milne, Nordic Correspondent, 'Norway's oil fund urged to boost ethical credentials', Financial Times, Aug 8, 2013. http://www.ft.com/intl/cms/s/0/735865bc-ef07-11e2-9269-00144feabdc0.html?siteedition=intl#axzz2df47Caai

[36] UN Guiding Principle 31 sets forth criteria for the effectiveness of such nonjudicial grievance mechanisms that provide relevant guidance for investors to assess whether companies are addressing grievances appropriately.

remedies and to set up a grievance mechanism to prevent and hear future grievances. There have already been many circumstances of investors prompting portfolio companies to take just such steps, where the company's actions have prompted such a level of grievance as to threaten the profitability of operations.[37]

5 What Should Investors Expect from the Companies in Which They Invest?

In addition to getting their own house in order, investors will want to know how well the companies they invest in are also prepared to address and manage human rights as such investments are the main source of their operational risk. The same principles and steps set out above apply equally to the investee company: use a systematic and forward-looking approach to focus on preventing human rights impacts in the first place. To do so, companies need both the capacity to manage and an understanding of and expertise to deal with the social landscape their operations are likely to encounter.

Environmental management systems are by now a well-accepted approach to identifying and managing environmental issues. The same is now demanded for human rights—companies are expected to put in place or integrate into existing enterprise risk management systems the policies, capacities, resources and expertise to identify and manage human rights issues. While an enterprise risk management system typically focuses on risks to the company, a management system to deal with human rights issues should focus on identifying and managing the risks the company creates for others and their human rights—its workers, the surrounding community and its customers. Increasingly, the two types of risks are intertwined—serious risks the company creates through its operations or its relationships create risks for the company itself. This is a core source of the 'business case' for human rights.

The UN Guiding Principles provide a useful benchmark for investors to understand whether the companies they invest in have the appropriate commitment, management and systems in place to address human rights issues.[38] For example, the existence of a policy commitment on human rights helps investors differentiate between companies that publicly acknowledge that they may have human rights impacts and those that do not. Companies that carry out human rights due diligence

---

[37] See Novethic, 'Controversial Companies: Do Investor Blacklists Make a Difference?', June 2013, www.novethic.fr/novethic/.../2013_controversial_companies_study.pdf or GMIRatings, CSR Concerns at Vedanta Resources, Sept 10, 2010, http://www3.gmiratings.com/home/2010/09/csr-concerns-at-vedanta-resources/

[38] For more explanation of the application of the UN Guiding Principles on Business and Human Rights and their relevance for investors, see Institute for Human Rights and Business, 'Investing the Rights Way: A Guide for Investors on Business and Human Rights'. http://www.ihrb.org/publications/reports/investing-the-rights-way.html

demonstrate that they are taking active steps to determine existing and potential human rights risks to people and the related reputational, financial and operational risks to the company.

6   Where to Go from Here?

This chapter has laid out the kind of systemic approach to managing human rights that provides a thorough and rational approach to managing risks, builds on familiar approaches to measuring and managing other types of non-financial issues material to business and is based on well-developed international law and globally accepted moral principles. It has also highlighted the attention already given by some investors to particular human rights topics—child rights, labour issues in supply chains, water use and investments in Sudan, to name just a few.

ESG service providers are increasing attention to human rights as a routine part of their research. All these various strands contribute to building experience and expertise in assessing and managing human rights issues as part of investment decision-making and management and build a stronger basis to integrate human rights considerations into a wider range of products.

With the UN Guiding Principles, investors have a set of benchmarks to understand whether companies they invest in are putting the management systems in place to take a systematic approach to human rights. What is currently lacking is a clear set of benchmarks around human rights outcomes that would be key to the content of human rights and thereby provide a clearer measure of whether the company is actually reducing its negative impacts on human rights and augmenting its positive impacts.[39]

Such a benchmark would give investors a quick way of understanding relative human rights performance among companies. More and better data can help companies and investors benchmark company performance with the goal of improving performance. Recognising the challenge of quantifying core concepts such as human dignity that are at the heart of international human rights standards, there are nonetheless many promising approaches inside and outside the human rights field that could be built on to bring human rights considerations further into the core of ESG quantitative methodology.

Human rights do not need to be nor can be entirely reduced to numbers—other ESG benchmarks are based on a useful combination of qualitative and quantitative indicators where appropriate. This will be an important next step in a progression towards solidifying consistent attention to human rights as a core part of the S in ESG.

---

[39] See Corporate Human Rights Benchmark, http://business-humanrights.org/en/corporate-human-rights-benchmark

Another logical next step involves identifying systemic human rights risks inherent in specific assets classes that may create material risk across the whole class. This is not a new concept for investors but is new when applied to considering human rights issues. For example, in the environmental area, the concept of 'stranded assets' is now being applied to a whole group of assets—oil and gas. The appellation highlights the longer-term risk that these environmentally unsustainable assets may become so heavily regulated as to become unviable and therefore worthless as a longer-term investment.[40] The push to internalise externalities that began with internalising environmental costs is now rightly expanded to consider a broader set of externalised costs imposed on society. As a recent article in the financial markets section of the Financial Times noted, 'privatisation of profits and socialisation of costs is increasingly unacceptable to the public'.[41]

There are human rights risks—and opportunities—similarly inherent in particular asset classes that investors, analysts and service providers will want to explore with a view to long-term profitability across their portfolios:

- For real estate investments in emerging markets, investors will need to consider more carefully the risks around their key asset: land. Outside of developed markets, land titling and land acquisition are often characterised by legal uncertainty at best or lack of law altogether. For example, throughout sub-Saharan Africa, it is estimated that only 2–10 % of land is officially titled, and usually in urban settings.[42] This raises questions about the legality and human rights risks surrounding acquisition of real estate in Africa. Large-scale land acquisitions are now under the spotlight from a wide range of players: governments, international organisations, civil society and increasingly business and investors[43] themselves. While attention began with large-scale land purchases often by sovereign wealth funds, inevitably, questions are being asked about land acquisition more generally in emerging markets, focused on ensuring that local inhabitants are not squeezed off their lands without some measure of due process and compensation, even in the absence of legal title. Where governments take

---

[40] See, for example, Smith School of Enterprise and the Environment, University of Oxford, Programme on Stranded Assets, http://www.smithschool.ox.ac.uk/research/stranded-assets/

[41] Jack McGinn, 'Green bookkeeping shows real business costs', Financial Times, Financial Markets Supplement, 24 June 2013. The article highlighted the move by Puma to account for its environmental costs—145 million euros of environmental damage compared to its 202 million euros of net profit, noting that if the true costs of its environmental damage were expensed, its recognised earnings would fall by more than two-thirds.

[42] Most titled properties are in cities and towns, which account for less than one per cent of the land area of sub-Saharan Africa; only one-third to one-quarter of Kenya's land is subject to formal title. Rights and Resources, Briefs on Reviewing the Fate of Customary Tenure in Africa (2012). www.rightsandresources.org/documents/files/doc_4699.pdf

[43] The World Bank works on large-scale land acquisitions, http://www.worldbank.org/en/news/press-release/2013/04/08/world-bank-group-access-to-land-is-critical-for-the-poor, PRI, Principles for Responsible Investment in Farmland, http://www.unpri.org/areas-of-work/implementation-support/the-principles-for-responsible-investment-in-farmland/

advantage of lacunae in their own legal regimes to forcibly evict residents from their land, the focus and protests are increasingly turning on the companies that have profited from accepting such lands without appropriate due diligence and consideration of the circumstances behind their licences.[44] This increased attention to the details and equity of land acquisition in emerging markets can create risks right across the entire asset class.

- Infrastructure funds face the same land risks and more, as infrastructure projects typically create a much wider range of risks beyond land acquisition. More questions are being asked about the scope and depth of what is covered in the cost-benefit analysis that underpins the economics of these sometimes vast projects with a growing recognition that the cost calculations must include the wider environmental and social costs that accompany the projects.[45] Addressing access to public infrastructure for the most vulnerable and impacts on food and water are all human rights issues that are relevant to and given increasing attention in connection with large infrastructure projects.[46] The water sector is very familiar with the long-term discussions around the right to water and the power of those concerns to materially affect, and even shut down, water privatisation projects.
- Commodities, particularly agricultural commodities, raise issues of the rights to food, water and health as well as the same land issues identified above. The 2008 food crisis highlighted the role of the financialisation of food commodities in contributing to the crisis.[47] Since then, there has been consistent pressure to eliminate harmful speculation such as through index commodity funds, including from G20 governments.[48] Several financial institutions have withdrawn from trading in food commodities.[49]

---

[44] See, for example, the land matrix which records land acquisitions, http://www.commercialpressuresonland.org/land-matrix and the Land Rights and the Rush for Land: Findings of the Global Commercial Pressures on Land Research Project, http://pubs.iied.org/X00053.html?a=Lorenzo%20Cotula

[45] See, for example, Nicholas Hildyard, 'More than Bricks and Mortar, Infrastructure-as-asset-class: Financing Development or developing finance? A critical look at private equity infrastructure funds', 2012. At: http://www.thecornerhouse.org.uk/resource/more-bricks-and-mortar

[46] See, for example, M. Wachenfeld (2011), 'The Hidden Impact of Large Infrastructure Projects on Children', http://www.theguardian.com/sustainable-business/children-large-infrastructure-hon eypot-effect

[47] See the UN Special Rapporteur on the Right to Food, http://www.srfood.org/en/speculation

[48] Cannes Summit Final Declaration: 'Building our common future: Renewed collective action for the benefit of all', November 2011. http://www.g20civil.com/documents/Cannes_Declaration_4_November_2011.pdf; and UNCTAD, Price formation in financialized commodity markets, June 2011. http://unctad.org/ en/Docs/gds20111_en.pdf; and Institute for Agriculture and Trade Policy, More evidence on speculators and food prices, June 2011. At: http://www.iatp.org/blog/201106/more-evidence-on-speculators-and-food-prices

[49] See: Farms and Funds—Investment Funds in the Global Land Rush, http://pubs.iied.org/17121IIED.html?a=Lorenzo%20Cotula

- Sovereign credit ratings may provide an example where attention to human rights issues provides a positive incentive to the asset class rather than a negative one. Few governments would argue against the right to education, yet even in developed countries, governments struggle to extend that right to their increasingly diverse populations. It is exactly this kind of measure, building a nation's full complement of human capital, that is crucial to the long-term prospects for a nation that are—or should be—figured into more positive sovereign credit ratings. A government's ability to deliver on[50] other economic and social rights, such as health care and stable labour markets that are based on respect for worker's rights, figure into prospects for stability and growth.

Developing these approaches would help build the experience and expertise to take on the challenge of more systematically integrating human rights considerations into a wider range of products that are interposed between a shareholder and their investment, such as indices. On an even longer-term basis is the more profound and complex issue of addressing the financialisation of many sectors. Just at the time when the business and human rights movement developed a strong emphasis on accountability to individuals whose human rights have been abused, the financialisation of many sectors has been moving the world in the opposite direction where accountability of a particular company for the impact of operations becomes harder and harder to pin down. How to reconcile these approaches will require innovative thinking.

References

Buxton, A., Campanale, M., Cotula, L. (2012). *Farms and funds—Investment funds in the global land rush*. http://pubs.iied.org/17121IIED.html?a=Lorenzo%20Cotula

Cotula, L. (2012). *Rush for land: Findings of the global commercial pressures on land research project*. http://pubs.iied.org/X00053.html?a=Lorenzo%20Cotula

European Commission. (2012). *Sector guides on implementing the UN guiding principles on business and human rights (for the employment and recruitment, ICT and oil and gas sectors)*. http://ec.europa.eu/enterprise/policies/sustainable-business/corporate-social-responsibility/human-rights/

G20 (2011). Cannes summit final declaration: *Building our common future: Renewed collective action for the benefit of all*, November 2011. http://www.g20civil.com/documents/Cannes_Declaration_4_November_2011.pdf

GMIRatings (2010). *CSR concerns at Vedanta resources*, Sept 10, 2010. http://www3.gmiratings.com/home/2010/09/csr-concerns-at-vedanta-resources/

Godelnik, R. (2011). *Shareholder resolutions receive record levels of support in 2011*, 17 Aug 2011. http://www.triplepundit.com/2011/08/shareholder-resolutions-2011/

Hildyard, N. (2012). *More than bricks and mortar, infrastructure-as-asset-class: Financing development or developing finance? A critical look at private equity infrastructure funds*. http://www.thecornerhouse.org.uk/resource/more-bricks-and-mortar

---

[50] In human rights terminology, this is referred to as 'respecting, protecting and fulfilling' human rights.

Institute for Agriculture and Trade Policy (2011). *More evidence on speculators and food prices*, http://www.iatp.org/blog/201106/more-evidence-on-speculators-and-food-prices

Institute for Human Rights and Business (2013). *Investing the Rights Way: A Guide for Investors on Business and Human Rights*. http://www.ihrb.org/publications/reports/investing-the-rights-way.html

Institute for Human Rights and Business and the Global Business Initiative on Human Rights (2012). *State of Play: The Corporate Responsibility to Respect Human Rights in Business Relationships*. http://www.ihrb.org/publications/reports/state-of-play.html

International Bar Association, *Interview with Professor John Ruggie, Special Representative of the UN Secretary-General on business and human rights*—transcript. http://www.ibanet.org/Article/Detail.aspx?ArticleUid=4b5233cb-f4b9-4fcd-9779-77e7e85e4d83

International Standards Organisation (2010). *Guidance on social responsibility*. http://www.iso.org/iso/home/standards/iso26000.htm

NEI Investments (2011). *Letter to UN working group on human rights and transnational corporations and other business enterprises*. http://www.google.be/url?sa=t&rct=j&q=&esrc=s&source=web&cd=1&ved=0CDAQFjAA&url=http%3A%2F%2Fwww.ohchr.org%2FDocuments%2FIssues%2FTransCorporations%2FSubmissions%2FBusiness%2FNEIInvestments.pdf&ei=xTubUu-NFYShyQPq34GAAw&usg=AFQjCNFIKDuKWq5fOKgJsnPuMnhtz71gSA&bvm=bv.57155469,d.bGQ

McGinn, J. (2013). Green bookkeeping shows hidden costs of business as usual, *Financial Times*, Financial Markets Supplement, 24 June 2013. http://www.ft.com/intl/cms/s/0/0b708b78-d751-11e2-a26a-00144feab7de.html?siteedition=intl#axzz2mElfK99z

Milne, R. (2013). Norway's oil fund urged to boost ethical credentials, *Financial Times*. http://www.ft.com/intl/cms/s/0/735865bc-ef07-11e2-9269-00144feabdc0.html?siteedition=intl#axzz2df47Caai

Norwegian National Contact Point for the OECD Guidelines for Multinational Enterprises (2013). *Final statement, complaint from Lok Shakti Abhiyan, Korean Transnational Corporations Watch, Fair Green and Global Alliance and Forum for Environment and Development v Posco (South Korea), ABP/APG (Netherlands) and NBIM (Norway)*, 27 May 2013. http://oecdwatch.org/cases/Case_262

Novethic (2013). *Controversial companies: Do investor blacklists make a difference?*. www.novethic.fr/novethic/. . ./2013_controversial_companies_study.pdf

Organisation for Economic Cooperation and Development (2011). *Guidelines on Multinational Enterprises*. http://mneguidelines.oecd.org/text/

Principles for Responsible Investment *Annual Report 2011, 2012*

Principles for Responsible Investment *Annual Report on Progress 2011*

Principles for Responsible Investment in Farmland. http://www.unpri.org/areas-of-work/implementation-support/the-principles-for-responsible-investment-in-farmland/

Red flags—Liability risks for companies operating in high risk zones. www.redflag.info

Rights and Resources (2012). *Briefs on reviewing the fate of customary tenure in Africa*. www.rightsandresources.org/documents/files/doc_4699.pdf

Smith School of Enterprise and the Environment, University of Oxford, Programme on Stranded Assets. http://www.smithschool.ox.ac.uk/research/stranded-assets/

Sullivan, R., Vines Fiestas, H. (2013). *How institutional investors can tackle poverty and development*. http://www.ethicalcorp.com/print/36858?utm_source=http%3A%2F%2Fuk.ethicalcorp

Umlas, E. (2009). *Human rights and SRI in North America: An overview*. www.reports-and-materials.org/Umlas-Human-Rights-and-SRI-Jan-2009

UN Special Rapporteur on the Right to Food. http://www.srfood.org/en/speculation

UNCTAD, *Price formation in financialized commodity markets*, June 2011. http://unctad.org/en/Docs/gds20111_en.pdf

Universal Declaration of Human Rights (1948). http://www.ohchr.org/EN/ProfessionalInterest/Pages/UniversalHumanRightsInstruments.aspx

Wachenfeld, M. (2011). *The hidden impact of large infrastructure projects on children*. http://www.theguardian.com/sustainable-business/children-large-infrastructure-honeypot-effect

World Bank, *Work on large scale land acquisitions*, http://www.worldbank.org/en/news/press-release/2013/04/08/world-bank-group-access-to-land-is-critical-for-the-poor

The Social Reform of Banking

Cynthia A. Williams and John M. Conley

> *The idea that there is something called 'the economy' that is separable from the welfare of society and its citizens is silly.*
> Prof. John Kay, *Financial Times*, 11 (May 30, 2012)
> *The economic power in the hands of the few persons who control a giant corporation is a tremendous force which can harm or benefit a multitude of individuals, affect whole districts, shift the currents of trade, bring ruin to one community and prosperity to another. The organizations which they control have passed far beyond the realm of private enterprise—they have become more nearly social institutions.*
> Adolf A. Berle, Jr. & Gardiner C. Means, *The Modern Corporation and Private Property*, 46 (Harcourt, Brace & World 1967; orig. 1932).

Abstract Recent developments in banking, including high-profile prosecutions for illegal activities, suggest further regulatory interventions on both sides of the Atlantic. Yet the structure of much banking regulation requires banks to make good faith determinations of the type of risks to which their loans give rise—determinations that can be and, in some cases have been, manipulated. Rather than evaluating specific regulatory interventions, this chapter will focus on the culture within financial institutions themselves, particularly the global entities that are explicitly or implicitly too big to fail, and on approaches to regulation that might affect and be affected by that culture. Our analysis is informed by the perspectives of anthropology, organizational and social psychology, and new governance regulatory theory.

C.A. Williams (✉)
University of Illinois College of Law, Champaign, IL, USA
e-mail: CWilliams@osgoode.yorku.ca

J.M. Conley
University of North Carolina College of Law, Chapel Hill, NC, USA
e-mail: jmconley@email.unc.edu

© Springer International Publishing Switzerland 2015
K. Wendt (ed.), *Responsible Investment Banking*, CSR, Sustainability, Ethics & Governance, DOI 10.1007/978-3-319-10311-2_14

1 Introduction

When the great and the good gathered to discuss the state of the world economy at the World Economic Forum in Davos in January of 2011, the prevailing mood ranged from optimistic to exuberant. The apocalypse had been averted and it seemed that the financial system and the world economy were both recovering. But there was an ant at the picnic: Barrie Wilkinson, an analyst from the international consulting firm Oliver Wyman, whom a Bloomberg report dubbed the "Loneliest Man in Davos" (Harper 2011). Wilkinson (whose lower-rung credentials kept him out of the celebratory elite events) had written a report for his company that concluded:

> For all the rhetoric about a new financial order, and all the improvements made or planned, many of the old risks remain. The basic regulatory framework—of bank debtor guarantees and regulatory bank capital and liquidity minima (that is, of risk subsidies and compensatory risk taxes)—has been maintained albeit with tweaked parameters. And within this system, bank shareholders, bondholders and executives still have incentives that might herd them towards excessive risk taking" (Oliver 2011).

In its analysis, the Oliver Wyman report emphasized a number of fundamental problems that it argued had not been solved. A particular concern was that shareholders' unwillingness to accept the lower returns on equity that higher capital requirements would produce would either lead banks to shift resources into commodities or emerging markets with expectations of higher returns, thus fueling new asset bubbles, or cause banks to continue to shift banking functions into the less-regulated interstices of the shadow banking system.

By today, however, especially after a particularly scandal-plagued summer of 2012, that analysis seems understated. For not only is it now clear that the old risks remain, it is becoming increasingly clear that there are additional, deeper problems to confront. Thus, in rapid succession came public charges that traders at up to 16 of the too-big-to-fail global banks, including Barclays, Citigroup, UBS, and HSBC, had engaged for at least 5 years in global manipulation of the London interbank offered rate, or Libor, which is referenced in trillions of dollars of credit instruments (Eaglesham and Enrich 2012); that HSBC subsidiaries had been knowingly laundering money for drug cartels, terrorists, and pariah states for over a decade (U.S. Senate 2012); that the vaunted risk mitigation systems at JPMorgan Chase had been insufficient to prevent US$5.8 billion worth of surprise losses in synthetic derivatives hedging (Silver-Greenberg 2007); that between US$21 trillion and US$30 trillion had been stashed away in tax havens by the global super-elite, which could not have happened without banks' assistance (with UBS, Credit Suisse, and Goldman Sachs alleged to have been centrally involved) (Henry 2012); and that Standard Chartered had been engaged in a scheme to hide about 60,000 transactions involving US$250 billion with Iranian citizens and government officials, in violations of long-standing American sanctions (Braithwaite and Goff 2012).

If even some of these charges are true, people in elite, global, too-big-to-fail banking entities have harbored and assisted global criminal conspiracies and enabled tax evasion on a staggering scale, even as their core functions continue to have the potential to produce unexpected, outsized financial risk. So damaging have these revelations been that the banking public relations machine, led until recently by JPMorgan's Jamie Dimon, has been temporarily knocked off stride. Opinions are being expressed on both sides of the Atlantic that it is time to reinstate Glass–Steagall's separation of commercial and investment banking (Zingales 2012); that the Volcker Rule limiting proprietary trading by banks and the Vickers Commission's "ring-fencing" of retail banking are insufficient Jenkins 2012a); that investment banks should be once again required to be private partnerships (see Jenkins 2012b); that it is time to look more carefully at alternative banking systems, such as coops and ethical banks (Jenkins 2012b); and that the too-big-to-fail banks need to be broken up (Mallaby 2012). That last opinion was, astonishingly enough, publicly expressed in late July of 2012 by Sandy Weill, architect of the Citigroup series of mergers that was the coup-de-grace to Glass–Steagall in 1999, which ushered in today's era of too-big-to-fail ("TBTF") universal banks (Braithwaite and Nasiripour 2012).

These developments portend further regulatory interventions to reform finance, on both sides of the Atlantic. Yet, given market participants' propensity to engage in regulatory arbitrage, one can feel a bit pessimistic about the ability of regulation alone to wring excessive leverage, fragility, and risk out of the system. Indeed, as this paper is being written, the New York Times is reporting on a new fund, called the Ovid Regulatory Capital Relief Fund, which is investing in "capital relief trades" or "regulatory capital trades," which allow banks to shift assets off their books by buying credit default swaps being sold by the Fund (Craig 2013). Even without regulatory arbitrage, the risk-adjusted capital adequacy requirements at the core of Basel II and III allow banks to make good faith determinations of the kinds of risks to which their loans give rise. There is concern that these determinations can be, and in some cases have been, manipulated. And even if the banks do act in good faith, the leverage ratio of Basel III, requiring equity of at least 3 % of total assets, will not go into effect until January 1, 2019, and has already been called "outrageously low" by prominent academic critics (Admati and Hellwig 2013: 177).

Regulatory interventions may well be necessary, but they are not likely to be sufficient. Therefore, rather than evaluating specific regulatory proposals that are now on the table, this paper will focus instead on another piece of the reform puzzle: the culture within the financial institutions themselves, particularly the global entities that are explicitly or implicitly TBTF, and will explore approaches to regulation that might affect that culture. We do so with some trepidation, not only because it is not obvious at the outset how deeply firm cultures can be influenced by outside factors such as regulation but also because "culture" as the problem within financial firms seems to be something of a reformist fad.

In the wake of the LIBOR scandal, the UK Parliament has established a Parliamentary Commission on Banking Standards that is investigating "professional standards and culture in the UK banking industry." 2013 started with the CEO of UBS, Andrea Orcel, telling the Commission that UBS was overhauling its culture and "was serious about putting integrity over profit" (Jenkins and Saigol 2013: 1). This announcement was prompted by the role of UBS in LIBOR manipulation

(18 employees involved have been fired and an additional 40 others disciplined); its failures in risk oversight, leading to losses of US$38 billion in credit derivatives in 2008 and US$2.3 billion from rogue trader Kweku Adoboli; and its payment of a US$780 million fine to US authorities for its role in assisting tax evasion by some of its wealthy clients (Jenkins and Saigol 2013). UBS was followed by Barclays, which was centrally implicated in both LIBOR manipulation and insurance mis-selling in the UK (Augar 2013). Bob Diamond lost his job as CEO over those scandals, and the new CEO, Antony Jenkins, quickly acted to set a more ethical tone at the top, writing a "stern e-mail" to all employees in an effort that one editorial writer described as a "strong start to reforming the bank's culture," while recognizing that "as Barclay's recent history shows, the problem with values statements is making them stick." Barclays then engaged Anthony Salz to do an independent review of its business practices and published the results. That review, which emphasized that the problems "faced at Barclays were to some extent industry problems—though Barclays should take no comfort from this," included both a chapter on Barclay's culture and an Appendix on what culture is and how it can go wrong (Salz Review).

Yet firm "culture" is more than this season's buzzword, and we think is an important factor in either undermining or enhancing the efficacy of regulation. In considering how regulation might affect firm culture, this article is informed by the perspectives of anthropology, organizational and social psychology, and new governance regulatory theory. Anthropologists now study corporate culture much as they used to study cultures of far-flung Pacific Islands: by participant observation and fine-grained qualitative analysis. Those observations have started to develop a picture of what life is like inside Wall Street or City institutions. The perspective from organizational psychology on which we rely is nicely summarized Jonathan Haidt: "Moral systems are interlocking sets of values, virtues, practices, identities, institutions, technologies, and evolved psychological mechanisms that work together to suppress or regulate self-interest and make cooperative societies possible" (Haidt 2007). As will be discussed below, a number of theories in social psychology can be used to develop insights into regulatory approaches that might better harness cooperative, pro-social orientations of the people within banking, that is, to affect their "values, virtues, practices, [and] identities." If these approaches were combined with structural reforms of banking, and changes in accounting to reinforce positive psychological mechanisms, there might be some forward progress toward finance that more fully advances social welfare.

2   The Anthropology of Corporate Culture

"Corporate culture" has become a ubiquitous term, a label for just about everything on the "soft" side of business analysis. When something cannot be explained by numbers, it is attributed to corporate culture. In this sense, the term has come to refer to established ways of doing something within a company, or a part of a company, that seem driven by tradition, habit, group psychology, or history. Such cultural ways of doing things may or may not be consistent with the practices that economic rationality would seem to dictate. In fact, sometimes the term is applied specifically to practices that seem to contradict economic prescriptions, as when business people speak of "norms" in opposition to quantifiable explanations for behavior.

But this is not to say that corporate culture is not real. The anthropological study of corporations as cultural entities has a substantial and growing pedigree. To an anthropologist, culture is the set of shared norms, beliefs, and practices that define a social group's way of life, the mental map that guides individual members of the group through the otherwise baffling complexity of daily life. In the economic sphere, anthropologists "have drawn attention to the practices, rituals, beliefs, and political motivations of the people who self-consciously create and maintain the institutions that engender the market" (Riles 2011: 14). To contemporary anthropologists, culture is more of a toolkit, a network of resources, than a body of deterministic rules or constraints. A group of people is said to share a cultural perspective when their responses to stimuli—whether an eclipse of the sun or an opportunity to participate in a shady financial transaction—draw on similar resources and follow roughly similar patterns. Finally, the shared beliefs and practices that identify a culture are usually in a state of negotiation, contestation, and resistance. Change, or at least the prospect of change, is a part of the cultural status quo.

A few examples will illustrate the anthropological approach to business culture. All involve ethnography, anthropology's basic method. It employs participant observation, "a sustained and engaged form of study based on relations of trust with one's subjects, often for long periods of time" (Riles 2011: 11). The ethnographer traditionally has lived among the subjects, observing while participating in their daily lives, and conducting wide-ranging interviews, all in an effort to see the world through their eyes. The method is intensive, fine-grained, qualitative, and unapologetically interpretive, and its ultimate goal is "thick description" rather than grand explanatory theory, what Clifford Geertz called an "ant's eye view" as opposed to a "bird's eye view" (Geertz 1973: 23). As these examples illustrate, while ethnography's roots lie in the study of Pacific islands, African tribal communities, and other small-scale societies, it has proven adaptable to the contemporary business world.

One of us (Conley) participated in an early exercise in financial anthropology, a study of large pension funds as institutional investors (O'Barr and Conley 1992). The study revealed that even in these multi-billion dollar entities, decisions were more driven by such factors as company traditions, the expressed values of leaders, and even the corporate equivalent of "creation myths" than by rigorous financial analysis. In fact, finance itself emerged as a kind of cultural practice that varied from setting to setting, with financial analysis as one of its constituent rituals.

More recently, Karen Ho has examined the day-to-day workplace culture of Wall Street firms, with a particular focus on downsizing and restructuring (Ho 2009a). Ho began pursuing the topic as an employee of Bankers Trust, where, 6 months into her tenure, she was "canned" (Ho 2009a: 15). She was then called back to work as a "collaborator" or "fellow axe man" in another downsizing project, and ultimately followed up this unusual participant observation with a more formal interview study (Ho 2009a: 16). She became intrigued with what she calls "the cultural production of liquidation" (Ho 2009a: 4), in particular the ways in which Wall Street culture creates models for corporate restructuring that are exported to the broader economy. The larger point is that the intensive, ant's eye examination of an ostensibly high-level economic phenomenon like "corporate restructuring" can reveal deeper and different realities, including the ways in which such practices are propagated into the broader economy. Ho's work is directly relevant to our topic, and we discuss it in more detail in Sect. 3.1.

A similar focus on mundane, taken-for-granted details is central to Annelise Riles's study of the use of collateral in international finance. As Riles aptly puts it, "[t]he starting premise of an anthropological approach is that markets are not abstract machines to be reduced to a few equations or theorems, but messy contexts, full of contradictory forces and elements, actors, languages, institutions, ways of living and knowing" (Riles 2011: 11). To a lawyer or economist studying markets, "collateral" will be a well-defined technical detail that everyone is assumed to understand. But for Riles, it becomes a problem that is itself worthy of investigation, one of "a set of routinized but highly compartmentalized knowledge practices" that actually comprise global financial governance (Riles 2011: 10). Our argument here is similar: to understand recent banking scandals, and to propose reforms that have a chance to succeed, one must understand—from the "ant's eye-view"—the "messy contexts, full of contradictory forces and elements." That is, one must understand banking culture and use that understanding to advantage in improving banks' institutional behavior.

3   Challenges from the Current State of Financial Institution Culture

There are a number of influences within global, complex, TBTF financial institutions that can normalize behavior that has the potential to create excessive social risk. All are cultural in nature, or at least have a strong cultural component. First is the very notion of too big to fail, and the implicit and explicit government guarantees that notion implies. Second is the atmosphere of insecurity and market-driven churning among employees. And third is the structure of compensation, particularly within the investment banking subculture.

3.1   The "Too Big to Fail" Problem

Five general concerns can be identified with continuing to permit TBTF banks to exist. First is the serious moral hazard: actors within TBTF entities may be encouraged to take on excessive risk, particularly using high levels of leverage and relaxed credit standards, with the expectation of government bailouts (Admati and Hellwig 2013; Wilmarth 2011). Second, given the expectation of government bailouts, credit rating agencies give TBTF entities higher credit scores than they would without that backstop, which distorts TBTF banking entities' cost of capital and thus leads to an unfair competitive advantage (Wilmarth 2011). This advantage, combined with the size of TBTF banks within the economy, then leads to the third problem, that of excessive political influence (Hirsh 2010). Fourth, the banks as a whole may become strategically reckless, seeking to "grow fast by expanding their borrowing without seeing their borrowing rates increase" because creditors "expect their investments to be safe because of the guarantees" (Admati and Hellwig 2013: 145). Fifth, there is a corrosive effect on social cohesion where perceptions become widespread that the financial system privatizes gains and socializes losses.

At the societal level, TBTF must be understood as a market failure; as such, it will not be solved by market mechanisms, and we have yet to see sufficient regulatory solutions. As an economic matter, TBTF banks may seem more profit-able than they actually are, benefiting as they do from subsidized funding (Admati and Hellwig 2013), which gives rise to allocative inefficiencies. Smaller (up to US$10 billion in assets) community banks, with superior loan quality, greater resilience during the financial crisis, and higher operating efficiencies, nonetheless find it difficult to compete for market share given the subsidies available to TBTF banks (Federal Reserve Bank of Dallas 2012). Within the TBTF banks, implicit and explicit government guarantees and subsidies have led to cultures that are prone to excessive risk-taking and speculation, to what the Salz Review described as a "winning at all costs" attitude with an atmosphere suffused with "rivalry, arro-gance, selfishness and a lack of humility and generosity" (Salz Review: 83).

3.2   A Culture of Insecurity

The second feature of life within global, TBTF financial institutions, particularly on their trading floors and in investment banking generally, is the volatility of employ-ment and the insecurity that can create, especially at lower and middle levels of employment. Karen Ho, an anthropologist, did field work on Wall Street by getting a job at an investment bank and then finding herself downsized. That experience allowed her both to observe and to participate in the brutal culture of employment that characterizes Wall Street, a culture that investment bankers have exported to corporate America through their efforts to sell their clients on serial acquisitions, divestment, reorganizations, mergers, and consolidations. As one of her informants put it, echoing the sentiments of many:

> I think that every single day you realize that your job could be gone the next day. You have a downturn in the market and they lay off hundreds of people or you have a downturn in just your desk's [particular product area] performance; all of sudden they need to lay off people. Your company decides they don't want to be in that product anymore; they lay off an entire department. I just think that's part of life here (Ho 2009b: 182).

Not only is employment volatile, but it is subject to daily accountability by the only metric that matters on Wall Street: how much money have you made for me lately? As one of Ho's informants put it: "I didn't realize just how short-sighted they were at that point. They are literally: it is all about today and it's whether you can make money today and if you can't make money today, you are out of there" (Ho 2009b: 182). Finally, these sackings are public: a flotilla of people from HR (human resources) march onto the floor with cardboard boxes and tap people who are losing their jobs on the shoulder—pack up and get out. Colleagues also receive a message: this could be you next time. Ultimately the environment is one of fear, insecurity, and potential humiliation. That environment has endured because of the possibility of great economic rewards for the winners, but with the consequence that survival at any cost becomes the dominating motivation for many participants.

3.3   Compensation Structures that Exalt Risk and Self-Interest

Much has been written about the problems of bankers' compensation. From a social risk perspective, the problem with executive compensation in banking arises from two factors. First, there has been a shift in banking from an "originate-and-hold" approach to lending to an "originate-to-distribute" model that relies on securitization (UK Treasury Committee 2008). In the latter approach, bank fees and bankers' performance-based compensation are increased by the volume of transactions. The shift to this approach has increased the cumulative risk in the global financial system, because the distribution of credit risk via securitization has undermined the banks' incentives to be as rigorous in credit evaluation as they would have been in the "boring" world of originate-and-hold banking (Bebchuk and Spamann 2010; Landskroner and Raviv 2009). The economic self-interest of bankers under this model—which lies in maximizing transactions and bank fees—thus directly conflicts with the goals of prudence and global systemic stability.

Within individual banks, these factors work in conjunction with the insecurity of employment to promote a "get it while the getting is good" mentality. This leads in turn to a frantic and unending search for deals and trades and volume of transactions. Since individual financial contribution—itself based largely on volume of transactions—is the "overwhelming determinant of discretionary bonuses" (Salz Review) within many TBTF financial institutions, a hypercompetitive, individualistic culture is an almost-inevitable result. In such an atmosphere, risk management and legal compliance can come to be seen as unnecessary grit slowing down deal flow.

Second, the sheer scale of bankers' compensation allows bankers (and the banks for which they work) to exercise a disproportionate influence in the political arena. This is particularly true in the United States, where legislative restraints on corporations' use of their funds for electioneering were declared unconstitutional by the United States Supreme Court in 2010 (*Citizens United* 2010). Even before that decision, as stated by the U.S. Financial Crisis Inquiry Commission, "[f]rom 1999 to 2008, the financial sector expended US\$2.7 billion in reported federal lobbying expenses; individuals and political action committees in the sector made more than US\$1 billion in campaign contributions" (Financial Crisis Inquiry Commission Report). A number of analyses of the influence of the finance industry on economic policy in the United States have recognized this as an increasingly serious problem, particularly as bankers' interests and financial contributions to campaigns constrain policy choices (Hacker and Pierson 2010; Johnson and Kwak 2010).

4 Organizational Psychology

In addition to these general conditions that foster a culture of risk, there are examples of more specialized units within banking that have demonstrated particularly pernicious behavior. One example is the Structured Capital Markets (SCM) group within Barclay's investment banking unit, which is being disbanded. The SCM group was established to develop and promote tax avoidance techniques for corporate clients. Although it endeavored to develop *legal* tax avoidance strategies, the Salz Review indicated that the group became increasingly aggressive about its work and hostile to tax authorities. The Guardian newspaper paints an extraordinary picture:

> Whistleblowers described to us a management style that depended on fear, summary sackings, ritual humiliations and group social events that outdid any 1980s fictional tales of macho banking excess.... On one occasion a secretary was said to have been fired for booking an executive a taxi that was a Volvo rather than an S class Mercedes... Team-building events included free-flowing champagne and cigars, poker games involving hundreds of thousands of pounds in bets and a "motivation" exercise in which an executive was strapped to a mock electric chair to the soundtrack of a rap song with the line "I hate you and I hope you die" (Lawrence 2013).

In a comprehensive review of the literature on behavioral ethics in organizations, Trevino, Weaver, and Reynolds suggest a number of reasons that such pathological work groups can develop (Trevino et al. 2006). First, research in accountancy has shown that managers and partners in public accounting firms "have lower moral reasoning scores than those at lower organizational levels in the firm" (Trevino et al. 2006). We can hypothesize that client-driven professions such as accounting, law, and finance will put pressure on individuals to identify more closely with clients, and thus minimize moral quandaries, as they take on more responsibility in the firm—particularly if such moral insensitivity is also consistent with the managers' financial self-interest. Second, while people's self-identity as moral agents and their cognitive evaluations of the morality of situations clearly have an effect on their behavior, so do organizational contexts. "Overt on-the-job pressures to act unethically clearly have an effect" (Trevino et al. 2006), as do unmet organizationally defined goals, especially where an individual employee is "just slightly removed from the achievement of a goal" (Trevino et al. 2006). Other contexts that can encourage unethical behavior include situations of "moral muteness" where practices and language within the firm, particularly among those with whom people work closely, do not recognize moral dilemmas. Finally, "organizational cultures and practices also can normalize unethical behavior" (Trevino et al. 2006). Trevino, Weaver, and Reynolds describe this process as "one of initial cooptation of newcomers, incremental increases in unethical behavior by the newcomer (leading to changes in attitude), and repeated moral compromises that similarly bring about ultimate attitude change" (Trevino et al. 2006).

But organizational and social psychology resists the view that such trajectories are inevitable. Although the notion of *homo economicus* has dominated social science theory in the past decades (Rupp and Williams 2011), in particular in law and in economics, a number of disciplines have come to embrace the view that it is not self-interest alone that drives human behavior (Cropanzano et al. 2005). The literature presents many examples of individuals acting against their own self-interest and instead acting in the name of norms (Fehr and Gächter 2002), cooperation (Bolton and Ockenfels 2000), fairness (Kahneman et al. 1986), empathy (see Batson 1995), and moral duty (Turillo et al. 2002). Thus, it is not illusory to suggest that banking cultures could be shaped to better advance social as well as individual goals, although admittedly the task is daunting. The social context for action must be structured to encourage other-regarding behavior, which social psychology suggests is possible.

Empirical and theoretical research in psychology shows three kinds of human motives for action: (1) instrumental motives, such as self-interest, which are based on the psychological need for control of one's life and environment; (2) relational motives, which are based on the need to belong to groups (such as families, firms, industries, and countries); and (3) moral motives, which are based on the need for a meaningful existence (Cropanzano et al. 2001). Research suggests that all three types of motives influence people at work as they react to multiple contextual factors, including the systems of power and influence within which they operate; the transparency of communications within the firm; the quality of relationships with peers and superiors; the opportunities for exercising autonomy, competence, and control; and the structures that enable a secure sense of attachment to and identification with the values of the firm. An influential psychological theory called self-determination theory (Deci and Ryan 1985) posits that the optimal human condition is one where individuals develop a sense of positive motivation and responsibility, and that the contextual factors that best promote this condition are autonomy, feelings of competence, and relatedness. This is hardly a description of the environment at a TBTF financial institution. Could it ever be so?

5 The Efficacy of Regulation as a Function of Psychological Fit

On the basis on the contextual factors that self-determination theory has identified as important for people's development of positive motivations and responsibility for their actions, we suggest that some aspects of "soft law" or "new governance" approaches (such as transnational private regulation) may lead to deeper engagement with the values and goals of any particular rule than will "hard law." One of us (Williams) has so argued in prior work with Deborah Rupp (Rupp and Williams 2011). Self-determination theory shows that external punishment and reward structures can thwart individuals' pursuit of activities for their intrinsic value, the so-called "crowding out" problem. Even if individuals perceive legal structures as just and agree with the moral foundation of a rule, if behaviors are narrowly regulated by threats of punishment or promises of rewards, such regulation can undermine the development of more psychologically-based motivations to conform fully to the spirit as well as the letter of the law. When regulation develops in principles-based fashion, with cooperative relationships between regulator and regulated becoming part of the regulatory environment, as in many new governance initiatives, the theory would suggest that values-based behaviors are more likely to evolve (Gunningham and Sinclair 2009).

This hypothesis about the potential efficacy of new governance is also based on another influential strand of research in organizational psychology, the justice and behavioral ethics research that emphasizes the multiple motives for human action (instrumental, relational and moral) described above. As Rupp and Williams (2011: 592) have argued previously, "when the regulatory context creates a state of shared values and mutual problem-solving among parties, then transformative change" may be possible. We turn next to an example in the banking context.

5.1 An Example of Social Regulation in Banking

In a less-publicized corner of global banking a different picture of bank social responsibility is emerging, an initiative that aims to mitigate the potentially negative social and environmental consequences of infrastructure development in politically unstable or environmentally fragile landscapes. The vehicle for doing this is a voluntary agreement among the major global banks called the Equator Principles ("EPs") (Conley and Williams 2011). The EPs create social and environmental standards for project finance. This sector is defined as the private financing of large, revenue-producing infrastructure projects constructed by private companies in the developing world. The project finance sector is vitally important because the decisions on whether, how, and on what terms infrastructure projects are undertaken in poorer countries can have tremendous economic, social, and environmental consequences.

There are also broader implications: because the sector is by definition both private and transnational, it has largely avoided meaningful regulation at either the national or public international level. Contrary to the expectation that the private protagonists would prefer to avoid any kind of regulation, something else has occurred: for a variety reasons, including risk and reputation management, the control of competition, the preemption of "hard" regulation, and even principled belief in corporate social responsibility, the global banks that are the leaders in project finance lending have agreed on an elaborate transnational private regulatory regime. The EPs commit the participants (the Equator Principles Financial Institutions, or EPFIs) to screening potential projects for social and environmental impact, rejecting those that fall short, and imposing ongoing and enforceable social and environmental standards on those projects that are financed. These social and environmental standards track those promulgated by the International Finance Corporation (IFC), the private-sector lending division of the World Bank Group.

The EPs were first promulgated in 2003, were initially revised in 2006, and revised again in 2011–2012. The latest revised version, EPs III, took effect on June 4, 2013. Since the EPs are taken directly from the IFC's Safeguard Policies and Performance Standards, the EPs are revised as the IFC revises its policies and standards. In the first two iterations, the EPs applied only to project finance as defined above. Project finance loans are nonrecourse, meaning that lenders are repaid only through the revenues generated by the project. So even if the project sponsor (the borrower) is consistently one of the world's most profitable companies, the lending banks face particularized financial risks from anything that might slow down or derail the project. As a result, the banks have become concerned about human rights and labor issues, community relationships, indigenous people's rights, environmental issues, and political turmoil generally. The EPs emerged in part as a way to manage these concerns. The just-promulgated EPs III apply to a broader set of financial arrangements, including project finance, project finance advisory services, project-related corporate loans, and bridge loans.

The EPs rely on self-enforcement by the participating banks. Each institution that adopts the EPs declares that it has or will put in place internal policies and processes that are consistent with the EPs. Those processes include using a common framework to identify infrastructure investments as posing high, medium, or low environmental and social risk, on the basis of an Environmental and Social Impact Assessment that is typically done by outside consultants. For projects in developed countries, an environmental impact assessment will probably already have been required by law, but in many developing countries that assessment will be performed only because the lending bank requires it to be pursuant to its agreement to participate in the EPs. Where a project is identified as medium or high risk, participating banks must require their clients to have a management plan designed to mitigate the risk, and loan covenants that require clients to comply with the management plan or be declared in default.

Academic research on the effects on the ground of the EPs is so far very limited, so the following observations must be understood in light of that substantial caveat. First, the single most important economic fact about the EPs is that project finance loans are nonrecourse, meaning that they are repaid (or not) solely from the income generated by the project. Consequently, the project must succeed or the lender will not get its money back. As a result, risk management is a vital concern and a leading motivation for joining the EPs for just about every participating bank. Because every project must be economically self-supporting, social and environmental fallout that might threaten its economic performance must be avoided. Thus, social, environmental, and human rights risks that normal accounting treats as externalities are effectively internalized. We consider this internalization factor to be highly salient in thinking about how better to instantiate positive social values within TBTF (and other) banks. In short, accounting must be changed.

Second, given the opprobrium heaped on global banks in recent years by politicians, voters, the media, and the NGO community, the reputation management potential of participation in the EPs is also highly valued. Transnational private regulation in the form of the EPs presents itself as an ostensibly benevolent cartel that seems superior both to doing nothing (and perhaps inviting hard regulation) and to taking individual action. The EPs permit a bank to manage risk and reputation and fend off prospective regulators without worrying about what its competitors are doing.

Notwithstanding the primacy of these self-interested motives, a real and growing commitment to corporate social responsibility cannot be dismissed. In particular, many EPFIs perceive the most important aspect of the EPs to be the increasing awareness of sustainability issues within the credit committees in these institutions, which can then spill over into general commercial lending, and in some cases underwriting. The EPs specifically require that there be outside monitors doing in-depth analysis of social and environmental risks at the planning stage and throughout the development of every project, and throughout a projects' development. This changing of procedures at EPFIs, and increasing the breadth of information being considered, may be creating a positive "social contagion," with potential to change the scope of some bankers' thinking about the social implications of their credit decisions.

Can this positive social contagion spread beyond project finance and commercial lending? Perhaps, but so far it seems not to have. In fact, the banks with the strongest evidence of EPs values influencing other commercial lending—HSBC, Barclays, JPMorgan Chase, Citibank, and UBS—are the same banks highlighted in the rogues' gallery at the beginning of this paper. A number of our informants have stated that project finance "guys" are different: they're "really making things," they can tell their children at night about the windmills they "made" at work that day. (Probably they are not emphasizing the Sakhalin II oil and gas pipeline that was also an EPs project.) So this observation emphasizes a point also made in the Salz Review: different parts of TBTF banks exhibit different cultures.

Third, one of the important features of the EPs is the interaction between the IFC and the 71 EPFIs. While the IFC is the private-sector lending arm of the World Bank, it is an explicitly public-regarding entity with public development objectives. The IFC's Social and Environmental Performance Standards are serious, are specific to specific industries, and are evaluated and changed through multiyear, multistakeholder collaborations. There are close working relationships between the IFC and the EPFIs, especially at the leadership level, including IFC workshops around the world and communications among participants concerning best practices. Through this iterative process at the IFC and among the EPFIs, the reach of the IFC's Performance Standards is extended, while the range of factors considered important by participants within the EPFIs is similarly stretched. In the EPs III, the most recent iteration of the EPs, indigenous people's rights are treated with more seriousness, for instance, with a requirement of free, prior, and informed consent before a project proceeds, and projects' greenhouse gas emissions are brought into the analytic and mitigation framework. Moreover, through constant communication among project bankers and reevaluation of the standards, moral challenges are made explicit, and discussions of values and norms enabled. This whole process is marked by a striking convergence of motives: fostering peer relations (without, thus far, engendering antitrust concerns), pursuing moral goals, and, in addition, self-interestedly managing risk and reputation, and creating a level competitive playing field. Perhaps the moral vacuum that psychologists have seen in so many work environments is being addressed.

Conclusion

So the question with which we conclude is this: could procedures like those found in the EPs be generalized? In fact, there are many similar examples of public–private standard setting to evaluate and, perhaps, to emulate. In evaluating the potential of such initiatives to affect cultures within groups and institutions, the relevant criteria should include: Does the initiative fulfill peoples' relational needs by encouraging them to build toward positive social values? Does the process involve enough ongoing communication to enable serious discussion of competing views of justice, morality, other peoples' needs and perspectives? Is the "moral muteness" characteristic of so many workplaces being addressed? Are people's autonomy interests, and their ability to be self-regulating, being enabled?

One example worth closer examination is the Australian Securities and Investments Commission ("ASIC"), led by Greg Medcraft, who is also the current chair of IOSCO. ASIC was divided into 11 industry sectors, and in each sector ASIC employees work with the relevant professional organizations and self-regulatory organizations to develop regulatory standards of best practice. The professions are responsible for developing the standards initially, but subject to ASIC's oversight so that there is public input into the standards, and ASIC can ask for revisions where standards are not high enough. Beyond the specifics, Commissioner Medcraft has articulated "integrity" as an over-arching goal. At least on paper, such a structure has real potential to allow the cultural power of industry self-regulation, with all of its advantages (expertise, autonomy, engagement with the goals of standards ultimately developed), but with public oversight to ensure that broader, public interests are given proper attention.

References

Admati, A., & Hellwig, M. (2013). *The bankers' new clothes*. Princeton, NJ: Princeton University Press.

Augar, P. (2013). It will take more than a stern email to make bankers behave. 9. *Financial Times*. January 29, 2013.

Batson, C. D. (1995). Prosocial motivation: Why do we help others? In A. Tesser (Ed.), *Advanced social science* (p. 332). Boston: McGraw-Hill.

Bebchuk, L. A., & Spamann, H. (2010). Regulating bankers' pay. *Georgetown Law Review, 98*(2), 247–297.

Bolton, G., & Ockenfels, A. (2000). ERC: A theory of equity, reciprocity, and competition. *American Economics Review, 90*, 166.

Braithwaite, T., & Goff, S. (2012). StanChart accused of hiding Iran dealings. *Financial Times*. August 7, 2012.

Braithwaite, T., & Nasiripour, S. (2012). Ex-Citi chief weill urges bank break up. *Financial Times*. July 25, 2012.

Citizens United v. Federal Election Comm'n., 130 S. Ct. 878 (2010).

Conley, J. M., & Williams, C. A. (2011). Global banks as global sustainability regulators?: The equator principles. *Law and Policy, 33*(4), 542–575.

Craig, S. (2013). Seeking relief, banks shift risk to murkier corner of market. *New York Times*. April 11, 2013.

Cropanzano, R., Goldman, B., & Folger, R. (2005). Self-interest: Defining and understanding a human motive. *Journal of Organizational Behavior, 26*, 985.

Cropanzano, R., Rupp, D. E., Mohler, C. J., & Schminke, M. (2001). Three roads to organizational justice. *Research in Personnel and Human Resource Management, 20*, 1.

Deci, E. L., & Ryan, R. M. (1985). *Intrinsic motivation and self-determination in human behavior*. New York: Plenum.

Eaglesham, J., & Enrich, D. (2012). Libor probe expands to bank traders. *Wall Street Journal*. July 24, 2012.

Federal Reserve Bank of Dallas. (2012). Financial stability: Traditional banks pave the way.

Fehr, E., & Gächter, S. (2002). Altruistic punishment in humans. *Nature, 415*, 137–140.

Financial Crisis Inquiry Commission Report. *Executive Summary* xviii. http://www.fcic.gov/report. Accessed 1 August 2012.

Geertz, C. (1973). *The interpretation of cultures*. New York: Basic Books.

Gunningham, N., & Sinclair, D. (2009). Organizational trust and the limits of management-based regulation. *Law and Society Review, 43*, 865–867.

Hacker, J. S., & Pierson, P. (2010). *Winner take all politics*. New York: Simon and Schuster.

Haidt, J. (2007). The new synthesis in moral psychology. *Science, 316*, 998–1002.

Harper, C. (2011). Loneliest Man in Davos Foresees 2015 Bank Crisis While Global Elites Party. Bloomberg. January 31, 2011. http://www.bloomberg.com/news/2011-01-31/lonely-analyst-warns-of-2015-bank-crisis-amid-upbeat-davos.html. Accessed 1 August 2012.

Henry, J. S. (2012). The price of offshore revisited: New estimates for "missing" global private wealth, income, inequality and lost taxes. Tax Justice Network. http://taxjustice.net/cms/upload/pdf/Price_Of_Offshore_Revisited_120722.pdf. Accessed 1 August 2012.

Hirsh, M. (2010). *Capital offense: How Washington's wise men turned America's future over to Wall Street*. Hoboken, NJ: Wiley.

Ho, K. (2009a). *Liquidated: An ethnography of Wall Street*. Durham: Duke University Press.

Ho, K. (2009b). Disciplining investment bankers, disciplining the economy: Wall Street's institutional culture of crisis and the downsizing of 'Corporate America.'. *American Anthropologist, 111*(2), 177–189.

Jenkins, P. (2012a). Inside business: Banks, the historical and the ethical. *Financial Times*. July 16, 2012.

Jenkins, P. (2012b). Bank investors should push for simplicity. *Financial Times*. July 23, 2012.

Jenkins, P., & Saigol, L. (2013). UBS chief calls on 'arrogant' bankers to change. *Financial Times*. January 9, 2013.

Johnson, S., & Kwak, J. (2010). *13 Bankers: The Wall Street takeover and the next financial meltdown*. New York: Random House.

Kahneman, D., Knetsch, J. L., & Thaler, R. H. (1986). Fairness and the assumptions of economics. *Journal of Business, 59*, 285.

Landskroner, Y., & Raviv, A. (2009). The 2007-2009 financial crisis and executive compensation: An analysis and a proposal for a novel structure. http://www.ssrn.com/abstract=1420991. Accessed 1 August 2012.

Lawrence, F. (2013). Lucrative dark arts were practiced in the run-up to the banking crisis by the company's structured capital markets division. The Guardian. February 11, 2013. http://www. guardian.co.uk/business/2013/feb/11/barclays-investment-banking-tax-avoidance. Accessed 1 August 2012.

Mallaby, S. (2012). Breaking up banks will win investor approval. *Financial Times*. July 17, 2012.

O'Barr, W. M., & Conley, J. M. (1992). *Fortune and Folly: The wealth and power of institutional investing*. Homewood, IL: Business One Irwin.

Oliver W. (2011). The financial crisis of 2015: An avoidable history 24. http://www.oliverwyman. com/ow/pdf_files/OW_EN_FS_Publ_2011_State_of_Financial_Services_2011_US_Web.pdf. Accessed 30 January 2011.

Riles, A. (2011). *Collateral knowledge: Legal reasoning in the global financial markets*. Chicago: University of Chicago Press.

Rupp, D. E., & Williams, C. A. (2011). The efficacy of regulation as a function of psychological fit. *Theoretical Inquiries in Law, 12*, 581–602.

Salz Review. www.salzreview.co.uk. Accessed 1 August 2012.

Silver-Greenberg, J. (July 13, 2007). JPMorgan [Chase] says trading loss tops $5.8 billion; Profit for quarter falls 9%. *New York Times Dealbook*.

Trevino, L. K., Weaver, G. R., & Reynolds, S. J. (2006). Behavioral ethics in organizations: A review. *Journal of Management, 32*, 951.

Turillo, C. J., et al. (2002). Is virtue its own reward? Self-sacrificial decisions for the sake of fairness. *Organizational Behavior and Human Decision Processes, 89*, 839.

U.K. Treasury Committee. (2008). Financial stability and transparency. *House of Commons Report No. 6, Session 2007-08*.

U.S. Senate Permanent Subcommittee on Investigations. (2012). U.S. vulnerabilities to money laundering, drugs, and terrorist financing: HSBC case history. July 17, 2012. http://hsgac. senate.gov. Accessed 8 November 2012.

Wilmarth, A. E., Jr. (2011). The Dodd-Frank Act: A flawed and inadequate response to the too-big-to-fail problem. *Oregon Law Review, 89*, 57.

Zingales, L. (2012). Why I was won over by the merits of Glass-Steagall. *Financial Times*. June 11, 2012.

The Global Reporting Initiative Guidelines and External Assurance of Investment Bank Sustainability Reports: Effective Tools for Financial Sector Social Accountability?

Niamh O'Sullivan

Abstract This chapter will examine the progression of financial sector social accountability since the late 1990s. In particular, it explores the role of the Global Reporting Initiative Financial Services Sector Supplement, as well as the external assurance of financial sector sustainability reports, in the evolution of investment bank social accountability. Specific attention is paid to the perceived effectiveness of the GRI guidelines and external assurance mechanisms to ensure the consistency and quality of environmental, social and governance disclosures across banks and hence whether these tools have enhanced investment bank social accountability to date.

1 Introduction

Demand for private financial sector social accountability emerged following non-governmental organisation (NGO) campaigns against international commercial and investment bank involvement in environmentally and socially destructive projects from the mid-1990s onwards (see, e.g. O'Sullivan and O'Dwyer 2009). Since then, increased transparency surrounding lending and investment risk management and decision-making frameworks; the integration of environmental, social and governance (ESG) criteria within these processes; and consistent reporting and auditing of the same have been recognised as important prerequisites for better financial sector social accountability.

This chapter examines the progression of financial sector social accountability since the late 1990s. In particular, it explores the role of the Global Reporting Initiative Financial Services Sector Supplement (GRI FSSS), as well as the external assurance of financial sector sustainability reports, in the evolution of investment bank social accountability. Special attention is paid to the perceived effectiveness

N. O'Sullivan (✉)
University of Amsterdam Business School, Amsterdam, The Netherlands
e-mail: niamh.osullivan@sustainalytics.com

© Springer International Publishing Switzerland 2015   251
K. Wendt (ed.), *Responsible Investment Banking*, CSR, Sustainability, Ethics &
Governance, DOI 10.1007/978-3-319-10311-2_15

of the GRI FSSS and external assurance to ensure the consistency and quality of ESG disclosures across banks.

The chapter begins by explaining the notion of accountability and social accountability. It then discusses the emergence of financial sector social accountability and how why the GRI FSSS was developed. It proceeds by providing an overview of sustainability reporting trends in the finance sector and the influence the GRI FSSS has had, and could have, on this. It then presents the results of a unique study into the use of the GRI FSSS by a sample of leading financial institutions and also considers the status of external assurance of financial sector sustainability reports. Finally, the chapter concludes by offering an informed opinion as to whether the GRI FSSS and external assurance of investment bank sustainability reports are effective tools for financial sector social accountability.

2   The Concept of Accountability

Whilst the definition of accountability is highly contested (Sinclair 1995; Shearer 2002; Cooper and Owen 2007), there is some general consensus within the academic literature regarding its basic attributes.

This literature informs us that the concept of accountability 'in its broadest sense simply refers to the giving and demanding of reasons of conduct' (Roberts and Scapens 1985, p. 447). More specifically, accountability is said to entail 'identifying what one is responsible for and then providing information about that responsibility to those who have rights to that information' (Gray 2001, p. 11). Accordingly, accountability is seen as dependent upon 'the free flow of appropriate information and on effective forums for discussion and cross-examination' (Mulgan 2000, p. 8). Being called to account for one's actions 'requires one to explain and justify what was done' (Ibid, p. 9), whilst 'the question of whom to hold to account for what raises immediate issues of personal responsibility and internal values' (Ibid, p. 10). Thus, according to Roberts (1991, p. 365), 'at the heart of accountability is a social acknowledgement and insistence that one's actions make a difference both to self and others'. It is this 'intersubjectivity' (Shearer 2002), or interdependence, between self and others that leads some to consider accountability 'as a moral phenomenon that both can and should be subject to ethical reflection' (Shearer 2002, p. 545; Schweiker 1993). Hence, they claim that it is the notion of 'moral responsibility that grounds the accountability of the entity with respect to [a] community' (Shearer 2002, p. 543) and may prompt organisations to scrutinise their 'mission, goals and performance' (Ebrahim 2003, p. 194).

As Ahrens (1996, p. 168) suggests, 'a defining feature of organisational processes of accountability is the alignment of organisational rhetoric and practice with wider public discourses'. Hence, the literature is dominated by research on why and how organisations attempt to 'evidence' their accountability and at the same time gain societal legitimacy (or a 'social licence to operate'), through the production of sustainability reports (O'Donovan 2002; O'Dwyer 2002; Deegan and Gordon 1996;

Deegan 2002, 2007; Deegan et al. 2002; Gray et al. 1995; Hogner 1982; Milne and Patten 2002; Patten 1992). From an organisational perspective, the concept of accountability is aligned with that of legitimacy as both concepts are concerned with societal values and expectations of organisations.

In this chapter, accountability is primarily interpreted as 'identifying what one is responsible for and then providing information about that responsibility to those who have rights to that information' (Gray 2001, p. 11). In addition, 'social accountability' will collectively refer to notions of environmental and social accountability throughout.

3   The Emergence of Financial Sector Social Accountability

From the mid-1990s onwards, a number of international NGO financial sector campaigns brought the notion of social accountability and legitimacy to the attention of large commercial and investment banks. Financing of controversial dam, mining, forestry and oil and gas pipeline projects[1] led NGOs to call banks to account for the environmental and social impacts of those projects, as well as their overall activities, in order to gain and repair their 'social licence to operate' (see O'Sullivan and O' Dwyer 2009).

The reputational and financial risks posed by these projects, and related NGO campaigns, catalysed leading commercial and investment bank awareness of sustainability issues, promoted them to develop voluntary initiatives such as the Equator Principles in 2003 to help address their environmental and social responsibilities and increased their recognition of the growing societal demand for greater transparency and reporting about their operations as a whole.

Partially influenced by this and following the move of some pioneering banks to produce environmental and later sustainability reports about their direct, in-house ecology impacts from the mid-1990s,[2]   the United Nations Environment

---

[1] Such as the Three Gorges Dam in China, the Freeport-McMoRan/Rio Tinto gold and copper mining project in Indonesia, Asian Pulp and Paper's (APP) forestry projects in Indonesia, palm oil plantations in Indonesia, the OCP oil pipeline in Ecuador, the Camisea gas pipeline in Peru, and the Chad–Cameroon oil pipeline (FoE EWNI 2002; FoE Netherlands 2006; RAN 2005; Spitzeck 2007; Steen 2008; Van Gelder 2003; Wright 2009).

[2] Some of these early reporters from, for example, 1996 onwards, included: Allianz SGD, Bank of America, Credit Suisse, Deutsche Bank, Lloyds TSB, Natwest Group and Swiss Re. They produced reports on their direct ecological impacts such as paper, energy and water use; waste; CO_2 emissions; recycling; and transport, associated with their offices and staff. These banks were amongst those involved in the development of, and/or later signatories to, the United Nations Environment Programme Finance Initiative (UNEP FI) in 1991/1992. UNEP FI's 1992 *Statement by Banks on the Environment and Sustainable Development* required financial signatories to periodically report on how they were integrating environmental considerations into their operations and thus acted as an influential catalyst to early sustainability reporting by these banks and the finance sector as a whole (Coulson 2001; Tarna 2001; www.unepfi.org).

Programme Finance Initiative (UNEP FI) and the Global Reporting Initiative (GRI) organised a multi-stakeholder working group to develop a set of indicators for financial sector sustainability reporting.

Between 2003 and 2005 the working group—comprised of financial sector, civil society, rating agency and academic representatives—produced a draft set of environmental indicators to assist reporting on the *indirect* impacts of banking, asset management and insurance activities. These indicators were to act as a supplement to the generic GRI 'G2' sustainability reporting guidelines as launched in 2002.[3] Subsequently, between 2006 and 2008, an additional UNEP FI–GRI working group pilot-tested this draft set of environmental indicators, helped combine them with a set of social performance indicators produced earlier by SPI-Finance in 2002[4] as well as updated the (now) combined set of indicators to the GRI 'G3' reporting framework (as launched in 2006). The result was the GRI Financial Services Sector Supplement (FSSS), consisting of 16 indicators, aimed at assisting retail; corporate and commercial bankers; and insurers and asset managers' report on the environmental and social performance of their products and services (GRI 2008; see Table 1). Whilst the FSSS became operational in 2008, its use became obligatory for reporters to be recognised as a GRI 'A'-level[5] reporter as of January 1, 2010 (GRI 2008; Lie 2012).

The effectiveness of the GRI FSSS in enhancing the quality of investment bank sustainability reporting and overall discharge of accountability to society is discussed further below. Prior to that, recent sustainability reporting trends within the finance sector, and the influence the GRI FSSS may have had on this, is discussed the next section.

---

[3] See www.globalreporting.org

[4] See http://www3.uji.es/~munoz/SPI_Finance_2002.pdf

[5] The GRI G3 (2006) reporting framework differentiated between three levels of reporting, A, B and C, in order for a report to be deemed 'in accordance' with the GRI Guidelines. The application level was dependent on the number and type of disclosures made. For example, an A-level application reporter was required to report on *all* criteria listed for G3 'Profile Disclosures', 'Disclosures on Management Approach' and 'Performance Indicators and Sector-Specific Supplement Performance Indicators'. With regard to the latter, reporters were specifically requested to 'respond on each core and sector supplement indicator with due respect for the [GRI] materiality Principle by either: (a) reporting on the indicator or (b) explaining the reason for its omission' (GRI 2008: *Application Levels*, p. 2). Reporters could self-declare themselves an A-, B- or C-level reporter, which then required third-party and/or GRI checks. If the reporter obtained formal assurance on their sustainability report, they could declare themselves an A+-, B+- or C+-level reporter. The G4 reporting framework launched in 2013 no longer includes A(+), B(+) or C(+) application levels. These have been replaced by two levels: 'core' and 'comprehensive', where, for example, all of the indicators for identified prioritised issues must be reported against to be regarded as a comprehensive level report (see GRI 2013a, b, c, d; Baker 2013).

Table 1 The GRI Financial Services Sector Supplement indicators

Performance indicators		No. of disclosure requirements
Category: Product and service impact		
Aspect: Product portfolio		
FS1	Policies with specific environmental and social components applied to business lines	6
FS2	Procedures for assessing and screening environmental and social risks in business	6
FS3	Processes for monitoring clients' implementation of and compliance with environmental and social requirements included in agreements or transactions	3
FS4	Process(es) for improving staff competency to implement the environmental and social policies and procedures as applied to business lines	2
FS5	Interactions with clients/investees/business partners regarding environmental and social risks and opportunities	5
FS6	Percentage of the portfolio for business lines by specific region, size (e.g. micro/SME/large) and by sector	5
FS7	Monetary value of products and services designed to deliver a specific social benefit for each business line broken down by purpose	5
FS8	Monetary value of products and services designed to deliver a specific environmental benefit for each business line broken down by purpose	2
Apect: Audit		
FS9	Coverage and frequency of audits to assess implementation of environmental and social policies and risk assessment procedures	6
Aspect: Active ownership		
FS10	Percentage and number of companies held in the institution's portfolio with which the reporting organization has interacted on environmental or social issues	2
FS11	Percentage of assets subject to positive and negative environmental or social screening	4
FS12	Voting policies applied to environmental or social issues for shares over which the reporting organization holds the right to vote shares or advises on voting	6
Category: Social		
Sub-category: Society		
Aspect: Local communities		
FS13	Access points in low-populated or economically disadvantaged areas by type	5
FS14	Initiatives to improve access to financial services to disadvantaged people	4
Sub-category: Product responsibility		
Aspect: Product and service labeling		
FS15	Policies for the fair design and sale of financial products and services	4
FS16	Initiatives to enhance financial literacy by type of beneficiary	4

Adapted from GRI (2008)

4 Sustainability Reporting Trends in the Finance Sector

The KPMG international surveys of Global Fortune 250 company corporate responsibility reporting highlight a general increase in financial sector sustainability reporting between 1999 and 2011. This ranges from 15 % of the financial institutions surveyed in 1999 producing reports to 24 % in 2002, to a more than twofold increase to 57 % in 2005, a slight decrease to 49 % in 2008 and an increase again to 61 % in 2011 (Tarna 2001; KPMG & WIMM 1999; KPMG and University of Amsterdam (2002); KPMG 2005, 2011).[6]

The increase in reporting between 1999 and 2005 may be attributed to the development of the GRI Guidelines for sustainability reporting in 1999 and their relaunch in 2002, as well as the (then) growing experience of banks regarding this form of reporting. In addition, bank involvement with sustainable finance initiatives, such as the Equator Principles from 2003 onwards, also increased their need for greater transparency and disclosure of, in this instance, project financing but simultaneously increased their awareness of heightened civil society scrutiny of their credit and investment activities in general and the demands for social accountability of the same (O'Sullivan 2010). Ironically, the latter might also be attributed to the slight decrease in reporting between 2005 and 2008, with some banks possibly cautious to report information they felt may be criticised by, for example, NGO stakeholders.[7] Whilst the increase in reporting again between 2008 and 2011 may be attributed to the introduction of the GRI Financial Services Sector Supplement (FSSS) in 2008 but, perhaps more significantly, the increased scrutiny of financial institutions post-2007; when their social accountability and legitimacy came under serious disrepute during the recent financial crisis.

Whilst an increase in financial sector sustainability reporting since 1999 is to be commended, more reporting does not necessarily mean better reporting. The content, quality and overall materiality of financial sector sustainability reports have been an ongoing stakeholder concern, with fears that reports are produced without due stakeholder engagement, and thus inadequately reflect stakeholder interests (see, e.g. Ernst and Young 2012). From a range of financial sector stakeholders, including inter alia investors and shareholders, employees and civil society, NGOs continue to request more detailed environmental, social and governance (ESG) information relating to financial sector business lines, products and services (see, e.g. GRI, 2013b). These demands in fact mirror the purpose and scope of the GRI FSSS. Yet, whilst NGOs, such as Friends of the Earth, were involved in the development of the GRI FSSS and related NGO coalitions such as *BankTrack* have advocated the use of the GRI FSSS to improve financial sector transparency and reporting, they have also bemoaned the fact that 'banks can choose to respond

---

[6] These are the most recent figures available from KPMG. The forthcoming *KPMG International Survey of Corporate Responsibility Reporting 2013* was not released at the time of writing.

[7] No informed opinion has been offered by KPMG to explain this slight decrease in reporting between 2005 and 2008.

to GRI indicators in brief and minimal ways, which results in poor disclosure' (BankTrack 2010, p. 93).

In turn, based on surveys conducted by BankTrack on financial sector sustainability reporting in 2007 and 2010, they have specifically requested more transparency regarding: first, the scope, content and application of bank sustainability policies; second, clients' material non-compliance with these policies and how the banks have addressed this; and third, more detailed information on deals being financed, beyond that required for Equator Principles-conditioned project finance reporting and *across* their portfolio (BankTrack 2007, 2010). In addition, BankTrack have, inter alia, called for greater institutional accountability, in the form of internal and external audits of environmental and social risk management systems and the public reporting thereof (BankTrack 2007, 2010).

The GRI FSSS makes provision for many of these transparency and disclosure requests (see Table 1, indicators: FS1, FS2, FS3, FS5 and FS9). A careful look at the indicator protocols stipulating the reporting requirements for each of the 16 indicators shows ample provision is made for detailed levels of reporting to be achieved (see GRI 2008). The issue is that, whilst some banks have made some good progress in this vein, it appears that many are currently either not paying enough attention to the specific reporting requirements of these indicators or just not choosing to do so. This is reflected in the results of an in-depth survey of a sample of leading financial institutions' use of the FSSS, as now discussed in the following section.

5 The Use of the GRI Financial Services Sector Supplement

According to the GRI, the 'Financial Services were the leading sector in GRI reporting in 2010, with 14 % of all GRI reports coming from the sector' (Lie 2012). In addition, the GRI database indicates that, of a total of 405 financial sector sustainability reports completed in 2012, 208 (51 %) used the GRI Financial Services Sector Supplement (FSSS), whilst thus far in 2013,[8] 89 of the 142 reports received (62 %) have also used the FSSS (GRI 2013c).

Despite the fact that the development of the FSSS was somewhat groundbreaking—regarding the reporting of *indirect* financial sector sustainability impacts—the actual use of the FSSS and whether it has enhanced the consistency and quality of investment bank ESG disclosures are highly questionable. A study of the use of the FSSS[9] in 21 major financial institution sustainability disclosures in 2012 raises some cause for concern (see Lie 2012; Lie and O'Sullivan 2013). The 21 institutions included in the study represented those financial institutions who participated in the development of the FSSS, were applying it to their most recent sustainability

---

[8] As per September 2013.

[9] That is the 2008 version used in conjunction with the GRI G3 sustainability reporting guidelines and not the slightly amended 2013 version to complement to new G4 reporting framework.

Table 2 Financial Sector use of the GRI Financial Services Sector Supplement

		Disclosure level		
Bank	Application level	Full disclosures	Partial disclosures	No disclosures
Bank of America	B+	4 (25 %)	2 (13 %)	10 (63 %)
BMO Financial Group	B	1 (6 %)	4 (25 %)	11 (69 %)
Calvert Group Ltd	B	1 (6 %)	6 (38 %)	9 (56 %)
Confederación Esnafiola de Cajas de Ahorros (CECA)	A	2 (13 %)	3 (19 %)	11 (69 %)
Citigroup	B	5 (31 %)	4 (25 %)	7 (44 %)
Credit Suisse Group	A+	3 (19 %)	3 (19 %)	10 (63 %)
Deutsche Bank AG	A+	3 (19 %)	2 (13 %)	11 (69 %)
Insurance Australia Group (LVG)	B	0 (0 %)	2 (13 %)	14 (88 %)
National Australia Bank	A+	2 (13 %)	3 (19 %)	11 (69 %)
Nedbank	A+	1 (6 %)	2 (13 %)	13 (81 %)
Rabobank	A+	3 (19 %)	3 (19 %)	10 (63 %)
Standard Bank of South Africa	B+	0 (0 %)	3 (19 %)	13 (81 %)
State Street Corporation	B+	0 (0 %)	1 (6 %)	15 (94 %)
Swiss Reinsurance Company (Swiss Re)	B	2 (13 %)	2 (13 %)	12 (75 %)
Tapiola Insurance Group	A	0 (0 %)	0 (0 %)	16 (100 %)
The Co-Operative Bank	A+	9 (56 %)	3 (19 %)	4 (25 %)
The Netherlands Development Finance Company (FMO)	B+	5 (31 %)	4 (25 %)	7 (44 %)
UBS AG	A+	3 (19 %)	5 (31 %)	8 (50 %)
Yancity Bank of Canada	A	3 (19 %)	7 (44 %)	6 (38 %)
Westpac Banking Corporation	A+	0 (0 %)	2 (13 %)	14 (88 %)
Zürcher Kantonalbank	A+	0 (0 %)	1 (6 %)	15 (94 %)

Lie and O'Sullivan (2013)

disclosures (as per June 2012) and had declared themselves a GRI 'B'-level reporter, *at least* (see Table 2).

The study involved a content analysis of the 21 institutions' use of the FSSS's 16 performance indicators and their related protocols.[10] Disclosure of the indicators was analysed on the basis of how many of the disclosure requirements for each indicator (as stipulated in the indicator protocols) were applied. The number of disclosure requirements for each indicator differs but ranges from 2 to 6, dependent on the indicator (see Table 1).[11] If all of the disclosure requirements were disclosed,

---

[10] This content analysis included *all* of the reporting mediums where disclosures on the Supplement's 16 indicators were made (as indicated by the GRI content index provided by the institutions themselves), such as sustainability reports, supplementary and more specific sustainability documents, various web pages and, on occasion, financial and integrated reports.

[11] See the GRI (2008) for detailed information on the specific number and content of each of the indicator protocols.

the indicator was considered 'fully disclosed'; if at least half of the disclosure requirements were disclosed, the indicator was considered 'partially disclosed'; and if none of the disclosure requirements were disclosed, the indicator was considered 'not disclosed'.[12] What emerged was that *none* of the financial institutions in the sample managed to provide full disclosure on all performance indicators (see Table 2; Lie and O'Sullivan 2013).

In fact, the financial institution that provided the highest level of disclosure,[13] the Co-operative Bank, only provided full disclosure on just over half of the performance indicators (9 of 16; 56 %). Due to the voluntary nature of GRI reporting, the application of the FSSS, and the disclosure of specific indicators therein, is of course at the discretion of the individual banks. However, what is most worrying from these results are the 12 instances where institutions declared themselves an A− or A+-level reporter yet failed to disclose all the FSSS indicators to their full extent, as was required to be a GRI (G3) A-level reporter. Of these, 9 declared themselves an A+ reporter which means that their report was externally assured and thus also raises concerns about the assurance process and providers that confirmed these institutions as A-level reporters (Lie and O'Sullivan 2013).

Furthermore, the study highlights that an A+-level reporter did not necessarily guarantee a higher level of disclosure than a B+-level reporter. *For example*, Citigroup and FMO both self-declared themselves B+ reporters, disclosing 5 performance indicators fully (31 %) and partially disclosing 4 (25 %). However, Westpac, a self-declared A+-level reporter, disclosed none of the performance indicators fully.

On average, only 14 % of the 16 performance indicators were fully disclosed by the 21 institutions, whilst 18 % were partially disclosed, meaning 68 % of the indicators were undisclosed (see Table 3; Lie and O'Sullivan 2013). These are quite unexpected results, particularly when one considers that these institutions were involved in the actual development of the GRI FSSS.

Of all FS1 and FS2, related to environmental and social policies and assessment procedures, were disclosed the most; but the number of reporters is still low, with only 8 and 9 of the 21 institutions disclosing these respectively. Considering that these indicators are, arguably, some of the most material indicators to help banks monitor, assess and report upon the integration of sustainability issues within core banking operations, these results are surprising (Lie and O'Sullivan 2013).

Equally surprising is that, from the indicators where no full disclosures were made (FS9, FS11, FS13 and FS14), none of the 21 institutions provided full disclosure on FS9: the 'coverage and frequency of audits to assess implementation of environmental and social policies and risk assessment procedures', with only four institutions doing so partially. From a social accountability perspective, a lack of (re) assurance that the sustainability policies and procedures that a bank claims to

---

[12] More specific information on the methodology applied in this study can be obtained from the author upon request.

[13] Measured by the highest amount of full and partial disclosures.

Table 3 Disclosure of GRI Financial Services Sector Supplement indicators

Performance indicator		Fully disclosed	Partially disclosed	Undisclosed
FS1	Policies with specific environmental and social components 1 applied to business lines.	8 (38 %)	4 (19 %)	9 (43 %)
FS2	Procedures for assessing and screening environmental and social risks in business lines.	9 (43 %)	1 (5 %)	11 (52 %)
FS3	Processes for monitoring clients' implementation of and compliance with environmental and social requirements included in agreements or transactions.	2 (10 %)	1 (5 %)	18 (86 %)
FS4	Process(es) for improving staff competency to implement the environmental and social policies and procedures as applied to business lines.	4 (19 %)	5 (24 %)	12 (57 %)
FS5	Interactions with clients, investees /business partners regarding environmental and social risks and opportunities.	1 (5 %)	2 (10 %)	18 (86 %)
FS6	percentage of the portfolio for business lines by specific region, size (e.g. micro SME. large) and by sector.	1 (5 %)	4 (19 %)	16 (76 %)
FS7	Monetary value of products and services designed to deliver a specific social benefit for each business line broken down by purpose.	6 (29 %)	4 (24 %)	10 (48 %)
FS8	Monetary value of products and services designed to deliver a specific environmental benefit for each business line broken down by purpose	4 (19 %)	3 (14 %)	14 (67 %)
FS9	Coverage and frequency of audits to assess implementation of environmental and social policies and risk assessment procedures	0 (0 %)	4 (19 %)	17 (81 %)
FS10	Percentage and number of companies held in the institution's portfolio with which the reporting organization has interacted on environmental or social issues	1 (5 %)	2 (10 %)	18 (86 %)
FS11	Percentage of assets subject to positive and negative environmental or social screening	0 (0 %)	7 (33 %)	14 (67 %)
FS12	Voting policies applied to environmental or social issues for shares over which the reporting organization holds the right to vote shares or advises on voting.	2 (10 %)	2 (10 %)	17 (81 %)
FS13	Access points in low-populated or economically disadvantaged areas by type	0 (0 %)	6 (29 %)	15 (71 %)
FS14	Initiatives to improve access to financial services to disadvantaged people.	0 (0 %)	7 (33 %)	14 (67 %)

(continued)

Table 3 (continued)

Performance indicator		Fully disclosed	Partially disclosed	Undisclosed
FS15	Policies for the fair design and sale of financial products and services	3 (14 %)	6 (29 %)	12 (57 %)
FS16	Initiatives to enhance financial literacy by type of beneficiary	6 (29 %)	3 (14 %)	12 (57 %)
Total		47 (14 %)	62 (18 %)	227 (68 %)
Average		3 (14 %)	4 (18 %)	14 (68 %)

Lie and O'Sullivan (2013)

have implemented—which can be obtained through internal and external audit channels—can seriously hamper societal confidence and trust in financial institution sustainability disclosures. Consequently, banks run the risk of societal (mis) perceptions of their sustainability efforts as being mere rhetoric (Lie and O'Sullivan 2013). This will now be discussed further in the following section.

6 External Assurance of Financial Sector Sustainability Reports

Sustainability assurance has long been considered an important, yet controversial, aspect of the corporate social accountability process. Whilst acknowledged as an essential mechanism to ensure the reliability of reported information and to demonstrate accountability with key stakeholders (AccountAbility 2008), concerns over corporate 'managerial capture' of the scope of assurance engagements (Owen 2007), the preference to request and award 'limited' as opposed to 'reasonable' levels of assurance, the subsequent frequency of 'negatively' worded assurance statements,[14] the independence and competence of the assurance providers and the lack of stakeholder engagement in the assurance process have led to extensive academic critique (see Edgley et al. 2010; Owen 2007; O'Dwyer and Owen 2005; O'Dwyer et al. 2011).

The KPMG surveys of corporate responsibility reporting show an increase in the external assurance of financial sector sustainability reports in their G250 company sample, from 37 % in 2005 (out of a total of 57 % financial sector reporters) to 44 % in 2008 (out of a total of 49 % financial sector reporters)[15] (KPMG 2005, 2008).

---

[14] Referring to the International Standard for Assurance Engagements (ISAE) 3,000 classifications of assurance scope (narrow or broad), level of engagement as limited or 'reasonable' (i.e. detailed) and 'negatively' (i.e. cautiously) as opposed to 'positively' worded assurance statements (IAASB 2011).

[15] Sector-specific information on sustainability assurance is not included in the 2011 KPMG survey of corporate sustainability reporting, and KPMG data for 2013 is currently unavailable. KPMG do mention, however, in the 2011 report, that only 46 % of all of the G250 companies in their survey used assurance as a strategy to verify and assess their corporate responsibility data (KPMG 2011).

Whilst the GRI database indicates that, of a total of 405 financial sector sustainability reports completed in 2012, 154 (38 %) were externally assured, 50 of the 142 financial sector sustainability reports received thus far in 2013 (35 %) have been externally assured (GRI 2013c).

Despite these developments, the assurance of financial sector sustainability reports is susceptible to the same, if not increased, societal concerns about the credibility of the sustainability assurance process and industry in general, as outlined above. This became strikingly obvious when Big Four accountancy firm Ernst and Young (EY) came under fire for its assurance of Barclays' corporate responsibility report, prior the Libor interest rate scandal in 2012. Public commenters criticised Barclays for discrediting corporate responsibility reporting and EY for failing to expose the banks' involvement in, inter alia, such interest rate rigging (see, e.g. Confino 2012). Whilst acknowledging that EY was requested to provide a limited assurance engagement on Barclays report, the question still asked was 'whether independent social auditing is ever going to do more than gloss over the surface of a company's affairs' (Confino 2012).

What becomes clear from such scandals, apart from the fact that some banks need to act more ethically, is that the sustainability assurance standard setters, the assurance providers and the corporates requesting assurance need to make a concerted effort to make reasonable (or more detailed) levels of assurance the norm, as opposed to exception, in order to enhance the legitimacy and credibility of the assurance process for all parties involved. This is particularly pertinent, given the need to restore societal trust in financial sector activities in the aftermath of the recent crisis. In the interim, better attention to the scope, and related transparency and clarity, of, even limited, assurance engagements of financial sector sustainability reports is needed. When one examines assurance statements in financial sector sustainability reports, it is often difficult to decipher what *exact* internal sustainability policies and procedures have been assured, if they are not *explicitly* outlined. For example, in the case of the implementation of the Equator Principles (EP) for project financing, it is still rare to find financial sector assurance statements that clearly outline that EP implementation has formed part of the assurance scope and what exactly that entailed.[16] All of this makes the relevance and importance of GRI FSSS indicator FS9, the 'coverage and frequency of audits to assess implementation of environmental and social policies and risk assessment procedures', even more prevalent as a helpful tool to assist such financial sector transparency and disclosure.

Whilst the new GRI G4 framework launched in May 2013 no longer requires external assurance for reporters to be deemed 'in accordance' with the GRI guidelines, GRI do recommend that reporters seek external assurance of their reports and

---

[16] It should be noted, however, that some pioneering banks, such as HSBC, have conducted assurance of their EP implementation either separately or as part of their sustainability report assurance process in recent years. In addition, the Equator Principles Financial Institution (EPFI) Association is currently engaged in ongoing debate about the introduction of an assurance requirement for EPFIs as an extension of the recent Equator Principles III (EP III) reporting requirements (see www.equator-principles.com/index.php/ep3).

disclose exactly which disclosures have been assured if they do so (GRI 2013). It remains to be seen however how this will affect the quality and reliability of reported information and the credibility of the same for external stakeholders.

Conclusion

There is no denying that the number and quality of sustainability reports from the financial sector has dramatically increased since the late-1990s. However, this chapter has revealed the need for further improvement. The Global Reporting Initiative Financial Services Sector Supplement (GRI FSSS) is currently not being used to its full potential to improve the transparency, consistency and in some cases accuracy of investment bank environmental social and governance (ESG) disclosures (Lie and O'Sullivan 2013). This can be viewed as a missed opportunity, particularly given the financial sector's need to rebuild societal trust and legitimacy in the aftermath of the recent crisis.

Regardless of the amount of time it takes to compile a sustainability report, or the internal capacity and commercial confidentiality constraints faced by many banks, the reporting process has to be attended to more carefully, with more qualified attention being paid to the relevance and importance of, for example, GRI FSSS indicators to core business operations. Hopefully, with the recently launched GRI G4 sustainability reporting framework, and its new emphasis on materiality in organisational selection and reporting of GRI indicators, international investment banks will make a more concerted effort to better choose and utilise the (now G4-refined) FSSS indicators. This is in order to meet both their material needs to monitor and assess the integration of ESG considerations into core business lines, products and services, as well as societal material demands for greater transparency and accountability of the same. The recent movement towards integrated reporting,[17] as well as more stringent reporting requirements of both the Equator Principles (EP) for project financing and the Principles for Responsible Investment (PRI),[18] could complement these efforts. Whilst it remains to be seen whether the emerging Sustainability Accounting Standards Board (SASB) indicators, for US-listed company filing of 10-K and 20-F forms with the Securities and Exchange Commission (SEC),[19] may act to complement or compete against the GRI framework in the future.

With all of these reporting developments comes the need for equal progression in sustainable assurance standards and the sustainable assurance industry in general. Here, more reasonable (detailed), purposeful and

(continued)

---

[17] See http://www.theiirc.org/

[18] See http://www.unpri.org/areas-of-work/reporting-and-assessment/reporting-framework/

[19] See http://www.sasb.org/sasb/

stakeholder-inclusive forms of assurance need to become the norm, to enhance the reliability of investment bank ESG disclosures and overall discharge of accountability to relevant publics.

Yet, in the advent of the recent financial crisis, what has become very clear is that any advance in investment bank sustainability reporting and assurance processes can only go so far to improve financial sector social accountability as a whole. This has to be accompanied by a genuine shift in the overriding culture of the banks towards better corporate social responsibility, if they truly wish to gain, repair and maintain their social licence to operate.

References

AccountAbility. (2008). *AA1000 Assurance Standard*. London: AccountAbility.

Ahrens, T. (1996). Styles of accountability. *Accounting, Organizations and Society, 21*(2/3), 139–173.

Baker, M. (2013). Generation materiality. *Ethical Corporation*, July-August, London, pp. 11–14.

BankTrack. (2007). *Mind the Gap: Benchmarking credit policies of international banks*. Utrecht: BankTrack.

BankTrack. (2010). *Close the Gap: Benchmarking investment policies of international banks*. Nijmegen: BankTrack.

Confino, J. (2012). Has Barclays brought corporate social responsibility reporting into disrepute. *The Guardian*, July 2nd, available at: www.theguardian.com/sustainable-business/barclays-corporate-responsibility-reporting-disrepute (last accessed, September 30, 2013).

Cooper, S., & Owen, D. (2007). Corporate social reporting and stakeholder accountability: The missing link. *Accounting, Organizations and Society, 32*, 649–667.

Coulson, A. (2001). Corporate environmental assessment by a bank lender—the reality? In J. J. Bouma, M. Jeucken, & L. Klinkers (Eds.), *Sustainable banking: The greening of finance* (pp. 300–311). Sheffield: Greenleaf Publishing.

Deegan, C. (2002). The legitimising effect of social and environmental disclosures—a theoretical foundation. *Accounting, Auditing and Accountability Journal, 15*(3), 282–311.

Deegan, C. (2007). Organisational legitimacy as a motive for sustainability reporting. In J. Unerman, J. Bebbington, & B. O'Dwyer (Eds.), *Sustainability accounting and accountability* (pp. 127–149). London: Routledge.

Deegan, C., & Gordon, B. (1996). A study of the environmental disclosure practices of Australian corporations. *Accounting and Business Research, 26*(3), 187–99.

Deegan, C., Rankin, M., & Tobin, J. (2002). An examination of corporate social and environmental disclosures of BHP from 1983-1997. *Accounting, Auditing and Accountability Journal, 15*(3), 312–343.

Ebrahim, A. (2003). Making sense of conceptual perspectives for Northern and Southern non-profits. *Nonprofit Management and Leadership, 14*(2), 191–212.

Edgley, C., Jones, M., & Soloman, J. (2010). Stakeholder inclusivity in social and environmental report assurance. *Accounting, Auditing and Accountability Journal, 23*(4), 532–557.

Ernst and Young. (2012). *The Path Forward Continues: The European and Dutch financial sectors viewed from a non-financial perspective*. Rotterdam: Ernst and Young.

Friends of the Earth (FoE) England, Wales and Northern Ireland (EWNI). (2002). Bank exposed at AGM, available at: www.foe.co.uk/resource/press_releases/0422barc (last accessed September 30, 2013).

Friends of the Earth (FoE) Netherlands (Milieudefensie). (2006). *People, plant, palm oil? A review of the oil palm and forest policies adopted by Dutch Banks*. Amsterdam: Milieudefensie.

(The) Global Reporting Initiative (GRI). (2008). *Financial services sector supplement*, available at: www.globalreporting.org/resourcelibrary/FSSS-Complete.pdf (last accessed September 30, 2013).

(The) Global Reporting Initiative (GRI). (2013). G4 *Sustainability reporting guidelines*, available at: www.globalreporting.org/reporting/g4/Pages/default.aspx (last accessed September 30, 2013).

(The) Global Reporting Initiative (GRI). (2013a). G4 *Sector disclosures financial services*, available at: www.globalreporting.org/resourcelibrary/GRI-G4-A4-SectorPublicationFinancial Services-final.pdf (last accessed September 30, 2013).

(The) Global Reporting Initiative (GRI). (2013b). *Sustainability topics for sectors: What do stakeholders want to know?* Amsterdam: GRI.

(The) Global Reporting Initiative (GRI). (2013c). *GRI Database*, available at: www.database. globalreporting.org/pages/about (last accessed, September 30, 2013).

Gray, R. (2001). Thirty years of social accounting, reporting and auditing: What if anything have we learnt? *Business Ethics: A European Review, 10*(1), 9–15.

Gray, R., Kouhy, R., & Lavers, S. (1995). Corporate social and environmental reporting: A review of the literature and a longitudinal study of UK disclosure. *Accounting, Auditing and Accountability Journal, 8*(2), 47–77.

Hogner, R. (1982). Corporate social reporting: Eight decades of development at US steel. *Research in Corporate Performance and Policy, 4*, 243–250.

(The) International Auditing and Assurance Standards Board (IAASB). (2011). *International Standard for Assurance Engagements (ISAE) 3000*. New York: IAASB.

KPMG. (2008). *KPMG International Survey of Corporate Responsibility Reporting 2008*. Amstelveen: KPMG.

KPMG. (2011). *KPMG International Survey of Corporate Responsibility Reporting 2011*. Amstelveen: KPMG.

KPMG and Institute for Environmental Management (WIMM). (1999). *KPMG International Survey of Environmental Reporting 1999*. Amstelveen: KPMG.

KPMG and University of Amsterdam. (2002). *KPMG International Survey of Corporate Sustainability Reporting 2002*. Amstelveen: KPMG.

KPMG and University of Amsterdam. (2005). *KPMG International Survey of Corporate Responsibility Reporting 2005*. Amstelveen: KPMG.

Lie, Y. (2012). Enhancing the quality of sustainability reporting in the financial services sector: Towards a better discharge of accountability, Unpublished MSc thesis, Amsterdam Business School, Universiteit van Amsterdam.

Lie, Y. & O'Sullivan, N. (2013). Social accountability and the finance sector: The effectiveness of the Global Reporting Initiative Financial Services Sector Supplement (2008), Working paper, Amsterdam Business School, Universiteit van Amsterdam.

Milne, M., & Patten, D. (2002). Securing organisational legitimacy: An experimental decision case examining the impact of environmental disclosures. *Accounting, Auditing and Accountability Journal, 15*(3), 372–405.

Mulgan, R. (2000). 'Accountability': An ever-expanding concept? *Public Administration, 78*(3), 555–573.

O'Donovan, G. (2002). Environmental disclosures in the annual report: Extending the applicability and predictive power of legitimacy theory. *Accounting, Auditing and Accountability Journal, 15*(3), 344–71.

O'Dwyer, B. (2002). Managerial perceptions of corporate social disclosure: An Irish story. *Accounting, Auditing and Accountability Journal, 15*(3), 406–436.

O'Dwyer, B., & Owen, D. (2005). Assurance statement practice in environmental, social and sustainability reporting: A critical evaluation. *The British Accounting Review, 37*, 205–229.

O'Dwyer, B., Owen, D., & Unerman, J. (2011). Seeking legitimacy for new assurance forms: The case of assurance on sustainability reporting. *Accounting, Organizations and Society, 36*(1), 31–52.

O'Sullivan, N. (2010) *Social Accountability and the Finance Sector: The case of Equator Principles (EP) institutionalisation.* Unpublished PhD thesis, Amsterdam Business School, Universiteit van Amsterdam.

O'Sullivan, N., & O' Dwyer, B. (2009). Stakeholder perspectives on a financial sector legitimation process: The case of NGOs and the Equator Principles. *Accounting, Auditing and Accountability Journal, 22*(4), 553–587.

Owen, D. (2007). Assurance practice in sustainability reporting. In J. Unerman, J. Bebbington, & B. O'Dwyer (Eds.), *Sustainability Accounting and Accountability* (pp. 168–183). London: Routledge.

Patten, D. (1992). Intra-industry environmental disclosures in response to the Alaskan oil spill: A note on legitimacy theory. *Accounting, Organizations and Society, 15*(5), 471–475.

(The) Rainforest Action Network (RAN). (2005). *Citigroup 2000-2004*, (last) available at: http://www.ran.org/what_we_do/global_finance/hist/citibank/ (last accessed August 31, 2007).

Roberts, J. (1991). The possibilities of accountability. *Accounting, Organizations and Society, 16* (4), 355–370.

Roberts, J., & Scapens, R. (1985). Accounting systems and systems of accountability. *Accounting, Organizations and Society, 10*(4), 443–456.

Schweiker, W. (1993). Accounting for ourselves: Accounting practices and the discourse of ethics. *Accounting, Organizations and Society, 18*(2/3), 231–252.

Shearer, T. (2002). Ethics and Accountability: From the for itself to the for-the-other. *Accounting, Organizations and Society, 27*, 541–573.

Sinclair, A. (1995). The chameleon of accountability: Forms and discourses. *Accounting, Organizations and Society, 20*(2/3), 219–237.

Spitzeck, H. (2007). Innovation and learning by public discourse: Citigroup and the Rainforest Action Network. Center for Responsible Business working paper series, University of California, Berkeley

Steen, M. (2008). Iryan mine sparks green approach. *Financial Times Special Report: Sustainable Banking*, June 3rd, London, p. 3.

Tarna, K. (2001). Reporting on the environment: Current practice in the financial services sector. In J. J. Bouma, M. Jeucken, & L. Klinkers (Eds.), *Sustainable banking: The greening of finance* (pp. 149–165). Sheffield: Greenleaf Publishing.

Van Gelder, J. (2003). *The financing of the OCP pipeline in Ecuador: A research paper prepared for Urgewald and environmental defense.* Castricum: Profundo.

Wright, C. (2009). Setting standards for responsible banking: Examining the role of the International Finance Corporation in the emergence of the Equator Principles. In F. Biermann, B. Siebenhüner, & A. Schreyögg (Eds.), *International organizations and global environmental governance.* London: Routledge.

Are the Equator Principles Greenwash or Game Changers? Effectiveness, Transparency and Future Challenges

Ariel Meyerstein

Abstract This chapter will focus on an overall assessment of implementation of the Equator Principles ("EPs") based on survey research from participating banks—Equator Principle Financial Institutions ("EPFIs"). It documents both how individual institutions have changed their organizational structures, policies and procedures following their decisions to adopt the EPs and how they have contributed to the growth and evolution of the regime. These measures, however, are not perfect proxies for "on the ground" performance, so the chapter also addresses the related issues of transparency and enforcement and proposes additional institutional structures that the EPFIs could adopt to enhance the EPs' effectiveness.

1 Introduction

The contributions to this volume all consider the various risk management frameworks and soft law standards that allow us to speak of a growing trend in 'responsible banking'. The Equator Principles are emblematic of these developments over the past decade: a code of conduct voluntarily adopted first in 2003 by many of the most profitable banks in the world that collectively held more than 30 % of the global project finance market (Meyerstein 2013b, 580). The Principles were adopted to ensure that the projects financed by the banks were 'developed in a manner that is socially responsible and reflect sound environmental management practices'. They were intended to serve as a common baseline and framework for the implementation by each adopting institution of internal social and environmental policies, procedures and standards related to its project financing activities (Equator Principles, Preamble). As has been widely recognised, there is a strong business case for the banks to enhance their risk assessment and management practices, which help minimise credit risk and reputational risks arising from

A. Meyerstein (✉)
Vice President, Labor Affairs, Corporate Responsibility and Corporate Governance,
United States Council for International Business, New York, NY, USA
e-mail: ariel.meyerstein@gmail.com

© Springer International Publishing Switzerland 2015
K. Wendt (ed.), *Responsible Investment Banking*, CSR, Sustainability, Ethics &
Governance, DOI 10.1007/978-3-319-10311-2_16

problematic projects becoming the focus of public advocacy campaigns and media attention (Macve and Chen 2010, 894; Lozinski 2012).

This all speaks to risk management, but the Principles also speak about responsibility over social issues historically the provenance of governments and public policy: the Preamble declares that the adopting banks 'recognise the importance of climate change, biodiversity, and human rights, and believe negative impacts on project-affected ecosystems, communities, and the climate should be avoided where possible', and, if unavoidable, these impacts 'should be minimised, mitigated, and/or offset'. The Preamble also acknowledges that financial institutions have 'opportunities to promote responsible environmental stewardship and socially responsible development'. To that end, the adopting institutions promise to 'not provide loans to projects where the borrower will not or is unable to comply with our respective social and environmental policies and procedures that implement the Equator Principles'.

There is no doubt that the Principles have grown rapidly in terms of membership, geographic scope and the stringency of the requirements they impose on adopting institutions and are now a project finance industry standard. This tremendous growth, however, is not the only measure of the regime's impact. More important questions must be asked about the quality of the regime's governance and its effectiveness. Have the adopting institutions executed on the promises in the Preamble? What impacts are they having on the actual practice of adopting institutions and, more importantly, on the ground in the lives of the communities affected by these projects. Have they been an exercise in corporate greenwash—an effort to boost reputations without any substantive change in practices—or have they been game changers?

After a decade of engagement, the Banktrack network of NGOs, which designated themselves the watchdogs of Equator Principle Financial Institution (EPFI) implementation, still views the EPs' fulfillment of their promise as a half-filled glass on a number of fundamental issues. While this view perhaps minimises the tremendous impact of the EPs, the complaints of the NGOs have some merit, particularly on the all-important issue of transparency, the cornerstone for all other implementation. The recent expansion of the EPs to cover other project-related modes of finance and to address human rights and climate change creates the potential for them to be even more relevant to responsible finance in their second decade, but only if the banks deliver on these commitments and continue to make them more rigorous. This may prove difficult, however, if the swelling of the ranks of regime's membership and their commitment to adopting rules by consensus threaten to ultimately undermine the brand's value.

2 The Origins of the Equator Principles

Large-scale infrastructure has been big business and the dominant economic development strategy of multilateral development institutions for more than half a century, although it dipped in popularity along with global financial crises in the 1990s and between 2007 and 2008. Most countries, however, have struggled to balance the contribution of large-scale infrastructure projects to economic development and their environmental and social impacts on local populations (Scott-Brown and Iocca 2010, 6). This challenge is exacerbated in developing economies where population growth and underdevelopment have placed the highest demand for infrastructure development in the coming decades (Orr and Kennedy 2008).

Unfortunately, effective project-level impact assessment remains a distant dream in most of these countries. A World Bank survey of 32 oil-producing developing countries found that most of the countries surveyed had a 'sufficiently appropriate, but largely theoretical, environmental policy and legal framework' in place for managing impacts of the oil and gas industry, including dedicated institutions such as a ministry of environment. However, the survey showed that these systems existed primarily on paper, and the institutions were found generally to be empty boxes lacking sufficient resources (budget, staff, training, technology, information systems, etc.) to implement their strategies effectively and to fulfil their regulatory mandate (Scott-Brown and Iocca 2010, 11–14). The survey found that in many countries, much of the emphasis of any impact assessment process 'appears to be directed toward regulatory approval of oil and gas projects rather than toward developing a life cycle approach for minimising environmental and social impacts across the entire project life' (Scott-Brown and Iocca 2010, 11).

After decades of these projects imposing great social and environmental costs on local populations, development finance institutions, such as the International Bank for Reconstruction and Development (IBRD), spurred on by NGO public advocacy campaigns, finally made some progress in incorporating sustainable development principles and accountability mechanisms, such as the World Bank's Inspection Panel, into their financing activities (Sarfaty 2009). But just as this progress was achieved, loans to private sector entities began to supplant direct loans to governments. The emergence of a global market for private investment in infrastructure was spurred on by privatisation and deregulation of many industrial sectors all over the world and the continued globalisation of financial markets through harmonising of tax regimes, lowering of restrictions on foreign capital and the conclusion of bilateral investment treaties (Sorge 2004; Esty 2007). The World Bank Group's private lending arm, the International Finance Corporation (IFC), picked-up the IBRD's increasing slack in this area, often lending to private entities as part of syndicates in concert with commercial banks from OECD countries (Wright 2007). Overall, annual project finance volumes for infrastructure in developing countries multiplied tenfold in developing countries between 1990 and 1997 (World Bank 2006, fn. 55).

With an increase in project investments came an increase in attention from civil society and, eventually, the internal reforms initiated at the IBRD began to bleed over to the IFC, which eventually incorporated nine of the World Bank's 10 Environmental and Social Safeguard Policies and other guidelines on environmental and social impact assessment into its own operational procedures. The IFC then created an oversight mechanism called the Compliance Advisor Ombudsman (CAO) to oversee the institution's compliance with these new policies. The Inspection Panel and the CAO have contributed to the architecture of accountability at the World

Bank Group, but they remain highly problematic mechanisms for achieving true accountability for project-affected populations (Bradlow 2005; Bridgeman and Hunter 2008).

Even though commercial banks often participated directly in project finance alongside the IFC, a gap remained between the level of scrutiny applied to project finance transactions by development banks and the processes (or lack thereof) for environmental and social risk review deployed by commercial banks. NGOs sought to bridge this gap with several very public advocacy campaigns against the leading project finance lending institutions (O'Sullivan and O'Dwyer 2009, 562). In response, in late 2002, a core group of four banks—ABN Amro, Barclays, Citi (then Citigroup) and West LB—created a working group, with guidance from the IFC, to explore the creation of an industry standard for environmental and social risk assessment. On 4 June 2003, after further refinement, the senior executives of 10 commercial banks met at the IFC in Washington, DC, and formally adopted the Equator Principles. Unrelenting pressure from the NGO community and the link between the EPs' normative content and the IFC's Performance Standards (which have been updated twice since the EPs were created) caused the regime to spread beyond its initial core group of banks and ratchet up its requirements twice in the past decade.

The 10 Equator Principles correspond to the various phases of the project finance lending cycle and aim to fill the gaps between what is required by national regulation in many developing countries and the IFC's Performance Standards, which are taken by many as global best practice for the assessment and management of project impacts.

All requirements flow from Principle 1 (EP1) on the categorisation of projects, as the scope of borrower and bank due diligence will turn upon the categorisation of projects as either Category A (projects with potential significant adverse social or environmental impacts that are diverse, irreversible, or unprecedented), Category B (projects with potential limited adverse social or environmental impacts that are few in number, generally site specific, largely reversible, and readily addressed through mitigation measures) or Category C (projects with minimal or no social or environmental impacts). For each Category A or Category B project, EP 2 requires the borrower to have 'conducted a Social and Environmental Assessment (Assessment) process to address, as appropriate and to the EPFI's satisfaction, the relevant social and environmental impacts and risks of the proposed project', which Assessment 'should also propose mitigation and management measures relevant and appropriate to the nature and scale of the proposed project'.

EP 3 then defines the scope of responsibilities of EFPIs and the borrowers based on the income and governance levels of the host country: for projects built in designated countries (countries 'deemed to have robust environmental and social governance, legislation systems and institutional capacity designed to protect their people and the natural environment'), borrowers' environmental and social risk assessment need comply only with national law, whereas for projects built in non-designated countries, the EPs insist that project sponsors also take into account the International Financial Corporation's Performance Standards on Social and

Environmental Sustainability and the IFC's sector-specific Environmental, Health and Safety (EHS) Guidelines. There has been concern, though no solid evidence of any systematic practice, that because the banks' discretion in project assessment is not checked externally, an EPFI's downgrading of the risk of a project would lighten the environmental and social requirements it must impose on sponsors (Amalric 2005; Richardson 2008 at 415; Wright 2012, 68).

Based on the impact assessment conducted pursuant to EP 2, EP 4 requires the borrower to develop an 'Action Plan' and a 'Social and Environmental Management System' to address the issues identified by the impact assessment through monitoring and/or corrective actions commensurate with the project's potential impacts and risks. Among these measures is stakeholder engagement, which is detailed in Principle 5. To capture lingering concerns or those that develop during project construction, EP 6 requires the borrower to establish a grievance mechanism 'scaled to the risks and adverse impacts of the project' that will allow the borrower to 'receive and facilitate resolution of concerns and grievances about the project's social and environmental performance raised by individuals or groups from among project-affected communities'. Principle 7 requires that 'an independent social or environmental expert not directly associated with the borrower will review the Assessment, A[ction] P[lan] and consultation process documentation in order to assist EPFI's due diligence, and assess Equator Principles compliance'.

Principle 8 recognises that an 'important strength' of the EPs is the inclusion of various environmental and social covenants in loan documentation which condition issuance of project financing on the borrower complying with 'all relevant host country social and environmental laws, regulations and permits' and the Action Plan 'during the construction and operation of the project'. Covenants should also require the borrower to periodically report on its compliance with the Action Plan and relevant laws and, where applicable and appropriate, to decommission facilities in accordance with an agreed decommissioning plan. 'Where a borrower is not in compliance with' these covenants, EP 8 requires EPFIs to 'work with the borrower to bring it back into compliance to the extent feasible'. If a borrower fails to attain compliance 'within an agreed grace period', EP 8 provides that 'EPFIs reserve the right to exercise remedies, as they consider appropriate'. In the case of such 'events of default', the principal remedy is repayment of the loan, although typically the banks prefer to work with borrowers to get them into compliance (EPFIs Guidance Note).

Principle 9 requires EPFIs to require the appointment of 'an independent environmental and/or social expert, or require the borrower to retain qualified and experienced external experts to verify [the] monitoring information' the borrower shares with the EPFIs. Finally, Principle 10 imposes a separate reporting requirement on each EPFI 'to report publicly at least annually about its Equator Principles implementation processes and experience, taking into account appropriate confidentiality considerations'. The reporting requirement is discussed in further detail below.

3 The Evolution of the Equator Principles

When they were first introduced, the original 10 EPFIs represented more than 30 %
of the 2002 project finance market (Meyerstein 2013a, b, 580). The number of
adopting institutions has steadily grown over the years and now totals 80 institutions
from 34 countries that lend to projects in more than 100 countries. The EPFIs' ranks
include commercial banks, export credit agencies and development finance institutions that, according to the EP website, finance more than 70 % of project finance
in emerging markets, which is, after all, the area of greatest importance in terms of
the Principles' intended effects of raising global standards of project regulatory
review on both sides of the Equator. In 2009, there were 26 EPFIs among the top
50 Global League Leaders, ranked by the total amount financed by market share,
and 40 of the top 224 League Leaders were EPFIs, accounting for more than 50 %
of the total capital flows in the global project finance market (PFI 2010).

The EPFIs have tried continually to expand their reach through sponsorship of
conferences in geographic areas not known for heightened attention to sustainability, including India, Russia, China and the Middle East. The EPFIs 'coordinate
closely' with the IFC 'on outreach activities in the emerging markets', (Aizawa and
Yang 2010, 129) which, according to an IFC staffer, allows the IFC to extend its
reach with commercial banks in those regions more easily. This strategy has
worked partially but has not kept pace with the dramatic rise of project financing
in key emerging markets in the past few years. For example, in 2010, there were
42 EPFIs in the top 233 League Leaders, covering 40 % of the project loan market
(PFI 2011), and in the first quarter of 2011, the top 25 lending banks were split
almost evenly between the EPs and Indian and Chinese institutions: Indian and
Chinese banks covered 38.6 % of the market and EPFIs covered 33.9 %. Notably,
the top three banks by project finance volume in 2010 were not EPFIs (Wright 2012,
at 62). Moreover, the largest individual projects sponsored in the first quarter of
2011 were nearly all in either India, China or Russia, with the exception of one
project each in the UK, Australia and Singapore (PFI 2011). This trend continued in
2012, in which 6 of the top 10 global lenders (by volume) were based in Asia
(Dealogic 2013), although only 2 of these (Suitomo Mitsui Financial Group and
Mizuho Financial Group, both of Japan) were EPFIs (there were 2 other EPFIs in
the top 10 from Europe and North America). And yet, to date, only one bank from
Russia, India and China have adopted the EPs. This shows that as much as the EPs
have gone global, they have thus far not successfully penetrated key emerging
markets that have been home in recent years to both the top lenders and the biggest
projects. Thus, while the EPs have expanded tremendously in their 8 years of
existence, the global playing field is still uneven in patches. To their credit,
however, the EPFIs have responded to these trends: in November 2013, the EP
Association's annual meeting chose Tokyo as the site of its first meeting outside of
Washington, DC, for the explicit purpose of engaging Asian financial institutions.

4 Ratcheting Up Standards and Ongoing Concerns

Uneven patches also remain in terms of the stringency of the requirements imposed on adopting institutions and their implementation of them. From the start, there were concerns that the EP regime did not go far enough in meeting the ideals expressed in the Collevecchio Declaration, a manifesto announced by 100 NGOs at the World Economic Forum in 2003, which called for financial institutions to recognise their role and responsibility for financing unsustainable projects and other global social problems, ranging from global warming to armed conflicts (Collevecchio 2003). The complaints of the NGOs about the Principles have remained fairly constant from the start, although some of their criticisms have been addressed over time to various degrees (such as the creation of an official governance structure and the recent expansion of the Principles to cover project-related corporate loans under certain conditions).

The perceived legitimacy of the regime has waxed and waned over time in the eyes of its main interlocutors (O'Sullivan and O'Dwyer 2009, 576), which, if anything, can be traced to a clash of paradigms: the focus of the NGOs on the environmental and social outcomes of projects and expect 'dodgy deals' (as they define them) not to be financed—period. The banks (and the language of the Equator Principles) emphasise their internal processes of project review and management of risks during the project planning phases. To this, the NGOs reply, as Banktrack noted in its 2011 report 'The Outside Job' and reiterated in its 2012 report on the draft EP III, '[t]he world does not need improved risk management as a goal in itself; it needs fewer supersized dams blocking life-supporting rivers, less mining projects scarring entire mountains and polluting community water sources with their tailings, no oil exploration projects destroying our seas and last remaining wilderness areas, no coal power plants belching out millions of tons of greenhouse gases into our already fatigued atmosphere' (Banktrack 2012).

The last revision of the EP IIIs came out in draft form in August 2012 and, after a 60-day public comment and engagement period and a finalisation and launch period, were finally released in May 2013 and became effective on 1 June 2013. The EP III represents a decade of maturation of the regime and arguably goes a considerable distance in responding to the NGOs long-standing concerns regarding transparency, the limited scope of the EPs' application only to project finance loans, and the EPs' previous failure to address climate change. Nonetheless, on these and other issues, the Banktrack network remains dissatisfied (Banktrack 2013), which is explored below.

But even with EP III, the banks have been unwilling to categorically exclude the development of coal projects, mountain top removal mining or projects in sensitive ecosystems (Wright 2012, 66). With EP III, the EPFIs have imposed new requirements related to carbon emissions, but the NGOs have dismissed these as ineffective.[1] In addition, only in July 2013, with the update to EP III, have they come closer to enabling communities affected by projects to not only be 'consulted' but also to have the power to give or withhold 'consent' to project development, but this remains a matter of considerable controversy, as the status and specific requirements of the international legal norm of 'free, prior and informed consent' that undergirds the EPs 'consultation' requirement remain hotly contested (Meyerstein 2013a, b, 560–563).

The particularly long period of internal consultation and engagement that this last revision required (and perhaps some of the perceived laxity in the requirements) is symptomatic of one of the key stress points in the EP regime—the diversity of participants (Lazarus 2012, 2015) and possible levels of implementation. Banks that adopt the EPs become members to the Equator Principles Association, which was established in July 2010. The Association is an unincorporated membership organisation and governance structure complete with bylaws, voting mechanisms and membership dues led by the Steering Committee, whose decisions are binding on the members (EP Association 2010). This enhanced formalisation also responded in small part to another of the NGOs' concerns, as it introduced a de-listing procedure for removing EPFIs not compliant with the annual reporting requirement in EP10 (although that is substantially different to a fully-fledged accountability mechanism based on non-compliance with the EPs' norms). Participation in the governance structure, general adoption levels across countries and reported levels of implementation by banks from different regions points to a bit of the tension that has accompanied the evolution of the regime and will continue to guide its future growth.

The overall membership of the Association is heavily tilted towards Western banks and those from advanced economies: more than 60 % of members are from North America, Australia and Western Europe, with 11 % from Africa and 6 % from Asia. The Association is governed by a 14-bank Steering Committee, which has consistently been comprised of mostly North American and Western European banks and, with the exception of the brief tenure of B, has routinely been chaired by one of the founding four banks (Barclays, Citi and now ING which subsumed ABN Amro in the wake of the financial crisis). Similarly, its various working groups focused on the substantive aspects of maintaining and enhancing the EP regime have historically also been Eurocentric. It is perhaps also revealing that of the banks that recently formed the Thun Group to address the implementation of the United Nations Guiding Principles for Business and Human Rights, most were EP Steering Committee members, comprising roughly half of the Committee (Barclays, BBVA,

---

[1] With respect to climate change, the NGOs are concerned that the analysis for less Greenhouse Gas (GHG) intensive alternatives to be conducted for projects with more than 100,000 tonnes of CO_2 omissions does not *obligate* project developers to choose the less GHG-intensive alternative. They also note that the threshold for reporting (100,000 tonnes annually) to be 'far higher' than the 25,000 tonnes threshold in the IFC Performance Standards. Moreover, '[g]iven the absence of any obligatory reduction targets over time, such reporting requirements alone will also do little to nothing to reduce emissions' (Banktrack 2012).

Credit Suisse AG, ING Bank NV, RBS Group, UBS AG and UniCredit). None of this should be particularly shocking, but the question is, what stresses it puts on governance of the regime and adoption of new standards, considering that the governance rules establish that the Principles attempt to govern by consensus, striving for decisions to be adopted by a majority of the banks.

5 Policy Adoption and Organisational Change

The lack of transparency regarding project level information has relegated most discussion of the banks' compliance to focus on the implementation of policy and procedures. Several studies demonstrate that, on the whole, EPFIs have dramatically enhanced their environmental and social risk management policies and review procedures for credit decisions and auditing processes and have implemented substantial staff training programmes (Meyerstein 2013a, b, 553–557; Banktrack 2010; Scholtens and Lammertjan 2007; Aizawa 2007; Freshfields 2005; Macve and Chen 2010, 897–898). My previous study found this to be true not only among banks from high-income OECD countries, which face the most reputational pressure from civil society (Wright and Rwabizambuga 2006), but also among other institutions, in roughly equal proportion to the distribution of these institutions in the larger pool of EPFIs. Notably, based on survey responses from 24 of the then 65 EPFIs, 'prior to the EPs' creation, there were virtually no ESRM systems in place, and those systems that were in place were perhaps rudimentary compared to what is in place now' (Meyerstein 2013a, b, 587). While roughly 40 % of these banks would discuss environmental and social issues with potential clients before adopting the EPs, only about a quarter of them benchmarked their environmental and social risk review to existing World Bank standards, and even fewer did so in a rigorous systemised fashion (Meyerstein 2013a, b, 587). Following their adoption of the Principles, however, 75 % reported having institutionalised changes of varying degrees in their project review practices, typically by designating personnel or creating specific departments for environmental and social risk review, standardising procedures in a more formal process that linked project review to the EPs and IFC benchmarks and incorporating these standards in detailed loan covenants (Meyerstein 2013a, b, 588).

In addition, a few banks have gone beyond what the Equator Principles require, both by applying more rigorous review procedures to non-project finance transactions (before this became a requirement for certain qualifying project-related loans in the 2013 update) (Meyerstein 2013a, b, 588) and by implementing policies addressing sustainable forestry practices, management of toxic chemicals, exclusion of financing of controversial weapons production and trade and higher standards on carbon emissions (Wright 2012, 63). There also has been steady progress in the EPFIs' obligation to report annually on their implementation of the Principles under Principle 10, although what is actually conveyed by the reporting information needs to be put into proper context (Meyerstein 2013a, b, 557–564; Banktrack 2010, 185).

If it is true that, by and large, EPFIs have changed their practices and procedures, this is a considerable step in the right direction, amplified by the nature of the project finance market. Because of the relatively small number of players and the pooling of the debt financing, whereby a single financial institution (mandated arranger) typically engages with the project sponsor and then collects additional financing from syndicates comprised of other banks, if the mandated arranger is an EPFI, then all of the lending to the project from the syndicate must be subject to the EPs (Meyerstein 2013a, b, 551). Others have reported that non-EPFIs chosen as mandated arrangers have voluntarily subjected particular deals to the EPs in their loan agreements to gain access to additional capital from EPFIs (Wright 2012, 69), that could not participate in the syndicate unless it was governed by the Principles. Some project sponsors may select EPFIs as arrangers because of their enhanced capacity for environmental and social risk management (Freshfields 2005, 118–121; Richardson 2008, 420). The prevalence of the Equator Principles is also reflected in part by anecdotal evidence of the drastic increase in the average fees paid to consultants for environmental impact assessments (at least for mining projects): in 1992, these fees could range between US$20,000 to US$160,000, but by 2010 these costs (Anckorn 2010) had escalated as high as more than US$2 million. Thus, even if policy implementation is not perfect and there are clearly defined subsets of leaders and laggards (those 'free riding' off the EP name), the structure of the project finance industry may minimise the impact of the uneven adoption levels.

If the regime has thus far relied on the structure of the project finance market to neutralise effects from potential disparities in adoption and implementation levels, this will not be operable when the Principles are applied in the future to general project-related corporate loans. With the release of EP III, in addition to applying to financing or advisory activities for projects of more than US$10 million, the EPs now apply to 'project-related' corporate loans so long as:

1. 'The majority of the loan is related to a single Project over which the client has effective operational control (either direct or indirect)'.
2. 'The total aggregate loan amount is at least US$100 million'.
3. 'The EPFI's individual commitment (before syndication or sell down) is at least US$50 million'.
4. 'The loan tenor is at least 2 years'.

The EP III also extends the EPs to 'bridge loans' that are financial instruments extended to cover short-term needs, so long as they have a 'tenor of less than 2 years' and 'are intended to be refinanced by a Project Finance or Project-Related Corporate Loan that is anticipated to meet the relevant criteria described above'. The capacity of individual banks not known for their EP-excellence to manage these projects will be one of the true future tests of the Principles, both because individual banks will be on their own to implement the Principles and because the leverage banks have with corporate loans is a bit more attenuated than with project finance loans.

6   Reporting and Transparency

In evaluating compliance with the Equator Principles, different metrics and sign-posts can be used, although by and large there is a paucity of information on both internal institutional practices and on the ground effects. Evaluation of policy adoption and institutional change has thus far been the principal approach because, as difficult as it is to gain an inside look at organisational structures and policies, it is even more difficult to assess compliance on the project level because the banks have long argued that project-level disclosure clashes with the banks' fiduciary duties: revealing project information, they claim, would be highly unprofessional, if not illegal (Gaskin 2007, 61). This is problematic and is likely the one element of the regime that will account most for its success or failure in the future.

Although the EP reporting requirement comes in the least credible fashion (first-party auditing) (Prakash and Potoski 2007, 790 n.18), research has shown that 70 % of the institutions reported using external auditing firms to verify the disclosures in their CSR reports, which Prakash and Potoski characterise as the gold standard among voluntary programmes.

Generally, assurance auditors from large accounting firms read EPFIs' corporate social responsibility reports, among other reports, to verify that the contents disclosed are accurate. An assurer for a major EPFI has argued, however, that the value of assurance is sometimes limited by the roles played by a bank in different syndicates: if a bank that has hired an assurer has not acted as the lead arranger or the 'environmental bank' for the deals on which it is reporting, it makes limited information available to the assurer regarding project implementation data. After the financial close, however, the agent bank is supposed to update all syndicate members of any issues reported by consultants, so all syndicate members should have this information, but it may come in summary and, therefore, less than helpful, form (Rodriguez 2011). In addition, the EP Strategic Review observed that '[t]here are no agreed standards for audits' and accordingly recommended that the EPFIs develop an 'EP assurance standard to use for third party auditing of EPFIs' internal implementation processes', including 'an audit procedure for verification of imple-mentation capacity of new members' (Lazarus and Feldbaum 2011, 7). These recommendations were not implemented in the EP III update.

Even assuming that the figures on rejection of projects reportedly annually are accurate, they must be taken with a grain of salt. Before the EP III upgrade, Principle 10 required adopting banks to disclose annually their categorisation of projects and results of their reviews of them, with the option of further breaking this down in the aggregate in terms of either/or both the sector and the geographic region. Although some might gleam from this a sense of how stringently a given institution has applied its environmental and social risk management policies, credit decisions are almost never made on these grounds alone and, thus, 'an absolute no would be unlikely based on the Principles alone' (Gaskin 2007, 63).

Credit approval committees often reject projects because the background of project sponsors not only raises questions about their capacity for environmental and social risk management, but also about their credit histories and general business practices. The two often go hand-in-hand. Others have noted that even 'getting to a no stage is pretty unlikely because few banks would let negotiations progress to that point' if warning signs had already manifested themselves (id.). Rather, '[o]nce the assessment has been done, if there are elements of a project that breach the standards, the response is not to refuse the project but to put processes in place to manage it so it does become compliant' (id.) Survey data, however, is more equivocal. It shows that the banks surveyed (24 of the then 63 EPFIs) were evenly split on whether they had ever rejected a project primarily because of ESRM issues (Meyerstein 2013a, b, 564).

Even if the overall content of the information currently disclosed in the banks' reporting is not particularly revealing in and of itself (compared to disclosure of project-level information well in advance of financial closure), it is nevertheless revealing because this reporting is costly to produce and even greater resources are expended in hiring external auditors to certify the disclosures. Thus, although the reporting does not provide concrete evidence that banks made certain funding decisions on particular projects *solely* in observance of their commitments under the Equator Principles, what the reporting does evidence is that their entire approach to credit decisions was informed by a process of categorisation and consideration of environmental and social risks as called for by the Equator Principles—something that only a handful of banks did prior to the EPs, and when they did so, it was not systematised in any fashion (Meyerstein 2013b, 553–554; Jeucken 2001; Scholtens 2009; Wright 2012).

Beyond aggregate reporting lies the Holy Grail for assessing the effectiveness of the Principles: project level data. Unfortunately, before EP III there were no requirements for either EPFIs or project sponsors to reveal project level information. What has emerged through other sources—principally NGO activism—has led to a mixed review of individual project implementation that varies depending on whom you ask. There have been instances where the EPs appeared to play a determinative role in project finance decisions, such as the withdrawal of financing for paper pulp mills along the Uruguay-Argentina border and the decision by several EPFIs not to finance the Belo Monte Dam in the Brazilian Amazon (Meyerstein 2015). There have also been instances where the Principles appear to have been ignored by the banks, such as the Rapu Rapu copper mine in the Philippines, or several other projects labelled by the Banktrack network as 'dodgy deals' (Banktrack 2007; Wright 2012, 65–66).

The test of the banks' commitment to enforcing the Principles lies not only in initial credit decisions, but also when they are confronted with information that they are funding a project that does not comply with applicable laws or the IFC Performance Standards. Principle 8 recognises that an 'important strength' of the EPs is the inclusion of various environmental and social covenants in loan documentation that condition issuance of project financing on the borrower complying with 'all relevant host country social and environmental laws, regulations and permits' and the Action Plan 'during the construction and operation of the project'.

Covenants should also require the borrower to periodically report on its compliance with the Action Plan and relevant laws and, where applicable and appropriate, to decommission facilities in accordance with an agreed decommissioning plan. 'Where a borrower is not in compliance with' these covenants, EP 8 requires EPFIs to 'work with the borrower to bring it back into compliance to the extent feasible'. If a borrower fails to attain compliance 'within an agreed grace period', EP 8 provides that 'EPFIs reserve the right to exercise remedies, as they consider appropriate'. In the case of such 'events of default', the principal remedy is demand for immediate repayment of the loan. However, survey research of bank practices has also shown that once financing has been extended to a project, the decision about what to do with a non-compliant borrower is not cut and dry: once a project is underway, most EPFIs (more than 80 %) prefer to massage the situation with the borrower and bring them into compliance, rather than take the drastic step of call a material default (Meyerstein 2015).

This decision is also complicated by the fact that defining project success or failure is often a very difficult one that is politicised by the relevant parties. This makes judging the EPs by project outcomes difficult to study without more objective, on the ground information. This state of affairs has been exacerbated on the one hand by the banks' refusal to discuss their successful projects (Watchman et al. 2007, 96–97) and, on the other, by Banktrack's emphasis on the 'dodgy deals' over the successful ones (Wright 2012, 65).

The perceived and actual persistence of dodgy deals can only be combated by fixing the major persisting criticisms of the EPs: insufficient transparency on the project, institution and regime levels (Banktrack 2013, 5–7) and the related lack of an independent monitoring, verification, or enforcement mechanisms on a regime level (Banktrack 2013, 7–9).

Although the EPs have always required project sponsor to create effective grievance mechanisms, with the advent of the United Nations Guiding Principles on Business and Human Rights and its calls for corporations to 'establish or participate in effective operational-level grievance mechanisms for individuals and communities who may be adversely impacted', there is already increased pressure on banks *themselves* to provide grievance mechanisms beyond those that are supposed to be established by project sponsors. Despite this increased awareness and the EPs' own referencing of the Guiding Principles in their new Preamble, it is highly unlikely that the EP banks will at any time establish a collective independent grievance mechanism. It is far more likely that NGOs will continue to creatively file Equator Principles Complaints to address what they consider to be 'dodgy deals' and will file them directly with the relevant institutions, who will then need to determine how to respond (Meyerstein 2015).

The continued ability of NGOs to identify these projects and intervene in a timely manner will depend on the EPFIs' implementation of the new requirement under EP 5 and also to some extent under EP 10 to facilitate the disclosure of project level information. Project level information is important functionally for risk avoidance related to stakeholder engagement and securing community support. Principle 5 is intended to make sure that project sponsors, governments and banks respect the norm of 'free, prior and informed consent' (FPIC), something governments, particularly in developing countries, struggle to ensure (Scott-Brown and Iocca 2010, 11).

Although FPIC is enshrined in international treaties and has been integrated into national legislation or recognised in national jurisprudence in many countries, sporadic implementation of FPIC in state practice has hindered its elevation to the status of customary international law. The 2012 revision of the IFC Performance Standards came to a considered, but controversial conclusion that '[t]here is no universally accepted definition of FPIC' (IFC 2012).

Under the new EP III, Principle 5 requires that for all Category A and, where appropriate, Category B projects developed in non-designated countries, 'the government, borrower or third party expert' must have 'consulted with project affected communities in a structured and culturally appropriate manner'. In the case of projects with 'significant adverse impacts', the process must occur 'early in the Assessment process and in any event before the project construction commences, and on an ongoing basis' and must 'ensure their free, prior and informed consultation and facilitate their informed participation as a means to establish, to the satisfaction of the EPFI, whether a project has adequately incorporated affected communities' concerns'. In the case of indigenous populations, the Principle requires compliance with national laws, including those implementing international obligations, and in the special circumstances, as recognised in IFC Performance Standard 7, these processes will require these marginalised populations' FPIC.

In addition, under the revised EP III, every EFPI must now also report project finance transaction names to the EP Secretariat, subject to obtaining client consent at any point prior to financial close. The EPFI must submit the name to the EP Association for publication on its website, including the calendar year in which the transaction closed, the sector of the project and the country where it is located. Since EP III is effective from 4 June 2013 and EPFIs have 1 year to fulfil their reporting requirement, it remains to be seen how compliant the EPFIs will be with these new obligations and also whether the very lean EP Secretariat staff is has sufficient resources to keep the website fully up to date. With enhanced project information should come not only new opportunities for NGOs to enforce the Principles but also enhanced opportunities for the entire community of banks to learn from each other's experiences and further refine best practices.

7   The Next Decade of the EPs

The true long-term impact of the EPs will likely be demonstrated in the coming decade, which will provide opportunities for EP banks to prove their commitment to the significantly upgraded Principles. The increased stringency in the project-level transparency requirements—while still not completely mandatory—provide a new level of expectations on adopting institutions and their borrowers. There will also now be many more opportunities to implement the Principles with the expansion in EP III to certain qualifying project-related corporate loans, which addresses the complaints long held by NGOs that too many projects escaped the EPs' scope of application. This expanded scope, however, does risk leading to some confusion over exactly which loans are covered. In addition, from an organisational perspective, corporate loan officers may have less experience in conducting the level of environmental and social risk assessment that is typical for a project finance transaction. If risk assessment is not centralised within a given bank, there will be a need to upgrade capacity in this regard.

There will also likely be further developments related to the application of the consultation requirements and grievance mechanisms, which overlap substantially with the UN Guiding Principles on Business and Human Rights' requirements for human rights due diligence and access to an effective remedy. As noted, half of the EP Steering Committee comprises most of the Thun Group of banks, which formed in order to address the financial sectors' responsibilities to respect human rights under the UN Guiding Principles. The Thun group released a discussion paper in October 2013 to address these responsibilities in detail. While the Thun group discussion paper was a major step forward and will greatly assist banks—particularly those not already engaged in Equator Principles environmental and social impact risk assessments—it was not without its faults.

For one, the Guiding Principles call on all companies—which unquestionably includes banks, as the Thun Group recognises,—to 'establish or participate in effective operational-level grievance mechanisms for individuals and communities who may be adversely impacted' and to 'provide for or cooperate in' remediation if they have caused or contributed to human rights abuses. The Thun Group's paper did not address this requirement because, as Mercedes Sotoca, head of environmental and social risk at ING, said, most of the time, when a bank is linked to a human rights issue, it's caused by the client rather than by the bank. In that case, she said, the client would be 'in a better position to provide access to remedy' (Meyerstein 2013a).

This interpretation of the banks' responsibilities under the Guiding Principles is questionable and bleeds into the other difficulty with the Thun Group's paper, which is that it may under-estimate the banks' leverage over their clients on certain transactions. (Id.) The Thun Group's paper suggested that '[w]here a transaction entails little leverage and no ongoing relationship, the capacity for engagement with the client is likely to be very limited'. This would not apply to project finance transactions, but may speak to corporate loans. Given the widespread adoption of the EPs, which now apply to corporate loans, the Thun Group's position may be somewhat undermined—if it were not the case that the Thun Group's members are some of the institutions at the avant-garde of applying the EPs.

Another area in which the EPs may soon need to re-evaluate their approach is climate change. As noted, EP III did address carbon emissions for the first time, although not at levels that NGOs had hoped (nor does the text of the EP IIIs appear to require choosing the least carbon intensive option identified). However, since the EP III came out, two leading development institutions—the European Bank for Reconstruction and Development and the International Bank for Reconstruction and Development at the World Bank—have announced new policies that curtail their financing of coal-fired power plants. If other development banks join them, the EPs will need to reconsider their climate policy stance sooner rather than later to keep pace with best practices.

Conclusion

The EPs have evolved constantly over a decade, continually responding to stakeholder pressures to improve the stringency of their requirements and the geographical scope, although this success and big tent approach has recently made consensus and even more stringent requirements harder to achieve. While new sources of project finance in Asia have been slow to embrace the EPs, the regime's expansion to cover corporate loans of US$100 million or more will both expand its reach beyond project finance and also complicate bank compliance with transactions in which they might have less leverage than project finance. Most importantly, the true test of the EPs in their next decade will be whether they live up to the new project level disclosure requirements and enforce the enhanced community engagement criteria. Enhanced transparency should soon dramatically improve compliance, both by creating new opportunities for direct engagement with lagging banks and sponsors and by creating broader and more refined understandings of what proper implementation requires.

References

Aizawa, M. (2007). The equator principles in action—Creating a community of learning. *Infrastructure Journal, 42*, 10–14.

Aizawa, M., & Yang, C. (2010). Green credit, green stimulus, green revolution? China's mobilization of banks for environmental cleanup. *Journal of Environment and Development, 19*, 119.

Amalric, F. (2005). *The equator principles—A step towards sustainability?* Working Paper 01/05, Center for Corporate Responsibility and Sustainability, University of Zurich

Anckorn, F. Are impact assessments creaking under the strain? *Mining, People and The Env't.* 22 Dec 2010. http://www.mpe-magazine.com/tailings/are-impact-assessments-creaking-under-the-strain?SQ_DESIGN_NAME=print_friendly

Banktrack. (2007). http://www.banktrack.org/download/mind_the_gap/0_071221_mind_the_gap_final.pdf

Banktrack. (2010). Closing the gap—Benchmarking credit policies of international banks. http://www.banktrack.org/download/close_the_gap/close_the_gap.pdf, accessed.

Banktrack. (2012). *Tiny steps forward on the outside job: Comments on the equator principles III.*

Banktrack. (2013). New equator principles to have deeply underwhelming impact on people and planet—Commitments on community safeguards and climate change far below what is required. June 4, 2013. http://www.banktrack.org/show/news/new_equator_principles_to_have_deeply_underwhelming_impact_on_people_and_planet. Last accessed 23 Oct 2013.

Bradlow, D. D. (2005). Private complainants and international organizations: A comparative study of the independent inspection mechanisms in international financial institutions. *Georgetown Journal of International Law, 36*, 403.

Bridgeman, N. L., & Hunter, D. B. (2008). Narrowing the accountability gap: Toward a new foreign investor accountability mechanism. *Georgetown International Environmental Law Review, 20*(2), 187–236.

Collevecchio Declaration. (2003). The Collevecchio declarations on financial institutions and sustainability. http://www.evb.ch/es/p25001979.html

Dealogic. (2013). *PF Archive. Dealogic first quarter League tables 2013—tables.* London: IJ Global.

Equator Principles Association. (2010). The Equator Principles Association—Governance and Management. http://www.equator-principles.com/resources/ep_governance_rules_december_2013.pdf

Esty, B. C. (2007). *An overview of project finance and infrastructure finance—2006 update.* Harvard Business School.

Freshfields. (2005). Banking on responsibility: Part 1 of equator principles survey 2005: The banks. http://www.banktrack.org/manage/ems_files/download/banking_on_responsibility/050701_banking_on_responsibility.pdf

Gaskin, K. (2007). A question of principles. *Infrastructure Magazine, 2007*, 59–64.

International Finance Corporation. (2012). IFC Performance Standard 7

Jeucken, M. (2001/2002). *Sustainable finance and banking: The financial sector and the future of the planet.* London: Earthscan.

Lazarus, S. (2012). *Finding Principles That Fit,* Environmental Finance, Nov. 22, 2012. http://www.environmental-finance.com/features/view/800

Lazarus, S. (2015). The equator principles: Retaining the gold standard. A strategic vision at 10 years. In K. Wendt (Ed.), *Responsible investment banking: Risk management frameworks and softlaw standards.* Cham: Springer.

Lazarus, S., Feldbaum, A. (2011). *Equator principles strategic review—Final report.* http://www.equator-pfinciples.com/resources/exec-summary-appendix-strategic-review report.pdf

Lozinski, A. (2012). The equator principles: Evaluating the exposure of commercial lenders to socio-environmental risk. *German Law Journal, 13*, 1487.

Macve, R., & Chen, X. (2010). The "equator principles": A success for voluntary codes? *Accounting, Auditing and Accountability Journal, 23*(7), 890–919.

Meyerstein, A. (2013a) "Are big banks short-selling their leverage over human rights?" *Guardian Sustainable Business.* October 31, 2013. http://www.theguardian.com/sustainable-business/banks-short-selling-leverage-human-rights

Meyerstein, A. (2013b). Transnational private financial regulation and sustainable development: An empirical assessment of the implementation of the equator principles. *New York University Journal of International Law and Politics, 45*, 487.

Meyerstein, A. (2015). Global private regulation in development finance. In M. Audit & S. Schill (Eds.) *The Transnational Law of Public Contracts,* Bruylant.

O'Sullivan, N., & O'Dwyer, B. (2009). Stakeholder perspectives on a financial sector legitimation process: The case of NGOs and the equator principles. *Accounting, Auditing and Accountability Journal, 22*(4), 553–587.

Orr, R. J., & Kennedy, J. R. (2008). Highlights of recent trends in global infrastructure: New players and revised game rules. *Transnational Corporations, 17*, 99.

Prakash, A., & Potoski, M. (2007). Collective action through voluntary environmental programs: A club theory perspective. *Policy Studies Journal, 35*(4), 773–792.

Project Finance International. (2010). Global Project Finance League Leaders Tables.

Project Finance International. (2011). Global Project Finance League Leaders Tables (First Quarter).

Richardson, B. (2008). *Socially responsible investment law—Regulating the unseen polluter.* New York: Oxford University Press.

Rodriguez, E. (2011). The reality of the equator principles—Reporting and assurance, carbon smart. http://www.carbonsmart.co.uk/wp-content/uploads/2011/02/Article-The-Reality-of-the-EP-v45-Assurance-andEP.pdf

Sarfaty, G. (2009). Why culture matters in international institutions: The marginality of human rights at the World Bank. *American Journal of International Law, 103*, 647–683.

Scholtens, B., & Lammertjan, D. (2007). Banking on the equator. Are banks that adopted the equator principles different from non-adopters? *World Development, 35*(8), 1307–1328.

Scholtens, B. (2009). Corporate social responsibility in the international banking industry. *Journal of Business Ethics, 86*(2), 159–175.

Scott-Brown, M., Iocca, M. (2010). Environmental governance in oil-producing developing countries: Finding from a survey of 32 countries. World Bank, Washington, D.C.

Sorge, M. (2004). The nature of credit risk in project finance, *BIS Quarterly Review*.

Thun Group of Banks. (2013). The guiding principles: An interpretation for banks—A discussion paper for banks on principles 16–21 of the UN guiding principles on business and human rights. http://www.business-humanrights.org/media/documents/thun_group_statement_final_2_oct_2013.pdf

Watchman, P., Delfino, A., & Addison, J. (2007). EP2: The revised equator principles: Why hard-nosed bankers are embracing soft law principles. *Law and Financial Markets Review*. http://www.equator-principles.com/resources/ClientBriefingforEquatorPrinciples_2007-02-07.pdf

World Bank. (2006). *Infrastructure: Lessons from the last two decades of world bank engagement*. Washington, DC: World Bank Group.

Wright, C. (2007). Setting standards for responsible banking: Examining the role of the international finance corporation in the emergence of the equator principles. In F. Biermann, B. Siebenhüner, & A. Schreyrogg (Eds.), *International organizations and global environmental governance*. London: Routledge.

Wright, C., & Rwabizambuga, A. (2006). Institutional pressures, corporate reputation, and voluntary codes of conduct: An examination of the equator principles. *Business and Society Review, 111*, 89.

Wright, C. (2012). Global banks, the environment, and human rights: The impact of the equator principles on lending policies and practices. *Global Environmental Politics, 12*(1), 56–77.

An Investigation on Ecosystem Services, the Role of Investment Banks, and Investment Products to Foster Conservation

Sonal Pandya Dalal, Curan Bonham, and Agustin Silvani

Abstract As they have done in the past with global challenges such as rebuilding in the aftermath of WWII and financing the industrial revolution, banks have a central role to play in helping society meet their development goals in a resource-constrained world. In preparing for the challenges of this next century, society will need to manage issues such as population growth, food and water scarcity, and climate change while preserving the ecosystem services that underpin economic growth. "Sustaining innovations" in a banks' business model are required—those that transform banking products to generate environmental and societal benefits. Banks can manage risk and seek opportunities by deploying latent capital into revolving funds, leverage public-private partnerships to develop the absorptive capacity of potential clients (particularly private equity investors), and establish innovative financial products that conserve ecosystem services in support of healthy, sustainable societies.

1 Introduction

1.1 Recognising the Link Between Ecosystem Services and Economic Growth

Unbeknown to many, nature is often at the heart of many of today's cutting-edge industries and discoveries, with nature-based products accounting for an estimated 42 % of the world's top-selling pharmaceutical drugs sales (KPMG and NVI 2011). Natural products, such as penicillin, provide companies in the field with "a competitive advantage, by providing access to the active ingredients that would not be synthesized in a lab", according to Frank Petersen from Novartis.

S.P. Dalal (✉) • C. Bonham • A. Silvani
Conservation International, Arlington, VA, USA
e-mail: spandya@conservation.org; cbonham@conservation.org; asilvani@conservation.org

© Springer International Publishing Switzerland 2015
K. Wendt (ed.), *Responsible Investment Banking*, CSR, Sustainability, Ethics & Governance, DOI 10.1007/978-3-319-10311-2_17

In addition to medicines, nature provides a host of tangible benefits to society, known collectively as ecosystem services. Simply put, ecosystem services are the services that we need to grow and prosper as an economy. Food and timber are the most obvious benefits we receive from nature, but so is clean water, livable climates, regulation of disease, recreation and eco tourism, and sustainable forms of energy.

Ecosystem services are also at the heart of our society's impending resource challenges. According to Food and Agricultural Organization (FAO), in preparing for a global population of 9 billion, our society will require 30 % more water, 45 % more energy, and 50 % more food, by just 2030 (FAO 2009; Hoff 2011). Meanwhile, detrimental agricultural practices and climate change together could reduce food productivity by 25 % and compromise access to freshwater, a key input to food production, energy production, industrial processes, and meeting basic human needs such as drinking water and sanitation (FAO 2009).

The Millennium Ecosystem Assessment noted that approximately 60 % of the Earth's ecosystem services have been degraded in the past 50 years, with human impacts being the root cause (MEA 2005). In economic terms, US$ 2–4.5 trillion per year is lost from deforestation and degradation of this natural capital (TEEB 2010).

Capital flows are central to the way ecosystem services are better protected and managed. The loss of ecosystem services and their resulting resource constraints pose a risk for environmental protection and economic growth. Protecting ecosystem services is critical to charting a development path that promotes healthy, sustainable societies—those that simultaneously support sustainability and economic growth at scale. Protection of watersheds, for example, is central to meeting human needs for food and energy. Conservation of forests and oceanscapes is key to regulating emissions of greenhouse gases and mitigating climate change. Getting capital into the hands of smallholders, entrepreneurs, and supply chain partners to invest in new technologies and equipment and to produce responsibly sourced goods will be critical to global stability and sustainable sourcing (UNEP 2009).

As they have done in the past with global challenges such as rebuilding in the aftermath of WWII or financing the industrial revolution, banks can play a central role in raising capital, reducing risk, and efficiently financing these solutions. In a resource-constrained world, societies are moving towards a new understanding of value, leading to increased quantification of the benefits nature provides and greater accountability for those business models that degrade it. By understanding the links of their business interests to healthy ecosystem services, banks and their clients can take advantage of emerging business opportunities arising from this paradigm shift and position themselves for sustainable growth. Opportunities exist, for example, in helping achieve deep and resounding efficiencies throughout the supply chain, target investments in high-risk areas (e.g. raw material sourcing), and successfully integrate sustainable production practices (the optimum use of resources to maintain the planet's valuable goods or services) with the growing movement in sustainable consumption.

By designing mechanisms to better direct capital flows and encourage institutions to make investments in innovative financial products and services, banks can simultaneously promote environmental sustainability and economic growth and help realise healthy, sustainable societies.

1.2 Banks and Ecosystem Services: Lessons in Disruptive Innovations

Historically, commercial banks have not been involved in financing the protection of natural resources, due to the high-risk and long maturity periods associated with such products. Over the last few decades, however, we have begun to see examples of how banks are making strides in designing financial vehicles by taking advantage of *disruptive innovations*[1] which have created new market opportunities.

Starting in the 1980s debt for nature swaps arose from the recognition that the world's biodiversity "hotspots"—areas with the highest levels of endemic plants and animals—were also in the same countries that faced foreign debt burdens (Resor 1997). Modelled after debt-equity swaps—in which private sector interests buy discounted debt and exchange it for local currency investments in the indebted country—debt-for-nature swaps are financial transactions in which a portion of a government's or private sector entity's foreign debt is forgiven in exchange for local investments in environmental conservation measures. The swaps were attractive for banks, for although they did not provide a profit for the investor, they provided an avenue for banks to remove high-risk claims from their books and promote the protection of forest ecosystems. Swaps established by multilateral agencies such as the International Finance Corporation (IFC) that took up the majority of risk were also highly attractive. In all, between 1987 and 2000, debt-for-nature swaps generated more than US$1 billion in conservation financing (Sheikh 2010).

Debt swaps were the starting point for the development of a number of new approaches for long-term financing for conservation (Resor 1997). In doing so, they also demonstrated the value case for investments by banks.

Conservation Trust Funds are financing mechanisms that provide sustainable financing for long-term management costs for a country's protected area (PA) system. CTFs are in effect public-private partnerships in which a large portion of the financing comes from government bodies and half of the governing board is from civil society. Banks have traditionally played the role of investment advisor or asset manager for CTFs. To some degree that has boosted investment performance. The Conservation Trust Investment Survey Analysis (2008) showed that the weighted average return for 19 CTFs was 10.19 % for all years and 10.57 % for

---

[1] Pioneered by Clayton Christensen, disruptive innovation brings disruptive solutions to the market that serve a new population of consumers.

2003 through 2006—performance similar to those of US colleges and universities. Worldwide there are now 58 CTFs, having raised US$810 million in capital (CFA 2008).

Banks must now take these initial successes to scale these innovations and provide better value to their clients and themselves. In this way, they can be more relevant to the marketplace and help provide solutions to some of the most pressing societal issues that will be acute in the next 15–20 years.

1.3 Barriers

High-risk, low-return issues remain the key barrier for many of the world's banks. It has been said that a bank's business model does not allow for innovation. By assuming the status quo, however, banks are prone to undervaluing or misplacing risks as they did with the 2008 financial crisis. In the same way that house prices cannot increase indefinitely, banks need to realise that a continuation of current "business as usual" unsustainable business models simply cannot exist in a resource-constrained world. Banks that understand this shift are able to appreciate that assets deemed "credit worthy" today (such as a fossil fuel fired power plant) may well become "stranded" as the world moves towards managing climate change and ensuring security for food, water, energy, and society.[2]

Achieving business success with products and services that protect ecosystem services, particularly in emerging markets, is not without its pitfalls. As most investors plan and focus their investments on achieving their exit strategy in the short term, for conservation-based investments this focus may not be appropriate. High-priority ecosystem services under significant threat are disappearing quickly and are often in places with limited infrastructure and market development. The lack of local capacity, a strong regulatory environment, and inadequate infrastructure present barriers to investor confidence. Although these regions are of interest from a conservation perspective, they often do not support a robust business enabling environment, which has historically limited investment. Even venture capital funds that have had the flexibility to develop opportunities in structuring finance vehicles have found challenges in bringing this investment to scale and catalysing a market segment due to the lack of a sufficient pipeline of viable deals, sound policy signals, and lower-profit margins.

Recognising these barriers, a landscape review of financial institutions has shown that there are ways that banks can evolve existing products, manage risks, and realise opportunities with clients while serving an important role in protecting critical natural capital and managing dangerous climate change.

---

[2] In 2013, the US Export–import Bank, the World Bank, and European Investment Bank publicly pledged to drop support for coal projects. These banks have pumped more than US$10 billion into such initiatives in the past 5 years.

2 Sustaining Innovation

Sustaining innovations generate growth by offering better performance in existing markets (Enders et al. 2006). E-banking established by brand name commercial banks has been called a sustaining innovation, taking advantage of the bank's brand and trust value to close the gap between what clients need and the risk associated with working with a nontraditional institution.

In the case of ecosystem services, a landscape analysis of financial institutions has found there are three ways that banks can currently transform banking products to generate environmental and societal benefits. These are categorised as risk avoidance, market development, and public-private partners.

2.1 Risk Avoidance

Spurred on by guidance from the Equator Principles (EP), International Finance Corporations (IFC) Performance Standards, and UN Principles for Responsible Investment/Sustainable Insurance, commercial banks and insurance companies are establishing a systematic evaluation of environmental and social risks in transactions as standard practice.

With the newly released third guidance of the Equator Principles (EPIII), for example, seventy-seven financial institutions are now building in environmental and social safeguards into a larger number of loans and project finance products (Equator Principles Association 2013). EPIII looks to tackle some critical environmental and social issues, including climate change, biodiversity, and human rights. For projects that emit more than 100,000 tonnes of carbon dioxide equivalent annually, borrowers will be required to conduct an "alternatives analysis" to evaluate low carbon-intensive alternatives. For the first time, guidance is provided to integrate free, prior, and informed consent, a key hallmark of human rights, into due diligence practices. Investments that offset impacts where they cannot be avoided, minimised, and mitigated (aka the mitigation hierarchy)[3] are also encouraged.

The Natural Capital Declaration has organised a group of signatories from the financial sector to integrate natural capital considerations into lending, investment, and insurance products and services. Being developed over the next 5 years, the

---

[3] The mitigation hierarchy guides an approach for development planners to limit any the negative impacts through a phased approach of avoiding and minimising any negative impacts and then restoring sites no longer used by a project, before finally considering offsetting residual impacts.

The IFC recognises the mitigation hierarchy as inclusive of:

(a) Avoidance: measures taken to avoid creating impacts from the outset, such as careful spatial or temporal placement of elements of infrastructure, in order to completely avoid impacts on certain components of biodiversity.

(b) Minimisation: measures taken to reduce the duration, intensity, and/or extent of impacts (including direct, indirect, and cumulative impacts, as appropriate) that cannot be completely avoided, as far as is practically feasible.

framework will look to encourage banks to integrate value and account for natural capital (the resources derived from ecosystem services) in a company's business operations by means of disclosure, reporting and fiscal measures.

Discussions have also begun on using tax breaks, natural capital credit ratings, and private debt instruments to build incentives for companies that integrate natural capital into their corporate profit and loss accounting and reporting. Similar incentives are being discussed for assisting companies in transitioning to sustainably managed commodities that protect, enhance and restore natural capital (IUCN 2014).

Finally, clients themselves recognise the risks to issues such as climate change. During the shareholder proxy season in 2013, a new record 110 shareholder resolutions were filed with 94 US companies on hydraulic fracturing, flaring, fossil fuel reserve risks, and other climate—and sustainability—related risks and opportunities (CERES 2013). The proliferation of sustainability rating indices (at last count almost 100 according to the Global Initiative for Sustainability Ratings) has also spurred corporate clients to seek out way to mitigate risk and meet their sustainability commitments.

The key challenge to all these initiatives is transparency and reporting. Banks need to transparently report on how risk avoidance guidance has impacted the banks transactions, particularly for those ranked as the EPs Category A—with "potential significant adverse social or environmental impacts which are diverse, irreversible or unprecedented".

Banks also need to establish an internal system for routinely measuring the impacts of these investments and to use this information to move clients from mitigating negative impacts to helping them generate net positive impacts. Improving transparency and their own internal system for measurement will also help banks to better develop key performance indicators (KPIs) which can assist them in improving business performance and integrating ecosystem services protection mechanisms into all parts of their business.

2.2   Market Development

Major financial institutions such as Bank of America, Citi, and others have made multibillion dollar commitments to stimulate green economic development. Morgan Stanley has an "investing with impact" offer for its wealthiest customers, and UBS along with the Swiss private equity investor, Obviam, launched an impact

---

(c) Rehabilitation/restoration: measures taken to rehabilitate degraded ecosystems or restore cleared ecosystems following exposure to impacts that cannot be completely avoided and/or minimised.

(d) Offset: measures taken to compensate for any residual significant, adverse impacts that cannot be avoided, minimised, and/or rehabilitated or restored, in order to achieve no net loss or a net gain of biodiversity. Offsets can take the form of positive management interventions such as restoration of degraded habitat, arrested degradation, or averted risk, protecting areas where there is imminent or projected loss of biodiversity.

investing fund of funds in 2013. Wells Fargo Bank has committed to awarding US$100 million to nonprofit organisations (focusing on the USA) and universities by 2020 in sustainable agriculture and forestry, conservation of land and water resources, restoration of urban ecosystems, and clean energy infrastructure.

Most of these financial products would fall into a category of investments known as impact investments. Impact investing is catching on among investors who want to use finance to stimulate positive change in the world by making more food, cleaner water, better health care, smarter children, and a richer bottom of the pyramid.

The impact investing industry is still in its infancy with an estimated market capitalisation of US$36 billion but is entering a phase of rapid growth, with approximately 2,200 impact investments worth US$4.3 billion in 2011, US$8 billion in 2012, and planned US$9 billion in 2013 (Martin 2013). According to Morgan (2010), this segment of the market offers the potential over the next 10 years, for invested capital of US$400 billion–US$1 trillion and profit of US$183–US$667 billion.

However, despite these positive trends in the growth of the impact investing industry, barriers such as below market returns and lack of deal flow exist, which challenge the industry's ability to attract investment at scale. The role of financial intermediaries to bridge this gap by brokering deals and reducing risk could add additional value to the industry which has yet to reach its full potential.

The market for payments for ecosystem services (PES) should be able to leverage capital currently under management by impact investors. Historically, payment for ecosystem services (PES) schemes have been built around four major ecosystem services (carbon sequestration, watershed services, biodiversity conservation, and scenic beauty or recreation) and structured in one of three ways: public payment schemes through dedicated government programmes, formal markets created by regulatory caps, and private, self-organised deals brokered between resource users and resource providers (Forest Trends, the Katoomba Group, UNEP 2008).

While PES mechanisms differ according to the local regulatory context, all PES projects are underpinned by the sustained provision of an ecosystem service to a resource user by a resource provider. As noted in the graphic below, the transaction between the buyer (i.e. ecosystem service user) and the seller (i.e. ecosystem service provider) is the foundation from which all PES projects are derived. Each of these mechanisms has specific financing requirements that can be met by investment banks but as of yet has not garnered scaled investment from traditional lending institutions.

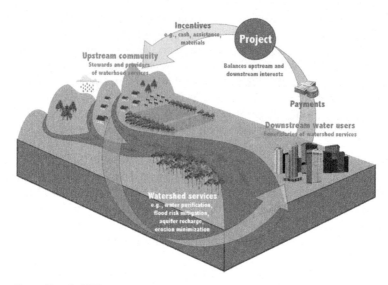

Source: Forest Trends 2008

According to the Katoomba Group's Ecosystem Marketplace, the total market size for direct buyer PES mechanisms such as carbon, biodiversity, and water along with certified agricultural and forest commodities could top US$427 billion by 2020. Looking at the additional service-oriented markets such as recreation and climate and water funds, the market could be valued at US$670 billion by 2020 (Katoomba's Ecosystem Marketplace 2013) (Table 1).

Table 1 Market size and growth projections for PES (2013–2020)

	Size of Market, 2013 (US$M, USD)	Potential Size, 2020 (US$M, USD)
Carbon		
Compliance forest carbon	US$52M	US$2,200M
Voluntary forest carbon	US$185M	US$1,200M
Water		
Compliance water quality trading	US$7.7M	US$10M
Voluntary private sector watershed payments	US$4.5M	US$10M
Biodiversity		
Compliance biodiversity compensation	US$3,000M	US$6,000M
Voluntary biodiversity compensation	US$25M	US$70M
Ag and forest products		
Certified ag. products[a]	US$64,000M	US$190,000M
Certified forest products[b]	US$20,000M	US$228,000M

[a]Coffee, cocoa, banana, tea, palm oil, marine fisheries, and organic
[b]Forest Stewardship Council only

2.3   Public-Private Partnerships

Public-private partnerships (PPP) have provided investments to the marketplace with innovative products to tackle issues such as climate change and invest in clean energy. With US$4.8 billion in financing, the UK Green Investment Bank (GIB) is enabling low carbon investment in the UK, beginning with investments in waste and energy efficiency. The State of Connecticut set up a green bank in the USA in 2011 as a quasi-independent public-private partnership to use US$8.5 million in repurposed stimulus funding to support residential use of clean energy.

A particularly robust example of PPPs in action comes from the Southern Agricultural Growth Corridor (SAGCOT) in Tanzania, which was initiated at the World Economic Forum on Africa in 2010. This initiative has brought together a number of large agribusiness corporations such as Syngenta, bilateral donors such as USAID, and the Government of Tanzania to form what is expected to be a US$100 million Catalytic Trust Fund, which will target small holder value chains with the objective of providing financing to commercially viable agricultural business that incorporates small holder farmers.

PPPs provide large financial institutions with a tremendous and largely untapped opportunity to play a role in managing, brokering, and underwriting large-scale investment in sustainable development. These partnerships in principle could allow banks and lending institutions to tap into new revenue streams while sharing risk among a variety of stakeholders. Investments in mechanisms that protect ecosystem services, which would not normally be explored due to the high risk and low returns, could be effectively engaged through the PPP model.

2.4   Experiences in Sustaining Innovations

Among the groups working with the private sector to design nontraditional investment products are nongovernmental organisations (NGOs) such as Conservation International (CI). With a mission focused on protecting natural capital and promoting human welfare, CI has designed trust funds and lending mechanisms which have invested more than US$150 million and leveraged more than US$200 million to protect more than 100 million hectares (240 million acres) of land in 27 countries, often the result of public-private partnerships and collaboration with the banking sector.

CI's Verde Ventures, an investment fund focused on providing finance to small- and medium-sized enterprises (SMEs) that contribute to healthy ecosystems and human well-being, is a prime example of investing—profitably—in nature. Founded on the belief that the only sustainable business model is one that delivers "triple bottom line" (people, planet, profit) results, Verde Ventures has disbursed over US$22 million in loans and enabled partners to help protect and restore more than 1.15 million acres (464,144 hectares), while supporting the employment of more than 55,000 local people in 13 countries. Its clients include businesses involved in agroforestry, ecotourism, sustainable harvest of wild products, and marine initiatives, and investors in the fund include Starbucks, the International Finance Corporation (IFC), and the Overseas Private Investment Corporation (OPIC).

A second unique financing platform developed by CI is its Carbon Fund. Launched in 2009 and capitalised at US$36 million, the fund was designed to enable transitions to healthy, sustainable, societies in target landscapes by supporting environmental pay-for-performance programmes and aiding in the commercialisation of carbon credits through voluntary partnerships. Private sector partners in the fund include Disney, Dell, and JPMorgan Chase, among others, which contribute to help reach a goal of reducing 100 million tons of CO_2 while providing alternative livelihoods to local communities and protecting critical natural habitat.

These two funds have worked together with numerous public and private partners in Peru to efficiently deploy capital in order to conserve a critical watershed, headwater to the Amazon River.

3 Case Study

3.1 Impact Investment in the Alto Mayo Region of Peru

Tropical deforestation is recognised as one of the major environmental issues of our time, both as a driver and key solution to climate change, with impacts ranging from biodiversity and livelihood loss to risks associated with globally important commodity supply chains. In reaction to this crisis, large public and private bodies have publicly stated goals of achieving zero-net deforestation by 2020 and have developed a market-based payment for ecosystem services called REDD+ (Reduced Emissions from Deforestation and Forest Degradation) to help them achieve it.

In 1987 the Peruvian government designated the headwaters of the Rio Mayo as a protected forest that would conserve the region's endangered species and ensure a sustainable supply of freshwater for its 250,000 local inhabitants for agriculture, human consumption, and energy (hydropower). The Alto Mayo Protection Forest (see map) encompasses a total forest area of over 300,000 hectares. In addition to it being home to some of the world's most endangered species such as the yellow-tailed wooly monkey, the region is also valued for its role in acting as a carbon sink.

Although legally protected, in practice the area is under immense threat from deforestation. With limited government budgets, two rangers were assigned to patrol an area roughly equivalent to the size of Manhattan—on foot. In 2009, CI partnered with the Government of Peru and worked with local communities to try and reverse this unsustainable situation by applying a variety of innovative financial mechanisms and tools, including REDD+ (Fig. 1).

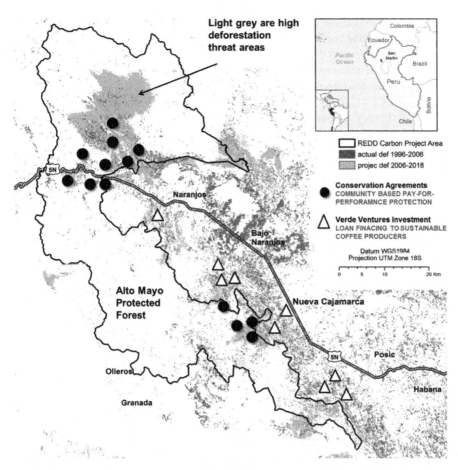

Fig. 1 The Alto Mayo Protected Forest in Peru is an important source of freshwater for the region and home to many threatened species. Deforestation pressure occurs in an east-to-west pattern, following a recently upgraded highway. Conservation finance, including carbon payments and low interest loans to farmers, is used to create a buffer around the highway and work with communities in and around the park to stop any new clearing of land

In the Alto Mayo region, the major driver of deforestation is the burning and clearing of forest by small farmers for establishment of non-shade-grown coffee plantations—leading to a loss in biodiversity, reduced water quality, and a huge release in CO_2 emissions. Although clearing intact forest to unsustainably plant short-rotation cash crops is a common activity in the Alto Mayo (and many parts of the tropics), a new wave of coffee producers were interested in improving farming techniques through plantation renewal, organic fertilisation, and erosion control programmes, which support rather than undermine native forests and generate higher incomes for participating farmers along the way. A major bottleneck hampering the uptake of these more sustainable practices was the upfront cost associated with making the transition (including opportunity costs). By quantifying and monitoring the environmental benefits these actions produced and linking them to global environmental markets, the project was able to access lending facilities and PES mechanisms to introduce additional financial resources that could be used to promote the long-term conservation of the area.

In 2009 CI's Carbon Fund entered into a historic US$7 million agreement with the Walt Disney Company to help it meet ambitious net-zero greenhouse gas emission target, in part by reducing deforestation in various tropical countries. The partnership provided much needed start-up financing to dramatically increase the number of rangers in the protected forest and implement local development programmes directly tied to the conservation of the forest. This pay-for-performance programme linked the well-being of the forest and its local inhabitants to an international need to reduce emissions in the most cost-effective way. Complementing this core conservation work and following an integrated landscape approach, Verde Ventures provided over US$800,000 in revolving credit lines to sustainable coffee producers in the Alto Mayo area to effectively create a "buffer" around the park and help stop an ever-expanding agricultural frontier.

This mix of conservation and production has led to sharp drops in emissions and improved livelihoods and also created a working, bankable model of nature-based investment which has attracted numerous sources of public and private financing since its inception. Rigorous independent monitoring against leading impact standards[4] assures that progress is being made against ambitious climate, community, and biodiversity targets. Between 2009 and 2012, the project has generated almost three million tons of emissions reductions—the equivalent of taking over 500,000 cars off the road for a year.

Conclusions and Recommendations

Financial mechanisms that support ecosystem services products need to take a long-term view and be supported by banks and financial institutions to help transform healthy sustainable societies. Traditionally, ecosystem services have been "paid for" by an ecosystem service user. But many times, the members of an ecosystem service user's value chain—banking clients, corporations downstream, supply chain partners, and consumers—may benefit and therefore may be incentivised to contribute payments. Mechanisms that can monetise payments from all the actors in the value chain will be more likely to provide the payments needed to realise more impactful returns on investment.

(continued)

---

[4] The Alto Mayo REDD+ project was successfully validated under the Verified Carbon Standard and the Climate, Community, and Biodiversity Standards through an independent audit of the project's design and methodology.

We recommend four approaches to capitalise on these potential opportunities for the banking sector.

Deployment of Latent Capital into a Revolving Fund for Use in Long-Term Projects to Finance PES

With over US$600 trillion in financial assets under management in 2010, the world is awash in available investment capital (Deloitte 2013). Now what is needed is the will and mechanisms to unlock that capital and route it into pro-environment investments. An interesting example of the utilisation of latent capital comes from the UK's Big Society Capital (BSC). Leveraging the UK's Dormant Bank and Building Society Accounts Act 2008, unclaimed assets from dormant accounts are used to fund impact investments.

What is needed is a pool of patient capital that is targeted for PES investment, flexible enough to allow for long-term commitment, tolerant and accepting of below market returns, and readily deployed as investment opportunities arise. The recent growth in the impact investing sector is indicative of the increasing appetite among investors to deploy capital in pursuit of both financial returns and environmental impact. Investment banks should be more than bystanders in this process and actively pursue portfolio development along these lines. Private equity firms may also play a critical role here, providing both technical assistance and long-term capital to nurture the expansion of these markets.

Development of Absorptive Capacity of Potential Clients

Currently, the amount of investment capital greatly outstrips the amount of available investment opportunities, not because of the lack of investment opportunities but because of the lack of awareness of bankable opportunities. It is estimated that in order for a venture fund to close one deal, 80–100 deals need to be sourced. This low rate of deal closure requires a large volume of potential investment opportunities. A key factor needed for this emerging sector to mature and to be able to respond to this challenge is an appropriate marketplace that provides education, coordination, and alignment between businesses searching for financing and investment funds looking to deploy capital. Financial intermediaries, business incubators, and accelerators are receiving more support and attention from development finance institutions and bilaterals. Banks should leverage these initiatives and work with these actors in order to bridge the information and deal flow gap.

Development of Innovative Financial Products

New products are needed in order to tap existing opportunities and mitigate risks associated with long-term investment in ecosystem services. Over the last decade there has been a growing demand for environmentally friendly

(continued)

investment products, starting with high-net-worth individuals and quickly spreading to endowments and pension funds, driven in part by increased pressure from stakeholder groups and mandates that reflect a growing climate risk. Banks have responded to this need from their client base by developing Green Bonds, specifically designed financial products used to raise capital for projects considered "green", typically focused on renewable energy infrastructure. Strong backing from development and private investment banks, combined with increased standardisation through the Climate Bonds Initiative, has helped to rapidly mature the market and provide products to a client base that is demanding higher environmental performance from their investment portfolios. Climate-themed bonds grew from virtually nothing in 2008 to US$74 billion in issuance last year, moving a fringe market once deemed too risky closer to the institutional mainstream (HSBC 2013).

This scenario is repeating itself in forest conservation. As the Alto Mayo initiative demonstrates, new products, partnerships, and investment approaches that properly value forests' contribution to society can have dramatic impacts on a region. With companies such as Unilever, Walmart, and Nestle all making pledges to reduce deforestation and countries such as Norway and the USA already pledging billions of dollars to help the market develop, the timing is right for banks to take a larger role in helping their clients meet these goals. Although existing demand has been growing and solutions to deforestation exist, the market is still patchy and not dissimilar to where climate bonds were several years back. Taking a similar approach, banks have begun to design Forest Bonds that respond to the needs of their clients to reduce risk from transactions, standardise investments, and guarantee a level of impact. As products evolve and multiply over time, a whole range of Environmental Impact Bonds will be developed to tackle everything from deforestation to overfishing, by efficiently pooling capital and spreading risk between public and private actors.

Development of Enabling Environments

Realising returns in investment grade products that support the development of healthy, sustainable societies in a resource-constrained world requires that financial institution find opportunities that fulfil three key criteria: financial return to investors, net benefits to local communities, and positive environmental outcomes. Any financial product or service will need to ensure economic benefits to local communities. These beneficiaries, often stewards of ecosystems services, must be incentivised to offset the opportunity cost of short-term gains when they choose to protect natural systems. For this to be truly effective, the economic value of ecosystem services must be integrated into any mechanism. Local capacity building, business development, and monitoring must be integrated as key components of investments products.

(continued)

It must be recognised that compensation mechanisms for beneficiaries do not only take the form of direct payments and financial compensation but also in-kind payments such as provision of social service benefits, livelihood support and capacity building, and access to resources or markets. Banks can improve performance and reduce risk by supporting the integration of local stakeholder interests and environmental considerations into the terms and conditions included in investment transactions.

References

CERES. (2013). http://www.csrwire.com/press_releases/35939-110-Shareholder-Resolutions-Related-to-Climate-Change-and-Fossil-Fuel-Use-Yield-Strong-Results-During-2013-Proxy-Season

Climate Bonds Initiative. (2013). *Bonds and climate change: The state of the market in 2013*. Commissioned by HSBC Climate Change Centre of excellence. Authors: Padraig Oliver.

Conservation Finance Alliance (CFA). (2008). *Rapid review of conservation trust funds*. Prepared for the CFA Working Group on Environmental Funds by Barry Spergel and Philippe Taïeb.

Deloitte Center for Financial Services. (2013). *2013 Financial services industry outlooks*. http://public.deloitte.com/media/0146/us_fsi_OutlooksConsolidatedDocument_021813.pdf

Enders, A., König, A., Jelassi, T., & Hungenberg, H. (2006). The relativity of disruption: E-banking as a sustaining innovation in the banking industry. *Journal of Electronic Commerce Research, 7*(2), 2006.

Equator Principles Association. (2013). http://www.equator-principles.com/resources/equator_principles_III.pdf

Food and Agricultural Organization. (2009, October 12–13). *How to feed the world in 2050*. High-level Expert Forum. Rome. http://www.fao.org/fileadmin/templates/wsfs/docs/expert_paper/How_to_Feed_the_World_in_2050.pdf

Forest Trends, The Katoomba Group, UNEP. (2008). *Payments for ecosystem services getting started: A primer* (66 pp). Nairobi: UNON Publishing Services Section.

Hoff, H. (2011). *Understanding the Nexus*. Background Paper for the Bonn2011 Conference: The water, energy and food security Nexus. Stockholm: Stockholm Environment Institute.

IUCN. (2014). *Integrating the value of natural capital into private and public investment and development practice*. IUCN. Retrieved from http://cmsdata.iucn.org/downloads/bellagio_meeting_short_report.pdf

Katoomba's Ecosystem Marketplace. (2013). *Mapping ecosystem markets: The matrix*. http://www.ecosystemmarketplace.com/documents/acrobat/the_matrix.pdf

KPMG and The Natural Value Initiative. (2011). *Biodiversity and ecosystem services – Risk and opportunity analysis within the pharmaceutical sector*. http://www.naturalvalueinitiative.org/content/005/501.php

Martin, M. (2013). *Making impact investible* (Impact Economy Working Papers Vol. 4).

Millennium Ecosystem Assessment. (2005). *Ecosystems and human well-being: Biodiversity synthesis*. Washington, DC: World Resources Institute.

Morgan, J. P. (2010). *Impact investments: An emerging asset class*. http://www.rockefellerfoundation.org/uploads/files/2b053b2b-8feb-46ea-adbd-f89068d59785-impact.pdf

Mulder, I., Mitchell, A. W., Peirao, P., Habtegaber, K., Cruickshank, P., Scott, G., & Meneses, L. (2013). *The NCD roadmap: Implementing the four commitments of the natural capital declaration*. UNEP Finance Initiative. Oxford: Geneva and Global Canopy Programme.

Resor, J. P. (1997). Debt-for-nature swaps: a decade of experience and new directions for the future. *Unasylva, 48*(188), 1.

Sheikh, P. (2010). *Debt for nature initiatives and the Tropical Forest Conservation Act: Status and implementation.* Congressional Research Service Report, March 30, 2010.

TEEB. (2010). *The economics of ecosystems and biodiversity ecological and economic foundations.* Edited by Pushpam Kumar. London and Washington: Earthscan.

UNEP. (2009). The environmental food crisis – The environment's role in averting future food crises. A UNEP rapid response assessment. In C. Nellemann, M. MacDevette, T. Manders, B. Eickhout, B. Svihus, A.G. Prins & B.P. Kaltenborn (Eds.). Arendal: United Nations Environment Programme, GRID. http://www.grida.no.

Mobilising Private Sector Climate Investment: Public–Private Financial Innovations

Shally Venugopal

Abstract Public financial resources alone will not be adequate to limit greenhouse gas emissions to safe levels and build resilience to the impacts of climate change. Recognising this financial gap, public actors, such as governments, development finance institutions, and aid agencies, are considering how best to harness and redirect private sector investment towards activities that address climate change.

This chapter profiles trends and innovative public interventions used or considered to mobilise private sector investment, including policy and technical support, supplying incremental finance, de-risking investments, and fostering public–private partnerships. It draws on a mix of primary research and analysis, case studies, and consultations to identify innovative means that the public and private sectors can collectively pursue to foster climate-friendly markets.

1 Introduction

Under a 'business as usual' growth scenario, the Organisation for Economic Co-operation and Development (OECD) estimates that US$5 trillion will be required each year until 2020 to meet the projected global demand for infrastructure.[1] An additional US$0.7 trillion each year will ensure that this future infrastructure—whether in the energy, transportation, forestry, or other sectors—is 'green'

This chapter defines climate-friendly markets to include renewable energy (excluding large hydropower projects), energy efficiency, agriculture, transportation, water infrastructure and treatment, forestry, sustainable land use, adaptation infrastructure (e.g. against extreme weather events and sea level rise), and other sectors that promote greenhouse gas emissions reductions or assist in adaptation to climate change impacts with minimal negative impact to ecosystems and communities.

[1] This chapter defines developing countries as Non-Annex I countries per the United Nations Framework Convention on Climate Change. Broadly, non-Annex I countries exclude industrialised countries (i.e. members of the Organisation for Economic Co-operation and Development (OECD) countries and economies in transition, e.g. Turkey, Malta, and Russia).

S. Venugopal (✉)
World Resources Institute (WRI), Washington, DC, USA
e-mail: svenugopal@wri.org

© Springer International Publishing Switzerland 2015
K. Wendt (ed.), *Responsible Investment Banking*, CSR, Sustainability, Ethics & Governance, DOI 10.1007/978-3-319-10311-2_18

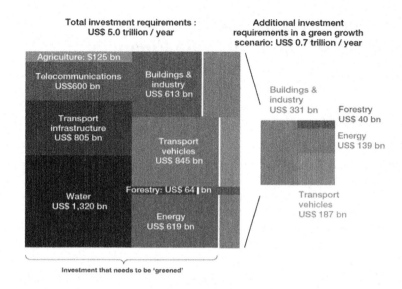

Sources: OECD[2,3], IEA[4], Food and Agriculture Organization of the United Nations (FAO)[5], United
Nations Environment Programme (UNEP)[6]
Note: All data converted to $ 2010 equivalents

Fig. 1 Total estimated investment requirements under business as usual and estimated additional costs under a 2 °C scenario. Source: The World Economic Forum (2013)

enough to prevent average global temperatures from rising beyond 2 °C above pre-industrial levels[2] (see Fig. 1).

Much of the projected infrastructure demand will come from developing countries. These countries will need US$300 billion annually by 2020 and up to US$500 billion annually by 2030 to mitigate greenhouse gas emissions to acceptable levels[3] and another US$70–100 billion annually to adapt to the impacts of climate change (World Bank 2010).

While raising an additional US$0.7 trillion sounds challenging, to put it in perspective, the estimated damage attributable to Hurricane Katrina in 2005 alone is estimated at more than US$0.1 trillion in 2012 dollars (Porter 2012). Reconstruction costs after the 2013 typhoon Haiyan struck the Philippines is estimated to be US$15 billion (The Economist 2013).

---

[2] Estimates from 'The Green Investment Report: The ways and means to unlock private finance for green growth'—a report of the Green Growth Action Alliance, produced by the World Economic Forum (2013).

[3] Through "mitigation" activities that reduce greenhouse gas emissions. Based on projections of upfront investment needs, these projections were released in 2008 or 2009 by McKinsey & Company, International Institute for Applied Systems Analysis, International Energy Agency, and Potsdam Institute for Climate Impact Research. Estimates are for stabilisation of greenhouse gases at 450 ppm CO_2e, which would provide a 22–74% chance of staying below 2 °C warming by 2,100, according to the Intergovernmental Panel on Climate Change (IPCC).

Funds from governments and publicly supported financial institutions such as development banks[4] are not only critical to addressing extreme weather events such as Katrina and Haiyan after they happen but are also central to ensuring that global warming is slowed to prevent similar events in the future. But the public sector cannot do it alone. Although industrialised nations have committed[5] to mobilising US$100 billion annually by 2020, this level of funding is still far from what is required to meet developing country investment requirements.

To fill the growing gap between finance needs and funding sources, governments will have to find creative and efficient ways to make their public dollars go further—harnessing private sector investment is one important path forward (see Fig. 2). The private sector,[6] which consists of project developers, investors, financial service providers, and other market facilitators, not only controls large pools of capital but also has the capability to manage complex projects, scale up renewable technologies, and coordinate expertise to create new and innovative solutions to environmental problems.

Governments, development banks, aid agencies, and dedicated climate change funds have started to consider and test what types of public interventions are most effective in mobilising private investment. Meanwhile, the private sector has increasingly embraced climate-conscious investments for several reasons, including avoiding material risks in supply chains and operations, embracing new market opportunities created by policy and consumer demand, and demonstrating corporate social responsibility.

This chapter highlights some innovative types of policy support and financial instruments the public sector can use to mobilise private investment from private sector investors, project developers, financial service providers, and other market facilitators. It considers innovations for developing countries, where finance is often hardest to access for climate-friendly projects[7]; however, some of these

---

[4] Development finance institutions typically intermediate finance on behalf of governments—whether industrialised countries channelling money to developing countries or national governments channelling money domestically. This set of institutions includes multilateral development banks (supported by multiple donors), bilateral development banks (supported by one donor country), and national development banks (supported by one country, typically in a developing country).

[5] Through negotiations under the United Nations Framework Convention on Climate Change, industrialised countries pledged to mobilise—from both public and private sector sources—US$100 billion annually by 2020.

[6] This chapter focuses on three types of private sector actors: capital providers (investors), project developers (including corporations, small- and medium-sized enterprises, and contract project developers), and market facilitators (including banks, rating agencies, credit/liquidity providers, and information/data providers). These private sector actors may be based in developed or developing countries, but this chapter focuses on their activities in developing countries.

[7] This chapter defines climate-friendly markets to include renewable energy (excluding large hydropower projects), energy efficiency, agriculture, transportation, water infrastructure and treatment, forestry, sustainable land use, adaptation infrastructure (e.g. against extreme weather events and sea level rise), and other sectors that promote greenhouse gas emissions reductions or

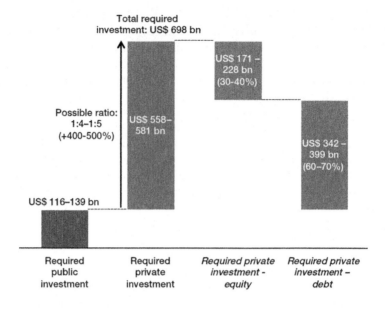

Fig. 2 Potential public–private finance mobilisation to close the cost gap for climate-specific investment. Source: The World Economic Forum (2013)

models are already in use, or are also applicable, to industrialised countries. The chapter first provides an overview of how public interventions can address investment barriers through policy, project, and financial support. It then details some examples of recently employed or potential innovative financial instruments and models. Finally, the chapter describes some of the operational steps the public sector can take to improve the way it mobilises finance, whether through policy support or finance.

2 Public Interventions to Mobilise Private Investment

The intended recipients of climate finance[8] from industrialised governments range from rapidly growing economies such as Brazil, India, and China to some of the world's poorest economies such as Rwanda, Bangladesh, and Haiti. Clearly, there is a wide variation between developing countries' political, regulatory, and

---

assist in adaptation to climate change impacts with minimal negative impact to ecosystems and communities.

[8] Climate finance (or public climate finance/climate-relevant finance): Public finance from developed countries used to support climate-friendly projects in developing countries projects.

low-carbon investment conditions and also the ease of mobilising private sector capital flows. Effectively harnessing private sector flows for climate-friendly activities across these geographies will, therefore, require donor governments to align their support with on-the-ground needs in developing countries thoughtfully, taking into consideration all the requirements of national governments, civil society, communities, and the private sector (Polycarp et al. 2013; Venugopal and Srivastava 2011).

A key challenge is to use public money to address structural market barriers that impede both small- and large-scale private finance flowing to climate-friendly projects. These barriers include:

1. Macroeconomic Risks: Political and macroeconomic risks affect climate-friendly projects just as they would any other sector. These risks, including political violence/instability, the risk of expropriation, currency convertibility, and interest rate/exchange rate fluctuations, can be managed through insurance and guarantees in some cases. However, accessing these products from less-developed countries can be particularly challenging (Ward et al. 2009).
2. Unsuitable or Uncertain Policies: Climate-friendly projects sometimes require a supportive policy framework to create a level playing field against greenhouse gas-intensive projects. Uncertain or short-lived policies, including legislation and regulation either at the national or international level, create risks (Brown et al. 2011). For example, in 2010 Spain implemented a retroactive cut in feed-in tariffs (FiTs) for solar photovoltaic schemes, with the ostensible aim of moderating energy prices. While this policy change may have reduced unnecessary subsidies of a growing solar market, the implementation rendered some projects unexpectedly unprofitable (Mulligan 2010).
3. Technology Risks: Renewable energy and other climate-friendly markets are often dependent on newer technologies. Even when these markets and their associated technologies are financially viable, investors may still be concerned about technology performance, obsolescence, and the challenge of reselling/divesting assets dependent on these technologies (Venugopal and Srivastava 2011).
4. Inadequate Access to Finance: Accessing finance for climate-friendly projects can be challenging due to the limited track record of these markets, and as a result there is limited investment awareness of and comfort in these markets from the private sector (Venugopal and Srivastava 2011).

The interrelated barriers above, while significant, can be addressed using a combination of broad public support mechanisms and targeted public financing instruments. When used effectively, these interventions can create markets with sufficient scale, transparency, liquidity, and an attractive risk-reward ratio as summarised in Fig. 3.

Specifically, public funds can be used in two distinct ways:

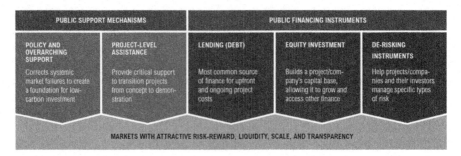

Fig. 3 Public interventions to support low-carbon markets. Source: World Resources Institute (Venugopal and Srivastava 2011)

2.1 Public Support Mechanisms

Funding and technical assistance to governments and projects are integral to creating and growing climate-friendly markets. These foundational support activities often influence the development of appropriate policies, regulations, and laws that promote low-carbon and climate-resilient investments. For example, public funds can provide monetary support and technical assistance to develop feed-in tariffs, tax credit programmes, certificate schemes, and other support for national, regional, and local government incentives and regulation. In addition, project support can be targeted to innovative projects to demonstrate technical and commercial feasibility, enable technology transfer, and help coordinate efforts between different financial actors.

For example, tailored policy support was critical to getting the Walney Offshore Windfarms (WOW) project in the United Kingdom off the ground. As a 367.2 MW wind farm, WOW was the largest offshore wind farm in the world as of early 2012 and produces 1,383 GWh of clean energy per annum (Hervé-Mignucci 2012). This output translates to 8.3 $MtCO_2$ and 193,000 tons of SO_2 avoided over the project's lifetime, which supports the UK government's emissions reduction targets; the project is also expected to pay GBP 400 million in taxes, benefitting the UK government (Hervé-Mignucci 2012).

The massive capital requirement (£1–1.2 billion) and the complex nature of the project were significant challenges that were overcome with targeted policy support and smart financial engineering. Specifically, the Climate Policy Initiative's analysis of the project highlights how the UK government established incentives for the project through a green tradable certificate mechanism (Hervé-Mignucci 2012). This mechanism provided tradable green certificates for each megawatt hour of energy WOW produced; the generated power and associated benefits of the certificates could be sold to regional energy companies, creating a secure revenue stream for the project. Furthermore, the project developers, DONG Energy (Denmark's largest energy company), and project investors including PGGM (a Dutch pension fund) and Ampere Equity Fund (a private equity firm specialising in European clean energy projects) were able to reduce the risk of fluctuations in the value of these green tradable certificates by negotiating three 15-year fixed-price power purchase agreements (Hervé-Mignucci 2012).

2.2   Public Financial Instruments[9]: Debt, Equity, and De-risking Instruments

Beyond providing a market's foundational support through policies and project development assistance, governments and public financial institutions[10] can support specific projects and companies using targeted financial instruments that reduce investment barriers. These instruments—sometimes provided at concessional terms—are designed to encourage private co-investment by assuming certain risks associated with the investment barriers previously outlined, as shown in Fig. 4.

For climate-friendly private sector projects in developing countries, finance may be sourced from both public and private sector sources. Public sector sources include national, regional, and international development banks and aid agencies, as well as dedicated climate finance funds such as the Clean Technology Fund or Global Environment Facility. Private sector sources include venture capitalists, private equity funds, commercial banks, investment banks, and institutional investors. However, private sector sources are not limited to financial actors. For example, philanthropists may provide grant funding to push forward an innovative and untested structure, or to ensure that a project is executed with adequate concern for the surrounding communities, or to achieve other social or environmental benefits.

Mexico's large-scale wind industry showcases how powerful public dollars can be in mobilising private investment, if the right policy and project support is complemented with tailored financial instruments from the public sector. Between 2003 and 2011 a mix of supportive domestic renewable energy policies and sector reform—particularly the 2008 Law for the Use of Renewable Energy (LAERFTE)—helped transform Mexico's fledging wind industry from 2 small projects with less than 1 MW in combined capacity to an industry boasting

---

[9] Public financial instruments: Tools available to public institutions to provide financial support for public and private sector projects. These generally take one of three main forms: (i) debt/loans, the most common source of finance for upfront and ongoing project costs; (ii) equity, an ownership stake in a project or company (builds a project or company's capital base, allowing it to grow and access other finance); and (iii) de-risking instrument includes insurance, guarantees, liquidity facilities, swaps, and derivatives and helps projects, companies, and their investors manage specific types of risk.

[10] Public financial institutions: Public institutions that provide finance to support public and private sector projects as well as policies and programmes that serve the public good, whether for economic, environmental, or social benefit. Examples include donor governments; export credit and aid agencies; multilateral, bilateral, and national development banks; and international entities.

Fig. 4 Public interventions to support climate-friendly markets. Source: WRI, with information
from UNEP report "Catalysing Low-Carbon Growth in Developing Economies" (2009); Standard
& Poor's report "Can Capital Markets Bridge the Climate Change Financing Gap (2011); ODI
Background note "Leveraging Private Investment: the Role of Public Sector Climate Finance"
(2011); McKinsey Sustainability & Resources Productivity "Energy Efficiency: A Compelling
Global Resource" (2010)

17 projects and total investments of US$1.14 billion (Polycarp et al. 2013;
Venugopal et al. 2012).

Despite these policy reforms, the country's first private sector wind projects still
had to contend with a range of policy, financial, and regulatory barriers. The
experiences of the 67.5 MW La Mata-La Ventosa project—the country's third
large-scale private sector wind project, conceived through a cooperation agreement
between Électricité de France (EDF), Asociados PanAmericanos (APA), and a
Mexican national—demonstrate how accessing public sector finance can be critical
to making private sector projects viable (U.S. Agency for International Development 2009).[11]

The La Ventosa project faced two important challenges. First, while the private
sector has been allowed to participate in power generation in Mexico since 1992,
the offtakers[12] of privately generated power can only include the generators themselves, municipalities, or the federal electricity commission (CFE) (OECD 2013).
This requirement led to a complex shareholding arrangement in La Ventosa, with
the US-based company Walmart (as the sole offtaker of the electricity) taking a
0.08% participation in the project through a joint venture with EDF. The agreement

---

[11] See the following report on "Public Financing Instruments to Leverage Private Capital for
Climate-Relevant Investment: Focus on Multilateral Agencies" for additional information. Available online at http://pdf.wri.org/public_financing_instruments_leverage_private_capital_climate_
relevant_investment_focus_multilateral_agencies.pdf

[12] Purchasers of future power generated by the yet-to-be constructed wind facility.

provided Walmart with electricity at a price higher than wholesale rates but lower than the retail rates at which it was originally purchasing electricity (Venugopal et al. 2012).

Second, the project was unable to secure domestic financing, largely due to the aftermath of the global financial crisis. Multilateral development banks and climate finance mechanisms[13] stepped in retroactively as the project broke ground, providing important commercial and concessional finance as well as de-risking shareholders' investments. Finance included long-term senior debt from the International Finance Corporation (IFC) of 280 million Mexican pesos (MXN\$), a MXN\$275 million senior loan from the Inter-American Development Bank (IDB), a US\$81 million dollar-denominated loan from the US Export-Import Bank (Wind Power Intelligence 2010), and a US\$15 million dollar-denominated concessional loan at a flat rate from the Clean Technology Fund—a climate finance mechanism that funds projects through several intermediaries and, in this case, through the IFC (Inter-American Development Bank 2009; International Financial Corporation 2009). Finally, the IFC also provided interest rate and currency hedges to offset macroeconomic risks.

Since the financing of this project, a further 1.2 GW of wind capacity has been installed or commissioned. Furthermore, the two subsequent wind projects financed by the Clean Technology Fund have required a lower concession and are without any subsidies, demonstrating the catalytic potential of public finance (Climate Investment Funds 2011).

3 Innovative Public–Private Financial Instruments

As the La Ventosa project demonstrates, public financial instruments can scale climate-friendly markets, particularly when complemented with a sound set of domestic policies and regulatory frameworks. The following sections outline some recent trends and innovative uses of public financial instruments.

3.1 Thematic Green or Climate Bonds

In recent years, the public and private sectors have increasingly used bonds to finance climate-friendly projects and business activities. The Climate Bonds Initiative and HSBC estimate that the number of climate-themed[14] bonds outstanding in

---

[13] Climate finance mechanisms: Dedicated international climate funds that channel finance from developed to developing countries for climate-relevant projects. Examples include the Global Environment Facility, the Climate Investment Funds, and the proposed Green Climate Fund.

[14] Includes a subset of bonds within the transportation, agriculture and forestry, energy, climate finance, water, waste and pollution control, and buildings and industry, sectors that the Climate

2013 totalled US$364 billion, up from their 2012 estimate of US$174 billion (Climate Bonds 2013). By and large this universe of bonds consists of public sector issuances—for example, China's Ministry of Railways is responsible for US$117 billion of the outstanding bonds.

Development banks have increasingly tapped fixed income markets through 'green bonds', that is, bonds whose proceeds are committed to financing green, including climate-friendly, activities. For example, since 2008, the World Bank has issued approximately US$3.7 billion in green bonds (rated Aaa/AAA) through 57 transactions with J.P. Morgan, Bank of America Merrill Lynch, and HSBC among others acting as managers. The World Bank Bonds support low-carbon projects that use new technologies to reduce greenhouse gas emissions, reforestation, and other climate-friendly investments in World Bank member countries (World Bank 2013).

A notable feature of these green bonds is that they allow major institutional investors, such as the California State Treasurer's Office, the New York Common Retirement Fund, the UN Joint Staff Pension Fund, and the Second and Third Swedish National Pension Funds (AP2 and AP3) in the World Bank's case, gain exposure to climate-friendly sectors (World Bank 2013). Though outstanding bonds only totalled US$7 billion in 2013, this number is likely to increase (Climate Bonds 2013). For example, Zurich Insurance Group recently announced their intentions to invest US$1 billion in green bonds, bringing further scale and liquidity to the market (Flood 2013).

The issuance of green bonds is certainly not limited to the public sector. In November 2013, Bank of America issued US$500 million (Baa2) in green bonds earmarked for environmental projects—the first green bond from a private US financial institution (Kidney 2013a, b). For some time now, larger private sector renewable energy companies—mostly in Europe—have also issued bonds to finance climate-friendly projects. While these bonds are often oversubscribed, it is still challenging for most renewable project developers and companies to achieve investment-grade credit ratings, and as a result, accessing debt capital can still be expensive. To promote infrastructure financing more broadly, the European Investment Bank and the European Commission recently introduced the Europe 2020 Project Bond Initiative. This initiative recently helped a UK wind bond enhance its ratings by one notch to achieve an A3 rating from Moody's, demonstrating how the public sector can provide credit enhancement to increase accessibility to fixed income capital markets (Kidney 2013a, b).

Bonds Initiatives defines as climate themed. See http://www.climatebonds.net/files/Bonds_Cli mate_Change_2013_A3.pdf, p 6–7 for more information.

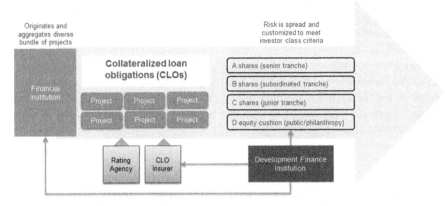

Fig. 5 An indicative collateralised loan obligation (CLO) structure for a renewable energy. Source: WRI

3.2 Asset-Backed Securitisation

The growing presence of the climate theme within fixed income markets may be driven by a number of different factors, including the greater commercial viability of certain low-carbon technologies, greater institutional investor interest in climate-friendly themes, and bonds' capacity to provide upfront and long-term financing—critical requirements for green infrastructure (Climate Bonds 2013).

However, tapping into fixed income markets is also becoming a necessity for many project developers and companies that previously secured financing from commercial banks. The Institute for Sustainable Development and International Relations (IDDRI), along with other experts, has highlighted how Basel III regulatory pressures on banks to recapitalise can reduce renewable energy project lending and long-term credit (Spencer and Stevenson 2013). To bridge the long-term financing gap for green projects, IDDRI, the Climate Bonds Initiative, and others have suggested the public sector find ways to arrange asset-backed securities and also provide refinancing guarantees.

While the asset-backed securities market has yet to fully recover since the global financial crisis, this type of instrument could bring the economies of scale and aggregation required to redirect institutional investment towards more climate-friendly and other green activities, similar to the field of microfinance.

As illustrated in Fig. 5, a public or private financial institution could originate and pool loans to several renewable energy projects and then structure this into a financial product with several different tranches of risk, to meet different investor tolerances for risk and return. To further customise or de-risk this security to attract a wider range of investors, a development finance institution or a philanthropist could provide an equity or first-loss cushion to reduce investment risk in other tranches and/or bond insurance (e.g. from a private sector monoline insurer or a public mechanism like the proposed Green Climate Fund) to increase the credit rating of the entire security (Karmali 2012).

There do not appear to be any securitised structures to finance or refinance green projects/assets in developing countries to date. But there are examples in industrialised countries. For example, in November 2013, SolarCity—a US residential and commercial solar service company—completed what is likely the first securitisation of distributed solar photovoltaic assets, raising US$54.4 million through a private placement (led by Credit Suisse) with an interest rate of 4.8% and a maturity of 2026 (SolarCity 2013).

3.3   Results-Based Structures: Development (or Environment) Impact Bonds and Tradable Put Options

Policymakers have increasingly considered results-based financing, also called pay-for-performance or performance-based financing, as a means to achieving development and climate change mitigation results. In these types of schemes, the public sector typically contracts with private sector service providers (whether commercial or nonprofit) to achieve development or other socially beneficial goals, but only promises payment upon delivery of results. There are several variations of these instruments, but the basic premise remains that (1) the private sector, and not the public sector, assumes the risk of failure or low performance, and as a result, theoretically, (2) the private sector and other parties can act more nimbly to test and implement innovative solutions (Social Finance 2013). As Ghosh et al. explain, these instruments combine the use of ex ante public funding with ex post payments for emissions reductions (Ghosh et al. 2012a, b).

One variation is the proposed Development Impact Bond, or DIB, which could be structured to achieve environmental goals (Environmental Impact Bonds—EIBs). The DIB concept (see Fig. 6), introduced by Social Finance and the Center for Global Development, builds on the successes of Social Impact Bonds (SIBs)—a model first implemented by the United Kingdom in 2010 (still in progress) to reduce prison recidivism (Social Finance 2013). SIBs are created through a public commitment to pay a group of private sector investors for social successes—that is, positive social impact outcomes as measured by predefined metrics.

For example, in 2012, New York City, Goldman Sachs, and others entered into a Social Impact Bond-style arrangement. In this arrangement, MDRC—a social services provider—was lent US$9.6 million by Goldman Sachs to design and oversee a programme to reduce prison recidivism among adolescent men incarcerated in Rikers Island (Chen 2012). The City of New York will make payments to MDRC based on the success of the programme in reducing recidivism and on a capped, sliding scale (Mike Bloomberg 2012). MDRC in turn agreed to pay Goldman Sachs and other investors based on this scale. Under this arrangement,

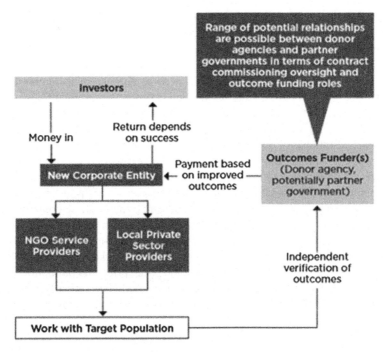

Fig. 6 Model for development impact bonds. Source: Center for Global Development and UK Social Finance

if recidivism decreases by 10%, the City of New York would pay MDRC US$9.6 million, and MDRC would then repay Goldman Sachs its US$9.6 million loan, allowing Goldman Sachs to break even on its investment. Goldman could also gain as much as US$2.1 million in profit if recidivism rates drop more than 10%. Separately, Bloomberg Philanthropies is providing a US$7.2 million grant to MDRC, which will be held in a guarantee fund to back a portion of Goldman's loan repayment, allowing Goldman losses from the arrangement to be capped at US$2.4 million (Mike Bloomberg 2012).

Considering the squeezed climate finance budgets of many countries, such a model may prove to be politically viable option for financing climate-friendly activities. Though it has yet to be tried, an indicative model could include a donor country—perhaps in conjunction with a developing country city or national government—paying to reduce greenhouse gas emissions in order to meet emissions reduction targets. This structure could be further enhanced, for example, in the case of climate proofing (adaptation), if an insurance company and city government agreed to copay for success considering their shared interest in protecting infrastructure assets.

Of course, there are important challenges in implementing these kinds of programmes. Among the many challenges are establishing a baseline from which to measure performance and instituting appropriate metrics to measure success. For example, in the case of climate proofing activities, how can a government be assured that success was achieved? And how can it determine what it would have otherwise paid for a similar level of climate proofing? In the case of developing countries, where macroeconomic and political conditions can be challenging and legal systems fragmented, how easy will it be to enforce such a complex legal arrangement between multiple parties and potentially across borders? Nevertheless, these kinds of models could create win-win situations for both the public and private sector, while tackling climate change, and are thus worth exploring.

Another results-based instrument variation put forward by Ghosh et al. through the Center for Global Development, are tradable put options. The put option structure would entail creating contracts for vendors that establish a right to sell to the public funder a specified amount of emissions reductions at a certain agreed price ('strike price') at a certain point in time. Importantly, these contracts can be bought and sold: if the current holder decides they are unlikely to use the contract, they can sell it to someone else who will use it (Ghosh et al. 2012a, b). Box 1 explains how these contracts could work when the market price falls below the strike price. If the market price rises above the strike price, the put option is moot, because the vendor can sell its allowance to the market. Theoretically, tradable put options will tend to end up in the hands of those who can most inexpensively achieve mitigation.

Box 1: Put option structure for CO_2-equivalent emissions reductions
Context: Government auctions off a tradable put option for 1 ton of CO_2-equivalent emissions reductions

- Vendor 1 purchases option at auction with strike price of US$30.
- Vendor 2 does not purchase option.

Scenario I
Six months later, Vendor 1 can reduce 1 ton of emissions for US$25. At the same time, Vendor 2 can reduce 1 ton of emissions for US$20. The put option is worth US$5 to Vendor 1, but US$10 to Vendor 2, and thus could be sold by Vendor 1 to Vendor 2.

Scenario II
12 months later Vendor 1 can reduce 1 tone of emissions for US$35, and Vendor 2 can reduce 1 ton of emissions for US$25. For Vendor 1, the put option may be worth trading because it would lose money by undertaking the emissions reductions even if it sold the allowance. And since the US$25 cost to Vendor 2 of reducing 1 ton of emissions is below the US$30 strike price, Vendor 2 would be better off financially by buying the put option at any price below US$30.

However, if at some other point down the road, no vendors in the market can reduce emissions for less than the strike price, then the tradable put option is moot.

Source: Based on Ghosh et al.

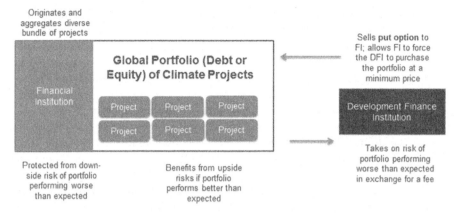

Fig. 7 Selling a put option on projects

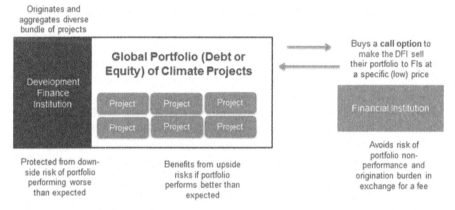

Fig. 8 Buying a call option on projects

3.4   Puts and Calls to Promote Origination and Scale Early-Stage Markets

Put and call options can also be employed to incentivise origination (including for asset-backed securitisation) and bring liquidity to climate-friendly projects as illustrated in Figs 7 and 8. Both these instruments give private financial institutions an extra layer of security in the form of a safe exit option, should the prospects of the portfolio weaken or strengthen.

A public financial institution, for instance, can sell a put option to incentivise private sector financial institutions to originate a portfolio of climate-friendly investments. This put option would allow the private sector financial institutions to force a development finance institution to purchase a portfolio of projects at a specified price, thus transferring the risk of the portfolio performing worse than expected in exchange for an upfront fee. If returns on the portfolio are higher than expected, the private sector financial institution would keep the profitable portfolio, sell to it to other parties, and/or tranche the portfolio to sell to multiple investors. A put option where FIs take on the origination burden is particularly useful for late-stage markets where private financial institutions may be interested in, but hesitant to, originate and/or pool projects.

For projects in earlier-stage markets, where investment comfort is low, a concessional call option may work better. A call option would allow a private sector financial institution to buy a portfolio from a development finance institution if the portfolio of projects is performing well, in exchange for a fee (which could be reduced as a form of concessionality). Through these options, the private sector financial institution gains exposure to a new market in which it may not yet feel comfortable investing while still limiting its risk exposure.

3.5 Tailored Political and Regulatory Risk Insurance

As mentioned in this chapter, policy and political uncertainty—whether driven by illegitimate or legitimate factors—can deter investment in climate-friendly markets, particularly in less-developed countries. Currently, political risk insurance and guarantees are offered to projects in developing countries through insurers such as Lloyds, Munich Re, or through public institutions such as the World Bank Group's Multi-Lateral Investment Guarantee Agency (MIGA). These political risk guarantees typically cover losses from: (1) political violence/civil war, (2) expropriation risk, (3) currency convertibility risk, and (4) government breach of contract (Venugopal and Srivastava 2011).

In June 2011, the US Overseas Private Investment Corporation (OPIC) tailored its traditional political risk insurance contract to create a new product to protect Terra Global Capital's investment in the Oddar Meanchey Reduced Emissions from a Reforestation and Degradation (REDD) [15] project in Cambodia. The result was a first-of-its-kind intervention for climate-friendly markets. OPIC provided Terra Global Capital—a forest land-use carbon advisory and investment company—with US$900,000 of expropriation and political violence insurance coverage over a five-year term for its REDD project. REDD projects are particularly challenging as REDD carbon credits are currently traded in voluntary emissions reductions markets, but these markets may change depending on the outcome of international political negotiations. It is possible that a new international agreement will require that some or all of these REDD credits be traded in compliance markets instead. As international and national REDD frameworks evolve, projects may be nested within

---

[15] Reduced Emissions from Deforestation and Degradation (REDD) is an international mechanism that uses market and financial incentives to promote sustainable forest management; the mechanism gives a financial value to the carbon stored in forests' trees, and developed countries then pay developing countries carbon offsets for their standing forests.

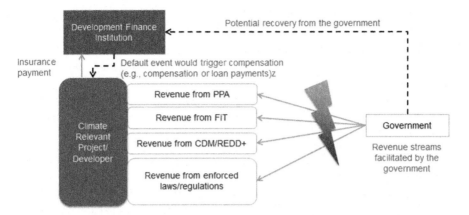

Fig. 9 Policy risk insurance

state or national-level REDD accounting systems that change the way REDD targets are measured, potentially preventing projects from earning carbon credits (Christianson et al. 2013).

Terra Global Capital has a grandfathering clause in its contract with the Cambodian government, but as its investment in the project grew, the company felt it prudent to insure that investment against political risk that could undermine this clause. OPIC's insurance provides coverage that protects against governmental breach of contracts, which can include risk protection for actions that rise to the level of an expropriation. The insurance also protects against damage to the project caused by political violence. Tailoring insurance instruments in this manner is particularly important for climate-friendly projects because if the insurance policy is not drafted to fit unique aspects of the project or climate policy, the investor and project sponsors may find filing and settling an insurance claim challenging (Christianson et al. 2013).

A few public financial institutions, including the US Overseas Private Investment Corporation (OPIC), are exploring how 'regulatory risk' insurance products can protect financiers against unexpected, but *legitimate*, policy changes. Theoretically, as shown in Fig. 9, such a product could guarantee investment returns if and when current or projected losses are triggered by specific types of legitimate policy changes such as a change in feed-in tariffs.[16] However, pricing such a product affordably can be challenging, particularly given the uncertainty of international as well as domestic climate change-related policies.

---

[16] A feed-in tariff (FIT) is a policy instrument that makes it mandatory for energy companies or utilities responsible for operating electricity grids (whether national, regional, or local) to purchase electricity from renewable energy sources at a predetermined price for a fixed period (usually 10–20 years) that is sufficiently attractive to stimulate new investment in the renewable sector. For more information, see GET FiT Program in the report 'Global Energy Transfer Feed in Tariffs for Developing Countries by the Deutsche Bank Climate Change Advisors' at http://www.dbcca.com/dbcca/EN/_media/GET_FiT_Program.pdf

3.6 Public–Private Climate Fund Models

Larger institutional investors such as pension funds, insurance companies, and sovereign wealth funds have assets under management representing US$71 trillion globally (OECD Global Pensions Statistics 2010).

Unsurprisingly, policymakers are eager to understand how public finance can leverage these actors' assets and redirect their investment towards climate-friendly activities. One key barrier to unlocking institutional money, particularly in developing countries, is the lack of scale and liquidity in many climate-friendly markets (Kaminker et al. 2012). In addition to green bonds and asset-backed securitisation, aggregating investments into a fund can help achieve this required scale and liquidity. Recently, two public funds successfully secured sizeable private sector investment at the fund level from institutional investors: (1) the Climate Catalyst Fund (from the State Oil Fund of Azerbaijan and an unnamed German Pension Fund) and (2) the Global Climate Partnership Fund [from Deutsche Bank and the German pension fund Ärzteversorgung Westfalen-Lippe (ÄVWL)].

The Global Climate Partnership Fund (GCPF) is a publicly and privately financed investment fund supported by the German Federal Ministry for the Environment, Nature Conservation and Nuclear Safety, KfW (a German development bank), IFC, the Danish Ministry of Foreign Affairs, ÄVWL, and the Deutsche Bank Group. The GCPF's tiered structure, and specifically the contributions of donor governments to the riskiest position (C-Shares) in the fund, de-risks returns for other private sector investors and has been critical to the GCPF's role in attracting securing US$30 million in investment from ÄVWL (Polycarp et al. 2013).

According to the fund's annual report, since its inception in 2009 the GCPF has disbursed US$152.8 million, US$102.8 million of which was disbursed in 2012 (Schneider et al. 2012). It currently focuses on Brazil, Chile, China, India, Indonesia, Mexico, Morocco, South Africa, the Philippines, Tunisia, Turkey, Ukraine, and Vietnam. GCPF is currently managed by a private sector financial institution—Deutsche Bank Group—which is also a co-investor in the fund.

The GCPF provides direct financing to project developers, energy service companies (ESCOs), and small-scale renewable energy and energy efficiency service and supply companies and indirect financing through local commercial banks, leasing companies, and other selected financial institutions for renewable energy and energy efficiency projects. To date, 98 % of the fund's investments has been provided indirectly through partner financial institutions, and only 2 % directly. The fund has used eight partner/intermediary institutions: Cronimet Mining AG in South Africa, XacBank in Mongolia, VietinBank in Vietnam, Ukreximbank in the Ukraine, Şekerbank in Turkey, Banco ProCredit and Banco del Pichincha in Ecuador, and Banco Pine in São Paulo (Schneider et al. 2012). As the GCPF is relatively new, it is hard to evaluate its overall performance, but its success in attracting institutional investors indicates that a fund model backstopped with public grants or first-loss investment can help attract institutional investment.

4 Overcoming Operational Challenges to Mobilising Investment

As public assistance budgets tighten and the investment needs of recipient developing countries grow, donor governments will need to ensure that their limited finance is effectively and accountably mobilising investment. As described earlier in this chapter, creating the right enabling conditions for investment through policy support and deploying public financial instruments to harness new sources of finance are both critical to success.

But implementing these two types of interventions is easier said than done. The public sector has to tailor these interventions to specific geographies, sectors, and technologies, as well as coordinate their execution among multiple public actors. For example, public sector arms of development finance institutions like the World Bank may be central to ensuring that appropriate policy and regulatory frameworks are in place within a country, the Global Environment Facility may provide critical research and development support to a burgeoning technology, the Clean Technology Fund might provide concessional finance to fund a demonstration project, and a bilateral development finance institution like the US Overseas Private Investment Corporation may increase a project's access to finance through its loan guarantees. Additionally, funding agencies and entities within developing country governments—that is, recipients of international climate finance—will need to coordinate with international public sector sources of finance and also ensure that its own finance is effectively deployed. Finally, all of these public sector actors will need to interface effectively with domestic and international private sector actors.

The paragraphs below highlight four examples of institutional challenges the public sector faces in implementing the interventions described in this chapter and also offer some solutions to overcome these challenges. It draws from the anecdotal experiences and reflections of both private sector and public sector actors as detailed in the World Resources Institute's Climate Finance series and specifically in its forthcoming publication 'Raising the Stakes'.[17]

1. **Increasing Private Sector Awareness:** Navigating the complex landscape of public pots of money can be daunting for both the public and private sector. Given the limited information available, private sector actors still seek finance in a relatively ad hoc and relationship-driven manner and require deep pockets to sustain business activities until finance is secured. This obstacle especially hurts small companies and applicants from poorer countries, but even larger companies and funds often struggle to understand where to go for public finance sources and how to meet the associated requirements. To ensure equitable access to public finance, public actors must ensure that the private sector, recipient

---

[17] See the following website for a listing of publications within the WRI Climate Finance Series: http://www.wri.org/our-work/project/climate-finance, and to access the December 2013 forthcoming publication, "Raising the Stakes."

governments, peer finance providers, and development finance institutions are aware of available public money and can access this money efficiently. Passive information tools like online databases can help the private sector navigate the complex landscape of public finance, but active tools such as relationship managers within public institutions and pro-bono advisory services can be particularly impactful.

2. **Improving Access to Public Finance:** Even with adequate information, unlocking public money can be cumbersome given the varying requirements of public institutions and the multitude—albeit limited volume—of public sources of money. Some of this difficulty and redundancy may be fixed by streamlining and harmonising processes among public institutions. However, due diligence concerns and institutional inertia might make it hard for institutions to come to a consensus. Furthermore, trimming processes could undermine environmental and social safeguards and the financial longevity of and confidence in public institutions. Nevertheless, recommendations to government agencies and development banks to improve private sector access and public sector processes include:

   • Providing collective information to the private sector on the availability of funds, co-investment timelines, basic access requirements, and internal contacts to help navigate the unique requirements of public pots of money.
   • Consolidating and co-investing in funds where requirements and processes are clearly defined at the outset and redundancies among institutions are minimised.
   • Co-syndicating to minimise work for both the public and private sector.
   • Agreeing on harmonised reporting indicators, approval procedures, and negotiation terms—or at least principles—among public sector institutions, in close consultation with the private sector.

3. **Monitoring and Evaluating Success:** Measuring the contribution and impact of public interventions on mobilising private investment is a complex task. Not only is data sparse on private sector projects and cofinance in climate-friendly projects (partly due to confidentiality issues), but there is also currently no standardised set of reporting methodologies to evaluate how public monies mobilise private monies. Subsequently, setting a baseline from which to improve, metrics to evaluate success, and identifying optimal sets of interventions are all challenging tasks.

   Thus far, development finance institutions and climate finance mechanisms like the Clean Technology Fund have measured their successes through metrics like how each dollar of public money leveraged private sector co-investment in a particular project. But policy, institutional, industry, and regulatory support are equally, if not more, central to mobilising private investment, especially at an early stage of a market (Polycarp et al. 2013). In fact, where well-defined and enforced regulatory frameworks exist, fossil fuel subsidies are retracted, and climate-friendly policies are in place, public finance and concessional funding may not be required for long.

Currently, a group of public and private sector institutions, through the OECD's Tracking Private Climate Finance Research Collaborative (OECD et al. 2013), are exploring ways to improve data collection and measurement of mobilised private climate finance flows and hopefully address some of the data and measurement challenges outlined. In addition, public sector institutions should provide aggregated data on private sector projects to promote learning from experiences, while still maintaining individual project confidentiality requirements.

4. **Building Robust Institutions:** Setting up appropriate governing and operating structures within development finance institutions and climate finance mechanisms like the proposed Green Climate Fund are important to ensuring public sector institutions can effectively engage with the private sector. For example, Sierra suggests that ensuring private sector participation on the Boards of funds can enhance the likelihood of achieving goals of 'scale-up, transformation, and leverage' (Sierra 2012). With regard to operational structures, Polycarp et al. find through a review of 27 existing public climate funds and initiatives that aim to mobilise private capital that some multi-donor funds are limited in their activities (including deploying innovative financial instruments) because of the limited flexibility of financial inputs from donors. Thus, donor countries should consider providing a reasonable amount of *grant* funding into public funds to ensure that a suite of financial instruments—including those described in this chapter—can be used flexibly as needed to most effectively mobilise private sector investments.

At a broader level, given the complex task of coordinating between multiple actors and deploying multiple interventions, landscaping the unique role and comparative advantage of each public financing institution, funds, and initiatives in the climate finance architecture is an important next step for public sector institutions.

Conclusion

Given the growing climate change financing gap globally, and particularly in developing countries, it is imperative that the public and private sectors work together to invest in climate-friendly projects. Without a doubt, enabling, promoting, and scaling investment is a huge task that requires not only instituting policy changes, supporting industry, and deploying innovative financial instruments but also making fundamental changes to the way public institutions interact with the private sector. If done right, mobilising private sector investment can create new investment opportunities, reduce business risk, and create a safer world for future generations.

Acknowledgement The author would like to thank Jawahar Shah, Aman Srivastava, and Sara Jane Ahmed for their research assistance.

References

Brown, J., & Jacobs, M. Leveraging private investment: the role of public sector climate finance. *Background Note*, Overseas Development Institute, April 2011. http://www.odi.org.uk/sites/odi.org.uk/files/odi-assets/publications-opinion-files/7082.pdf

Chen, D. Goldman to invest in city jail program, profiting if recidivism falls sharply. *The New York Times*, 8 August 2012. http://www.nytimes.com/2012/08/02/nyregion/goldman-to-invest-in-new-york-city-jail-program.html

Christianson, G., Venugopal, S., & Patel, S. (2013). Unlocking private climate investment: Focus on OPIC and Ex-Im bank's use of financial instruments. Working Paper, Installment 3 of *Public Financial Instruments* series. Washington, DC: World Resources Institute. wri.org/publication/unlocking-private-climateinvestment-focus-on-opic-and-ex-im-bank.

City of New York. NYC announces nation's first social impact bond program. *Mike Bloomberg*, 2 August 2012. http://www.mikebloomberg.com/index.cfm?objectid=E791E137-C29C-7CA2-F5C2142354A09332

Climate Bonds. (2013) Bonds and climate change: The state of the market in 2013, pp. 6–7. http://www.climatebonds.net/files/Bonds_Climate_Change_2013_A3.pdf

Climate Investment Funds. Climate investment funds: Lessons learned from private sector interventions through MDB intermediaries, November 2011. http://www.climateinvestmentfunds.org/cif/sites/climateinvestmentfunds.org/files/Joint%20CRP%201%20-%20IF%20ppt%20CIF%20Lessons%20Learned%20private%20sector.pdf

Flood, C. Zurich pledges $1 bn to go green. *Financial Times*, 17 November 2013. http://www.ft.com/intl/cms/s/0/43e36770-4e05-11e3-8fa5-00144feabdc0.html#axzz2m9Ly81fB

Ghosh, A., Müller, B., Pizer, W., & Wagner, G. Mobilizing the private sector quantity-performance instruments for public climate funds. *Oxford Energy and Environment Brief*, August 2012. http://www.oxfordenergy.org/wpcms/wp-content/uploads/2012/08/Mobilizing-the-Private-Sector.pdf

Ghosh, A., Müller, B., Pizer, W., & Wagner, G. Mobilizing the private sector: Quantity-performance instruments for public climate funds. *Environmental Defense Fund*, August 2012. http://www.edf.org/sites/default/files/Ghosh_et_al_2012_EDF_Mobilizing_the_Private_Sector.pdf

Hervé-Mignucci, M. San Giorgio Group Case Study: Walney Offshore Windfarms. *Climate Policy Initiative*, June 2012. http://climatepolicyinitiative.org/wp-content/uploads/2012/06/Walney-Offshore-Windfarms.pdf

Inter-American Development Bank. Project abstract: Structured and corporate finance, October 2009. http://idbdocs.iadb.org/wsdocs/getdocument.aspx?docnum=2202496

International Finance Corporation. EDF La Ventosa: Summary of proposed investment, December 22, 2009. http://ifcext.ifc.org/ifcext/spiwebsite1.nsf/0/81ACEB3C99869A77852576BA000E32E3

Kaminker, C., Steward, F., & Upton, S. The role of institutional investors in financing clean energy. *OECD Round Table on Sustainable Development*. London: OECD, 26 April 2012. http://www.oecd.org/sd-roundtable/papersandpublications/50363886.pdf

Karmali, A. Innovative financial mechanisms to make the UN Green Climate Fund's Private Sector Facility operational. *Submission to the Green Climate Fund*. October 2012.

Kidney, S. (2013a). Bank of America closes their own 3 yr, Baa2, $500 m green bond—a US first. *Climate Bonds Initiative*, 20 November 2013. http://www.climatebonds.net/category/green-bonds/

Kidney, S. (2013b). UK Greater Gabbard wind-grid bond, 19 yr £305 m ($496 m), is 3 x oversubscribed. Whacko! EIB Proj Bonds Initiative helps it get magic A3 rating; shows the way for future Proj Bonds credit enhancement. *Climate Bonds Initiative*, 27 November 2013. http://www.climatebonds.net/2013/11/uk-greater-gabbard-wind-grid-bond-19yr-305m-488m-is-3-x-oversubscribed-whacko-eib-proj-bonds-initiative-helps-it-get-magic-a3-rating-shows-the-way-for-future-proj-bonds-credit-enhancement/

McKinsey & Company. (2010). *Energy efficiency: a compelling global resource.* New York: McKinsey & Company.

Mulligan, M. Spain pressed over solar tariff cuts. *Financial Times*, 23 June 2010. http://www.ft.com/intl/cms/s/0/3a7ac61c-7ee0-11df-8398-00144feabdc0.html#axzz1mZkcTkP4

OECD. (2013). *OECD Environmental performance reviews: Mexico 2013.* OECD. http://dx/doi.org/10.1787/97892641801809-en

OECD Global Pensions Statistics. (2010). Global pensions statistics. *OECD Database.* http://www.oecd.org/finance/financial-markets/globalpensionstatistics.htm

OECD et al. OECD research collaborative. OECD, 2013. http://www.oecd.org/env/researchcollaborative/

Polycarp, C., Brown, L., & Fu-Bert, X. (2013) Mobilizing climate investment: The role of international climate finance in creating readiness for scaled-up low-carbon energy. *WRI Report.* Washington DC: World Resources Institute. http://www.wri.org/sites/default/files/pdf/mobilizing_climate_investment.pdf

Porter, D. Hurricane sandy was second-costliest in U.S. history, report shows. *The Huffington Post*, 2 February 2012. http://www.huffingtonpost.com/2013/02/12/hurricane-sandy-second-costliest_n_2669686.html

Schneider, M., Hölter, M., Kern, S., Klinker, M. Mitigating climate change together: Global Climate Partnership Fund Annual Report 2012. *Global Climate Partnership Fund*, 2012. http://gcpf.lu/tl_files/downloads/annual_reports/GCPF_AR-2012_web.pdf

Sierra, K. *The green climate fund's private sector facility: The case for private sector participation on the board.* Brookings Institution, August 2012. http://www.brookings.edu/~/media/research/files/papers/2012/8/green-climate-private-sector-sierra/08-green-climate-private-sector-sierra.pdf

Social Finance and Center for Global Development. Investing in social outcomes: Development impact bonds—The report of the development impact bond working group, p. 2, October 2013. http://www.socialfinance.org.uk/sites/default/files/cgd-sf-dibreport_online.pdf

SolarCity. SolarCity completes industry's first securitization of distributed solar energy. *Global Newswire*, 21 November 2013. http://globenewswire.com/news-release/2013/11/21/591675/10059078/en/SolarCity-Completes-Industry-s-First-Securitization-of-Distributed-Solar-Energy.html

Spencer, T., Stevenson, J. EU low-carbon investment and new financial sector regulation: What impacts and what policy response?. Working Papers No. 5/2013, IDDRI, 2013. http://www.iddri.org/Publications/EU-Low-Carbon-Investment-and-New-Financial-Sector-Regulation-What-Impacts-and-What-Policy-Response

The Economist. Typhoon Haiyan: Worse than hell. Cebu, Hanoi and Manila, 16 November 2013. http://www.economist.com/news/asia/21589916-one-strongest-storms-ever-recorded-has-devastated-parts-philippines-and-relief

The World Economic Forum. (2013). The Green Investment Report: The ways and means to unlock private finance for green growth—A Report of the Green Growth Action Alliance. http://www3.weforum.org/docs/WEF_GreenInvestment_Report_2013.pdf

United States Agency for International Development. (2009). Mexico wind farm case study. http://www.energytoolbox.org/gcre/wind_case_study.pdf

Venugopal, S., & Srivastava, A. (2011). Moving the fulcrum: A primer on public climate financing instruments used to leverage private capital. WRI Working Paper, World Resources Institute, Washington, DC. http://www.wri.org/publication/moving-the-fulcrum

Venugopal, S., Srivastava, A., Polycarp, C., & Taylor, E. (2012). Public financing instruments to leverage private capital for climate-relevant investment: Focus on multilateral agencies. Working Paper. World Resources Institute, Washington, DC. http://www.wri.org/project/climate-finance-private-sector

Ward, J., Fankhauser, S., Hepburn, C., Jackson, H., Rajan, R. Catalysing low-carbon growth in developing economies: Public Finance Mechanisms to scale up private sector investment in climate solutions. *Press Release*, UNEP and Partners, October 2009. http://www.unep.org/PDF/PressReleases/Public_financing_mechanisms_report.pdf

Wind Power Intelligence. EDF Secures Financing for La Mata La Ventosa Wind Farm. 15 December 2010. http://www.windpowerintelligence.com/article/aW7SPD9w0iY/2010/12/15/mexico_financing_secured_for_675_mw_oaxaca_wind_farm/

World Bank. (2010). *Economics of adaptation to climate change—Synthesis report*. Washington, DC: World Bank. http://documents.worldbank.org/curated/en/2010/01/16436675/economics-adaptation-climate-change-synthesis-report

World Bank Treasury. (2013). Green bonds issuances to date. http://treasury.worldbank.org/cmd/htm/WorldBankGreenBonds.html

Implementing ESG in the Financial Sector in Russia: The Journey Towards Better Sustainability

Alexey Akulov

Abstract While environmental and social considerations have become a standard practice within many national and international financial institutions over the past decade, the Russian financial sector is still only taking its first steps towards better sustainability. Environmental matters in Russia have traditionally been a prerogative of state regulatory bodies. The philosophy of industrial companies, therefore, was, and in many cases still is, to comply with environmental regulation. Financial institutions lending to and investing in industrial companies preferred to distance themselves from their clients' environmental issues. Social aspects, as currently understood within the ESG concept, received even less consideration. Tighter environmental regulation, however, and, more importantly, better enforcement, political developments, wider international cooperation, increased public awareness, and promotion of sustainability standards by major international finance institutions acting in Russia have now instigated a change of approach by financial sector companies to address ESG issues. This chapter will discuss what is happening, and why, and the key challenges to implement sustainability strategies into the financial sector operations in Russia.

1 Introduction to Russia

Russia is the world's largest country in terms of land, ninth in terms of population. It is eighth largest economy in the world by GDP nominal value (2012) (International Monetary Fund 2013). The Russian economy is currently labelled as high income: non-OECD by The World Bank (2013). Russia takes membership in BRICS, G8 and G20. In 2012, Russia became a member of WTO.

Since the dissolution of the Soviet Union in 1991, Russia has undergone significant changes, moving from a centrally planned economy to a more market-based and globally integrated economy.

A. Akulov (✉)
Vnesheconombank, Responsible Finance Unit, Moscow, Russia
e-mail: aleksey.akulov@gmail.com

© Springer International Publishing Switzerland 2015
K. Wendt (ed.), *Responsible Investment Banking*, CSR, Sustainability, Ethics & Governance, DOI 10.1007/978-3-319-10311-2_19

The modern Russia inherited the banking system of the Soviet Union, with a few large banks where the state is the main or the only shareholder including Sberbank, VTB Bank (former Vneshtorgbank), Gazprombank and Vnesheconombank. After more than 15 years of reform, there are now more than 900 financial institutions (Central Bank of Russian Federation 2013). The only development bank in Russia is State Corporation Vnesheconombank (VEB), where the Russian government is the only shareholder.

2   Russian Environmental Regulatory Framework

The history of Russian environmental regulation dates back to the seventeenth and eighteenth centuries, with the majority of development occurring in the 1700s under the rule of Peter the Great. He was the first to introduce formal regulation in areas such as subsurface resource use, forest use and conservation, soil protection, surface water body use and protection, and others. Development and strengthening of environmental regulations continued until 1917.

The development progress slowed down upon the Soviet regime setup, and little attention was paid to environmental matters until the 1970s. It is important to mention that no state regulatory body dedicated to environmental issues management existed in the USSR until 1988 when the State Committee on Environmental Protection was established. The change in understanding of the importance of the environmental issues in the 1970s–1980s resulted in the development of a series of key legislation that are considered to have laid down the basis for the current Russian environmental regulation. During that period, the following main regulatory documents were introduced: Land Code, Water Code, Subsurface resource Code, Forest Code, Law on atmospheric air protection.

After the collapse of the Soviet Union, the development of the environmental regulation continued—the existing laws were amended to reflect changes in economic and regulatory environment, while new important regulation was enforced including laws on environmental impact assessment, on state environmental expertise, on specially protected areas, on wildlife, on Red Book of Russia, on wastes management and on environmental protection.

3   Environmental Impact Assessment in Russia

Adoption of the law on state environmental expertise in Russia in 1995 introduced the procedure of environmental impact assessment for all projects that could potentially have a negative impact on the environment.

The project approval cycle provided for two sequential stages: (1) predesign stage that included preparation of declaration of intent and technical and economic justification of the project (feasibility study) and (2) design stage that included project design and detailed (working) project documentation.

As per the legislation, the EIA was to be carried out at the predesign stage and was subject to the state environmental expertise review and approval. At the design

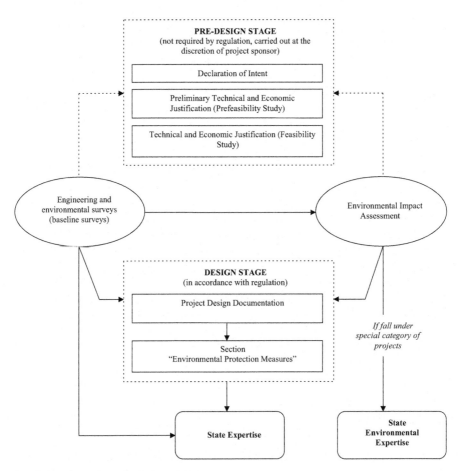

Fig. 1 EIA in project preparation cycle

stage, development of an Environmental Protection section was required based on the approved EIA report to further detail environmental and social impacts associated with the project and to develop appropriate mitigation measures. The design documents were again subject to the stage environmental expertise review, and the positive conclusion of the expertise was required to obtain a construction permit.

However, in 2006 the new Town Planning Code was adopted in Russia that changed the above-mentioned stages of the project approval. Since 2007, the predesign stage of the project is no longer within the scope of state expertise review. All projects are currently required to pass the US Expertise, which covers the environmental issues. The dedicated state environmental expertise is only obligatory for certain types of project, e.g. those implemented in the specially protected nature areas, in the coastal shelf, etc.

The principal flow chart of the current project approval cycle and the EIA is indicated in Fig. 1 (Ineca-Consulting 2009).

Although the project design documentation submitted to the State Expertise should contain the Environmental Protection section, which in turn should be based on the EIA, given the lack of dedicated state environmental review procedures, the EIA is often conducted in a formal way and does not ensure proper impact assessment and development of appropriate mitigation measures.

Therefore, despite the long history of environmental regulation in Russia, its enforcement is still considered weak compared to the developed western countries. Many environmental professionals agree that it has got weaker since 2007 when the scope of state environmental expertise was limited to certain types of projects.

In addition, due to continuous reforms of environmental regulations, it became very complex and bureaucracy driven. This meant that the environmental units of industrial companies had to spend most of their time and energy ensuring they were complying with environmental laws and standards and demonstrating it clearly through dozens of documents and approvals, rather than focusing on actual environmental performance. In most cases, the compliance was first achieved on paper and then (if at all) on the ground.

Weakness of Russian environmental regulation especially in the EIA areas stipulates significant environmental and social risks for financial institutions operating in Russia. While environmental and social considerations have become a standard practice within many national and international financial institutions over the past decade, the Russian financial sector is still only taking its first steps towards better sustainability.

4 Paradigm

Rooted back in the history of Soviet time, a strong paradigm has been established and in fact still persists in Russia with regard to environmental issues and environmental protection. It can be briefly expressed as 'environmental issues are between regulators and industrial companies'. It is general public opinion that environmental issues are the subject for state regulatory bodies and that industrial companies are the only ones that have to accept responsibility and take action towards a better environment.

Given the above, it is no surprise that Russian financial sector companies have traditionally remained, and in many cases still are, distant from environmental, health and safety and social issues associated with the projects and clients they finance. In addition, due to the generally low level of environmental regulation enforcement, there have been almost no cases so far in Russia where banks' financial performance was significantly affected by environmental or social issues experienced by the banks' clients or projects—the case that would be the main driver in introducing ESG Risk Management Framework.

The concept of sustainable development historically lacked attention in Russia—the Soviet regime did not allow a slot for the idea of sustainability, while during the 1990s, the newly established Russian Federation was entirely focused on political reforms and economic growth, leaving no room for 'theoretical' concepts such as sustainability.

5 The Beginning of ESG in Russia

Fast development of international cooperation and Russian integration into the world commodity and financial markets introduced new practices to Russia, including those within the ESG and sustainability area.

The first practice was the EHS due diligence approach employed by foreign trade and investing companies upon acquisitions and equity investments.

The EHS due diligence procedures—a standard practice for western companies making deals—was very new to Russian companies and financial institutions. International finance institutions such as EBRD and IFC applied their environmental and social requirements to projects and investments they financed in Russia promoting the practices of environmental and social due diligence, environmental and social impact assessment and community engagement. Gradually, this raised awareness among Russian businesses, including financial sector companies, about environmental and social risks and their implication on business financial performance.

The second idea to penetrate Russia along with international integration was the concept of corporate social responsibility. Obviously, the industrial companies were the first to adopt the CSR principles with the leading role taken by major companies and those promoting their products and services to or seeking funding from outside Russia. The key target of introducing CSR policies was to build better relationship with companies' internal and external stakeholders and to improve image and reputation. The CSR concept initiated the practice of non-financial reporting within Russian companies as a tool to demonstrate companies' environmental and social responsibility and commitment to sustainable development to a wider group of stakeholders. The non-financial reporting has become one of the key attributes of the CSR-committed companies. As of December 2013, as many as 132 companies issued their non-financial reports accounting for a total of 463 reports issued since 2000 (Russian Union of Industrialists and Entrepreneurs 2013).

That is how Russian financial sector companies became involved with sustainability—through adopting CSR strategies and engaging in non-financial reporting.

6 From CSR to Sustainable Banking

The CSR strategies that were the starting point for Russian FIs towards sustainability were at first mainly focused on social aspects such as internal company-employee relationship, local communities support and charity. The word 'environment' initially drew little attention from the banks because of the paradigm mentioned at the start of the chapter—environmental issues are the responsibility of industrial companies and regulators. However, increased awareness of ESG risks in financial sector, promotion of the idea of socially and environmentally responsible investments, political developments and further international cooperation have resulted in integration of socially oriented CSR policies and ESG risk management approaches creating a so-called responsible finance practice.

In 2012, the Russian national development bank Vnesheconombank—one of the leading financial institutions in the area of CSR—under its CSR strategy for 2012–2015 committed to implement the responsible finance practice into its credit and investment operation (Vnesheconombank 2012). Vnesheconombank defines the responsible finance as the approach to credit and investment operations that provide for adequate consideration of environmental and social risks and impacts associated with financed projects and clients and appropriate management system to mitigate these risks and impacts, and allows for financing environmentally and socially important projects under special terms.

Given its role of the national development bank, Vnesheconombank is best positioned to take the lead in promoting the responsible finance into the Russian business community. It believes it may serve as an example for other leading financial institutions in Russia to introduce ESG practices into its operations.

2013 has become an important year for the Russian financial sector in terms of mainstreaming responsible finance and ESG practices: the first two Russian banks joined the internationally recognised initiatives in the sustainability area—Vnesheconombank joined the UNEP Finance Initiative and bank 'Otkrytie' adopted the Equator Principles. Regional Russian bank 'Center-Invest Bank' was awarded the special commendation for Leadership in Eastern Europe of the 2013 FT/IFC Sustainable Finance Award.

7 The Way Forward

The Russian financial sector still has further to go to widely embed the sustainability concept and ESG practices into a standard flow of business performance. The major state and leading private financial institutions need to play a key role in the process of moving towards better sustainability. Russia's further integration into the process of global development and cooperation with international communities, the recognition of environmental and social issues as key global challenges and sustainability as one of the priorities to focus on may become a good driver for the Russian government to introduce new regulation fostering sustainability mechanisms and practices. The increasing number of strong and successful business cases should become the key driver for Russian businesses, both in financial sector and industry sector, to implement ESG and sustainability considerations into its day-to-day operations.

Raised public awareness of the issue, supported by the active position of NGOs, should also play a significant role in mainstreaming sustainability and ESG aspects in Russia.

Given the current state of understanding and developments within the sustainability area, as well as the possible drivers mentioned, we would hope that over the next 3–5 years, more financial institutions in Russia will implement sustainability policies and ESG-related practices into their operations.

References

Central Bank of Russian Federation. (2013, December). *Notice on the number of credit organizations and its subsidiaries.*

Ineca-Consulting LLC. (2009, February). *Ineka Eco-bulletin № 1 (132).*

International Monetary Fund. (2013, April). *World Economic Outlook Database.*

Russian Union of Industrialists and Entrepreneurs. (2013, December). *National register of corporate non-financial reports.*

The World Bank. (2013, October). *World Bank Open Data.*

Vnesheconombank. *Corporate social responsibility strategy of Vnesheconombank for 2012–2015.*

Implementing International Good Practice Standards: Pragmatism Versus Philosophy

L. Reed Huppman

Abstract Mainstreaming environmental and social considerations is something people have been working on for many years, and still are. For economists, the environment was considered an externality—if you cannot quantify it, you cannot incorporate it into your economic model. This is an ongoing problem, though tremendous strides have been made. John Dixon at the World Bank was one of the first to tackle this divide. Two years prior to the creation of the original Equator Principles, the four founding banks—Citibank, Barclays, WestLB and ABN Amro, each experienced a reputational crisis fomented by NGOs that led them to found what later was to become the Equator Principles. The four banks—Citi, Barclays ABN Amro and West LB—eventually got together, and this was the catalyst for the Equator Principles. They discussed that they needed some sort of environmental and social policy framework for project finance lending across the board. Although it was a cautious approach, it was a brave move. It took two more years of lobbying to recruit another six banks to have a critical mass of 10 for the original launch in June 2003. It has taken another 10 years to exceed 75 members.

Regarding E&S Considerations and Development Worldwide in Emerging Markets, Can You Take Us Back to the Origins of the World Bank Safeguards? The World Bank was created as the International Bank for Reconstruction and Development (IBRD) in July 1944 by the allies to rebuild Europe by lending money to governments. After Europe was largely rebuilt, it shifted its operations to the emerging markets with a mandate to improve economies, raise living standards and alleviate poverty. The World Bank generally finances only public sector projects, while its affiliate, the International Finance Corporation

---

Interview by Nicola Pearson: Reed Huppman was a director at Environ International but is now director of sustainability at a Canadian mining company. He worked as an environmental specialist at the World Bank between 1994 and 1996 and was seconded for 2 years to the International Finance Corporation as an environmental specialist, in 1996–1997 and again in 2000. He has worked with Equator Principle Financial Institutions on environmental and social due diligence since the launch of the EPs in June 2003 and provided training on the IFC Performance Standards since 2006.

L.R. Huppman (✉)
Guyana Goldfields Inc., 141 Adelaide St W #1700, ON M5H 3L5 Toronto, Canada
e-mail: lrhuppman2@icloud.com

© Springer International Publishing Switzerland 2015   333
K. Wendt (ed.), *Responsible Investment Banking*, CSR, Sustainability, Ethics &
Governance, DOI 10.1007/978-3-319-10311-2_20

(IFC) founded in 1956, finances private sector projects. The original purpose of the first umbrella Safeguard Policy, OP 4.01 Environmental Assessment, was to improve decision making, to ensure that project options under consideration by the client country and the Bank were sound and sustainable and that communities likely to be affected are properly consulted. OP 4.01 drew on the National Environmental Policy Act of the USA, promulgated around 1970 and which invented the concept of environmental impact assessments or statements (EIAs or EISs). I believe OP 4.01, or OD 4.01 as it was originally termed, was originally developed in the early 1980s. In the ensuing years, the Bank developed the nine other Safeguard Policies (Natural Habitats, Forestry, Involuntary Resettlement, Indigenous Peoples, Cultural Property, International Waterways, Safety of Dams, Disputed Areas and Pest Management).

By about 1956, the infrastructure of Europe was partially recovered, but many economies were still lagging behind. The IFC was created as the private sector arm of the World Bank Group to advance economic development by investing in private, strictly for-profit, commercial projects, still with the ethos of reducing poverty and promoting development.

The IFC therefore had a very different mandate, with a different culture and very different personality. The IFC was much slower than the World Bank to adopt the Safeguard policies. By the mid-1980s, it was just starting to incorporate environmental policies and trying to apply them. In 1989, IFC had hired its first environment director, Martyn Riddle, who grew the department over time.

The World Bank created OP 4.01 as a result of a growing awareness in developed countries of environmental concerns and in response to pressure from NGOs (nongovernmental organisations). NGOs have protested against the World Bank's development projects for many years. Even when the Bank had these safeguard policies in place, it took years to mainstream the safeguard policies, that is, to get the loan officer staff on board. Mainstreaming environmental and social considerations is something people have been working on for many years and still are. For economists, the environment was considered an externality—if you can't quantify it, you can't incorporate it into your economic model. This is an ongoing problem, though tremendous strides have been made. John Dixon at the World Bank was one of the first to tackle this divide.

How Big an Impact Did the Cut the Card Campaign Have on the Development of Sustainable Investing and the Development of the EP? Huge! It was a very clever campaign.

Two years prior to the creation of the original EP, the four founding banks—Citibank, Barclays, WestLB and ABN Amro—each experienced a reputational crisis fomented by NGOs that led them to found the EPs. For Citi, it was campaign that resulted in boxes of cut-up credit cards being sent to the chairman, Sanford Weill by cardholders.

At the time, Citi was the largest issuer of credit cards, certainly in the USA, if not globally. NGOs and, in particular, the Rainforest Action Network (RAN) were criticising the Citi for funding projects that were allegedly destroying rainforests.

RAN delivered 2,500 letters, supposedly written by schoolchildren, to Citigroup, asking the institution to protect the environment. Later the same year, RAN announced that 20,000 people had cut up their Citibank credit cards and sent the debris to RAN's offices to voice their disgust with Citigroup. In 2003, RAN started running TV ads criticising Citigroup featuring celebrities such as Susan Sarandon and Richard Gere. This proved too much for the Bank and it realised it had to rethink how and what it was financing.

The four banks, Citi, Barclays, ABN Amro and WestLB, eventually got together, and this was the catalyst for the EPs. They discussed that they needed some sort of environmental and social policy framework for project finance lending across the board. Although it was a cautious approach, it was a brave move. It took two more years of lobbying to recruit another six banks to have a critical mass of 10 for the original launch in June 2003. It has taken another 10 years to exceed 75 members. So, yes, you could say that the Cut the Card campaign was a game changer.

Are There Areas Where the Standards Are Limited, Even for Banks and Their Clients Invested in Them? One limit is the project finance focus, but this limitation is now being addressed in the third iteration of the EPs and the focus has expanded. But perhaps the greatest weakness is that an EA/EIA, now ESIA, is effectively a permitting document in emerging market countries, and/or a lending approval document for lenders, whereas EIA is, in theory, intended to be a planning process. Second, the original WB 4.01 guidance called for scoping prior to preparation of the EIA ToR. Application of the mitigation hierarchy and avoidance of major risks or impacts has to take place early in site selection and project design and planning to be effective. In my experience, ESIAs are typically tendered when the site has been selected and the project is well into preliminary design; hence, the greatest opportunities to avoid environmental and social risks and impacts may not be fully realised.

How Can Private Companies, Such as Oil and Gas Companies, Deal with Cross Cutting Issues Such as Human Rights, Biodiversity and Ecosystem Services? Do They Have the Required Leverage on Their Projects? Generally no or at best with difficulty as good management of these aspects to be truly effective must be conducted at a regional or national scale. In the case of a given project, it depends to a great extent on an individual host country's regulatory and environmental planning framework, or lack thereof, and the environmental and social geography and the extent of the project including associated facilities and cumulative impacts, and the area of the developer's concession or area of control. For example, it is rare that a developer will have full control over a catchment or river basin, and hence it cannot control all the other potentially deleterious activities in that basin that can have adverse effects on human rights, biodiversity and ecosystem services. This is why pre-ESIA screening and scoping is so important as they represent critical opportunities to identify potential risks and impacts, which, with additional lead time, can hopefully be mitigated through changes to the project's siting and design and coordination with the relevant government ministries.

Is There a Risk of Creating a Double Standard When Attempting to Implement E&S Standards in Some Host Countries in Developing Markets? There is already a double standard between many emerging market country EIA regulatory requirements versus international good practice, for example, IFC PSs and EHS Guidelines versus emerging market national standards.

The World Bank\IFC EHS Guidelines are typically more stringent than those of the host country with regard to standards for emissions, noise, sewage, waste from a factory and so on. Similarly, the IFC Performance Standards for impact assessment are generally far more comprehensive in scope than what is required in most emerging market countries. Because of this dichotomy in ESIA or EIA requirements, we have often recommended that an international developer consider preparing an EIA to meet the host country standards in order to obtain the development licence and plan to prepare a second ESIA to meet international standards (e.g. the IFC Performance Standards).

In some countries, an EIA may be a fairly straightforward document to meet various permitting requirements of different government ministries, whereas the international impact assessment will typically be a longer and more comprehensive process, demanding more environmental and social baseline information, stakeholder mapping and consultations and, if resettlement is involved, extensive analysis of affected households to determine appropriate compensation. Resettlement needs to be carried out in a very detailed manner, and it's not always done well. Failed or poorly carried out resettlement programmes were exactly the type of problem the World Bank faced, which led to the protests and the gradual development of the Safeguard Policies and subsequent IFC Performance Standards. In the old days, a village would just have been moved. Period. The battle to get everyone on board to do things properly is still going on.

In Some Emerging Market Countries, Enforcement of Standards Is Weak. What Does That Mean for Developers, International Banks Financing the Deal and the Affected Communities Since Impacts Often Are Irreversible and Poorly Mitigated, Leaving the Client Caught in the Middle with the Community the Loser? In remote and/or relatively undeveloped areas, the impacts of the Project are not necessarily the problem; the conundrum is when the developer follows best practice and conducts extensive stakeholder consultations, which, even if very carefully carried out, result inevitably in expectations of benefits. In such cases, the developer may be forced to act as a surrogate government. In remote areas, where there is very little in terms of infrastructure, health care, education and so on, how much is enough—how much should that company do? Most multinationals are willing to contribute quite a bit to improve the local economy, infrastructure and health conditions, but this can be a very slippery slope. Typically, the lenders don't have to worry about the potentially large associated costs over the life of the Project, long after the loan is paid back.

Should Investment Banks and Clients Be Wary of Strategic Development Plans of Countries and Changes in National Policies Towards Less Responsible Practices? In my opinion, investors and lenders should certainly be aware of what is beginning to happen in an area and incorporate it into their investment decisions. The case of a major Brazil hydro project is quite alarming. As I understand it, the Brazilian government reduced pre-existing protected areas and indigenous peoples' territories to allow a mega hydro to be built. In mining, oil and gas, the deposit is fixed, and it should be the government's responsibility to establish concession boundaries in a manner that avoids protected areas or at least recognises the value of certain areas for biodiversity or indigenous people. However, this is often not the case. For example, the Petroperu website used to show the entire Amazonas portion of Peru divided into future concession blocks for oil and gas exploration. Whether there are oil and gas reserves there and whether these will ever be of interest to developers is uncertain. But from a national biodiversity/ecosystem services management/indigenous peoples' perspective, it would appear that those considerations were not incorporated in the concession delineation process.

When considering whether to bid for a concession, the larger extractive multi-nationals will often evaluate the potential risks of a concession area in terms of biodiversity, rare species, communities, etc. But what should they do if they bid and win the concession? The government has granted them the concession, and to develop it will inevitably result in certain impacts. In effect, managing the development to avoid, minimise or mitigate the impacts becomes their dilemma. This is the conundrum of international development. There is always the trade-off: to develop natural resources to improve a nation's economy and living standard often results in loss of wild areas.

Ideally, the government would be well aware of the non-extractive natural resources of their own country and have a well-conceived master plan in place that balances development and preservation or protection. National mitigation banks that preserve exceptional areas and which are firmly protected and financed by natural resource development projects in other areas may be one possible solution.

Unfortunately, things appear to be going backwards in Brazil. What was a protected area, with an indigenous people territory, has now had chunks sliced off to allow the project to go through. It has become a joint responsibility between the government and the developer, but it would be better if governments protected the country's biodiversity so that private sector didn't have to wrestle with the dilemma.

Regarding the Brazil example, it is often true in the emerging markets that protected areas are on occasion somewhat randomly delineated and in many instances aren't strategically located in terms of biodiversity or cultural values. Drawing on the knowledge of academics and nonprofits to identify the most important areas for biodiversity or cultural heritage preservation to develop national master plans is a critical need. In theory, this could be combined with the mitigation bank concept mentioned above to develop a more proactive system to balance natural resource exploitation and protection.

Is It Unrealistic to Think that Environmental Issues Are not Linked to Economic and Political Change? Are There Any Solutions to Radical Pendulum Swings in Sustainable Finance When, for Example, Anti-hydro and Antinuclear Suddenly Become Pro-hydro and Pronuclear? Obviously, this an issue far larger than sustainable finance, but the pendulum swing or paradigm change evidenced by the popularity of hydroelectric projects is exemplary and striking and demonstrates how great the uncertainty regarding planetary management and the relative importance of issues continues to be.

Hydroelectricity was full speed ahead in the 1960s, 1970s and 1980s, and then the Narmada Dam project in India turned the tables. The World Bank was heavily involved in the early days of the Narmada project (circa 1994–1995) but decided not to finance it in the end because of the enormous resettlement requirements. There had been much prior NGO opposition to big dams, in particular International River Network, but post Narmada, the World Commission on Dams, was created and the anti-hydro period began, the general consensus being that the negative impacts of most large hydro projects far outweighed the benefits.

Now, with concerns over GHGs and climate change, all renewable energy projects, including hydropower dams, are in vogue and hydro projects are being developed at a very high rate all over the world. Though the modern hydro projects tend to be smaller in scale, the impacts can still be significant, in particular from a cumulative and ecosystem services perspective. The takeaway is how new concepts can rapidly and totally reverse prior paradigms of what is good environmental management.

Can the IFC Standards Be Applied More Widely? To IPOs? To Any Finance? To Equity Investments? I think they can be applied at a corporate level and to asset management with some adjustments that would allow their application to IPOs, mutual fund portfolios and other types of financing or investment. In the end, it depends on demand from the investors. Europe, in particular the Nordic countries, has done a considerable amount in this area using various metrics and the GRI initiative. This has been driven by a combination of investor demand and government support. However, the relative demand in the USA and Canada appears to be far less.

The biggest risk I see in the asset management side is 'black box' technology, that is, entities selling their recommendations regarding which publically traded companies are superior in terms of environmental and social performance without revealing their methods for making such a determination. However, I do believe that good environmental and social management is in the end in any corporate's best interest, but it may not always translate directly to profits. The relative performance of many green funds, created originally as 'socially responsible' anti-apartheid funds that morphed into antitobacco and then green funds, has demonstrated that being 'green' doesn't always generate the best performance. But this problem is a result of the arbitrary definitions of 'green' rather than the benefits of good environmental and social management.

Tipping Points: Learning from Pain

A Commentary by Herman Mulder

Herman Mulder

Abstract At this year's OECD Global Forum on Responsible Business Conduct (June 2013), the terrible tragedy of the collapse of the Rana Plaza garment factory in Bangladesh that killed more than 1,000 workers rightly took centre stage. It reminded us all—governments, factory owners, product off-takers, but also financial institutions (investors and banks)—that we must take responsibility for the value chains of our businesses. The sustainability agenda is progressing with regard to public and private sector stakeholders, including the financial sector, and current momentum is irreversible in eliminating the short-termism that has dominated the financial sector for too long: the Working Party conclusions at the OECD forum re-confirmed that the financial sector is now part of the OECD MNE Guidelines, and European Commissioner Michel Barnier's structural reform of banks has indicated that "corporate transparency is key to a prosperous and sustainable future". Barnier's "report or explain" proposal that insists large companies disclose information on the major economic, environmental and social impact of their businesses as part of their annual reporting cycle is also of major importance. Unfortunately, the uncomfortable truth is that pain is often the driver of gain and many of the successes of the sustainability agenda have relied on a push from a major crisis or serious wake-up such as Rana Plaza. It is my opinion, that there could be another serious crisis around the corner that will emanate from the workers in the value chain upon whom we, the affluent society, increasingly depend and continue to ignore, even exclude, and whose natural environment and GDP we are seriously affecting. The warning signals are there and, if we take our feet off the accelerator this, too, could be a global game changer.

Interview by Nicola Pearson

H. Mulder (✉)
Executive Fellow Duisenberg School of Finance, Gustav Mahlerplein 117,
1082 MS Amsterdam, The Netherlands

Chairman True Price Foundation, Barbara Strozzilaan 201, 1083 HN Amsterdam,
The Netherlands
e-mail: mrhermanmulder@gmail.com

© Springer International Publishing Switzerland 2015
K. Wendt (ed.), *Responsible Investment Banking*, CSR, Sustainability, Ethics &
Governance, DOI 10.1007/978-3-319-10311-2_21

During my 15 years of working with the sustainability agenda, originally as a banker and risk manager at ABN Amro bank until 2006, to my current involvement with Inter Alia, the Dutch National Contact Point (NCP) for the OECD Guidelines for Multinational Enterprises (OECD MNE Guidelines), experience has taught me that it often takes a serious wake-up call to push the movement forward and convince us that it is no longer possible to live unsustainably and carry on doing business as usual.

These wake-up calls are often unexpected, shocking, sometimes tragic and always painful when we ask ourselves in hindsight, as I had to following the financial crisis of 2008, 'why did I not see this coming?'

The uncomfortable truth is that pain is often the driver of gain. At this year's OECD Global Forum on Responsible Business Conduct in Paris (June 2013), the terrible tragedy of the collapse of the Rana Plaza garment factory in Bangladesh that killed more than 1,000 workers, mostly women, rightly took centre stage and united us, governments, business, unions and others, in considered, collective action to determine that this must never happen again, anywhere. It reminds us there are fundamental flaws in our society and that everyone—governments, factory owners, product off-takers and also financial institutions (investors, banks) that have been slow to come to the table—must take responsibility for the value chains of their businesses.

There is a message coming from Nature and from the workers in these value chains that 'Not good is bad', that nature has to be preserved for current and future generations and that 'Not enough is not enough', and we should be listening.

The 'reward' for innovation and globalisation seems largely to be benefitting the affluent few, still leaving too many underprivileged poor in our societies (who are often working at the beginning of our own supply chains, on which we are dependent), excluded from our 'common goods'—decent wages, work, safety and health, free association, etc.—and being directly affected by our lack of environmental and social stewardship, even seriously at risk.

Rana Plaza was yet another 'canary in the coal mine', a wake-up call about a broader issue that we all need to address: how on earth can we, all 9 billion of us BY 2050, live together sustainably, in peace and in prosperity? How do we realise the world we 'need' (rather than the one the Rio+20 'want'), incorporating well-being and social justice for all, within planetary boundaries?

This terrible accident in Bangladesh will hopefully prove an inflection point for the broader recognition of the importance and urgency of the sustainability agenda and provide further impetus to, in particular, a comprehensive Post-2015 Agenda of the UN.

Practical and anecdotal calculations suggest that major crises often happen on a Monday, in September or October, 7 years apart. In 1994, we witnessed the Mexican Tequila crisis following the devaluation of the peso; in 2001, the dotcom bubble burst, followed by the collapse of Enron and Global Crossing; and in 2008, it was the turn of Lehman and AIG.

My guess, therefore, is that the next crisis could hit us on Monday (always), October 12 (very often), 2015 (biblical logic?), and that it will emanate from the workers in the value chain upon whom we, the affluent society, increasingly depend and continue to ignore, even exclude, and whose habitat (i.e. natural environment) and GDP we are seriously affecting. The warning signals are there and this, too, will be a global game changer.

Momentum for the sustainability agenda is building irrevocably, and as such, we may allow ourselves a moment to 'celebrate' (or at least acknowledge) some of the pain that got us here. We should, however, do so quietly out of respect for all victims of tragedies such as Rana Plaza, and we should do it with our minds focused on a better world and our feet firmly on the ground.

1 Inflection Point, 2013

Three things have happened thus far in 2013 to convince me that we have passed an inflection point with the sustainability agenda for all public and private sector stake-holders including the financial sector and that current momentum is also irreversible in eliminating the short-termism that has dominated the financial sector for too long.

First, the Working Party conclusions at this year's OECD forum in June 2013 reconfirmed that the financial sector is now part of the OECD MNE Guidelines. There is more practical work to be done in implementing this, but it sets the stage for banks, pension funds and other investors to take on board that, though they might not physically contribute to any damage, they are directly linked to the operations of their clients and investees and thereby to any footprint and impact. Even as a minority shareholder, these financial institutions must, in their own and society's interest, perform proper due diligence and risk management and, where they have leverage, use it to improve practices with their clients.

Second, nowhere is this clearer than in the landmark case in which the Dutch NCP has recently fostered an agreement between the large Dutch pension fund ABP/APG and a number of international and local NGOs over a complaint about their involvement with the South Korean steel company POSCO.

In autumn 2012, the Netherlands, Norwegian and South Korean NCPs received a complaint directed at POSCO over allegations of breaches of human rights and land-grabbing within planned iron mining and steel production in the Indian state of Odisha, one of the largest planned foreign investments in India.

The fact that the Dutch NCP has been able to foster such an agreement with APG and the NGOs about how to resolve these issues and major, responsible investors such as APG will commit to using their leverage with clients to improve practices gives vital kudos to the work of NCPs. NCPs are an essential part of the Guidelines, and as such, it is a priority to enhance their credibility worldwide so that more cases such as POSCO can be brought to light.

NCPs in the UK, Norway and the Netherlands currently enjoy the most consistent backing from their government and are the most engaged with NGOs and stakeholders, with those in Canada and Denmark improving rapidly. A lack of commitment, so far, from governments in other countries to allow NCPs to function independently hinders development of others. In the USA and Korea, for example, the NCPs operate as part of the government. Run by bureaucrats, willing as they may be, they do not necessarily then have the balanced influence to impact on business practices.

I also regard as positive that lobby groups, essentially subsectors of stakeholders, are lobbying the NCPs on broader issues and that certain NGOs are also using the lobbying power of the Guidelines to target companies that wield influence in their sector.

The recent agreement reached with Netherlands-based agricultural MNE Nidera is a case in point. The company was called upon by NGOs to develop and implement an effective company-wide human rights policy and due diligence procedural commitment. The successful outcome has seen Nidera strengthen its human rights policy, formalise human rights due diligence procedures for temporary rural workers, to allow the NGOs to monitor its Argentine corn seed operations via field visits, and, importantly, engage with peers in its sector. The agreement also included an improvement in Nidera's supply chain approach and operational-level grievance mechanism.

And third is European Commissioner Michel Barnier's statement in April 2013 regarding the structural reform of banks that 'corporate transparency is key to a prosperous and sustainable future' along with his hugely important 'report or explain' proposal that insists large companies disclose information on the major economic, environmental and social impact of their businesses as part of their annual reporting cycle. As Chairman of the Global Reporting Initiative (GRI), I am particularly pleased with this proposed directive, currently before the European Parliament. Should a company decide not to disclose information on any of six key topics, including human rights, anticorruption and bribery, it would be required to explain why not.

2   Inflection Point, 1998

Personally, my first inflection point came in 1998 when I was working as director general/head of group risk for Dutch bank ABN Amro. As one of the newest appointees at the top of the bank, I had also been made chair of the Group Risk Committee.

The bank received a letter from Friends of the Earth (FOE) criticising our financial involvement with a copper project in West Irian in Indonesia, for a long list of problems, including human rights, corruption and ecosystem degradation.

At that time, NGOs were not taken seriously, and we, as the first bank to be approached by FOE, might have ignored the letter had it not been backed by 800 of our client's signatures. As the person who had brought the West Irian project into the bank in my previous capacity as head of global structured finance, I was instrumental in creating something now considered a sin.

I asked a colleague in Indonesia to visit West Irian, and he reported back that FOE was right, that our due diligence had not sufficiently incorporated human rights nor environmental impacts.

We realised we had made a mistake, and, with the support of the ABN Amro Board, I went back to the FOE and told them they could go public with our admission and that we were now embarrassed to be associated with the credit and intended to sell it on. I also asked them to advise us with improving our mining risk analysis policy.

FOE was surprised by our approach, and their response was indeed to go public that our due diligence had been lacking. They declined to help us progress our policy and asked that, rather than sell on the credit, we use our leverage to encourage the Indonesian company to amend their practices. It was this wake-up call that gave us the kick start to develop our sustainability polices.

3 The Right People at the Right Time

At this year's OECD Global Forum (2013), I was impressed that several of the panellists originated from our ABN Amro school of sustainable finance.

The sustainability agenda is heavily dependent on the right people involved at the right time to implement change. Around the time of my FOE wake-up call, I'd hired an assistant whose MBA thesis was on palm oil. She persuaded me that we needed to upgrade our forestry policy, with advice from NGOs such as Oxfam, but the problem was how to go about it.

At that time, relationship managers were loath to involve themselves with potentially sensitive client business, but a courageous colleague in Canada offered to try the approach with one of her clients. The CFO of the company she chose was impressed that, rather than talking about her business, she'd spoken to him specifically about his business, something he'd never experienced before. He then went on to admit that the company had their own legacy issues and asked her to act as a go-between with one of the Canadian NGOs to set up talks. Companies rarely had conversations with NGOs, so, at the time, this was a big step. When she called me in the middle of the night to ask what she should do, I told her it was another wake-up call and to make the phone call.

4 Inflection Point, 2002: The Creation of the Equator Principles

At ABN Amro, as chairman of the Group Risk Committee, I was faced with a proposal to finance an oil project in Venezuela. The company asked us to waive the independent environmental assessment study, which had to be made as part of our company policy.

The fees involved were around US$3 million, and I was told that if I refused, there was a US bank ready and waiting to waive the independent study and ABN

Amro would lose the deal. If I said yes, the sustainability momentum I was creating within the bank would be lost.

Amro's chairman backed me, telling me to decide whether I wanted to be principled or practical and how far I valued the credibility issue within the bank if I gave in. We made the decision not to waive.

Shortly thereafter, I happened to have a conversation with Peter Woicke, chief executive of the IFC (International Finance Corporation), telling him I knew I was doing the right thing, but that I might win the battle and lose the war. Peter admitted over a cup of coffee that he had problem of his own, in that, as a small bank, the IFC needed to increase its lending and non-lending leverage for more sustainable finance.

We decided to convene a meeting of the 12 largest banks to see if we could find common ground for the issues that all of us must be experiencing. We invited the largest project finance banks, including Barclays, WestLB and Citigroup, to London and asked them to come up with a case study with which they were struggling involving stakeholders, communities or unions. Every bank had such a case.

The people at the table were not, on the whole, from investor relations but were practitioners and the people responsible for the credit. By the afternoon, we realised that, yet again, the right people were together at the right time to do something for a common cause. Out of that meeting, the Equator Principles were formed and signed by ten banks.

This was social responsibility in its early stage. There was an awareness that we not only had a common responsibility to ourselves but also to our sector and society. The Equator Principles of 2003 were a landmark—the first global, voluntary set of sector standards agreed (now adopted by 79 banks and FIs). We had taken a risk that relied on the media and the NGOs recognising that we were at least trying.

My favourite quote is, 'Nothing is impossible, particularly when it is inevitable': It is what I believe and I consider myself lucky to have been there at the right time. In hindsight, of course, one could ask why we had not started it earlier.

5   Inflection Point, 2002/2003, OECD Wake-Up Call

While still working at ABN Amro, in 2003 I experienced another wake-up call when I received a letter from the unions in the Netherlands complaining that, despite the OECD Guidelines, a union in the USA, Unitus, was not recognised by a client of the bank, Angelica Corporation, which was a client of LaSalle National Bank of Chicago, a subsidiary of ABN Amro.

At that time, we tended to ignore the OECD Guidelines, not considering them applicable to the financial sector. I also believed we had been doing good work with the Equator Principles, with sustainability and our clients, so I was taken aback to receive this complaint about Unitus.

This did not go on to become a case because American legislation was deemed effective enough on these issues of labour representation, leaving no need for our involvement. What this case did prove, however, was the strength of the OECD Guidelines, proof that they offered an effective mediation process whereby a local client in St. Louis could come to us in Amsterdam and tell us we were not good enough. Yet another call to the bank that it had to perform its due diligence and look at the boundaries to better understand what was happening in the value chain of its clients and, hence, of its own, not least from a risk management point of view. A serious indication that the Guidelines were something the financial sector should be involved with and should have to deal with.

Yes there was scepticism, ignorance and reluctance, but it was the right thing to do because, even holding a meaningful minority interest, a bank (or any other financial institution) could be held accountable through a link to operations.

6   Dreaming with My Feet on the Ground: Moving Forward

In June 2013, IDFC became the first Indian financial institution to become a member of the Equator Principles, preceded at an earlier stage by the Industrial Bank of China. Several initiatives continue to develop in Nigeria.

It is essential that China and India in particular become part of the OECD Guidelines as two of the countries where the infrastructure of the future will take place.

My retirement from ABN Amro gave me the opportunity to work on making EP practice mainstream. I spent time in India with micro finance and community development, talking at board level to the Indian banks to persuade them that the EPs were something they should take seriously because of the Performance Standards of the IFC.

I largely failed here because the response from the banks in India was that the EPs were developed by 12 western banks so were not applicable here, a common complaint outside of Europe. They also felt that if they signed the EPs, they would incur a liability they were unsure they could meet in practice. In other words, the more I publish, the more I make myself responsible and liable, so it's easier not to sign.

My argument was that all financial risk today will inevitably become financial risks of the future and suggested the banks create their own set of principles to discuss with us.

I consider imperative that more institutions in India and China will accept both the EPs and the OECD MNE Guidelines, but it may take time. They understand that we are discussing the right things. They may not like it, they may not be ready for it, but the realisation is that it's the right thing to do.

China's relationship with the USA is casting a shadow, but practitioners in China, more so than the government, are keeping an open mind. Some Chinese institutions, including the banks, are improving their practices in relation to climate change and environmental degradation, although human rights remain an issue.

This year (2013), India attended the OECD Global Forum as an observer, and although the Chinese were not present, I believe they are showing keen interest. They are cautious, since it might not be in their own interest, but momentum is building, capital markets are recognising the work and hopefully the Chinese and Indian governments will realise they need a level playing field of some sort. At some point in time, if they want to be involved in mining projects in Peru and Chile, both adhering countries to licensing agreement, the Guidelines will come into play so they know it's better to be at the table and to have some influence, rather than remaining on the outside and not having access to natural resources their countries need.

The sustainability movement is moving forward at an unstoppable pace. The USA is slow, but is coming. There will be companies and countries who feel the OECD MNE Guidelines go against their interests because of cost or some other mundane reasons, but sector leaders are coming to realise it's the essential way forward.

7   Drivers for Change

Unintentional blindness has obscured our vision on values and value. This is changing. We are increasingly able, prepared and even required to identify and value nontraditional assets, liabilities, returns and costs. Measuring is an essential part of managing change for better.

In this context, new, advanced initiatives are being taken: the creation of IIRC (integrated reporting; co-founded by GRI), G4 Guidelines from GRI (with particular focus on due diligence and materiality) and various initiatives to develop methodologies to measure and monetise environmental and social externalities (EP&L and SP&L: TEEB for Business Coalition, B-team, True Price Foundation). Zero impact coalitions (on climate, water, biodiversity, etc.) are spreading. Impact investing is attracting increasing interest from large investors.

Risk management and policy development may only be done adequately if the relevant data are known and the medium/long-term broader context is considered. Due diligence is of the essence, as well as focusing on material issues, possible impacts beyond the direct control of an organisation, taking preventive remedial actions and/or setting conditions for engagement.

'Making markets work' for a sustainable economy and society is a challenge: markets are not perfect (failing regulation, asymmetric information, short-term focus); prices are not right (holistic valuations, incorporating natural, human, social capital are hardly considered); the lenses of many investors and most consumers are predominantly focused on short-term profits and lowest costs, without considering the real intrinsic value or the harm done to others—for example, the working conditions and subsistence wages in Rana Plaza.

Key drivers for change are (GRI-style) structured disclosure of nonfinancial issues in company reports and product information; government baseline regulations on industry—and disclosure—standards; social media; disciplined application by large corporations of their high standards into their full value chains (even beyond local requirements; directly affecting SMEs in their operations); procurement and contracting practices by governments; and active sharing and learning of good practices.

I recently attended a presentation from Dutch company Philips that highlighted the purchasing behaviour of 15- to 29-year-olds and their increasing demand to be able to make informed decisions about what they buy and from whom. This is echoed by a nonprofit organisation with which I'm involved, True Price, which works to help front-running companies uncover the social and ecological costs of products and services and recognises that increasingly investors want to choose companies that make explicit their standards and costs with regard to human rights, equal opportunities and the environment.

As always, the focus now is on passing the mantle onto the next generation and further increasing their awareness of sustainability. They will share the future, and their use of social media will play a big part in influencing their attitudes and habits.

The lessons from the Rana Plaza tragedy must be extended to other unions and to other governments until workers have the confidence to say I have the right not to go into that building and that not enough is not enough. Sadly, there are plenty more Rana Plazas of the world that need to be addressed. The warning signals are there that there are more 'canaries in the coal mine'.

Celebrate, or rather commemorate, momentarily then the pain that got us this far, but we must not fall asleep afterwards and allow our feet to ease off the accelerator.

References

www.oecdguidelines.nl
www.trueprice.org
www.worldconnectors.nl

Sustainable Private Equity Investments and ESG Due Diligence Frameworks

Gavin Duke

Abstract Conventional wisdom states that ESG is a necessary cost centre that reduces reputational risk, whereas this chapter introduces ESG as a framework for profit creation and strategic direction. Drawing on experience of a private equity fund that looks for environmental companies and grows them into viable international enterprises, this chapter also showcases how detailed ESG due diligence can add value to portfolio companies throughout the investment process from selection and structuring to portfolio management and profitable exits. Continuous improvement highlights the mechanisms through which ESG drives the bottom line.

1 Introduction

A simplified view of the Private Equity business model has three stages: investing in/acquiring companies, growing/adding value to the portfolio of companies and, finally, exiting/selling said companies. Superior Environmental, Social and Governance (ESG) due diligence adds value to each of these stages and thus delivers financial outperformance. Robeco (2012) states, "Empirical evidence shows that sustainable businesses outperform their non-sustainable counterparts over the long term, especially during and after crisis periods". In addition, a broad Deutsche Bank (2012) literature review of approximately 162 published papers concluded that "CSR and most importantly, ESG factors are correlated with superior risk-adjusted returns at a securities level". This chapter includes strategic frameworks for ESG management, due diligence, investment decision-making and portfolio management.

Aloe Private Equity (www.aloe-group.com) manages a number of Environmental and Socially Sustainable Funds and is dedicated to investing in companies that provide solutions to environmental and social problems, whilst also delivering superior financial returns for its investors. Aloe achieves these sustainable solutions by investing in industrial companies that have a high integrity corporate culture. The following frameworks have evolved from Aloe's focus on sustainable investing and continuous improvement.

G. Duke (✉)
Aloe Private Equity, 8 High Street, Twyford, Reading, UK, RG10 9AE
e-mail: gavin.duke@aloe-group.com

© Springer International Publishing Switzerland 2015
K. Wendt (ed.), *Responsible Investment Banking*, CSR, Sustainability, Ethics & Governance, DOI 10.1007/978-3-319-10311-2_22

High ESG Impact	**Risk Reduction**	**Continuous Improvement**
Low ESG Impact	**Risks Unknown**	**ESG system failing**
	ESG is a Cost Centre	ESG is a Profit Driver

Fig. 1 ESG strategic framework

Private Equity generally acquires majority shareholdings in targeted companies. This provides considerable influence to drive enhanced corporate social governance, improved environmental performance and better safety reporting as well as the traditional corporate restructuring associated with Private Equity. This influence, which is underpinned by legal rights, is key to embedding a high impact ESG culture within portfolio companies. In addition, the viewpoint a company adopts towards ESG factors determines whether ESG is viewed as a cost centre or profit driver. The following diagram provides an analysis of different strategic approaches to ESG within a portfolio company (Fig. 1).

When ESG is viewed solely as a business cost and ESG considerations have limited impact from the shop floor to the boardroom, then there is the potential for a serious incident with severe reputational and financial damage due to **unknown risks**.

The traditional view of ESG factors is that the assessment and management of ESG is a cost centre; however, a high focus on ESG serves to **reduce business risk**.

The Aloe view is that ESG can be viewed as a profit driver, and when coupled with a high impact focus on ESG, a continuous improvement culture emerges with ESG benefits driving improved profitability. For example, environmental monitoring of air, effluent and solid discharge informs business decisions regarding the loss of feedstocks, products or production yields. Improvements in social factors such as health and safety reduce sick days and improve staff retention. Governance factors such as regular board meetings and minutes provide reassurance to the future acquirers of a business and may lead to improved exit valuations.

There is a possibility of standards slipping, and although ESG is viewed as a profit driver, ESG factors may have a low impact with a company. In this case, the ESG system is failing and the company is drifting back to unknown ESG risks.

The following frameworks provide management tools that help maintain a continuous improvement culture.

2 Starting Point: UN Global Compact

There is a substantial body of work on ESG standards for various industries and sectors; however, the most universally accessible is the UN Global Compact. These 10 guiding principles can provide the cornerstones to any ESG Framework. Aloe requires that all portfolio companies abide by these principles and would not invest in any company which indicated it could not follow these principles.

Human Rights

Principle 1: Businesses should support and respect the protection of internationally proclaimed human rights.
Principle 2: Make sure that they are not complicit in human rights abuses.

Labour

Principle 3: Businesses should uphold the freedom of association and the effective recognition of the right to collective bargaining.
Principle 4: The elimination of all forms of forced and compulsory labour.
Principle 5: The effective abolition of child labour.
Principle 6: The elimination of discrimination in respect of employment and occupation.

Environment and Social

Principle 7: Businesses should support a precautionary approach to environmental and social challenges.
Principle 8: Undertake initiatives to promote greater environmental and social responsibility.
Principle 9: Encourage the development and diffusion of environmentally and socially friendly technologies and options.

Anti-corruption

Principle 10: Businesses should work against corruption in all its forms, including extortion and bribery.

The value of these ten principles is their simplicity, each principle makes sound business sense and any hesitation or resistance to them provides a warning that there could be significant ESG issues within a business.

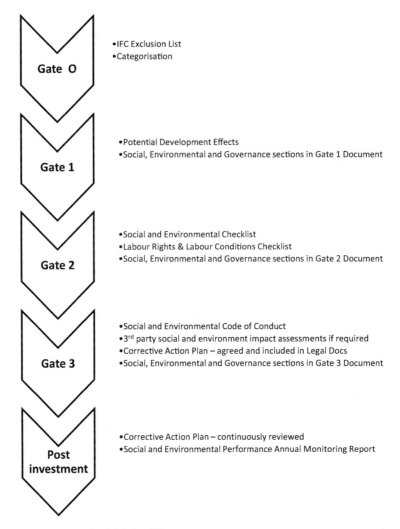

Fig. 2 Gating process for ESG due diligence

3 Investing in/Acquiring Companies: Due Diligence

The investment decision-making process at Aloe is a series of decisions from Gate 0, an exclusion gate, to Gate 3, final investment decision. At each Gate, the required investment documentation and justification becomes more thorough and comprehensive and any issues be they ESG, financial, legal or recruitment raised at the previous Gate must be resolved before the investment opportunity can progress to the next Gate. Aloe has procedures covering financial, legal, technical, IT and marketing; however, this chapter will only document the ESG frameworks. An overview of the Gating Process for ESG is shown below (Fig. 2).

3.1   Gate 0

This is a simple Gate which excludes Aloe from investing in certain sectors. The International Finance Corporation, IFC, is a cornerstone investor in Aloe's funds and the IFC's Exclusion List is incorporated into the fund by-laws to legally prevent Aloe from investing in these excluded sectors.

The categorisation is a simple high, medium or low assessment of the potential environmental and social impacts of the investing opportunity, which serves as guide to the intensity of the future ESG due diligence.

High: The investment opportunity is likely to have significant adverse environmental and social impacts that are irreversible, diverse or unprecedented, such as the loss of a major natural habitat, affecting vulnerable groups or ethnic minorities, involving involuntary displacement and resettlement or affecting significant cultural heritage sites. A full Environmental and Social Impact Assessment (EIA) is required. Investment opportunities with high ESG risk tend to be forestry, mining, hazardous waste disposal, oil and gas and large infrastructure projects.

Medium: The investment opportunity may result in specific environmental and social impacts, but these impacts are site specific and are not irreversible. An Environmental and Social Impact assessment according to the IFC Performance Standards is required. Investment opportunities with medium ESG risk tend to be general manufacturing plants, food processing, paper mills and textile plants.

Low: The investment opportunity is likely to have minimal or no adverse environmental and social impacts. The Social and Environmental Checklist and Labour Rights and Labour Conditions may be sufficient, provided that no issues are identified. Investment opportunities with low ESG risk tend to be office-based, consultancy-type, service businesses.

3.2   Gate 1

The **Potential Development Effects questionnaire** is used by Aloe to understand the positive benefits of the investment opportunity and to determine whether the opportunity fits with Aloe's sustainable investment objectives. The answers to the questionnaire form the basis of the Social, Environmental and Governance sections in the Gate 1 Document, which is a formal Board paper that provides the necessary information for the Gate 1 investment decision.

During the initial Gate 1 due diligence site visits, observations of social and environmental standards as well as governance are made. In addition, Aloe's social, environmental and governance standards as well as the UN Global Compact are introduced.

3.3   Gate 2

The **Social and Environmental Checklist** and **Labour Rights and Labour Conditions Checklist** are used to collect comprehensive information on the environmental and social aspects of the potential investment opportunity. Within Aloe's investment process, these checklists must be completed before the Gate 2 document, as part of the ESG due diligence on the company. This Gate 2 due diligence will include extended periods onsite of approximately 1 month to document and analyse the E&S performance as well as operations, finance, HR, sales and marketing. The ESG gaps and areas of concern will be summarised in the ESG section of the Gate 2 document.

3.4   Gate 3

The outcomes of the Social and Environmental Checklist and Labour Rights and Labour Conditions Checklist will identify whether a **third party Environmental Impact Assessment**, EIA, or **Social Impact Assessment**, SIA, is required. Due to the complexity of operations, environmental discharge requirements or potential severity of an incident, an independent expert may be required to review the ESG impacts of the potential investment opportunity. This is comparable to using an independent accountancy firm to review the financials or an independent legal firm to review the legal status. The outcomes and areas for improvement from all the ESG reviews are incorporated into the **Corrective Action Plan**. This document will summarise any social and environmental deficiencies, the agreed actions and time frames to remedy these and will be developed in conjunction with the new potential portfolio company. The Corrective Action Plan will provide pre-closing conditions and post-completion conditions that will be included in the legal documents.

Aloe may reject an investment opportunity on the grounds of irregularities found in the company's ESG procedures identified by the checklists or must work with the management of the opportunity to solve these issues and condition the investments upon effectively tackling them.

As part of the Gate 3 due diligence, Aloe mandates that all potential investment opportunities sign a **Social and Environmental Code of Conduct**, which is approved by the Board of Directors of the opportunity. In most cases, this is based around the UN Global Compact.

Having completed the Gate 3 due diligence and with the agreed Corrective Action Plan, incorporated into the legal documents, Aloe will then proceed with the final investment decision.

Including the ESG requirements and Corrective Action Plan in the legal documents is necessary to provide legal remedies for ESG non-compliance. Punitive steps could include withdrawing future investment tranches, delaying bonus payments to the senior management, increasing the interest rate of debt or equity

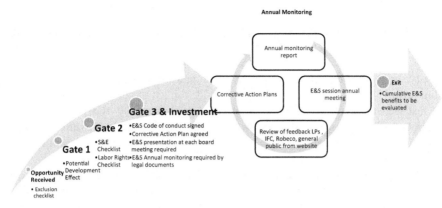

Fig. 3 Overall ESG process from investment to exit

instruments and formal written warnings to senior management potentially leading to dismissal.

4 Growing/Adding Value: Portfolio Management

An overall view of the ESG framework which is between Aloe, as the Private Equity firm, and its portfolio companies is shown below (Fig. 3).

The Corrective Action Plan and post-closing conditions form the basis of the ESG management within the first year of investment. Tasks will be on 1-, 3-, 6- or 12-month delivery schedules depending on their complexity. Aloe has weekly discussions with its portfolio companies and will track the progress of these tasks through the year.

Aloe requires all portfolio companies to complete an **Annual Monitoring Report** to document ESG performance of their company and the progress with implementing the Corrective Action Plan. The report is an annual summary; Aloe's objective and what is truly important is that companies measure and note their performance daily, weekly and monthly. This forms the basis of the well-known management mantra "what gets measured gets managed". This data will allow a company to create an economic justification based on a simple Net Present Value or Payback calculation, i.e. an economic case to demonstrate an improvement to the bottom line for the ESG capital expenditure or ESG operational change.

The first section of the Annual Monitoring Report is a simple overview of who prepares the report, their responsibilities for ESG, their background in ESG and training as well as a description of the management systems within the company, such as ISO 14001, ISO 9000, OHSAS 18001 and SA 8000. This basic information provides a guide to depth of focus on ESG; does it go all the way to the Board or is it a middle-management issue?

The second section is the environmental performance for emissions to air, liquid effluent, solid waste and hazardous materials. The company performance is recorded against the national legal requirements and the IFC Performance Standards. Emissions in excess of national laws require immediate improvement and justify capital investment to remedy the situation as the company is at risk of being shut down. Measurements of emissions provide the data to understand the amount of lost feedstock/product and the amount by which the yield of a process can be improved. The monetary value of the lost feedstock or yield improvement can be used to justify the payback of a capital expenditure, thus improving the profitability of a company.

The third section of the report is the social performance: numbers of employees and contractors, male to female ratios, number of trade unions, number of strikes and lost output, employee turnover, incident statistics, lost workdays, vehicle collisions and employee training. Investment in employees, be it health and safety, training or new facilities, can be economically justified based on reductions in employee turnover, less lost time due to incidents and improved relations with trade unions. Thus, enhanced social policies can be proven to improve profitability.

The fourth section of the report focuses on community relations, activities where the company has engaged with the local community and grievances lodged by the local communities. The Aloe methodology for the economic justification for these expenses is still evolving, and Aloe is involved in sharing best practices with our peers to understand a robust economic mechanism to evaluate these benefits. Currently, the Aloe methodology follows the pricing model for a Public Relations firm, where the value is determined by the number of media mentions of a company, the quality of the media channel and its circulation.

After the Annual Monitoring Report, Aloe will organise a working session with senior management of the company to review the report, to tackle any identified deficiencies and to update and agree the Corrective Action Plan for the next 12 months. A focus on continuous improvement improves profitability as well as ESG performance. In addition, Aloe will source benchmarking information on the industrial sector, so that the company and Aloe can understand whether the performance is ahead, comparable or behind its peers. This information is useful for setting targets, for example, health and safety statistics for the EU are freely available. The use of ESG measurement to provide a baseline and then a focus on continuous improvement over future years is also the model of the UNPRI (United Nations Principles for Responsible Investing).

This process of the Annual Monitoring Report, annual review and updating of the Corrective Action Plan should be incorporated in the legal documents at the time of investment. This provides the legal framework for punitive measures if these work processes are not implemented in portfolio companies. In most cases, punitive measures are not required. However, the ability to force behaviour change is useful in dire ESG situations.

5   Exiting/Selling Companies

During exit negotiations, the seller wishes to push the valuation up and buyer wishes to drive the valuation down. Both parties will analyse the risks within a company to justify their position and influence the valuation. Full ESG compliance with supporting evidence will support the sellers' positions that there are no unknown ESG risks and negate any arguments from the buyer to reduce the valuation. On the other hand, a pending law suit will have a negative impact on the valuation. Some buyers may walk away whilst others may insist on a reduction in the valuation equivalent to the maximum possible damages claim. Private Equity funds have a fixed term; therefore, Private Equity investors know that at some point in the future, they will have to sell the company. Since PE investors are ultimately focussed on the exit, requiring good ESG performance in their portfolio companies from the date of investment is important to achieving the highest possible exit valuation.

6   External Reporting

ESG reporting now follows a similar pattern to Financial Reporting whereby the results at a portfolio company level are consolidated at the fund level, multiple funds' results are consolidated together into a "fund of funds" and ultimately consolidated results are reported to the assets owners.

Aloe uses the Annual Monitoring Reports from its portfolio companies to provide consolidated reports to its investors who require ESG reporting. Some such as the IFC and Robeco will then report consolidated ESG results over all their operations. Robeco also ranks all of its Private Equity investments in terms of their ESG performance. In general, people who work in financial services are competitive, and it is Aloe's view that this ranking and individual assessment of ESG performance encourages Private Equity firms to try and outperform their peers. Nobody likes coming last and everyone likes being in the top quartile.

In addition, Aloe publically reports its conduct and performance in relation to the UN Global Compact.

> **Conclusion**
> The Aloe ESG framework is based on continuous improvement. The initial pre-investment due diligence phase is a progressively deeper dive into the ESG issues of each potential investment. This results in a Corrective Action Plan, CAP, which is developed in conjunction with the management of the new potential portfolio company and incorporated into the legal documentation for the investment. This provides a legal mechanism for Aloe to enforce

(continued)

good ESG performance, if necessary. The CAP is reviewed annually to provide new benchmarks and targets to drive ESG outperformance. The measurement of key performance indicators provides the economic justification for ESG expenditure and evidence that a high systematic focus on ESG enhances long-term profitability.

References

Aloe. Accessed August 23, 2013 from http://www.aloe-group.com/en-gb/our-ethics

Deutsche Bank. (2012, June). *Sustainable investing: Establishing long-term value and performance*. Accessed September 17, 2013 from http://www.dbcca.com/dbcca/EN/_media/Sustainable_Investing_2012.pdf

EPP EU. Accessed September 13, 2013 from http://epp.eurostat.ec.europa.eu/portal/page/portal/health/health_safety_work/data/main_tables

IFC. Accessed August 24, 2013 from http://www.ifc.org/wps/wcm/connect/Topics_Ext_Content/IFC_External_Corporate_Site/IFC+Sustainability/Sustainability+Framework/IFC+Exclusion+List/

IFC. Accessed August 24, 2013 from http://www.ifc.org/wps/wcm/connect/Topics_Ext_Content/IFC_External_Corporate_Site/IFC+Sustainability/Sustainability+Framework/Sustainability+Framework+-+2012/Performance+Standards+and+Guidance+Notes+2012/

Kool, A (2013). The search for sustainable returns: Pension fund managers in conversation with Robeco. ISBN 978 9080 582545

UN Global Compact. Accessed August 23, 2013 from http://www.unglobalcompact.org/aboutthegc/thetenprinciples/

UN Global Compact. Accessed September 13, 2013 from http://unglobalcompact.org/participants/detail/11803-Aloe-Private-Equity

In Principle Good: The Principles for Responsible Investment

Rolf D. Häßler and Till Hendrik Jung

Abstract More than 1,200 institutional investors, asset managers and financial institutions have committed themselves by recognising the Principles for Responsible Investment (PRI) to integrate sustainability criteria into their investment. Together they manage more than US$30 trillion, representing a share of around 45 % of global investments. A success story, then? This chapter gives an overview of the aims and development of the PRI, introduces the contents of the six principles and highlights the opportunities and risks of signing the PRI for investors and asset managers. The updating of the success story requires—according to the authors—a dual strategy: outreach and enlarging the membership and opinion leaders supporting responsible investments and, at the same time, going deeper—focusing on improving the quality of implementation of the PRI by the signatories in addition to further expansion. The chapter is a starting point for the development of the PRI and concentrates on evolution and development of the PRI in terms of 'broadening and deepening'.

1 Development and Structure of the Principles for Responsible Investment

Even if—as opposed to in their early years—they now have to do without the symbolic prefix 'UN', for United Nations, the Principles for Responsible Investment (PRI) are a financial initiative supported by the United Nations and linked to the United Nations Environmental Programme Finance Initiative (UNEP FI) and the UN Global Compact. In 2005, a group of institutional investors met at the invitation of the then UN Secretary General Kofi Annan to formulate the principles for sustainable investment. The investor group consisted of 20 people representing

R.D. Häßler (✉)
Institut für nachhaltige Kapitalanlagen GmbH, Corneliusstraße 10, 80469 München,
Deutschland
e-mail: rolf.haessler@nk-institut.de

T.H. Jung
Oekom Research AG, Goethestr. 28, 80336 Munich, Germany
e-mail: jung@oekom-research.com

© Springer International Publishing Switzerland 2015
K. Wendt (ed.), *Responsible Investment Banking*, CSR, Sustainability, Ethics &
Governance, DOI 10.1007/978-3-319-10311-2_23

institutions from 12 different countries and was supported by a 70-member expert group, in which, among others, representatives of the investment industry and civil society were present.

The PRI were presented to the public in April 2006 at the New York Stock Exchange. The total of 68 initial signatories included the BT Pension Scheme, CalPERS, the Government Pension Fund of Thailand, Munich Reinsurance, the New York City Employees Retirement System and the powerful Norwegian Government Pension Fund.

1.1 Sustained Growth

The number of signatories has increased significantly since then. As of November 2013, more than 1,200 institutions have signed the declaration on voluntary consideration of the six PRI principles presented in chapter "Editor's Contribution". Three groups of signatories can be distinguished: the asset owners (i.e. institutional investors who invest capital); investment managers, managing on behalf of asset owners of capital; and the so-called professional service providers, providing required consulting services, information and data. The third category includes sustainability rating agencies such as oekom research, who already signed the PRI in 2007. There are also so-called network supporters. See Diagram 1 for the structure and number of PRI signatories.

Between July 2012 and June 2013 alone, more than 190 new organisations have signed the PRI, including 26 asset owners, 141 investment managers and 26 service providers. During the same period, 70 signatories have been deleted from the directory. The reason was that these signatories either did not pay their annual fee for financing of the PRI or have not been reporting on progress in the confines and to the extent prescribed in the PRI guidelines. Some signatories have also left at their own request, for example, because the company was acquired by another signatory of the PRI. Unfortunately, the PRI do not further track or differentiate the reasons for resigning, apart from the voluntary resignations, and do not make transparent which signatories were delisted for what reasons.

All in all, however, there has been an increase of 120 signatories for the aforementioned 12-month period. This shows the continued high dynamics in recruiting new signatories. Compared to the number of potential signatories, the group is, however, still modest. For comparison, in Germany alone there are around 150 pension funds with business activities and 40 unincorporated foundations with assets of more than 100 million euros, both groups of institutional investors that could potentially commit to implement the PRI. The current signatories dispose of a combined capital of more than US$30 trillion.

1.2 Leadership Structure

The work of the network is coordinated by the PRI Secretariat, which oversees the daily operations of the initiative and organises the implementation of the strategy.

Diagram 1 Number and structure of PRI signatories (November 2013; *Source*: www.unpri.org/signatories/signatories/)

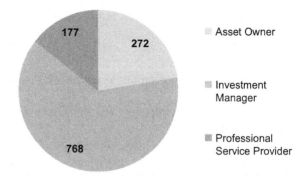

The Secretariat is financed by an annual fee paid by the signatories to the PRI, the amount depending on size and capital under management. In addition, the initiative receives financial grants from governments and international organisations.

Although the investment managers today represent nearly two-thirds of the signatories, the leadership structures of the PRI focus strongly on the main target group of the PRI, the asset owners. They are represented by nine members in the central decision-making body, the PRI Advisory Council (PRIAC), and with nine out of 16 members, they have absolute majority. Four seats in the PRIAC are reserved for investment managers and service partners, two for representatives of the UN and one for the chairman.

The second important body is the PRI Association Board (PRIAB) to oversee and support the work of the PRI Secretariat. It consists of seven members. Recently, there has been dispute and controversy over the selection of those members within the PRI. According to information from the information service 'Responsible Investor', mainly Scandinavian signatories have questioned the selection methodology for appointment of members to the PRIAB. Instead of having members to the PRIAB elected by the dominated asset owners' board PRIAC, the members of PRIAB should be elected by the PRI signatories. In connection with this dispute over the leadership structure within the PRI, six Danish PRI signatories withdrew from the initiative in December 2013. The controversy shows that there are quite different views about management structure and objectives of the PRI among the PRI signatories.

2   The Principles and Their Implementation

2.1   The Six Principles

With their signature under the PRI, the signatories commit to the systematic application of the following six principles:

1. We will incorporate ESG issues into the analysis and decision-making processes.
2. We will be active owners and incorporate ESG issues into our ownership policies and practices.
3. We will seek appropriate disclosure on ESG issues by the entities in which we invest.
4. We will promote acceptance and implementation of the Principles within the investment industry.
5. We will work together to enhance our effectiveness in implementing the Principles.
6. We will each report on our activities and progress towards implementing the Principles.

The PRI emphasises that recognition of the Principles is not a 'non-binding letter of intent', but should be only pursued if the signatory is seriously willing to gradually implement the principles. For the first five Principles, the signatories can define themselves, in what form, to what extent and at what strategic speed they are pursuing those principles. The PRI are to be understood in this regard as a framework that can be applied in a flexible manner in accordance with the profile and circumstances of the individual signatory. The situation is different with regard to Principle 6, annual reporting. There are binding specifications and criteria to be met for the asset owners and investment managers.

The six principles are increasingly criticised for their open and non-binding formulation. They were formulated, however, in the context of a comprehensive, consensus-based discussion process with multiple stakeholders with many different culturally influenced views and definitions. The PRI are therefore the result of the equilibrium between as ambitious goals as possible and the widest possible support in the financial industry. Proposals for implementation (possible actions) given by the PRI are intended to increase content value; collaboration on content, sharing best practice and benchmarking between signatories are intended to engender a race for the best performance in implementing the PRI and therefore shall provide dynamic and momentum.

The substantive work on content is done in particular in the working groups that exist for different asset classes (see Table 1). They serve the exchange of experiences and the development of methods and best practice in implementing the principles. The so-called Engagement Clearing House offers the signatories to the PRI a platform for a coordinated pursuit of their interests as owners towards the companies they invest in as part of a so-called coordinated engagement strategy. The objective is to eliminate deficiencies in sustainability management implementation and strategy through dialogue with the target companies to be invested in.

The organisational structure of the PRI also includes an academic network and a public policy network, which brings together the signatories with scientists and government officials to discuss the implementation of the PRI.

Numerous German signatories to the PRI are also members of the Forum for Sustainable Investments (FNG), the industry association for sustainable

Table 1 Thematic working groups of the PRI, October 2013

Shareholdings	Hedge funds	Bonds
Private equity	Natural resources	Infrastructure
Small funds	Inclusive finance	Immobilien
Impact investing		

Source: German Ministry for Environment (2013), p. 9

investments in the German-speaking countries. Its more than 150 corporate members include banks, investment companies, insurance companies, rating agencies, investment companies, asset managers, financial advisers and NGOs. Its responsibilities include increasing the awareness of sustainable investments in the financial sector and the public; helping to shape the political, legal and economic conditions; and the active promotion of development, transparency and quality of sustainable financial products. Comparable 'Social Investment Forum' (SIF) exists also in other countries or regions. An integration of the activities between the SIF and the PRI has, so far, however, hardly taken place.

> **Supplement: Principles for Sustainable Insurance**
> Analogous to the PRI for capital investment at the +20 conference in Rio de Janeiro, the Principles for Sustainable Insurance (PSI) were presented in the summer of 2012. They were developed by the finance initiative of the UN Environment Programme (United Nations Environment Programme Finance Initiative, UNEP FI). Insurers from all over the world and other players in the industry have contributed in a consultation process to the emergence of the four principles in the insurance industry.
>
> The PSI shall be established as worldwide, voluntarily principles on sustainability within the insurance industry. By signing, the insurer undertakes to consider environmental and social and governance issues along the entire value chain and include them systematically in its activities. In accordance with the four principles, the insurance company sets individual goals and formulates concrete measures. Signatories undertake to report about the progress regularly.
>
> More information is available at www.unepfi.org/psi/

2.2 Opportunities and Risk for Investors and Investment Managers

Accession to the PRI opens up a whole range of support services to the signatories. These include:

- Obtaining support on implementation of the six principles and optimisation of owners' investment practices through participation in the PRI working groups as well as access to PRI publications, seminars and webinars

- Being part of an international network with many opportunities to collaborate and exchange knowledge and experience
- Obtaining access to important decision-makers and stakeholders within and outside the financial sector

The application of the Principles can bring particular benefits to the signatories. Not only the signatories to the PRI, but the majority of sustainable investors are convinced that the systematic integration of ESG criteria leads to a better understanding of the risks and rewards of various investment opportunities and of the profile of issuers. In this context, we can distinguish two levels: On the one hand, investors believe that the quality and performance of the ESG management system is an indicator for the quality of the overall management system of a target company. A company that controls its energy and raw material consumption treats its employees, suppliers and customers fairly and pays attention to the environmental and social quality of its products and is assumed to be led and operated in an overall responsible manner.

The sustainability management thus becomes an indicator of the quality of the overall management. Conversely, the following applies: A poor sustainability rating is indicative of a poor corporate governance and thus increased risks. There are numerous examples evidencing this: Enron (Insolvency 2001), Worldcom (Insolvency 2002), Parmalat (Insolvency 2003), Lehman Bothers (Insolvency 2008) and Hypo Real Estate (Nationalization 2009) received very bad ratings from oekom research, long before the economic difficulties became public.

Second, the rating of sustainability performance allows the identification of management deficits in key operational areas of companies. For example, when in the case of Tepco, the operator of the nuclear power plants in Fukushima, or in the case of BP glaring deficits in the area of plant security are identified, these deficiencies constitute simultaneously huge risks for financial performance and share price. The key risk areas have to be defined and identified for in each industry and correlated to the concrete industry background. For example, firms in resource- and energy-intensive industries that do not trim their energy and resource consumption efficiency will suffer cost disadvantages compared to their competitors and are more dependent on the evolution of commodity prices. Companies in consumer-related sectors, whose products do not meet the increasing demands of consumers on the social and environmental quality, produce products that will not survive on the markets and go down the food chain.

Investment managers are allowed to comply with their fiduciary duties more robustly and comprehensively by integrating ESG criteria. Numerous studies and meta-studies have shown that the consideration of ESG factors can have a positive impact on risk and return of investments. The consequence of this statement seems not yet clear to many investment managers: If the consideration of ESG issues has positive effects on the assets managed by them for their customers, then they need to be committed to the inclusion of appropriate ESG criteria into asset management in order to fulfil their fiduciary duty. This represents a reversal of the previous argument that sustainability criteria are an optional addition to capital allocation.

This logical conclusion leads to the statement that today the majority of investment managers violates their fiduciary duty when not considering ESG.

All signatories gain opportunities to present themselves as a responsible market actor towards business partners, customers and the public by signing up to the PRI. This positive effect on the reputation of the investor can however prove to be a boomerang, if not followed suit by robust implementation. Who has bound themselves with a signature to the PRI publicly to responsible investment must expect to be measured against this promise. Even before signing of PRI, asset owners and investment managers therefore need to familiarise themselves with how they can contribute to the success of the initiative and what they want to contribute. Motives, goals and actions must be transparent and comprehensible to the inside and outside world.

This does not mean that, even by signing, all six principles must be implemented to perfection. The very notion of 'progress report' for the annual reporting suggests that it is assumed that the implementation of PRI evolves progressively over time.

Nevertheless, the question of how far one must have come in the field of sustainable investments to be 'legitimised' to sign the PRI is subject to cultural differences. The comparatively small number of German signatory has possibly to do with the fact that German investors do not sign until all the 'homework' is done, while other members understand the signing of PRI rather as 'work in progress'.

Regardless of this, at the time of signing, each signatory must be aware that he has to face the abundance of the Principles and demonstrate that he is serious about their implementation. Anyone who does not risks the danger of being 'delisted' and harming their reputation. This is particularly true for investment managers who have regarded signing the PRI, primarily in the early years, as a marketing tool to be compared favourably by the asset owners and to position themselves as a suitable contractor. With regard to the 'quality assurance' effect of delisting, it would be desirable if the PRI communicate in future more clearly, which signatory for what reason has been removed from the list, for financial or other substantive aspects.

3   Perspectives and Evolution: Deepening and Broadening

How will the PRI evolve? The number of signatories has grown dynamically in recent years, and the same applies to the assets managed by them. Compared to the number of potential signatories, the support of the PRI is still comparatively low. At the same time, answers to criticism of the quality, content and implementation gaps of the PRI need to be found.

Starting Points for Further Proliferation of the PRI

As the 'first mover' advantages of signing the PRI no longer exist, the PRI are no longer self-perpetuating. It will be more important than ever to combine the membership to PRI with manifest benefits for the signatories. A key starting point for this is a more regionally or even nationally oriented structure for recruitment and support of the signatories. Currently, the following regional networks exist:

1. Australia Network	2. Nordic Network
3. Brazil and South America Network	4. Southern Africa Network
5. Canada Network	6. South Korea Network
7. Continental Europe Network	8. United States Network
9. Japan Network	

Regional network managers often have little resource capacity available, partly because the networks are organised without appropriate support from the PRI organisation itself. It is foreseen that continental Europe will, in the future, be looked after by just one single network manager, which does not correspond to the significance of the financial industry in Europe. France, as the country with the highest asset volume managed on the basis of the PRI worldwide and more than 100 signatories, is expected to get along without a dedicated network manager and the same applies to Germany, where, despite some progress in recent years, there is still room for improvement in increasing the number of signatories.

Likewise, it would be desirable to deal with regional or national network managers in other regions that are so far underrepresented in the PRI, as, for example, the Asian region with the financial centres of Hong Kong and Singapore and the USA, with a focus on broadening the membership. The regional network manager will understand the particular characteristics of these markets and be able to overcome cultural and language barriers (Diagram 2).

At the same time, the offer for assistance in implementing PRI can be further enhanced. While the signatories of the first phase have often been dealing with the challenges of sustainable investment long before the existence of PRI and recruiting them was for PRI like 'harvested low-hanging fruits', potential future signatories today often face greater challenges. To win them as a signatory, they will need to be offered concrete and enhanced support in the implementation of the PRI.

The establishment and expansion of support by regional or national network managers and the expansion of support from the PRI will cost money. These additional funds, however, can be procured through a successful acquisition of new members and by adjustment of the fee structure for existing members—to the extent necessary.

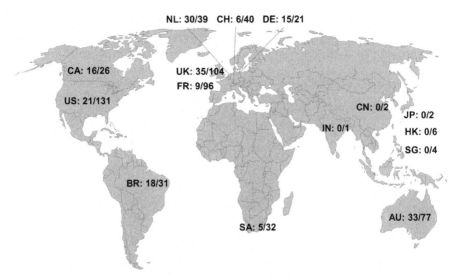

NL: 30/39   CH: 6/40   DE: 15/21

CA: 16/26

UK: 35/104
FR: 9/96

US: 21/131

CN: 0/2
JP: 0/2
IN: 0/1
HK: 0/6
SG: 0/4

BR: 18/31

AU: 33/77

SA: 5/32

Diagram 2 Number of signatories to the UN PRI in various countries; *first number*, asset owner; *second number*, investment manager (November 2013; *Source*: www.unpri.org/signatories/signa tories/)

Quality Improvement in Implementing PRI

In its early years, the PRI focused on achieving the widest possible support from the investment community and winning signatories. To achieve this objective, the PRI have decided on very general formulation of the principles and given the signatories the greatest possible freedom in the implementation of these principles. To keep the 'barrier to entry' for new signatories as low as possible, there is still no defined minimum requirements for integration of sustainability criteria. This strategy is very similar to that followed by the UN Global Compact in the early years.

Similar to the UN Global Compact a few years ago, the PRI have now reached a stage of development where the calls are getting louder for better quality in the implementation of the Principles. So for the credibility of the initiative, a crucial phase has begun. In response to these higher expectations, the PRI have introduced a new 'reporting framework' for the progress reports to be given by asset owners and investment managers. This reporting is already mandatory for the signatories, but what is new is that the reports need to be published and are therefore open to the public. The reform of reporting has been one of the key projects of the PRI in recent years (Diagram 3).

The starting point of the reorganisation of the reporting system was a comprehensive survey of members, which resulted in a first version of the new reporting guidelines in 2012. After a pilot phase, the guidelines have been thoroughly revised. The first officially mandatory reporting season based on the new reporting requirements was initiated by the PRI in October 2013. A transition period applies to new

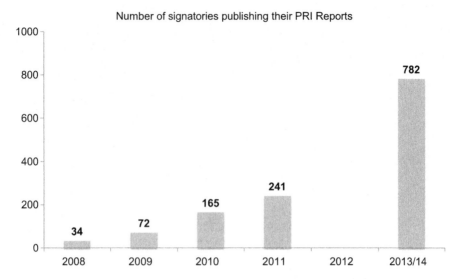

Diagram 3 Number of signatories publishing their progress report. Estimate for 2013/2014; source: PRI Annual Report 2013, S. 25

members. Members who have only become signatories within the last year and service provider are exempt from the new reporting requirement.

The new reporting framework pursues several objectives: First, the framework is intended to provide asset owners and investment managers a better basis for assessing their own progress in implementing the Principles. The so-called assessment report primarily serves this purpose and is automatically created in the reporting database based on the input of the signatories. The report supports the signatories in the identification of strengths and weaknesses in the implementation of the PRI and creates the opportunity for comparison with other signatories. This report is confidential and is intended only for the respective signatories.

Second, the new reporting format is designed to provide the asset owner with an enhanced information basis for the selection and evaluation of its external investment managers. Thus far, investors only needed to rely on the reports of investment managers, which show little standardisation, if such reports existed at all. In the future, the reporting framework will facilitate this process considerably by providing a comparable overview of the development of investment managers in the field of sustainable investment. Hopefully, the increased transparency will influence the selection of investment managers by asset owners and enhances competition for sustainability performance among investment managers. An appropriate benchmark process is also supported by the fact that the new reporting framework records the performance of the signatories and therefore also the investment manager for each asset class separately. Thus, in the future, asset owners will be able to compare the performance of different asset managers per asset class, particularly in the area of government bonds or shares.

Supplement: The Structure and Content of the New Reporting Framework

The new reporting framework for mandatory reporting comprises 12 modules of which three are applicable for each signatory in general, while the others relate to individual asset classes. These other modules can only be completed if the signatory is significantly active in the respective asset class. The three mandatory parts refer to the following areas:

1. In 'Organisational Overview', the signatory presents itself, e.g. the business model and assets under management.
2. The 'Overarching Approach' provides general information about the ESG policies of the signatory, about the appropriateness of organisational structures and resources.
3. The 'Closing Module' presents the extent to which the information and data in the report were reviewed internally by signatory or externally by independent third parties.

Overall, the reporting framework comprises 224 indicators, and the signatory must provide on average information on 75 indicators, according to calculations of the PRI.

The most important objective of the new framework is to ensure the integrity of the initiative and establish lost trust in the sincerity and effectiveness of the PRI again. The well-intentioned declarations of intent from the start-up phase now must be translated into concrete and demonstrable progress in implementing the PRI. The 'Responsible Investment Report' ensures transparency to stakeholders and the public must be created by all signatories and will be publicly accessible. However, there is the possibility for signatories to exclude certain specific answers to individual questions from publication due to confidentiality requirements or for sustaining competition, in consultation with the PRI. It remains to be seen how comprehensive the rapporteur will make use of this possibility. Overall, the newly enacted transparency is designed to ensure that the interested public and affected individuals, entitled to a pension fund or insurance, can get a better idea of the investment decisions of their managers and the extent to which the signatories do implement the various principles and how far they progress on an annual basis.

The introduction of the new 'reporting framework' has consequences. Members who refuse to report will have to leave the initiative. The PRI itself assume that 5–10 % of current signatories will leave the PRI or be 'delisted'. However, this bloodletting is likely to be outweighed by a significant gain in credibility.

Conclusion

The only way is up was a hit by Yazz and the Plastic Population in 1998. This was true for the PRI measured by the number of signatories and funds under management in recent years. Following the solution of structural and governance-related issues and the further expansion of the signatory base, the initiative is now facing the challenge to develop a strategy to preserve the credibility of the PRI. The magic bullet for this is high as possible and continuously increasing quality in the implementation of the PRI and ensuring transparency.

The new 'Reporting Framework' is a good way to preserve the credibility of the organisation and to underpin the long-term success, if not too many signatories pull the 'confidentiality joker' for avoiding publication of their report. But it is in the interest of all signatories actively to participate in the credibility of the PRI and put pressure on the signatories that do not demonstrate the required commitment in implementation or transparency—as perceived shortcomings of the PRI directly fall back on their signatories. Against this background, the PRI still offer the perspective to which they owe their origin. And this is no more and no less than the plan to make the capital market a pillar of sustainable development.

Bibliography

See PRI Annual Report 2013 (pp. 49–51).
See www.responsible-investor.com on 16 October 2013: Nordic investors threaten to leave over PRI governance/public policy concerns.
See http://www.responsible-investor.com/home/article/six_danish_pension_funds_pri/
See Federal Ministry for the Environment, Nature Conservation and Nuclear Safety (2013): *Responsible investing—a guide. The UN principles for responsible investment* (PR) (p. 12). Berlin: Author.
See http://www.unpri.org/about-pri/the-six-principles/
See www.forum-ng.org
See Federal Ministry for the Environment, Nature Conservation and Nuclear Safety. (2013). *Responsible investing—a guide. The UN Principles for Responsible Investment (PR)* (p. 12). Berlin: Author.
See, for example, Research Center for Financial Services, Steinbeis University Berlin. (2013). *Sustainable investments from the point of view of science: promise and reality*. Munich: Author.
See http://www.unpri.org/areas-of-work/reporting-and-assessment/reporting-framework/ and PRI (2013, October). *A snapshot of the new PRI reporting framework. Including in 'AT–A–GLANCE' guide to its mandatory indicators*.
See www.responsible-investor.com from 01 October 2013: *RI Interview: Principles for responsible investment MD Fiona Reynolds*.

Investing in the ESIA and Stakeholder Engagement Process to Improve Project Bankability

Elizabeth van Zyl

Abstract Twenty years ago, engagement with communities affected by projects was limited, even non-existent in some parts of the world. Today, Project Sponsors invest in stakeholder engagement programmes with affected communities and stakeholders with varying degrees of effort and success. Environmental and Social Impact Assessments (ESIA) and stakeholder engagement programmes are a regulatory requirement for many development projects and a condition of the majority of project financiers who require the Project Sponsor to comply with international environmental and social standards. These can be referred to as "soft laws" or "performance benchmarks", and include the Equator Principles, IFC's Environmental and Social Sustainability Framework and EBRD's Environmental and Social Policy. Compliance with regulatory and international standards should not be the only driver for undertaking ESIA and stakeholder programmes. Such activities can broadly reduce and control environmental and social project risks and improve project bankability. Environmental and social risks and impacts can result in delay, cost increase and can affect the Project Sponsor's ability to repay existing project finance and access further capital at a reasonable cost. Many Project Sponsors, however, remain unconvinced. This chapter demonstrates that ESIA and stakeholder engagement are not just about compliance with regulations and international standards but an essential part of project risk management. Drawing on practical experience, it gives examples of how risks can be reduced or increased depending on the adopted approach. The chapter concludes with a summary of the business case for using the ESIA and stakeholder engagement processes to support risk management and timely project delivery.

1 Introduction

Twenty years ago, engagement with communities affected by development projects was extremely limited, even non-existent in some cases. Today, stakeholder engagement is recognised as key to a project's success and sustainability. This

E. van Zyl (✉)
Citrus Partners LLP, London, UK
e-mail: elizabeth.vanzyl@citrus-partners.com

© Springer International Publishing Switzerland 2015
K. Wendt (ed.), *Responsible Investment Banking*, CSR, Sustainability, Ethics & Governance, DOI 10.1007/978-3-319-10311-2_24

change has been brought about through the development of national and international legal requirements and local community expectations, through the onset of Environmental and Social Impact Assessment (ESIA) and through growing concerns with reputation management.

Obtaining and maintaining the support of affected people who live and work in the area of impact of a project is now referred to as having a 'social licence to operate' or as achieving 'broad community support'. Engagement and consultation with affected people is a core activity when seeking such a licence. Failure to obtain and maintain a social licence can result in delays, conflict and cost increases for projects, impacting both project sponsors and lenders.

Whilst many companies increasingly recognise the need to invest in social performance programmes corporately as part of an overall business strategy, convincing some project sponsors of the need for such a 'social licence' for some projects can be challenging. Often citing examples of where things 'went wrong' is needed to scare them into submission. Simply asking a project sponsor the following question can demonstrate the value of seeking a 'social licence': 'Do you want to run a project for the next 25 years inside a large fence, with the local community opposing you, or do you want them to be part of the project, supporting you?'. Most project sponsors want the best project they can have with the least risk profile they can achieve within the resources they have available.

Environmental and Social Impact Assessments (ESIAs) and stakeholder engagement programmes are a regulatory requirement for many development projects and a condition of the majority of project financiers who require the project sponsor to comply with international, environmental and social standards. These can be referred to as 'soft laws' or 'performance benchmarks' and include the Equator Principles, IFC's Environmental and Social Sustainability Framework and EBRD's Environmental and Social Policy.

Compliance with regulatory and international standards should not be the only driver for undertaking ESIA and stakeholder programmes. Such activities can broadly reduce and control environmental and social project risks and, in turn, improve project bankability. Environmental and social risks and impacts can result in delay and cost increase and affect the project sponsor's ability to repay existing project finance and access further capital at a reasonable cost. Many, however, remain unconvinced.

This chapter describes the key components of ESIA and how the stakeholder engagement programme fits into this process. It describes how both ESIA and stakeholder engagement can be used as part of a project's risk management framework, moving beyond the requirements of basic compliance. Drawing on a series of indicative case study scenarios, it discusses how risks can be reduced or increased depending on the adopted approach.

The focus of the chapter is on stakeholder engagement during the ESIA phase. It must be recognised, however, that consultation should span the life of a project, from very early planning through to decommissioning. The chapter provides visibility into how the involvement of stakeholders in the ESIA process and in the wider project development can result in a reduction of overall risks and result in benefits. The chapter concludes with a summary of the business benefits for investing in the ESIA and stakeholder engagement processes to support risk management.

2 Background

Environmental Impact Assessment (EIA) was introduced, initially, under the National Environmental Policy Act (1969) in the USA. Following this, many countries developed formal EIA systems often using environmental legislation and EIA regulations as implementation tools.

The scope of EIAs has developed significantly during the past decade to encompass and address an increasing level of detail on social and socio-economic aspects. In international standards and practice, the term now commonly used is 'Environmental and Social Impact Assessment' (ESIA). However, different countries and regions of the world have varying degrees of regulatory requirements and practice, and the process in some jurisdictions still tends to focus on biophysical environmental issues with limited consideration of social issues.

There are often gaps between international standards, such as IFC Performance Standards, and regulatory requirements and EIA/ESIA practice in some countries. Moreover, project ESIAs may receive a national approval, though this does not necessarily imply compliance with international standards as applied by lenders. Lender standards have evolved to go beyond domestic national compliance, moving towards wider governance concepts and seeking to mainstream environmental and social risk management within the normal transaction process. For example, the Equator Principles III distinguishes the standards it applies to financial products in certain countries. In designated countries,[1] compliance is evaluated against host country law, regulations and permits. For non-designated countries evaluation is against the applicable IFC Performance Standards (IFC PS) and World Bank Environmental, Health and Safety (EHS) Guidelines.[2] Sometimes this can catch out project sponsors when applying for finance.

Lenders have developed and adopted standards as part of their overall risk management frameworks, with many appraising environmental and social risks during the process of deciding on and structuring transactions. Project sponsors, therefore, are becoming increasingly used to having to demonstrate compliance with these environmental and social standards through processes such as Environmental and Social Due Diligence (ESDD) before financial close and ongoing monitoring. For some projects this can become a major challenge and result in risks of delay and of achieving project financing. Some project sponsors have

---

[1] http://www.equator-principles.com/index.php/ep3/324: 'Designated countries are those deemed to have robust environmental and social governance, legislation systems and institutional capacity designed to protect their people and the natural environment'.

[2] Equator Principles III (June 2013), Exhibit III: IFC Performance Standards on Environmental and Social Sustainability (1 January 2012) and the World Bank Group Environmental, Health and Safety Guidelines.

responded proactively by investing in structuring their projects during the early planning stages to meet the environmental and social standards. This can be done partly by investing in the ESIA and stakeholder engagement programmes.

2.1 Key Components of the ESIA Process and Good Practice

In its simplest form, ESIA is a risk assessment and management process that:

- Identifies the project's potential significant environmental and social impacts and risks on the baseline environment and local community/stakeholders.
- Sets out how a project sponsor has avoided, minimised and mitigated these impacts and risks.
- Explains how they intend to manage these risks going forward.

ESIA legislative requirements and processes vary around the world, although there are some fundamental components and phases recognised as good ESIA practice, indicated in Fig. 1.

Baseline investigations should reduce uncertainty over environmental and social risks through the:

- Identification of features of the physical and social environment that may be vulnerable to change (termed receptors).
- Preparation of baseline maps and maps of constraints.
- Identification of potential impacts on resources and receptors.
- Provision of benchmark data against which to monitor future project impacts.

2.2 Mitigation Hierarchy

The ESIA process identifies potential **significant** impacts on the environment and local communities and helps to develop appropriate options for their mitigation. The purpose of mitigation is to develop a project that seeks to achieve 'no net loss' on the environment and local communities, minimise the residual adverse effects and, if possible, provide enhancements/maximise benefits. The application of mitigation in a project should be a continuous one, from site selection and optioneering through to project design and delivery.

A key element of ESIA practice is the application of the *Mitigation Hierarchy* (see Fig. 2[3]), which is embodied in regulatory frameworks to degree[4] in some jurisdictions.

---

[3] Terminology on 'Mitigation Hierarchy' varies but generally is formed around the stages indicated herewith.

[4] For example, the EC EIA Directive requires 'a description of measures envisaged in order to avoid, to reduce and if possible remedy significant adverse effects'.

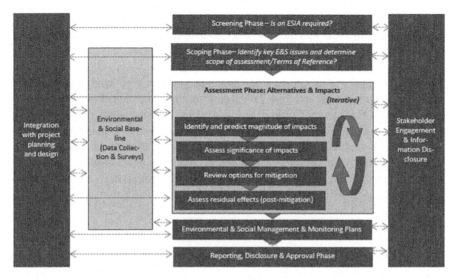

Fig. 1 ESIA process—key components and phases

Mitigation Hierarchy – Options:
- ➤ **AVOID:** *avoiding or 'designing out' impacts first;*
- ➤ **REDUCE:** *consider alternatives/design modifications/measures to reduce significant impacts;*
- ➤ **REMEDY:** *apply mitigation measures if possible to remedy significant impacts;*
- ➤ **COMPENSATE, REMEDIATE & OFFSET:** *as a last resort identify fair compensation, remediation and offsetting measures to address potentially significant residual effects.*

Fig. 2 Mitigation hierarchy

A guiding principle of ESIA is to aim for a mitigation option towards the top of the hierarchy. This is in accordance with the fundamental principles on the protection of the environment as contained within the EU policies[5] and those of other jurisdictions (*e.g. precautionary principle, preventative action should be taken, environmental damage should be rectified at source and the polluter should pay*).

2.3 Principles of Good Stakeholder Engagement

Stakeholder engagement involves the communication of project information to interested and affected parties to enable them to express opinions and have direct involvement in the process. It is also the foundation for achieving a 'social licence

---

[5] Including: *European Principles for the Environment* (EPE), which consist of the guiding environmental principles enshrined in the EC Treaty and practices and standards incorporated into the EU's secondary legislation on the environment.

to operate'. Engagement is part of the process to establish community support and understanding, to avoid and mitigate risks, to help the community achieve access to the benefits of the project and to avoid objections and delays.

Legislative requirements for stakeholder engagement within ESIA frameworks and other regulatory instruments and planning systems vary across jurisdictions. There are also international laws[6] regarding public information and consultation requirements. Engagement often needs to go beyond the legal requirements to comply with international standards and, more importantly, to manage risks. The international standards, as referred to here, contain Performance Standards and requirements for stakeholder engagement and information disclosure, supported by many guidance documents. Some key components of good stakeholder engagement are represented in the Fig. 3.[7]

3 What Are Environmental and Social Risks?

Real and perceived environmental and social impacts can, in turn, create material risks to their project sponsors (i.e. owners/developers) and the financial institutions that provide financial products to these projects. Environmental and social risks both 'inside' and 'outside' the fence of a project can result in delays, cost increases and reputational risks. These can impact the ability of a project sponsor to access finance at reasonable cost. Figures 4, 5 and 6 outline examples of environmental and social impacts and the associated risks that project sponsors and financial institutions may be exposed to.

4 The Problem

The early stages of a project are primed to avoid environmental and social impacts and reduce risk, particularly during the decision-making process on project siting and the selection of alternatives (e.g. for project location, layout, infrastructure and associated facilities). Case studies cited below illustrate the application of the mitigation hierarchy and the incorporation of stakeholder views into early project planning decisions (*see Case Study Scenarios 1, 4, and 5*).

ESIAs and stakeholder engagement are early-stage project activities that commence prior to income-generating activities. Convincing some project sponsors of the need to invest in the ESIA and stakeholder engagement programmes early in a project's development is often a challenge. Project sponsors may be willing to do

---

[6] For example, the Aarhus and Espoo Conventions.

[7] Reference, Stakeholder Engagement: A Good Practice Handbook for Companies doing Business in Emerging Markets; International Finance Corporation (IFC) (First Printing: May 2007).

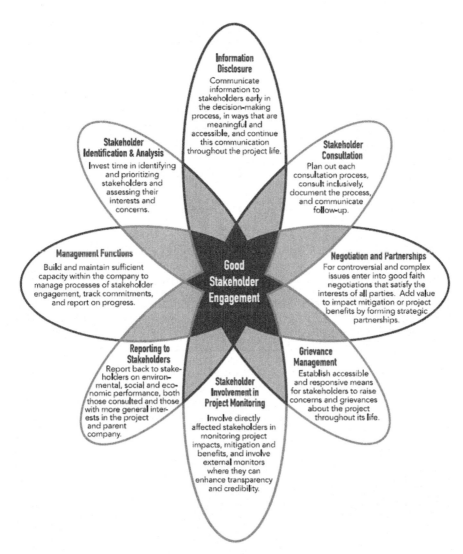

Fig. 3 Key components of good stakeholder engagement. *Source* Stakeholder Engagement: A Good Practice Handbook for Companies doing Business in Emerging Markets; International Finance Corporation (IFC) (First Printing: May 2007)

this as a means to gain regulatory approval but are often less willing to embrace engagement as part of a project's overall risk management framework.

Poor ESIA and stakeholder engagement practice during the planning stages of a project can contribute to delays and risks to achieving financial close. Some of the case studies below show how a poor ESIA approach and/or the lack of stakeholder engagement resulted in delays to achieving financial close (*see Case Study Scenario*

Examples of Environmental & Social Project Impacts	
Environmental	**Social**
WATER: ➢ Pollution of water resources ➢ Diversion/alteration of surface and groundwater flows ➢ Reduction on water availability for local communities AIR QUALITY: ➢ Increase in dust in atmosphere ➢ Emission of air pollutants ➢ Emission of greenhouse gases NOISE & VIBRATION: ➢ Increase in ambient noise levels causing impacts on local communities and wildlife ➢ Impacts on buildings from vibration effects VISUAL & LANDSCAPE: ➢ Visual impacts and destruction/alteration of topographical/landscape features SOIL: ➢ Contamination and reduction of soil resources ➢ Increased erosion risks HABITATS, FLORA & FAUNA: ➢ Direct loss, disturbance and fragmentation of habitats (including terrestrial and marine) ➢ Loss of biodiversity ➢ Disturbance/fragmentation/destruction of protected habitats/areas/flora & fauna species	LAND: ➢ Loss of land resulting in effects on livelihoods and displacement of communities; ➢ Disproportional impacts on vulnerable people and indigenous people LIVELIHOODS: ➢ Disturbance to livelihood of communities NATURAL RESOURCES: ➢ Loss of natural resources/ecosystems for local communities CHSS: ➢ Community health, safety and security (CHSS) issues ➢ Influx of workers and employment seekers can place pressure on local services and communities WORKFORCE: ➢ Labour and working conditions issues ➢ Employment opportunities ECONOMY: ➢ Economic improvements ➢ Taxation income etc. CULTURAL HERITAGE: ➢ Disturbance to cultural heritage and archaeology ➢ Disturbance/destruction of protected cultural heritage sites/resources

Fig. 4 Examples of environmental and social project impacts

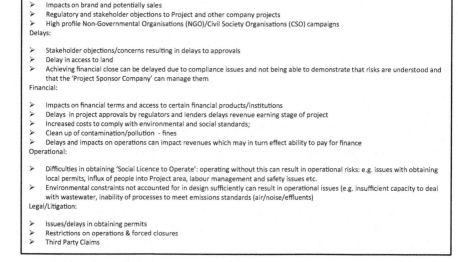

Examples of Potential Risks Project Sponsors may be exposed to due to E&S Impacts:
Reputational risks: ➢ Impacts on brand and potentially sales ➢ Regulatory and stakeholder objections to Project and other company projects ➢ High profile Non-Governmental Organisations (NGO)/Civil Society Organisations (CSO) campaigns Delays: ➢ Stakeholder objections/concerns resulting in delays to approvals ➢ Delay in access to land ➢ Achieving financial close can be delayed due to compliance issues and not being able to demonstrate that risks are understood and that the 'Project Sponsor Company' can manage them Financial: ➢ Impacts on financial terms and access to certain financial products/institutions ➢ Delays in project approvals by regulators and lenders delays revenue earning stage of project ➢ Increased costs to comply with environmental and social standards; ➢ Clean up of contamination/pollution - fines ➢ Delays and impacts on operations can impact revenues which may in turn effect ability to pay for finance Operational: ➢ Difficulties in obtaining 'Social Licence to Operate': operating without this can result in operational risks: e.g. issues with obtaining local permits, influx of people into Project area, labour management and safety issues etc. ➢ Environmental constraints not accounted for in design sufficiently can result in operational issues (e.g. insufficient capacity to deal with wastewater, inability of processes to meet emissions standards (air/noise/effluents) Legal/Litigation: ➢ Issues/delays in obtaining permits ➢ Restrictions on operations & forced closures ➢ Third Party Claims

Fig. 5 Examples of potential risks that project sponsors may be exposed to due to E&S impacts

Examples of Potential Risks Financial Institutions may be exposed to due to E&S impacts/risks:
Reputational:
➤ High profile NGO/CSO campaigns ➤ Damage to financial institution brand image ➤ Impact on reputation through association with project/company that is the subject of environmental and social criticism
Financial:
➤ Loan defaults due to delay in revenue, increased operating or capital expenditure ➤ Devaluation of project/investments ➤ Liabilities for clean-up costs or damages
Delay:
➤ Delays in investment decisions and return on investments

Fig. 6 Examples of potential risks financial institutions may be exposed to due to E&S impacts

2), negative impacts on operational revenue, reputational risks and project delays (*see Case Study Scenarios 3 and 7*).

5 Case Studies: Reducing and Increasing Environmental and Social Risks

A selection of case studies[8] is provided below. Observations have been drawn regarding how approaches to the various components of ESIA and stakeholder engagement have contributed to reducing or increasing the environmental and social risk of a project.

Within the limits of this chapter, it has not been possible to present case studies on how approaches to **all** the components of ESIA and stakeholder engagement can contribute to reducing or increasing environmental and social risks.

5.1 New Major Port in Area of Sensitive Coral Reef

Case Study Scenario 1: New Major Port in Area of Sensitive Coral Reef
A government authority decided a US$500 m new port was required along a geographically restricted coastline and a Design-Build-Finance-Operate (DBFO) model was prepared with the aim of attracting investment. The authority recognised the need to accommodate trade, industry and tourism concurrent with environmental conservation, notably the important coral reef.

(continued)

---

[8] These are 'indicative' case study scenarios.

They recognised, early on, that any risk to conservation of the reef may result in reputational issues for potential investors and reduced investor interest. Whilst the DBFO investor would be ultimately responsible for the full ESIA, the authority adopted a 2-stage 'ESIA' strategy; they commissioned a strategic study looking at siting options for the port and the coral risk, their aim being to avoid and reduce impacts to the coral reef, as far as possible, in the siting of the port.

Early baseline studies on the key issues of the coral reef were undertaken, the findings of which were fed into the siting options analysis and redesign of the layout of the port, which significantly reduced the amount of coral impacted. Engagement on options and coral risk was undertaken with affected and interested parties. A compensation and offset package for the impacts to the coral reef was designed and agreed with relevant parties. This approach reduced the uncertainty for potential DBFO investors regarding potential damage to the coral reef, whilst letting them develop the full ESIA, addressing the more predictable risks of the proposed port, at a later date.

The approach of focusing on the key significant risk early and applying the mitigation hierarchy early in the project planning, along with integrating the environmental and social disciplines as part of the overall design team, avoided and reduced environmental risks and uncertainty for investors. Identification and early consultation with key stakeholders and interested parties regarding the coral reef and options for siting the port supported the management of potential risks associated with impacts to the sensitive resource of the coral reef (e.g., reputational risks due to international NGO campaigns, delays in achieving consents, etc.).

5.2   Railway in Europe

Case Study Scenario 2: Railway in Europe
A scheme to develop a regional European railway corridor included a section comprising the rehabilitation of an old railway line. An ESIA was commissioned and scoped to meet national regulatory requirements and ESIA practice which included limited consideration of social issues.

The route ran alongside and through a number of urban areas and villages. However, limited social baseline investigation or consultation with local communities was undertaken along the old existing railway line during the development of the original ESIA. There appeared to be a presumption that,

(continued)

given the land was already in the railway easement, negligible social impacts would occur in this section.

The project sponsor determined that project financing would need to be sought during the development of the ESIA. Before finalisation of the ESIA, further reviews were undertaken by prospective lenders. These reviews revealed that certain key environmental and social aspects as required under their lender E&S standards had not been sufficiently covered in the project planning and ESIA process. One of the significant social impacts being the presence of an informal vulnerable community partially living within the existing railway corridor. Further surveys and consultation with the families were then undertaken to determine mitigation and appropriate compensation measures. This issue and other issues delayed the disclosure of the draft ESIA, which significantly delayed achieving financial close.

5.3 Wind Farms in Southwestern Europe and MENA

Case Study Scenario 3: Wind Farm in Southwestern Europe
During the initial period of operation of the wind farm, a relatively high number of one scavenging bird species were killed due to collisions with the turbines. This species was protected under the EU Birds Directive and known to be highly vulnerable to potential impacts from wind energy development. The wind farm was located in the vicinity of a scavenging food source (e.g. cattle carcass landfill). There were protests by a number of NGOs and a temporary closure order issued. The project planning and EIA process had not considered the conflict potential. The EIA proponent had received the necessary approvals and the project had all required permits for operation. This risk therefore was to a degree hidden from investors. The interim solution agreed was to allow the wind farm to operate only at night, thus resulting in a substantial loss of energy revenue whilst closure of landfill could occur and alternatives to food source sites/strategies identified.

Case Study Scenario 4: Proposed Wind Farm in MENA
As part of the EIA scoping phase, early consultation was undertaken with environmental conservation organisations. This along with reviews of available information identified that the project lay on an important route for migratory soaring birds. However, the exact route and flight altitudes of the migrating birds across the project area and the significance of the potential risk to birds were unknown. A 12-month ornithological survey was

(continued)

commissioned to map the routes and species. The scope of the survey was agreed with key stakeholders. The siting of the turbines within the wind farm development was then informed by the outcomes of the surveys in order to reduce risks to birds. The ESIA was approved and the project successfully tendered to a consortium for the development.

Effective scoping of significant issues triggered the early investigation (survey and consultation) of the potentially significant bird conflict issue and the review of the siting of turbines to avoid and reduce this risk at source. The early application of the mitigation hierarchy by integration of the ESIA with the design process reduced the risk and uncertainty associated with this issue. Whereas in Case Study Scenario 3, even with an approved EIA, insufficient scoping of potentially significant issues, poor investigation of baseline and limited consultation with interested stakeholder, along with other aspects, appear to have possibly contributed to risk which resulted in loss of revenue and reputational damage.

5.4   Onshore Oil and Gas Project in MENA

Case Study Scenario 5: Onshore Oil and Gas Project in MENA
During the scoping of the ESIA, a walkover survey and initial consultations identified significant cultural heritage and archaeological sites. Further consultations with the local community and archaeological protection authority revealed that the sites were too important to damage and needed to be preserved. The project layout was altered to avoid impacts on the sites and allow for the retention and protection of the cultural heritage and archaeological resources. Environmental and social constraint maps were developed. These were provided to the wider team to prevent the location of further project infrastructure in the constraint areas and to prevent accidental damage. The stakeholders and local community also participated in the monitoring of the sites. This participation helped to build trust and support for the project.

5.5   Natural Resources (Mining) Project in Central Africa

Case Study Scenario 6: Natural Resources (Mining) Projects in Central Africa
Mining Company 'A' secured a large mining concession containing a few urban centres, over 50 villages, large and small scale agriculture and

(continued)

undeveloped forestry areas. The estimated population of the concession was 130,000. All land in the concession was state owned; however, a customary and traditional land system had been operated in the region for many generations. Occupants of land were viewed by the state as 'informal' with no security of tenure and no right to compensation for loss of access to land or resettlement. Under the mining concession issued by the state, the mining company had the right to use the land as it seemed fit. Within the legal framework there were certain very limited rights for compensation for loss of crops, etc.

In the same region in Central Africa, other mining concessions had been issued and mining commenced by other companies on a number of these projects with little consultation with local communities during the project planning and development of the ESIA and land acquisition planning. Negligible compensation and resettlement planning was undertaken by some of these mining companies with the state clearing land and forcing eviction of local communities who had resided and farmed the land for many generations. Some community livelihoods were also dependent on artisanal mining activities. International NGO-backed campaigns and protests from local communities arose, resulting in the potential for significant reputational damage for some mining companies/investors along with impacts to their actual mining operations.

Mining Company 'A', understanding the value of obtaining broad community support, implemented a continuous programme of stakeholder engagement to establish community participation in the decision-making process. The company recognised during the scoping phase that land acquisition and effects on local communities would be a significant issue for the project. Specifically, they engaged with the local affected communities' resettlement committees who participated in the development of resettlement plans and livelihood restoration packages for affected people. One of the key livelihood restoration measures was the provision of training and jobs. Whilst the state prevented Mining Company 'A' from paying compensation for the loss of land, with negotiation, they agreed to the mining company providing land replacement allowances and livelihood restoration packages to affected people.

By investing early in the stakeholder engagement programme and using it to deal with community concerns, the company avoided some of the key risks evident in other mining projects in the region related to impacts on customary land tenure.

Consultation needs to be managed carefully so as not to cause distrust due to a lack of information and understanding on the project, balanced with not raising expectations. Companies face many challenges during the external engagement process during the planning of a project. One which is common

(continued)

in mining projects, often due to the fluctuations in the market place, is ensuring and enabling continuity of the stakeholder engagement programme during periods when a project's development slows and in some cases is put into a care and maintenance phase. Establishing a local community relations team, operating through the project's life cycle, is an approach that some companies have adopted.

5.6   Mixed-Use Development Project in MENA City Centre

Case Study Scenario 7: Mixed-Use Development Project in City Centre—Middle East and North Africa (MENA)
A development authority prepared a master plan and associated studies, for the redevelopment of an area of the old town in the city into a high-end mixed-use development. The authority needed to make the land available for the new developments and investors. Low-income, semi-informal, poverty-stricken vulnerable communities had been living in the area for many generations. The project therefore required the relocation of these communities.

The authority undertook very limited social baseline assessment and no consultation. Without any community engagement or participation, it commissioned the design and construction of a new housing development outside the city centre; it then announced this to the local affected community and prepared the anticipated timetable for their relocation. Having not been consulted, the communities resisted the move. The lack of examination of the social impacts on this local community meant that the proposed relocation would in itself potentially result in other significant effects, which had not been accounted for in the authority's plans. The local community's livelihoods were dependent on the local area including specifically the local market area. Not only would the proposed development result in their involuntary resettlement but would impact their livelihoods.

The key risk of the project was the involuntary resettlement of the local vulnerable community. The lack of social impact assessment, affected communities consultation, information disclosure and community participation in decision-making in relation to the involuntary resettlement resulted in severe delays to the project and long-term distrust between communities and the development authority. Retrospective assessment and consultation was undertaken with the support of international development agencies and civil society organisations to achieve community participation in decision-making over the relocation of the community. However, the distrust resulted in lasting negative impacts on community support and perceptions of the development giving rise to the potential for reputational risks of future developers and investors.

Conclusion

Effective ESIA and stakeholder engagement are proactive participatory project management tools that look ahead at future risks and provide decision-makers with options, commonly referred to as mitigation measures, to avoid or reduce environmental and social (E&S) damage. If implemented early in the project cycle, they can encourage the consideration of alternatives that can avoid and reduce environmental and social impacts (*see Case Studies 1, 4 and 5*).

Development projects inherently face many potential environmental and social risks and it is not possible to solve them all early on. Some risks are more critical than others and adopting an approach that enables the identification and examination of the critical and significant ones early in project planning can provide downstream benefits and reduce the overall risk profile of the project.

One of the keys to reducing risks appears to be establishing an ESIA and a stakeholder engagement strategy and resources early in the project cycle, focusing on the significant critical environmental and social issues. Investing time and resources in understanding these issues, carrying out baseline investigations and consultations on these issues and applying the mitigation hierarchy early in the process to avoid, reduce and remedy these issues reduce both the uncertainty associated with them and the risk on the project.

The ESIA, related land acquisition and stakeholder engagement activities can be most valuable when applied and integrated into the decision-making processes early in the planning of a project. Integration of the key players in ESIA (design team, land acquisition and resettlement planning team, community relations team) will have obvious benefits in the identification and application of appropriate mitigation measures.

The case studies illustrate some of the benefits of early consultation in risk reduction. Failure to undertake consultation may not only lead to breaches of legal compliance but is likely to exacerbate social concerns, leads to social objections to the project and may ultimately result in project delay and a delay to financing.

Building structured communication channels for early and continuous engagement will help to achieve trust and build community support. It should be recognised, however, that stakeholder engagement must run beyond the temporal limits of the ESIA, given that the majority of ESIA tasks will be undertaken prior to commercial activity. Each project's approach to ESIA and stakeholder engagement also needs to be relevant to a specific project's social context, geographical setting and industry sector.

(continued)

The Business Case

The carrot and stick idiom is based on the reward of a *carrot* (the incentive) and the punishment of a *stick* to encourage a horse to move along. Legislation is undoubtedly the stick for undertaking ESIA and the related stakeholder engagement and disclosure process. Increasing the search for compliance with international standards adopted and established by the International Financial Institutions (IFIs) has been a driver for change that provides both a stick and some carrot incentives. Moving away from compliance and viewing investments in the ESIA and stakeholder engagement programmes as part of the overall risk management framework for projects can provide benefits and further carrot incentives, as explored in this chapter.

There are many things on the shopping list that project sponsors need to purchase to achieve an operating project. Investing in ESIA and stakeholder engagement can be an effective way to improve a project and minimise risks.

This chapter outlines some of the potential benefits of investing in ESIA and stakeholder engagement processes, particularly during the early stages of a project's planning, to enable the avoidance and reduction of environmental and social impacts and risks. The potential benefits realised by reducing environmental and social risks underpin the business case for using these processes to support risk management. A summary business case for using ESIA and stakeholder engagement to support risk management is represented in the Fig. 7.

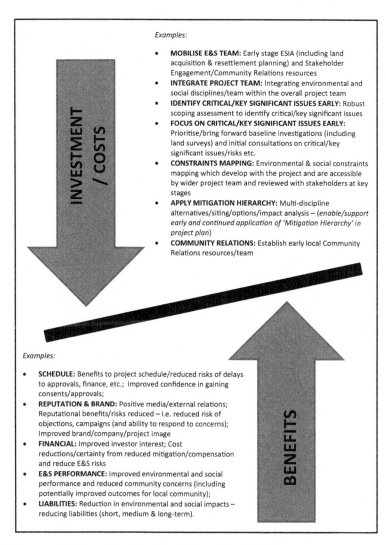

Fig. 7 Summary business case for using ESIA and stakeholder engagement to support risk management (indicative)

Reference

National Environmental Policy Act (1969) Pub. L. 91-190, 42 U.S.C. 4321-4347, January 1, 1970, as amended by Pub. L. 94-52, July 3, 1975, Pub. L. 94-83, August 9, 1975, and Pub. L. 97-258, § 4(b), Sept. 13, 1982

Positive Impact Business and Finance: A Challenge for Industries and Services, A Preeminent Role for the Financial Sector

Denis Childs

Abstract Positive Impact Business (PIB) has to be integrated into the mainstream strategy of industry and services, since the growth of the population to nine billion by 2050 will create great business opportunities. PIB will have to address the market with the basic needs of the population (housing, access to energy and water, food security, transportation, health, education), while consideration of the limits of the planet will require new technologies and business models. But the main hurdle (and that is the primary environmental and social responsibility of the financial community) will be the huge, anticipated, long-term financial gap at a time when the United Nations estimates the need for annual investment of between US\$1,300 billion and US\$9,600 billion. Fundamentally, this is what the creation of a successful long-term debt PIB asset class is all about.

1 Sustainable Development: Hope and Concerns

Since the Rio Summit in 1992, international institutions, and, namely, the United Nations (UN), have made significant progress in their promotion of sustainable development. Governments have strengthened their social and environmental regulations and incentivised sustainable sectors such as energy transition. Multilateral agencies and development finance institutions, supported by governments, have increased their work at public and private levels and via international agreements such as the Kyoto Protocol and the Convention on Biological Diversity, which both demonstrate the international efforts to coordinate initiatives.

For many, the Rio Summit was the starting point of hope. Hope that a cohesive approach by institutions and governments could be found to meet the sometimes conflicting demands of a growing population and the capacity of our planet to sustain it.

D. Childs (✉)
Positive Impact Finance and Environmental and Social Advisory, Société Générale Corporate & Investment Banking, Global Finance, Paris, France
e-mail: denis.childs@sgcib.com

© Springer International Publishing Switzerland 2015
K. Wendt (ed.), *Responsible Investment Banking*, CSR, Sustainability, Ethics & Governance, DOI 10.1007/978-3-319-10311-2_25

But 20 years later at RIO+20, concerns were growing that the original targets would be missed and hope was increasingly replaced by disappointment. This, coupled with the 'sovereign' financial crisis that had forced many governments to scale down their level of subsidy to the 'green economy', meant that we still face many of the same planetary challenges as at the Rio Summit. It will take the mobilisation of governments, institutions and the private sector to address these planetary challenges. The key question is, why should the private sector be interested in addressing these challenges and how can the finance sector become a driving force to achieve it?

2 Private Sector Contribution

During the past 20 years, the private sector has been adapting to new environmental regulations set by governments and has started to establish green/responsible methods. During this period, extra financial obligations have been set in the form of compulsory CSR reports. 'Sustainable development' has been positioned very differently from one company to the next and only a handful of companies have considered it as a 'mainstream issue' at the heart of their strategies.

More recently, World Business Council for Sustainable Development (WBCSD) in 'Vision 2050: the new agenda for business' report published in February 2010 was clear that what was at stake was the strategies of industries and services:

> We hope to challenge companies to rethink their products, services and strategies, envisioning new opportunities that put sustainability at the center, to communicate with and motivate employees and their boards, and to develop leadership positions in the wider world.

The basic challenge being that, according to WBCSD estimates, the nine billion people on the planet by 2050 would consume 2.3 times the ecological resources of the planet on a 'business as usual model'.

WBCSD considers 2010–2020 the 'turbulent teens', the time to introduce ideas and new attitudes in order to prepare for the 2020–2050 'transformation time'.

In a nutshell, the issue is to address the basic needs of the population and how many of the nine billion people should be considered as clients while taking into consideration the limits of the planet.

3 From Sustainable Development to Positive Impact Business

Even though the three pillars of 'sustainable development' (environmental, social and economic convergence) are always mentioned, it is a fact that the environmental issues have so far always taken the lead.

Attention has been focused on addressing the negative environmental impacts linked to the development of industry and agriculture (and namely pollution) in order to avoid the foreseeable disasters affecting the planet and its population.

Taking the social aspect as the key driver creates more business opportunities and is probably a better vector of dialogue for governance to be built between different stakeholders (governments, local communities, financial institutions, philanthropic institutions, NGOs, etc).

Sustainable development is the reconciliation of the three pillars, but has generally been defined as the intersection of the positive impacts of the three pillars.

Using this strict definition could mean one ends up in a void perimeter: any human activity has generally both positive and negative impacts.

Negatives impacts have to be addressed, even for an investment generating highly positive impacts.

Positive Impact Business (PIB) is derived from sustainable development concept. PIB consists of a wider perimeter including any business that has positive impact(s) on one or more of the pillars of sustainable development while correctly addressing negative impacts.

Another difficulty is to take impacts as a basis to define a business perimeter. From a business point of view, sources of positive impacts, such as sectors of activities, technologies and countries, are better concepts.

Using sources of impacts to define the PIB perimeter will also help government set their policies.

One of the targets of the Positive Impact Business initiative is to clarify business perimeters and the methodology to identify, evaluate and address both negative and positive impacts.

4 Finding New Sources of Finance Is the Main Hurdle: 'Positive Impact Finance'

Given the Magnitude of Demand, Financing Positive Impact Business Needs Access to New Sources of Finance and Thinking Out of the Box.
New cities will be developed for the doubling of the urban population by 2050. Urbanisation, population increase and a rise in income levels will all lead to an increase in the demand for food, estimated between 60 and 70 % by 2050, with an even bigger increase in demand for meat and processed food.

This will put a fundamental stress on resources, magnifying the scarcity of energy and water.

Planetary limitation means that existing technologies and business models are in many cases no longer efficient.

In the same time, the number of countries and people able to afford services and products is increasing.

Needs are growing rapidly and the UN estimates that the annual investment requirements are US$1,300G, reaching US$9,600G by 2050.

This magnitude leads to the financial hurdle that is the growing inability to provide long-term debt to support such investments.

The current efforts of the multilateral agencies and development finance institutions and of governments to match these financials needs are reaching their limits, and a huge long-term debt financing gap is anticipated, which outstanding could be as high US$8,600G by 2020 according to our own estimations.

Addressing this financing gap is not only a matter of magnitude but also a matter of:

- Correctly securing the credits
- Minimising the administrative costs of such credits
- Designing the proper financial instrument to attract private investors
- Making sure that the E&S targets are reached
- Putting into place a proper governance

The private finance industry has a preeminent role to play in making PIB real. It is crucial that this industry that is not currently focusing on the matter will do so in order to lift the anticipated financing hurdle. This is possible, but the finance industry has to 'think out of the box'.

Société Générale's contribution is to propose a 'four-step programme' for defining PIB perimeter and methodologies in order to align and focus stakeholders on implementation.

The ultimate goal is to create a PIB community with platforms to address specific PIB issues, with a specific focus on finance [Positive Impact Finance (PIF)].

5 The Positive Impact Business Programme: Perimeter, Methodologies and Implementation

A four-step programme proposes:

1. **To clarify the general definition of common target**
2. **To precise the scope of Positive Impact Business (PIB) to allow easy identification of potential business**
3. **To determine a methodology to qualify for PIB**
4. **To create a PIB community**

This programme is meant to guide individuals, companies, institutions and governments willing to contribute to the PIB debate, development of PIB and creation of PIB Community.

5.1 Proposed Definition

Positive Impact Business (PIB) has a positive impact on at least one of the three pillars of sustainable development (human needs, environmental preservation or economic convergence) and can be considered holistically sustainable in that any potential negative impacted pillar has been correctly mitigated or off-set.

This definition recognises that any human activity where potentially 'positive' also has some inherent negative aspects that need to be addressed.

5.2 Scope of Positive Impact Business (Identification)

Identification goes through the definition of sectors, transversal subjects, countries and the size of enterprises that can be anticipated as having at least one positive impact on one of the pillars of sustainable development (NB, final qualification for PIB cannot occur at this stage).

This constitutes referential sources of potential positive impacts (and potential associated negative impacts):

5.2.1 Sectors

A list of sectors is proposed reflecting the 10 sectors of focus mentioned in the UNEP Towards a Green Economy report published in 2011 and other added sectors, which are detailed with 1 level of subsectors:

- Agriculture, buildings, energy (supply), fisheries, forestry, industry, tourism, transport, waste and water (UNEP sectors)
- Energy and power, infrastructure (including telecom/networks), education, healthcare and web/social networks (added sectors)

These sectors are associated with their **potential impacts** (positive and negative) including, but not limited to:

- **Social impacts**: access to water; access to energy, education level, transport and communication; and access to housing, food security, labour creation and physical or economic resettlement (generally estimated in number and quality of people impacted)
- **Environmental impacts**: air, water, soil, biodiversity, climate, resources efficiency and waste efficiency (generally estimated through appropriate measurement)
- **Economic convergence** (estimated through GDP or more comprehensive indexes)

The UN International Standard Industrial Classification of All Economic Activities drives all the regional and national nomenclatures. This nomenclature is currently not detailed enough to reflect the above-mentioned key sectors and should be amended accordingly. This would help clarify PIB perimeter and ease identification and follow-up. A working group of professionals created within ORSE (Observatoire pour la Responsabilité Sociétale des Entreprises) is currently analysing the gap in order to make precise proposals to progress in the direction of a UN (and in parallel regional and national) nomenclature that would be aligned to UN Millennium goals

5.2.2 Transversal Subjects

Certain transversal subjects given their objective will be considered as potential PIB, such as resource efficiency (water, energy, waste, emissions), labour/human rights improvement and biodiversity improvement.

5.2.3 Countries

What is proposed is the adoption of the World Bank Atlas Method system for country classification, GNI per capita in USD, to target the lowest two tiers ('low income and lower-middle income' categories with revenue per person under US$3,945 per annum).

5.2.4 Small and Medium Enterprises

Proposal is derived from IFC criteria but reduced to three levels only of turnover depending upon the countries. Specific cases have been made for USA and China. A definition for those of cooperatives to be included in scope needs to be elaborated.

5.3 Evaluation Methodology

5.3.1 E&S Human Evaluation

With the help of identification tools derived from the above, the type of impacts and their materiality have to be evaluated against recognised international standards on a case by case by environmental and social specialists.

Valuation of negative impacts should result in defining mitigation or off-set plans.

Positive impacts should be measured (harmonisation of measurement should be pursued).

5.3.2 Transparency

For the sake of transparency, the process for evaluation should be such that it can be further audited. Discrepancies in above perimeters or methods are acceptable as long as it is transparent to other stakeholders, reported and audited.

5.4 Positive Impact Business Community

5.4.1 Targeted Stakeholders

A number of stakeholders are already involved in PIB/PIF. The purpose in creating a PIB community is to accelerate the dialogue and debate among stakeholders but as quickly as possible to set up the right organisations to implement PIB.

- **Policymakers:** governments and local authorities and international and regional institutions
- **Companies(State owned companies or private sector companies):** those involved in industry or services contributing to PIB, a specific attention should be given to the 'new economy' that will be the primary beneficiary of PIB (since solutions coming from broadband, access providers, research engines, devices providers, social networks, etc. will need to be incorporated in solutions coming from 'classical' industries and services)
- **Financial institutions:** private finance institutions: IB and retail banks, insurers, asset managers, pension funds, hedge funds, private equity, public or multilateral finance and foundations/philanthropy
- **Other stakeholders:** consultants/auditors, NGOs, media, research and universities, working groups/clubs/associations, etc.

5.5 Contribution to New Governance

Governance is needed to adopt a wider view in order to find solutions and, namely, to incorporate consideration externalities. Governance goes beyond cooperation and is necessary when the interests of different stakeholders are apparently not aligned. It is a way to address situations in a more holistic way and to optimise solutions. It is a kind of an 'economic democracy'.

5.5.1 Identification of Barriers and Incentives to PIB

Lobby should be organised to have a PIB-friendly regulation, namely, for the financial aspects.

Identification of geographical/technical hurdles is a starting point to find solutions. Special attention should be given to financial matters because of the anticipated financial gap (PIF).

5.5.2 Constitution of Platforms

Platforms should correspond to the different stages of development of PIB:

1. Research and development phase, where the concept needs to be shared and discussed. Pilot phase, where some specific actions take place (certain countries, certain sectors or transversal issues). Pilots could both consist of consulting (namely, when dealing with less developed countries or energy efficiency) or finance mandate for a specific project or programme.
2. Industrial phase that will, namely, need specific consultancy and powerful financing platforms.

The ultimate target, from a financing point of view, would be to have the finance industry focus on financing PIB (PIF) that corresponds to the Millennium Development Goals (post 2015 Agenda under discussion).

6 PIF: The Creation of a New Asset Class

6.1 Magnitude of Finance to Be Raised

Given the magnitude of the financial needs, the addition of finance coming from host countries, multilateral and development agencies, export credit agencies, local banking system, international banking system and philanthropy is far from sufficient. In order to close the gap, it is necessary to attract a much larger type of investor, including insurance companies, pension funds, asset managers, hedge funds, sovereign wealth funds and strategic investors.

The lack of private finance will concentrate on long-term debt (loans) given the timeframe of financial returns of the projected investments. Difficulties will also be faced for equity and short-term debt, but long-term debt will be the most difficult subject to address

6.2 Investigate New Routes to Secure Underlying Loans/ Portfolio of Loans

The question is how to attract the private finance industry to new areas of business. The starting point is that PIB contributes to economic prosperity.

New basic finance technology has to be developed to transfer this economic wealth into sound finance structures with attractive returns.

In some way, the finance industry is primarily looking to the finance rationale and then looks to a broader economic rationale.

PIF will do the reverse in capitalising on any situation that brings economic value to find the appropriate financing solution.

6.3 Establish Over-Performing Assets That Match UN Millennium Goals

The intrinsic financial value of the asset (good SHARPE ratio) is the only credible driver that will attract 'classic' investors that initially are neutral to the Millennium Goals. Governments, MLA/DFIs and foundation/philanthropy whose targets are converging with Millennium Goals should aim at leveraging their intervention with the private finance sector. The target of PIF is to satisfy the Millennium Goals while bringing a new attractive asset class to the markets.

6.3.1 PIF Is a Huge Volume of Assets for the Market

The prospective of volume for this type of assets can be expressed in terms of in X1000 G of USD, given the exponentially growing financial gap.

PIF assets are not 'a small niche' and need to be developed as a full 'asset class'.

6.3.2 PIF Has a Clear PIB Perimeter Aligned with Millennium Goals

- PIB corresponds to the Millennium Goals (post 2015 Agenda discussion) given its strong social content in addressing the need of the growing population while integrating the pressure it puts on the planet.
- PIB considers the three billion increase of the population as potential clients and business opportunities and not as a matter of charity.
- PIB is business innovation to adapt to planetary constraints: new technologies, new sustainable cities, integration of 'new economy' in industrial and services solutions.
- PIB is all that goes with urbanisation (housing, energy, water, education, healthcare, transportation, food security, leisure, security, etc.):
- PIB is agribusiness.
- PIB is resource efficiency.

6.4   PIF Controls the Achievement of E&S Targets

- PIF identifies both positive and negative impacts (social, environmental and economic development).
- PIF evaluates positive and negative impacts and aims at the best in class remedies or off-set.
- PIF is not reached when negative impacts are not correctly remedied (positive does not compensate negative).
- PIF needs transparency and third party assessment (audit).

6.5   PIF Covers Existing Financing Solutions but Addresses also Sectors/Countries/Transversal Issues

PIF considers that all economically viable investment must find its financing solution, thus also addressing investment not (or insufficiently) producing cash flows but with a strong economic rationale, smaller investments/programmes, resources efficiency, SMEs and poorest countries.

6.6   PIF Uses Same Standard Principles to Secure Risk on Underlying Loans (or Other Financing Instruments) and Optimising Return for Investors

- Use of direct or indirect externalities to secure finance
- Mitigating the risk in creating portfolios of transaction or clients
- Tranching the risk according to the target of the different stakeholders participating in the finance, namely, combining underlying finance with host countries, multilateral agencies, development finance institutions and philanthropy

6.7   PIF Aims to Optimise Financing Costs for Issuers

- Simplification of underlying credit structure
- Programme financing
- Distribute to originate approach considering investors as partners

6.8 PIF: A Good Sharpe Ratio to Attract Financial Investors

These assets should be over-performing other debt asset classes in order to attract investors on a purely financial return ground. These assets will over-perform for a series of reasons:

- For underlying assets, the current difficulty for private financing institutions to bring new sound financing solutions creates an arbitrage between real risk (once correctly secured) and perceived risk: underlying risk/return ratio is good.
- Volatility of return will be low due to the various risk mitigation factors included in underlying credits.
- Governance brings an alignment of all parties involved in credit.
- Combination of private finance with action of governments, MLA/DFIs and philanthropy can bring value to the private investor share in many ways.

6.9 Expertise to Be Combined to Produce PIF Asset Class, A Barrier to Entry to Be Addressed

Expertise to combine to bring these asset classes to the market is diverse:

- **On the investors' side**: a good understanding of classical financial investors, which are not yet ready to invest in PIF asset class, and a proximity to the specialised investors (governments, MLA/DFIs, foundations) and structured finance
- **On the issuers' side:** E&S expertise, underlying loans collaterisation through future revenues monetisation and governments advising

7 Where We Stand, What Has Been Achieved, What Is the Agenda?

7.1 Where We Stand, What Has Been Achieved

Internal development started within Société Générale in 2010 to set the fundamentals of 'Why PIB is needed and will turn out in a huge volume of attractive assets'.

In 2012, a working group was set with ORSE (Observatoire pour la Responsabilité Sociétale des Entreprises) including various private institutions (IB banks, retail banks, insurance companies, asset managers), public finance institutions (local and development finance institutions) and UNEP.

7.2 What Is the Agenda?

- To form a more international group of 'PIB partners' that would highly contribute to the R&D phase, would work to bring the initiative to the pilot phase and then be able to constitute a powerful group of investors for PIB/PIF
- To begin pilots that could consist of private development finance, energy efficiency finance and farmer financing (in emerging/developing countries)
- To organise and develop the debate over PIB/PIF

Contribution from additional stakeholders is key. Significant efforts have been undertaken so far by Société Générale; however, wider communication and input from other stakeholders are needed for further progress.

The ORSE (Observatoire pour la Responsabilité Sociétale des Entreprises) working group with the support of UNEP-FI is a first step in this direction.

PIB/PIF initiative should not be considered purely as an E&S initiative but simply as an adaptation of finance and business to the new business environment driven by the growth of the population and the limits of the planet.

PIF is a way to better serve clients that have understood where the business of today and tomorrow is developing.

Adopting EP in India: Challenges and Recommendations for Future EP Outreach

Alok Dayal and Ashok Emani

Abstract Throughout the world, environmental and social concerns are increasingly integrated voluntarily by businesses into their operations and interaction with stakeholders as part of sustainable and long-term business models. This has led to greater emphasis on disclosure, evident from business participation in forums such as the CDP, UNGC, UNPRI and UNEPFI. Environmental and social issues cannot be ignored in the pursuit of greater economic development. This is particularly relevant to emerging economies such as India where building infrastructure and the utilisation of natural resources are imperative for the development of the economy. Industry insiders look for a balance between these two seemingly contradictory requirements, often exacerbated by poor governance and enforcement of regulations. One of the main concerns for investors in India is the lack of proper infrastructure. Growth of infrastructure is imperative for the long-term growth of the Indian economy and, as such, has been spearheaded through the PPP model under the project financing framework. This necessitates the large-scale acquisition of land and use of natural resources, making the principles of sustainable development assume greater importance. Internationally, financial institutions have met the ESG challenges posed by project financing activities by adopting the Equator Principles, often driven by brand reputation, best in class commitment, globally aligned systems and procedures, new financial business opportunities and access to low-cost funds. Regional disparity, however, means that few organisations from emerging economies have joined the EP association, particularly from the big emerging economies of China and India. This chapter examines the reasons behind the lack of EP adoption in India. It will attempt to answer the basic questions: What are the challenges in adopting EP for Indian banks and financial institutions? What are the opportunities? How can ESG concerns in the project financing operations of banks and financial institutions in India become mainstream?

A. Dayal (✉)
IDFC Ltd, Mumbai, Maharashtra, India
e-mail: alok.dayal@idfc.com

A. Emani
IDFC Alternatives Ltd, Mumbai, Maharashtra, India

© Springer International Publishing Switzerland 2015
K. Wendt (ed.), *Responsible Investment Banking*, CSR, Sustainability, Ethics &
Governance, DOI 10.1007/978-3-319-10311-2_26

1 Indian Environment and Social Landscape and Related Regulatory Scenario

India is one among the 17 mega-diverse countries in the world, sustaining 17 % of the world population on merely 2.4 % of the world's total land area.

India's diverse economy encompasses traditional village farming; modern agriculture; fisheries; small, medium and modern industries; and a multitude of services. The structure of the Indian economy has undergone considerable change over the past few decades, particularly since the economic reforms of the 1990s. That decade witnessed fundamental economic reforms that led to the removal of entry barriers, reduction of areas reserved for the public sector and liberalisation of the foreign investment policy and import policy for intermediates and capital goods, all of which contributed to an upsurge in industrial growth. India's GDP growth rate increased rapidly to reach a peak of 9.5 % during Economic Survey, 2005–2006. However, following the global financial crisis of 2008, Indian GDP growth rates have moderated considerably due to a variety of internal and external factors.

Indian environmental legislations are more than a century old. The initial acts[1] were intended for extracting forest resources, primarily wood, during the colonial period. New legislation changed from general to specific with the enactment of the Environment Protection Act (EPA), 1986. EPA 1986 is the umbrella act that consolidated all the legislation pertaining to environmental aspects in the country. The Constitution of India[2,3] guarantees every citizen[4] the fundamental right to life and personal liberty (Constitution of India. Accessed at http://india.gov.in/mygovernment/constitution-india).[5] The essence of Indian environmental regulation has been to make public goods (such as the environment) take precedence over private economic interests through the creation of bureaucracies[6] equipped with legal sanctions to regulate economic activities.

The Bhopal gas tragedy in 1984, which led to the release of toxic gas in the city of Bhopal in central India, killing more than 4,000 people, was a watershed in the development of Indian environmental legislations. Prior to this incident, most of the environmental regulations in India were based on criminal justice where fines were

---

[1] 1865—British taking forest lands from Princes, 1927 Forest Act and subsequent amendments.

[2] Article 21 of the Constitution of India guarantees Fundamental Right to Life.

[3] Article 48-A of the Constitution of India states that the state shall endeavour to protect and improve the environment and to safeguard the forest and wild life.

[4] Article 51-A (g) of the Constitution of India states that the fundamental duty of every citizen of India is to protect and improve the natural environment including forests, lakes, rivers and wild life and to have compassion for living creatures.

[5] Which would include the right of a decent environment.

[6] Under the influence of the UN Conference on the Human Environment (Stockholm 1972) declaration, the National Council for Environmental Policy and Planning within the Department of Science and Technology was set up in 1972. This Council later evolved into a full-fledged Ministry of Environment and Forests (MoEF) in 1985, which today has been renamed as the Ministry of Environment, Forest and climate Change (MoEF&CC) is the apex administrative body in the country for regulating and ensuring environmental protection.

used to penalise the firms not complying with pollution control regulations. After the Bhopal gas tragedy, the Indian government adopted different legislation with regard to environment, health and safety. The Dock Workers (Safety, Health and Welfare) Act, 1986; the Factories (Amendment) Act, 1987; the Hazardous Waste (Management and Handling) Rule, 1989; the Manufacture, Storage and Import of Hazardous Chemical Rule, 1989 and as amended in 2000; the Public Liability Insurance Act, 1991; Rules on Emergency Planning, Preparedness and Response for Chemical Accident, 1996; etc. were all enacted in India after the Bhopal gas tragedy.

Under the EPA, 1986, the key legislation on environment and social management was the enactment of the EIA notification in 1994, later revised in 2006. The EIA 2006 notification elaborates the process of securing environmental clearance for various projects developed in the country.

Environmental clearances are accorded to projects based on the thresholds defined in the EIA notification. All the major projects in the country now have to go through a public hearing process. The issuance of the Policy Statement for Abatement of Pollution by the MoEF&CC in 1992 introduced a completely new set of instruments in the form of legislation and regulation, fiscal incentives, voluntary agreements, educational programmes and information campaigns in order to prevent, control and reduce pollution.

With regard to forests, a new style of governance was introduced in the form of Joint Forest Management where both the government and the local community participate in managing the forest resources. The roles and responsibilities of the centre and the state are clearly delineated in providing the environment and forest clearance. Social issues pertaining to land acquisition, which were being dealt with under the archaic Land Acquisition Act, 1884, amended in 1994,[7] and the national policy on resettlement and rehabilitation are now sought to be regulated through the Right to Fair Compensation and Transparency in Land Acquisition, Rehabilitation and Resettlement Bill 2013 (new Land Acquisition and RR Bill). The aforementioned Indian regulations on environment, health, safety and social aspects have been drawn on par with the legislations of other countries, for addressing the issues of industry and project development in India.

The industrial development of India has involved massive expansion of energy and resources, intensive industrial activity and major developmental projects such as large dams, use of forest land, mining, power generation and energy-intensive agriculture. This has inevitably led to social conflicts with the local communities. The Chipko movement in the Himalayas, where people protested against the contractors' indiscriminate felling of trees in the hill district of Uttarakhand (formally United Uttar Pradesh), is perhaps the best-known community conflict over natural resources, and it marked the beginning of the era of public protest in India.

---

[7] Government of India approved a new bill on land acquisition reforms and rehabilitation titled the Right to Fair Compensation and Transparency in Land Acquisition, Rehabilitation and Resettlement Bill, 2013 (new Land Acquisition and RR Bill), in September 2013. The bill is the key legislation in India for the rehabilitation and resettlement of families affected by land acquisitions for developmental projects.

Inspired by the success of the Chipko movement, the Appiko movement kicked off in the south of India against the illegal felling of forests and challenged large dams, mining and other destructive development projects in the ecologically fragile Western Ghats of India. The ecological protest over bauxite mining in Odisha is reminiscent of the former movement in Gandhamardhan hills and the current movement in Niyamgiri hills of Odisha (a state in eastern India). Narmada, Tehri, Koel-kara and Bodhghat saw similar public protests and conflicts over planned hydro projects and related development agenda pursued by the government. The 73rd amendment to the Constitution of India in 1992 tried to address this issue by entrusting the local communities with the responsibility of becoming more closely involved in the planning and monitoring of the development activities in their neighbourhood. Local communities in India are today much more aware of their rights and are willing to actively take up issues related to developmental activities impacting on their lives.

2   International Sustainability Initiatives

The 1987 Brundtland report introduced for the first time an integrated approach for addressing economic development, natural resources management and protection along with social equity and inclusion. The report provided the classic definition of sustainable development as 'development that meets the needs of the present without compromising the ability of future generations to meet their own needs'. The subsequent 1992 UN Conference on Environment and Development held at Rio de Janeiro was a milestone event that resulted in Agenda 21—an action plan for addressing environmental and developmental problems for a sustainable future. In 1993, the UN General Assembly established the Commission on Sustainable Development as the UN high-level political body entrusted with monitoring and promotion of the implementation of Rio outcomes including Agenda 21.

In 1994, when the action points of Agenda 21 were being debated, a further proposal in terms of considering triple bottom line for financial entities was put forward. Triple bottom line takes into account people and planet along with economic value. The triple bottom line measures a company's economic, social and environmental responsibility value. It advocates that businesses should prepare their triple bottom line—instead of focusing solely on their finances, thereby giving consideration to the company's social, economic and environmental impact. The 2002 World Summit on Sustainable Development (WSSD) advanced the agenda of mainstreaming the three dimensions of sustainable development—economic, social and environment—in development policies at all levels through the adoption of the Johannesburg Plan of Implementation (JPOI).

In the past few years, a number of initiatives such as UNEP Finance Initiative (UNEP FI), UN Global Compact (UNGC), UN Principles for Responsible Investing (UNPRI), Carbon Disclosure Project (CDP) and so on have evolved. The response of businesses to these initiatives has been overwhelming. As illustrated by Table 1,

Table 1 Business participation across various sustainability initiatives

Initiative	Inception year	Members	Members in 2013	Members from India
UNEP FI	1991	5+	200+	2
UNGC	2000	47+	7,000+	280
CDP	2003	35+	755+	53
UNPRI	2003	65	1,220	3

Source: Compilation by authors from respective websites, August 2013

there has been significant increase in the number of businesses subscribing to such sustainability forums over the years.

3 Sustainability Initiatives in India

India has also played an important role in the evolution of an international consensus to tackle major global environmental issues. India is party to numerous multilateral conventions that contribute to the protection of the environment and social aspects in meeting a sustainable development agenda. These include the UN Framework Convention on Climate Change (1992), the Convention on Biological Diversity (1993), the Vienna Convention on the Protection of the Ozone Layer (1985), the Montreal Protocol on Substances that Deplete the Ozone Layer (1989), the Ramsar Convention on Wetlands of International importance (1971), the Basel Convention on the Transboundary Movement of Hazardous Wastes (1989), the Convention on Combating Desertification (1994) and the Convention on the International Trade in Endangered Species of Wild Flora and Fauna (1973).

India is a founding member of the International Labour Organisation and has ratified 43 conventions. India is also party to a number of international treaties on human rights, including the International Convention on Elimination of all forms of Racial Discrimination (1968), International Covenant on Civil and Political Rights (1979), among others. India is also an active member of the Commission on Sustainable Development that was set up after the Rio Conference to monitor the implementation of Agenda 21.

Since the introduction of economic reforms in the 1990s, sustainable development has become a part of India's planning process. India's Ninth Five-Year Plan (2002–2007) explicitly recognised the synergy between environment, health and development and identified the need for ensuring environmental sustainability through community participation.

Subsequent to WSSD in 2002, the Indian government initiated a process of addressing the key elements of sustainable development in the five-year plan documents starting with the Tenth Five-Year (Plan Planning Commission 2011).

India is signatory to 93 multilateral environmental agreements[8] including United Nations Framework Convention on Climate Change (UNFCCC). It became a signatory to the UNFCCC in 1992 and since then has undertaken numerous response measures that are contributing to the objectives of the UNFCCC. India has adopted the National Action Plan on Climate Change to provide guidance in addressing its climate change-related issues. The government's commitment to sustainable development was reflected in the specific targets established for key indicators of human development and conservation of natural resources that became part of the Tenth Five-Year Plan. Similarly, the Eleventh Five-Year Plan focused on inclusive growth aimed at increasing the forest and tree cover, attaining international standards in all major cities pertaining to air emissions, treating urban waste water and cleaning river waters and increase energy efficiency by 20 %. The approach to the Twelfth Five-Year Plan released by the Planning Commission[9] is 'faster, more inclusive sustainable development' taking further steps towards sustainable and inclusive growth (Planning Commission, Government of India, 12th Five Year Plan (Vol. 1), accessed at http://planningcommision.nic.in).

4 Sustainability Initiatives Adopted by Indian Businesses, Banks and Financial Institution

Harmony with nature has always been an integral part of the ethos of Indian business. Many Indian businesses have realised the importance of addressing sustainability in their operations and have taken the necessary initiatives. Many large Indian businesses such as Hindustan Unilever Ltd (HUL), Associated Cement Company Ltd (ACC Ltd) and Wipro have been pursuing a sustainable development agenda for a long time. For example, HUL, a leader in the FMCG space, has reported a 22 % reduction in CO_2 emissions and a 77 % reduction in waste generated from manufacturing between 2008 and 2013, respectively (Hindustan Unilever Ltd 2012–2013).

ACC Ltd has managed to cut down its carbon footprint to 31 % of 550 kg of CO_2 per tonne of cement today (ACC 2011). Godrej, another FMCG company, has crafted a long-term vision focused on carbon neutral, zero waste, water positive and energy-efficient business. Sustainability principles are being applied by many Indian businesses across their entire value chain, including vendor suppliers. Many of them are publishing their sustainability reports in which information pertaining to economic, environmental, social and governance performance is reported and publicly disclosed (Sujit 2012).

Indian banks and financial institutions have also joined others in addressing sustainability issues. One of the leading Indian public sector banks, through its Green Banking policy, has come up with a plan to develop green power to substitute

---

[8] http://sedac.ciesin.columbia.edu/entri/countryProfile.jsp?ISO=IND

[9] Planning Commission has since been replaced with the National institution for Transforming India (NITI Ayog).

its own consumption of thermal power. Furthering their endeavours to reduce carbon footprint, through their vast network of branches and establishments, the banks have adopted several measures such as energy-efficient lighting systems; installation of energy savers such as intelligent switches, water harvesting and efficient water and waste management systems; gradual migration to paperless banking in internal operations; and so on. In 2012, some 80 Indian businesses, including banks, reported on their internal sustainability goals and disclosed their performance on the targets achieved to wider audiences through their sustainability responsibility reports.

Indian banks and financial institutions are also providing opportunity for innovation in the sustainability sphere to their employees and encouraging them to come up with solutions. This type of engagement has led to the development of innovative green solutions and products, which are later scaled up. Instabanking[10] is one such product that has evolved through such engagement. Direct Instabanking has reduced the carbon footprint of consumers by cutting the travel and paper requirement. The Indian parliament has recently promulgated the Companies Act, 2013, which promotes gender equality on company boards and makes spending on corporate social responsibility (CSR) by companies mandatory (Ministry of Corporate Affairs 2012a). Companies with a net worth of more than Rs. 500 crore or turnover of more than Rs. 1,000 crore or net profit of more than Rs. 5 crore are required to spend at least 2 % of annual net profit on corporate social responsibility activities.

The Indian market regulator, the Securities and Exchange Board of India (SEBI), is also playing a key role in furthering the sustainability agenda in India. In 2012, it directed the top 100 listed companies based on market capitalisation at Bombay Stock Exchange (BSE) or National Stock Exchange (NSE) as on March 31, 2012 mandatorily to submit an annual business responsibility report disclosing compliance to various environmental, social and governance aspects defined in the National Voluntary Guidelines (NVG).[11] Thus, many banks and financial institutions in India have begun to report on sustainability metrics and are disclosing the same through their sustainability/annual reports and through forums such as the CDP and UNGC.

5   Environment and Social Risk Management Frameworks in Banks

Globally, banks and financial institutions such as OECD, EXIM Bank of United States, European Bank for Reconstruction and Development (EBRD), the African Development Bank, the Asian Development Bank and the Inter-American Development Bank have developed internal Environment and Social (ESG) Risk

---

[10] InstaBanking is a way of undertaking banking anytime, anywhere through simpler, faster and more convenient banking modes. The Instabanking channels are Internet banking, mobile banking, bank ATMs, instant voice response (IVR) banking and iMobile.

[11] National Voluntary Guidelines on Socio-Economic and Environmental Responsibilities of Business prepared by Ministry of Corporate Affairs, GoI 2012a, b.

Management Frameworks and Guidelines that they follow as part of their due-diligence process and compliance requirements. By doing so, they have also been able to mainstream sustainability in their lending operations and deal with ESG risks in their lending portfolios.

The degree of diligence and sophistication of procedures varies from firm to firm. The IFC Performance Standards on Social and Environmental Sustainability are a well-recognised benchmark on which many of these guidelines are based. Many international commercial banks and institutions have also adopted the Equator Principles (which are based on the IFC Performance Standards) for addressing ESG issues in their project financing activities. In the past, most banks and institutions in India have relied on the national environment and regulatory approvals to take care of ESG issues in their financed portfolios. There is no commonly accepted ESG Framework and Guidelines that banks in India ascribe to as part of their lending process. As seen above, Indian businesses have responded enthusiastically to the various international sustainability initiatives and thus increased their prevalence throughout the country. However, with regard to ESG Frameworks, Indian banks and financial institutions still have a long way to go. We will explore this aspect in greater detail below and suggest ways forward.

6 Infrastructure Financing and the Equator Principles

One of the main concerns voiced by investors in India is the lack of proper infrastructure. It is widely accepted that growth of infrastructure is imperative for the long-term growth of the Indian economy. In India, during the Twelfth Five-Year Plan period (2012–2017), the total investment in infrastructure is expected to be 8.2 % of India's GDP, up from 7.2 % during the period of the Eleventh Plan. The investment by the private sector in the Twelfth Five-Year Plan is envisaged to be 48 %[12] of the total required investment, substantially more than the 36.6 % expected during the period of the Eleventh Plan (2007–2012) and 22 % throughout the Tenth Plan (2002–2007). In fact, during the Eleventh Plan period, certain infrastructure sectors such as ports and telecom received more than 80 % of total investments from the private sector. This number was closer to 50 % for the electricity sector. These numbers show that private participation through the public–private partnership (PPP) mode continues to play an important role for infrastructure development in India. By necessity, infrastructure projects involve large-scale acquisition of land and use of natural resources. In this context, the principles of sustainable development assume great importance for a country such as India that is trying to balance the development needs of its people with the conservation of its natural resources and the social inclusion of its masses.

---

[12] Planning Commission, Government of India, Twelfth Five-Year plan Vol 1 (accessed at http://planningcommision.nic.in). The Planning Commission has since been replaced with the National institution for Transforming India (NITI Ayog)

Banks and financial institutions play a central role in financing infrastructure projects in the country and are therefore key stakeholders in the area of sustainable development.

Internationally, financial institutions have stepped up to meet the ESG challenges posed by project financing activities by adopting the Equator Principles.

There are several factors that have driven the adoption of the EP across the world. They became popular with project financiers who were looking to adopt a common ESG risk mitigation framework for projects across the globe. The genesis of EP was partly in response to intense NGO criticism relating to lax environmental standards in projects financed by global banks in developing countries. Another objective for their formulation was to develop a banking industry framework for addressing environmental and social risks in project financing that could be applied globally and across all industry sectors. As more international banks have started following EP, these guidelines have become part and parcel of a majority of the international project finance deals.

Over the years, financial institutions in many developing economies such as Brazil and South Africa have adopted EP. The drivers for adoption of EP in many such countries were the following:

1. Participation in international deals and diversification to new geographies
2. Requirement of a sound ESG risk management system in their credit appraisal process globally recognised as a best practice
3. Transactions with multilateral institutions such as World Bank and IFC and lines of credit from other multilateral agencies that emphasize the need to mainstream ESG risk management in project finance deals
4. Civil society pressure on Banks to address adverse environmental and social impacts and need for transparency and stakeholder consultation in project development
5. Experience of projects being delayed and cancelled because of inadequate and improper resolution of environmental, ecological, social and cultural concerns

7   Challenges and Opportunities in Adopting EP by Indian Banks and Financial Institutions

In the Indian context, none of the drivers mentioned in the previous section on EP exist for Indian banks to be motivated in adopting enhanced ESG risk management standards in their credit appraisals. Investment for projects in the Indian economy has until now largely been driven by internal domestic sources. The Twelfth Plan period envisages funding from debt sources, 85 % of which is expected to come from domestic sources.

The project finance space in India is dominated by domestic banks and institutions, predominantly owned by the government. These government-owned institutions are more focused on following Indian regulatory requirements and do not feel the need to adopt any global ESG standards that are not mandated by Indian regulations. A lack of public participation in examining environmental and social issues associated with project development in India has similarly not helped the cause of Indian banks in adopting global benchmarks such as EP.

This has resulted in many of the Indian institutions not being focused on ESG issues and therefore not building internal capacities and capabilities to analyse and address such risks in their projects. Over the past few years, project execution risk has emerged as a major concern for all stakeholders. Mostly these execution risks are straightjacketed as delays due to land acquisition, securing regulatory approvals and cost and time overruns in projects and are increasingly quoted as reasons for delayed or subpar performance of projects by project financiers and project developers alike. Furthermore, many of them rely on a compliance-driven 'check the box' approach where obtaining requisite regulatory clearances is assumed to be sufficient to take care of ESG issues.

There is little appreciation among banks and financial institutions to understand the underlying environment and social requirements in projects that later crystallise and take the shape of challenging execution risk and lead to significant project delays in the first place. For example, delay in land acquisition could be due to lack of a proper consultation process with the local community or due to lack of fair compensation being awarded to those affected by the project or even inadequate restoration of lost livelihoods. Most project financiers in India today, however, are not capable of understanding and analysing these issues as potential risk to their projects.

There are three reasons Indian project financiers take such a stand. First, environment and social issues are always considered external to the project and carry a preconceived notion of being able to be 'managed' by project developers. Second, hiring trained in-house ESG experts is considered an additional expenditure that is avoidable. Third, tackling such situations is always in firefighting mode. Many project financing lenders therefore equate ESG risks to project development issues best left to the project developer to handle. A lack of understanding and focus on such issues has led Indian financiers to blindly rely on the ability of the project sponsor to deal with such 'execution issues' and bail out the project.

What many fail to realise is that ESG risks in India can no longer be treated in 'business as usual' mode. Blindly relying on the project sponsors to 'manage' ESG issues and relying on a 'check the box' compliance of regulatory approvals for ESG-related matters is no longer sufficient for insulating project lenders from such risks. A greater appreciation and analysis of ESG risks early on in the project life cycle is essential for ensuring that proper mitigation measures are adopted in a timely and effective manner and become part and parcel of the project's development and execution. This helps in preventing issues that may appear minor at the initial project funding stage from blowing up and later becoming major risks.

Many in Indian industry and the banking community feel that adopting a framework such as EP will involve taking on onerous commitments that go far beyond what the Indian national regulations require. As stated earlier, frameworks such as EP actually help project financiers analyse ESG risks material to their projects and therefore play a crucial role in mitigating risk in their lending business. Having said that, we do not believe there are material gaps between what Indian regulations warrant from projects and what frameworks such as EP require us to do except for the proper implementation of the regulations in spirit as well as in law.

Some of the major perceived gaps are attributed to areas of land acquisition and resettlement and rehabilitation (R&R). It is perceived that land purchases in India are not carried out at 'fair' prices and in a free and prior informed manner with the local community as required by international ESG Frameworks such as EP. Indian laws in this regard, however, have been evolving over time. Today, the process of land acquisition, public consultation and consent and requirements imposed by regulations such as the new Land Acquisition and R&R Bill on large projects provides sufficient checks and balances for dealing with all such related issues. What is required instead is to ensure that the various conditions imposed as part of the regulations and clearance process are followed in true spirit. The same is true with regard to labour welfare issues pertaining to health and hygiene, worker amenities as well as worker safety. Frameworks such as EP are immensely beneficial here. These frameworks help project financiers segregate such issues based on materiality and ensure effective implementation and monitoring of projects on such critical ESG aspects. The so-called gaps in requirements between frameworks such as EP and the Indian regulations are therefore more to do with implementation issues on the ground rather than any additional regulatory requirements.

Another reason often cited to explain the non-popularity of EP in India is the additional requirements with regard to disclosures that have to be followed. This may have been true in the past, but going forward, we do not see much merit in such arguments. Increasingly, many businesses are adopting additional disclosure requirements in the ESG space voluntarily by virtue of being affiliated to internationally acclaimed sustainability foras. A case in point are the signatories to the CDP and the numerous corporate entities issuing sustainability reports. There is a significant increase in CDP signatory investors from 39 in 2007 to 53 in 2012.[13] The recent SEBI Guidelines also make it mandatory for the top 100 listed entities in the BSE and NSE to submit a Business Responsibility Report (based on the National Voluntary Guidelines on Social, Environment and Economic Responsibilities of Businesses released by the Ministry of Corporate Affairs, GoI in August 2012a, b). Indian industry is thus becoming increasingly comfortable with the idea of increased disclosures.

The Ministry of Environment, Forest and Climate Change (MoEF&CC) has also begun to insist on online disclosure of assessment documents, environment performance and other compliance-related reports for projects. The process of public consultation as well as the process of awarding the terms of reference and final environmental clearance by MoEF&CC contains many stages where related documents are published on the MoEF&CC website. The new Land Acquisition and R&R Bill also requires public disclosure of social impact assessment reports and

---

[13] https://www.cdproject.net/en-US/Results/Pages/All-Investor-Reports.aspx

R&R schemes for projects. We believe, therefore, disclosure requirements as part of EP will not pose a significant hurdle for Indian firms in the future.

Another misplaced perception is that additional documentation required by EP is too onerous. Projects in India go through extensive legal and technical studies and due diligence for which detailed documentation is drawn up. Why, therefore, shouldn't the ESG due diligence, also an important part of the project appraisal process, not warrant some documentation? Once project developers and financiers start looking at ESG due diligence as being on par with the legal and technical due diligence of a project and an essential part of the project's appraisal, then the issue will cease to exist and will be dealt with automatically.

What many project financiers today fail to appreciate is that a proper ESG due diligence at the initial stage of a project will help identify important environmental and social issues and prevent them from snowballing into a major risk at a later stage. Local communities are increasingly becoming aware of their rights and are vocal in demanding the same from authorities and project proponents. Under India's constitutional provision of Article 21, citizens of India are entitled to a healthy environment. The creation of the National Green Tribunal (NGT) in October 2010 is a step in this direction. The NGT is a fast-track court that handles the expeditious disposal of the cases pertaining to environmental issues. Anyone can challenge the decisions of the MoEF&CC by approaching the NGT for expeditious disposal and redress of cases pertaining to environmental issues. This gives anyone affected by a project the right to make their voice heard. With courts becoming more active with respect to Public Interest Litigations (PILs), there is greater activism in the civil society with regard to ESG issues. There is, therefore, a growing and urgent need for building greater awareness of ESG issues among project financiers and developers.

Project financing in India is dominated by the domestic banks. Increasingly, however, we see that foreign debt and equity funds are playing a crucial role in financing projects. Many of the contributors to these funds are international institutional players who have a much greater appreciation of the ESG risk mitigation requirements for projects financed by them. Such players increasingly demand better disclosure as well as assessments of ESG risks from funds or institutions to whom they lend. Multilateral institutions are also investing in and funding projects as well as lending to Indian financial institutions through lines of credit. This presents another opportunity for Indian banks and institutions to learn and adopt ESG practices and institutionalise the ESG risk management procedures, thereby mainstreaming ESG appraisal in their credit due diligence process. This should hopefully motivate more people in the Indian industry and financial institutions to begin building capability in earnest to effectively deal with ESG issues.

8   The Way Forward

Indian banks and institutions need to develop a much greater appreciation of the ESG risks in the projects which they finance. As a first step, they need to develop capabilities to assess such risks in their portfolio. Setting up an environment team with personnel of relevant qualifications and background within their institutions to analyse ESG risks will be a crucial step in this direction. They should also employ external consultants to help with such assessments, just as they do today for technical and legal due diligence of projects. This will help ascertain the real reasons behind some of the execution delays that plague industry and infrastructure projects. Once banks are able to identify the ESG risks, they will be able to take concrete measures to minimise them. Adopting well- established and proven risk mitigation frameworks for ESG risks such as the EP will then be a logical progression for Indian banks. Institutions such as IDFC Ltd have demonstrated that this can be done in the Indian context. IDFC has a dedicated environment risk group that conducts a detailed due diligence of ESG risks for all category A and category B projects it finances. Suitable loan covenants are drawn up, and there is regular monitoring of projects to make sure that projects comply with the requisite ESG conditions. IDFC also recently became the first Indian financial institution to sign up to the Equator Principles. There is no reason why other Indian banks and institutions should not be able to follow IDFC's example and mainstream ESG risk assessment and mitigation in their day-to-day business operations.

Indian bankers also need to adopt a common framework for addressing ESG issues so that a level playing field is established and everyone is speaking the same language. This should be done by adopting a uniform framework towards identifying and addressing ESG risks and its impacts for projects in India. EP is one such framework that readily meets such a requirement and has been widely accepted and practised the world over.

EPFIs who have a presence in India can also help by ensuring that funds provided by them either directly to projects or routed through other financial intermediaries in India, both in form of debt and equity, are deployed in projects that are compliant with their global ESG risk management practices.

External funds in the form of external commercial borrowings and equity will continue to play a crucial role in meeting the funding requirements for infrastructure development in India in the near future. Equity funds for infrastructure projects are a risk capital that is scarce in India. Providers of equity funds in Indian projects therefore have greater leverage with project developers than anyone else. They are associated with a project at an earlier stage than a debt provider of funds. It will therefore be a good idea for the EP Association to enlist the support of foreign equity funds that are involved in project financing in India for propagating better ESG practices in Indian projects. By monitoring the end use of their funds, EPFIs and equity funds will help speed up the process of transferring their knowledge and expertise in ESG risk management issues to their Indian counterparts.

As is true for the entire banking sector in India, project financing is dominated by funding from public sector banks. Most of these public sector banks would be more comfortable with direction from the Reserve Bank of India (RBI) before adopting enhanced ESG risk mitigation frameworks such as the EP.

We believe that the Indian Banking Association with the help of RBI should take the initiative of building a working group comprising of leading Indian banks to explore ways to enhance the ESG risk mitigation measures within the banking community. As part of this process, the committee should formulate a common ESG Framework along the lines of the EP that will be used by all Indian banks for their project financing activities in India.

Failure to meet the challenges posed by ESG risks in project financing may lead to a situation whereby banks avoid taking such risks completely in their portfolios. This would be a shame as it would prevent them from participating in many project financing deals and lead to a range of lost opportunity for financing in India.

Indian banks should also realise that as financial intermediaries, the biggest impact they have on the natural environment and on society is through the business activities of their clients. It is therefore imperative that they take the initiative of enhancing their ESG assessment and mitigation capabilities. They need to understand and mitigate the ESG risks in their projects and also demonstrate their commitment to sustainable development not only through participation in various sustainability foras and also by adopting a comprehensive ESG Framework such as the EP.

References

ACC Limited. (2011). *Sustainable development report*

Carbon Disclosure Project. https://www.cdproject.net/en-US/Results/Pages/All-Investor-Reports. aspx

Constitution of India. Accessed at http://india.gov.in/my-government/constitution-india

CPCB. (2010). *Pollution control acts, rules, notifications issued thereunder* (6th ed.). New Delhi: CPCB.

Economic Survey, Government of India (2005–2006).

Economic Survey, Government of India (2012–2013).

Hindustan Unilever Ltd (2012–2013) *Making sustainable living common place—business responsibility report*

Ministry of Corporate Affairs. (2012). *National voluntary guidelines on socio-economic and environmental responsibilities of business*

Ministry of Corporate Affairs. (2012). The company bill

Ministry of Environment and Forests. www.envfor.nic.in/

MoEF. (2011). *Sustainable development in India: stocktaking in the run-up to Rio 20+*

Our Common Future. (1987). Electronic version, accessed at http://www.un-documents.net/wced-ocf.htm

Planning Commission, Government of India, 12th Five Year Plan (Vol. 1), accessed at http://planningcommision.nic.in

Planning Commission, Government of India. (2011). Faster, sustainable and more inclusive growth: An approach to Twelfth Five Year Plan

Sujit, J. (2012) 80 Indian companies are now doing sustainability report, *Times of India*

Sustainability Outlook, accessed at http://www.sustainabilityoutlook.in/news/sbi-become-signa tory-carbon-disclosure-project#sthash.PaHAa6VU.dpuf

(2013) *The right to fair compensation and transparency in land acquisition, rehabilitation and resettlement bill.* Government of India.

CSR Reporting and Its Implication for Socially Responsible Investment in China

Olaf Weber and Haiying Lin

Abstract Corporate social responsibility (CSR) reporting has grown significantly in China during the past decade. This chapter assesses the status of Chinese CSR reporting and its main drivers as well as firms' subsequent social, environmental and financial performance. Employing data from 130 Chinese listed companies, we assessed the development trend of CSR reporting and suggest that such a growth is mainly driven by external pressure (e.g. regulations). Our statistical testing found positive associations between CSR reporting and firms' subsequent social, environmental and financial performance. Our results have important implications for social responsible investors who focus on both financial and social returns. They, therefore, can leverage firms' CSR reports as indicators for their investment decisions.

1 Introduction

This contribution describes the development of corporate social responsibility (CSR) reporting and its connection with corporate social performance (CSP) as well as with the financial performance of firms in China. Since CSR reporting increased significantly over the last decade, it can provide helpful information for socially responsible investing. The paper will demonstrate that CSR reporting affects both CSP and financial performance positively. Consequently, socially responsible or responsible investors may use CSR reports of Chinese companies in order to analyse whether a company meets the non-financial criteria of (socially) responsible investing. Furthermore, we suggest that socially responsible investing in China is attractive from a financial perspective because CSR reporting and CSP positively influence the financial performance of firms.

The data presented in this chapter is for securities of Chinese corporations that are traded at one or more of the big Chinese stock exchanges, the Hong Kong stock

O. Weber (✉) • H. Lin
School for Environment, Enterprise and Development, University of Waterloo, Waterloo, Canada
e-mail: oweber@uwaterloo.ca

© Springer International Publishing Switzerland 2015
K. Wendt (ed.), *Responsible Investment Banking*, CSR, Sustainability, Ethics & Governance, DOI 10.1007/978-3-319-10311-2_27

exchange and Shanghai and Shenzhen stock exchanges. The analysis is important from a responsible investment point of view because investments in emerging countries, and particularly in China, are becoming increasingly attractive financially and from a sustainable development point of view.

2 Background

China's economic miracle comes with huge environmental costs. To boost GDP growth and support the expansion of the manufacturing sector as a world factory, China consumed excessive energy resources and produced large amount of environmental pollution (Wang, Qin and Cui 2010). In 2007, China overtook the USA in becoming the world's largest emitter of greenhouse gases. Series of environmental scandals occurred lately, which include the foggy capital, cancer villages, toxic milk powder and coal mining accidents. Most of these environmental issues are related to business operations (Olivier et al. 2012).

We therefore focus our research on Chinese firms, particularly the listed firms, because they are under increasing institutional pressure to report their environmental initiatives and demonstrate their effort in advancing their environmental performance. Despite the significant environmental impacts of Chinese companies, firms' level of CSR reporting has been very low in the early 2000 (Wong et al. 2010). Chinese firms tend not to conduct or disclose any CSR practices (Liu and Anbumozhi 2009) since they perceive CSR as a trade-off to their bottom line (Winn et al. 2012). It has been the external pressure from government agencies that motivated firms to report their CSR activities. But often both firms and investors are unaware of the connection between CSR reporting and their subsequent environmental and financial performance.

We aim to examine the development of CSR reporting in China and investigate whether firms that report their CSR activities tend to be associated with better environmental and financial performances. We test these associations with data collected from 130 Chinese listed companies. Among them, 40 firms are listed in Hong Kong, 50 in Shanghai and 40 in Shenzhen stock exchanges. They constitute the index of the respective stock exchange.

2.1 Reporting of Key Performance Indicators

We examined whether the firms in the sample published a CSR report and whether they report about the key performance indicators (KPI) of their industry. KPIs are the most important indicators to measure the impact of an industry (Hesse 2010). KPIs are an indicator for focusing on CSR issues that are crucial for an industry and thus indicate the validity of a CSR report. Our results suggest that CSR reporting in China grew significantly since 2005, and such growth is mainly driven by government influence and regulations. Our statistical testing demonstrated that CSR reporting is positively associated with firms' subsequent environmental and financial performance.

3 The Development of CSR Reporting in China

CSR refers to the social and environmental impact and responsibilities that businesses should consider to include in their business operation (Wang, Qin and Cui 2010). CSR reporting is an activity to present the performance of a firm and a means of communication to stakeholders such as shareholders or investors (Chan and Welford 2005; Ziek 2009), employees, clients or communities. CSR reports are mainly published to communicate positive achievements of the publishing company (Niskanen and Nieminen 2001; Spence 2009). They are also useful tools for both the reporting firm and stakeholders, such as investors, and are clearly an indicator of the importance of CSR in a firm.

Chinese firms did not disclose any CSR information (Liu and Anbumozhi 2009) prior to 2000. The growing environmental pressure in China and the need for an efficient use of resources, however, caused a change in the attitudes from pure financial goals to a more integrated model of growth that integrates environmental risks. In 2001, Chinese listed firms were required to disclose their environmental risks in the prospectus for initial public offering (IPO). Responding to this requirement, the China National Petroleum Co Ltd released China's first CSR report in 2001 (Wang et al. 2010). Between 2001 and 2004, CSR reporting in China developed very slowly (Ying Xu and Jie Niu 2010), and there was still lack of transparency, reflected by the relatively low amount of CSR reporting, in Chinese firms. Some CSR studies showed that about 40 % of the sampled companies did not disclose substantial environmental data to the public (Kuo et al. 2011; Noronha et al. 2012), which could partially be explained by firms' intent to maintain business confidentiality (Kimber and Lipton 2005).

This stagnate phenomenon changed in 2005, however, when China CSR Association developed its first China CSR Standard and released China CSR Beijing statement. This agency started to rate and publish the environmental performance of Chinese companies (Liu and Anbumozhi 2009). Further, a Chinese Company Law in 2006 required companies to conduct social responsibility in their businesses. The Chinese Ministry of Environmental Protection also regulated environmental reporting and introduced mandatory environmental reporting for heavy-polluting companies. During the process, more attention has been paid to corporate CSR systems, and there is a growing public awareness and expectation regarding companies' roles and responsibilities in addressing social and environmental problems (Wang et al. 2010). These series of regulations and policies, and heighten public awareness, put significant pressures on Chinese firms to report their CSR performance. CSR and connected reporting activities have experienced increasing

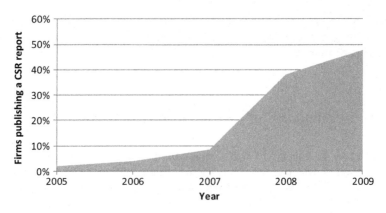

Fig. 1 Percentage of Chinese firms publishing CSR reports

growth in China (Moon and Shen 2010), with most of the growth concentrated on year 2005 onwards.

Our data analysis of the 130 Chinese listed firms between 2005 and 2009 also suggests a similar, remarkable development trend. The percentage of CSR reporting among Chinese listed companies increased significantly from below 5 % in 2005 to more than 80 % in 2009 (see Fig. 1). Along with the growth in the number of firms that conduct CSR reporting (quantity), we simultaneously observed the improvement of their reporting quality. In 2009, about 96 % of Chinese listed firms disclosed information related to one of their industry's key performance indicators, 39 % disclosed two key performance indicators, while 38 % disclosed three key performance indicators.

In line with other Asian countries, international reporting frameworks are increasingly used in China (Gill et al. 2010). Frameworks such as the Global Reporting Initiative (GRI) and third-party verification help enhance the quality of CSR reports (Fonseca 2010; Lober et al. 1997) in China. As we described above, many Chinese companies use the global GRI reporting standard for their CSR reporting. According to the latest statistics of the Global Reporting Initiative (www. globalreporting.org), 203 Chinese companies report their sustainability performance using the Global Reporting Initiative (GRI) Framework in 2011. This is 5.8 % of all reporting organisations worldwide.

4 CSR Reporting in China: External Pressures as the Main Driver

Cultural, developmental, market, regulative, and political influences play an important role in firms' activities, and this is also valid for activities such as CSR reporting (Husted and Allen 2006; Jennings and Zandbergen 1995). Environmental and sustainability management in Chinese corporations are mainly externally driven (Wing-Hung Lo et al. 2010; Wong 2009). In the case of CSR reporting, our study suggests that the growth, both in frequency and in quality of CSR reporting in China since 2005, is mainly driven by external pressures such as government regulations.

Along with regulation, government control and ownership play significant roles in influencing Chinese firms' likelihood to report CSR. Compared to other Asian Pacific countries, China's economy is dominated by state-owned enterprises (SOEs), and governments have strong influence over SOE's operations (Kimber and Lipton 2005). In 2008, the State-Owned Assets Supervision and Administration Commission of the State Council (SASAC) released a guideline on Social Responsibility Implementation for about 150 government-controlled enterprises (Lin 2010). Such regulation explained why state-owned corporations tend to disclose more environment, social and governance (ESG) information than other corporations (Tagesson et al. 2009). Our data analysis of 130 Chinese listed firms also suggested that government-controlled corporations are more likely to publish a CSR report than non-government-controlled firms.

Further, our data analysis of CSR reporting shows significant variances among the three stock exchanges and that companies listed in Hong Kong stock exchange tend to report CSR less than companies listed in two other stock exchanges. Such CSR reporting variances can be explained by regulation. In 2008, the Shenzhen Stock Exchange and the Shanghai Stock Exchange both introduced social responsibility instructions (Noronha et al. 2012) and published guidelines on ESG and environmental disclosure for listed companies (Lin 2010; Siddy 2009). The Hong Kong Stock Exchange, however, did not introduce such guidelines until 2013 (Hong Kong Stock Exchange 2012). As such, the introduction of CSR Guidelines at Shenzhen and Shanghai Stock Exchange has significant impact over their listed firms' likelihood to report CSR.

We use firms' size as a proxy of firms' external pressures. Our data analysis results suggest that larger firms that are subject to stronger external regulatory forces tend to report their CSR performance more than smaller firms. The partial explanation of this phenomenon is that smaller firms are not aware of positive benefits associated with CSR reporting (Wong et al. 2010) as such their CSR reporting behaviour is less likely to be internal driven. There is limited research assessing the association between firms' CSR reporting and their subsequent environmental and financial performance. In the following section, we will fill this literature gap by assessing these associations.

5 The Association Between CSR Reporting and the Subsequent Corporate Social and Financial Performance

Would CSR reporting send authentic signal regarding firms' corporate social performance (CSP)? Previous literature shows controversial results regarding the association between firms' CSR reporting behaviour and their subsequent social and environmental performances. In general, CSR reporting is seen as an important tool to improve CSR management and environmental or social performance (Sumiani et al. 2007). While Clarkson et al. (2008) found a positive association between environmental performance and the level of discretionary environmental disclosures, Patten (2002) indicated a negative relation between CSP and the disclosure for the corporations.

A recent China study by Liu et al. (2010) found that companies publishing environmental information under the government-oriented disclosure programme improved their environmental performance because the publication encourages the corporations to manage their environmental problems. In line with this study, we further tested the association of CSR reporting and firms' CSP using the China Top 100 Green Companies Report (China Entrepreneur Club, 2012) data. This report uses proprietary methods and different criteria from CSR reporting to rank the sustainability performance of Chinese companies. It thus provides an independent measurement of CSP compared to CSR reporting. We tested whether companies that frequently report CSR are more likely to be listed as Top 100 Green Company. Our statistical tests suggest that CSR reporters are more likely to have greener environmental performance. The likelihood to be listed in the Top 100 Green Companies list was 7 % lower for non-reporters than for those that have published CSR reports.

Furthermore, frameworks such as the Global Reporting Initiative (GRI) and third-party verification contribute to the quality of reports (Fonseca 2010; Lober et al. 1997) and to their transparency (Kolk and Perego 2010) in China. As we described above, many Chinese companies use the global GRI reporting standard for their CSR reporting.

5.1 The Development and the Quality of CSR Reporting

Before we report on the connection between CSR reporting and financial returns, we further assess whether firms' CSR reporting is associated with higher financial performance. CSR reporting often comes with a cost. CSP, which involves stakeholder management and environmental management, requires significant resources (Orlitzky et al. 2011), and Chinese corporations are not an exception to this rule (Zeng et al. 2010). As such, it is important for firms and investors to become aware of whether CSR reporting may associate firms with higher long-term financial benefit.

In order to analyse the connection between CSR reporting and financial returns, we used data for the years 2007–2009 for CSR reporting, and we applied a 1-year lag in measuring these firms' subsequent financial returns. Adopting such a data collection method (1-year time lag) is due to the time interval that is needed for the market to react to the publication of a CSR report. We also control for market capitalisation, risk (covariance), government control and industry in our models.

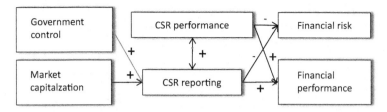

Fig. 2 Connection between CSR reporting, firm size, CSP and financial indicators

Our statistical model suggests that CSR reporting is positively associated with firms' subsequent financial performance, and 24.4 % of the variance in firms' financial performance can be explained by firms' prior CSR reporting behaviour. The result suggests that the financial return of firms that published CSR reports are 2 % higher than the return of those not publishing CSR reports. The only control variable that had an impact in addition to CSR reporting was covariance, representing risk. As expected, higher financial risks were correlated with lower financial returns.

Conclusions

Our assessment of the correlation between CSR reporting and the subsequent corporate social performance (CSP) not only contributes to the academic literature but also enhances the knowledge of socially responsible investors; it is important to know whether good CSR reporting corresponds to high CSP.

We assessed the development of CSR reporting in Chinese corporations and its relation to financial market returns. The analysis was based on data of members of the three main Chinese stock exchanges indexes SZSE Component Index, Hang Seng Index and SSE Composite Index. Our results demonstrated a significant increase in both the frequency and quality of CSR reporting in Chinese companies since 2005. While in 2005 only 4 % of the corporations in our sample published CSR reports, in 2009 more than 80 % of the corporations published CSR information.

These findings have important managerial contributions. CSR reporting increased significantly over the last decade and therefore provides helpful information for socially responsible investing. Whether firms publish a CSR report signals to socially responsible investors the firms' subsequent environmental and financial performance. As such, these investors may have more confidence in using CSR reports of Chinese companies for analysing whether these firms comply to the non-financial criteria of (socially) responsible investing. Furthermore, knowing that CSR reporting may enhance investors' confidence and lead to positive financial returns will also motivate Chinese firms to report their CSR practices.

The connection between CSR reporting and the different variables analysed in this study is presented in Fig. 2.

(continued)

Our results suggest that CSR reporting is influenced by the size of a firm (e.g. proxy of external pressures) and by their government ownership. Bigger firms and those that are government controlled are more likely to publish CSR reports. Our results also suggest that CSP is positively associated with CSR reporting. CSR report helps communicate CSP to stakeholders, which consequently increases the transparency of the firm. CSR reporting thus reduce corporate financial risks, because they are means to manage corporate risks and opportunities.

As such, CSR reporting is a tool that helps (socially) responsible investors to analyse Chinese firms. Through the analysis of CSR reports, investors are not only able to gather information about the corporate social performance, but also enhance their awareness of corporate financial risks and opportunities. The growing number of CSR reports also enables socially responsible investors to invest in Chinese securities.

References

Chan, J. C., & Welford, R. (2005). Assessing corporate environmental risk in China: An evaluation of reporting activities of Hong Kong listed enterprises. *Corporate Social Responsibility and Environmental Management, 12*, 88–104. doi:10.1002/csr.088.

Clarkson, P. M., Li, Y., Richardson, G. D., & Vasvari, F. P. (2008). Revisiting the relation between environmental performance and environmental disclosure: An empirical analysis. *Accounting, Organizations and Society, 33*(4–5), 303–327. doi:10.1016/j.aos.2007.05.003.

Fonseca, A. (2010). How credible are mining corporations' sustainability reports? A critical analysis of external assurance under the requirements of the international council on mining and metals. *Corporate Social Responsibility and Environmental Management, 17*(6), 355–370. doi:10.1002/csr.230.

Gill, A., Allen, J., & Powell, S. (2010). *CG Watch 2010—Corporate governance in Asia* (p. 6). Hong Kong: Credit Lyonnais Securities Asia in Cooperation with the Asian Corporate Governance Association.

Hesse, A. (2010). *SD-KPI standard 2010–2014*. Muenster, Germany: Dr. Axel Hesse.

Hong Kong Stock Exchange. (2012, August 31, 2012). *The exchange publishes consultation conclusions on environmental, social and governance reporting guide*. Retrieved October 24, 2012, from http://www.hkex.com.hk/eng/newsconsul/hkexnews/2012/120831news.htm

Husted, B. W., & Allen, D. B. (2006). Corporate social responsibility in the multinational enterprise: Strategic and institutional approaches. *Journal of International Business Studies, 37*(6), 838–849.

Jennings, P. D., & Zandbergen, P. A. (1995). Ecologically sustainable organizations: An institutional approach. *Academy of Management Review, 20*(4), 1015–1052.

Kimber, D., & Lipton, P. (2005). Corporate governance and business ethics in the Asia-Pacific region. *Business and Society, 44*(2), 178–210. doi:10.1177/0007650305275300.

Kolk, A., & Perego, P. (2010). Determinants of the adoption of sustainability assurance statements: An international investigation. *Business Strategy and the Environment, 19*(3), 182–198. doi:10.1002/bse.643.

Kuo, L., Yeh, C.-C., & Yu, H.-C. (2011). Disclosure of corporate social responsibility and environmental management: Evidence from China. *Corporate Social Responsibility and Environmental Management, 19*(5), 273–287. doi:10.1002/csr.274.

Lin, L.-W. (2010). Corporate social responsibility in China: Window dressing or structural change? *Berkeley Journal of International Law, 28*(1), 64–100.

Liu, X., & Anbumozhi, V. (2009). Determinant factors of corporate environmental information disclosure: An empirical study of Chinese listed companies. *Journal of Cleaner Production, 17*(6), 593–600. doi:10.1016/j.jclepro.2008.10.001.

Liu, X., Yu, Q., Fujitsuka, T., Liu, B., Bi, J., & Shishime, T. (2010). Functional mechanisms of mandatory corporate environmental disclosure: An empirical study in China. *Journal of Cleaner Production, 18*(8), 823–832. doi:10.1016/j.jclepro.2009.12.022.

Lober, D. J., Bynum, D., Campbell, E., & Jacques, M. (1997). The 100 plus corporate environmental report study: A survey of an evolving environmental management tool. *Business Strategy and the Environment, 6*(2), 57–73. doi:10.1002/(sici)1099-0836(199705)6:2<57::aid-bse81>3.0.co;2-e.

Moon, J., & Shen, X. (2010). CSR in China research: Salience, focus and nature. *Journal of Business Ethics, 94*(4), 613–629. doi:10.1007/s10551-009-0341-4.

Niskanen, J., & Nieminen, T. (2001). The objectivity of corporate environmental reporting: A study of Finnish listed firms' environmental disclosures. *Business Strategy and the Environment, 10*(1), 29–37.

Noronha, C., Tou, S., Cynthia, M. I., & Guan, J. J. (2012). Corporate social responsibility reporting in China: An overview and comparison with major trends. *Corporate Social Responsibility and Environmental Management, 20*(1), 29–42. doi:10.1002/csr.1276.

Olivier, J. G. J., Janssens-Maenhout, G., & Peters, J. A. H. W. (2012). *Trends in global CO2 emissions—2012 Report. Background studies* (p. 40). The Hague, Ispra: PBL Netherlands Environmental Assessment Agency and European Commission's Joint Research Centre.

Orlitzky, M., Siegel, D. S., & Waldman, D. A. (2011). Strategic corporate social responsibility and environmental sustainability. *Business and Society, 50*(1), 6–27. doi:10.1177/0007650310394323.

Patten, D. M. (2002). The relation between environmental performance and environmental disclosure: A research note. *Accounting, Organizations and Society, 27*(8), 763–773. doi:10.1016/s0361-3682(02)00028-4.

Siddy, D. (2009). *Exchanges and sustainable investment* (p. 44). Paris, France: World Federation of Exchanges.

Spence, C. (2009). Social and environmental reporting and the corporate ego. *Business Strategy and the Environment, 18*(4), 254–265. doi:10.1002/bse.600.

Sumiani, Y., Haslinda, Y., & Lehman, G. (2007). Environmental reporting in a developing country: A case study on status and implementation in Malaysia. *Journal of Cleaner Production, 15*(10), 895–901. doi:10.1016/j.jclepro.2006.01.012.

Tagesson, T., Blank, V., Broberg, P., & Collin, S.-O. (2009). What explains the extent and content of social and environmental disclosures on corporate websites: A study of social and environmental reporting in Swedish listed corporations. *Corporate Social Responsibility and Environmental Management, 16*(6), 352–364. doi:10.1002/csr.194.

Wang, J., Qin, S., & Cui, Y. (2010). Problems and prospects of CSR system development in China. *International Journal of Business and Management, 5*(12), 128.

Wing-Hung Lo, C., Fryxell, G. E., & Tang, S.-Y. (2010). Stakeholder pressures from perceived environmental impacts and the effect on corporate environmental management programmes in China. *Environmental Politics, 19*(6), 888–909.

Winn, M. I., Pinkse, J., & Illge, L. (2012). Case studies on trade-offs in corporate sustainability. *Corporate Social Responsibility and Environmental Management, 19*(2), 63–68. doi:10.1002/csr.293.

Wong, L. (2009). Corporate social responsibility in China: Between the market and the search for a sustainable growth development. *Asian Business and Management, 8*(2), 129–148.

Wong, A., Long, F., & Elankumaran, S. (2010). Business students' perception of corporate social responsibility: The United States, China, and India. *Corporate Social Responsibility and Environmental Management, 17*(5), 299–310. doi:10.1002/csr.216.

Xu, Y., & Niu, J. (2010). CSR evaluation index system. *Cooperative Economy & Science, 3*, 12.

Zeng, S. X., Xu, X. D., Dong, Z. Y., & Tam, V. W. Y. (2010). Towards corporate environmental information disclosure: An empirical study in China. *Journal of Cleaner Production, 18*(12), 1142–1148. doi:10.1016/j.jclepro.2010.04.005.

Ziek, P. (2009). Making sense of CSR communication. *Corporate Social Responsibility and Environmental Management, 16*(3), 137–145. doi:10.1002/csr.183.

Sustainability on Planet Bank

Heffa Schücking

1 Introduction

The past decade has seen an enormous growth of sustainability initiatives in the banking sector. Acronyms such as CSR (corporate social responsibility) and ESG (environmental and social governance) have become standard bank vocabulary. Most large commercial banks have signed on to a multitude of voluntary commitments such as the Equator Principles, the Global Compact or the UNEP FI Statement on Sustainable Development, to name a few. Many banks produce regular CSR reports to document their achievements, and a new class of consultants has sprung up to analyse banks' environmental management systems. Commercial banks now compete among each other to receive favourable environmental ratings or to be included in so-called ethical indices. Sustainability has become a financial industry standard.

But has this made banks' lending more environmentally sensitive, their investment banking more responsible, their portfolios more sustainable? We explore this question on the background of an unfolding planetary crisis in which banks—for better or for worse—have a major role to play.

2 The Highway to Hell

In 2010, almost 200 nations agreed that global warming must be limited to 2 °C to avoid worst-case climate change scenarios. Reports from the world's leading climate scientists, the International Energy Agency (IEA) and the World Bank, however, all concur that we are currently heading towards a global temperature rise

H. Schücking (✉)
Urgewald, Sassenberg, Germany
e-mail: heffa@urgewald.de

© Springer International Publishing Switzerland 2015
K. Wendt (ed.), *Responsible Investment Banking*, CSR, Sustainability, Ethics & Governance, DOI 10.1007/978-3-319-10311-2_28

of **more than double** the 2 °C limit. In its "Turn Down the Heat" report, the World Bank warns that if current emission trends continue, we could be living in a 4 °C world as early as the 2060s. Some of the predicted impacts are a 50 % drop in water availability in many regions, large-scale displacement of populations, an increase in epidemic diseases, rising sea levels and extreme heat waves "expected to potentially exceed the adaptive capacities of many societies and natural systems". In short, a world the report calls "unmanageable".[1] The report also estimates that if this scenario comes to pass, "a further warming to levels over 6 °C would likely occur over the following centuries".[2]

Even the current "modest" global temperature rise of 0.8 °C is already evoking real and significant changes to the Earth's climate and ecosystems. Arctic sea ice reached a record minimum in September 2012, halving the area of ice covering the Arctic Ocean in summers over the past 30 years. The past decade has seen an exceptional number of extreme heat waves around the world such as the 2012–2013 drought in the United States, which impacted 80 % of the nation's agricultural lands. Since 1980, extreme weather events have tripled worldwide. At the opening session of the 2013 UN Climate Summit, Yeb Sano, a civil servant from the Philippines, struggled to find words to describe the destruction that the hellstorm Haiyan had brought to his country. "Super Typhoon Haiyan was nothing we have ever experienced before, or perhaps nothing that any country has experienced before. To anyone who continues to deny the reality that is climate change, I dare you to get off your ivory tower", said Sano.[3] His is one of many testimonies that millions of people around the world are already suffering the impacts of a changing climate.

3 The Culprit Is Coal

The single greatest source of the carbon dioxide (CO_2) emissions heating up our planet is coal. Each ton of coal burned produces around 2.4 tons of CO_2, and each molecule of CO_2 stays in the atmosphere for hundreds and sometimes even thousands of years.[4] Yet, perversely, the more we talk about climate change, the more we mine and burn coal. Since 2000, global coal production has grown by more than 69 % and now amounts to a staggering 7.9 billion tons annually.[5] Since 2005, the

---

[1] "Turn Down the Heat—Why a 4 °C World Must be Avoided", World Bank, 2012.

[2] "Turn Down the Heat—Why a 4 °C World Must be Avoided", World Bank, 2012.

[3] http://www.rtcc.org/2013/11/11/its-time-to-stop-this-madness-philippines-plea-at-un-climate-talks/

[4] "Nasa Scientists on 400 ppm CO_2", Countercurrents.org, May 22, 2013.

[5] The World Coal Association (WCA) provides an estimate of 7.831 billion tons global production for 2012. Its estimate for China is, however, 111 million tons lower than the data provided by the China National Coal Association. Data for Australia also seems too low by 39 million tons, based on the statistics of the Australian Bureau of Resources and Agricultural Economics. When taking these figures into account, the corrected total is 7.981 billion tons.

year the Kyoto Protocol came into force, the installed capacity of coal-fired power plants increased worldwide by 35 %.[6] Coal has been the fastest growing energy source for every year of the past decade.

The frightening fact is that we have very little time left to change course. The International Energy Agency's chief economist Fatih Birol warns that "we need to change our way of consuming energy within the next 3 or 4 years" because otherwise "in 2017, all of the emissions that allow us to stay under 2 °C will be locked in".[7] As public policy responses to climate change are woefully slow, and even optimists expect that an international climate agreement will not come into force before 2020, the development of the coal sector over the next crucial years will, to a large degree, be determined by the financial decisions of investors and banks.

4   The Power of the Finance Sector

New coal investments require huge amounts of capital. The construction of a 600 MW coal-fired power plant can cost up to US$2 billion. Cost estimates for developing new mines vary from location to location but can also be extremely capital intensive. The costs for developing the Alpha coal mine in Australia's Galilee Basin are, for example, estimated at US$4 billion, while the construction costs for the associated rail and port infrastructure to transport the coal are expected to top US$6 billion.[8]

Banks play a key role in enabling these developments by providing loans or underwriting bond and share issues to mobilise financial resources for the coal sector. Even the largest mining companies or utilities typically rely on banks to provide or mobilise the lion's share of capital for their investments. By the same token, banks, of course, also play a key role in mobilising financial resources for the renewable sector and energy efficiency investments. Through their allocation of financial resources, banks are therefore in a unique position to either help or hurt our climate.

---

[6] "International Energy Statistics Database", US Energy Information Administration.

[7] "Fatih Birol: Our Global Energy Future", Forbes, August 3, 2013.

[8] "Stranded—A Financial Analysis of GVK's proposed Alpha Coal Project in Australia's Galilee Basin", Institute for Energy Economics and Financial Analysis, 2013.

5 Banks and Climate

In contrast to many big players in the coal industry (who are still in a state of climate change denial), banks do generally recognise that climate change is happening. Surfing the web pages of the world's largest commercial banks, there is an abundance of statements about "combatting climate change". But when a bank says it is committed to "reducing its carbon footprint", it is not talking about its portfolio, but about the operational emissions resulting from lighting, heating and air conditioning its offices or from the car and air travel of its employees. With few exceptions, these are the only emissions that banks report on and take responsibility for.

A 2013 study by the World Development Movement on the Royal Bank of Scotland (RBS) puts this into perspective. In 2012, RBS reported operational emissions of 735,000 tons of CO_2 equivalent. The World Development Movement analysed the fossil fuel deals in the bank's lending portfolio and concluded that RBS' true carbon footprint is up to 1,200 times as high. RBS' financed emissions were possibly 1.6 times as high as the entire CO_2 emissions of the United Kingdom in 2012.[9]

While most large commercial banks provide figures on their annual investments into renewable energy, they neither track nor publish their support for dirty fossil fuel investments. When it comes to their core business, banks are still in a state of denial regarding their climate responsibility.

6 Banking on Coal

To understand which institutions are bankrolling the enormous expansion of the coal sector, Urgewald, BankTrack, the Polish Green Network and CEE Bankwatch recently analysed the financing of 70 coal mining companies. Collectively, these companies account for 52 % of global coal production. Our study "Banking on Coal" shows that 89 commercial banks channelled more than 118 billion euros into these companies between 2005 and mid-2013. The lion's share of this finance— 71 %—was provided by only 20 banks. The following chart shows the top 20 "coal mining banks" identified in our research (Fig. 1):

Ironically, these banks are quite vocal regarding their concern about global warming and the importance of tackling climate change. The complete disconnect between banks' statements on climate change and their actual portfolios leads to the impression that they are suffering from a split personality disorder. How else to explain that Bank of America believes it is "financing a low-carbon economy", that

---

[9] "RBS's true carbon emissions 2012: An estimate of emissions resulting from energy loans made during that year, and the shortcomings of the existing reporting framework", World Development Movement, 2012.

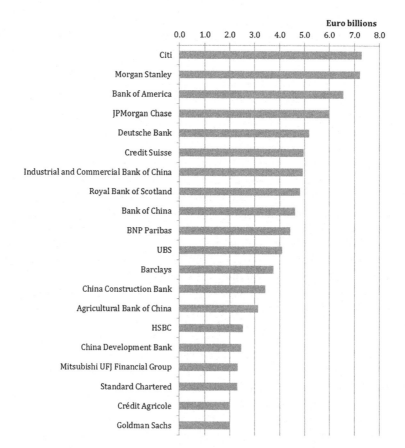

Fig. 1 Top 20 coal mining banks 2005 to mid-2013

Credit Suisse claims to "care for climate" or that BNP Paribas thinks it is "combatting climate change"?

7 Subprime Carbon

To compound the picture, what do banks' research departments say about coal investments? Analysts from several of the largest commercial banks such as Citibank, Deutsche Bank, HSBC and Goldman Sachs have recently begun to question the business rationale for further investments in coal. A 2013 Citibank report, for example, states that half of the value ascribed to the thermal coal assets of large mining companies such as BHP Billiton and Rio Tinto could be lost if the world took decisive action on climate change by 2020.[10] Analysts from Goldman Sachs warn equity investors that "an ice-free summer at the North Pole" or a single extreme weather event could swing public opinion and force governments "to respond with drastically tighter environmental regulations that would further erode the long-term demand for coal".[11] These reports also mention other threats to coal investments such as clean air regulation, conflicts around water availability and increased competition by renewables and shale gas, to mention just a few. They all concur that investments in so-called "pure" coal companies are most at risk.

But the business departments of the same banks are not listening. In its May 2013 research report, Deutsche Bank writes "most thermal coal growth projects will struggle to earn a positive return for their owners". Four months later, in September 2013, Deutsche Bank nonetheless took a decision to underwrite a share offering for Coal India, the world's largest "pure" coal company. Other participating banks are Goldman Sachs, Bank of America, Credit Suisse and three Indian investment banks. Together, these banks aim to raise 1 billion euros for Coal India and help the company turn some of the country's most valuable forests and few remaining tiger habitats into open-cast coal mines.[12] Among the banks that also (unsuccessfully) bid on the Coal India deal were Citibank and HSBC—banks whose research departments have been particularly outspoken about the risks of investing in coal.

If we have learnt anything from the subprime mortgage crash that triggered the current global recession, it is that banks are not good learners. They are deal driven and notoriously short-term in their perspective. Even if some bank analysts are starting to read the writing on the wall regarding subprime carbon, this isn't stopping decision-makers in the banks' business departments and boardrooms from jumping onto the next coal deal.

One of the most alarming results of our study "Banking on Coal" is the rapid growth rate of banks' financial contributions to the coal mining sector. Since 2005—the year the Kyoto Protocol came into force—commercial banks' financing for coal mining companies has increased by 397 %! While governments are still debating a regulation of the coal sector, commercial banks are speeding ahead with investments that are undermining our common future.

8   Banks as Coal Traders

Banks do not just lend money to the coal industry – in some cases, they **are** the coal industry. A case in point is Goldman Sachs. Through its subsidiary, Colombian Natural Resources, the US investment bank owns two coal mines and a coal port in

---

[10] "Unburnable Carbon—A Catalyst for Debate", Citi, April 2013.

[11] "The window for thermal coal investment is closing", Goldman Sachs, July 2013.

[12] "Goldman and Deutsche Bank back Coal India despite their environmental standards", The Guardian, sustainable business, October 1, 2013.

Colombia. The La Francia and El Hatillo coal mines jointly produced more than 5.5 million tons of coal in 2012 and are highly controversial because of their extreme water and air pollution impacts. The inhabitants of El Hatillo have appealed to the UN Special Representative for the right to food as the mine has completely destroyed their livelihoods.[13] No wonder the Public Eye Award for the world's worst corporate offender went to Goldman Sachs in 2013.

Several of the biggest banks are also involved in trading coal, both physically and on paper through derivatives. This includes proprietary trading (from the bank's own capital) as well as trading on behalf of clients. Banks involved in trading coal include Morgan Stanley, Goldman Sachs, Credit Suisse, Deutsche Bank, Société Générale, Barclays, Standard Chartered, the Macquarie Group and Bank of America (via Merrill Lynch Commodities).[14] In practice, this means that Merrill Lynch Commodities transports coal around the world on vessels chartered by its own in-house shipping brokerage, while Standard Chartered sells coal it bought in Indonesia via an off-take loan agreement[15] and Deutsche Bank agrees to buy a fixed amount of coal from Latin American suppliers each month in order to help mining companies realise their growth plans.[16]

It's bizarre to see how the very same banks that are wheelers and dealers in the international coal trade pride themselves on their climate commitments. Deutsche Bank offers a typical example of this schizophrenia: It calls itself a "climate ambassador"[17] on its webpage, but is also proud to have been designated "Coal House of the Year" in 2013.

9   Public Banks Moving Away from Coal

While commercial banks continue to expand their coal portfolios, a number of international public banks have recently taken decisions to move out of the coal sector. In July 2013, the World Bank acknowledged the devastating impacts of coal on our climate and stated in its new "Energy Sector Directions Paper" that the bank will no longer fund new coal-fired power plants "except in rare circumstances".[18]

One day after this announcement, the **Export–import Bank of the United States** said "no" to an application for financing the construction of a new coal-

---

[13] Open letter from FIAN International to Colombian president Juan Manuel Santos and to Olivier de Schutter, UN Special Rapporteur for the Right to Food, February 13, 2013.

[14] "Fact box: The world's top coal trading companies", Reuters, May 19, 2009 and "JP Morgan Looks to trade Physical Iron Ore and Coal", Money news, June 15, 2012.

[15] "Commodity Derivatives House of the Year—Standard Chartered", Risknet, October 18, 2012.

[16] "Leading the Pack: Deutsche Bank wins a hat-trick of prizes at the Energy Risk Awards", Energy Risk, June 2013.

[17] https://www.db.com/cr/en/concrete-energy-and-climate-strategy.htm

[18] "Toward a Sustainable Energy Future for All: Directions for the World Bank Group's Energy Sector", World Bank, July 2013.

fired power plant in Vietnam.[19] This was in the wake of President Barack Obama's commitment to put "an end to US government support for public financing of new coal plants overseas".[20]

Next in line was the **European Investment Bank (EIB).** With a portfolio of 72 billion euros, the EIB is a much bigger lender than the World Bank. In July 2013, the EIB announced the adoption of a new Emissions Performance Standard (EPS)[21] of 550 g of carbon dioxide per kilowatt hour (CO_2/kWh) to be applied to all fossil fuel generation projects.[22] This standard effectively excludes the financing of most coal-fired and lignite-fired power projects. Since 2010, the EIB has also begun putting a "shadow carbon price" of 28 euros on each ton of CO_2, with the price going up each year to reach 45 euros by 2030.

But this is not all. In September 2013, the Nordic countries stated that "the leaders of Denmark, Finland, Iceland, Norway, and Sweden will join the US in ending public financing for new coal-fired power plants overseas, except in rare circumstances".[23] In late 2013, the **European Bank for Reconstruction and Development** (EBRD) followed suit. It not only pulled out of financing the controversial Kolubara B lignite power plant in Serbia but also revised its energy strategy. According to this document, the EBRD will not finance new coal-fired power plants, "except in rare circumstances, where there are no economically feasible alternatives".[24]

The public financial institution that has adopted the most comprehensive climate policy is probably the **US Overseas Private Investment Corporation (OPIC)**, a government-owned institution, which provides financing and guarantees for US companies abroad. In 2008, OPIC adopted a greenhouse gas cap that limits the emissions it can have on its books for any fiscal year. This policy requires a 30 % reduction in portfolio greenhouse gas (GHG) emissions by 2018 and a 50 % reduction by 2023. OPIC must account for the direct GHG impact of any project it finances and count it against this target. Due to accumulated emissions from old projects in its portfolio, OPIC in 2011 financed US\$1.3 billion in clean energy and not a single fossil fuel project.

Some of the most important international development institutions and the export banks of the United States and Nordic countries now recognise that coal-

---

[19] "Ex-Im Bank Halts U.S. Funding Review for Vietnam Coal Plant", Bloomberg News, July 18, 2013.

[20] "The President's Climate Action Plan", The White House, June 2013.

[21] Emission Performance Standards are requirements that set specific limits to the amount of pollutants that can be released into the environment from power plants.

[22] "European Investment Bank to reinforce support for renewable and energy efficiency investment across Europe", EIB, July 24, 2013.

[23] "Joint Statement by Kingdom of Denmark, Republic of Finland, Republic of Iceland, Kingdom of Norway, Kingdom of Sweden, and the United States of America", The White House, September 4, 2013.

[24] "EBRD gives up Kolubara B lignite power plant project in Serbia", CEE Bankwatch, September 9, 2013.

fired power projects are harmful to the climate and should not receive financing. While their decisions set important precedents, this will have little impact on the climate crisis if private banks' financing for the coal sector continues to grow. According to the World Coal Association, 1,199 new coal-fired power plants are on the drawing board and global coal demand is expected to increase by 50 % by 2035.[25] By continuing to provide the financial resources for the coal industry's reckless expansion plans, commercial banks are in effect pushing our climate over the brink.

10   Private Bank Policies: Mostly Hot Air

While leading public banks have begun to move away from coal, private commercial banks have yet to act. Although many private banks have developed standards or policy statements of some kind over the years, these are often weak or even meaningless when it comes to coal.

For the coal power sector, the most stringent policy to date is HSBC's 2011 energy policy,[26] which includes an Emissions Performance Standard (EPS) of 550g CO_2/kWh—the same level applied by the European Investment Bank. However, HSBC only applies this standard to developed countries. For developing countries, an EPS of 850 g CO_2/kWh applies. Other private bank standards are based on thermal efficiency thresholds. BNP Paribas[27] and Société Générale,[28] for example, require an efficiency ratio of 43 % in high-income countries and 38 % elsewhere. From our viewpoint, these standards are incredibly low: modern gas-fired power plants can, for example, reach an efficiency level of 60 %. We also do not understand the reasoning for having different emissions performance or efficiency standards for developed and developing countries. Can developing countries better afford an inefficient use of fuel or higher emissions? We don't think so. All of these standards fall far short of the European Investment Bank's Emissions Performance Standards and the World Bank's policy on new coal power plants.

While some commercial banks do have general mining sector policies, these are for the most part so weak that they do not exclude even the blackest sheep in the corporate mining herd. When it comes specifically to coal mining, hardly any bank standards exist. The only policies and statements that directly relate to coal mining are mostly about mountaintop removal. Mountaintop removal or MTR is a highly

---

[25] "The Public Image of Coal: inconvenient facts and political correctness", Milton Catelin, World Coal Association, 2013.

[26] "Energy Sector Policy", HSBC, January 2011.

[27] "Corporate Social Responsibility—Sector Policy—Coal-Fired Power Generation", BNP Paribas, September 2011.

[28] "Corporate Social Responsibility—Coal-Fired Power Sector Policy", Société Générale, May 2011.

controversial mining technique in which the tops of mountains are literally blown up to reach the coal seams beneath.

Following many years of campaigning by Rainforest Action Network (RAN), some US banks adopted sector thresholds or enhanced due diligence processes for financing this type of coal mining.[29] But as RAN revealed in its latest Coal Finance Report Card,[30] the same banks remain heavily involved in financing mountaintop removal companies. In Europe, however, Credit Suisse adopted a mining policy in 2010 that seemed much more solid: it lists mountaintop removal mining as one of seven "excluded activities".

Unfortunately, it is also a prime example of what we call the big policy lie. Increasingly, banks are issuing new commitments and policy statements that look good at first glance. For example:

> Credit Suisse does not directly finance or provide advice on operations to extract coal or other resources where mountaintop removal mining practices are used.[31]

The trick word that allows Credit Suisse to feel that this policy is in no way an impediment to channelling millions of euros to companies practising mountaintop removal is "directly". It allows the bank to argue that it is not giving loans to blow up mountains (a purpose that would likely be frowned upon in Switzerland). Credit Suisse is instead simply providing a "general corporate loan", to a company that does mountaintop removal, which (surprise, surprise) may be using this loan to blow up mountains—or, to be fair, for other activities. No one really knows, but this policy lets Credit Suisse do all the financing it wants for mountaintop removal companies while telling the public it has "strict" standards.[32]

We have randomly picked Credit Suisse as an example, but the problem is generic among commercial banks. As a reaction to customer concerns and environmental campaigns, more and more banks have developed new and stricter standards on the kinds of projects they will under no circumstance finance. The big policy lie is based on the fact that banks, in reality, do very little targeted project financing. The coal sector is symptomatic for this trend. The results of our most recent study "Banking on Coal" shows that direct project finance only accounts for around 2 % of financial flows to the coal mining industry. Ninety-eight percent of financial flows are in the form of corporate finance, i.e. corporate loans or investment banking.

The nicely worded environmental and social policies of commercial banks are thus often "paper tigers" as controversial projects are financed "indirectly" through

---

[29] A threshold standard, in this case, prohibits lending to companies with more than a certain percentage of coal production from Mountaintop Removal mining.

[30] "Extreme investments: US banks and the coal industry", Rainforest Action Network, May 2013.

[31] "Summary of Mining Policy", Credit Suisse, October 2010.

[32] Since Credit Suisse published this policy in November 2010, it has provided loans and investment banking services of over 260 million euros to the four companies practising MTR that we included in our research. It is likely that if we had researched more companies, we would have found an even higher amount.

general corporate finance. When banks give companies blank checks in form of revolving credit facilities, corporate loans or raise money for companies through share or bond issues, they can pretend not to know that their money is being invested into nasty activities.

Most large commercial banks claim to care deeply about our climate, but as long as they have no real exclusion policies or standards that are applied to corporate finance, their money will continue to be used for investments that are turning up the heat, blowing up mountains, displacing communities and destroying jungles to extract coal.

11 Ethical Indices: What Are They Measuring?

So-called ethical indices and CSR (corporate social responsibility) rating agencies play a key role in helping banks maintain this divide between policy and practice.

Like most companies, commercial banks want to praise themselves for their achievements in sustainability. They frequently mention their inclusion in one of the main "sustainability indices", such as the Dow Jones Sustainability Indices, the FTSE4Good Indexes, the ASPI Eurozone Index or the Ethical Sustainability Index. These indices are linked to CSR rating agencies, which evaluate publicly listed companies based on their environmental, social and governance performance.

The ethical rating agencies' evaluation of the banking sector is problematic. For the indices, banks are required to report only on their direct impacts, such as office paper consumption, direct CO_2 emissions from heating, air conditioning and business travel. The indices, however, ignore that banks' major climate impact is through their core business activities: financing and investment. While CSR rating agencies do also have a category called "controversial deals", there is no real analysis of banks' lending or investment portfolios. Instead, CSR rating agencies often simply rate a bank's communication skills: CSR reports, policy commitments and self-evaluation on the basis of questionnaires.

In our view, the methodology of these rating agencies is deeply flawed and superficial, when it comes to the finance sector. The rating agencies themselves have become part of the problem. They are partially to blame that among banks, "sustainability" has come to mean publishing the best CSR report, instead of having a cleaner portfolio.

How else to explain that Bank of America was included in the Dow Jones Sustainability Index in September 2013—at the moment the bank had just committed to underwriting a new share issue for Coal India, the world's second largest producer of coal.[33] Around the same time, Australia-based ANZ was chosen as the new "Industry Group Leader" in the banking sector, although it is Australia's

---

[33] "Sustainable" badge for Bank of America stretches credibility of Dow Jones Sustainability Index", BankTrack, September 13, 2013.

biggest lender to a series of coal and gas export terminal projects threatening to destroy the Great Barrier Reef.[34]

Ethical and sustainability index providers must exclude the most carbon intensive banks from their indices. Our research shows that a very small number of banks provide 71 % of the finance that is fuelling a coal boom with disastrous local and global impacts. Any index that includes **even one** of the world's top 20 climate killer banks surely cannot be serious about "sustainability" in any sense of the word.

12   Sustainability on Planet Bank and Planet Earth

In the banking world, "sustainability" has become a synonym for regular CSR reporting, running greener office buildings and signing on to toothless voluntary commitments. For the most part, it hasn't led banks to manage or even assess the environmental and social impacts of their portfolios in the real world.

If we want to keep 80 % of coal reserves in the ground—as the International Energy Agency says we must in order to avoid run-away climate change—banks must begin taking responsibility for the climate impacts of their portfolios. In their glossy CSR reports, most banks highlight their investments in renewable energy. And yes, it is true that banks' renewables finance has grown significantly. But as long as the very same institutions are also expanding their money flows to high-carbon sectors, that added percentage in renewables finance is not going to make much difference to our climate.

One of the most frightening figures to emerge from our research is the almost 400 % increase in coal mining finance over the past 8 years. Asking banks to move away from coal or to reduce their fossil fuel portfolio is not a popular idea in the institutions. Banks hate doing **less** of something, as everything (climate change included) is seen as a "business opportunity". But this is the change that civil society movements around the world are demanding. We want banks to say no when the Australian coal industry asks for that next coal terminal loan or when Indonesian companies want a financial push for their coal rush into central Borneo. Banks must stop seeing coal as a business opportunity. Bankers must realise that they live on the same planet as the rest of us, and on that planet, coal is an opportunity for climate suicide.

---

[34] "ANZ awarded Australia's biggest lender to Great Barrier Reef-destroying coal and gas", Market Forces, May 2, 2013.

Sex Matters: Gender Differences
in the Financial Industry

Alexandra Niessen-Ruenzi

Your research looked for an explanation as to why there are so few women working in the US mutual fund industry. Could you sum it up? For the past 20 years, the number of women working as fund managers in the US equity mutual fund industry has hovered at around 10 %, which is surprisingly low. While there are probably some self-imposed factors that contribute to this, such as career interruptions and the choice to work in other industries, our evidence shows that investors discriminate against funds run by women, investing less in them, making it less attractive for companies to employ women and less appealing for women to work in the sector.

Is there any practical reason for this discrimination? No. In our data, we could not find any gender specific differences in fund performance. This means that, although there seems to be a strong view that women can't be trusted to deliver as good an investment performance as men when it comes to money management, there is no reason not to trust women in asset management. The growth rates of female-managed funds are about a third lower than male-managed funds, but this has nothing to do with the women's performance. If women fund managers underperformed or showed bad investment decisions, it would be rational not to invest in their funds, but they don't. If anything, the investment style of female fund managers is more persistent over time than male fund managers—women tend to follow more stable and therefore more reliable investment styles—and average performance is pretty much identical. This should mean, if anything, that investors should prefer female fund managers, if they are looking for consistent management styles, but they don't. Female-managed funds experience much lower inflows, which impacts of the perceived success of those women. Fund flows also drop

Interview by Nicola Pearson

A. Niessen-Ruenzi (✉)
University of Mannheim, Mannheim, Germany
e-mail: niessen@bwl.uni-mannheim.de

© Springer International Publishing Switzerland 2015
K. Wendt (ed.), *Responsible Investment Banking*, CSR, Sustainability, Ethics &
Governance, DOI 10.1007/978-3-319-10311-2_29

439

significantly—by about 13 %—if a woman manager replaces a male manager, while a manger change per se has little impact. This ultimately means that the decision of whether to invest in a fund run by a women has nothing to do with the success of her performance.

Your research study was in the USA. Does the same apply to Europe? There is a lack of research across Europe in this subject. But some survey evidence of European fund managers suggests the answers would be pretty similar to what we found in our study.

Do women have a different approach to risk, risk culture and governance? Do they have a different approach to investment? That depends on the group of women you investigate. There are several studies showing that female retail investors are more risk averse than male retail investors. Their portfolios are less volatile and they tend to trade less. We did not find these differences among professional money managers. This might not be surprising as these managers have similar educational backgrounds and investment objectives as compared to the more heterogeneous group of retail investors. However, women tend to follow their investment styles more closely and deviate less from announced investment styles. Given that investors have to rely on a fund manager following his investment style and not deviating, this should be a good signal to investors.

If they are just as good at the job as men, why do investors mistrust women fund managers? There might be an overriding view that women can't be trusted with money management or to deliver a good investment performance when it comes to money management. There are some professions that are considered to be 'male professions', and money management is one of them. And it becomes self-perpetuating—prejudice against women in financial markets makes investors continue to believe they are less qualified than men. It takes time to change the mindset that male nurses and female money managers, for example, are as trustworthy as their counterparts.

Is that partly to do with the traditional male environment of the investment world, where who you socialise with is an important part of business? Yes, male managers certainly have better access to male-dominated networks of institutional investors, and it's probably fair to say that women might feel less comfortable in circles in which a lot of business is done. A past survey conducted by Wang has also suggested a certain amount of 'machismo' among brokers, meaning they target men as customers rather than women.

With regard to the working environment, research by Niederle and Vesterlund shows that women generally don't like competition—if you give them the choice of working in a competitive environment or in an environment where there is no competition, they generally prefer no competition. Men, on the other hand, really enjoy competition and like to work in a competitive environment. Even low-qualified men will select a competitive environment, while highly qualified women don't. Women tend to trade less, which is often interpreted as evidence for less overconfidence.

Media coverage also has a positive impact on fund flows, and research shows that the press focuses on male fund managers significantly more than female managers.

Playing devil's advocate here, does it matter if some industries remain male dominated and others female? Obviously there are some jobs for which you need a high degree of physical strength where women are biologically constrained, but for most jobs, you have to differentiate between the knowledge that is needed to do that job and the environment in which it's done. In none of the studies, I'm aware of there is difference in the qualifications that can be achieved by men and women, for example, in maths. In fact, some recent studies show that girls do even slightly better than boys in maths. So other factors come into play, such as the way children are brought up and how they perceive themselves and the environment around them. And maybe there are differences in preferences in things such as working hours and working environment, but for the highly paid jobs we are talking about here, I don't see there is any difference in the qualification to do the job between men and women.

What does gender inequality have to do with sustainability? Female fund managers follow less extreme patterns of investing, so you could argue that women in the financial sector would enhance sustainability as they're not taking such extreme bets. Historical data show that there is no difference in risk taking and performance between female and male professional money managers on average. What we do find, however, is that male fund managers are more likely to follow extreme investment styles (individual style bets). These bets sometimes work out, sometimes they don't so that on average you do not find a difference in performance. But male money managers are more likely to rank in extreme (high or low) performance ranks. So for institutional investors there might be a point then in selecting a fund managed by a women, if he wants more stability.

On the other hand, research suggests that top-level women approximate to men—that is, they may start to work in the same way as men. So with a woman managing a fund, you might get the short-term effect of better sustainability, but there are no studies that have looked at the long term. It may be that women start to behave differently if they work with top-level men for a period of time, which could cancel out their impact on sustainability.

How about if you interpret sustainability in connection with women's and workers' rights, in that the finance industry tends to be a high-paying industry so if women are discriminated against, it affects their ability to earn as much as men? Part of sustainability should look at gender equality as well. This has not necessarily anything to do with economic considerations, but is more of an ethical question. You could also make an economic argument that a lot of managerial talent is lost if you don't look at gender equality. And, yes, women do have less access to being high earners.

Do financial companies who implement quotas or a diversity policy in their employment of women do well? Experiments conducted as part of our research

show that there is a minority of investors (typically women) who do not discriminate against female managers so it makes sense from the fund company's point of
view to hire female fund managers to specifically cater to this group of investors.

Some institutional investors in the USA require their business partners to report
explicitly on their diversity policies before they invest in them, and the Dodd-Frank
Act requires federal agencies to do business only with firms that 'ensure the fair
inclusion of women'. So for mutual fund companies to win business from these
clients, they have to employ at least some female fund managers.

What this means in practice, however, is that these companies only have to
ensure that the companies with whom they invest *employ* women; it doesn't mean
they then actually have to *invest* in the funds run by the women. In other words, just
having the presence of women in the company means that the company does better,
without the women attracting better flows into their own fund—they simply provide
a positive spillover effect into other funds managed by men. And although male-
managed funds grow by more than 6 % if the fund company employs at least one
female manager, there is no additional benefit of adding more female managers, just
so long as there is at least one female-managed fund in the company.

In Norway, when they introduced a mandatory quota of women on the board, the
share price of the companies affected dropped sharply immediately following the
announcement. So it appears the owners of these companies, the shareholders, don't
like the idea of having women on the board of these firms, which is why they sold
the stock, making the price drop. However, you can't say that proves quotas do or
don't work as this was a short-term effect assessed on the day of the announcement,
and it's not whether having women on the board will add value in the long term.
One of the reasons the quotas were negatively received in Norway is that there were
not too many women who were qualified to sit on these boards, which meant those
who were would have to spread themselves across too many different companies
and not give sufficient time to each company. As a shareholder, this would probably
seem like a bad thing, but it has little to do with being female and more to do with
being too busy.

*Would the financial world be different if women were equally represented
on the boards of financial institutions?* This question probably goes back to a
statement made by Harriet Harman in 2009 that the financial crisis would have been
less severe if Lehman Brothers had been Lehman Sisters, when she was asked
whether the turmoil would have been avoided if more women were in senior
positions. She made the point that women make up half the workforce of insurance
companies and banks, so why shouldn't they have a say on boards as well.

Just five of the 61 board places in Britain's 'big four' banks were at the time
occupied by women, and the boards of Barclays and Royal Bank of Scotland were
entirely male.

Based on the empirical literature, though, it is hard to make a prediction. There
are several studies that looked at the general impact of board diversity on firm
performance. Some of them find a (weakly) positive effect of female board representation on firm value; others do not find a difference. There is some evidence by

Adams and Ferreira that female board members are better monitors and attend board meetings more frequently than male board members (interestingly, male board members are more likely to attend the meetings if female members are present). Regarding financial institutions, a recent study conducted by Finish researchers suggests that smaller banks with female CEOs or chairwomen were less likely to fail during the financial crisis. But I think it is too early to make a decisive statement about whether women on boards of financial institutions would largely change the financial world.

Presumably, though, if there were more women working in the financial industry per se, women fund managers would do better because there would be more women investors? Yes. We conducted an experiment with students and found it was the male students who did not invest with female fund managers, not the female students, so this is something I would definitely expect. Diversity literature shows that if you only add one or two women, or one or two African-Americans, it doesn't really help because these people just become a subgroup. It needs a significant range, not simply a minority, to really make a change.

Are tougher diversity policies using quotas the way to implement change to this traditional mindset? What we're actually talking about is changing the working environment of the financial industry, and I do believe quotas can help in the long term even if their short-term impact is negative. I think quotas might help to promote role models for young girls and the development of their ambitions and educational choices.

The role model effect is very important. A recent study published in the Science magazine that was conducted in India has shown that young girls grow much higher ambitions if they see there are women in high-ranked positions, meaning they too can achieve such a position. So at the cost of maybe having less qualified women at the margin today (which, by the way, is not clearly shown so far), the next generation that starts working in the industry will increase female presence by even more because it observed women in these jobs, which changes their mindsets, and that feeds into the next generation after that. It's a slow process, but it might be a good way to start.

Women on Board: Female Supervisory Board Members in Shareholder Circles and Their Role in Changing Risk Culture and Sustainable Management

Monika Schulz-Strelow

From 2016, Germany will introduce a legal quota requiring listed companies and companies subject to codetermination legislation to fill 30 % of open supervisory board seats with female candidates. Ms Schulz-Strelow, have you achieved what you set out to in terms of gender equality in the boardroom? Does it feel good? We are still a long way off, but at least one thing will be achieved through this new legal requirement: There will be no going back. Because, unfortunately, the number of women in top management has actually gone down again. This is something we have seen time and time again in recent history, contrary to loud assurances that there will be gender equality.

This is exactly what has happened on the boards of DAX companies over the past months, correct? Yes, unfortunately. There may well be a whole host of individual reasons for this, but there is one general assumption that can be made: A single woman in an entirely and exclusively male-dominated sphere is a disrupting influence that is rejected like a foreign body in a perfectly functioning immune system.

The introduction of a legal quota should bring about a psychological-behavioural change then? In the future, companies will have to make more of an effort to retain women because they are legally obligated to meet the quota, and, therefore, they will have to actively try to enable women access to top management. Unfortunately, the legal requirement affects too few companies. It should apply to all listed, co-determined and public companies. Then there would be a much broader and longer-lasting change, and the social development so desperately needed would happen more quickly.

So, this is just a small victory? After such a long stalemate during the last legislative period, the decision to introduce a quota makes me much more hopeful

An interview with Monika Schulz-Strelow by Gisela Maria Freisinger.

M. Schulz-Strelow
Präsidentin FidAR e. V., Kurfürstendamm 61, D-10707 Berlin, Germany
e-mail: monika.schulz-strelow@fidar.de

© Springer International Publishing Switzerland 2015
K. Wendt (ed.), *Responsible Investment Banking*, CSR, Sustainability, Ethics & Governance, DOI 10.1007/978-3-319-10311-2_30

than I have been in recent years. We can count the quota as a big success. All of the parties involved have acknowledged that it would not have been achieved without FidAR and its political commitment. Now, we will very carefully monitor the new coalition government's implementation of the quota.

FidAR, Frauen in die Aufsichtsräte, is a very well-known and respected organisation, of which you are both president and co-founder. The organisation's strength also lies in the fact that many members are women in top management positions. They didn't need a quota to make it to the top, so why are they demanding legal support when they're at the height of their power? Because their stories are a series of similar experiences that demonstrate how hard the road to the top is for women, how alone they often are and why there are so few women actually getting there. Being the infamous "token woman" might be an acceptable position for some, and one they're not even aware of, but for most, it's a very difficult and unsatisfactory state of affairs. Only a more balanced and diverse combination of men and women can ensure sustainable management strength and, with it, a more successful implementation of a company's goals.

You have been fighting for a quota of female supervisory board members in shareholder circles for seven years now. At the beginning, you were demanding a modest 25 %. Now it's 30 %. Why so easily satisfied? A host of studies, including those from the large consulting firms, have come to the conclusion that corporate culture begins to change and mixed top teams start being perceived as normal from upwards of 30 % female representation in top management. ...

...yes, that is well known.

And this is exactly why we are using this line of reasoning. Demanding equal representation on boards was not something we believed to be a particularly realistic goal. It would simply have caused people to put up barriers, and that includes FidAR members. During our first years of existence, we just placed importance on getting companies to realise that having women on boards at all was a necessity.

That was courageous in view of actual developments.

Indeed. And we really did lose patience in the end because experience taught us something different. The quota isn't the last word on the subject, but we couldn't help recognising that things only change under pressure. Although we knew then and definitely still believe that we need strong men on our side to achieve our demands. These men exist, and that is something we need to shout about into closed management circles. They have a broader perspective and some are involved in FidAR or deeply sympathise with our cause. Getting them on our side was easier with a 30 % quota than if we had come at them with the threat of 40 or even 50 %.

Even the German President, Joachim Gauck, honoured you with the Federal Cross of Merit for standing up for gender equality in the economic sphere. Surely this means that the whole country profits from your commitment to this cause? Personally, and on behalf of all FidAR members, I'm honoured to have received this recognition. When such a prestigious man of his generation recognises that more women are needed on supervisory and management boards, then, hopefully, it will have woken up decision-makers with a bang. One thing I want to be really clear about, however, is that achieving an exact quota is not my main priority at FidAR.

What is it then? It is about change in corporate culture. That is at the core of both gender and sustainability debates. It can't be about turning business women into (better) men, as still happens now, be it consciously or subconsciously.

What are the three most important experiences that you have gained in your work with top executives over the past years? First, second and third: That my Rheinish humour has helped me to work through it all with a positive attitude. It also protects me from the kinds of hostility that, unfortunately, cannot be avoided in such a controversial area, and given the media attention that FidAR receives.

Let's stick with the (male) "masters of the universe". Are they afraid of you, or do they perceive you as some sort of "court jester" in the business world? FidAR is very well known and is taken seriously as a network. I am respected by many business representatives, admired by others, even if they are against having a quota for women on boards, but I'm sure others reject me. An HR consultant once put it very aptly: "FidAR divides the nation". To which my response is, well, at least 50 % are on our side.

You (and FidAR) invented the WoB, the "Women on Board Index", that examines the 160 listed DAX companies with regard to how many women are on their management boards, supervisory boards and the various board committees. Why? We wanted to create transparency: one that names those involved and shows development. And we have succeeded. In the WoB Index, every company can now see where it stands according to clearly defined criteria. This attracted a positive response in politics and the media, but the business world also closely watches this ranking. In the first year of the Index, 74 of the 160 listed DAX companies were in the "women-free" zone, meaning they did not have a single woman on their management or supervisory boards. In October 2014, when it was last updated, this figure had more than halved: There were only 31 companies still "women-free".

"Only"? Isn't that rather euphemistic, a bit of forced optimism perhaps? Of course that is still far too many, particularly considering DAX companies' function as important role models. But we did not achieve much by simply pointing fingers at the fact that there are far too few women on supervisory boards. By taking a close look at every company, publishing names and listing them in a transparent ranking, we have achieved a noticeable and enormous effect. When it comes to scores, we all want to be the best, no one wants to be last, let alone branded a "failure", which is how companies with no women in top management are ranked.

So psychology trumps good arguments? Psychology supports our good arguments, and it gets the job done. That's how I see it. The WoB Index has been closely watched by politicians. Over the years, it was said that if there was no improvement by 2011, the legislators would have to take action. This rhetoric was repeated in 2012 and most recently in 2013 until a legal requirement was finally formulated. The WoB Index made it very obvious how little progress had been made. In fact, progress was so small that one didn't even dare say it out loud. That is the entire secret to the success; it doesn't take a rocket scientist to work it out.

When you introduced the WoB Index, did you believe it would become the extraordinarily effective "weapon" that it has? It was clear to me that in publishing it with a strong media partner, the "manager magazin", we would attract a different kind of attention than if we had done it alone. The economic elite are reflected in the "manager magazin", and there, with no polemic, the black sheep among them are laid bare. Of course, the ranking also presents the "heroes", the modern, progressive thinkers who are forward-looking in their company's interests. All of a sudden, the "failures" are paraded in public as outdated stuck in the muds that missed the boat and caused their companies to fall behind, because mixed teams are simply more successful. On top of that, the lack of skilled workers created by demographic change is increasingly causing companies staffing problems. Incidentally, each political party wanted to see WoB figures during the electoral campaign and it played a decisive role in the coalition negotiations.

Does the magic of the WoB Index also come from the fact that it sparks a race to be the first among business leaders? In football, they say it's the result that counts. Numbers can't be disputed, and that equally impresses both women and men. The real success is the effect the ranking has on people. The media, which has strongly focused on the WoB Index, plays an important role there, too. Whether it is a young female graduate looking at the opportunities for career advancement from a potential employer, or an investment fund that places importance on diversity criteria, or policymakers whose large amount of patience was based on companies' promises that there will be improvement, one quick look is enough to see where everyone stands.

Did the financial crisis and the ensuing economic crisis also play a role? You bet! When the power and decision-making structures were revealed in 2008 and 2009, and when the absurd and apocalyptic scenarios that were being cooked up behind the scenes in the financial sector came to light, it created an unstoppable desire for change both in Germany and worldwide, one that is still very much felt today. All of a sudden, bankers stood there looking like conmen. They seemed to have succumbed to the belief in the emperor's new clothes or at least selling this belief at high prices to their audience. And we all know how that ended.

Trust in their top leaders vanished rapidly. And this loss of trust also transferred to the top management of nonfinancial corporations. No one believes in the stereotypical strong guy anymore, in the man who can use his authority and masculinity to sort it all out and move the world with nothing more than a healthy dose of testosterone. No one wants to relive this horror because we looked into the abyss long enough, afraid of the final fall. The anecdote from Archimedes about moving the world is a metaphor that is no longer associated with archaic, healthy (male) drive but with pathological megalomania. I think, subconsciously, that all has to do with finally wanting to see women in the top management of banks. Women are perceived as being more prudent and responsible.

It's often said that the financial crisis would have never happened if there had been more women in top management positions in the banks. Do you agree with this assumption? No, I can't agree with that statement. But I think it is safe to assume that women would have asked more questions and not fallen into the compulsive "no risk, no fun" pattern of behaviour so quickly. Without pointing fingers, an adrenalin rush played and perhaps still plays a role there, one that rather reminds you of substance abuse. Compared to that, the Hollywood film Wall Street that was once perceived to be the most shocking of all documentary films now seems like a lame and boring Sunday afternoon show.

Following on from that, can we assume that having more women at the top would automatically guarantee more sustainability? Yes, I would largely agree with that. According to many studies, men are more focused on short-term returns, while women place more importance on long-term security and are, more often than not, more socially competent.

In technical sectors, it is often claimed that there is a lack of women in top management because there are simply too few female engineers or technically adept women. But in the financial sector, the numbers are quite different: Far more than half the employees in banks are women, for example, yet the bottom line is the same—they're nowhere to be found in top management. How is that possible? This is exactly where it becomes apparent that the small number of women in top management in sectors with a large proportion of female employees has nothing to do with logic. Across all sectors, we find the frequently mentioned male-dominated corporate structures that have developed "naturally" over time and, as many studies have shown, persist and perpetuate. Successors in top management are chosen based on the principle of similarity. That is one of the decisive reasons that power is male and appears sealed off to women; it is simply impossible for women to break through into these circles. They can be as successful as they like, but they will always fail when it comes to actually resembling their predecessors.

Evidently, this applies to Germany much more than other European countries. Research data from the well-respected executive search firm Egon Zehnder International demonstrates this clearly. And, unfortunately, the banking sector is far behind other sectors even though they have a higher number of female employees. Investment banks are even a couple of percentage points worse than commercial banks in this area That doesn't surprise me at all. As mentioned, the "no risk, no fun" attitude or rather the puffed-out chest that goes with the "my house, my car, my boat, my swimming pool" materialistic insanity is not really a female thing.

In the corporate world, it seems as if there is a programme for the support of women hiding around every corner. How seriously should we take these when they quite obviously don't bring much success? According to studies by McKinsey, these programmes are only successful when the advancement of women, which is often found under the guise of diversity, is one of the primary strategic goals pursued by top management. Otherwise, these programmes don't have much effect. They are often used to present a company in a positive light externally, while internally, they don't produce much change.

Shouldn't we be thinking more fundamentally about whether such programmes make sense at all? They seem to be based on the assumption that women are like developing countries—far behind and need to catch up. But in fact it's quite simple: Men and women are different. What are women supposed to be catching up with? Wouldn't it be more appropriate to actually promote them, rather than to just have programmes supporting them? I have been saying for years that "women are supported, while men are promoted". Women need to be included equally in promotion logic; otherwise even the best performance goes unnoticed. Some companies have committed themselves to this goal and not put it under the umbrella of support for women but instead called it sponsoring programmes. Also, if the success of these programmes is a consideration in bonus payments, they are definitely more effective.

Assuming these programmes actually mean well, are they not also a form of progressive discrimination that should be warned against? Why aren't men being taught to understand women's language and behaviour in companies to an equal extent? I think there is a great necessity for creating awareness and understanding for and from both men and women, so that they recognise the new challenges in dealing with each other. This is an enormous task for both parties but also essential to the much-needed process of change.

Sheryl Sandberg, chief operating officer of Facebook, describes in her bestseller *Lean In* all the stereotypes that still make it almost impossible to achieve leadership equality between men and women. Would the learning process (in terms of gender) be more promising if every aspiring executive were given this book as required reading? That would probably be helpful, but this topic is about more than just understanding; it is also about power. Existing structures won't just be argued away with a bestseller.

Academic gender research speaks of an "unconscious bias" or stereotypes that we all carry around with us, irrespective of how progressive our thinking. Stereotypes aren't negative per se: They allow our survival by helping us quickly and subconsciously sort through and classify the huge amount of information that bombards us daily. Without them, we would have to screen and judge each and every piece of information individually every time. But in places where we want to see change, they are a handicap. How can we avoid falling into this preprogrammed trap? Two approaches are needed for change: a top-down and a bottom-up approach. Top management needs to take the lead; otherwise an initiative will have no effect. Language is a way of measuring the credibility of management behaviour in this area. Furthermore, female role models in upper management are essential for young women looking to reach the top.

In almost every discussion about gender and diversity, fortunately, there are bosses who show how much they want change and demonstrate this in a credible way. The same men are, however, also unaware of the "unconscious bias" that can be a barrier to them. With this in mind, how can change take place? Only by having more women on board. Changing thought patterns, and with it culture, can only happen through the power of numbers. If change in thought doesn't occur, then women will leave the company sooner or later. On the other hand, women also need to think about their role in the change in corporate culture and actively take part in defining new standards. I think it is imperative that they have the right training for this. Men often get support from consultants or coaches and I would recommend every woman do the same.

Is it possible that programmes for the support of women include a type of literacy campaign that assumes that the language of power is masculine and should remain so? The language of power will remain masculine for as long as women reject the term "power". As all top management positions are also synonymous with a power monopoly, and women want to and will enter into top management, they need to seriously think about what it means to them and make a decision. Without power or influence—a word more likely to be accepted by women—they won't be able to achieve change. That decision-making process creates two groups: those who want to reach the top and those for whom it is too uncomfortable there.

As an organisation that represents the interests of top women in the economy, why aren't you demanding "half the sky", as the saying goes, or, as we should be asking with regard to this book, why aren't you demanding half the accounts and portfolios? We'd happily take half the accounts. But for half the sky, we need the young, highly qualified female graduates and career entrants. And unfortunately, some of these do not necessarily see their life's fulfilment in their own independent bank account, but rather prefer to depend on half of the joint account. This tendency really gives us food for thought.

Corporate Social Responsibility in Modern Central and Eastern Europe

Heidrun Kopp

Abstract Central and Eastern Europe (CEE) is a region made up of various countries. A statement made for one country is not necessarily true for another. Corporate Social Responsibility (CSR), therefore, has to be translated to serve local requirements and expectations. The political, economic, historical and cultural backgrounds of society all have an impact on these requirements. The socialist-communist era after World War II has shaped the mindset of society and subsequently built the base for the outstanding economic growth of the region after the fall of the Iron Curtain. Foreign direct investment plays a major role in this context. The decision of foreign companies to do business in CEE is based on various advantages of location, for example, economic backlog demand and the tax regime, but also on social and environmental legislation. What is a modern corporation's current understanding of its social and environmental responsibility? Why is it attractive to corporates to take CSR seriously: as an additional risk measure, as an innovative approach to deal with future economic and societal requirements or purely as green branding? In any of these cases, CEE has a unique opportunity to learn from CSR-relevant initiatives active in economically advanced countries and to present itself as a relevant socio-ecological global player.

1 Introduction

Corporate Social Responsibility (CSR) is a concept that was developed in a US environment based on the assumption that a sustainable consideration of economic, social and ecological factors in corporate decision-making is not only beneficial to the economy but also to society.

What does such a business-society model mean for the countries of the Central and Eastern Europe (CEE) region, with economic and social models that changed profoundly with the political upheavals after the fall of the Iron Curtain in 1989? What role do eco-social considerations play in an economic environment where

H. Kopp (✉)
Institut für nachhaltiges Finanzwesen, Vienna, Austria
e-mail: heidrun.kopp@inafina.org

© Springer International Publishing Switzerland 2015
K. Wendt (ed.), *Responsible Investment Banking*, CSR, Sustainability, Ethics & Governance, DOI 10.1007/978-3-319-10311-2_31

453

formerly state-owned companies (that also used to fulfil a social function) are integrated into a system that is subject to commercial interests and the rules of the market? We will also ask who the relevant stakeholders are and what particularities should be considered in this context.

The CEE region is comprised of numerous countries that, apart from sharing some similarities, also exhibit specific historical and cultural features. In consideration of the findings of established cultural theories, we will discuss what role CSR can play as an innovative tool to support a sustainable and competitive economic, social and societal model in this region.

2 Regional Focus

Before discussing the specifics of CSR in Central and Eastern Europe, it is necessary to define which countries of the region are covered by the contribution. CEE refers to a region whose geographical scope is defined differently by various sources (OeNB 2013; Bussière et al. 2005; IMF 2010; Raiffeisen Research 2013). This chapter focuses on the area comprising Central Europe (CE), South-Eastern Europe (SEE) as well as Russia and Ukraine, which are both embraced under the term CIS region. The country list is presented in Table 1.

Table 1 Overview of CEE countries

Central Europe (CE)	South-Eastern Europe (SEE)	Commonwealth of Independent States (CIS)
Czech Republic (CZ)	Albania (AL)	Russia (RU)
Hungary (HU)	Bosnia and Herzegovina (BH)	Ukraine (UA)
Slovakia (SK)	Bulgaria (BG)	
Slovenia (SI)	Croatia (HR)	
Poland (PL)	Kosovo (KO)	
	Romania (RO)	
	Serbia (RS)	

3   Definition and Origins of CSR

Corporate Social Responsibility is a concept that serves to describe the role of business within society. Originating in a US context, it has been much discussed over the past decades.

The book *Social Responsibility of a Businessman* by Howard R. Bowen (1953) is often stated as the starting point for a scientific approach towards the term CSR. Milton Friedman believes that firms' responsibility is singularly defined by enhancing shareholder value within the framework of law. Allegedly, he also made the pointed statement 'the business of business is business' (Friedman 1962).

Broader discussions of the concept of CSR suggest that companies have a responsibility towards society that extends beyond any legal requirements. They have to integrate social and environmental considerations into their business practices and standards. An important categorisation is provided by Archie B. Carroll (1979/1991) who distinguishes four areas of interaction between business and society, namely, economic, legal, ethical and philanthropic responsibility (Matten and Moon 2005). For a better overview, his model is presented in pyramid form (Graph 1).

Even though the discussion has shifted from a mere shareholder value perspective towards a stakeholder value perspective, there is still no common understanding of the meaning of CSR. Votaw delivers a sharp characterisation, saying: 'this term [CSR, acc. to author.] is a brilliant one, it means something but not always the same thing, to everybody' (Votaw 1972, p. 25). The theoretical problem of CSR lies in the blurred boundaries of understanding a company's duties towards society.

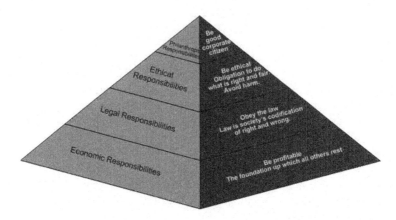

Carroll's CSR Pyramid

Graph 1 Carroll's CSR pyramid. *Source*: Carroll A., 1991, The Pyramid of Corporate Social Responsibility: Toward the Moral Management of Organizational Stakeholders, in: Business Horizons, 34, pp. 39–48 (see also http://www.csrquest.net, accessed 15 November 2013)

Furthermore, differing perceptions of the concept of CSR exist both on the micro level of companies and on the macro level of countries and regions. On the company level, the scope of CSR can range from a mere marketing initiative for shaping a more positive corporate image all the way to a comprehensive, integrated implementation of eco-social standards in all business practices and procedures. On the regional level, CSR is strongly dependant on the historical, cultural, legal and institutional context to understand the perception of business-society relations.

Campbell proposes a pragmatic definition when he talks of a 'minimal behavioural standard with respect to the corporation's relationship to its stakeholder' (Campbell 2007, p. 951). He suggests that a certain economic practice may be seen as normal in one region while in another region the same practice might be considered particularly ethical. Any allocation of meaning to the term CSR, therefore, has to be viewed within the geographical as well as historical-cultural context (Koleva et al. 2010).

4   CSR Debate Reaches Europe

During the 1990s, the concept of CSR entered public debates in continental Europe and became increasingly important. Landmarks of this evolution are the foundation of the first sustainability rating agency oekom research (1993), the establishment of CSR Europe (1995), the introduction of a Ministry of Corporate Social Responsibility in the UK (2000), the adoption of the Social Policy Agenda of the Nice Council (2000) and subsequently the EU Sustainable Development Strategy (European Council 2006) (Steurer et al. 2012).

In 2001, the European Commission published the Green Paper on Promoting a European framework for Corporate Social Responsibility that defines CSR as 'a concept whereby companies integrate social and environmental concerns in their business operations and in their interactions with the stakeholder on a voluntary basis' (Commission of the European Communities 2001, p. 6). This definition is again based on the understanding that 'being socially responsible means not only fulfilling legal expectations, but also going beyond compliance and investing "more" into human capital, the environment and the relations with stakeholder' (Commission of the European Communities 2001, p. 6). In Europe, there is a long-standing tradition of business involvement in society issues, which is now associated with responsible corporate behaviour. The reason that the European countries have only recently begun to deal with the concept of CSR may be that many issues (e.g. working hours, minimum wage, health and social security benefits) related to CSR are already settled within the legal and institutional frameworks in (Western) Europe (Matten and Moon 2005).

The concept of CSR was developed in market-oriented economies with a stable democracy and an established civil society. American and European countries can rely on a stable and mature economy and an active civil society. Corporate, legal and institutional organisations usually enjoy a high level of trust within the public opinion. The civil society, often represented by NGOs that aim to address societal and environmental issues, is prepared to act as stakeholder—among other stakeholders—in the dialogue with enterprises. In this context, CSR assumes the role of a basic ethical standard when applying legal norms and regulations (Lewicka-Strzalecka 2006). Similarly, in the early 1990s, the countries of the CEE region experienced profound political upheavals that led to a radical transformation of the role of the state, the economy and society in general (Matten and Moon 2005). The following paragraphs look at the evolution of CSR within the context of an ongoing transformation process in an emerging market economy.

Before making a deeper analysis, we have to ask whether it is even possible to create an assessment of CSR in the CEE region. According to Gasparski (Gasparski 2005) we have to deal with a fragmented picture based on different historical and cultural experiences on the one hand and simultaneously many similarities on the other hand. The countries share a 'transitional socio-economic model' (Steurer et al. 2012) in which a redefinition of the role of business, the institutional framework and eventually the engagement of civil society has to be newly agreed upon. This transition phase is accompanied by difficult economic situations, dysfunctional legal environments, high unemployment and poverty rates and low public social expenditures in comparison with the EU average (Lewicka-Strzalecka 2006; Steurer et al. 2012).

In the following we will make a deeper analysis of the institutional context in which local and foreign companies are embedded in CEE. A few phases can be distinguished: the socialist era with complete negligence of market forces; the transitional phase whose negative traits laid a foundation of distrust towards governmental institutions and market-oriented economy within large parts of the population; and the contemporary phase where the unfinished transition has been shaken by the global financial and sovereign debt crisis since 2008, with partly increasing corruption ratios (CPI) as well as rising unemployment and poverty rates (Gasparski 2005).

5   Business and Society in a Socialist Context

The centrally planned economy was based on the principle of a job for all citizens. Social benefits were provided by the socialist productive unit and consisted of nurseries, kindergarten, social security, housing, etc. In providing the social infrastructure, the relationship between a state-owned company and its employees was patron-like and not only shaped the daily life of people and families but often defined the local community.

This fact is highlighted by the absence of independent trade unions (Lewicka-Strzalecka 2006). In return for this basic economic security, employees received wages with low purchasing power on the market and a very limited assortment of goods which were often not even available. This model of social benefits for employees was in place for decades and was therefore strongly rooted within the local population (Koleva et al. 2010).

The objective of state-owned firms was primarily to provide employment and ensure a certain level of well-being for their employees and subsequently the local community, while economic efficiency and maximised profits were not an objective. In general, the multiannual economical plans were drafted in ministries in distant Moscow, with the result that regional requirements, long-term considerations and environmental concerns were not taken into account (Vorobey 2005). This patron-like 'management' style of state-owned firms and the related social security measures could be considered as CSR to a certain extent when applying the definition of Campbell (Koleva et al. 2010). This is an important consideration treated in more detail in the CSR rhetorics. Long-standing indoctrination and experience had a strong impact on the public's mindset and was thus the starting point for the economic transformations from the 1990s onwards.

6   Business and Society in a Post-Socialist (Transformation) Context

As a consequence of the political changes initiated in 1989, the economic and social systems in the CEE region also changed dramatically (complete breakdown of societal governance). State-owned firms gradually became privately owned and were transformed into businesses within a market-oriented economy. This principle was followed in all CEE countries, even though they took different approaches to the implementation.

Poland is a country among others where the financial assets and properties were often transferred directly to the managers and employees of the formerly state-owned companies in the first privatisation phase. Occasionally, co-ownership models were arranged between the private owners and the state. These structures often led to misuse, with costs and liabilities remaining in the state-owned part of the company and assets being externalised into the private part (Lewicka-Strzalecka 2006). In Hungary, to give a different example, privatisation was used to maximise profits for the government, and to achieve this, the government tried to attract strategic investors and encourage the inflow of foreign direct investment (Fekete 2005). Generally, there was a lack of transparency regarding the way the privatisation process was carried out in the 1990s, which did not promote trust in the market-oriented business structure (Vorobey 2005).

Along with enhancing economic efficiency and clearly separating the economic from the social role of the corporations, the workforce was downsized and the social functions originally carried out by firms were no longer fulfilled, as this was considered a hindrance to survival in the new competitive environment (Lewicka-Strzalecka 2006). Most companies did not consider the social and environmental impacts of their activities. And the environmental deterioration inherited from the socialist past was further intensified by ignorance during the transitional period (OECD 1999).

Many entrepreneurs tried to take advantage of new opportunities and a dysfunctional legal infrastructure with numerous loopholes and wanted to accumulate wealth as fast as possible (Bohata 2005).

6.1   Corruption

Malfunctioning, bloated bureaucracy, out-dated laws and officials lacking know-how and experience in market-oriented economy completed the picture of an inefficient, overstrained legal environment (Bohata 2005). High temptations for public administrators with low income and a high degree of responsibility encounter profit-oriented firms and managers, for whom the transferred sums are simply irrelevant. And all of this is supported by a weak political will to address the problem on a public level (Koleva et al. 2010).

There is literature to argue that corruption is related to economic and social prosperity and subsequent decline (Lewicka-Strzalecka 2006). Transparency International regularly provides the so-called Corporate Perception Index, which ranks countries based on how corrupt the public sector in the respective country is perceived. A comparison of the years 2012 and 2008 shows that the rates of perceived corruption in nearly half of the investigated regions have followed a downward trend since the outbreak of the financial and sovereign debt crisis in late 2008 (Table 2).

A high level of corruption is considered a critical factor for CSR. In a highly corrupt environment, position and success of business people depend more strongly on public administrators who grant necessary licenses and access to the market. This fact discourages an active dialogue with other stakeholders such as employees, customers, business partners, NGOs and the local community (Lewicka-Strzalecka 2006).

It is assumed that unethical practices are temporary and are gradually forced back by a general evolution of business and also by various initiatives and educational measures such as classes for business ethics at universities (Bohata 2005). The Anti-Corruption Program from the Batory Foundation in Poland is a good example of this development. Its objective is to analyse mechanisms that support corruption, observe the conduct of public institutions and, last but not least, successively change peoples' behaviour with an increased flow of information (Lewicka-Strzalecka 2006).

6.2   Legal Environment

In the CEE region, excessive (new) legal regulations and slow court proceedings have become a reality. The red tape requirements are challenging, particularly for small companies, which makes them cut corners and overlook legal rules. Business

Table 2 Corruption development in CEE according to the Corporate Perception Index (CPI)

Rank		Country	Tendency/based on rank
2012	2008		
1	1	Denmark	Stable
25	12	Austria	Decreasing
37	26	Slovenia	Decreasing
41	58	Poland	Increasing
46	47	Hungary	Increasing
54	45	Czech Republic	Decreasing
62	62	Croatia	Stable
62	52	Slovakia	Decreasing
66	70	Romania	Increasing
72	92	Bosnia and Herzegovina	Increasing
75	72	Bulgaria	Increasing
80	85	Serbia	Increasing
105	n/a	Kosovo	n/a
113	85	Albania	Decreasing
133	147	Russia	Increasing
144	134	Ukraine	Decreasing
174	180	Somalia	Increasing

Note: High-ranked countries are considered less corrupt than those on the lower end of the range
Note: Denmark, Somalia and Austria listed as references
Source: Transparency International, www.transparency.org
Composition: author

people then took advantage of the collapse of the legal system, information chaos and ambiguity of ownership during the transformation (Lewicka-Strzalecka 2006).

The pressure of transformation has led to the development of two different economic spheres: a prosperous one and one with increasing economic hardships. According to Kostjuk, an estimated 20 % of all people in the CEE region live under extremely difficult economic conditions, with illegal employment relationships and insufficient access to health and pension services (Kostjuk 2005).

The accession to the EU of numerous CEE countries (2004, 2007, 2013) was a main driver for most institutional reforms in many of these countries in order to integrate into the European institutional framework (Koleva et al. 2010).

During the transition period, companies strived for efficiency and increased productivity and placed little emphasis on managing their human resources fairly. Companies still tend to accept a certain reputational risk. Illegal and unfair treatment and disobedience of employment rights and labour laws have to be viewed within the context of high unemployment rates. Employees do not defend themselves against bullying in the workplace for fear of losing their job (Table 3).

An example from Poland illustrates that a poorly developed civil society is not yet ready to stand up for the rights of other stakeholder groups. According to a survey, 65 % of the customers of a supermarket chain are not prepared to change their shopping behaviour when faced with information about unfair treatment of the

Table 3 Development of the unemployment rate 2008–2013

Country	2008	2009	2010	2011	2012	2013
Albania	12.55	13.62	13.60	13.30	15.00	13.00
Belarus	0.80	0.90	0.70	0.60	0.60	0.60
Bosnia and Herzegovina	23.41	24.07	27.20	27.60	28.00	27.00
Bulgaria	5.66	6.88	10.31	11.35	12.38	12.38
Croatia	8.27	9.05	12.21	13.68	15.00	15.20
Czech Republic	4.39	6.66	7.28	6.70	7.03	8.10
Hungary	8.00	10.50	10.90	11.00	11.00	10.47
Kosovo	.	.	.	.	.	.
Poland	7.12	8.17	9.64	9.63	10.35	10.97
Romania	5.79	6.86	7.28	7.40	7.00	7.03
Russia	6.40	8.40	7.50	6.60	6.00	5.50
Serbia	14.70	17.40	20.00	24.40	23.10	22.98
Slovak Republic	9.58	12.12	14.49	13.61	14.00	14.33
Slovenia	4.39	5.89	7.27	8.21	9.03	9.80
Ukraine	6.36	8.84	8.10	7.86	8.05	8.24

Source: International Monetary Fund, World Economic Outlook Database (April 2013). http://www.imf.org/external/pubs/ft/weo/2013/01/weodata/index.aspx
Composition: author

supermarket employees. Since there is no 'voting with your feet', companies do not have to worry that their customers will change their habits even when they are confronted with a poor public image (Lewicka-Strzalecka 2006).

However, in the context of CSR, an important group of a company's stakeholders are their own employees. This is linked to the ever-increasing importance of corporate image to the public, which is why a company's risk management will also aim at avoiding any reputational risks (e.g. fair treatment of the staff, human resource policies).

6.3 Civil Society and NGOs

CSR management policies are usually a response to the corporate environment such as expectations or even pressure expressed by relevant stakeholder groups. This requires a strong civil society that is capable of formulating and enforcing expectations towards companies in an organised way. In the CEE countries, consumers are often unaware that they can articulate expectations either themselves or through an NGO. Civil engagement is not yet well rooted, and interest groups are slow to articulate their respective interests (Losoncz 2005). Thus far they have had low impact on corporate decision makers (Vorobey 2005).

NGOs are often unknown to the public, suffer from a lack of financial resources and are unable to provide a sufficient track record of their actions to gain trust from a wider public (Koleva et al. 2010). And yet, despite a lack of financial resources and a limited range of action, the number of NGOs is rising. NGO representatives articulate the expectations of their respective interest groups and become increasingly relevant stakeholders in the dialogue with corporations. The Czech Donor Forum, an NGO serving the Czech donor community, recorded more than 1,200 foundations and thousands of civic association in 2005 (Czech Donors' Forum 2013).

In Russia, on the other hand, civil society initiatives (e.g. Pussy Riot Trial 2012) and foreign NGOs are hitting the headlines and causing worldwide debates as they are accused of interfering in Russian politics by government officials. With new legislation, the work of NGOs is significantly restricted:

> 'The Russian State Duma has passed a bill that requires all non-governmental organizations engaged in politics that receive funding from abroad to register with the Justice Ministry as "foreign agents." (. . .) According to the bill, a non-governmental organization is categorized as foreign agent if it receives financial funding from other countries or their public agencies, international and foreign organizations, non-citizens or their representatives. All NGOs will have to submit financial records and semi-annual reports on their activities to Russia's authorities. In addition, the bill permits NGOs to be inspected based on individual complaints or publications about extremism in their activities.' (Russia beyond the headline, 28 Sept 2013)

Along with globally active environmental NGOs such as Friends of the Earth and Greenpeace, a large number of local NGOs are actively addressing social issues and delivering charitable support to less-advantaged parts of society. Following the inflow of foreign direct investment (FDI) in the region, there are also a number of non-profit organisations from abroad that have become engaged in the CEE region. One of them is the volunteer-led United Way Charity that has US roots and established units in the CEE region a few years ago, namely, in Hungary, Poland, Romania and Russia. Their aim, working with companies, civil society organisations and many volunteers, is to strengthen the self-organisation of society and implement necessary community projects for the handicapped, single parents and elderly citizens (United Way Worldwide 2013).

Ideally, an active CSR dialogue is held with various external stakeholders, e.g. stakeholders representing interest groups such as NGOs, business associates, trade unions, etc. However, if civil society institutions are not well established, the corporate dialogue is left mainly to the government and other institutional bodies, which could be interpreted as corporate intervention into politics (Steurer et al. 2012). Without any social control of these procedures, the company's commitment may be reduced not just merely to an advertising exercise but, worse, to nicely wrapped attempted corruption.

6.4   Local Firms and Multinational Companies

The economy in the countries of the CEE region in question is made up of small and medium-sized companies. Many of these companies were only founded in the 1990s. A lack of business know-how and a difficult economic environment often led to the adoption of unethical and also illegal business practices, e.g. illegal employment and payment backlogs to cope with the day-to-day economic hardship. Irrespective of the size of the enterprises, local firms are often not aware of the importance to acting responsibly due to a lack of insight to the full range of CSR measures. Although there is evidence that voluntary CSR measures are applied (even if they are not necessarily labelled as such), whereby they clearly resort to their past experience with social benefits for employees and communities. This leads to the fact that too many firms consider their employees the only relevant stakeholder group for their CSR considerations (Koleva et al. 2010).

What is the situation regarding local entrepreneurs? A study has revealed that even if they formally have CSR rules in place, they often establish them to meet international investors' expectations rather than to initiate a sustainable stakeholder dialogue (Koleva et al. 2010).

Along with the privatisation of formerly state-owned companies, many multinational corporations settled in the CEE region in the form of foreign direct investments. Their motivation was, first and foremost, to achieve profit by exploiting a new market potential and the locational advantages, such as cheap and well-trained labour and also deficiencies of the post-social institutional context, e.g. tax regime, social and environmental policies, etc. (Fekete 2005; Koleva et al. 2010).

On the other hand, multinational corporations brought long-standing experience with, e.g. gender issues, labour integration, employee training and CSR standards as well as the formulation of Codes of Conduct (Losoncz 2005).

It should be stressed that multinational corporations hardly ever address the requirements of local stakeholders in their CSR communication. Corporate philanthropy and cause-related marketing, particularly with sport and culture, often targeted at children, are often the central aspects of the CSR measures. These measures are usually taken in order to improve the brand image and not necessarily to develop a strategic management tool for CSR. Or, as Fekete appropriately remarks, 'the substantive accomplishment of CSR does not appear to be an intrinsic part of their corporate agenda' (Fekete 2005, p. 147).

6.5   Similarities on a Business-Society Level

In summary, we can say that an assessment of CSR in the CEE region has to be made in a context that is characterised by a negative image of the economy due to a high level of corruption, a difficult economic situation for many companies, high unemployment rates and a dysfunctional legal environment. When considering the already-mentioned CIP, we can talk of a lack of business ethics (Lewicka-Strzalecka 2006; Vorobey 2005).

7   Challenges for the Inception of CSR in Contemporary CEE

In view of the challenging economic and social frameworks in the CEE countries, it is not possible to transfer the concept of CSR, which originates from a stable economic, social and democratic environment, one to one to an emerging market with a transformational economy as well as evolutionary institutional and societal frameworks. CSR requires a well-developed civil society and actively involved NGOs, since CSR management practices are often a response to expectations and even pressure by the corporate environment (Steurer et al. 2012).

A trivial reason is linguistics. In many countries, the concept of CSR is familiar, but it is a trend that is strongly connected to an academic discourse and has little to do with the 'real' life of the people (Fekete 2005).

CSR—socialistic idea via the backdoor? Lewicka-Strzalecka has introduced an important idea to the discussions surrounding the difficulties of embedding CSR in CEE. The concept of CSR often uses a language which addresses idealistic values such as common good and sustainable behaviour. But the people in the CEE region have worked for the common good and a better world for decades. Since the 1990s, they have learnt to find their way in a market-oriented environment and put individual before collective interests. They have learnt to distrust socialist party propaganda and they are familiar with optimistic plans and reports that have little to do with reality. With a population that shares such experience, CSR finds it difficult to integrate as a serious concept that adds a social and ecological component to economic decisions of corporations (Lewicka-Strzalecka 2006).

7.1   Despite These Challenges, a Number of Initiatives Exist to Promote CSR

Nevertheless, there are numerous CSR initiatives that support the concept of CSR and make it better known and contribute to the redefinition of business-society relations. To give a few examples, it can be referred to the foundation of the Academy for the Development of Philanthropy (1988) and Responsible Business Forum (2000) in the Czech Republic. The initiative Business Fair Play and Approved Partner aims to highlight fair and ethical business practices and make them more visible to customers by awarding certificate to the participating companies (Lewicka-Strzalecka 2006). The Belgrade Chamber of Economy organised a

CSR round table to promote the implementation of ethical codes with Serbian companies (Losoncz 2005). In Russia, there are also a number of organisations that differ in their respective target groups, e.g. small and medium-sized businesses for OPORA RUSSIA. A pioneer in this field is the Association of Managers in Russia. This Association carried out a comprehensive survey about 'Corporate social responsibility: public expectations' with Philip Morris International (Litovchenko and Korsakov 2003). The survey covering the opinion of several stakeholder, e.g. general people, business people, politicians and media representatives, is particularly valuable since it is a comparative investigation covering Eastern European countries including Hungary, Poland, Czech Republic and Ukraine. The results clearly show that the concept of CSR is confronted with: a lack of trust towards business. 46 % distrust their local companies, 36 % distrust foreign companies and an alarming 87 % do not believe that companies' CSR declarations are trustworthy and sincere (Kostjuk 2005).

7.2 Differences on Country Level

At the same time, the countries of the CEE region show many differences that are partly due to different linguistic meanings but also have historical and cultural reasons (Vorobey 2005; Steurer et al. 2012):

- For non-EU countries, there were fewer incentives to harmonise with EU standards and norms, particularly in a social and environmental context.
- Apart from not being an EU member state, Russia also influences civil-societal measures at a political level (NGO legislation).
- Ukraine is still trying to find its national identity. It is a divided country in linguistic terms as well as in its economic orientation: eastern Ukraine speaks Russian with an economy that relies on large industrial conglomerates. In the west, the population speaks Ukrainian, and there are many small and medium-sized companies.
- In some former Yugoslavian countries, the impacts of war and the outcomes of the post-war economy and society still play a major role.

7.3 Cultural Differences Impacting the Inception of CSR in CEE

We have established that there are a number of similarities among the CEE countries concerning business practices and procedures; at the same time, the cultural differences must also be stressed. The best-known theories on cultural differences as a framework for understanding the role of business in different societies were developed by Hofstede with his five value-oriented, bipolar dimensions and by Tromenpaars with the so-called seven dimensions of culture (Hofstede 1984, 2013; Trompenaars 1997).

Based on Hofstede's definition, 'Culture is the collective programming of the mind distinguishing the members of one group or category of people from others' (http://geert-hofstede.com/national-culture.html, Accessed 15 September 2013), the following cultural dimensions have been established:

1. Power distance (PDI)
2. Individualism versus collectivism (IDV)
3. Masculinity versus femininity (MAS)
4. Uncertainty avoidance (UAI)
5. Long-term orientation (LTO)–which was added based on the research by Michael Bond (1991)
6. Indulgence versus restraint–which was added based on the research by Michael Minkov (2010)

Applying this categorisation to the cultures in the countries of the CEE region creates a very diverse, inconsistent image. It highlights that the countries exhibit significant cultural differences even though they also share many historical, political and economic similarities (Table 4) (Hofstede 1984, 2013; Reynaud et al. 2007).

Table 4 Hofstede's cultural dimensions applied to CEE countries

Countries	Cultural dimensions				
	PDI	IDV	MAS	UAI	LTO
AUT	11	55	79	70	31
BG	70	30	40	85	n/a
CZ	57	58	57	74	13
CR	73	33	40	80	n/a
HU	46	80	88	82	50
PL	68	60	64	93	32
RO	90	30	42	90	n/a
RU	93	39	36	95	n/a
Serbia	86	25	43	92	n/a
Slovakia	104	52	110	51	38
Slovenia	71	27	19	88	n/a
AL	n/a				
Bosnia	n/a				
UA	n/a				

Note: High scores show that a cultural dimension is common. Analyses covering the countries of Albania, Bosnia and Ukraine were not available. Austria listed as reference

Source: The Hofstede Centre, (http://geert-hofstede.com/austria.html), Accessed 15 September 2013

Composition: author

Table 5 CSR-related criteria based on the cultural factors

	PDI	UAI	IDV	MAS
Consumer activism	Lower	Lower	Higher	Lower
Environmental activism	Lower	Higher	Lower	Lower
Employee activism	Lower	Lower	Higher	Lower
Governmental activism	Lower	Higher	Lower	Lower
Community activism	Lower	Lower	Lower	Lower

Source: Lenssen and Vorobey (2005, p. 360f)

Katz et al. (1999) and Katz and Nelson (2001) have investigated the cultural influence on CSR in more detail based on Hofstede's work and have identified the following criteria: consumer activism, environmental activism, employee activism, governmental activism and community activism (Table 5) (Lenssen and Vorobey 2005).

With this research in mind, a stable framework for a structured implementation of CSR can be established which considers both the socio-economic relations and the cultural particularities regarding CSR-relevant criteria.

Based on the above analyses, four main systems can be identified that help to explain the link between cultural tendencies and the role of business in society: from the Anglo-Saxon system (UK, Ireland) to the Dutch/Scandinavian system, the Latin system (France, Belgium, Italy, Spain) and the German system (Germany, Austria, German-speaking regions of Switzerland) (Lenssen et al. 2005).

Within the German cultural model, CSR is embedded in the understanding that each community member has a say in joint matters. CSR is often referred to under the topic Corporate Citizenship, though with a strong tendency towards the welfare state. The French cultural model sees companies in their role as profit maximisers within the frameworks provided by the state. Engagement beyond legal requirements could lead to allegations that public opinion is manipulated (Lenssen and Vorobey 2005). These different assessments show the diverse tendencies in the perception of the role of business and CSR in society. Segal (2004) has discovered how CSR is depicted in the sociopolitical systems. In this context we have to emphasise that CSR has its origins in the protestant Anglo-Saxon system, with freedom and independence as central values, with society voluntarily accepting responsibility. Moreover, it is assumed that the key question is to what degree CSR can contribute to profitability and competitiveness of a company (Lenssen and Vorobey 2005).

Matten and Moon (2005) distinguish between implicit and explicit CSR, whereby explicit CSR stands for corporate programmes and policies issued by corporations voluntarily. Here they address issues that they consider relevant for their stakeholders and society in general. This model is practised in the US context. Implicit CSR on the other hand stands for a framework where a country's legal mandatory requirements based on values, norms and rules constitute the environment for companies to address issues that are considered economically, environmentally and socially relevant for customers, employees and society in general.

Implicit CSR describes the situation in the continental, Western European countries (Matten and Moon 2005).

CEE is still in a process of ongoing transition that entails transformations into a market-oriented business model and throwing most social functions of the socialist system overboard. It can be assumed that while the role of business within society is still being negotiated by society, the region finds itself in a phase that is very similar to the Anglo-Saxon model with methods that can be understood as explicit CSR.

Conclusion

To assess CSR in the CEE region, its status and future requirements, it can be said that the countries show large **similarities** regarding the fact that people's expectations towards the economy and the state are deeply shaped by the socialist and post-socialist phases.

The market economy was depicted in an exclusively negative way by socialist propaganda. State-owned firms, in contrast, also provided social service. Particularly during the first phase of the transformation into a market and private economical system, the dynamics of the situation and the lack of preparation on the side of the legal and institutional authorities together with an underdeveloped tradition of business ethics led to unethical, illegal and even corrupt practices. This, in turn, coined the public's assessment of the economy and the state. The now-privatised companies no longer provided social benefits, and hence they were either offered by the state or commercial providers, or they were cancelled altogether. A UNDP baseline study on CSR found that 'Due to the socialist heritage, there is a general perception, both in the business community and the public at large, that social responsibility and social caring is the primary role of the government' (UNDP 2007, p. 23f).

Apart from the local companies, multinational corporations very often import their general expertise in dealing with CSR relevant topics and establishing a dialogue with relevant stakeholders into the region: the relationships towards employees but also customers, NGOs and municipal as well as national institutions. Despite numerous newly founded local and international non-governmental and non-profit organisations, civil-society initiatives are still fairly rare due to a lack of tradition, financial resources and the chance to influence the system. The region is also united by the fact that the concept of CSR cannot be transferred one to one to countries that are still undergoing transition. Even the understanding of CSR is not uniform: while the majority of the established CSR literature (see CSR definition of the European Commission) sees CSR as something that goes beyond legal requirements, there are voices within the CEE region who believe that responsible, sustainable business methods mean adhering to the law and paying taxes.

(continued)

In addition, the CSR concept has inherited a heavy burden since its terminology is sometimes associated with socialist ideas (Lewicka-Strzalecka 2006) so not only the concept itself but also its trustworthiness is viewed with scepticism.

At the same time, there are big **differences** between the countries of the CEE region, which are demonstrated by Hofstede's cultural dimensions and which were caused by the distinct transition phases to a market and private-economic system. While the countries in Central Europe and CIS saw a peaceful transition, large parts of former Yugoslavia were drawn into war. Several CEE countries are already EU member countries that harmonised their legal and institutional frameworks during the accession negotiations and are thereby integrated into the European economic and social understanding.

For the CEE region, CSR can be recommended as an important, innovative and future-oriented tool for establishing an economic culture shaped by business ethics with the help of all stakeholders and supported by initiatives of the EU (Steurer et al. 2012; Bartol 2008), the respective government and also multinational corporations, with different measures for each country, to varying degrees and at a different pace depending on the national requirements.

There is potential to establish another location advantage for the region and attract national and international investors to the benefit of society. Or, to put it in the words of the American economist **Peter F. Drucker** (1984) who originates from Austria and pleads for a new understanding, an entrepreneurial approach and for adopting a management diction that states that social-societal initiatives should be considered as economic opportunities, as business case so to speak:

> 'But the proper ‚social responsibility' of business is to tame the dragon, that is to turn a social problem into economic opportunity and economic benefit, into productive capacity, into human competence, into well-paid job, and into wealth.' (Drucker, 1984 p. 62 quoted in Carroll 1999, p. 286)

Acknowledgments I would like to thank Simone Sattler (graduate of University of Vienna in international business administration) for her valuable support in research and providing tables and graphs clearly arranged and intelligible. Sources were quoted and put together with best care and attention.

References

Bartol, L. (2008). *Three CSR models in new European Union member states and candidate countries* (CSR Paper 43).

Bussière, M., Fidrmuc, J., et al. (2005). *Trade integration of Central and Eastern Countries.* Lessons Learned from a Gravity Model, ECB Working Paper Series, No 545. Frankfurt: European Central Bank.

Bohata, M. (2005). Discovering a new concept of authority. In A. Habisch et al. (Eds.), *Corporate social responsibility across Europe.* Berlin: Springer.

Bowen, H. R. (1953). *Social responsibilities of the businessman.* New York: University of Iowa Press.

Carroll, A. (1991). The pyramid of corporate social responsibility: Toward the moral management of organizational stakeholders. *Business Horizonts, 34,* 39–48. (see also http://www.csrquest.net, accessed 15 November 2013)

Carroll, A. B. (1999). Corporate social responsibility. Evolution of a definitional construct. *Business & Society, 38*(3), 268–295.

Campbell, J. L. (2007). Why would corporation behave in socially responsible ways? An institutional theory of corporate social responsibility. *Academy of Management Review, 32*(3), 946–967.

Czech Donors' Forum. (2013). Accessed September 22, 2013, from http://www.expats.cz

Commission of the European Communities. (Ed.) (2001). *Green paper, promoting a European framework for corporate social responsibility.* Accessed September 22, 2013, from http://europa.eu/documents/comm/green_papers/index_de.htm

Commission of the European Communities. (Ed.) (2002). *Corporate social responsibility: A business contribution to sustainable development.* Accessed September 22, 2013, from http://europa.eu/documents/comm/green_papers/index_de.htm

Der Spiegel online. Russland: Angriff auf Pussy-Riot-Aktivistinnen Aljochina und Tolokonnikowa. Accessed September 14, 2014, from http://www.spiegel.de/politik/ausland/russland-pussy-riot-aktivistin-aljochina-bei-angriff-verletzt-a-957235.htm

Drucker, P. (1984). The new meaning of corporate social responsibility. *California Management Review, 26,* 53–63.

European Commission. (Ed.) (2011). *A renewed EU strategy 2011–14 for corporate social responsibility.* Accessed September 22, 2013, from http://europa.eu/documents/comm/green_papers/index_de.htm

Fekete, L. (2005). Social welfare lagging behind economic growth. In H. André et al. (Eds.), *Corporate social responsibility across Europe.* Berlin: Springer.

Friedman, M. (1962). *Capitalism and freedom.* Chicago: University of Chicago.

Gasparski, W. (2005). Business expectations beyond profit. In H. André et al. (Eds.), *Corporate social responsibility across Europe.* Berlin: Springer.

Habisch, A., Jonker, J., et al. (Eds.). (2005). *Corporate social responsibility across Europe.* Berlin: Springer.

Hofstede, G. (1984). Cultural dimension in management and planning. *Asia Pacific Journal of Management, 1*(2), 81–99.

International Monetary Fund. (2010, January). *Central and Eastern Europe regional resident representative site.* Accessed September 21, 2013, from http://www.imf.org

Katz, J., Swanson, D., & Nelson, L., (1999). *Culture based expectations of corporate citizenship.* Accessed May 20, 2004, from http://info.cba.ksu.edu/Katz/Working%Pagers/culture.pdf (quoted in Lenssen et al. 2004).

Katz, J. P., & Nelson, L. K. (2001). Culture-based expectations of corporate citizenship: A propositional framework and comparison of four culture. *The International Journal of Organizational Analysis, 9*(2), 149–171.

Koleva, P., Rodet-Kroichvili, N., et al. (2010). Is corporate social responsibility the privilege of developed market economies? Some evidence from Central and Eastern Europe. *The International Journal of Human Resource Management, 21*(2), 274–293.

Kostjuk, K. (2005). The thin line between small business and big politics. In A. Habisch et al. (Eds.), *Corporate social responsibility across Europe.* Berlin: Springer.

Lenssen, G., & Vorobey, V. (2005). The role of business in society in Europe. In A. Habisch et al. (Eds.), *Corporate social responsibility across Europe*. Berlin: Springer.

Lewicka-Strzalecka, A. (2006). Opportunities and limitations of CSR in the postcommunist countries: Polish case. *Corporate Governance, 6*(4).

Litovchenko, S., & Korsakov, M. (Eds.) (2003). *Corporate social responsibility: Public expectations*. Moscow.

Losoncz, A. (2005). Confronting a leadership vacuum. In A. Habisch et al. (Eds.), *Corporate social responsibility across Europe*. Berlin: Springer.

Matten, D., & Moon, J. (2005). A conceptual framework for understanding CSR. In A. Habisch et al. (Eds.), *Corporate social responsibility across Europe*. Berlin: Springer.

OECD. (1999). *Environment in the transition to a market economy: Progress in Central- and Eastern Europe and the New Independent States*. OECD

Oesterreichische Nationalbank. (2013). Accessed September 15, 2013, from http://www.oenb.at/isaweb/report.do?lang=DE&report=950.1.2

Raiffeisen Research. (May 2013). *CEE banking Sector Report*. Raiffeisen Research

Reynaud, E., Egri, C. P., et al. (2007). The differences in values between managers of the European Founding Countries, the new members and the applicant countries: Societal Orientation or Financial Orientation? *European Management Journal, 25*(2), 132–145.

Segal, J.-P. (2004). *Pluralite des lectures politiques de la responsibilite sociale de l'enterprise en Europe*. Unpublished paper. ENPC, CNRS, Gestion et Societe.—quoted in Lenssen et al., (2004).

Steurer, R., Martinuzzi, A., et al. (2012). Public policies on CSR in Europe: Themes, instruments, and regional differences. *Corporate Social Responsibility Environment Management, 19*, 206–227.

The Hofstede Centre. (2013). Accessed September 15, 2013, from http://geert-hofstede.com/austria.html

Transparency International, Corruption Perception Index 2008 and 2012. Accessed September 23, 2013, from http://www.transparency.org

Trompenaars, F. (1997). *Riding the waves of culture*. London: Nicholas Brealey.

United Way Worldwide. (2013). Accessed September 28, 2013, from http://worldwide.unitedway.org/pages/what-is-united-way

UNDP (Mark Line, Robert Braun). (2007). *Baseline study on CSR practices in the New EU Member States and candidate countries*. UNDP

o.V., *Russia beyond the headlines*. Accessed September 28, 2013, from http://rbth.co.uk/npo_law

Votaw, D. (1972). Genius becomes rare: A comment on the doctrine of social responsibility. *California Management Review, Winter 1972*, 25–31.

Vorobey, V. (2005). In search of national identity. In H. André et al. (Eds.), *Corporate social responsibility across Europe*. Berlin: Springer.

10 Years' Equator Principles: A Critical Appraisal

Manuel Wörsdörfer

Abstract 4 June 2013 marked the formal launch of the third generation of the Equator Principles (EP III) and the tenth anniversary of the EPs—enough reasons for evaluating the EPs initiative from an economic ethics and business ethics perspective. This chapter deals with the following questions: What has been achieved so far by the EPs? Which reform steps need to be adopted to further strengthen the EPs Framework? Can the EPs be regarded as a role model in the field of sustainable finance and CSR? The first part explains the term EPs and introduces the keywords related to the EPs Framework. The second part summarises the main characteristics of the newly released third generation of the EPs. The third part critically evaluates EP III from an economic ethics and business ethics perspective. The chapter concludes with a summary of the main findings.

1 Introduction

The Equator Principles (EPs) aim for environmental protection (i.e. the protection of project-affected ecosystems), the promotion of environmental and social stewardship and corporate environmental and social responsibility (CESR)—including human rights.

The EPs are officially described as a voluntary and self-regulatory finance industry benchmark in project finance. In particular, they are a finance industry standard for environmental and social risk management or, as it is often referred to, a 'credit risk management framework for determining, assessing, and managing environmental and social risk in Project Finance transactions'[1] (EP website). The Equator Principles Association (EPA) refers to the principles as the 'gold standard' (Lazarus and Feldbaum 2011: i) and good business practice in environmental and social risk management for project finance.

---

[1] cp. EPA (2013b).

M. Wörsdörfer (✉)
Goethe Universität, Frankfurt, Germany
e-mail: woersdoerfer@wiwi.uni-frankfurt.de

© Springer International Publishing Switzerland 2015
K. Wendt (ed.), *Responsible Investment Banking*, CSR, Sustainability, Ethics & Governance, DOI 10.1007/978-3-319-10311-2_32

The EPs impose obligations on both lenders—the so-called Equator Principles Financial Institutions (EPFI)—and borrowers (EPFIs' clients) with regard to environmental and social impact assessment, public participation and stakeholder engagement, risk management, compliance, enforcement and monitoring. For example, lenders are accountable to implement responsible and sustainable lending practices. They are liable for negative social and environmental externalities of their clients. While the participating EPFIs have adopted the EPs and help enforce and monitor them, it is the client or borrower who is expected to fulfil and adhere to the laid-down requirements. These obligations are imposed by the lender upon the borrower, and they are formalised as covenants that are part of the loan documentation or investment agreement between the financial institution and the project developer (cp. the eigth Equator Principle on Covenants).

The term Equator represents the balance between 'developed countries', 'developing countries' and emerging markets, a balance between the southern and the northern hemisphere, between East and West. The EPs apply *globally* on both sides of the Equator. The third generation of the EPs (EP III) in particular applies to four financial products, namely project finance, advisory services related to project finance, project-related corporate loans and bridge loans. They apply where total project capital costs exceed US$10 million. They are adopted by so-called EPFIs, financial institutions that are active in project finance or project-related advisory services.

2   Equator Principles: The Third Generation

The updated third generation of EPs (EP III) consists of ten principles.[2] The first principle (*Review and Categorisation*) requires the EPFIs to categorise each proposed project 'based on the magnitude of its potential environmental and social risks and impacts'.[3] The screening process is based on the environmental and social categorisation process of the International Finance Corporation (IFC).[4] Category A projects are 'projects with potential significant adverse environmental and social risks and/or impacts that are diverse, [cumulative] irreversible or unprecedented'. Category B projects are 'projects with potential limited adverse environmental and social risks and/or impacts that are few in number, generally site-specific, largely reversible and readily addressed through mitigation measures'. Category C contains 'projects with minimal or no adverse environmental and social risks and/or impacts'. The categorisation process is crucial due to the decision on which environmental and social standards and procedures are subsequently applied. The following EPs apply to Category A and B projects only. Category C projects do not

---

[2] cp. EPA (2013a).

[3] The following quotes refer to the third generation of the EPs (EP III): cp. EPA (2013a: 5).

[4] cp. International Finance Corporation (2012a, b).

fall into the EPs Framework since they are socially and environmentally inoffensive; they can be classified as safe from an environmental, social and human rights perspective.

Principle 2 (*Environmental and Social Assessment*) requires the client to conduct for all Category A and B projects an environmental and social assessment process to address all relevant environmental and social risks and impacts of the proposed project. The Environmental and Social Assessment Documentation should include 'measures to minimise, mitigate and offset adverse impacts'. It should also include an Environmental and Social Impact Assessment (ESIA) and an alternatives analysis for projects emitting more than 100,000 tonnes of CO_2 equivalents annually.[5] For these projects, an alternatives analysis has to be conducted to evaluate less greenhouse gas (GHG)-intensive technologies and procedures.

Which environmental and social standards are applicable depends on the location of the particular project. In 'designated countries'—i.e. mainly industrial and (high-income) OECD countries—compliance with host country laws, regulations and permits pertaining to environmental and social issues is required. In 'non-designated countries', however, compliance is also required with the IFC Performance Standards and the World Bank's Environmental, Health and Safety (EHS) Guidelines (Principle 3: *Applicable Environmental and Social Standards*).

Principle 4 (*Environmental and Social Management System and Equator Principles Action Plan*) demands that the client develops and maintains an Environmental and Social Management System[6] (ESMS) as well as an Environmental and Social Management Plan (ESMP). The overall aim is to comply with the applicable environmental and social standards. In case that the applicable standards are not met, the client and the EPFI will develop a joint EP action plan.

Principle 5 asks for an encompassing and constant *stakeholder engagement* process. Project-affected communities and other stakeholder groups must have rights to information, consultation and influence. Of particular importance is the 'informed consultation and participation' (ICP) process, a process that ideally takes place in a 'culturally appropriate manner'. Information has to be readily and publicly available to the affected communities in their local languages. The disclosure of information (e.g. assessment documentation) should occur as early as possible in the assessment process—ideally within the planning stage and before construction commences—and on an ongoing basis. Project-affected communities must have the right to participate in decision-making (i.e. notion of *Teilhabe* and inclusion). Their voices have to be heard and the interests and needs of disadvantaged and vulnerable groups taken into consideration. The whole stakeholder engagement process should be free from external manipulation, interference,

---

[5] This includes Scope 1 and Scope 2 emissions: Scope 1 emissions are direct GHG emissions from the facilities themselves while Scope 2 emissions refer to the indirect GHG emissions associated with the off-site production of energy used by the infrastructure or industry project (cp. EPA 2013a: 19).

[6] cp. for more information on E(S)MS: Wood (2003a, b), Wood and Johannson (2008).

coercion and intimidation. Projects with adverse impacts on indigenous peoples even require 'free, prior, and informed consent' (FPIC).

The client is also required by Principle 6 to establish a (project-level and worker) *grievance mechanism* (as part of the ESMS), which is 'designed to receive and facilitate resolution of concerns and grievances about the Project's environmental and social performance. [...] It will seek to resolve concerns promptly, using an understandable and transparent consultative process that is culturally appropriate, readily accessible, at no cost, and without retribution to the party that originated the issue or concern'.

In order to assess compliance with the principles, independent monitoring, reporting and reviewing are required. Principles 7 and 9 deal with these topics. Principle 7 requires that an *independent review* of the assessment documentation (including ESMP, ESMS and stakeholder engagement process) is conducted by an independent environmental and social expert or consultant who is not directly linked with the client. Moreover, the consultant can propose a suitable action plan for the projects that are not in compliance with the EPs. Projects which cause potential adverse impacts on indigenous peoples, critical habitats and cultural heritage and/or involve large-scale resettlement are the most crucial ones.

Principle 9 is devoted to *independent monitoring and reporting*. Here, an independent consultant or a 'qualified and experienced external expert' is required in order to assess project compliance with the EPs. The consultant or expert is responsible to verify monitoring and reporting information after financial close and over the life of the loan.

Principle 8 (*Covenants*) also deals with compliance: It requires the client to 'covenant in the financing documentation to comply with all relevant host country environmental and social laws, regulations and permits'. The client has the covenant to comply with the ESMP and EP action plan, to report publicly in an appropriate format (i.e. provide public reports) and to decommission facilities where applicable. Finally, '[w]here a client is not in compliance with its environmental and social covenants, the EPFI will work with the client on remedial actions to bring the Project back into compliance to the extent feasible. If the client fails to re-establish compliance within an agreed grace period, the EPFI reserves the right to exercise remedies, as considered appropriate'.[7]

Principle 10 deals with accountability in the form of *reporting and transparency* requirements both for clients and EPFIs. The client ensures that a summary of the ESIA is made publicly available and readily accessible (e.g. online disclosure). Principle 10 also requires the client to report publicly on GHG emission levels for projects emitting more than 100,000 tonnes of CO_2 equivalents annually.[8] The

---

[7] cp. Meyerstein (2013: 26).

[8] Interestingly, the new IFC Performance Standards require annual reports for projects emitting over 25,000(!) (and not 100,000) tonnes of CO_2 equivalent annually. The EPs' threshold is much higher than the one on the IFC Performance Standards. Thus, the EPs fall behind the commitments made by the IFC Performance Standards. 'EP III does not contain any commitments on issues that are beyond what is included in the IFC Performance Standards. In some cases the commitment in EP III is even below what is required in IFC PS (such as reporting requirements on CO_2

EPFI is required to report publicly on an at least annual basis on 'transactions that have reached Financial Close and on its EP implementation processes and experience, taking into account appropriate confidentiality considerations'. The EPFI is further requested to provide additional information on the total number of deals financed under the EPs, the number of Category A, B and C projects, the sector, region and country of financed projects as well as information with regard to EP implementation (i.e. credit and risk management policies), independent review, role of senior management, internal preparation and (ongoing) staff training, etc. Project names are conveyed to the EPA. Given the client's approval, this information may be made public on the EPA website in the near future.

The Governance Rules as well as the legal *Disclaimer* state that 'the Equator Principles do not create any rights in, or liability to, any person, public or private'. EPFIs adopt and implement the EPs on a voluntary, legally nonbinding basis. The EPs Framework is, therefore, voluntary in use relying purely on self-enforcement and the goodwill of EPFIs; no mandatory obligations or direct punitive actions can arise from the principles themselves (i.e. exclusion of liability).[9]

3 A Critical Economic-Ethical Evaluation

The following paragraphs critically examine and evaluate the EPs from an economic ethics and business ethics perspective. They weigh the pros and cons and investigate what has been achieved so far and which necessary reform steps should be adopted in the near future. The main aim is to provide a baseline for a revision of EP III and pave the way towards EP IV.

3.1 Limited Scope of the EPs

A major flaw of the EPs is that they only apply to project finance, bridge to project finance, project-related corporate loans and project advisory. Yet the project finance and project-related corporate loans sector is a small segment for multinational financial institutions. The sector commonly accounts for up to 5 % of the overall turnover of major multinational banks. Therefore, project finance portfolios are small and, worse, that portion is declining.[10] It has become clear in recent years that

---

emissions)' (cp. BankTrack 2012: 8). The EPs should ideally go above and beyond the IFC Performance Standards and not fall behind.

[9] cp. Andrew (2009: 306).

[10] On the other hand, the still ongoing trend towards privatisation of state-owned enterprises and the deregulation of state monopolies and key industry sectors (e.g. electricity and telecommunication sectors) in developing countries and emerging markets in combination with the overall trend towards globalisation boost the project finance sector (cp. Scholtens and Dam 2007).

multinational banks have shifted their banking activities towards the highly profitable investment banking sector. Consequently, the EPs apply only to a small
fraction of major bank's total activities.[11] What is required from a business ethics
perspective is a deeper engagement: The application of the EPs should be extended
to other business segments and departments within a firm. The 'Spirit of the Equator
Principles' (Conley and Williams 2011: 547) should ideally be embedded throughout the whole company and across product categories; it should be internalised in
that it is part of the core activities of multinational banks and insurance companies.
What is required is outreach to neighbouring fields, with spillover to other finance
areas. As a minimum requirement, the EPs should be extended to cover not only
project finance, reserve-based lending and project-related corporate loans but any
transaction with a potential significant adverse impact on the socio-ecological
environment, local communities and in particular indigenous peoples. Here, the
third generation of the EPs with its inclusion of project-related corporate loans
and bridge loans is a major step forward to 'Go Beyond Project Finance' (Lazarus
and Feldbaum 2011: iii/8),[12] although it remains to examine whether this extension
of scope has any practical meaning.[13] A future reform of the EPs (EP IV) should
include (all forms of) export finance and other forms of corporate lending and
financing (including IPOs and the issuance of bonds). To put it differently, the
scope of the EPs should at minimum be 'extended from "project finance" to
"financing projects"' (BankTrack 2011: 11).

3.2 Special Case: The BRIC Countries

So far, a high number of BRIC countries' banks are not members of the EPA.[14]
Particularly, the new economic powerhouses, China and India, are underrepre-
sented. In January 2014, only one Chinese (Industrial Bank Co), one Indian
(IDFC Limited) and one Russian bank (Otkritie) have joined the EPA. In particular,
the major Asian players are still missing, e.g. Agricultural Bank of China, Bank of
China, China Construction Bank, ICICI Bank, Industrial and Commercial Bank of

---

[11] cp. Lazarus and Feldbaum (2011: iii).

[12] EP I was solely restricted to project finance. EP II included advisory services related to project
finance. EP III goes one step further and incorporates project-related corporate loans and bridge
loans. EP IV ideally extends the scope and goes beyond project finance including all forms of
corporate financing, export financing, etc.

[13] cp. BankTrack (2012: 8).

[14] One noteworthy exception is Brazil. Here, five financial institutions joined the EPA. Another
exception, although the country is not part of the BRIC countries, is South Africa. Here, three
financial institutions have adopted the EPs.

China (ICBC), Sberbank, State Bank of India, etc.[15] China is of major importance since it is a major cross-border lender even larger than the World Bank Group.[16]

In total, only five Asian banks—one Chinese, one Russian and three Japanese—are members of the EPA and represent only a tiny fraction of all EPFIs (6.4 %); Equator banks from emerging markets represent around 25–35 % of EPFIs (depending on the definition of emerging markets), while there is still a high concentration of Western European, North American and Australian EPFIs accounting for up to 65 % of all EPFIs.[17] Fifty-two out of 79 EPFIs are from industrialised countries—a heavy contrast with the regional distribution of project finance markets and the tremendous growth of project finance transactions in Asia.

The most recent financial market crisis and the Eurozone crisis have caused fundamental shifts in the global project finance markets. The share of North American and European banks in project finance markets has dropped dramatically, due to limited liquidity, constrained risk appetite, mergers and acquisitions (by governments). As a consequence, reduced or closed project finance business activities—the share of project finance activities in emerging markets has rocketed—accounted for up to 45 % of the market in 2012, up from 22 % in 2008. By 2012, the top five project finance banks were all Asian.

Two of the top ten project finance banks were not EPFIs, namely the State Bank of India and the Korea Development Bank.[18] Moreover, most of the Chinese financial institutions displaying huge growth rates in all financial market segments are not (yet) Equator banks—which allows criticism that various non-EP deals are carried out in BRIC countries with detrimental consequences for the environment and the people affected by project finance transactions.

One of the biggest problems in developing or emerging countries is that environmental and social governmental regulations are often inadequate. In addition, these countries face the problem of 'environmental shopping' (Nwete 2005: 178): Borrowers and clients unconcerned with the environmental and social impacts of their projects can easily reduce their transaction costs by shopping the project around until they find a lender with the lowest environmental and social standards and requirements.[19] If bank A—an EPFI—refuses to finance a particular project, non-Equator bank B, C or D might do so, and Equator bank A loses lucrative

---

[15] Other global players which have not yet joined the EP club are the Deutsche Bank, Morgan Stanley and the Swiss UBS.

[16] cp. Meyerstein (2013: 20).

[17] Most of the member institutions are from high-income OECD countries such as Australia (4 EPFIs), Canada (7), France (4), Germany (4), Spain (5), the Netherlands (6), the United Kingdom (5) and the United States (5). One reason is that Western European and North American financial institutions face strong reputational pressure to become 'green' and to behave in a socially responsible manner.

[18] cp. Thomson Reuters (2012), Lazarus (2014).

[19] cp. Hardenbrook (2007: 212).

business, causing a dilemma. As a consequence of environmental shopping, environmental and social standards are circumvented and undermined.[20]

This is emphasised by the geographical limitations and the missing global coverage of the EPs that threaten their de facto impact in the global project finance market. With some major project finance lenders not being part of the EPA, the playing field is not completely levelled.[21] Chinese, Indian and Russian banks have the potential to undermine the whole project by financing 'dirty projects', making it crucial to win them over. The status quo needs to change to prevent disadvantages for member banks, to minimise the problem of environmental shopping and to secure global socio-environmental standards, requiring a broader geographic diversification and outreach to BRIC countries. A major task of the EPA in the upcoming years is to promote the EPs in other geographical areas.[22]

Expanding EP membership in emerging markets and developing countries could, however, create tension[23]: When more financial institutions from different regional areas, different cultural backgrounds and heterogeneous financial interests become members of the EPA, consensus building becomes increasingly difficult. The danger is that only the lowest common denominator is found (which seems already to be the case).[24] One way out of the dilemma between deepening and broadening might be a tiered membership structure reflecting different aspirations. This reform proposal by Lazarus/Feldbaum is discussed later.

3.3   Lack of Transparency

A major problem concerning the EPs is the lack of publicly disclosed information (i.e. limited or no disclosure). Public consultation and public disclosure of information are often prevented by confidentiality duties towards clients.[25] In some

---

[20] The EPs as an industry-wide standard theoretically help to prevent 'environmental shopping' by creating a level playing field. The greater uniformity and commonality among project financiers make it harder for corporations to pit one financial institution against the other and to negotiate or water down environmental and social standards (cp. Hardenbrook 2007: 211). Yet the missing global coverage and outreach to BRIC countries impedes the (entire) abolition of 'environmental shopping'.

[21] cp. Lazarus (2014).

[22] cp. Lazarus and Feldbaum (2011: 6), Conley and Williams (2011: 557/566).

[23] cp. Lazarus and Feldbaum (2011: iii).

[24] BankTrack (2012: 4) criticises the EP III (draft) for being a 'watered down compromise between parties with a widely divergent view on matters, with those Equator banks aiming for a more ambitious new "gold standard" clearly loosing the debate from those who are fine with a little tinkering on the edges'.

[25] On the one hand, breaches of client confidentiality 'can entail civil or criminal sanctions and damage relationship between a lender and its client' (Richardson 2005: 287). On the other hand, 'NGOs have complained that this caveat [appropriate confidentiality considerations] is a hindrance to disclosure and transparency. They have found that banks are characterising many relevant issues as "commercially sensitive" and, as such exempt from disclosure for reasons of confidentiality' (Mikadze 2012: 1406).

cases, banks 'hide behind excessive interpretations of "client confidentiality" to withhold information to stakeholders and the public' (BankTrack 2011: 5).[26] It is, however, in the bank's own interest not to hide behind confidentiality issues and to be more open-minded towards stakeholder dialogue and engagement. Inclusion rather than secrecy as well as a spirit of transparency could help restore public trust in the banking sector.

Another problem related to lack of transparency is the lack of consistent reporting standards and a lack of agreed standards for audits..[27] It remains to be seen whether the new reporting requirements of EP III (Principle 10) will help to overcome the lack of transparency and accountability. The EP III reporting requirements with more detailed information on the EP portfolio (i.e. detailed composition, regional and sectoral breakdown) appear to be a step in the right direction. Mandatory revelation and online disclosure of all project names and project sponsors financed under the EPs are still missing, but there will be a list of the projects financed by EPFIs on the EPA website to demonstrate that EPs have been applied by EPFIs. This is, however, subject to client consent. Project level disclosure has likewise been strengthened with the new EP Principle 5. Yet (more) detailed information on the EP implementation and compliance should be made public: which projects were approved and which declined, and for what reasons. In the case of noncompliance, what corrective measures have been adopted to bring the project back to compliance.[28]

An encompassing stakeholder dialogue and engagement process is crucial to transparency at project level. Locally affected communities and particularly indigenous peoples should have full rights to information, consultation/participation and influence and full access to all relevant information.[29] This is tackled by the updated Principle 5 and its 'informed consultation and participation' and 'free, prior, and informed consent' paradigms. The challenge is how to implement it in reality. Different interpretations of what FPIC entails might prevent its full realisation. For example, who is affected, who gives consent and what constitutes consent? For IFC consent constitutes at least the agreement of indigenous peoples to the impact assessment and to the action plan to ensure that impacts are stated correctly and actions address indigenous peoples' concerns. Currently, FPIC applies only for projects impacting indigenous peoples. Should there be a universal application of FPIC to all projects? Who counts as indigenous peoples—is the definition in the IFC Performance Standards clear enough? Are their concerns adequately represented in terms of gender, age and societal structure? How many focus

---

[26] cp. Wright (2012: 64).

[27] cp. EPA (2011).

[28] cp. BankTrack (2011, 2012).

[29] cp. the 1989 ILO's Convention No. 169 on Indigenous and Tribal Peoples, the 1992 Rio Declaration on the Environment and Development, the 1998 Aarhus Convention on Access to Information, Public Participation in Decision-making and Access to Justice in Environmental Matters as well as the 2007 UN Declaration on the Rights of Indigenous Peoples.

group consultations will be set up? Who is responsible for seeking FPIC—the state or the company? Does FPIC require a binding consultation or is an informative consultation sufficient? Does FPIC grant any veto rights (the answer is no—see below)? Does it require unanimity? If a majority is sufficient, which majority rule should be followed? Is two-thirds' majority approval sufficient for consent? Does 51 % approval constitute consent? And what happens in cases when consent cannot be reached and third-party mediation fails?

Stakeholder engagement also needs to be enhanced: A structural reform in the form of a creation of an EP advisory group with representatives from stakeholder and civil society groups and an EP forum for engagement on finance industry sustainability issues seems promising.[30] The inclusion of stakeholder groups and particularly NGOs in decision-making processes of the EPA could raise the legitimacy of the EPs and strengthen it. The feedback EPFIs will receive from various civil society organisations will help overcome practical challenges.

3.4 Lack of Accountability and Liability

The disclaimer of the EPs states that the principles do not create any rights or liabilities, which ensures there are no mandatory obligations or direct punitive actions that can arise. The EPs Framework is a voluntary, legally nonbinding governance system that relies on self-enforcement. Minimum entry requirements and absolute performance standards are lacking. Also lacking are clear, verifiable metrics that are transparently and independently monitored.[31]

This lack of accountability occurs at an individual project (micro level), organisational (meso level) and institutional level (macro level).[32] It brings negative effects on project-affected communities, local stakeholder groups as well as EPFIs: Irresponsible business activities negatively affect the organisational legitimacy of financial institutions. They might open or widen the legitimacy gap between organisational and social values respectively between current business practices and societal expectations and perceptions. In the end, they might threaten the reputational capital of a company.[33] If EPFIs are truly committed to the 'spirit of the EPs', then they need to implement effective measures (including complaint and remedy mechanisms) that ensure external accountability to the public, project-affected communities, shareholders *and* stakeholders.

---

[30] cp. Lazarus and Feldbaum (2011: 10), BankTrack (2011: 10), BankTrack (2012).

[31] cp. Schepers (2011: 101).

[32] cp. O'Sullivan and O'Dwyer (2009: 556).

[33] cp. Haack et al. (2010: 23), O'Sullivan and O'Dwyer (2009).

Some commentators even go as far as to claim *third-party beneficiary rights for project-affected communities*[34] in order to enhance accountability and liability. These rights would allow non-signatories to a contract (i.e. project-affected communities) to enforce their rights against the contracting parties (i.e. lender and borrower). A third-party beneficiary status would provide a right to a promised performance enforceable by a non-signatory to a contract. This approach proposed by Marco[35] would hold both borrowers and lenders accountable for failing to adhere to the EPs. Borrowers and lenders as promisors owe duties of performance to project-affected communities as local stakeholders that if breached are enforceable by the respective communities. EPFIs and clients that violate the EPs could be sued[36]: Project-affected communities would be able to assert their third-party beneficiary rights through breach of contract actions in US,[37] Canadian[38] or European courts. The overall aim is to curb negative environmental and social impacts on local communities and to ensure that project-affected communities and indigenous peoples maintain their livelihoods.[39]

---

[34] The *Alien Tort Claims Act* in the United States allows US companies to be sued by foreigners from the host country in US courts for torts committed abroad. Domestic courts become increasingly aware of human rights abuses committed on foreign soil and the need to grant legal standing for the victims. More and more litigations are brought before domestic courts for distant human rights violations perpetrated by governments or private actors such as multinational companies (cp. Imai et al. 2007: 137; Imai et al. 2012; Zumbansen 2004, 2005, 2006).

[35] cp. Marco (2011).

[36] If a lawsuit could be brought against an EPFI for violating the EPs, this would have significant consequences: EPFIs would have an increased incentive to strictly screen and monitor financed projects in order to avoid lawsuits (as well as the fines for violating environmental and social laws, the court fees for defending against these lawsuits and the damage to the brand reputation). Yet this possibility would also create a large disincentive for other banks to join the EPA, and already members of the EPs could leave the association to avoid being sued (cp. Hardenbrook 2007: 218). Nevertheless, accountability, liability and transparency are indispensable aspects of an effective governance regime: Global environmental, social and human rights standards can only be established and effectively monitored when the relevant actors can be held accountable for their practices. Moreover, third-party beneficiary rights and the possibility of lawsuits could also help to separate free-riders that are merely interested in gaining reputational benefits from those EPFIs that are truly committed to the 'spirit of the EPs'.

[37] cp. the 1789 US Alien Tort Statute/Alien Tort Claims Act: 'The district courts shall have original jurisdiction of any civil action by an alien for a tort only, committed in violation of the law of nations or a treaty of the United States' (28 U.S.C. § 1350).

[38] cp. Supreme Court of Canada (2013).

[39] cp. Marco (2011), Hardenbrook (2007: 218).

3.5 Inadequate Monitoring

So far, EP compliance relies mainly on passive or interactive monitoring.[40] NGOs, civil society organisations and other stakeholder groups function as watchdogs.[41] In case of apparent noncompliance—i.e. corporate governance scandals and serious violations of environmental, social and human rights standards—NGOs might start public naming and shaming campaigns. These protests often catch media attention and as a consequence might create negative publicity for the involved EPFIs and their clients. In fact, most of the founding members of the EPs have been targeted by NGO criticism and civil society organisations' advocacy campaigns. Therefore, it is in the EPFIs own best interest to take preventative measures and to boost their credibility and reputation relative to critics. To avoid reputational threats, an active and 'internal' form of monitoring is required. A mandatory, independent and transparent third-party assessment of compliance—e.g. in the form of an independent EP ombudsman[42]—is needed (Principles 7 and 9 deal with these particular requirements. It remains to be seen whether they are able to establish a properly working independent review and monitoring system). This impartial verification of conformity should be based on absolute performance standards as well as clear, verifiable metrics that are transparently monitored—both missing from the third generation of the EPs. Finally, official and joint project-level grievance mechanisms as well as third-party complaint (and dispute settlement) mechanisms[43] at the corporate or industry level are needed to address inadequate implementation and noncompliance. These compliance mechanisms should conform to the principles of legitimacy, accessibility, predictability, equitability, rights compatibility and transparency. It is important to examine whether Principle 6 of the third generation of the EPs might be able to establish effective and efficient project-level grievance and complaint mechanisms.

---

[40] cp. Sarro (2012: 1542).

[41] cp. O'Sullivan and O'Dwyer (2009).

[42] The IFC has already established an ombudsman and compliance officer; cp. IFC Compliance Advisor Ombudsman (2013).

[43] These third-party complaint mechanisms on the associational level could complement client's project-level grievance mechanisms. These mechanisms ideally help to enhance corporate credibility and reputation by fostering lender and client compliance. They also help to overcome the problem of freeriding (due to the fact that the detection of freeriding and cheating is more likely) and help to avoid *collective-action problems* (among EPFIs and within the EPA) and *principle-agent problems* [between lenders (EPFIs as principals) and sponsors/clients (as agents)]. Interestingly, EPFIs play a double role: They function as self-regulators and regulators; the EPs regulate Equator banks (being part of the regulating EPA) as well as EPFIs' clients via loan documentation and covenants (i.e. hierarchical relationship) (cp. Flohr 2014).

3.6   Lack of Implementation and Enforcement

The EPs are a set of voluntary guidelines without appropriate accountability, monitoring and auditing systems. The self-regulatory regime is ineffective since a credible deterrent, an 'enforcement pyramid' (including delisting[44] and exclusion of non-compliant EPFIs) and formal sanctions are absent (cp. Sect. 3.8 on sanctions). Loopholes, grey areas and a discretionary leeway also exist to circumvent the principles in myriad ways (cp. Sect. 3.9 on exit-door strategies).

The lack of committed resources to the implementation of the principles by the respective EPFIs is also a problem. The EPs need to be embedded throughout the whole organisation. All levels of an organisation should internalise the spirit of the EPs. Some of the important factors are environmental and social management systems, environmental and social risk management, monitoring and auditing systems as well as due diligence. Environmental and social risk management as well as CSR due diligence should ideally be integrated into the company's core businesses. Recruitment, outside consultation, staff and front-line training as well as awareness rising and sensitising are essential, as is top-level commitment: The CEO and other senior managers function as role models. A change in organisational culture also affects the incentive structures and in particular the bonus payment systems that should be long- rather than short-term oriented. Additionally, it is required to enhance funding and staffing of the EPA (i.e. reform of the EPA). The currently available financial and personnel resources are insufficient to guarantee proper assistance and advice to implement the principles and to effectively monitor compliance with standards.[45]

3.7   Practical Failure

EPFIs are still financing controversial projects, particularly in developing countries where investors try to maximise profits while shirking contractual responsibilities (covenants) in project-affected communities.[46] The funding of 'dirty projects' continues.[47] Some of the most controversial projects include large-scale oil and

---

[44] So far, a delisting is possible according to the EPA Governance Rules if an EPFI fails to report publicly within 18 months or if it does not pay the annual fee. Only in these cases will an EPFI be removed from the list and, thus, be no longer a member of the EPA (a read option, however, is still possible). Yet it is not planned to delist a company due to noncompliance.

[45] cp. Lazarus and Feldbaum (2011: iii).

[46] cp. Marco (2011: 453).

[47] Dirty projects are those projects that involve one or more of the following socio-environmental and human rights standards violations: environmental degradation; community health risks; destruction of community livelihoods, especially those of indigenous peoples; forced resettlements and displacements; forced labour/child labour; poor working conditions/violation of labour rights; unfair terms of employment; trade union intimidation and suppression; discrimination due to

gas projects (e.g. in the Arctic) and massive fossil fuel projects particularly those emitting GHG.[48] The aim of EP III is to limit GHG emissions and, in general, negative externalities of project finance. The EPA should reconsider whether significantly high-emitting projects succeeding a certain threshold should be automatically excluded from financing. So far, a categorical exclusion of projects and business activities with a high impact on climate change/global warming does not exist.

A further problem concerns the financing of nuclear power plants, which are, from an environmental perspective, highly destructive and unsustainable (i.e. the problem of finding an adequate permanent repository site for nuclear waste), leaving aside the inherent risks and dangers of nuclear energy.

In summary, non-compliance continues. The EPs are still violated in practice on both sides. Both borrowers and lenders fail to implement the EPs in practice. Reasons for EP breaches are the failure of an enforcement mechanism, the lack of formal sanctions, the lack of objective and verifiable metrics to measure performance, a lack of transparent monitoring and last but not least, an inconsistent EP implementation: The latter should be overcome by facilitating knowledge transfer, information sharing, and membership capacity building especially via the EPA. The website/intranet of the EPA is the ideal place to provide all EPFIs with case studies, training materials, guidelines, implementation tools and resources. Best practice workshops and regional workshops should be organised to help EPFIs with implementation.[49]

3.8 Sanctions

Monitoring, enforcement and sanctions form an indissoluble triangle. In all three regards, the EPs lack proper governance mechanisms. With regards to sanctions, do

---

gender, race, nationality, ethnicity, religion, disability, age or sexual orientation; use of coercion, intimidation and violence; obstruction of justice and intimidation of the free press; production of and trade with illegal and/or controversial weapons; trade with countries that abuse human rights; pervasive tax noncompliance; speculative investments, especially investments in food commodities; corruption, bribery and fraud; contribution to war crimes; collaboration with security forces/ paramilitary groups; and human rights violations committed by subsidiaries and (sub-)contractors along the labour and supply chain. By providing financial support to their clients (i.e. provision of corporate loans as well as managing, underwriting and/or assisting with the issuance of shares and bonds; financial institutions (FI) are also significant shareholders in many of the companies), FIs tacitly condone, promote and profit from the controversial business operations of their business partners—some of these harmful investments contribute directly to serious breaches of human rights and social and environmental regulation. FIs, thus, play a key role in determining the future existence of the aforementioned detrimental business practices: Through their investment and business decisions, they co-determine whether or not financial resources are used in an ethical and sustainable manner (cp. Facing Finance 2012, 2013: 4).

[48] cp. BankTrack (2011: 13), BankTrack (2012: 10).

[49] cp. Lazarus and Feldbaum (2011: 8).

the EPs have enough bite to penalise institutions that fall behind their voluntary commitments? Currently, EPFIs face few sanctions should they not comply with EP governance structures. So far, only public naming and shaming campaigns that cause media attention put EPFIs and their clients under pressure.[50] Especially NGOs functioning as watchdogs have a powerful position when it comes to reputational pressure. They help to ensure that non-state actors such as multinational companies abide by their voluntary commitments and guidelines (e.g. corporate human rights responsibility, responsibility for sustainable development and environmental stewardship). Nevertheless, this passive and ex-post way of monitoring is not sufficient to prevent non-compliance. What is needed is the establishment of a credible deterrent and an 'enforcement pyramid'. This pyramid should start with less coercive means such as an appeal to lender's and client's environmental and social responsibilities, warnings and deadlines for bringing projects back into compliance. Only when these fail should more coercive tactics such as formal sanctions and fines be employed. The final stage of such an enforcement pyramid should include the delisting of non-compliant institutions and an exclusion of EPFIs not meeting the standards.[51]

3.9 Exit-Door Strategies

The EPs are vaguely, even ambiguously, formulated leaving enough discretionary leeway for diverging interpretations. The language used is often declaratory rather than compulsory; some principles are conditional in nature; others contain mere recommendations. Words such as 'should', 'intend', 'aim', 'encourage',[52] 'make aware of' and 'commit' are used, while legal terminologies such as 'shall', 'must', 'will' and 'oblige' are more or less avoided. The EPs are written in 'should' not in 'shall' language, which implies no legal obligations. Loopholes and grey areas also exist. [53] Borrowers and lenders are able to circumvent the contractual obligations of the EPs to avoid being classified as high risk.[54] Banks can redefine their project finance activities as representing something else, such as corporate or export finance, and project financiers take the back-door option and classify their projects as Category B or C to avoid a stricter A classification.[55]

---

[50] cp. Lee (2008: 362).

[51] cp. Sarro (2012: 1549).

[52] What happens if 'encouraging' and 'awareness rising' do not lead to anything? Which formal sanctions exist?

[53] For example, the alternatives analysis requires 'the evaluation of *technically* and *financially* feasible and *cost-effective* options' leaving enough discretionary leeway for the involved EPFIs and their clients.

[54] cp. Marco (2011: 470).

[55] cp. Haack et al. (2010: 21), Wright (2012: 68).

3.10   Adoption Motives[56]

NGOs accuse EPFIs of green washing and window dressing[57]: An often-heard criticism is that the EP engagement is just a PR exercise (i.e. CSR as a mere rhetoric device). Multinational banks, so the argument goes, are merely interested in the branding benefits and the increased reputational capital. Their main aim is to avoid naming and shaming campaigns, negative media coverage and public criticism that might threaten banks' reputational capital. As such, adopting the EPs is just seen as a precautionary measure against the potential threat of public outcry and a form of managing nonfinancial risk (e.g. reputational risk management). Response to sociopolitical stakeholder pressure is seen here as the main motive behind the adoption of the principles, mainly motivated by strategic reasons rather than intrinsic motives.

Others criticise that the EPFIs aim to avoid mandatory and formal, state-run regulations and the costs accompanied with this potential future regulatory compliance. Firms use the freedom of self-regulation to pre-empt governmental regulations. By adopting the EPs, they can decrease this threat of potential regulation and the accompanied compliance costs.

The EPs are also criticised for their symbolic nature (i.e. 'economy of symbolism'): According to that, the EPs are a mere symbolic gesture leaving enough flexibility and discretionary leeway as well as a minimal appeasement strategy aiming to appease NGOs and other stakeholder groups.[58]

It is almost impossible to figure out the particular and concrete motives of EPFIs that made them adopt the EPs—most likely, it is an interdependent mixture of financial and nonfinancial rationales. Yet it is clear that the adoption process has to be followed by an adequate embedding and implementation process. The spirit of the EPs has to be internalised; otherwise, they remain a paper tiger (i.e. high-

---

[56] The main motives for financial institutions to adopt the EPs include the following ones: (1) level the playing field, (2) managing financial risks/credit risk mitigation and (3) reputational risk management/managing nonfinancial risks. Besides these economic and self-interested rationales for EP adoption (i.e. EPFIs are regarded as private profit-seeking entities that try to minimise financial, legislative and reputational risks and/or try to follow a differentiation-based strategy that allows them to achieve competitive advantages), altruistic motives also seem to play a (minor) role: Among them are good corporate citizenship, environmental consciousness, public goods preferences (i.e. CSR and environmental protection/sustainability as public goods), social preferences or warm-glow preferences of employees, investors and consumers, etc. (cp. Chan 2012; Conley and Williams 2011: 550; Kulkarni 2010; Macve and Chen 2010: 894).

[57] cp. for an opposing view (Scholtens and Dam 2007: 1308): 'We do not find support for the view that adoption of the Equator Principles is merely window dressing, since there are at least some costs involved' (e.g. larger operational, screening and implementation costs; EP compliance might also lead to a delay in project completion due to the time-consuming requirements). The costs, however, might be outweighed by the potential benefits of signing up (e.g. reduced reputational risk/better reputation, positive impact on (financial) risk profile, better market access, charging of premium prices, enhanced possibilities to recruit high-quality employees, etc.).

[58] cp. O'Sullivan and O'Dwyer (2009: 566).

minded commitments on paper that fail to be enforced in practice[59]) and a corporate PR tool for greenwashing and window dressing purposes only. In case that the EPs are (at least partially) backed by an intrinsic motivation (among other motives), voluntary codes of conduct such as the EPs can serve as signalling devices that demonstrate positive (ethical or green) credentials. They help to communicate environmental and business ethics commitments to external stakeholders with the aim to strengthen corporate reputation and organisational legitimacy.[60] In case that intrinsic motivation is lacking, the danger comes up that environmentalism is a 'rich man's game', i.e. compliance with environmental and social standards is only ensured in economically prosperous times. Thus, it is rather unlikely that voluntary codes of ethics will succeed in a weak economic climate. If this would be the case, then the future of the EPs would depend on the state of the global economy.[61]

3.11   Freeriding and Adverse Selection

The motives behind the adoption of the EPs bring us to our next point of criticism—the problem of freeriding and adverse selection.[62] EPFIs know that they potentially gain reputational benefits irrespective of their actual practices. Even EPFIs that do not intend to comply gain good publicity from their association with the EPs. They imitate or mimic the behaviour of good EPFIs, while project-affected communities suffer from a lack of effectiveness and practical failure of the EPs. In other words, irresponsible institutions might claim benefits of enhanced reputation and a reduced threat of government regulations with no intention of actually implementing their new commitments.[63] Strategic free-riders gain the benefits without bearing the implementation and compliance costs. The danger, therefore, comes up of attracting signatories that are not truly committed to the spirit of the EPs. Freeriding behaviour leads to competitive disadvantages for adopters, since they have to bear compliance costs while free-riding companies do not. Additionally, freeriding negatively affects the collective by lowering the standards of the code and by decreasing the level of compliance. In the end, the brand value of the EPs diminishes.[64]

---

[59] Due to a lack of adequate enforcement, monitoring and sanctioning mechanisms, the EPs (in their current version) seem to exist only on paper.

[60] cp. Wright and Rwabizambuga (2006: 90), O'Sullivan and O'Dwyer (2009).

[61] cp. Conley and Williams (2011: 564).

[62] 'Adverse selection results from corporations joining the collective, gaining the benefits of the collective, while at the same time negatively affecting the collective by lowering the standards of the code [...]. As the number of adoptees increases, the newer members are more likely attracted by the benefits while at the same time decreasing the level of compliance. Adverse selection reduces the incentive of strong performers to join or remain as members' (Schepers 2011: 94).

[63] cp. Wright and Rwabizambuga (2006: 91), Macve and Chen (2010: 895), Schepers (2011: 93).

[64] cp. Sarro (2012: 1532).

One proposed solution to overcome the problem of freeriding and adverse selection is to introduce entry criteria for the EP membership and absolute performance standards. Moreover, a two-tiered EPA membership structure[65] reflecting different aspirations would allow EPFIs to voluntarily apply the spirit of the EPs to fields other than project finance, thus moving beyond project finance. This European Union-like 'two-speed' or 'clubs within the club' structure would allow EPFIs to *proactively* respond to ethical and environmental issues and meet the demands of multiple stakeholder groups. EPFIs would have the strategic opportunity to 'over-comply' (Kulkarni), to go beyond what is formally/legally and informally required and gain first-mover advantages. They might boost their credibility and as a consequence gain (additional) reputational capital that directly adds to their brand value. In case that the spirit of the EPs is internalised and embedded throughout the whole organisation, this could also trigger a cultural change within banks and other financial institutions.

While a tiered membership structure once established would allow EPFIs to voluntarily comply with additional and strengthened environmental, social and human rights standards that go beyond the IFC Performance Standards, it would at the same time take into consideration that some EPFIs are not willing or able to comply with the respective strengthened standards (and to bear additional implementation and compliance costs). Nevertheless, these EPFIs would still be part of the EPA. This would ensure that at least minimum environmental, social and human rights standards are met (given that adequate monitoring and sanctioning mechanisms are established).

A tiered membership structure is particularly important when considering the rising tension between a *broadening* (i.e. outreach to BRIC countries) and a *deepening* strategy (i.e. further enhancement and strengthening of the principles): The decision-making process is already slow and complicated given the conflicting views and differing priorities especially between EFPIs from high-income OECD countries and those from 'non-designated countries'. The more financial institutions coming from heterogeneous cultural backgrounds and having (partially) conflicting interests adopt the EPs, the more difficult consensus building within the EPA gets.

---

[65] Such a two-tiered membership structure is de facto already in place. The so-called *Thun Group of Banks* consisting of seven leading international banks (Barclays, BBVA, Credit Suisse, ING Bank, RBS Group, UBS and UniCredit) recently published a working paper on banks and human rights (cp. Thun Group 2013). The paper is the result of 2 years of deliberations among the Thun Group members and provides a (first) guide to the banking sector for operationalizing the UN Guiding Principles on Business and Human Rights. The paper recognises that the UN Guiding Principles apply to all parts of a bank's business segments, including asset management, corporate and investment banking. The paper has been welcomed by BankTrack as a significant step towards recognising the relevance of human rights to banks' core business (cp. BankTrack 2013); yet the paper has also been criticised for its limited scope: the main problem is that it focuses solely on Principles 16–21 of the UN Guiding Principles (which are related to the corporate responsibility to respect human rights) leaving aside the foundational Principles 11–15 as well as all those principles devoted to operational-level grievance, complaint and remedy mechanisms (cp. Principles 22 and 29 of the UN Guiding Principles).

In several occasions in the recent past (cp. the most recent review and update process), only the lowest common denominator could be found. This process of consensus seeking with all its negotiations and bargaining is not only time-consuming and slow, it also inhibits the further advancement of the EPs in general.

3.12 Business and Human Rights

The EPs explicitly acknowledge John Ruggie's *Protect, Respect, and Remedy Framework* (PRR), which forms the basis of the United Nations' *Guiding Principles on Business and Human Rights*.[66] They also acknowledge the Universal Declaration of Human Rights; the International Covenants on Civil and Political Rights, and on Economic, Social and Cultural Rights; the core conventions of the International Labour Organization; and the UN Declaration on the Rights of Indigenous Peoples.

Human rights are closely related and interlinked with the inclusion of project-affected communities, particularly indigenous peoples, but also NGOs, civil society organisations and other local stakeholder groups. It is the aim of the EPs to establish an ongoing and culturally appropriate stakeholder engagement and informed consultation and participation process. Information has to be made readily and publicly available to the project-affected communities in their local languages.[67] The disclosure of information should occur as early as possible in the assessment process—ideally within the planning stage and before construction commences. Project-affected communities should be included in decision-making. Financial institutions and their clients have to make sure that the voices of local stakeholders are heard and that the interests and needs of disadvantaged, vulnerable and marginalised groups are taken into consideration. The whole stakeholder engagement process should be free from external manipulation, interference, coercion and intimidation. Projects with adverse impacts on indigenous peoples even require their 'free, prior, and informed consent' (FPIC). It should be noted that FPIC does not create any veto

---

[66] The UN Guiding Principles on Business and Human Rights is the first global standard for preventing and addressing the risk of adverse impacts on human rights linked to business activities. It encompass three principles: (1) 'the state duty to protect against human rights abuses committed by third parties, including business, through appropriate policies, regulation and adjudication'; (2) 'the corporate responsibility to respect human rights [. . .] acting with due diligence to avoid infringing on the rights of others, and addressing harms that do occur' (i.e. need for a human rights due diligence process that enables corporations to be aware of, prevent and address their adverse human rights impacts); and (3) 'access by victims to effective remedy [. . .] through judicial, administrative, legislative or other appropriate means' (United Nations 2011b; cp. UN 2011a).

[67] A huge problem in this regard that has to be tackled is the problem of illiteracy in developing countries.

rights nor does it require unanimity; however, it strives for consensus building and thus goes beyond the previous EP II consultation paradigm.[68]

The EPs, in theory, go beyond the pure shareholder value approach. They try to incorporate multiple stakeholder perspectives including those of project-affected communities, NGOs, civil society organisations and other stakeholder groups. The aim is dialogue between these groups, EPFIs and their clients. As such, the EPs ideally take a bottom-up approach that enhances democratic legitimacy. Stakeholder dialogue, public discourse and deliberation can be seen here as a source of organisational legitimacy.[69] The principles also allow (multinational) companies to adapt to the changing community expectations of corporate responsibilities and help to reframe their public identity as corporate citizens—going beyond pure profit-seeking entities.[70]

The protection of human rights—together with environmental protection and the fight against global warming/climate change—is, thus, at the heart of the third generation of the EPs. It is remarkable that it took exactly 10 years until the term 'human rights' was introduced into the EPs Framework for the first time. Only the latest version of the EPs contains direct references to corporate human rights policy and corporate human rights due diligence.[71] As such, EP III has to be considered a major step forward compared to EP II with regards to (environmental protection and) human rights. But the current version of the EPs needs to be improved: There is only one explicit reference to the PRR Framework in a footnote. The term 'human rights' is mentioned mainly in the preamble and the exhibit; the term 'human rights due diligence' is mentioned only once and with the addition of 'may be appropriate', while the terms 'Human Rights Impact Assessment (HRIA)' and 'human rights action plan' are lacking. EP III refers only once to gender issues and/or women's rights—tellingly in exhibit II.[72] Most importantly, a huge gap between

---

[68] This idea of inclusion (in the sense of *Teilhabe* and integration) bears some remarkable resemblances to the works of the Nobel Prize laureates Amartya Sen (2009) and Elinor Ostrom (1990) as well as to Kantian philosophy—including Kant's notion of positive freedom, autonomy, human dignity and the categorical imperative which demands that people are treated as ends in themselves and never merely as means to an end (cp. Kant 1797/2013; 1785/2002; 1781/2011).

[69] Haack et al. (2010: 33) speak of 'legitimation as deliberation' and the 'communicative sources of legitimation'; see also Scherer's and Palazzo's (2007) interpretation of Habermasian discourse theory.

[70] cp. Wright and Rwabizambuga (2006: 92), Andrew (2009: 302), Matten and Crane (2005), Moon et al. (2005).

[71] Human rights due diligence requires (1) the development of a human rights policy statement, (2) periodic assessments and reports of actual and potential adverse human rights impacts of corporations' activities and (stakeholder) relationships, (3) the integration of commitments and assessments into internal control and monitoring systems, and (4) reporting and tracking of human rights performance (cp. Torrance 2012).

[72] Principles 7 and 9 (on independent review and monitoring) as well as Principles 9 and 10 (on reporting) can be easily combined, thus creating space for a separate principle solely devoted to human rights issues. This principle should then precede all others and serve as an anchoring or guiding principle (cp. BankTrack 2012: 11; BankTrack 2011: 16).

theory and practice exists. In practice, socio-environmental and human-rights standards are (still) massively abused and undermined by the involved multinational companies, e.g., EPFIs and their clients (still) engage in (funding) 'dirty projects'.

One main reason for this is the inadequate governance structure of the EPs and its association (including ineffective enforcement, monitoring and sanctioning mechanisms). Another reason is that the EPs are mainly based on Ruggie's PRR Framework. They can therefore be qualified as a concept of 'human rights minimalism' (Wettstein 2012a: 745) as well. Ruggie (and the EPs) clearly favours an impact-based concept of negative corporate responsibility according to the motto 'do no harm', that is, avoid causing or contributing to human rights violations. Ruggie (and therefore also the EPs) rejects all forms of positive and leverage-based CSR.[73] States are considered to be the primary duty bearers: According to Ruggie, international human rights laws apply only to states, but not to non-state actors such as (trans- or multinational) corporations. Thus, any duty to protect and realise human rights is part of the exclusive domain of nation states (i.e. nation state-centred perspective). Corporations only need to fulfil the duty to respect human rights; exercising leverage to protect and realise human rights is regarded as an optional matter, not as a moral obligation.[74]

The problem is that Ruggie's (and the EPs') human rights 'voluntarism' clashes with the fundamental moral nature of human rights. Human rights (including social and economic rights) are moral rights or entitlements that are deeply rooted in human dignity and the moral equality of all human beings.[75] They are inalienable and universal moral rights that exist a priori and independently of nation states and legal laws. This status of human rights rules out any form of moral discretion, arbitrariness and human rights voluntariness. Thus, (multinational) corporations have direct moral obligations unconditionally to respect, protect and realise human rights. They are direct duty bearers—in other words: states are not the exclusive and only bearers of positive obligations. Multinational corporations' moral responsibilities must go beyond 'do no harm', and they must do more than merely respect human rights. Their scope of responsibility includes a positive duty to protect and realise human rights. Due to their political role and power (i.e. transnational corporations as political, quasi-governmental actors, de facto rule makers, and (co-)authors of regulations[76]), multinational corporations have a positive duty to speak out (i.e. avoidance of corporate complicity defined as 'aiding and abetting' in human rights violations committed by third parties), a duty to protect victims of human rights abuses, a duty to promote human rights-compatible institutions in home and host countries and a duty to foster change or to put pressure on oppressive governments.

---

[73] cp. Wood (2011a, b, 2012).

[74] cp. Ruggie (2007, 2008, 2009, 2013).

[75] cp. Wettstein (2009a, b, 2010a, b, 2012a, b), Wettstein and Waddock (2005).

[76] cp. Scherer and Palazzo (2008), Scherer et al. (2009).

The EPA would be well advised to take the critique of Ruggie's PRR Framework seriously: What is needed is a push for nonvoluntary, mandatory and legally binding rules for business in particular with respect to human rights as well as a comprehensive impact and leverage-based conception of responsibility (i.e. making use of financial institution's leverage/organisation's capacity to influence other parties' decisions and activities, especially those which are part of the supply and value chain) including positive human rights obligations for corporations and a corporate human rights advocacy and activism.

Conclusion

This chapter has dealt with the special role of financial institutions as (de facto) 'global sustainability regulators' (Conley and Williams 2011)[77] and standard setters in a transnational business context.[78] In many cases, these organisations have taken the lead in fostering CSR and sustainable development, particularly in politically unstable and/or socially and environmentally fragile contexts such as developing countries and emerging markets. By establishing world-wide applicable social and environmental standards, they have adopted the role of quasi-regulators.[79] Moreover, banks, insurance companies and the like are key factors in the transition towards a green economy. They ideally help to catalyse this process towards economic, ecological and social sustainability and CSR by voting with their money (i.e., leverage-based responsibility).[80] During this process, the EPs have an important function to fulfil: They ideally help to balance economic (profit),

(continued)

---

[77] '... lenders, owing to their expertise in the project finance sector and their understanding of existing norms on managing environmental and social risk [...] are relatively well-placed to set effective standards and to effectively monitor their borrowers' conduct. [...] [yet] lenders are currently not well-placed to enforce the [EPs]. Their short-term interest in the completion of the projects they finance impairs their ability to credibly threaten to withdraw financing in the face of persistent non-compliance by borrowers' (cp. Sarro 2012: 1524).

[78] This 'post-Westphalian world order' (Kobrin 2009) is characterised by the following characteristics: shift from government to governance (Foucault 2008); erosion of the regulatory power of the nation state; fragmentation of legal-political authority and power; existence of regulatory or governance gaps; increasing ambiguity of borders and jurisdictions; blurring of the separation between private and public spheres; and politicisation of non-state actors such as transnational corporations, civil society and nongovernmental organisations (cp. Kobrin 2009: 5; see also Jessup 1956; Zumbansen 2006, 2010a, b; Baur 2011: 21).

[79] cp. Conley and Williams (2011).

[80] cp. Conley and Williams (2011: 565).

ecological (planet) and ethical issues (people) (so-called 'triple P' Framework). They have the potential to equally promote self-interest and the common good: EPFIs and clients pursue their own economic (pecuniary) motives,[81] while the adopted principles make sure that environmental, social and human rights standards are met.

Last but not least the EPs have the ability to function as a catalyst for cultural change within banks.[82] Yet in order to fully do so, some necessary reform steps have to be adopted.

According to Jeucken (2001/2002: 72), four types of banking have to be distinguished: *defensive banking* ('... environmental laws and regulations are thought to be threats to its business. Only curative measures are taken. In this vision, care for the environment only adds to costs and there is certainly no money to be earned from it'), *preventive banking* ('... different from the previous phase in that potential costs savings are identified. [...] A bank does not want to go any further than the environmental laws that exist [...] it is somewhat passive, limiting external risks and liabilities and saving production costs internally'), *offensive banking* ('Banks see new opportunities in the marketplace, both in the area of specific products and new markets [...]. The bank is looking for profitable, environmentally sound opportunities in the market, which can compete with alternative investment and lending opportunities. The stance can be described as proactive, creative and innovative [...]. The extra steps are taken whenever there are win-win situations at the micro-level...') and *sustainable banking* ('... the bank lays down qualitative preconditions so that all its activities are sustainable [...] thanks to a consciously chosen policy [...] [and] the ambition to operate sustainably in every respect').

The current EPFIs fall either into the preventive or offensive type of banking category where a holistic and all-encompassing implementation of the spirit of the EPs is still lacking. What is required from an economic ethics perspective is the transformation from preventive/offensive banking towards sustainable banking. This implies that the spirit of the EPs needs to be embedded throughout the whole organisation. All levels of the organisation should internalise the spirit of the EPs. Environmental and social risk management as well as CSR due diligence should ideally be integrated into the company's core businesses. Recruitment, staff and front-line training as well

(continued)

---

[81] By reducing various forms of economic and noneconomic risks, the EPs can also help to make a project a more secure investment and a safer loan.

[82] cp. Conley and Williams (2011: 546). Whether such a change in organisational culture has already started remains doubtful as recent financial market crises, the EURIBOR and LIBOR scandals and other corporate governance scandals (especially in the investment banking sector) have shown.

as awareness and consciousness rising and sensitising are also essential. Of eminent importance is the top-level commitment: The CEO and other senior managers function as role models. A change in organisational culture (towards the ideal of the honourable (banking) merchant) also affects the incentive structures and in particular the bonus payment systems or compensation structures/packages that should be long- rather than short-term oriented. So far, investment managers are judged according to their quarterly or annual performance and not according to their multiple-years performance.[83]

In order to further strengthen the EPs as a true benchmark for responsible investment practices, this paper has identified the following ten necessary reform steps (i.e. top ten priorities towards EP IV[84]):

Ten Necessary Steps for Reform
1. Introduction of an anchoring and guiding principle solely devoted to human rights.
2. Extension of scope I: The spirit of the EPs should be applied to all banking activities (including investment banking) and not being restricted to project finance alone ('going beyond project finance').
3. Extension of (regional) scope II: An outreach strategy to BRIC countries is required in order to guaranty worldwide application of the EPs.
4. Introduction of an enforcement pyramid including automatic sanctions like delisting and exclusion of non-compliant EPFIs.
5. Introduction of absolute performance standards, i.e. clear, verifiable metrics that are transparently and independently monitored which help to assess environmental and social performance of EPFIs and their clients.
6. Introduction of minimum entry requirements that have to be met prior to becoming a member of the EPA (e.g. human rights due diligence, grievance/complaint and remedy mechanisms).
7. Tiered membership structure within the EPA that allows to bridge the gap between broadening and deepening considerations.
8. Reform of the EPA including enhanced funding and staffing, establishment of an EP forum and an EP advisory group as well as establishment of an EP ombudsman office.

(continued)

---

[83] cp. Chan (2012: 1345).

[84] EP III has to be considered as an improvement over EP II (cp. EPA 2006), but bigger steps must be taken by the EPFIs to further strengthen the EPs. Reform measures to fight global warming (climate change) and to fully realise corporate human rights responsibilities are important issues. Further fields of necessary reform include the extension of scope, an increase in transparency and accountability (see also BankTrack 2012).

9. Establishment of third-party beneficiary rights for project-affected communities.
10. Regulatory pressure: Stronger government oversight (including binding/ mandatory regulation) should be accompanied by increasing shareholder pressure (i.e. divestment from companies which violate social, environmental and human rights standards; shareholders filing lawsuits against CEOs and senior management) and market regulation pressure (i.e. denied market access by securities and exchange commissions; exclusion of companies from sustainability indexes).

Given that these reform steps are implemented in the near future (which imply a reform of the Governance Rules[85] as well), the EPs Framework can be seen as the starting point of developing hard(er) law through soft law (i.e. hardening of transnational norms).[86] The EPs have to be considered as an essential step forward in an unregulated and potentially destructive area of doing business, but they require further strengthening, especially strengthening of the governance system (i.e. enforcement, monitoring and sanctioning mechanisms), in order to enhance transparency, accountability and liability.

References

Andrew, J. (2009). Responsible finance? The equator principles and bank disclosures. *The Journal of American Academy Business, 14*(2), 302–307.
BankTrack. (2011). *The outside job. Turning the equator principles towards people and planet.* Accessed July 11, 2013 from www.banktrack.org/show/pages/equator_principles
BankTrack. (2012). *Tiny steps forward on the outside job. Comments on the equator principles III official first draft.* Accessed July 11, 2013 from www.banktrack.org/show/pages/equator_principles#tab_pages_documents
BankTrack. (2013). *BankTrack on the Thun Group Paper on banks and human rights.* Accessed January 8, 2014 from http://www.banktrack.org/download/banktrack_on_the_thun_group_paper_on_banks_and_human_rights/banktrack_thun_group_paper_131119_0.pdf
Baur, D. (2011). *NGOs as legitimate partners of corporations. A political conceptualization.* Dordrecht: Springer.
Chan, M. (2012). What about psychological actors? Behavioral analysis of equator principle adoption and its implications. *German Law Journal, 13*(12), 1339–1362.
Conley, J. M., & Williams, C. A. (2011). Global banks as global sustainability regulators? The equator principles. *Law and Policy, 33*(4), 542–575.
Equator Principles. (2006). *The "equator principles" (EP II).* Accessed July 11, 2013 from http://equator-principles.com/index.php/ep3/ep3
Equator Principles. (2010). *Governance rules.* Accessed November 11, 2013 from www.equator-principles.com/index.php/about/governance-and-management

---

[85] cp. EPA (2010).

[86] cp. Conley and Williams (2011: 565).

Equator Principles. (2011). *Guidance note on equator principles implementation reporting*. Accessed November 11, 2013 from http://equator-principles.com/index.php/reporting-requirements

Equator Principles. (2013a). *The equator principles (EP III)*. Accessed November 11, 2013 from http://equator-principles.com/index.php/ep3/ep3

Equator Principles. (2013b). *Equator principles website*. Accessed January 8, 2014 from www.equator-principles.com/

Facing Finance. (2012). *Dirty profits I* (Report on Companies and Financial Institutions Benefiting from Violations of Human Rights). Accessed January 8, 2014 from http://www.facing-finance.org/wp-content/blogs.dir/16/files/2012/12/ff_dirtyprofits.pdf

Facing Finance. (2013). *Dirty profits II* (Report on Companies and Financial Institutions Benefiting from Violations of Human Rights). Accessed January 8, 2014 from http://www.facing-finance.org/files/2013/12/DIRTY_PROFITS_II.pdf

Flohr, A. (2014). A complaint mechanism for the equator principles – and why equator members should urgently want it. *Transnational Legal Theory* 5(3), 442–463.

Foucault, M. (2008). *The birth of biopolitics. Lectures at the Collège de France 1978–1979*. Houndmills: Palgrave Macmillan.

Haack, P., Schoeneborn, D., & Wickert, C. (2010). *Exploring the constitutive conditions for a self-energizing effect of CSR standards: The case of the "equator principles"* (Working Paper Series Institute of Organization and Administrative Science, No. 115). Zurich: University of Zurich.

Hardenbrook, A. (2007). The equator principles: The private financial sector's attempt at environmental responsibility. *Vanderbilt Journal of Transnational Law, 40*, 197–232.

Imai, S., Mehranvar, L., & Sander, J. (2007). Breaching indigenous law: Canadian mining in Guatemala. *Indigenous Law Journal, 6*(1), 101–139.

Imai, S., Maheandiran, B., & Crystal, V. (2012). *Accountability across borders: Mining in Guatemala and the Canadian justice system* (Osgoode CLPE Research Paper 26/2012). Accessed July 31, 2013 from http://papers.ssrn.com/sol3/papers.cfm?abstract_id=2143679

International Finance Corporation. (2012a). *Performance standards on environmental and social sustainability*. Accessed July 11, 2013 from www.ifc.org/wps/wcm/connect/Topics_Ext_Content/IFC_External_Corporate_Site/IFC+Sustainability/Sustainability+Framework/Sustainability+Framework+–+2012/Performance+Standards+and+Guidance+Notes+2012/

International Finance Corporation. (2012b). *Guidance notes: Performance standards on environmental and social sustainability*. Accessed November 30, 2013 from http://www.ifc.org/wps/wcm/connect/e280ef804a0256609709ffd1a5d13d27/GN_English_2012_Full-Document.pdf?MOD=AJPERES

International Finance Corporation Compliance Advisor Ombudsman. (2013). *CAO annual report 2013*. Accessed November 11, 2013 from http://www.cao-ombudsman.org/publications/documents/CAO_AR13_ENG_high.pdf

Jessup, P. (1956). *Transnational law*. New Haven: Yale University Press.

Jeucken, M. (2001/2002). *Sustainable finance and banking: The financial sector and the future of the planet*. London: Earthscan Publications.

Kant, I. (1781/2011). *The critique of pure reason*. London: Penguin Classics.

Kant, I. (1785/2002). *Groundwork for the metaphysics of morals*. New Haven: Yale University Press.

Kant, I. (1797/2013). *The metaphysics of morals*. Cambridge: Cambridge University Press.

Kobrin, S. J. (2009). Private political authority and public responsibility: Transnational politics, transnational firms and human rights. *Business Ethics Quarterly, 19*(3), 349–374.

Kulkarni, P. (2010). Pushing lenders to over-comply with environmental regulations: A developing country perspective. *Journal of International Development, 22*, 470–482.

Lazarus, S. (2014). The equator principles at ten years. *Transnational Legal Theory, 5*(3), 417–441.

Lazarus, S., & Feldbaum, A. (2011). *Equator principles strategic review* (Final Report). Accessed July 11, 2013 from www.equator-principles.com/resources/exec-summary_appendix_strategic_review_report.pdf

Lee, V. (2008). Enforcing the equator principles: An NGO's principled effort to stop the financing of a paper pulp mill in Uruguay. *Northwestern Journal of International Human Rights, 6*(2), 354–373.

Macve, R., & Chen, X. (2010). The "equator principles": A success for voluntary codes? *Accounting Auditing & Accountability Journal, 23*(7), 890–919.

Marco, M. (2011). Accountability in international project finance: The equator principles and the creation of third-party-beneficiary status for project-affected communities. *Fordham International Law Journal, 34*(3), 452–503.

Matten, D., & Crane, A. (2005). Corporate citizenship: Towards and extended theoretical conceptualization. *The Academy of Management Review, 30*(1), 166–179.

Meyerstein, A. (2013). Global private regulation in development finance: The equator principles and the transnationalization of public contracting. In A. Mathias & S. Stephan (Eds.), *The internationalization of public contracts* (pp. 1–41). Brussels: Bruylant.

Mikadze, K. (2012). Public participation in global environmental governance and the equator principles: Potential and pitfalls. *German Law Journal, 13*(12), 1386–1411.

Moon, J., Crane, A., & Matten, D. (2005). Can corporations be citizens? Corporate citizenship as a metaphor for business participation in society. *Business Ethics Quarterly, 15*(3), 429–453.

Nwete, B. O. N. (2005). The equator principles: How far will it affect project financing? *International Business Law Journal, 2*, 173–188.

Ostrom, E. (1990). *Governing the commons. The evolution of institutions for collective actions.* Cambridge: Cambridge University Press.

O'Sullivan, N., & O'Dwyer, B. (2009). Stakeholder perspectives on a financial sector legitimation process. The case of NGOs and the equator principles. *Accounting, Auditing & Accountability Journal, 22*(4), 553–587.

Richardson, B. J. (2005). The equator principles: The voluntary approach to environmentally sustainable finance. *European Environmental Law Review, 2005*, 280–290.

Ruggie, J. G. (2007). *Business and human rights: Mapping international standards of responsibility and accountability for corporate acts* (Report of the Special Representative of the Secretary-General (SRSG) on the issue of human rights and transnational corporations and other business enterprises; A/HRC/4/035). Accessed October 8, 2013 from www.business-humanrights.org/Documents/RuggieHRC2007

Ruggie, J. G. (2008). *Protect, respect and remedy. A framework for business and human rights* (Report of the Special Representative of the United Nations Secretary-General on the issue of human rights and transnational corporations and other business enterprises). *Innovations: Technology, Governance, Globalization, 3*(2), 189–212. Accessed October 8, 2013 from www.mitpressjournals.org/doi/pdfplus/10.1162/itgg.2008.3.2.189

Ruggie, J. G. (2009). *Business and human rights: Towards operationalizing the "protect, respect and remedy" framework* (Report of the Special Representative of the Secretary-General on the Issue of Human Rights and Transnational Corporations and Other Business Enterprises; A/HRC/11/13). Accessed October 8, 2013 from www.refworld.org/docid/49faf98a2.html

Ruggie, J. G. (2013). *Just business. Multinational corporations and human rights.* New York: W.W. Norton & Company.

Sarro, D. (2012). Do lenders make effective regulators? An assessment of the equator principles on project finance. *German Law Journal, 13*(12), 1522–1555.

Schepers, D. H. (2011). The equator principles: A promise in progress? *Corporate Governance, 11*(1), 90–106.

Scherer, A. G., & Palazzo, G. (2007). Toward a political conception of corporate responsibility – Business and society seen from a Habermasian perspective. *Academy of Management Review, 32*, 1096–1120.

Scherer, A. G., & Palazzo, G. (2008). Globalization and corporate social responsibility. In A. Crane, A. McWilliams, D. Matten, J. Moon, & D. Siegel (Eds.), *The Oxford handbook of corporate social responsibility* (pp. 413–431). Oxford: Oxford University Press.

Scherer, A. G., Palazzo, G., & Matten, D. (2009). Introduction to the special issue: Globalization as a challenge for business responsibilities. *Business Ethics Quarterly, 19*(3), 327–347.

Scholtens, B., & Dam, L. (2007). Banking on the equator. Are banks that adopted the equator principles different from non-adopters. *World Development, 35*(8), 1307–1328.

Sen, A. (2009). *The idea of justice*. Cambridge: Harvard University Press.

Supreme Court of Canada. (2013). *Judgments of the Supreme Court of Canada: Ezokola v. - Canada*. Accessed July 25, 2013 from http://scc.lexum.org/decisia-scc-csc/scc-csc/scc-csc/en/item/13184/index.do

Thomson Reuters. (2012). *Project finance review full year 2012*. Accessed November 11, 2013 from http://dmi.thomsonreuters.com/Content/Files/Q42012_Project_Finance_Review.pdf

Thun Group of Banks. (2013). *UN guiding principles on business and human rights* (Discussion Paper for Banks on Implications of Principles 16–21). Accessed January 8, 2014 from www.csrandthelaw.com/wp-content/uploads/2013/10/thun_group_discussion_paper.pdf

Torrance, M. (2012). Human rights. In M. Torrance (Ed.), *IFC performance standards on environmental and social sustainability. A guidebook*. Markham, Canada: LexisNexis.

United Nations. (2011a). *The UN "protect, respect and remedy" framework for business and human rights*. Accessed July 11, 2013 from www.business-humanrights.org/SpecialRepPortal/Home/Protect-Respect-Remedy-Framework/GuidingPrinciples

United Nations. (2011b). *Guiding principles on business and human rights*. Accessed July 11, 2013 from www.ohchr.org/Documents/Publications/GuidingPrinciplesBusinessHR_EN.pdf

Wettstein, F. (2009a). *Multinational corporations and global justice. Human rights obligations of a quasi-governmental institution*. Stanford: Stanford University Press.

Wettstein, F. (2009b). Beyond voluntariness, beyond CSR: Making a case for human rights and justice. *Business and Society Review, 114*(1), 125–152.

Wettstein, F. (2010a). The duty to protect: Corporate complicity, political responsibility, and human rights advocacy. *Journal of Business Ethics, 96*, 33–47.

Wettstein, F. (2010b). For better or for worse: Corporate responsibility beyond "do no harm". *Business Ethics Quarterly, 20*(2), 275–283.

Wettstein, F. (2012a). Silence as complicity: Elements of a corporate duty to speak out against the violation of human rights. *Business Ethics Quarterly, 22*(1), 37–61.

Wettstein, F. (2012b). CSR and the debate on business and human rights: Bridging the great divide. *Business Ethics Quarterly, 22*(4), 739–770.

Wettstein, F., & Waddock, S. (2005). Voluntary or mandatory: That is (not) the question. Linking corporate citizenship to human rights obligations for business. *Zeitschrift für Wirtschafts- und Unternehmensethik zfwu, 6*(3), 304–320.

Wood, S. (2003a). Environmental management systems and public authorities in Canada: Rethinking environmental governance. *Buffalo Environmental Law Journal, 10*, 129–210.

Wood, S. (2003b). Green revolution or greenwash? Voluntary environmental standards, public law, and private authority in Canada. In Law Commission of Canada (Ed.), *New perspectives on the public-private divide* (pp. 123–165). Vancouver: UBC Press.

Wood, S. (2011a). Four varieties of social responsibility: Making sense of the "sphere of influence" and "leverage" debate via the case of ISO 26000. *Osgoode Hall Law School Comparative Research in Law and Political Economy, 07*(04). Accessed October 8, 2013 from http://papers.ssrn.com/sol3/papers.cfm?abstract_id=1777505

Wood, S. (2011b). The meaning of 'sphere of influence' in ISO 26000. In H. Adrian (Ed.), *Understanding ISO 26000: A practical approach to social responsibility* (pp. 115–130). London: BSI.

Wood, S. (2012). The case for leverage-based corporate human rights responsibility. *Business Ethics Quarterly, 22*(1), 63–98.

Wood, S., & Johannson, L. (2008). Principles for integrating non-governmental environmental standards into smart regulation. *Osgoode Hall Law Journal, 46*, 345–395.

Wright, C. (2012). Global banks, the environment, and human rights: The impact of the equator principles on lending policies and practices. *Global Environmental Politics, 12*, 56–77.

Wright, C., & Rwabizambuga, A. (2006). Institutional pressure, corporate reputation, and voluntary codes of conduct: An examination of the equator principles. *Business and Society Review, 111*(1), 89–117.

Zumbansen, P. (2004). Globalization and the law: Deciphering the message of transnational human rights litigation. *German Law Journal, 5*(12), 1499–1520.

Zumbansen, P. (2005). *Beyond territoriality: The case of transnational human rights litigation* (4 Constitutionalism Web-Papers 4/2005). Accessed July 31, 2013 from www.wiso.uni-hamburg.de/fileadmin/sowi/politik/governance/ConWeb_Papers/conweb4-2005.pdf

Zumbansen, P. (2006). Transnational law. In J. Smits (Ed.), *Encyclopedia of comparative law* (pp. 738–754). Cheltenham: Edward Elgar Publishing.

Zumbansen, P. (2010a). *Neither 'public' nor 'private', 'national' nor 'international'. transnational corporate governance from a legal pluralist perspective* (Osgoode Hall Law School Comparative Research in Law & Political Economy, Research Paper Series, Research Paper 22/2010). Accessed July 31, 2013 from http://papers.ssrn.com/sol3/papers.cfm?abstract_id=1626338

Zumbansen, P. (2010b). Transnational legal pluralism. *Transnational Legal Theory, 1*(2), 141–189.

The New Development Cooperation: The Importance of the Private Sector

Nanno Kleiterp

1 Introduction

The world is changing fast, but policies are changing slowly. In the past, development cooperation was mainly focused on the public sector and on poverty in low-income countries. Over the past two decades, we have seen **four important** trends, which should affect development cooperation policies.

The first is the shift of economic activity and political power from the West to the East and the South. This is changing the pattern of capital flows, with more commercial capital flowing to emerging markets. For example, foreign direct investment to sub-Saharan Africa has grown fivefold in the past decade. At the same time, it is flowing backwards.

Amazingly, Europe in crisis asked even China and Brazil for financial assistance. This is creating a multipolar world that fosters equality and reciprocity instead of dominance in dealings of the West with the East and South.

The second trend is the shift in the pattern of poverty. Twenty years ago, more than 90 % of the poor lived in low-income countries. Now, less than 30 % of the poor still live there. This is not because the poor have moved but because their countries have become richer.

Two recent low-income countries, Nigeria and Vietnam, are expected to be in the G20 by 2050. This is changing the core premise of the relationship between the old rich world and the developing countries. More and more developing countries have more means to tackle poverty in their own countries without grant money. As a result, the basis of development cooperation will be equality and reciprocity instead of conditionality; the new focus will be on doing sound business together.

It is clear that Official Development Assistance (ODA) has become less significant in the total flows to developing countries. Instead, we see growth in private

N. Kleiterp (✉)
FMO, Anna van Saksenlaan 71, 2593 HW, The Hague, Netherlands
e-mail: n.kleiterp@fmo.nl

© Springer International Publishing Switzerland 2015
K. Wendt (ed.), *Responsible Investment Banking*, CSR, Sustainability, Ethics & Governance, DOI 10.1007/978-3-319-10311-2_33

sector investment and private international foundations as well as tied aid from former developing countries such as China, India and Brazil.

The third trend is the continuing mismanagement of global public goods, such as carbon emissions, water and fisheries. This is fuelling climate change and posing the first genuine threat to humanity. At the forecast growth rates and given the growing middle class in emerging markets, we will need 2.4 planets in 2050 to sustain our lifestyles. We will have to change our ways of production and consumption in order to be able to live with scarcities of resources and avoid drastic climate change.

The fourth is the increasing scarcity of resources, which leads to price increases, and at the same time a change in policies of corporates and countries to get more control in important value chains. This control is important for them to keep access and to improve productivity and sustainability deep in their supply chain.

1.1 What These Trends Mean for International Cooperation

1. We head for a multipolar world, where equality and reciprocity are key in relations between nations. The world where the rich countries dictate which values are the norm and puts conditions on trade and aid is over.

   Apart from countries in conflict and the very poor countries, developing countries will not accept conditionality. More so because there are other important upcoming powers such as China and Brazil that are investing in Africa, Asia and Latin America in their own interest.

   They are looking for scarce resources and new markets for their products. The deals they make are based on business negotiations and equality and not on predominant moral values. Developed countries are already changing their policies and putting more focus on the private sector and loans instead of grants. Also, because of the crisis a growing number of countries focus more on their economic interest and are looking for more reciprocity.

2. The majority of the poor live in middle-income countries, and it is expected that several low-income countries will develop into the middle-income category in the coming years. Most of these countries have economic growth rates between 5 and 8 %. The poor in these countries have many more opportunities than in the past. The growth creates new jobs.

   But are these jobs paying enough wages? Are labour circumstances at a reasonable level?

   Such questions are becoming increasingly central to the debates on development. We see economic growth with increasing inequality but also with less poverty. One problem with increasing inequality is the danger of political instability. A strong and a growing middle class can counterbalance this danger of instability. The middle class wants better education, health services and better governance in return for the taxes they pay.

The big challenge thus is creating economic growth in middle-income countries with a relative decreasing environmental footprint and growing good quality employment.

In international cooperation of developed countries we see a growing emphasis on the private sector. The population with an income of less than US$2 a day will be concentrated in low-income countries in Africa and particularly in fragile states. For these countries, nobody has found a way to support them through the private sector. The first priority in these countries is peace and creating institutions and better governance. That should be the foundation for a more private sector-oriented approach.

3. It is necessary that the developed world takes drastic measures to fight climate change. The urgency to change is now here. Developed countries have to act first to adjust their ways of production and consumption. The private sector plays a key role, as wealth creation and pollution both come from the private sector. The most important measure that has to be taken is to create a carbon market where the price of CO_2 per ton is more than US$50. This would lead to a change in investment patterns. The countries that have used the space of carbon emissions since the industrial revolution should compensate the newly growing countries for the high CO_2 price. At this moment in time it seems impossible to create such a market at a global level. But we see positive signs on regional level in the United States, Australia, China and Europe.

Also the new Climate Fund to transfer financial flows from developed to emerging economies could be helpful. But it is crucial that we do not make the same mistakes as with aid programmes that focus on the public sector and grants only. At the same time we need to take urgent measures to protect nature and biodiversity. Invest, for example, in forestry and biodiversity services. We already see that in several countries, climate change is becoming a relevant part of the development cooperation budget. Governments have agreed to create a climate fund. In most countries this will be done out of the budget for development cooperation. In the coming years, the traditional development cooperation will more and more focus on financing climate adaption and mitigation.

4. The need for integration of sustainability and productivity increases in different value chains. BRIC countries (Brazil, Russia, India and China) are leading this trend in Africa. Still a lot of developed countries have not incorporated this trend in their policies. Here they can learn a lot from the Chinese approach in Africa. For developed countries it is essential to follow the example and copy this approach. There is a trend in most countries to focus development cooperation on their direct national interest, their national industry that invests in developing countries or their exporting companies.

At the same time, we see that because resources are becoming scarce and consumers are demanding more sustainable produced goods (i.e. goods produced without child labour, with decent working circumstances and with no loss for nature and biodiversity), companies are forced to take responsibility on how the inputs they buy are produced. There is a need to go further back into the value chain to control a sustainable way of production by local producers and to keep access to these resources.

When a company only buys goods in the harbour of, for example, Accra or Mombasa, they will lose access to scare resources. Using development cooperation funds to improve sustainability and efficiency deep in the value chain (with, e.g. small farmers) combines the interest of the companies in developed and developing countries. So we will see that more funds from developing cooperation will be used for value chain finance in order to combine the pressure to use the funds in the national interest and create positive impact in developing countries.

2   Economic Growth and the Private Sector

Looking at the trends it is clear that international economic cooperation needs to promote green inclusive economic growth.

To reduce poverty in the world, we need economic growth. Only through economic growth can sufficient jobs be created to provide decent living standards to the 600 million new planet inhabitants in this decade and the 200 million unemployed people worldwide. Fortunately, developing countries have been growing much faster than developed nations since 1990 and, as a result, poverty has come down dramatically in past decennia.

Income differences between countries have been reduced and this is a trend that will continue in the coming decade.

> The world has experienced a fast and impressive shift in wealth. That is the good news. The bad news is that income distribution within countries is becoming more and more skewed. There are still two billion people living on less than US\$2 a day and with the growing middle classes we will need 2.4 planets to sustain the way we produce and consume today.

So the world faces the challenge to create economic growth that makes it possible to live within the limits of our planet and reduce poverty at the same time. We cannot prioritise economic growth, poverty reduction or environmental sustainability only. We need to work on all three at the same time.

Economic growth can be stimulated by several measures, whereby the combination depends on the special characteristics of the country. Macroeconomic stability seems basic for long-term economic growth. And most developing countries have improved their macroeconomic management and controlled deficit on current account and government debt.

Countries also need to stimulate expenses for R and D and education in order to increase productivity and innovation. Investment climate and infrastructure (roads, schools, hospitals and access to financial services) are crucial for long-term economic growth.

> To live within the means of our planet, we need to:
>
> *Halve* the carbon emissions worldwide by 2050 (based on 2005 levels).
> *Double* agricultural output without increase of water usage.
> *Halt* deforestation and increase yields from planted forests.
> *Deliver* a four- to tenfold improvement in the efficient use of resources and
>   materials.

To reach these goals, countries need to invest in a circular economy, renewable energy, energy-efficient buildings, reforestation, protection of forest and new production processes with less and reuse of resources and materials.

To reduce poverty further, we need to create 800 million jobs over the coming decade. Developing countries need to increase their productivity, and therefore, product and process innovations are necessary. Ninety percent of all jobs are created in the private sector. And these jobs are created in large, medium, small and microenterprises. Studies show that most of the decent jobs, with a reasonable salary and labour conditions, are created in the formal sector. Those jobs help to reduce poverty.

In an IFC study on jobs, four findings stand out with regards to impediments for growth of companies:

- Informality is a major hindrance for SMEs in middle-income countries.
- Reliable power supply is most important for companies in lower-income countries and infrastructure in general (roads, ports) for all countries.
- Access to finance is particularly essential for SMEs.
- A shortage of skilled workers constitutes a key challenge for larger businesses.

Thus, for inclusive growth, it is vital to stimulate growth of the added value of SMEs.

This is crucial to create development impact through the private sector and reduce poverty, which is the highest goal in development cooperation.

> **Conclusion**
> It is clear that we need to review globally existing development and international cooperation policies to focus them more on the most urgent issues in the coming years: climate change, nature and biodiversity and poverty and a fair income distribution.
>
> The millennium goals have to be replaced by a new set of indicators. Global sustainability goals could be a starting point. A key success factor is

(continued)

that the private sector takes on a crucial role in the solution of the above-mentioned problems and that the public sector focuses on its role as a catalyser and enabler for the private sector.

Finally, equality and reciprocity should be the leading principle for nations when dealing with each other.

Respecting Human Rights in Investment Banking: A Change in Paradigm

Christine Kaufmann

It's not about risk, it's about doing the right thing.

1 Money, Markets, and Morals

1.1 From Homo Economicus to Homo sapiens[1]

One of the most frequently invoked arguments in discussions on human rights in investment banking is the alleged profit-driven attitude of investors and the related consequences on the fiduciary agreement and its underlying duties. In this concept, managing funds in the best interest of the investors is often interpreted as seeking maximum return on investments (Sandberg 2013).

However, new insights from neuropsychology and neuroeconomics indicate that the concept of a rationally acting homo economicus whose behavior is largely driven by utility maximization is rather outdated (Akerlof and Shiller 2010). It took more than 200 years after Adam Smith's early statement in 1790 that people were genuinely willing to cooperate beyond pure self-interest to back this insight with empirical evidence. In the 1990s James Buchanan and Bruno S. Frey were among the pioneers in recognizing and empirically proving that not only profit but also ethical considerations such as fairness or avoiding conflicts influenced market participants' decisions (Buchanan 1994, p. 132; Frey 1994, p. 139). Recent results from behavioral finance research identify several decisive elements for market participants' actions. In the context of investments, fairness, both in terms of substantial values and procedures, seems particularly relevant (for an overview see Singer 2012, p. 440, and for risk

---

[1] The title of this section has been borrowed from Richard Thaler. See Thaler (2000).

Ch. Kaufmann (✉)
University of Zurich, Centre for Human Rights Studies, Raemistrasse 74/5, CH-8001 Zurich, Switzerland
e-mail: Lst.kaufmann@rwi.uzh.ch

© Springer International Publishing Switzerland 2015
K. Wendt (ed.), *Responsible Investment Banking*, CSR, Sustainability, Ethics & Governance, DOI 10.1007/978-3-319-10311-2_34

behavior Baisch and Weber 2015, p. 163–167). Accordingly, an important role is attributed to so-called internal constraints motivated—among others—by ethical principles (Stringham (2011, pp. 101–102).

With regard to investment banking, new research results indicate that the archetype of a profit-driven rationally acting investor does not exist in reality. As a result, questions arise with regard to market functioning and the framework for bank-investor relations.

1.2 Markets and Their Limits

The fact that financial markets are not perfect has become clear at the very latest with the financial crisis of 2007/2008 (Koslowski 2012, pp. 8–11). Three key reasons for the crisis have been identified and largely agreed upon: the lack of information, the complexity of some financial (derivative) products, and remuneration systems that set the wrong incentives (Crotty 2009).

Complex financial products made it difficult both for supervisors and market participants to obtain accurate information on market developments and their impact on financial institutions. Along with highly sophisticated risk management models under the Basel II framework, a vicious circle started that included constantly developing new complex products combined with the illusion of efficiently managing their implied risks with even more intricate monitoring systems.

Not surprisingly, once the dimension of the financial crisis had become clear, the call for regulation followed quickly and loudly. Yet legal regulation has limited power to prevent undesired behavior. The financial crisis showed that asymmetric information is also a problem for supervisory authorities because the risks associated with new complex, structured, and derivative products can often only—if at all—be assessed ex post (see FINMA 2009, pp. 9, 27–28).

In addition, state regulation is notoriously slow and generally reactive because democratic lawmaking takes time. Apart from this lack of flexibility, there is an inherent risk of regulation for dynamic products and markets to be either too detailed and restrictive (over-inclusive) or too general and lax (under-inclusive). Finally, regulatory arbitrage can severely affect financial markets without an international consensus on the basics for a regulatory framework.

1.3 New Rules of the Game for Investment Banking: Myths and Facts

What remains if legislation does not seem capable to address all forms of undesired behavior while markets can still not be left all to themselves? Recent controversies in the context of investments show that activities may be considered objectionable even if they are completely legal (e.g., see Dirty Profits [Facing Finance 2013]). Therefore, a purely legalistic approach that every action is allowed as long as it is not explicitly prohibited cannot be the answer.

Similar considerations are at the heart of the "Renewed EU Strategy 2011–2014 for corporate social responsibility" which the European Commission issued in October 2011 (European Commission 2011). It defines corporate social responsibility very broadly as "the responsibility of enterprises for their impacts on society." In addition, the strategy deviates from the UN traditional dichotomy between hard law on the one hand and voluntary, industry-driven measures on the other. Instead it opts for a smart mix of both categories:

> "The development of CSR should be led by enterprises themselves. Public authorities should play a supporting role through a smart mix of voluntary policy measures and, where necessary, complementary regulation, for example to promote transparency, create market incentives for responsible business conduct, and ensure corporate accountability" [EU Strategy (European Commission 2011), para. 3.4].

This change in paradigm which results in a complementary state and business responsibility for implementing human rights has been initiated by the UN Guiding Principles on Business and Human Rights (United Nations Human Rights Council 2011) unanimously adopted by the Human Rights Council in 2011 and confirmed in the revised OECD Guidelines on Multinational Enterprises (OECD 2011). While the primary duty to actively *protect* human rights lies with the state, enterprises are responsible to *respect* human rights. This responsibility to respect has not (yet) been framed in legally binding terms—therefore, the UN Guiding Principles use the term *responsibility* instead of duty or obligation (for a critical view Wettstein 2012, p. 756). Despite its formally non-binding nature, the inclusion of such a responsibility in the UN Guiding Principles marks an unprecedented milestone and is largely due to an extensive 6-year consultation process with all stakeholder groups conducted by Professor John Ruggie (Ruggie 2013, pp. 148–150). Still, unanimity on business' responsibility to respect fundamental moral and ethical values does not imply an agreement on its concrete content. What exactly do the new rules of the game mean?

2   Change of Perspective: From Business Risk to Real People

2.1   "Principled Pragmatism"

For banks, the key relevance of the UN Guiding Principles lies in their implicit change of perspective. Contrary to the lengthy efforts within the UN to compile a set of rules which would overcome all conceptual obstacles in holding both states and private actors accountable, the UN Guiding Principles follow a much more modest approach with a focus on results. What they want to achieve is to improve the human rights situation for people affected by business activities—nothing more and nothing less. They are open for legally non-binding measures if they serve this purpose better than hard law. John Ruggie called this approach "principled pragmatism." What looks rather soft and seems to lack conceptual stringency at first glance turns out to be a change in paradigm, turning away from framing human rights as an element of risk management to a people-oriented approach (Kaufmann 2013).

2.2   From a Risk-Oriented to a People-Oriented Perspective

Typically, a bank's risk management will focus on *business risks* which result from human rights violations associated with its business activities. Examples include reputational risks, financial obligations, security risks for personnel and infrastructure, lawsuits, etc. Such a notion of risk can be found also in national banking laws, the Basel II and Basel III framework, or in due diligence requirements for the board of directors under corporate law. Clearly, members of a bank's management are under a legal obligation to avoid any risks for their own enterprise and to abstain from activities that may harm the bank. In such a concept, human rights infringements in the context of investments are relevant if they result in risks for the bank. If there is no risk for the bank, human rights infringements will not become part of risk management. An example is a situation where the victims are members of a group with low societal support or prestige, resulting in little negative reactions from the public against the bank. With such a risk-oriented approach, the severity of the human rights violation is irrelevant. While systematic serious human rights violations do not necessarily manifest themselves in reputational, financial, or other risks for the bank, an isolated incident may nevertheless amount to a substantial business risk, for instance, if the case is taken to court.

In contrast, a *human rights-oriented* approach will focus on the right holders and the respective state obligation to protect these rights against violations from third parties including private individuals and businesses. From such a perspective, bank-related risks are still an issue but not the only concern. In other words, human rights infringements in the context of business activities are relevant for the bank regardless of whether they amount to a business risk.

The UN Guiding Principles implement a change in paradigm while still taking into account business-related risks as a key element of corporate decision-making. What is truly innovative is their call for including both *risks for the human rights of affected people* and the *risks resulting from human rights infringements for the bank* in corporate due diligence procedures.

The new approach brings about a plethora of questions: Which human rights are to be considered and how far does corporate responsibility go, particularly if a business is not involved in human rights infringements with its own actions but rather through its clients or business partners which is typical for an investment bank?

2.3 Impacts Through Own Activities and Actions "Directly Linked by Business Relationships"

For decades, one of the most heatedly debated issues in the context of corporate responsibility for human rights had been the so-called *sphere of influence* for corporations and the resulting complicity with human rights violations. Given that all efforts to precisely define the sphere of influence failed, the UN Guiding Principles deliberately avoid any reference to this concept. Driven by the overall goal to improve the human rights protection for the affected people, they focus on facts rather than on legal or moral accountability. Which are the situations in a business context that are factually problematic from a human rights perspective? The answer of the UN Guiding Principles is clear: It is first a situation where an enterprise contributes to human rights infringements with its own actions. Examples in the financial services industry are rather rare but may include the disregard of an employee's labor rights by a bank. Much more relevant is the second constellation mentioned in the UN Guiding Principles: A bank may be associated with human rights infringements in the context of clients' and investors' activities or in their asset management operations. Both the UN Guiding Principles and the OECD Guidelines call on business to prevent and mitigate adverse human rights impacts that:

> "[. . .] are directly linked to their operations, products or services by their business relationships, even if they have not contributed to those impacts." (UN Guiding Principles, para. 13b and OECD Guidelines, para. IV.3)

The term "directly" was introduced at the very last stage of the drafting process in order to address concerns that the scope of business responsibility may otherwise be defined too broadly. Unfortunately, this well-meant decision added a new layer of complexity rather than clarifying the concept. Discussions in the financial services industry illustrate this finding: In linguistic usage negative human rights impacts which result from client activities would be called "indirect" impacts of a bank's business transactions rather than "directly linked to a business relationship." In addition, the notion of business relationship needs to be clarified in a financial context, a task which is currently being addressed in the OECD (see below Sect. 5.1).

An important departure from previous complicity concepts in both the UN Guiding Principles and the OECD Guidelines is often overlooked: Clearly, negative human rights impacts which occur within a business relationship by clients' or business partners' activities *cannot* be attributed to the bank. However, a bank is required to include its business partners' and clients' activities in its own due diligence procedure and to draw the necessary conclusions.

3 New Rules of the Game for Investment Banking: Myths and Facts

3.1 Financial Services: A Special Case?

It is often argued that financial services industry and in particular investment banking are different from other industries and therefore require regulations that are specifically tailored to their business activities. In addition, some business areas such as minority holdings should be completely excluded from the scope of the UN Guiding Principles and the OECD Guidelines.

In fact, financial services are a highly complex industry with a wide range of different products offered to variety of clients (Castelo 2013, pp. 141–148, 142). In a globalized market, financial institutions operate in many jurisdictions and are therefore subject to a complex web of international and national regulations. Moreover, human rights infringements in the context of financial services often result from private and institutional clients' activities rather than a bank's direct operations. Clearly, clients and investors remain responsible for their actions; this responsibility cannot be delegated to the respective bank.

These are all valuable arguments, yet the question remains: Are banks really that different compared to other industries to warrant a special treatment under the UN Guiding Principles and the OECD Guidelines? Many of the challenges that banks are faced with are equally relevant in other industries with highly complex supply chains. The products and services may be different, but the key challenges are not. Therefore, there is no reason why financial services and particularly investment banking should be excluded in whole or partially from the scope of the UN Guiding Principles and the OECD Guidelines. Rather, the distinctive industry features need to be taken into account when defining the specific due diligence requirements.

Adverse human rights impacts are relevant in investment banking not only when they are caused by the bank's own activities but also when they are *directly linked to its operations*, products, or services through its business relationships. The difference between these two types of human rights impacts is reflected in different due diligence requirements—not in the applicability or non-applicability of the UN Guiding Principles and the OECD Guidelines.

3.2 Focus on Risks

Neither the UN Guiding Principles nor the OECD Guidelines ban specific types of business transactions. Instead they ask for a mapping of potential human rights risks associated with business operations both in terms of own activities and business relationships. Once these risks have been identified, they need to be incorporated in due diligence procedures. Only after the completion of such a holistic due diligence can an informed and deliberate business decision be taken.

Unfortunately, a communication published by the Office of the UN High Commissioner for Human Rights (OHCHR) in the context of a proceeding before the Norwegian OECD National Contact Point concerning the Norwegian State Pension Fund (NBIM) created considerable misunderstandings (United Nations Office of the High Commissioner for Human Rights 2013): The issue at hand was whether minority shareholdings, such as the ones that NBIM has held in the Korean company POSCO, would fall within the scope of the UN Guiding Principles and accordingly also the OECD Guidelines. The OHCHR not only confirmed that the UN Guiding Principles would apply but also stated that a bank with minority shareholdings should aim at increasing its leverage in order to positively influence the human rights situation. If this were not possible, a bank should consider ending the business relationship. In its statement, the OHCHR referred to a matrix which was published in the UN Guiding Principles Interpretative Guide in 2012 (United Nations Office of the High Commissioner for Human Rights 2012) (Fig. 1).

The matrix offered by the OHCHR has limited value for investment banking and asset management for two main reasons: First, investment decisions are not being made by the bank only but also by the owners. Second, strengthening leverage and influence often implies increasing shareholdings, which is particularly delicate and difficult to communicate to the broader public when the company is involved in human rights infringements.

As a consequence, a different model developed by the Danish Human Rights Institute and the UN Global Compact has been applied by the financial industry: The Arc of Human Rights Priorities (Fig. 2).

Other than the UN matrix, the Arc of Human Rights Priorities refers to the *severity* of the human rights violation (vertical axis) and the *influence/leverage* (horizontal axis) that a company has. The business relationship is not a self-standing criterion yet it is of relevance for defining influence and leverage. Most importantly, the Arc of Human Rights Priorities reflects the mentioned shift in paradigm and change of perspective: A business relationship is considered problematic (dark) if it is associated with severe human rights violations, regardless of the influence/leverage a bank may have. Still, there is no general solution for such dilemmas: Every bank has to decide how to react on a case-by-case basis.

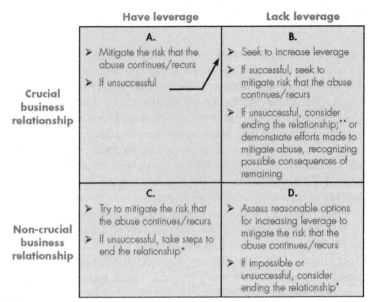

	Have leverage	Lack leverage
Crucial business relationship	**A.** ➤ Mitigate the risk that the abuse continues/recurs ➤ If unsuccessful	**B.** ➤ Seek to increase leverage ➤ If successful, seek to mitigate risk that the abuse continues/recurs ➤ If unsuccessful, consider ending the relationship;** or demonstrate efforts made to mitigate abuse, recognizing possible consequences of remaining
Non-crucial business relationship	**C.** ➤ Try to mitigate the risk that the abuse continues/recurs ➤ If unsuccessful, take steps to end the relationship*	**D.** ➤ Assess reasonable options for increasing leverage to mitigate the risk that the abuse continues/recurs ➤ If impossible or unsuccessful, consider ending the relationship*

* Decisions on ending the relationship should take into account credible assessments of any potential adverse human rights impact of doing so.

** If the relationship is deemed crucial, the severity of the impact should also be considered when assessing the appropriate course of action.

Fig. 1 United Nations, Office of the High Commissioner for Human Rights (2012). An Interpretative Guide to the Corporate Responsibility to Respect Human Rights, p. 50. Copyright: United Nations

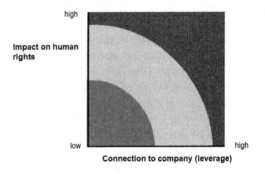

Fig. 2 Baab and Jungk (2011) The Arc of Human Rights Priorities, p. 14. Copyright: Baab/Jungk

4 The Thun Group of Banks

4.1 Motivation

By now it should have become evident that implementing the UN Guiding Principles effectively requires their translation into a language that can be understood in the business reality. The wish to take on this work themselves and in cooperation with other banks instead of waiting for regulators to become active was the key driver for the establishment of the Thun Group of Banks in May 2011. A small number of representatives of international universal banks met in the Swiss town of Thun to discuss the relevance of the UN Guiding Principles for banks.

Thun Group of Banks Discussion Paper (Thun Group of Banks 2013)

"The work of the Thun Group is motivated by the following drivers:

1. Acting responsibly: Respecting human rights as 'the right thing to do' and an integral part of responsible business conduct. All of the participating banks are committed to respect human rights in their business activities. The motivation for this commitment is twofold: it reflects responsible business practice by minimizing related risks and underlines the banks' desire to manage their impacts on society responsibly.
2. Acting instead of waiting for legal requirements [...].
3. Acting Jointly [...]".

The approach chosen by the Thun group may seem unusual for an industry in which risk is normally the key element in regulatory discussions. However, the participating banks deliberately decided to depart from the traditional risk-dominated approach and instead adopted an active strategy to integrate human rights into existing business models. Therefore, from the beginning human rights were seen as both an opportunity and—in case of infringement—a risk. As a result, the Thun group quite naturally applied the UN Guiding Principles' shift in paradigm.

4.2 From Shift in Paradigm to Policy Commitment

Changing the perspective implied adding a new dimension to corporate governance: Not only business risks were to be considered but rather a more holistic approach was developed which included a bank's impact on society as a whole and particularly on human rights.

As straightforward as this may sound, the operationalization of such a concept requires a substantial amount of "translation" to be undertaken by the respective banks. The three building blocks of the UN Guiding Principles—policy commitment, operational due diligence procedure, and creating remedy mechanisms— need to be interpreted and substantiated for all business areas within a bank. For a start, the work of the Thun group focused on Guiding Principles 16–21 and in particular on due diligence requirements.

The UN Guiding Principles emphasize the nature of a corporate human rights policy as a roadmap and "compass" for the business itself (Guiding Principle 16). Consequently, such a policy commitment should on the one hand be communicated transparently both with regard to internal and external stakeholders. On the other hand, its adoption by top management serves the purpose of fostering coherence among different corporate strategies and paves the way for the operational implementation, including the establishment of an accountability mechanism.

For banks, a policy statement as an instrument of self-commitment cannot easily be accommodated within the general regulatory environment. Depending on national law, voluntary commitments by banks may become part of internally binding corporate policies and eventually feed into the legally binding duty of care for bank management and/or lead to corresponding reporting obligations. An example can be found in the UK Action Plan for implementing the UN Guiding Principles which—in accordance with the EU Strategy (European Commission 2011)—calls on UK companies to:

> "[. . .] be transparent about policies, activities and impacts, and report on human rights issues and risks as appropriate as part of their annual reports." (Secretary of State for Foreign and Commonwealth Affairs 2013)

In addition, the new Directive on disclosure of non-financial and diversity information in the EU requires companies with more than 500 employees or which exceed either a balance sheet total of EUR 20 million or a net turnover of EUR 40 million, to provide the following information:

1. "[. . .] a non-financial statement containing information to the extent necessary for an understanding of the undertaking's development, performance, position and impact of its activity, relating to, as a minimum, environmental, social and employee matters, respect for human rights, anti-corruption and bribery matters, including:

   (a) a brief description of the undertaking's business model;
   (b) a description of the policies pursued by the undertaking in relation to those matters, including due diligence processes implemented;
   (c) the outcome of those policies;
   (d) the principal risks related to those matters linked to the undertaking's operations including, where relevant and proportionate, its business

relationships, products or services which are likely to cause adverse impacts in those areas, and how the undertaking manages those risks;

(e) non-financial key performance indicators relevant to the particular business.

Where the undertaking does not pursue policies in relation to one or more of these matters, it shall provide a clear and reasoned explanation for not doing so.

[...] In requiring the disclosure of the information referred to in the first subparagraph, Member States shall provide that undertakings may rely on national, Union-based or international frameworks, and if they do so, undertakings shall specify which frameworks they have relied upon. [...]"

(Directive of the European Parliament and of the Council, amending Directive 2013/34/EU as regards disclosure of non-financial and diversity information by certain large undertakings and groups, adopted 25 July 2014, Art. 1 introducing a new Art. 19a).

With the amended directive entering into force, the corporate human rights policy commitment as contained in the UN GPs will indirectly have legal effect because it will trigger binding reporting obligations.

Not surprisingly, with this dynamic background in mind, the Thun group's work does not aim at setting an industry standard but instead wants to foster further discussion. The discussion paper which was published in October 2013 (Thun Group of Banks 2013) does therefore not contain a general policy commitment but leaves this to each participating bank. In fact, participants chose different models. Most of the group members developed their own *human rights statement* (UBS, Barclays Group, BBVA—Banco Bilbao Vizcaya Argentaria, ING), a *human rights commitment* (UniCredit), or a *position statement on human rights* (RBS—Royal Bank of Scotland) with different degrees of detail, from very short statements (UBS, RBS) to more elaborated documents (Barclays, UniCredit). Credit Suisse included human rights in its *sustainability statement*.

Despite the different implementation within the participating banks, the Thun group's discussion paper emphasizes the importance of top management support both with regard to internal acceptance and coherence with other corporate strategies and policies. Particularly in asset management and investment banking, employees may often not be accustomed to including human rights in their operations and therefore require special training.

4.3   Human Rights as Part of a Bank's Due Diligence

In domestic corporate law, due diligence regularly refers to the corporation's interests which are to be safeguarded by the management and the members of the board. For banks there are additional requirements imposed by supervisory authorities and stock exchanges with a view to protecting investors.

Opening up the perspective of risks for banks and investors to include adverse human rights impacts broadens the scope of due diligence. However, expanding the scope of due diligence does not imply additional procedures. In this regard the Thun group's discussion paper contains an important clarification for banks by explaining that human rights considerations need not trigger new administrative hurdles but can (and should) be incorporated in existing due diligence requirements. As a first step, a bank needs to *identify areas* with a potential exposure to human rights issues in its operations (scope). It will then need to *assess the impacts* of its operations on human rights and based on the results identify the specific human rights-related risks. Finally, these *risks* need to be *translated* and *operationalized* to become part of regular due diligence and risk management procedures.

In a universal bank, each of the different business areas, retail and private banking, corporate and investment banking, as well as asset management, requires a specific analysis tailored to their business activities.

According to the UN Guiding Principles, due diligence applies to adverse human rights impacts caused by a bank's own actions as well as those directly linked to its business relationships (Guiding Principle 17). In investment banking due diligence will focus primarily on identifying potential adverse human rights impacts of investment products and services first in order to then take appropriate measures to prevent or mitigate these impacts.

Human rights risks may occur in investment banking for instance when products and services are offered to companies with a questionable human rights record or companies which operate in countries with a problematic human rights situation. Examples may include corporate clients doing business in conflict regions. Similar risks may be associated with services for fragile states. Moreover, regardless of a client's behavior, services for projects in industries with a high human rights exposure or projects in particularly exposed areas may bear human rights risks.

Categories of risk in investment banking:

1. Providing products and services to clients (companies, governments, and state-owned enterprises) with a challenging human rights track record
2. Providing products and services to projects in sensitive industries
3. Providing products and services to projects in sensitive locations

Based on these three categories—clients (private and states), industries, and location—potential human risks associated with investment banking need to be identified and mapped. In this regard it is essential for banks to not only rely on their own assessments but to have recourse to reliable indicators for human rights risks, an area which is still under-researched. Finally, business areas and operational units must be included and cooperate with each other in the implementation process. Putting the UN Guiding Principles into practice cannot be prescribed by a central

CSR unit but requires a cooperative effort. Business units play a particularly important role in the identification of potential risks, their severity, and their probability to manifest.

It cannot be emphasized enough that identification and mapping are of a *factual* not of a normative nature. The only purpose of this process is to understand how business operations impact human rights, not to attribute responsibilities or complicity. Only after the human rights map has been established can a bank assess its options in terms of leverage to ameliorate or mitigate the situation. Since there is no one size-fits all solution, the Thun group suggests a two-pronged approach.

First, the existing internal guidelines and procedures of a bank need to be reviewed with regard to the results of the mapping. There may be gaps that need to be filled. In addition, each bank will have to determine on a case-by-case basis depending on the concrete circumstances how it can prevent or mitigate negative human rights impacts. The UN Guiding Principles ask for steps to increase leverage and influence, which in an investment banking context may be rather difficult to realize especially since clients as the owners of their investments often decide on their investment strategy themselves (for pension funds see Sandberg 2013, pp. 440–441).

The implementation of the UN Guiding Principles in investment banking requires several steps:

1. Mapping of the facts: Which human rights are affected by investment banking activities?
2. Risk assessment: How severe are and how often do adverse human rights impacts occur? How likely do human rights risks manifest themselves?
3. Analysis of existing corporate policies and procedures with regard to their compatibility with risk assessment. Fill in potential gaps if the risk situation is not adequately reflected.
4. Options for the bank: In which areas does the bank have leverage to influence the situation?
5. Deliberate business decision on next steps: Identify measures to be taken or give reason for not becoming active.

Obviously, it is impossible for an investment bank to thoroughly analyze the human rights record of every single company and country in which its clients invest. What is, however, doable and requested is to include clients' and business partners' human rights responsibility in the bank's own due diligence procedures, for instance, by asking them for their human rights policy commitment.

5 Challenges

5.1 Relationships

"Rose is a rose is a rose is a rose" wrote Gertrude Stein in her poem Sacred Emily in 1922. She wanted to point out that different perceptions and ideas may nevertheless result in the use of the same word. In fact, the first experiences with the implementation of the UN Guiding Principles and the OECD Guidelines show that several provisions are interpreted differently and will need to be clarified from a conceptual point of view. At the heart of the discussion are the mentioned terms (see Sect. 2.3) "business relationship" and "directly linked" used in UN Guiding Principles 17 and para. IV.3 of the OECD Guidelines to define the scope of corporate responsibility.

While it is undisputed that a bank's own actions can trigger its human rights responsibility, it is more difficult to draw the line for actions in the context of business relationships. Of particular interest is currently the debate on central banks' and state funds' responsibility for adverse human rights impacts which occur in the context of their investments (see Sandberg 2013 for pension funds as a specific type of state funds). Unfortunately, the term "directly linked" which was added during the last phase of the negotiations rather adds to the confusion than clarifying it. The idea that not every (remote) link to a business operation should qualify as a business relationship and potentially trigger a human rights responsibility seems legitimate. However, in a banking environment, the term "directly linked" is rather misleading. A first step towards clarification has been undertaken by the OECD with the support of the UN Working Group on Business and Human Rights (OECD 2014). One important issue in this process is the Norwegian view—presented by the Norwegian Central Bank in the aftermath of the Norwegian National Contact Point's decision in the NBIM (manages the Norwegian Pension Fund on behalf of the government) case (Norwegian National Contact Point 2013a)—which suggests that sovereign wealth funds should be exempted from the scope of the OECD Guidelines and accordingly the UN Guiding Principles (cited in Norwegian National Contact Point 2013b).

5.2 Coherence

Apart from conceptual clarifications, coherent implementation of the UN Guiding Principles is one of the major challenges. John Ruggie's three pillar framework is based on the complementary responsibility of states and business. For an effective implementation of this shared responsibility, state and business instruments as well as policies should be coordinated. However, in reality we will find a plethora of state and business-driven instruments which are to a large extent launched and operated independently and thereby add to an already fragmented regulatory environment. Although the new EU CSR Strategy (European Commission 2011) provides for some guidance, member countries' national action plans not only considerably differ in the process by which they are developed but also in substance.

Businesses are required by law to keep up with regulatory developments, yet states may find it more difficult to stay informed on industry-driven initiatives with regard to human rights. Structural inefficiency such as different ministries involved in human rights issues in different areas as well as accommodating the business and human rights agenda in different government departments may be a reason that relevant information does not reach all actors involved. Given the many facets of the business and human rights agenda, it is not surprising that the multi-stakeholder dialogue among government, business, and civil society on its implementation is still in its infancy in most countries. This is particularly true for the banking sector where the notion of risk in prudential regulation is heavily influenced by investor protection and system stability which results in highly complex risk management systems. Adding another layer of complexity with the inclusion of human rights is therefore challenging. Thus, it is even more important for banks to participate and bring in their expertise in multi-stakeholder dialogues. Similarly, states will need to contribute their part by mapping the applicable regulatory environment (for Switzerland see Kaufmann et al. 2013).

6 The Road Ahead

The Thun group illustrates what potential industry-driven initiatives may entail despite their formally non-binding nature. In order to further advance the published discussion paper which has been developed among banks only, a broad dialogue which includes all stakeholders—state, civil society, and business—will be necessary. As much as investment bankers need to give up their reservations vis-à-vis human rights issues, states have to engage in a discussion about meaningful and implementable human rights standards for the financial sector. With the multi-stakeholder dialogue, the UN Guiding Principles set the tone and ask for a new approach which is still *terra incognita* for many countries, both with regard to substance and institutions. We do not know yet where the road ahead will take us. What we do know is, however, that the trend to hold business including financial institutions accountable for their human rights responsibility cannot be stopped anymore. Industry standards are currently being developed thus giving banks the opportunity to actively engage in their shaping. The Thun group's discussion paper is an important first step in the debate. Its implementation has brought about surprises with sometimes unexpected questions arising and some of the anticipated challenges just passing smoothly. It is hoped that more banks are willing to venture into this process and contribute to an effective implementation of the UN Guiding Principles and the OECD Guidelines.

References

Akerlof, G. A., & Shiller, R. J. (2010). *Animal spirits: How human psychology drives the economy, and why it matters for global capitalism*. Princeton, NJ: Princeton University Press.

Baab, M., & Jungk, M. (2011). *The arc of human rights priorities: A new model for managing business risk*. Copenhagen: Danish Institute for Human Rights and Global Compact.

Baisch, R., & Weber, R. H. (2015). Investment suitability requirements in the light of behavioural findings. In K. Mathis (ed.), *European perspectives on behavioural law and economics, Economic analysis of law in European legal scholarship series*, Vol 2, pp. 159–192. Heidelberg: Springer.

Buchanan, J. M. (1994). Choosing what to choose. *Journal of Institutional and Theoretical Economics, 150*, 123–135.

Castelo, B. M. (2013). Banks and CSR. In S. E. Idowu (ed.), *Encyclopedia of corporate social responsibility* (pp. 141–148). Berlin: Springer.

Crotty, J. (2009). Structural causes of the global financial crisis: a critical assessment of the 'new financial architecture'. *Cambridge Journal of Economics, 33*, 563–580.

European Commission. (2011). *A renewed EU strategy 2011-14 for Corporate Social Responsibility, COM(2011) 681 final*.

Facing Finance. (2013). *Dirty profits II*. Berlin: Facing Finance

FINMA, Swiss Financial Market Supervisory Authority. (2009). *Financial market crisis and financial supervision*. Bern: FINMA

Frey, B. S. (1994). Moral and institutional constraint, comment on Buchanan. *Journal of Institutional and Theoretical Economics, 150*, 136–141.

Kaufmann, Ch. (2013). Menschenrechte: Risiko oder Chance für Unternehmen? *Zeitschrift für Schweizerisches Recht ZSR, 132*, 497–516.

Kaufmann, Ch., Niedrig, J., Wehrli, J., Marschner, L., & Good, Ch. (2013). *Implementing human rights in Switzerland: A baseline study on the human rights and business situation*. Bern and Zurich: Weblaw.

Koslowski, P. (2012). *The ethics of banking, conclusions from the financial crisis*. Dordrecht: Springer.

Norwegian National Contact Point. (2013, May 27). *Forum for environment and development vs Norwegian bank investment management*. Final statement on breaches of the OECD guidelines.

Norwegian National Contact Point. (2013, September 12). *Background note from NCP Norway: Does Norges bank investment management fall under the OECD guidelines?* http://www.responsiblebusiness.no/en/

OECD. (2011). *Guidelines for multinational enterprises*. OECD Publishing

OECD. (2014). The terminology on 'directly linked' in the context of the financial sector. DAF/INF/RBC(2014)1/REV1.

Ruggie, J. G. (2013). *Just business: Multinational corporations and human rights*. New York/London: WW Norton.

Sandberg, J. (2013). (Re)-Interpreting fiduciary duty to justify socially responsible investment for pension funds? *Corporate Governance: An International Review, 21*, 436–446.

Secretary of State for Foreign and Commonwealth Affairs. (2013, September). *Good Business: Implementing the UN guiding principles on business and human rights* (Doc-. No. Cm 8695).

Singer, T. (2012). The past, present and future of social neuroscience: A European perspective. *NeuroImage, 61*, 437–449.

Smith, A. (1790). *Theory of moral sentiments*, 6th ed. London: A. Millar.

Stringham, E. P. (2011). Embracing morals in economics: The role of internal moral constraints in a market economy. *Journal of Economic Behaviour and Organization, 78*, 98–109.

Thaler, R. H. (2000). From Homo Economicus to Homo Sapiens. *Journal of Economic Perspectives, 14*, 133–141.

Thun Group of Banks. (2013). *UN guiding principles on business and human rights—Discussion paper for banks on implications of principles 16–21*. http://www.menschenrechte.uzh.ch/publikationen/thun_group_statement_final_2_oct_2013.pdf

United Nations, Human Rights Council. (2011). *Guiding principles for business and human rights (A/HRC/17/31)*. United Nations, Human Rights Council

United Nations, Office of the High Commissioner for Human Rights. (2012). *An interpretative guide to the corporate responsibility to respect human rights* (HR/PUB/12/02). United Nations, Office of the High Commissioner for Human Rights

United Nations, Office of the High Commissioner for Human Rights. (2013). *The issue of the applicability of the guiding principles on business and human rights to minority shareholdings*. Letter of 26 April 2013

Wettstein, F. (2012). CSR and the debate on business and human rights: Bridging the great divide. *Business Ethics Quarterly, 22*, 739–770.

Fiduciary Duty and Responsible Investment: An Overview

Christine Berry

Abstract The extent to which pension funds and other fiduciary investors can take account of environmental and social issues when making investment decisions has long been subject to debate. This chapter examines some of the key legal arguments and argues that fiduciary investors' scope for action on such issues is considerably wider than is often supposed. Although the primary focus is on the UK legal context, similar issues arise in various other jurisdictions. In 2013, the UK Law Commission was asked to review this area of law and make recommendations to policymakers with a view to addressing uncertainties among market participants. The chapter makes reference to the Law Commission's provisional findings where appropriate, but at the time of writing, its final report had not yet been published.

1 Setting the Scene: The Case of Cowan Versus Scargill

For many years, received wisdom has been that trustees have a legal duty to maximise returns and that taking account of "extraneous" environmental and social factors could leave them exposed to liability for breach of this duty.[1] This view derives largely from the 1984 case of *Cowan v. Scargill*. In this case, the union-nominated trustees of the mineworkers' pension scheme, led by Arthur Scargill, refused to approve an investment plan for the trust unless it excluded all overseas investments and all investments in industries directly competing with coal (e.g. oil

---

[1] The question of how far fiduciary duties apply to those acting on behalf of trustees, such as asset managers and consultants, is complex and is beyond the scope of this chapter. For a consideration of these issues, see UNEP-FI (A legal framework for the integration of environmental, social and governance issues into institutional investment. UNEP-FI, 2005), FairPensions (Protecting our best interests: Rediscovering fiduciary obligation. London: FairPensions, 2011) and Law Commission (Fiduciary duties of investment intermediaries: A consultation' (Consultation Paper No. 215). London: Law Commission, 2013)

C. Berry (✉)
New Economics Foundation (NEF), 10 Salamanca Place, London SE1 7HB, UK
e-mail: christine.berry@cantab.net; christine.berry@neweconomics.org

© Springer International Publishing Switzerland 2015
K. Wendt (ed.), *Responsible Investment Banking*, CSR, Sustainability, Ethics &
Governance, DOI 10.1007/978-3-319-10311-2_35

and gas). The court upheld the employer-nominated trustees' contention that this was a breach of fiduciary duty.

It is commonly argued that this finding demonstrates that trustees may be acting unlawfully if they take any account of "non-financial" factors in their decision-making. For example, Berry and Scanlan (2014) quotes the following response from a pension fund to an enquiry from a member about the fund's management of an environmental risk:

> The Trustees have a legal duty to not only invest, but to actively seek the best possible financial return ... even if it is contrary to the personal, moral, political or social views of the trustees or beneficiaries. This was demonstrated in the Cowan v Scargill (1984) court case.

However, as we shall see, this conventional interpretation of the law is unduly restrictive. The judgement rested on several specific facts of the case with limited relevance to modern-day debates about sustainable and responsible investment. The judge held that the union-nominated trustees were motivated by their personal views and a desire to pursue union policy and were not putting their beneficiaries' interests first—a clear breach of the fiduciary duty of loyalty; that the proposed policy was in breach of the fiduciary duty of impartiality because it would financially disadvantage all beneficiaries but would bring no positive benefit to those not working in the mining industry, such as widows and dependents; and that in any case, those benefits were "too speculative and remote", since the fund was not large enough to have a material impact on the health of the mining industry or the UK economy. In other words, the judgement in *Cowan v. Scargill* was founded not on the principle that any consideration of non-financial factors is unlawful, but on several specific breaches of particular fiduciary duties posed by the facts of the case.

2 Financially Material Risks: The Freshfields View

The first major challenge to the conventional interpretation of *Cowan v. Scargill* came from the "Freshfields report", commissioned by the United Nations Environment Programme Finance Initiative (UNEP-FI 2005). This report argued that there was good evidence that environmental, social and governance (ESG) issues could have an impact on financial returns and, therefore, that taking them into account clearly fell within the ambit of fiduciary obligations. Indeed, taking such issues into account was "clearly permitted, and arguably required" in all jurisdictions analysed. Specifically in relation to *Cowan v. Scargill*, the report concluded that "no court today would treat Cowan v. Scargill as good authority for a binding rule that trustees must seek the maximum rate of return possible with every individual investment and ignore other considerations that may be of relevance, such as ESG considerations".

The Freshfields report was influential and helped catalyse the mainstream acceptance of "responsible investment" approaches based on integration of financially material ESG issues. The UK Law Commission's 2013 consultation paper essentially endorses the Freshfields view, citing various studies which have found a positive relationship between ESG performance and financial returns (e.g. Deutsche Bank Group 2012; Eccles et al. 2013). It concludes that "trustees should consider, in general terms, whether their policy will be to take account of ESG factors" (Law Commission 2013). Despite near-universal agreement among legal experts as to the validity of this view, some confusion remains among smaller pension funds in particular—as illustrated by the quote above from a UK pension fund, which was given in response to a query about a financially material risk. On this basis, groups such as the UK responsible investment charity ShareAction have called for explicit legislative clarification (FairPensions 2012).

It is also worth noting that a "finance-only" approach to ESG integration allows for a range of interpretations. It can be construed narrowly in terms of ESG issues which are likely to affect returns at a *company* level (e.g. the operational risks associated with unconventional oil extraction, which had catastrophic financial consequences for BP following the Deepwater Horizon oil spill). Or it can be construed broadly in terms of ESG issues which are likely to affect returns at *portfolio* level (e.g. the potential economic impacts of climate change). On this second reading, there might be a case for fiduciary investors to act on ESG issues even if this *reduced* profits at an individual company level, if those profits relied on the generation of negative externalities for which the costs were borne elsewhere in the investor's portfolio. This applies particularly to "universal owners" with holdings across the entire economy—a description which applies to most pension funds (see Hawley and Williams 2000). For example, an investor might oppose the use of shareholder capital on unconventional fossil fuel extraction, irrespective of the risks or benefits at company level, because of the negative portfolio impacts of the associated carbon emissions. "Universal owners" have an inherent interest in the health of the economy and can therefore take a broad and enlightened approach to their fiduciary responsibility to protect their beneficiaries' financial interests. However, to date these ideas appear to have been more influential in theory than in practice.

3   A Broader Approach: The "Ethical Tie-Break"

A question that remains more controversial is how far fiduciary investors can take environmental and social issues into account for their own sake, regardless of whether doing so is expected to improve financial performance. This chapter argues that *Cowan v. Scargill* may not be as restrictive on this point as is often assumed (see also FairPensions 2011). Indeed, contrary to the common assumption that any consideration of purely non-financial factors is unlawful, the judge in this case explicitly stated, "I am not asserting that the benefit of the beneficiaries which a trustee must make his paramount concern inevitably and solely means their financial benefit, even in a trust for the provision of financial benefits". The question therefore is not whether non-financial factors can be taken into account, but to what extent and under what circumstances. Trustees must exercise their investment powers for the purpose for which they were given—which, in a pension scheme context, means they must not compromise their core objective of securing a decent pension for their beneficiaries (Law Commission 2013).[2] But, within these parameters, trustees do have latitude to take a broader, more enlightened interpretation of what will serve their beneficiaries' "best interests".

The judge in *Cowan v. Scargill* hinted at this in a subsequent lecture, in which he speculated on how the case might have been different had the union trustees proposed an "all things being equal" policy, rather than a blanket ban on certain investments, so that "no investment should be made overseas or in oil *if any other investment of equal merit were available*" (my emphasis). He concluded that this would have been "by no means a like case" and that it might "well be contended that an investment in A Ltd instead of in B Ltd made because the great majority of beneficiaries oppose investment in B Ltd and so gratifying the majority, will neither harm nor benefit the minority, and so will be for the benefit of the beneficiaries at large" (Megarry 1989). In other words, if the ethical views of some beneficiaries can be accommodated without financially disadvantaging beneficiaries who do not share those views, there will be no breach of fiduciary duties.[3] This has become known as the "ethical tie-break" principle. In principle, the "tie-break" can be applied not only to beneficiaries' ethical views but also to other non-financial interests they may hold: for example, their interest in a healthy environment or a safe and peaceful community (see Berry and Scanlan 2014). In other words, fiduciary investors can take into account the non-financial interests of their beneficiaries provided that by doing so they do not compromise their financial interests.

The tie-break principle appears to have been endorsed by subsequent cases. For example, in *Harries v. Church Commissioners*, the court held that the Church of England's ethical investment policy, which excluded around 13 % of UK listed companies by value, was lawful (while rejecting the plaintiff's claim that the Church should be taking an even more stringent approach, which would have excluded 37 % of UK listed companies by value). Although various special considerations apply due to the Church's charitable status [see FairPensions (2011) for a full discussion of these], the court's endorsement of the existing policy did not rest on these factors: the judge stated that he saw "nothing" in the Commissioners' ethical policy which was inconsistent with the general principles of

---

[2] See also FairPensions (2011) for a discussion of whether trustees are or should be permitted to take into account the 'underlying purpose' of the trust (i.e. to provide beneficiaries with a secure and prosperous retirement) rather than only the immediate purpose (i.e. to provide the largest possible pension pot as a means to that end).

[3] This is clearly more straightforward in a defined contribution (DC) pension scheme, where beneficiaries make their own choice of funds. However, the tie-break principle provides a framework for making ethical decisions in a defined benefit (DB) scheme, where all beneficiaries' assets are invested together.

trustee investment and that he believed his views to be in accordance with the judgement in *Cowan v. Scargill*.

4   Fiduciary Investment: Art or Science?

Critics such as Rosy Thornton have argued that this finding reflects the legal profession's lack of understanding of investment matters: according to modern portfolio theory (MPT), any restriction on a fund's investment universe must necessarily compromise its ability to diversify and hence have an effect, "however small", upon financial performance (Thornton 2008). The "ethical tie-break" will therefore never arise in practice, and the judge in *Harries v. Church Commissioners* (1993) was wrong to suggest that the Church's ethical investment policy met this test. But this argument hides an important assumption which goes to the heart of what fiduciary responsibility is about. Leaving aside the fact that MPT is increasingly being called into question in the wake of the financial crisis, which showed all too clearly the dangers of overreliance on mathematical risk models which might not correspond to reality, evidence shows that the benefits of diversification tail off rapidly above around 30 stocks (Elton and Gruber 1977). Even on purely financial grounds, the question of whether the tiny marginal benefit of additional diversification outweighs the dangers of reduced knowledge and oversight of investee companies is a subjective one on which reasonable people may disagree.

Ultimately, fiduciary duty is a matter of judgement. Fiduciary investors are expected to exercise their judgement in good faith in a context where the future is unknowable. When decisions are taken for the right reasons and in the right way, courts are unlikely to intervene. They recognise that the question of what course of action will best serve beneficiaries' interests is a complex and ultimately subjective one which may involve a range of factors—not one which can be objectively answered simply by running a model. This is perhaps what the judge in *Martin v. City of Edinburgh* (1988) (another landmark UK case) meant when he said:

> "I cannot conceive that trustees have an unqualified duty... simply to invest trust funds in the most profitable investment available. To accept that without qualification would, in my view, involve substituting the discretion of financial advisers for the discretion of trustees."

This view was echoed by the Law Commission's (2013) consultation paper, which summarised the position as follows:

> "The courts have not required trustees to restrict themselves to the metrics of modern portfolio theory. They do not demand that an efficiency frontier is improved through greater and greater diversification. As we have seen, trustees may instead make broad judgments based on a wide range of factors, including ESG factors and the effect of investments on the economy as a whole."

5   Broader Approaches in Practice

If taking non-financial issues into account for their own sake is permissible in principle, what does this mean in practice? How can trustees identify the issues to focus on and what should they do about them?

Legally speaking, the key principle is that any ethical policies must reflect the values and priorities of the beneficiaries rather than the personal whims of the trustees. How can these values and priorities be identified? It is sometimes argued that this is impossible in practice, since ethical issues are inherently subjective and there will never be sufficient agreement among beneficiaries on which to base a policy (see, e.g. Sandberg 2011). However, it is important to remember that the "tie-break" principle frees trustees from the need to identify *complete* consensus, since those who do not share the ethical views in question are not disadvantaged financially. It is enough to identify themes on which a significant proportion of beneficiaries seem to agree. As we shall see, this is far from impossible.

One starting point suggested by the Freshfields report (UNEP-FI 2005) is to use widely accepted social norms—for example, as expressed through international conventions—as a proxy for beneficiaries' values. The Law Commission appeared to endorse this approach in its 2013 consultation paper when it said that trustees should not invest in "activities which contravene international conventions", such as cluster bombs. Applying this approach to other international conventions such as the Universal Declaration of Human Rights or those of the International Labour Organization, it is clear that this alone offers sufficient grounds on which to build a substantive ethical investment policy.

Moreover, experience demonstrates that it is possible to identify shared priorities among groups of beneficiaries—particularly those who have certain common characteristics, as members of workplace pension schemes often do. For example, the Pensions Trust, a UK multiemployer pension scheme for the charitable sector, in 2010 surveyed 15,000 members about their ethical preferences (ShareAction 2013). While the issues which traditionally dominate ethically screened products—such as gambling and alcohol—ranked relatively low in members' list of priorities, there was a striking degree of consensus on the importance of issues like child labour, human rights and environmental impacts. Interestingly, these are all issues which may pose financial risks and which may be amenable to shareholder engagement approaches rather than traditional negative screening. Thus, as well as informing the choice of ethical fund for their DC scheme, the Pensions Trust has used the survey findings to inform the "themes" which they have directed their engagement overlay providers to focus on.

In Denmark—where the legal principles at issue are essentially similar to the UK—healthcare sector scheme PKA drew up a socially responsible investment policy in consultation with its "member delegates" (a group of elected representatives who sit in between the board and the membership at large). Staff acknowledge that disagreement between members was the biggest challenge in developing the policy, noting that any ethical principles agreed upon had to be broadly acceptable, since members are not able to leave the fund. The final policy reflects a combination of international norms and standards, such as the Geneva Convention on Forbidden Weapons and the UN Global Compact, and issues on which members felt strongly, such as armaments and tobacco (ShareAction 2013). The consultation also showed that, like the members of the Pensions Trust, PKA's delegates were particularly interested in protecting labour rights and in seeking out socially or environmentally positive investments (Berry and Scanlan 2014).

As these examples demonstrate, integrating non-financial considerations can be about more than the simplistic negative screening approaches which have tended to dominate legal debates. Indeed, it would be difficult or impossible to screen for many of the issues which most exercise today's beneficiaries. However, if fiduciary investors are willing to accept the principle that they may legitimately take a moral stance on what constitutes acceptable corporate behaviour based on their beneficiaries' values, other possibilities open up. Using shareholder engagement to advance beneficiaries' ethical concerns avoids some of the concerns discussed above about the potential financial impact of ethical screening. It may also have a greater direct impact on the real world, which is ultimately what many beneficiaries with strong ethical views would wish for.

The Pensions Trust example also demonstrates that the line between financially material ESG issues and purely ethical concerns may be fuzzier than legalistic debates about fiduciary duty often assume. Indeed, many of the biggest issues facing fiduciary investors today fall into many or all of the categories discussed in this chapter. For example, climate change will have significant impacts on individual companies' financial performance, on the economy as a whole and on beneficiaries' quality of life; many beneficiaries will also regard it as a moral issue. The best approach for pension schemes may be to develop a policy which synthesises their beneficiaries' ethical priorities and their own investment beliefs about the financial impacts of ESG. Indeed, given that the precise financial impact of a given ESG issue is notoriously hard to measure, and may only manifest itself in the long term, a more open-minded approach to non-financial factors—far from being financially dangerous—could leave pension funds better placed to manage financially material long-term risks.

Disclaimer The author is former Head of Policy and Research at ShareAction (formerly known as FairPensions) and authored the papers cited as ShareAction publications in that capacity. However, this paper is written in a personal capacity.

References

Berry, C., & Scanlan, C. (2014). The voice of the beneficiary. In J. P. Hawley, A. G. F. Hoepner, K. L. Johnson, J. Sandberg, & E. J. Waitzer (Eds.), *Handbook of institutional investment and fiduciary duty*. London: Cambridge University Press.
Cowan v. Scargill. (1984) 2 All ER 750, (1985) Ch 270

Deutsche Bank Group, DB Climate Change Advisors. (2012). *Sustainable investing: Establishing long-term value and performance*. New York: Deutsche Bank Group, DB Climate Change Advisors.

Eccles, R., Ioannou, I., & Serafeim, G. (2013). *The impact of corporate sustainability on organizational processes and performance* (Working Paper 12-035). Harvard Business School.

Elton, E. J., & Gruber, M. J. (1977). Risk reduction and portfolio size: An analytic solution. *Journal of Business, 50*, 415–37.

FairPensions. (2011). *Protecting our best interests: Rediscovering fiduciary obligation*. London: FairPensions.

FairPensions. (2012). *The enlightened shareholder: Clarifying investors' fiduciary duties*. London: FairPensions.

Harries v. Church Commissioners for England. (1993). 2 All ER 300

Hawley, J., & Williams, T. (2000). *The rise of fiduciary capitalism: How institutional investors can make corporate America more democratic*. Philadelphia, PA: University of Pennsylvania Press.

Law Commission. (2013). *Fiduciary duties of investment intermediaries: A consultation* (Consultation Paper No. 215). London: Law Commission.

Martin v. City of Edinburgh. (1988). SLT 329, 1988 SCLR 90

Megarry, R. (1989). Investing pension funds: The mineworkers case. In T. G. Youden (Ed.), *Equity, fiduciaries and trusts* (pp. 149–159). Toronto: Carswell.

Sandberg, J. (2011). Socially responsible investment and fiduciary duty: Putting the Freshfields report into perspective. *Journal of Business Ethics, 101*, 143–162.

ShareAction. (2013). *Engaging savers with stewardship and responsible investment: Best practice guide for pension schemes and asset managers*. ShareAction

Thornton, R. (2008). Ethical investments: A case of disjointed thinking. *Cambridge Law Journal, 67*(2), 396–422.

United Nations Environment Programme Finance Initiative (UNEP FI). (2005). A legal framework for the integration of environmental, social and governance issues into institutional investment. UNEP-FI

The Case for Environmental and Social Risk Management in Investment Banking

Olivier Jaeggi, Nina Kruschwitz, and Raul Manjarin

Abstract The debate about sustainable finance focuses mostly on responsible investment. Considerably less attention tends to be paid to the direct relationships between banks and their corporate clients. Some of these clients are associated with controversial business practices, sectors, projects, and/or countries that, in turn, are associated with detrimental environmental and social impacts. In the context of this article, environmental and social (E&S) risks are those risks that occur when investment banks engage with such clients. This article discusses five factors that put pressure on banks to address E&S risks more systematically. It makes the case that E&S issues harbour considerable potential for damage in the here and now and that investment banks take a risk if they underestimate them.

1 A Brief Introduction to E&S Risk Management

It seems surprising that the debate about sustainable finance focuses mostly on responsible investment. It is hard to understand why considerably less attention tends to be paid to the direct relationships between financial institutions and their corporate clients: banks provide cash, insurance companies provide insurance, and both provide advisory services. Investments, on the other hand, are made mainly in the secondary market. Although investors theoretically play an important role from a corporate governance perspective, in practice they primarily buy and sell securities that are already in circulation.

Investment banks fulfil many important functions in the economy. For their clients, they provide a wide range of financial services "including underwriting and

O. Jaeggi (✉) • R. Manjarin
ECOFACT AG, Stampfenbachstrasse 42, 8006 Zurich, Switzerland
e-mail: olivier.jaeggi@ecofact.com; raul.manjarin@ecofact.com

N. Kruschwitz
MIT Sloan Management Review, Cambridge, MA, USA
e-mail: ninakru@mit.edu

© Springer International Publishing Switzerland 2015   535
K. Wendt (ed.), *Responsible Investment Banking*, CSR, Sustainability, Ethics &
Governance, DOI 10.1007/978-3-319-10311-2_36

advising on securities issues and other forms of capital raising, mergers and acquisitions, trading on capital markets, research and private equity investments".[1] Also, "an investment bank trades and invests on its own account". This chapter focuses on the direct relationships between an investment bank and its corporate clients, in which the bank provides capital and advisory to its clients. These are mainly related to capital market transactions, M&A advisory, and the provision of loans.

Some of these clients are associated with controversial business practices (e.g. illegal logging), sectors (e.g. the defence industry), projects (e.g. large dams), and/or countries (e.g. autocratic regimes). This chapter uses the adjective *controversial* as a general term to describe business practices, sectors, projects, and/or countries that are—directly or indirectly, allegedly or actually—associated with detrimental environmental and social impacts. Such impacts often, but not only, occur in emerging markets and developing countries that tend to have less developed and less reliable sociolegal processes.

In banking, controversial issues are often summarised under the term "environmental and social" (E&S) issues. The latter usually also covers issues related to labour standards and human rights. In the financial sector, E&S issues are often combined with additional nontraditional issues under the umbrella term *ESG issues*: environmental, social, and governance issues. The "G" component may cover issues related to companies (e.g. poor corporate governance) or to countries (e.g. sociopolitical instability). In banking, however, governance issues are traditionally dealt with in compliance (e.g. money laundering), in credit risk management (e.g. corporate governance), or in political risk management (e.g. crisis potential). This is why, in banking, the term E&S is still more common.

In the context of this article, *E&S risks* are those risks that occur when investment banks provide financial services to companies that are associated with controversial issues. E&S risks can occur in multiple financial risk categories, such as credit risk, operational risk (including legal risk), and reputational risk.

The business case for managing E&S risks first builds on the observation that the risks a client is exposed to can translate into risks for the bank, such as credit risk. Imagine a firm operating a mine in Latin America that loses its operating license because it does not meet the expectations of the regulator. This building block of the business case addresses risks that are already material today.

Second, the business case for E&S risk management also builds on the assumption that investment banks expose themselves to risk if they engage in business relationships with entities that disregard (voluntary) minimum environmental and social requirements. Such requirements have been defined by supranational and multilateral institutions such as the World Bank Group (e.g. the IFC Performance Standards), the United Nations (e.g. the 10 principles of the UN Global Compact), and the OECD (e.g. the OECD Guidelines for Multinational Enterprises). Other minimum requirements are defined by voluntary initiatives, often driven by

---

[1] Financial Times Lexicon: lexicon.ft.com

non-profit organisations or by sector associations (e.g. the Roundtable on Sustainable Palm Oil, or the Equator Principles).

The remainder of this chapter focuses on the second building block of the business case, as it is here, that the materiality of these E&S risks is less obvious. This chapter makes the case that E&S issues harbour considerable potential for damage in the here and now and that investment banks take a risk if they underestimate them. Several factors are changing the risk landscape of banks, and, as a consequence, E&S risks will quickly become material.

The factors that drive this change are briefly outlined below. These changes put significant pressure on banks to address E&S risks more systematically. Unfortunately, based on research from private-sector companies such as ECOFACT[2] and MSCI,[3] only a handful of first-tier banks manage these risks systematically today.

2 Drivers of Change

Five main drivers in the risk landscape of investment banks increase the need for them to address E&S risks systematically (Fig. 1):

(a) The growing materiality of E&S risks.
(b) Changing perceptions and expectations.
(c) Greater transparency.
(d) New and stricter minimum requirements.
(e) Advances in business practices.

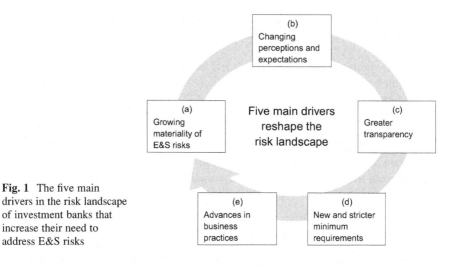

Fig. 1 The five main drivers in the risk landscape of investment banks that increase their need to address E&S risks

---

[2] ECOFACT AG, http://www.ecofact.com

[3] MSCI Inc., http://www.msci.com

These five drivers shape the risk landscape of any private-sector company. Many E&S risks are influenced by the sectors (e.g. mining) and the countries (e.g. weak governance zones) in which a company is active or with which it has business relationships. Some companies will therefore be exposed to greater and more material risks than others. Investment banks tend to be among the companies that are significantly exposed to E&S risks. This exposure is a result not only of their own actions but also of the actions of their clients.

The five drivers of change are highly interrelated, and, when discussed below, they overlap. One way to read the connections between the five factors might be that the growing materiality of E&S risks (a) changes how the risks and the underlying issues are perceived and influences expectations of private-sector companies (including banks) in addressing them (b). Greater transparency (c) makes it easier for NGOs, the media, and other actors such as ESG rating agencies and the general public to compare a company's business practices against benchmarks. These benchmarks are defined by new and stricter minimum requirements (d), mostly set by international standards and emerging regulation, as well as advances in business practices defined by the leaders in a specific sector (e). Deviations from these benchmarks—whether alleged or actual—expose investment banks to risks.

(a) The Growing Materiality of E&S Risks

A good indicator of how E&S risk are becoming more material is the fact that five of the "10 Global Risks of Highest Concern in 2014" collated in the World Economic Forum's "Global Risks 2014" report are related to E&S issues: water crises (ranked third); the failure of climate change mitigation and adaptation (fifth); the greater incidence of extreme weather events such as floods, storms, and wildfires (sixth); food crises (eighth); and profound political and social instability (tenth). The report was produced by the World Economic Forum in collaboration with a leading advisory firm, insurance and reinsurance companies, and academic institutions.[4]

Human rights-related issues are an ideal means of illustrating how E&S risks can no longer be ignored by the private sector.

The game changer came in the form of the "Guiding Principles on Business and Human Rights",[5] a document authored by the UN Secretary-General's Special Representative for Business and Human Rights, Harvard professor John Ruggie. The Guiding Principles were endorsed by the UN Human Rights Council in 2011. This framework aggregated existing international human rights norms laid down in international treaties, conventions and covenants, and customary international law, and their legal implications for different entities. It did not create any new norms or

---

[4] Marsh & McLennan Companies, Swiss Re, Zurich Insurance Group, National University of Singapore, the University of Oxford, and the Wharton School of the University of Pennsylvania.

[5] Report of the Special Representative of the Secretary General on the issue of human rights and transnational corporations and other business enterprises, John Ruggie—Guiding Principles on Business and Human Rights: Implementing the United Nations "Protect, Respect and Remedy" Framework, 21 March 2011.

provisions. However, the Guiding Principles clearly state that companies have the responsibility to respect all human rights. The key documents that require compliance are the International Bill of Human Rights and the Declaration on Fundamental Principles and Rights at Work issued by the International Labour Organization (for more details on the Guiding Principles, see below).

In the first phase, risks related to the infringement of human rights were seen as material at the client level. For example, the International Committee of the Red Cross (ICRC)[6] observed in the context of the extractive industries that "a 2008 study of 190 projects operated by the major international oil companies showed that the time taken for projects to come online has nearly doubled in the last decade, causing significant increase in costs. A confidential follow-up of a subset of those projects, conducted in support of Ruggie's mandate, found that non-technical risks accounted for nearly half of the total project risks faced by these companies, and that stakeholder-related risks constituted the single largest category". In other words, companies not successfully managing what is often termed their *social license to operate* had a high chance of delays and unexpected costs.

However, in the second phase, risks related to human rights are now material at the financial institution level. It is fair to say that human rights are one of the challenging issues facing leading financial institutions (see the work of the Thun Group,[7] e.g., or in Chap. 10).

It is important to realise that, according to the Guiding Principles, business activity is understood as both action and omission. Alongside its own activities, a company can impact adversely on human rights through the relationships it maintains with other businesses, provided they are linked directly to its operations, products, or services. Financial institutions, in particular, may contribute to human rights impacts in this way. The term "relationship" is a broad one and includes investee companies, project partners, and clients, in addition to other parties. In response to questions submitted by the OECD, the United Nations Office of the High Commissioner for Human Rights (OHCHR) also clarified that the concept of indirect impact—a term often used when the bank's client and not the bank itself violates human rights standards—is not supported by the Guiding Principles. There is either "a direct link (...) or there is no link".[8]

Recent related decisions by two government bodies in the Netherlands and Norway—both of whose National Contact Points (NCPs) are key elements of an OECD-wide mechanism that supports the implementation of the OECD Guidelines for Multinational Enterprises (MNE Guidelines)—reemphasised the responsibility of financial institutions in the human rights arena and set a precedent for what is expected from investors. The decisions, both published in 2013 and related to the

---

[6] International Review of the Red Cross, Volume 94, Number 887, Fall 2012.

[7] The Thun Group of Banks, "UN Guiding Principles on Business and Human Rights/Discussion Paper for Banks on Implications of Principles 16–21", October 2013.

[8] OHCHR, "Subject: Request from the Chair of the OECD Working Party on Responsible Business Conduct", 27 November 2013.

Korean steel producer POSCO, concluded that the MNE Guidelines also apply to minority shareholders. The decisions by the NCPs make investors accountable for human rights issues related to the companies in which they invest.

In summary, the Guiding Principles clearly apply to financial institutions. Principle 14 stipulates that all companies have a responsibility to respect human rights. Although the same principle also states that this responsibility may vary depending on the organisation's "size, sector, operational context, ownership, and structure", it appears evident that the Guiding Principles therefore also apply to a bank's client relationships.

In two working papers from the Harvard Kennedy School, Kytle and Ruggie (2005) determine that, for global companies, new risks are emerging from global operations and empowered stakeholders, among other factors, and that these risks cannot be mitigated by traditional means. In the context of human rights, Sherman and Lehr (2010) conclude that not conducting human rights due diligence presents significant risks to companies. The conclusion is simple: investment banks should not ignore the risks that result from engaging with clients that do not meet—or ignore—minimum requirements for E&S practices.

(b) Changing Perceptions and Expectations

In recent years, E&S issues have received significant attention from mainstream media. Even media that are often considered conservative or business-friendly, such as the Wall Street Journal, now regularly cover controversial issues. NGO action and the marketing campaigns run by companies that promote environmentally friendly or fair trade products constantly remind the public of E&S issues. The bottom line is that the general public is more aware of these issues and, as a result, more able to act if it disapproves of certain business practices. Today, E&S issues are also covered by academic research, in academic literature, in business school case studies, and in academic curricula.

Consequently, companies are more exposed to scrutiny, and there is the widespread expectation that they should be able to explain their business models to the public. This is perhaps especially true of investment banks in the wake of the financial market crisis. RepRisk, a Swiss-based ESG business intelligence provider,[9] has identified 375 NGOs that have criticised banks over the past few years, and roughly 20 campaigns that have specifically targeted banks. These have covered a wide range of E&S issues, such as the financing of mountaintop removal mining and coal-fired power plants, the financing of companies which produce or maintain controversial weapons such as nuclear weapons and cluster munitions, the trade in soft commodities (food speculation), the financing of companies that operate in disputed territories (such as the Western Sahara or the West Bank), and the financing of companies targeted by animal rights activists, among others.

For a while, there seemed to be a vicious cycle in which new controversial issues would emerge, NGOs would criticise banks for failing to address these issues

---

[9] RepRisk AG, http://www.reprisk.com

appropriately, and the banks would respond by drafting new policies and adapting their screening processes—until new controversial issues and new criticism arose. To break this cycle, many banks now maintain a more proactive approach. They monitor NGO criticism, they listen to their stakeholders' expectations, and they observe regulatory developments. Most importantly, they assess the materiality of issues in accordance with their criteria. This allows them to make their own informed decisions on what the relevant E&S issues are.

(c) Greater Transparency

There are at least five interconnected trends that have led to greater transparency. First, NGOs have established global networks that connect remote regions with the homes of concerned consumers. Second, the way NGOs and the public access and disseminate information has evolved in recent years, mainly because of new digital technologies. NGOs are able to reach their membership base or to launch a new campaign almost instantaneously thanks to social media. Third, as explained above, traditional media are reporting on E&S issues more frequently. Fourth, ESG rating agencies and specialised business intelligence providers assess and monitor corporate track records and performance. Note that these companies sell their data primarily to financial institutions. Fifth, multiple disclosure and reporting mechanisms lead companies to disclose details of their business practices, objectives, and levels of achievement. These mechanisms include the CDP,[10] which "represents 722 institutional investors holding US$87 trillion in assets, to help reveal the risk in their investment portfolio"; the Global Reporting Initiative (GRI),[11] which has established a reporting framework "to make sustainability reporting standard practice"; and specialised programmes such as the Extractive Industries Transparency Initiative (EITI),[12] which aims to improve the "accountable management of revenues from natural resources". This creates transparency among peers and increases the pressure on all to follow the sector leaders which shape new business practices (please also refer to (e) below).

(d) New and Stricter Minimum Requirements

New standards that aim to define minimum requirements for specific issues or sectors are mushrooming. Examples include the Voluntary Guidelines on the Responsible Tenure of Land, Fisheries and Forests and the Environmental, Health, and Safety Guidelines for 62 sectors developed by IFC, the private-sector arm of the World Bank Group. Please also refer to Sect. 1 above for additional standards that define minimum requirements.

---

[10] Originally: the Carbon Disclosure Project. Now, as the abbreviation has become a widely known brand and the CDP has broadened the scope of their work, "CDP" is used in abbreviated form only: http://www.cdp.net

[11] http://www.globalreporting.org

[12] http://www.eiti.org

There are also voluntary standards tailored to financial institutions. The best known of these are the Equator Principles (EP),[13] which originally concentrated on project finance and project finance advisory. Their scope has recently been extended (EP III) and now also covers project-related corporate and bridging loans. However, they do not yet include capital market transactions or corporate loans that provide funds for general corporate purposes.

At present, there is no comparable standard for investment banks. However, certain initiatives will influence the issues investment banking has to take into account. Two examples are the Sustainability Accounting Standards Board (SASB),[14] which "provides standards for use by publicly-listed corporations in the US in disclosing material sustainability issues for the benefit of investors and the public", and the Sustainable Stock Exchanges (SSE) initiative,[15] which is "a peer-to-peer learning platform for exploring how exchanges, in collaboration with investors, regulators, and companies, can enhance corporate transparency". SSE partner exchanges include NYSE Euronext, NASDAQ OMX, the Bombay Stock Exchange, the Brazilian BM&FBOVESPA exchange, Borsa Istanbul, the Johannesburg Stock Exchange, the Nigerian Stock Exchange, the Warsaw Stock Exchange, and the Egyptian Exchange.

It is crucial for companies to understand such voluntary standards, as compliance with legal requirements is often not enough, particularly if a company's senior management or its shareholders are aware of potentially detrimental side effects of its business operations. Changing perceptions, changing business practices, and changing judicial practices can result in risks in retrospect. This further underscores the importance of following certain best practices now, to avoid such risks in the future. One daunting example is the case of the now-defunct Italian company Eternit SpA, which specialised in asbestos products. In June 2013, the former key shareholder of the company was sentenced by an Italian court of second instance to 18 years in jail for negligence that had reportedly led to more than 2,200 asbestos-related deaths. Note that the company had gone under as far back as 1986, had met the relevant legal requirements, and the Italian authorities did not ban asbestos until 1992.

(e) Advances in Business Practices

Companies are responding to new expectations. The annual research that has been carried out over the past five years by the MIT Sloan Management Review and the Boston Consulting Group shows a steady increase in companies' willingness to address E&S issues. The last report,[16] released in December 2013, investigates how companies turn their attention to the most significant sustainability issues. Furthermore, although "many companies struggle to match their strong level of

---

[13] http://www.equator-principles.com

[14] http://www.sasb.org

[15] http://www.sseinitiative.org

[16] MIT Sloan Management Review and The Boston Consulting Group: "Sustainability's Next Frontier: Walking the talk on the sustainability issues that matter most", MIT Sloan Management Review, Research Report, December 2013.

sustainability concern with equally strong action", many companies are making progress in this respect.

As a result, business practices evolve, and what is considered acceptable at a certain point in time might not be so a few years later. Advances happen at the level of individual companies that push the boundaries within their sector, and at the level of entire sectors, often in the attempt to define common sector best practices that will eventually lead to a level playing field (please also refer to (d) above).

The ECOFACT Quarterly, a briefing for financial institutions, contains an overview of the policies, guidelines, and commitments financial institutions have issued with regard to controversial sectors or issues. According to the December 2013 issue, the 30 banks that are systemically important in the eyes of the Financial Stability Board, including the larger investment banks, mention 248 such sector or issue-specific documents on their websites (ECOFACT 2013). This indicates that first-tier banks are now defining best practices in E&S risk management.

Conclusions

In summary, the risk landscape is evolving owing to changes in the market and nonmarket environments. Even more importantly, the way that private-sector companies are addressing these risks is also evolving. Corporate social and environmental responsibility, "once regarded as a concern of a few philanthropic individuals and companies" (Clarke and Klettner 2007), has become critical to business development and risk management.

As outlined above, there is a clear business case that supports the implementation of E&S risk management in investment banking. When investment banks assess ESG issues in client relationships, they help their clients to manage ESG risks more effectively. Even more importantly, they manage important risks that are already material today. And, as always, thoroughly understanding risk will eventually make it possible to identify new business opportunities.

The minimum goal should be to not provide financial services to clients that violate those international standards that define acceptable business practices. In the future, ignoring such standards could be seen in retrospect as a deliberate decision which will eventually expose a bank to risk.

References

Clarke, T., & Klettner, A. (2007). *Tip of the Iceberg? Corporate Social Responsibility and Sustainability: the new business imperatives?* Financial Services Institute of Australasia (Finsia): Sidney.

ECOFACT AG (2013, December). The briefing for E&S risk experts. *The ECOFACT Quarterly,* (7)

Kytle, B., & Ruggie, J. G. (2005). *Corporate social responsibility as risk management—A model for multinationals* (Working Paper No. 10). Cambridge, MA: Corporate Social Responsibility Initiative, Harvard University: John F. Kennedy School of Government.

Sherman, J. F. I., & Lehr, A. (2010). *Human rights due diligence: Is it too risky?* (Working Paper No. 55). Cambridge MA: Corporate Social Responsibility Initiative. Harvard University: John F. Kennedy School of Government.

Responsible Investment Banking and Asset Management: Risk Management Frameworks, Soft Law Standards and Positive Impacts

Global Standards and Responsible Leadership: Reviewing the Role of ISO 26000 and Its Relationship with the UN Global Compact and the Global Reporting Initiative

Jonathon Hanks

Abstract The past 15 years has seen a proliferation of soft law standards aimed at promoting responsible business practice across all types of business sectors, including specifically within the banking and asset management sectors. Amongst this profusion of standards and initiatives, there are arguably three global standards that cut across all sectors and that enjoy prominence amongst those sustainability practitioners looking for international guidance: ISO 26000, the United Nations Global Compact (UNGC), and the Global Reporting Initiative (GRI). This chapter focuses on the potential contribution that ISO 26000 can play in promoting responsible business practice in the investment banking and asset management sectors. After providing a broad introduction to ISO 26000, identifying some suggested unique features that distinguish the standard from other social responsibility initiatives, the chapter reviews how ISO 26000 can and is being used to promote responsible investment practices. The chapter will argue that while these initiatives have a potentially significant role to play in promoting sustainable development, it is critical to recognise their limitations.

J. Hanks (✉)
Incite, Cape Town, South Africa
e-mail: jon@incite.co.za

© Springer International Publishing Switzerland 2015   545
K. Wendt (ed.), *Responsible Investment Banking*, CSR, Sustainability, Ethics &
Governance, DOI 10.1007/978-3-319-10311-2_37

1 Introduction

The past 15 years has seen a proliferation of voluntary 'soft law' standards aimed at promoting responsible practice amongst all business sectors, including within the financial sector. The most notable examples of such standards and initiatives in the banking and asset management sector include:

- The United Nations-supported Principles for Responsible Investment (PRI)—a set of principles developed by an international group of institutional investors that reflect the increasing recognition that environmental, social and governance issues can affect the performance of investment portfolios and that seek to better align investors' activities with the broader objectives of society (http://www.unpri.org).
- The International Finance Corporation's (IFC) Sustainability Framework and Performance Standards—these strive to promote sound environmental and social practices, encourage transparency and enhance the societal impacts of development projects (http://www.ifc.org/sustainabilityframework).
- The Equator Principles—a risk management framework adopted by financial institutions for determining, assessing and managing environmental and social risks in projects, with the aim of providing a minimum standard for due diligence to support responsible risk decision-making (http://www.equator-principles.com).

In addition to these financial-sector initiatives (each of which is reviewed in more detail elsewhere in this book), there are many cross-sector initiatives that provide social responsibility guidance and/or performance specifications for organisations across the public and private sectors. Of these cross-sector initiatives, there are three that arguably enjoy particular prominence amongst sustainability practitioners looking for global guidance: the ISO 26000 international standard on social responsibility, the United Nations Global Compact (UNGC), and the Global Reporting Initiative's (GRI) Sustainability Reporting Guidelines.

This chapter briefly reviews the role of each of these initiatives in promoting responsible business practice, with a particular focus on ISO 26000. After providing a broad introduction to ISO 26000 and identifying some suggested unique features that distinguish this standard from other social responsibility initiatives, the chapter briefly reviews the role of UNGC and GRI, before reflecting how each of these can be used to promote responsible business practices, identifying some of their potential benefits and shortcomings. The chapter argues that while each of these initiatives has a useful role to play in promoting more responsible business and contributing to sustainable development, it is important to recognise their limitations and that they are not a substitute for the more transformative business leadership that is required.

2 ISO 26000: An Ambitious Global Standard Promoting Sustainable Development

In November 2010, the Geneva-based International Organization for Standardization (ISO)[1] launched one of its most eagerly awaited standards: the ISO 26000 international guidance standard on social responsibility. Developed over 5 years, the standard provides guidance for all types of organisations on social responsibility principles and practices, with the explicit broader goal of contributing to sustainable development.

The publication of the standard was the culmination of the largest multistakeholder negotiating process ever undertaken by ISO, involving the participation of more than 450 experts and 210 observers from 99 countries and 42 'liaison organisations'. The participating organisations included international business, trade union, NGO and civil society bodies, intergovernmental organisations and the secretariats of various multinational social responsibility initiatives. The individual experts involved in drafting the standard represented six different stakeholder groups: industry, labour, government, consumers, nongovernmental organisations and a broad group comprising national standard bodies, academia, consultants and 'others'.

The 5-year negotiation process provided an extremely valuable opportunity for experts from different countries, cultures and stakeholder groups to develop a deeper understanding and build consensus on what constitutes 'socially responsible behaviour' across all cultures and regions. Although at times a difficult and contentious process—which was inevitable given the range and complexity of the issues under discussion—the negotiation process resulted in one of the highest levels of approval for any ISO standard, an important feature that adds legitimacy to the quality of its guidance.

In assessing the potential contribution of ISO 26000, it is critical to appreciate that it is a voluntary *guidance* standard. Unlike ISO 9001 (on quality management) and ISO 14001 (on environmental management), it is not a management system standard, nor is it intended or appropriate for certification purposes or regulatory or contractual use. The standard is quite explicit on this aspect and maintains that 'any offer to certify, or claims to be certified, to ISO 26000 would be a misrepresentation of the intent and purpose and a misuse of this International Standard'. Recognising that this is a guidance document—and not a certifiable standard—has a profound bearing on how this document should be used and on the value that it offers.

---

[1] ISO is an independent, non-governmental organisation made up of members from the national standards bodies of 164 countries, with a Central Secretariat based in Geneva, Switzerland. ISO is the world's largest developer of voluntary international standards that provide state-of-the-art specifications for products, services and good practice (http://www.iso.org).

3   What Guidance Does the ISO 26000 Standard Provide?

ISO 26000 provides guidance to all types of organisations—regardless of their nature, size, activity or location or whether they are from the public or private sector—on the following areas[2]:

- Key concepts, terms and definitions related to social responsibility.
- The background, trends and characteristics of social responsibility.
- Some fundamental principles and practices relating to social responsibility.
- An identified set of 'core subjects' and 'issues' of social responsibility.
- How to integrate, implement and promote socially responsible behaviour throughout the organisation and within its sphere of influence.
- Communicating commitments, performance and other information related to social responsibility.

The standard defines social responsibility as:

'The responsibility of an organisation for the impacts of its decisions and activities on society and the environment, through transparent and ethical behaviour that

- contributes to sustainable development, including health and the welfare of society;
- takes into account the expectations of stakeholders;
- is in compliance with applicable law and consistent with international norms of behaviour; and
- is integrated throughout the organisation and practiced in its relationships'.[3]

Given this definition, it is clear that 'social responsibility' should not be confused with an organisation's philanthropic and charitable activities, a misunderstanding that is arguably still prevalent within many organisations. While an effective social responsibility programme might include these activities, its focus will be much broader, with the emphasis on integrating relevant environmental, social and governance (ESG) considerations into all relevant aspects of the organisation's activities and throughout its sphere of influence.

In terms of this approach, social responsibility is about understanding and addressing an organisation's impacts and influence on such areas as human rights, labour issues, the environment and community development, as well as about responding to the expectations of its different stakeholders, with the goal of making a positive contribution to sustainable development. Ultimately, it's about improving an organisation's understanding of the changing risks and opportunities associated with operating in an ever-globalised world, where ESG issues are increasingly impacting on business competitiveness.

Undoubtedly the most useful part of the standard relates to the detailed guidance provided on the following seven 'core subjects' of social responsibility: organisational governance, human rights, labour practices, the environment, consumer issues, fair operating practices and community involvement and

---

[2] This list is a slight rephrasing of that provided in the Scope of ISO 26000 (2010), p. 1.

[3] ISO 26000 (2010), Clause 2.18, p. 3.

development.[4] Each of the seven core subjects includes a set of subject-specific 'issues' that an organisation should take into account when identifying its social responsibility expectations; there are a total of 37 issues across all seven subjects. While each of the seven core subjects is seen to have some relevance for every organisation, not all issues are necessarily applicable to all organisations. In considering its social responsibility, an organisation is expected to identify each issue that is relevant to its specific decisions and activities, informed by an assessment of its most significant impacts, and with consideration to the interests of its stakeholders.

The most useful feature of the guidance lies in the set of recommended 'actions and expectations' that are provided for each of the 37 issues. These provide a comprehensive, yet concise, description of the fundamental expectations of what constitutes socially responsible behaviour for all organisations in all jurisdictions. Most importantly, these actions and expectations are all derived from authoritative international instruments. For example, the detailed list of actions and expectations relating to the five issues under the core subject on labour practices[5] are all derived from relevant conventions and recommendations of the tripartite International Labour Organization (ILO), the most authoritative source of international standards on labour. Sixty-nine ILO conventions and recommendations are listed as references in the ISO 26000 bibliography. By providing a concise eight-page description of the principal implications of all of these authoritative international instruments, ISO 26000 provides organisations with readily available, easily understood guidance on the international expectations relating to labour.

Similarly, the clause on human rights provides succinct guidance based on the Universal Declaration of Human Rights and related UN instruments,[6] and it is very closely aligned with the subsequently released UN Guiding Principles on Business and Human Rights.[7] The clause on consumer issues derives mainly from the UN Guidelines for Consumer Protection, while the guidance on environmental issues is based on an array of recent multinational environmental agreements (and so on across all the subjects). This is the core strength of the standard: a concise articulation of the fundamental expectations and international norms of socially responsible behaviour derived from authoritative international instruments.

---

[4] ISO 26000 (2010), Clause 6

[5] ISO 26000 (2010), Clause 6.5, pp. 33–40. The five labour 'issues' are employment and employment relationships, conditions of work and social protection, social dialogue, health and safety at work and human development and training in the workplace.

[6] The list of core international human rights instruments that informed the clause on human rights is provided in Box 6 of the standard; p. 23.

[7] The UN Guiding Principles are available at http://www.ohchr.org/Documents/Publications/GuidingPrinciplesBusinessHR_EN.pdf; although these were agreed after the publication of ISO 26000, there was very close cooperation between the drafters of the human rights section of ISO 26000 and those responsible for developing the UN Guiding Principles developed by the Special Representative of the Secretary-General on the issue of human rights and transnational corporations and other business enterprises (Professor John Ruggie).

In addition to providing guidance on these core subjects and issues, the standard also provides general guidance on how to put social responsibility into practice within an organisation. The guidance covers issues such as conducting a due diligence process, determining the relevance and significance of social responsibility issues, undertaking internal awareness raising, setting appropriate policies and standards and communicating and reporting on social responsibility. The standard suggests that 'in most cases, organisations can build on existing systems, policies, structures and networks of the organisation to put social responsibility into practice, although some activities are likely to be conducted in new ways, or with consideration for a broader range of factors'.

Finally, an annex to the standard contains a non-exhaustive list of voluntary initiatives and tools for social responsibility that may offer additional guidance on the core subjects and integration practices of social responsibility. The annex briefly shows examples of additional guidance that is available on the various core subjects and/or practices for integrating social responsibility and provides a brief description and reference to the official website.

4   ISO 26000: Important Distinguishing Features

Given the plethora of existing soft law initiatives—including those targeting the finance sector—is there any additional value to be gained in using the guidance provided in ISO 26000? Some have argued that ISO 26000 has the potential to take its place 'at the apex of the burgeoning body of SR standards... a potential derived from the body's brand recognition, the broad stakeholder and geographic reach of its processes, and a business-led demand for convergence in the overall body of available guidance on social responsibility'.[8]

Assessing the potential value of ISO 26000, it is suggested that there are three principal features that distinguish this standard from other voluntary initiatives on social responsibility:

1. Its explicit focus in describing the fundamental expectations of socially responsible behaviour.
2. The breadth of the consensus-driven multi-stakeholder process in drafting the standard.
3. The global reach of the ISO brand.

Each of these features is briefly reviewed below.

---

[8] Ward (2011).

4.1 Describing the Fundamental Expectations of Socially Responsible Behaviour

From the outset, the ISO 26000 process had bold ambitions, both in terms of its subject matter and in the nature of the multi-stakeholder process used in its development. By venturing into the field of social responsibility and sustainable development, ISO entered into an area involving subjects and issues of broad public policy concern that are qualitatively different from the development of technical standards that the international standards body has traditionally dealt with.

Recognising this change of focus, the multi-stakeholder Advisory Group on Social Responsibility—established in 2002 to advise ISO's Technical Management Board on the merits and possible scope of work of a social responsibility standard—identified seven preconditions that it argued ISO should observe if it were to proceed with developing any deliverables in the social responsibility field.[9] These preconditions, which had a strong influence on the final design and content of the standard, included the advice that ISO should only proceed if 'ISO recognises that it does not have the authority or legitimacy to set social obligations or expectations which are properly defined by governments and intergovernmental organisations; (and) ISO recognises the difference between on the one hand, instruments adopted by authoritative global inter-governmental organisations (such as the UN Universal Declaration on Human Rights, international labour conventions and other instruments adopted by the ILO and relevant UN Conventions) and on the other hand, private voluntary initiatives that may or may not reflect the universal principles contained in the above instruments'.[10]

Informed by these recommendations, the standard explicitly strives to 'foster greater awareness and wider observance of an agreed set of universal principles as expressed in United Nations conventions and declarations' while ensuring that it is 'consistent with and not in conflict with existing documents, international treaties and conventions and existing ISO standards'.[11]

As argued earlier, a particular strength of the standard lies in its articulation of a set of international norms and expectations as to what constitutes socially responsible behaviour, regardless of the size or type of organisation or the location of its operations. The identification of these performance norms and expectations is based

---

[9] ISO/TMB AG CSR N32 *Recommendations to the ISO Technical Management Board* 2(2004-10-21); see also ISO Advisory Group on Social Responsibility (April 2004) *Working Report on Social Responsibility*. The terms of reference of the Advisory Group were 'To determine whether ISO should proceed with the development of ISO deliverables in the field of corporate social responsibility; if so to determine the scope of work and the type of deliverable'. The Advisory Group comprised 24 members, plus two representatives of the ISO Secretariat. Members included representatives from standards bodies, industry, academia, nongovernmental organisations, the international trade union movement, the UN Global Compact and the Global Reporting Initiative.

[10] ISO/TMB AG CSR N32 *Recommendations to the ISO Technical Management Board* 2(2004-10-21).

[11] ISO/TMB *New Work Item Proposal N26000* (2004-10-01), Annex B (f) and Annex A (1).

on a considered review by the participating subject experts and by relevant representative interest groups, of the implications of the requirements contained in authoritative intergovernmental instruments (all of which are listed in the standard's bibliography). This consolidated consensus-based view of the globally applicable norms of behaviour is outlined primarily in terms of the seven core subjects—and the associated 'issues' and 'actions and expectations'—presented in Clause 6.

4.2 The Consensus-Based Multi-stakeholder Process of Drafting the Standard

A second important distinguishing characteristic of ISO 26000 over other voluntary initiatives is the nature of the process of its development. As noted earlier, it was the largest multi-stakeholder negotiation process undertaken by ISO, involving the participation of more than 450 experts and 200 observers from 99 countries and 42 'liaison organisations'. Throughout the ISO 26000 process, steps were taken to promote a representative geographic and gender-based balance of experts, with a particular focus on facilitating the participation and contribution of developing-country experts.

A critical feature of the multi-stakeholder process was the fact that the process provided for double levels of consensus: firstly amongst the participating experts drafting the standard and secondly amongst the 163 ISO member countries who considered the final draft:

- In accordance with ISO Directives, the negotiation of the standard was based on decision-making by consensus amongst all the participating experts. For the purposes of the ISO 26000 process, consensus was defined as 'general agreement, characterised by the absence of sustained opposition to substantial issues by any important part of the concerns interest, and by a process that involves seeking to take into account the views of all parties concerned and to reconcile any conflicting arguments; note: consensus need not imply unanimity'.
- After passing this stiff test in reaching agreement on the text across all stakeholder groups, the final step was to ensure sufficient approval amongst ISO's member countries.[12]

The fact that the Final Draft International Standard (FDIS) passed both hurdles and secured 93 % of eligible votes in favour of the standard, across all regions,

---

[12] ISO/TMB/WG SR N196 *Result of ballot of ISO FDIS 26000*. To be approved the ISO standard required at least 66.66 % of P-members voting in favour of the standard, and not more than 25 % of total member bodies voting against the standard. The final vote on the standard was 93 % of P-members in favour and 6 % of total member bodies voting against. Only 5 P-members voted against the standard: Cuba, India, Luxembourg, Turkey and the USA.

suggests—as ISO Secretary General Rob Steele has argued—that ISO 26000 'distils a truly international consensus on what social responsibility means'.[13]

4.3 The Global Reach of the ISO Brand

A third distinguishing feature of ISO 26000 relates to ISO's broad international reach and credible brand recognition. As a worldwide federation of national standards bodies, the Geneva-based International Organization for Standardization has the institutional architecture, the global brand recognition and the credibility to play an influential role in promoting the social responsibility agenda and facilitating convergence in the overall body of guidance on social responsibility initiatives.

ISO's significant global reach and brand recognition is reflected in the fact that there are substantially more companies across all continents that have ISO 9001 (quality) or ISO 40001 (environmental) certification than there are companies that produce GRI-based reports or that are signatories to the UNGC. This global uptake of ISO standards suggests not only high levels of awareness of ISO standards but also implies confidence and credibility in the ISO brand. ISO standards are often included within supply chain requirements, referenced in international instruments and incorporated into national regulatory and governance standards.

At a national level, ISO standards have been used to inform the development of corporate governance standards. In South Africa, for example, the King Code of Governance for South Africa 2009 (King III)—recognised as one of the most progressive corporate governance standards globally, due in part to its strong focus on sustainability—specifically references ISO 26000 and draws on elements of the standard to inform key aspects of the code.[14]

5 The Other 'Charismatic' Cross-Sector Social Responsibility Initiatives

As argued above, of the various global cross-sector social responsibility initiatives,[15] there are two that stand out alongside ISO 26000 in terms of their application and uptake across sectors: the United Nations Global Compact (UNGC) and

---

[13] ISO Secretary General Rob Steele speaking at the ISO 26000 launch, November 2010 (Geneva).

[14] For example, the King III definition of corporate social responsibility draws directly from the ISO 26000 definition of social responsibility (Hanks, J. 2011a, March).

[15] Examples of other cross-sectoral standards and initiatives include: the OECD Guidelines for Multinational Enterprises, AccountAbility's AA1000 series of standards on accountability and stakeholder engagement, the CERES principles, the EFQM Framework for CSR and Excellence Model, the Ethical Trading Initiative and Social Accountability International (SAI) SA8000 standard (for further examples see, e.g. Annex A of ISO 26000).

the Global Reporting Initiative (GRI), both of which are referred to in the Principles for Responsible Investment (PRI).[16] These are each very briefly reviewed below.

5.1   The United Nations Global Compact

The UNGC describes itself as 'the world's largest corporate citizenship and sustainability initiative... with more than 10,000 participants, including more than 7,000 businesses in 145 countries'.[17] Launched in July 2000, the UNGC provides a principle-based framework, supported by a range of management tools, resources and programmes, with the aim of achieving two key objectives:

- Aligning business strategy and operations with 10 universally accepted principles in the areas of human rights, labour, environment and anti-corruption (Box 1).
- Catalysing actions in support of the broader goals of the United Nations, including the Millennium Development Goals.[18]

The 10 Principles of the United Nations Global Compact
The UNGC asks companies to 'embrace, support and enact, within their sphere of influence' the following principles:
Human Rights
1. Businesses should support and respect the protection of internationally proclaimed human rights; and
2. Make sure that they are not complicit in human rights abuses.
Labour
3. Businesses should uphold the freedom of association and the effective recognition of the right to collective bargaining;
4. The elimination of all forms of forced and compulsory labour;
5. The effective abolition of child labour; and

(continued)

---

[16] Principle 3 of the PRI states: 'We will seek appropriate disclosure on ESG issues by the entities in which we invest'. Suggested actions under the principle include: 'Ask(ing) for standardised reporting on ESG issues (using tools such as the Global Reporting Initiative)' and 'Ask(ing) for information from companies regarding adoption of/adherence to relevant norms, standards, codes of conduct or international initiatives (such as the UN Global Compact)'. http://www.unpri.org/about-pri/the-six-principles/

[17] http://www.unglobalcompact.org/ParticipantsAndStakeholders/index.html   (Accessed   on 30 December 2013).

[18] UNGC tools and resources are available at: http://www.unglobalcompact.org/AboutTheGC/tools_resources/general.html. A comprehensive self assessment tool is available at: http://www.globalcompactselfassessment.org/aboutthistool.

6. The elimination of discrimination in respect of employment and occupation.

Environment

7. Businesses should support a precautionary approach to environmental challenges;

8. Undertake initiatives to promote greater environmental responsibility; and

9. Encourage the development and diffusion of environmentally friendly technologies.

Anti-Corruption

10. Businesses should work against corruption in all its forms, including extortion and bribery.

Business participation in the UNGC involves a commitment by the company's chief executive officer, with the support of its highest-level governance body, to the implementation, disclosure and promotion of the 10 UNGC principles. By joining the initiative, a company is expected to make these principles an integral part of its business activities, to contribute to the achievement of broad development objectives through partnerships and to advance the case for responsible business practices through advocacy and active outreach to peers, partners, clients, consumers and the public at large. Signatory companies are also expected to publish an annual Communication on Progress describing the ways in which they are implementing the principles and supporting the broader development objectives.

The UNGC has come in for criticism from various civil society organisations for its lack of formal accountability and sanctioning mechanisms and for admitting signatories with dubious social responsibility records. Some have argued, for example, that signatory companies are using the UNGC for simple public relations purposes or as a means for countering more stringent social responsibility regulation and for increasing business influence within the United Nations process.[19]

The UNGC has produced a useful guidance document in which it reviews the link between the UNGC's 10 principles and ISO 26000's seven core subjects.[20] While not an exhaustive review of the various areas of alignment, the publication shows that there is strong consistency between the two initiatives and that each of the UN Global Compact Principles is included in ISO 26000. This consistency between the two initiatives is not surprising, given that both initiatives derive their guidance on the shared subjects of human rights, labour, the environment and corruption from the same authoritative international instruments. In terms of these shared subject areas, in essence ISO 26000 simply offers a more detailed articulation and a greater level of guidance regarding the expectations and practical

---

[19] See, for example, Knight and Smith (2008) and the website *Global Compact Critics* (http://www.globalcompactcritics.net/).

[20] UNGC (2010).

implications for organisations arising from these instruments. In doing so, by implication it reaffirms the UNGC's 10 principles.

While there is evident consistency between the relevant ISO 26000 core subjects and the UNGC principles, there are nevertheless some important process differences between the two initiatives. A principal difference is that the ISO 26000 is simply a guidance document for use by organisations and practitioners as they see fit. The UNGC, by contrast, involves a public commitment by the signatory CEO, as well as the publication of an annual Communication on Progress (CoP). To assist signatory organisations to deliver on these commitments, the UNGC offers participants a set of management tools, resources and programmes that provide further guidance on implementation of the principles and that maintain a continuing 'live' interest in and focus on the UNGC.

5.2   The Global Reporting Initiative

The GRI is a network-based nongovernmental organisation founded in 1997 by Ceres and the United Nations Environment Programme (UNEP) with the aim of promoting greater uniformity in the reporting of sustainability issues.[21] With its Secretariat based in the Netherlands, the GRI produces the world's most widely used sustainability reporting framework, developed through 'a consensus-seeking, multi-stakeholder process' involving participants from global business, civil society, labour, academia and professional institutions.[22]

The GRI's sustainability reporting framework defines the principles and performance indicators that organisations can use to measure and report their economic, environmental and social performance. The cornerstone of the Framework is the GRI's Sustainability Reporting Guidelines, with the most recent 'fourth generation' (G4) guidelines launched in May 2013. In addition to outlining a detailed set of environmental, social and economic performance indicators, the guidelines include provision for a CEO statement, a profile of the reporting entity, a description of the organisation's policies and management systems on environmental, social and economic issues and details on the organisation's approach to stakeholder engagement. These core guidelines are complemented by various Sector Supplements (containing unique indicators for different sectors), as well as by National Annexes

---

[21] Founded in the USA in 1997 by CERES and the United Nations Environment Program (UNEP), the GRI was originally based in Boston, Massachusetts. In 2002, it moved its central office to Amsterdam, where the Secretariat is currently located; it also has regional Focal Points in Australia, Brazil, China, India and the USA. Although the GRI is an independent NGO, it remains a collaborating centre of UNEP and works in cooperation with the UN Global Compact. See http://www.globalreporting.org/.

[22] A useful overview of the process involved in establishing the GRI is provided in Brown et al. (2007).

(with unique country-level information).[23] All of these are freely available from the GRI website (http://www.globalreporting.org).

Although they have different underlying purposes, there is clear synergy between ISO 26000 and the GRI, although ISO 26000's focus is clearly broader than that of the GRI. Not only does the ISO guidance standard seek to describe the globally acceptable norms of socially responsible performance (the GRI reporting criteria cannot be seen in the same vein as international norms, although some practitioners appear to treat them as such), but it also provides broad process guidance on the full spectrum of management activities, including reporting. The GRI, by contrast, limits its focus explicitly to providing process guidance on sustainability reporting issues, although understandably it does so on this issue with a greater level of detail than ISO 26000.

Although some might suggest (as the GRI has argued) that ISO 26000 'does not provide guidance on specific indicators',[24] it can be countered that the core subjects, issues and related actions and expectations outlined in Clause 6 of ISO 26000 provide an obvious and very comprehensive basis for organisations to develop their own set of indicators that are of material interest to them and/or their stakeholders. In some instances (e.g. on human rights), the set of suggested indicators provided in the ISO standard is more comprehensive and useful than those listed in the GRI, while in other areas (e.g. environmental performance) the GRI offers a greater level of specificity. The checklist format in which indicators are presented in the GRI Guidelines opens the GRI to the risk of being seen to promote a tick-box approach to reporting that undermines their explicit (and much needed) efforts to encourage a focus on identifying the material issues.

The GRI and ISO have produced a useful explanatory document on using the GRI Guidelines in conjunction with ISO 26000.[25] The document includes a detailed seven-page table that tracks each of the GRI's disclosure items against relevant subjects, issues and clauses in ISO 26000. This table is intended to assist organisations that are interested in using the ISO 26000 guidance when producing a sustainability report based on the GRI Guidelines.

An important distinction between ISO 26000 and the GRI is that ISO 26000 seeks to provide a normative framework for social responsibility, outlining a set of fundamental principles and/or substantive *performance* expectations against which to judge an organisation's performance; by contrast GRI focuses on providing guidance on a *process* issue (reporting) without defining the normative performance expectations that define whether or not an organisation is socially responsible. Looking at it another way, ISO 26000 defines the performance expectations in

---

[23] These framework documents are supported by a series of learning publications including a step by step handbook introducing the process of reporting (*The GRI Sustainability Reporting Cycle: A Handbook for Small and Not-So-Small Organisations*) as well as a guide on producing a sustainability report (*Let's Report! Step-by-step Guidance to Prepare a Basic GRI Sustainability Report*). See: http://www.globalreporting.org/LearningAndSupport/GRIPublications/LearningPublications/

[24] GRI and ISO (2014).

[25] GRI and ISO (2014).

terms of how social responsibility is *implemented*, while the GRI focuses on identifying performance indicators that should be *reported on*.

5.3 Promoting Responsible Business Practices: Recognising the Role for Each Initiative

This chapter has suggested that each of the three initiatives—ISO 26000, the UNGC and the GRI—has distinct characteristics and benefits that enable them to play a valuable role in assisting organisations to understand societal expectations and to identify and implement policies and practices that integrate these expectations more effectively throughout their activities.

In understanding the distinction between them, putting it simply:[26]

- ISO 26000 provides a comprehensive and credible normative framework of globally applicable social responsibility expectations derived from authoritative international agreements, with detailed guidance on the expected *performance*, as well as high-level guidance on *process* issues.
- The UNGC, through its focus on CEO commitment, annual reporting of progress and the provision of management tools and resources, offers a structured process for engaging organisations on a critical subset of social responsibility *performance* expectations, although it lacks the level of more specific detail available in ISO 26000.
- The GRI provides valuable guidance on the *process* of reporting on sustainability issues, identifying the principles and suggested performance indicators that organisations can use to report their economic, environmental and social performances (notwithstanding the current move to integrated reporting, for most organisations there will continue to be an important role for sustainability reports, as these reports target a different audience to integrated reports and are intended to provide greater detail on an organisation's sustainability performance).

For the investment banking and asset management sectors, these initiatives have a useful role to play in helping investors deliver on the first three of the *Principles for Responsible Investment*, which should be seen as the foundation of responsible investment banking and asset management practice:

- Principle 1: We will incorporate ESG issues into investment analysis and decision-making processes.
- Principle 2: We will be active owners and incorporate ESG issues into our ownership policies and practices.

---

[26] A more detailed typology for distinguishing between these voluntary SR initiatives is provided in Hanks, J. (2011b).

- Principle 3: We will seek appropriate disclosure on ESG issues by the entities in which we invest.

While there is an obvious potential role for the GRI in terms of Principle 3, for the purposes of delivering on all three of these principles, there is particular value to be gained from the detailed guidance provided in ISO 26000. Effective delivery of these three principles requires not only a good appreciation of the ESG issues that could affect the performance of investment portfolios but also a sound understanding of the normative expectations regarding socially responsible behaviour (or as the PRI puts it, 'aligning investors with the broader objectives of society').[27] For the reasons outlined earlier, this is where the ISO 26000 guidance is seen to be uniquely valuable. This particular attribute of the standard has been picked up, for example, by one of the leading asset managers in South Africa who drew on the ISO 26000 guidance when developing their Ownership Policy and Proxy Guidelines.[28]

From an investor's perspective, the potential role of these initiatives is further evidenced, for example, in the extent to which they are referenced in—and have informed—some of the leading codes of corporate governance practice (including most notably the King Code of Governance for South Africa 2009), as well their contribution in informing aspects of the global shift towards integrated reporting, an exciting global initiative that is specifically aimed at 'providers of financial capital'.[29] This uptake of integrated reporting—which is being driven in particular by the International Integrated Reporting Council (IIRC)[30]—seeks to foster a greater appreciation within the investment community of the strategic and financial implications of societal trends and to prompt more informed investor engagement in contributing positively to these trends. Each of the three initiatives have informed aspects of this shift towards integrated reporting, and each of them has a continuing role to play, particularly in terms of assisting organisations to identify the material societal issues.

---

[27] This wording comes from the chapeau to the six principles: http://www.unpri.org/about-pri/the-six-principles/

[28] Investec Asset Management *Ownership Policy and Proxy Guidelines* http://www.investecassetmanagement.com/en/investment-expertise/stewardship/#stewardship

[29] *The International <IR> Framework* (December 2013) states, for example, that '<IR> aims to improve the quality of information available to providers of financial capital. . .' (p. 2).

[30] The International Integrated Reporting Council (IIRC), an initiative that brings together a cross section of representatives from the corporate, accounting, securities, regulatory and standard-setting sectors in response to the recognised need for 'a concise, clear, comprehensive and comparable integrated reporting framework structured around the organization's strategic objectives, its governance and business model, and integrating both material financial and non-financial information'. Representatives from both the GRI and the UNGC serve as members of the IIRC Working Group (http://www.theiirc.org).

6 Recognising the Limitations: Looking for Leadership to Drive Change

Notwithstanding the potential benefits of these initiatives, it is important to recognise some of their limitations and to appreciate the implications this has in terms of the need for greater societal leadership from the business community in general and the financial sector in particular.

In the context of declining resources, growing disparity in access to resources and greater demand associated with increasing population and consumption—coupled with the challenge of global climate change—it is increasingly evident that 'business as usual' will not deliver on the necessary changes. This presents a challenge for social responsibility initiatives, particularly those such as ISO 26000 and the UNGC that (understandably) have sought to identify societal expectations by using international instruments as their yardstick. There is an evident delay between the acceptance of generally accepted societal values and their codification in law, especially at the international level where the collective efforts of international diplomats to protect national self-interest, coupled with their tendency to fall back on previously agreed text, result in a conservatism that is ill-suited to increasingly complex and rapidly changing societal challenges. Another potential constraint with voluntary initiatives, especially those that are certification-based, is their tendency to promote a compliance mindset, where ticking the box against a checklist of expectations is mistakenly seen as a substitute for real integration and innovation.

Recognising the specific role and limitations of these voluntary initiatives is the responsibility of the organisations and individuals that choose to use them. While these initiatives certainly have a role to play, without this recognition they will fail to contribute effectively to the transformative role that is needed if sustainable development is to be achieved. For this to happen we will arguably need to see uncommon (and far more widespread) levels of societal leadership, including most particularly from the investment banking and asset management sectors.

References

Brown, H., de Jong, M., & Lessidrenska, T. (2007) *The rise of the global reporting initiative (GRI) as a case of institutional entrepreneurship.* http://www.hks.harvard.edu/m-rcbg/CSRI/publications/workingpaper_36_brown.pdf

GRI & ISO. (2014) *GRI G4 Guidelines and ISO 26000:2010. How to use the GRI G4 Guidelines and ISO 26000 in conjunction.* Retrieved from http://www.iso.org/iso/iso-gri-26000_2014-01-28.pdf

Hanks, J. (2011a, March). *Attention SMOs: ISO 26000 makes good business sense in South Africa.* ISOFocus+

Hanks, J. (2011b). ISO 2600 and other standards. In: A. Henriques (Ed.), *Understanding ISO 26000: A practical approach to social responsibility.* BSI

International Integrated Reporting Council. (2013). *The International <IR> Framework.* http://www.theiirc.org

ISO 26000. (2010). *Guidance on social responsibility.* ISO

ISO Advisory Group on Social Responsibility. (2004). *Working report on social responsibility.* ISO Advisory Group on Social Responsibility

ISO/TMB AG CSR N32. (2004). *Recommendations to the ISO Technical Management Board* (2004-10-21)

Knight, G., & Smith, J. (2008). The global compact and its critics: Activism, power relations, and corporate social responsibility. In J. Leatherman (Ed.), *Discipline and punishment in global politics: Illusions of control.* Basingstoke: Palgrave Macmillan.

UN Global Compact. (2010). *An introduction to linkages between UN Global Compact Principles and ISO 26000 core subjects.* UN Global Compact

Ward, H. (2011). The ISO 26000 international guidance standard on social responsibility: Implications for public policy and transnational democracy. *Theoretical Inquiries in Law, 12*(2), 665–718.

How Private Equity Models and Practitioners Can Advance Impact Investing in Emerging Markets

EMPEA

1 Introduction

Recognising the growing importance of impact investing, the Emerging Markets Private Equity Association (EMPEA)[1] established an Impact Investing Council in 2013[2] to play a leading role in professionalising and scaling the industry, focusing specifically on market-based solutions to major global social and environmental challenges. EMPEA believes that private equity investors have much to contribute to impact investing in emerging markets. The private equity discipline lends commercial expertise and financial rigour, and private equity practitioners have years of experience operating in inherently impactful geographies, sectors (e.g. financial services, healthcare, education, agribusiness, and housing), and customer segments (e.g. low-income people and those excluded from traditional sources of finance).

This article summarises insights provided by firms on the Emerging Markets Private Equity Association's Impact Investing Council. Contributors include: • Patricia Dinneen, Chair of EMPEA Impact Investing Council • Arun Gore, President and CEO, Gray Ghost Ventures • Renana Shvartzvald, Head of ESG and Impact, Vital Capital Fund • Yasemin Saltuk, J.P. Morgan Social Finance • Vineet Rai, Founder and CEO, Aavishkaar • Jim Roth, Cofounder and Partner, LeapFrog Investments • Marcus Regueira, Founding Partner and CIO, FIR Capital • Joan Trant, Director of Marketing and Impact, TriLinc Global • Gloria Nelund, Chairman & Chief Executive Officer, TriLinc Global, EMPEA staff member Katryn Bowe served as an editor for this article.

[1] EMPEA is an independent, global membership association whose mission is to catalyse private equity and venture capital investments in emerging markets around the world. For more information, visit http://www.empea.org

[2] For more information on the Impact Investing Council, please visit http://www.empea.org/about/leadership-governance/impact-investing-council/. The council has gathered a library of useful resources, including a list of representative Impact Investing Funds, at http://www.empea.org/resources/third-party-resources/impact-investing-resources/

EMPEA (✉)
1077 30th St. NW, Suite 100, Washington, DC 20007, USA
http://www.empea.org

© Springer International Publishing Switzerland 2015
K. Wendt (ed.), *Responsible Investment Banking*, CSR, Sustainability, Ethics & Governance, DOI 10.1007/978-3-319-10311-2_38

563

Since its inception, EMPEA has contributed to the acceptance of emerging markets' private equity as a credible and attractive investment approach. In the past 6 years, for example, the asset class has attracted more than US\$213 billion[3] from institutional investors and provided capital for more than 4,000 companies in this time period. During the past 10 years, private equity has also generated attractive returns, outperforming benchmarks for public securities investments, such as the S&P 500[4]. And yet at the time of EMPEA's founding, private equity in emerging markets faced numerous challenges, including many of the same obstacles inhibiting the growth of impact investing today. Despite the vast potential for impact investing to unlock growth and reduce poverty in emerging markets, there is still much scepticism about its power to do so. The domain is fragmented, and the data available to investors on the institutional quality of investment managers as well as their performance are lacking.

The EMPEA Impact Investing Council is well positioned to help private equity impact investing overcome some of these obstacles and realise its potential. The council seeks to bring together leading impact investing practitioners and thought leaders to share best practices, support rigorous research, and assist in the development of innovative business/cost models and performance databases. In this chapter, several council members describe a range of private equity approaches to impact investing, explain how they add value and measure impact, and highlight the challenges still to overcome.

2   What Is Impact Investing?

Impact investing is a lens through which investors consider investment options across asset classes, such as bonds, listed equities, and private equity. Impact investors aim to generate a financial return for themselves and measurable benefits to society and/or the environment. In many cases, they do so by deploying capital to companies which sell products or services that improve the lives of low-income or vulnerable populations in a way that conserves and/or protects the environment.

Impact investing is also a process by which investment managers screen, evaluate, and monitor investments. Whereas "socially responsible investment" (SRI) screens to avoid portfolio exposure to socially or environmentally harmful investments, impact investing actively and intentionally seeks to create a positive, measurable impact through profitable businesses.

---

[3] All figures in this article are accurate, to the best of our knowledge, as of January 23, 2014.

[4] Cambridge Associates LLC Proprietary Index.

Spotlight on Aavishkaar

Aavishkaar is a pioneer in early-stage investing in India and has provided investment advice and support to four funds in the past decade. The firm is guided by its philosophy to build a financial ecosystem that nurtures entrepreneurs to build scalable rural-focused enterprises. Aavishkaar has built a track record of high impact scalable enterprises in its portfolio, of which two are featured below:

Vaatsalya: A healthcare service provider which offers quality and affordable healthcare to semiurban and rural populations. Since its investment in 2006, the firm has grown to establish a network of ten hospitals and has attracted successive rounds of equity from sources beyond Aavishkaar.

Servals Automation: A social enterprise that sells affordable and sustainable cooking solutions, such as a stove burner that saves up to 30 % kerosene and vegetable oil stove. The firm raised its Series B round from the Grassroots Business Fund in 2010.

2.1 What Is Unique About a Private Equity Approach to Impact Investing?

Private equity is one investment approach within impact investing. It employs the traditional private equity model that intends to generate an attractive financial return for fund managers and their investors. The private equity process is one in which investors structure an investment vehicle (private equity fund) to raise capital from major institutional and individual investors (such as pension funds, endowments and high net worth individuals), committing the commingled capital into private businesses to expand and improve their operations and ultimately, and usually after several years, to sell their stake in these businesses or to take them public on a stock exchange. Extending the traditional model, private equity impact investing deliberately and fully integrates intentionality, measurement, and accountability for social and environmental benefits into the investment process, in addition to and in equal measure to the emphasis placed on financial returns.

As a result, private equity impact funds, unlike standard private equity funds, tend to invest primarily in businesses that sell essential products or services to low-income people. They seek to create compelling business propositions in markets where low-income consumers are willing and able to pay for certain products/services that are affordable, accessible, good quality, and competitive with those offered by other suppliers, including the government and foreign companies. Such businesses may operate in sectors that include sustainable agriculture, healthcare, education, housing, communication technology, and financial services. The positive impacts are created by expanding access to a wide range of critical goods and services for the low-income populations that can improve their health, education, and employment prospects.

> LeapFrog Investments' Financial Inclusion Fund I is one example. It is a US$135 million fund that invests in insurance and financial services companies which offer tailored products to the "emerging consumer" in Africa and Asia—people who have moved or are moving from poverty to the middle class and are now in a position to purchase such services. The financial services firms in which the fund invests allow consumers who otherwise are excluded from mainstream financial institutions to access insurance and related financial tools. Insurance is inherently beneficial, as it provides a safety net to prevent people who have recently emerged as consumers from falling back into poverty. It also provides a springboard out of poverty. For example, farmers with insurance are able to manage their downside risk: this means they are more likely to plant crops that, although costly, have higher yields.

Private equity impact funds often invest in early- or growth-stage businesses that are immature and have not been able to reach critical scale. These businesses can include start-ups and occasionally may involve supporting entrepreneurs in creating businesses; for example, Brazil-based private equity firm FIR Capital has been working to perfect business models for several pipeline companies in parallel with raising a new fund that will focus on healthcare, education, housing, and financial services. Preparing these companies and investing in their restructured businesses require discipline and patience (with long enough duration to yield returns) and risk tolerance.

Spotlight on Vital Capital

Vital Capital Fund is a US$350 million private equity fund focused on urban communities building and affordable housing, commercial agriculture, healthcare, water, and education in sub-Saharan Africa. Vital's vision is to continue to deliver measurable improvement in the living and economic conditions for local populations by focusing primarily on building affordable and vibrant communities.

In parallel to financial review, Vital Capital screens projects for impact potential using the following criteria:

1. Impact is **local**. The firm is unlikely to invest in agricultural production for export as the primary market, and conversely production of quality import-substitutes is a key focus. Employees must also be locals.
2. Provides an **essential** service or product, such as affordable housing rather than commercial real estate.
3. Represents a **sustainable** use of natural resources.
4. Engages the local community and **partners** with local governments.

Other funds target investments in small and medium size enterprises (SMEs) in view of their inherently impactful role in driving job creation, GDP growth, and social stability. According to the International Finance Corporation, the private sector arm of the World Bank, formal SMEs contribute up to 45 % of formal employment in developing economies.[5] One such SME-focused fund is the TriLinc Global Impact Fund, a US$14.3 million debt fund that has been invested in South America and Indonesia. The fund's strategy is driven by the belief that impact objectives such as better-trained staff and energy efficiency can be intrinsic to the portfolio company's success as well as investor returns, in addition to creating societal benefits.

3   What Constitutes an *Impact Investing* Private Equity Fund?

Although many private equity funds in emerging markets generate a positive economic impact through their investments, this is not sufficient to qualify them as impact investors. These funds must also demonstrate that they have integrated impact considerations throughout their investment process[6] from initial screening through due diligence, closing, and post-investment monitoring with measurable results. They are therefore differentiated from purely financially driven private equity funds because of intentionality, measurement, and accountability.

> **Spotlight on FIR Capital**
>
> FIR Capital is a Brazilian venture capital firm founded in 1999. It believes there is a compelling business proposition in enabling low-income consumers to have access to high-quality products and services in education, healthcare, housing, and financial services. The firm sees an opportunity to respond to the high demand for quality services in these sectors because consumers in this demographic have discerning tastes and disposable income and are unsatisfied with the quality of services that the government provides. FIR Capital's new growth fund targets SMEs with intrinsically impactful businesses with the potential to achieve scale and deliver outstanding returns.

In practice, an impact investor must conduct relentless due diligence regarding the potential for impact in addition to the standard financial due diligence. TriLinc Global, for example, gathers baseline impact data on job creation, wage increase, revenue, profitability, and company taxes. LeapFrog Investments conducts

---

[5] International Finance Corporation (2010), *The SME Banking Knowledge Guide*, International Finance Corporation.

[6] To increase effectiveness, many impact investing PE funds embed this social mission in their investment thesis. According to TriLinc Global, integrating impact intent alongside financial goals allows funds to (1) integrate data gathering monitoring and analysis on both finance and impact performance, (2) formalise accountability to investors on impact, and (3) mitigate the potential trade-off between return and impact.

extensive research on the firm's behaviour towards its employees, customers, and other investors to ensure they share the same values, recognising that a fund aligned with its partners ensures the investment is more likely to attain commercial success.

They are therefore differentiated from purely financially driven private equity funds because they meet three criteria *simultaneously:* they intentionally create positive social impact, measure these outcomes, and are accountable to their investors in attaining this impact.

It may be further argued that intentionality alone is probably not an adequate criteria, given that large established enterprises also benefit society in the multiple things they do. An impact investing fund that invests early is prepared to take the risks associated with early-stage investment and would then need to be included while measuring the intentionality of the investor.

Once a private equity impact fund makes an investment, it monitors impact closely. Funds typically interact with their portfolio companies on a quarterly basis, tracking metrics that vary across sectors. Although multiple organisations are attempting to develop standardised metrics, such as Impact Reporting and Investment Standards (IRIS) and Global Impact Investing Ratings System (GIIRS), there is still no universally accepted approach. What is important is that the fund specifies to its investors the relevant metrics to track and is held accountable to this end.

4 Compared to Other Potential Funding Sources, What Advantages Does Private Equity Bring to Impact Investing?

Spotlight on J.P. Morgan Social Finance

Launched in 2007, J.P. Morgan Social Finance services and grows the nascent impact investing market through principal investing of JP Morgan Chase capital in impact investing funds, building a dataset and publishing analytical research for investors, and advising clients on implementing impact investment strategies.

Recent reports published by the firm include:

- Perspectives on Progress: The Impact Investor Survey (Jan 2013)
- A Portfolio Approach to Impact Investment: A Practical Guide to Building, Analyzing and Managing a Portfolio of Impact Investments (Oct 2012)
- Insight into the Impact Investment Market: An In-Depth Analysis of Investor Perspectives and Over 2,200 Transactions (Dec 2011)

With its rigorous focus on building commercial, scalable, and profitable businesses, private equity is well positioned to generate positive and sustainable impacts in such critical sectors as affordable housing, healthcare, and local food production. It is particularly poised to do so compared to other funding sources that are not driven by profitability, including government, foreign assistance, and philanthropic capital. Combining profitability with impact objectives can lead to mutually beneficial outcomes if there is intentionality, measurement, and accountability, as we have illustrated above.

An important attribute of private equity is that it can enable access to vast pools of financing through global capital markets. By comparison, funding sources such as government aid and philanthropic finance are often limited (and unpredictable) in low-income countries and represent only a fraction of what is potentially available from the capital markets. Funding from Development Finance Institutions (DFI) may be significant in scale and can play a catalytic role but is usually only available on the condition that additional private equity capital is committed.

Private equity is further set apart in its inherent focus on impact that is both profitable *and* sustainable. "If you want to reach millions of people, then you need to be able to invest in a business capable of attracting those people", explains Leapfrog's co-founding partner Jim Roth. Investors in private equity funds expect attractive financial returns, so the fund managers are incentivised to target businesses that they perceive to have the potential to grow. The private equity investors' incentives are therefore aligned with those of their investors. Of course this will preclude certain potentially impactful but unprofitable projects. But for those activities that have a positive social impact and may be profitable to expand, private equity is well positioned to support the growth.

Private equity is also distinguishable from other private, for-profit investment sources such as debt. For example, equity investment can be a more favourable capital base than debt for the many businesses with potential impact that are testing new business models to deliver products or services to consumers who have inconsistent and low incomes. "Some new business models require significant customer education, which can be capital intensive and can take some time to translate into revenues, which can make it challenging to service a debt investment", explained Yasemin Saltuk of J.P. Morgan Social Finance, which invests J.P. Morgan capital in impact investing funds, provides thought leadership on impact investing, and advises clients on implementing impact investment strategies.[7] In certain situations, particularly in frontier markets or early-stage businesses, portfolio companies can face volatile cash flows, unpredictable supply chains, poor infrastructure, or inefficient regulation. This can translate into volatile cash flows for the businesses, making debt payments a burden, especially at high interest rates.

---

[7] J.P. Morgan Social Finance further explores these dynamics in several publications, such as its January 2013 report "Perspectives on Progress: the Impact Investor Survey".

Spotlight on TriLinc Global
TriLinc Global is dedicated to creating a global platform for impact investments at competitive yields through alternative investment funds both retail and institutional investors. It manages the TriLinc Global Impact Fund, which seeks to make debt investments in growth-stage small and medium enterprises (SMEs) in developing economies. Among other investments, TriLinc provided financing to a sugar producer operating in the northeastern Brazilian state of Pernambuco, which allowed it to plant and fertilise its sugar crop and improve milling operations. TriLinc's financing also increases employees' knowledge and skills through training courses. Beyond employment and training, the borrowing company provides over 250 houses to employees rent-free and free medical services to employees and their families and covers building rent and maintenance costs for a local school.

Private equity offers more than capital to emerging market businesses; it seeks to improve the way firms do business. Any growth private equity fund—not just in the impact or emerging market space—seeks to transfer management and operational expertise to its portfolio companies. African-focused impact investing firm Vital Capital, for example, believes the operational expertise it brought to bear in financing Kora Housing, a 40,000 unit project in Angola, significantly enhanced the project's financial and impact performance. The fund understood the structural limitations of the Angolan housing market and developed a unique approach involving a lease-to-purchase mechanism. It enabled local families to acquire housing units gradually, thereby making it possible for a larger percentage of the Angolan middle class to own a home, which ultimately has the effect of contributing to economic growth.

Another way to improve business, according to FIR Capital's Marcus Regueira, is to "clean up the house" by improving management capacity, corporate governance, and legal compliance, so as to create a competitive advantage for the business. Arun Gore, President and CEO of Atlanta-based Gray Ghost Ventures, agrees that private equity funds inculcate discipline and execution—the hallmarks of private equity—in fast-growing businesses. The role of educating firms about private equity can be remarkably effective particularly in environments where informality is the norm. The educating role can, in Gore's words, "trigger a systemic change on how to develop an enterprise".

5 What Are the Main Challenges Facing Private Equity Impact Investing?

Attracting institutional capital remains a significant constraint to the development of emerging markets' private equity impact investing and is a top priority for the EMPEA Council. Although increasing in size and prominence during the past several years, private equity-style impact investing in emerging markets remains a "niche" investment strategy that mainstream institutional investors do not typically include in their portfolios. Attracting institutional investors will require evidence that it is possible to achieve both impact and financial returns *and* education of investors about appropriate opportunities in which to invest.

> **Spotlight on Gray Ghost Ventures**
> Gray Ghost Ventures (GGV) has been active in impact investing since 2003, when it established the Gray Ghost Microfinance Fund. It moved beyond microfinance to build a portfolio of mission-related investments on behalf of Gray Matters Capital in 2006. GGV's fund Gray Ghost DOEN Cooperatief has five investments in financial services, which intend to provide security, savings, opportunity, transactional reach, and access to financial products. The firm has invested in such firms as:
>
> - Babajob, a Bangalore-based start-up that uses the web and mobile technology to connect employers and bottom-of-the-pyramid informal sector workers (i.e. maids, cooks, drivers, etc.) with the goal of creating a scalable, replicable, and profitable solution to combat poverty.
> - M-Kopa, a mobile technology company based in Nairobi, Kenya. Since 2010 the firm has helped Kenyans acquire solar power products by offering innovative payment plans and a distribution model tailored to the needs of their customers.

These educational efforts will necessarily be aimed at investors and portfolio companies, but journalists represent another key audience, notes FIR Capital's Marcus Regueira, who observes that journalists are specially positioned to be key educators of the distinction among philanthropy, socially responsible investing (SRI), and impact investing. FIR Capital has raised awareness locally in Brazil by convening private wealth managers, the Brazilian private equity association, universities, pension funds, and journalists, with the support of the Brazilian private equity association ABVCAP.

One of the first steps in the education process is to provide a more nuanced description of "impact investing private equity" that differentiates among mainstream investors, market-based impact investors, and non-profit grant givers. EMPEA Council Chair Pat Dinneen emphasises that, in so doing, "it is vitally important to explain the risk-return characteristics and the possibly longer duration of investments—recognising that some impacts might require many years to fully materialise".

Another necessary milestone is the delivery of evidence that it is possible to achieve impact alongside risk-adjusted financial returns. Developing a comprehensive financial performance database would help enormously to identify critical success factors and to develop customised benchmarks. Many impact investing private equity funds are first generation and therefore early in their respective investment cycles. As funds mature and proliferate, however, more data will become available. In the interim, the EMPEA Council is working with potential partners to collect and analyse data on exits in an attempt to quantify financial returns and key impact metrics.

Another challenge is the need for deeper commercial and operational experiences among private equity impact fund managers generally, due in large part to the fact that many initially come from a non-profit background. This has been the most significant constraint to the sector achieving scale, according to Jim Roth at Leapfrog Investments, who attributes his firm's success in raising capital to the commercial orientation of the LeapFrog team.

Spotlight on LeapFrog

LeapFrog Investments manages the US$135 million Financial Inclusion Fund, which has invested in financial services firms in India, Indonesia, the Philippines, Kenya, Ghana, and South Africa. The fund invests US$5–20 million into expansion-ready companies for a 4–7-year partnership.

An example of a LeapFrog investment is **Express Life Insurance Company Ltd**, a firm that aims to provide over half a million low-income Ghanaians with affordable hybrid savings and risk products. LeapFrog is actively helping the firm expand its management team, train its sales force, upgrade IT systems, and launch innovative products. LeapFrog acquired a majority stake in the firm, which constituted the largest private foreign direct investment in the history of Ghana's insurance industry. The sector has grown 40 % per year over the past 5 years in Ghana and has high growth prospects, as only 2 % of the population has currently has access to insurance.

Furthermore, without relevant and robust metrics, it is difficult to demonstrate success in achieving social and environmental impact. The idiosyncratic nature of impact investing presents some specific challenges with respect to the development of metrics, including:

- Timescale. Whereas financial returns to investors end once the fund has exited the investment, the social impact continues after a project has been completed. Some projects create impact throughout the life of the investment such as an insurance company, whereas others such as housing or infrastructure deliver impact over the longer term but in many cases only beginning in the final stage of the investment. Vital Capital thus suggests differentiating immediate and long-term impact projects and measuring them differently.

- Differentiated value of outcomes versus outputs. Outcomes, such as poverty reduction, reflect the ultimate impact objective of impact investments, while output measure metrics such as units of housing are constructed. Yet outcomes are more difficult to measure; to the extent that it is possible to determine a causal link between a firm's operations and the outcome, it is expensive to do so. Attributing the outcome to a particular investment in the firm is a further challenge.

- Lack of comparability across impact investments. Each company and product creates impact in its own idiosyncratic way so generic indicators make it impossible to capture the complexity of the true impact. For example, one operational metric for insurance companies is the speed at which a claim is paid, which is not relevant for education where graduation rates would be a more appropriate measure. Even for metrics that appear on the surface to be comparable, variability in the methodology can create challenges. For example, a simple count of the number of jobs created obscures whether those were local workers or child labour or jobs offered at competitive wages. Further, cross-comparisons are extremely difficult for certain units of value that have an inherently subjective component such as valuing the life of one patient or the value of reducing one unit of fuel consumption. To accommodate the wide range of metrics, IRIS has developed a repository of over 400 metrics, recognising that no single combination will be right for all organisations. This effort by IRIS (as well as GIIRS) is helpful, but one aspiration among the EMPEA Council Members is to simplify the process and make it more practical by focusing on the key "metrics that matter". FIR Capital's Marcus Regueira recommends 4–5 indicators per industry to provide a balance between comparability and overload of indicators.

Finally, the scale in private equity impact investing is hindered by a mismatch between investors' preferences and realistic investment opportunities. JP Morgan Social Finance conducted a survey of leading institutional impact investors and found that absorptive capacity is a critical bottleneck. It is not unusual for mainstream pension funds, insurance companies, and asset managers to consider investing in only those funds that are of significant size (e.g. minimum of US$500 million). Furthermore, many investors have minimum commitment sizes (e.g. they want to commit more than US$100 million) and maximum ownership limits (e.g. they cannot represent more than 20 % of the fund's interests). By way of comparison, the average impact investing private equity fund is US$7 million, and the average underlying investment is US$2 million.

Another gap lies between investor preferences for the stage of the business in which they would like to invest and where the majority of impact investees are in the growth cycle. The JPMorgan survey "Perspectives on Progress" revealed an overwhelming focus on growth-stage businesses (78 %), while only 51 % indicated a focus on venture capital. Eighteen percent of respondents indicated an appetite in seed or start-up capital.

6 Conclusion

As EMPEA prepares to celebrate its tenth anniversary in 2014, it is important to reflect on the similarities between the opportunities and challenges facing emerging markets' private equity investors in the early 2000s and those facing impact investors today. The opportunities are to unlock growth and reduce poverty in emerging markets, serve the demand of billions of new consumers, and protect and improve the environment. The challenges are to expand the universe of institutional quality impact managers, develop practical and credible metrics, collect and analyse performance data, share best practices and proclaim more success stories. The EMPEA Impact Investing Council will seek to transfer relevant best practices and lessons learned from emerging markets' private equity, especially innovation, financial analysis and discipline, sustainable and scalable business models, risk mitigation techniques, access to institutional capital, and rigorous legal and commercial due diligence. And in return, EMPEA will seek to identify and adopt relevant best practices from impact investors to contribute to the evolution of emerging markets' private equity.

7 EMPEA Impact Investing Council Members

The following individuals are members of the EMPEA Impact Investing Council, as of January 2014. The examples and perspectives in this article do not represent the views of all council members:

- **Patricia M. Dinneen (Chair)**, Senior Advisor, EMPEA
- **Amy Bell,** Executive Director, Social Finance, J.P. Morgan
- **Monica Brand,** Managing Director, Frontier Investments Group, Accion
- **Aruz Gore,** President and CEO, Gray Ghost Ventures
- **Gloria Nelund,** Chairman and Chief Executive Officer, TriLinc Global
- **Vincent Oswald,** Co-founder and CEO, Azure Partners
- **Vineet Rai,** Founder and CEO, Aavishkaar
- **Marcus Regueira,** Founding Partner and Chief Investment Officer, FIR Capital
- **Jim Roth,** Co-founder and Partner, LeapFrog Investments
- **Eytan Stibbe,** Founding Director, Vital Capital Fund
- **Julie Sunderland,** Director, Program-Related Investments, Bill & Melinda Gates Foundation
- **Rik Vyverman,** Global Head Ventures Equity, responsAbility Investments AG
- **Adam Wolfensohn,** Managing Director and Investment Committee Member, Wolfensohn Fund Management

The Opportunity for Bonds to Address the Climate Finance Challenge

Sean Kidney and Bridget Boulle

Abstract 2014 saw a niche, thematic 'green bond' market becomes a new asset class and a talking point among mainstream and SRI investors alike. Over US$36bn was issued in 2014—more than triple any previous year. The development of this thematic asset class has the potential to marginally, but significantly, reduce friction and transaction costs for investors looking for a means of addressing climate change, helping to reduce the cost of capital and speed flows of that capital. This chapter describes how the growth of this new asset class can help direct capital to meet the vast financial requirements involved in a rapid transition to a low-carbon and climate resilient economy and sets out steps to grow the theme.

About the Climate Bonds Initiative

The Climate Bonds Initiative (CBI) is an investor-focused, international not-for-profit working to mobilise debt capital markets for climate change solutions. The Initiative is a charity registered in England with US charities registration being undertaken.

CBI promotes investments in assets and activities needed for a *rapid* transition to a low-carbon—and climate resilient—economy. It proposes policies and mechanisms for banks, developers and governments to tap bond markets and provides tools for investors to better understand and make decisions about climate change investment opportunities.

1 Introduction

The International Energy Agency (IEA) estimates that, on current trajectories, the world is, in the words of IEA Chief Economist Fatih Birol, 'barrelling' towards 6–7 °C warming and that this would have 'catastrophic' impacts.

The IEA also estimates that, worldwide, US$1 trillion of investment in energy, transport and building sectors is required each year—above business as usual—to

S. Kidney (✉) • B. Boulle
Climate Bonds Initiative, London, UK
e-mail: sean@climatebonds.net; bridget.boulle@climatebonds.net

© Springer International Publishing Switzerland 2015
K. Wendt (ed.), *Responsible Investment Banking*, CSR, Sustainability, Ethics & Governance, DOI 10.1007/978-3-319-10311-2_39

reduce energy-related carbon emissions in line with a 2 °C global warming scenario.[1]

Climate scientists now recognises that 2 °C warming is now very likely, leading to significant adaptation pressures. According to the UN Environment Programme, adaptation and the sustainable management of natural resources such as forests, fisheries, agriculture and water will require an average additional annual investment of US$1.3 trillion out to 2050.

Climate change is the dominant challenge of our times. It is central to other environmental challenges—without solving climate challenge, numerous other social and environmental problems will be exacerbated. Climate change will affect biodiversity, migration, human rights and welfare, forests, food prices and a plethora of environmental and social problems—if climate change is not addressed, many social and environmental problems will only get worse.

The scale of investment required is achievable in the context of global GDP, but large on such a sustained basis, and complicated by public sector balance sheets remaining constrained in many parts of the world.

The good news is that both the IEA and UNEP talk in terms of investment: the bulk of the spending required to address climate change can be constructed as investible propositions, from clean energy systems to flood protection built into new coastal property development.

Solution paths are largely understood: a rapid global shift from polluting to clean energy, energy efficiency measures to buy time until that shift can be completed and sequestering carbon through agriculture, forestry and other measures. This is distinct from numerous other environmental and social challenges whose solutions are not well understood and go far beyond the ability of the global economy to finance.

The other good news is that there is no shortage of capital available should investible propositions be available. In the corporate sector, cash reserves are at an all-time high as companies 'save their powder' to see which direction a global recovery will take and, perhaps more importantly, institutional investors with US$83 trillion of assets under management[2] continue to experience net cash inflows.

For the latter group, with 50–60 % of investments in fixed income, bonds as an instrument are potentially a good match for the high capital expenditure, low running cost of many of the investments required.

But the urgency of change is a challenge for investors. The speed of investment required for the deployment of new technologies required for mitigation, for example, is unprecedented, as is the scale required. In the absence of investment performance histories, investors and rating agencies see this as high risk. Investors will need governments and corporations to take on part of that risk before investments can be included in their largely risk-averse portfolios. Therein lies the forward agenda for this market.

---

[1] International Energy Agency, ETP World Energy Outlook 2012.

[2] OECD (2014).

> **A Note**
>
> This chapter will not cover the integration of ESG issues into fixed income. These are well covered through other channels. The thesis of this chapter is that bonds have a different role to play than equity investments—in directly addressing and financing environmental (although could equally be applied to social) challenges at scale, i.e. the role that bond markets can play in promoting solutions.
>
> Similarly, specialised bonds such as social impact bonds will not be covered. While specialised products are useful in many instances, many are not scalable and therefore do not the primary aim of the green bond market which scales up investment in a low-carbon economy.

2 Bond Basics

Bonds can be described as loans or debts. They are similar to bank loans, but often last longer; bond 'tenors' last from 1 year to over 30 years (there are even a few 100-year bonds around), but most are 3–7 years in term.

For companies, bonds provide a lower-cost form of capital raising than equity and, usually, bank loans; the trade-off is that bonds are 'senior debt' and have to be repaid before equity and, usually, bank loans. That can increase the relative risk profile of equity and loans and their costs to a company. It's a balancing act.

On the other side of the deal, investors buy bonds because they are lower risk and so more secure than equity investments—especially important to institutional investors, like insurance companies and pension funds that have to match forward liabilities with assets.

2.1 Bond Types

The main bond types relevant for this chapter are:

- Project bonds: A bond where the returns are based on the success of a particular project (e.g. bond issued to build a wind farm with repayments made from the revenue generated from selling power to the grid). An example is the US$1 billion bond issued by MidAmerican Energy in 2013 for solar farm developments in the south-west of the USA. Note that 5–10 % of project debt globally uses project bonds; the bulk is bank lending.
- Corporate bonds: Bonds issued by any entity (usually a company) that are backed by the full balance sheet of the issuer rather than a project or asset. The creditworthiness of the bond will be determined by the strength of the

company's balance sheet and its bond repayment history. Examples here would be bond issued by Vestas wind energy or by SNCF for rail investments.

- Use-of-proceed corporate treasury guaranteed bonds: These are simply corporate bonds where the funds have been earmarked to specified areas of investment. Examples will be water bonds, wind bonds from a utility and 2013/2014 green bonds from corporations like the 1.4 billion euros bond from Électricité de France and the 750 million euros bond from Unibail-Rodamco or various Climate Awareness Bonds from the European Investment Bank.
- Securitisation: A bond collateralised by one or more specific projects/assets such as a pool or mortgage loans. The first source of repayment is generally the cash flows of the assets. An example is SolarCity's securitisation in 2013 of rooftop solar lease cash flows.
- Sovereign bonds and municipal or 'city' green bonds: Bonds issued by a municipality or government. These are essentially the same as the 'use-of-proceed corporate treasury' bonds. Examples are the 'General Obligation' Green Bonds from the State of Massachusetts and the City of Gothenburg in 2013.

2.2   Bonds as a Refinancing Instrument

Only 5 % of the US$350 billion in global project and infrastructure debt raised in 2011 were in bonds; the bulk is bank lending.[3] Because of the risk assessment expertise required for pre-completion project lending, this is unlikely to change. Bonds should therefore be seen less as tool to raise money for a specific project and more as a tool for refinancing—and exit strategy for equity investors and bank lenders.

Refinancing allows organisations to take on short-term bank lending for the construction phase of a project and then pay the loan back by issuing bond once the construction phase is over. As construction is usually the highest risk part of a project, a bond provides a longer-term lower cost of capital once the construction phase is passed. This provides borrowers with that exit strategy and, given that few investors are willing to take on construction risk, this allows the smaller pool of investors with a higher-risk appetite, and banks with reduced internal allocations to project finance most recapitalisation, to more quickly recycle their funds into new projects.

The result is a reordering of the capital pipeline where each market participant focuses on risk levels they have the capability to deal with—for example, banks taking on short-term construction risk and pension funds taking on long-term post-construction risk.

---

[3] Dealogic.

Banks can use asset-backed securities backed to 'flip' their longer-term project loan portfolios to long-term investors. The easier it is for loans to be offloaded, the more likely they are to lend more and for longer terms.

2.3   Brokers/Underwriters

The life of a bond has two phases, primary and secondary. The primary phase is the gestation period of a bond before it is priced and launched into the markets. After its initial pricing, it enters its secondary phase.

The primary phase encompasses all the work leading up to the pricing and launching of a bond where several brokers work together to find investors for the bond, write the prospectus, etc. These are called lead and colead managers or arrangers or underwriters.

Having a number rather than one lead manager gives the bond the greatest possible exposure to potential buyers as each broker will have some nonoverlapping clients. The key objective for the brokers is to get the best (i.e. highest) price for the bond to raise the most amount of money for the client while also ensuring that all the bonds are sold.

The primary phase finishes when bonds have been allocated by the brokers to clients, 'switches'—where a broker agrees to buy an existing secondary market bond in exchange for sale of the new primary market bond on fixed terms—have been completed and the price set. The secondary phase then starts.

When a bond enters its secondary phase, it is open to be traded by all. Generally, the brokers, or lead managers, that brought the bond to market commit to making a two-way price (they commit to both offering to buy or sell the bond and 'make a market') in the bond for its life.

3   The Challenge

In order to meet the IEA's US$1 trillion target, the challenge is not to creating new capital but by shifting a portion of existing investment into low-carbon development.

Public sector balance sheets are severely constrained and are likely to remain so. The bulk of the money is going to have to come from the private sector, in particular from the US$83 trillion of assets under management by institutional investors.[4]

Although funds from the private sector are already the main source of investment in renewable energy and energy efficiency (e.g. about 94 % of the investment

---

[4] OECD (2014).

in sustainable energy in 2007 came from the private sector[5]), capital inflows are still small in comparison to what is required.

If structured correctly, the good news is that the US$1 trillion required is investment not cost. Investment in high capital expenditure projects can deliver stable returns over a long period. The key is using the right instruments to attract the appropriate levels of capital. Investments in climate resilient infrastructure, from renewable energy to energy efficiency, typically involve high capital expenditure that creates secure and predictable long-term assets—very close to what pension funds and insurance investors are looking for.

4 Bonds Are a Vital Part of the Solution

The global bond market, currently at US$80 trillion in size, can provide much of the capital needed but remains chronically underutilised in financing our low-carbon transition[6] as the financing of climate assets has so far been focused primarily on using equity.

This is in stark contrast to how governments have previously engineered investments for economic transformation (see section on capital steerage below) where bonds have been key.

Bonds are a suitable funding instrument for high capex, long-life projects (see Fig. 1) such as renewable energy. Renewable energy infrastructure requires high upfront capital costs but minimal and fairly stable running costs given that there are no fuel inputs as with coal and natural gas. Unlike nuclear, they also have minimal end-of-life costs as decommissioning costs for nuclear are uncertain. This is ideal for bond financing which provides substantial upfront capital and a long pay-back period.

There has been a marked shift towards bonds within both investment portfolios (including Specialist-Sustainable and Responsible Investment funds). Institutional investors that were overweight in equities at the time of the 2008 Crash have realised that consistency of high returns in equity can be illusory and have been busily increasing allocations to bonds.

In the UK, for instance, allocation to equities has dropped from approximately 68 % in 2003 to 30 % in 2013[7] (see Fig. 2), while allocation to bonds has risen from 31 to 47 %; the trend is similar across Europe and the USA.

A number of factors have driven this change, including the reduction of risk for pension schemes driven by asset liability modelling and accounting rules as well as the financial crisis.

---

[5] UNEP and SEFI (2007).

[6] BIS statistics, total debt securities year end 2012.

[7] Mercers, 2013, European Asset Allocation Survey, http://info.mercer.com/rs/mercer/images/ Mercer2013EuropeanAssetAllocationSurvey.pdf

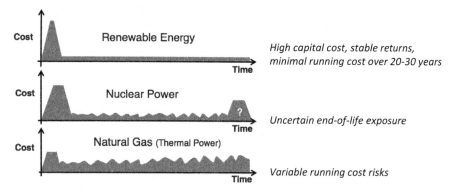

Fig. 1 Suitability of bond financing for renewable energy. Source: Jason Langley, AXA Real Estate

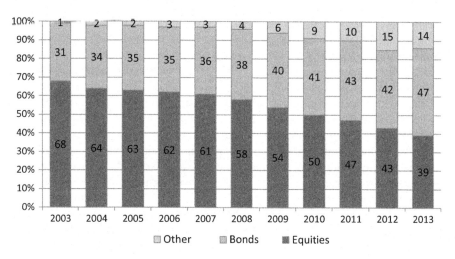

Fig. 2 Changes in broad strategic asset allocation for UK plans (Source: Mercer)

In the USA, many defined benefit funds have been put off by the impact that reduced equity values have had on their ability to meet forward commitments and have made huge shifts in their weighting to bonds. While an ongoing shift cannot be guaranteed, it is likely that investors will continue to reassess the risk associated with equities and the risk associated with their liabilities.

Assets are already shifting to fixed income, but this shift will only be accompanied by a shift in capital towards climate infrastructure if a thematic market is created.

5 A Thematic Bond Market Climate Change

A thematic market is a labelled bond market where use of proceeds is specifically devoted to a particular purpose, in this case climate change and environmental problems.

Many investors—for example, those representing US$23 trillion of assets under management that signed declarations in 2013 and 2014[8] about the urgent need to address climate change—express interest in green bonds, subject to their meeting existing risk and yield requirements. That interest in *equivalence* has been the key driver in sustained issuance and oversubscriptions of thematic green bonds in 2013 and 2014.

Green bonds do already exist—for example, as bonds from solar or rail companies—but the discoverability and the capability to do 'environmental' due diligence remain limited among investors. The development of a thematic market is key to reducing those transaction costs and in shifting capital towards low-carbon assets.

5.1 What Are Green/Climate Bonds?

Climate bonds are where the use of proceeds is used to finance—or refinance—projects addressing climate. They range from wind farms and solar and hydropower plants to rail transport and building sea walls in cities threatened by rising sea levels. Only a small portion of these bonds have actually been labelled as green or climate bonds by their issuers.

The term 'climate bond' is used interchangeably with the term 'green bond' in this chapter, although technically, the use of proceeds from a green bond could be allocated to wider environmental projects with no impact on climate. In practice, green bonds have mostly been the same as climate bonds, with proceeds going to climate change projects. For example, proceeds from World Bank Green Bonds are allocated to what they describe as 'climate' areas such as renewable energy and energy efficiency lending.

For operational purposes, thematic bonds largely function as conventional debt instruments. They are risk weighted and credit rated in the usual way based on the creditworthiness of the issuer and are tradable in the secondary market, market conditions permitting. Theoretically, they can be issued by any issuer including sovereigns, multilateral development banks (MDBs) and corporates.

In the early stages of development of thematic markets, there was some small-scale experimentation around bonds where the 'green' characteristics were provided by the nature of the coupon, with returns linked to green indices. These approaches were only ever successful for smaller-scale retail issuance in markets such as Japan and have generally been cast aside in recent years.

Climate-themed bonds are designed to:

– **Attract institutional capital**—while this was initially a niche SRI investment, the recent years (especially 2013) have seen substantial investment from institutional investors (e.g. ATP, Norwegian Global Fund, Skandia Life, Zurich

---

[8] http://globalinvestorcoalition.org/

Insurance), corporations (Microsoft, Ford) and government treasuries and central banks (California, German Bundesbank).

- **Mobilise governments**—bonds could provide a means for governments to direct funding to climate change mitigation; this is done either by choosing to provide qualifying bonds with preferential tax treatments (e.g. 'clean renewable energy' bonds in the USA) or by providing government guarantees to non-sovereign issues.
- **Send a political signal to other stakeholders**—government can use the announcement of their investment in green bonds to encourage other investors to support debt issuance related to climate change policy agendas. The German Bundesbank and California Treasurer are examples of government investors in green bonds.

The vast bulk of climate bonds have been bought by institutional investors like pension funds and fund managers. In the Netherlands and South Africa, banks have also offered green bonds to retail investors; and some fund managers have, using World Bank Green Bonds, created special funds that individuals can invest in—for example, Nikko Asset Management's World Bank Green Bond Fund.

More recently, mainstream investors have shown interest in green bonds for their additional green characteristics on top of their comparable returns—Microsoft, Apple and Ford have all purchased portions of recent issues as have central banks such as the German Bundesbank. In 2013, Zurich Insurance also announced that it had provided BlackRock with a mandate to invest US$1 billion towards green bond investing.[9]

5.2 History of the Green Thematic Market

The first major thematically labelled climate or green bond was issued in 2007 by the European Investment Bank (EIB)—a 'Climate Awareness Bond' where proceeds were specifically linked to renewable energy and energy efficiency. Since then, other issuers have joined this *labelled* market, including the World Bank, African Development Bank, the International Finance Corporation (IFC, a division of the World Bank) and the European Bank for Reconstruction and Development (EBRD). Until 2013, the market was limited to highly rated development bank issuers. By the end of 2012, approximately US$7.8 billion had been issued in this labelled market, US$6.2 billion of which was still outstanding.

From 2007 to 2012, the market grew slowly with only a small spike in 2010 (see Fig. 3). But in mid- to late 2012, three French provinces, Ile-de-France, Provence-Alpes-Côte d'Azur and Nord-Pas-de-Calais, issued green bonds that were heavily oversubscribed—this increased the market interested in thematic bonds. In 2013, the IFC issued a US$1 billion (benchmark size) green bond in February, and shortly after, the EIB issued a 650 million euros Climate Awareness Bond, which it then

---

[9] http://www.ft.com/cms/s/0/43e36770-4e05-11e3-8fa5-00144feabdc0.html?siteedition=uk#axzz2ktmERTSj

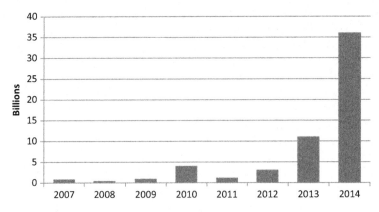

Fig. 3 The labelled bond market grew rapidly in 2013 and 2014

tapped again to make it a 900 million euros. The size of these bonds were a turning point in the market (up to that point, few bonds reached US$200 million) and stimulated interest from both banks and investors. Banks became interested in arranging similar deals while investors saw the market's potential to meeting size and liquidity requirements while at the same time meeting green mandates. Over 20 new green bonds followed in 2013 making it more than twice as large as any previous year and broadening both the issuer and investor base. By the end of 2013, the market stood at approximately US$15 billion outstanding, with most new bonds larger than US$250 million.

Growth continued into 2014 with total issuance over the year of US$36.6 billion, more than triple the 2013 figure. A number of new corporate issuers such as joined the market including Toyota, Unibail-Rodamco, GDF Suez and Iberdrola.

5.3 Key Features of Market Growth in 2013

1. **The first corporate-labelled green bonds were issued** by Électricité de France (EDF), Vasakronan and Bank of America Merrill Lynch. The entrance of corporates is important for the market to achieve genuine growth given the pool of capital available in comparison to MDBs. The size of the EDF bond demonstrates the potential for growth—their first foray into this space was the largest green bond issued to date at 2.5 billion euros.
2. **Bonds sizes increased**: The average bond size in 2012 was US$96 million vs. US$430 million in 2013. Of the 20 bonds issued in 2013, 13 were larger than US$200 million in size. Bonds that are large increase liquidity and enable institutional investors to meet sized and liquidity requirements (Fig. 4).

The pioneer issuers of 'labelled' green or climate bonds have undoubtedly been the European Investment Bank, with their Climate Awareness Bonds, and the World Bank and its sister organisation, the International Finance Corporation,

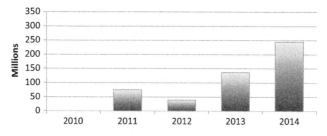

Fig. 4 Average labelled green bond sizes 2010—Q1 2014

with their green bonds. However, the successful entry of corporates to the market in 2013 and the fact that 2014 corporate issuance has outstripped that of the development banks suggests that companies will quickly become the dominant issuers. Along with corporate bonds, municipality and city bonds have also become a feature of the 2014 market with issuers across the world including Ile-de-France, Swedish cities Gothenburg and Stockholm, the City of Johannesburg in South Africa and US municipalities.

This labelled green bond market captures issuers who have actively labelled and marketed their bonds as green.

However, bonds have been issued to raise finance for low-carbon infrastructure for decades, particularly for rail, most of which have not been labelled as 'green' or 'climate'. The Climate Bonds Initiative estimates[10] that together the labelled and *unlabelled* markets linked to climate change stand at approximately US$500 billion outstanding, over US$460 billion of which is unlabelled and issued by companies. The bonds are predominantly in transport but also in energy, finance and agriculture. The study also showed that the vast majority of this market is investment grade product (89 %).

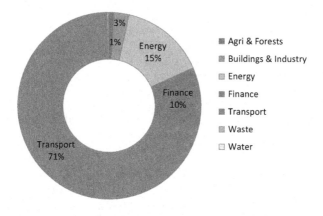

----

[10] Bonds and Climate Change: The State of the Market 2014. HSBC and the Climate Bonds Initiative.

6 Growing a Thematic Bond Market: A Guide for Stakeholders

If thematic bonds are to provide the scale of capital needed to address climate change estimated by the IEA, then the issuers will need to supply some US$5–10 billion per week on average during that time frame. While the current green bond marker is still a long off these levels, there is plenty of room to grow given the size of global debt markets. In 2013, the US corporates alone issued US$1.3 trillion—an average of US$26 billion per week—while US municipals issued approximately US$6.3 billion per week.[11]

In order for the market to grow anywhere near the levels required, the market needs to:

(a) Be capable of producing this debt
(b) Be capable of digesting such a supply of debt

---

1. Create deal flow: Bond investors need scale; projects (markets) should be aggregated into larger offerings suitable for the appetite of the big investors.

---

2. Engineer investment grade offerings: Where climate-related investmeent are still deemed as risky, governments and development banks need to engineer a stream of large scale investment opportunities and provide support to make them invesment grade

---

3. Create mechanisms for public sector risk-sharing: This could be through policy risk insurance and currency risk insurance

---

4. Form Green enabling institutions: e.g. Green Investment Banks

---

5. Provide Incentives for investors and issuers: where necessary Treasury should consider tax incentives that incur little loss to Treasury but provide a big boost to investment

---

6. Build an economic recovery narrative: the transition to a green economy revamps our economy across every sector and addresses the climate change threat

---

7. Use climate standards as a screening and preferencing tool: a tool that helps investors monitor and verify the climate effectiveness of their investments

---

8. Make it easy for politicians: bond investors and business issuers have to help politicians see how they can successfully sell plans to voters

---

To meet the US$1 trillion required, all stakeholders will be involved.

---

[11] SIFMA, https://www.sifma.org/research/statistics.aspx

6.1   Investors

To grow the market, investors need to:

- Signal demand by:
  - Buying green and climate bonds
  - Endorsing climate bonds as a good idea
  - Signing statements to express interest in more products (e.g. climatewise statement)
  - Publicly stating intention to purchase further product
  - Set aside a portion of investment portfolio to green products

- Engage in the debate by telling issuers what they will buy
- Demand standards for what can and can't be called a green bond

The primary role for investors in this market is to demand green and climate product (with the risk/yield characteristics they are looking for). Developments in 2014 indicate that there is more than enough demand for the current levels of green/climate debt. Demand is coming from both SRI and mainstream investors and central banks.

Indicators of demand have been the relentless oversubscription of climate and green bonds since 2012 and the number of buyers who have been public about their purchase of green bonds, including corporations such as Ford and Microsoft[12] and central banks. These mainstream investors are interested in the additional green benefits while still being comparable in terms of yield and risk as other products (e.g. the World Bank Green Bonds are issued with the same risk/return profile as their regular bonds). Of even greater value to the burgeoning market are the specific mandates or funds tied to green bonds. This includes the announcement made by Zurich Insurance Group in 2013 that it would be investing US$1 billion into purchasing green bonds that 'finance projects aimed at mitigating climate change and helping communities adapt to the consequences of global warming'.[13]

While all these factors are important, the nature of bond investing means that bonds can easily fit into mainstream investment portfolios without any specific mandate to buy them if they are included on indexes. This is therefore the goal if the market is to grow. As green and climate bonds are included on indexes, investors of all types will purchase them as they seek to track a benchmark.

Bonds that are large and liquid and issued in an appropriate currency will be included in relevant bond indices and, therefore, automatically included in

---

[12] http://www.businessgreen.com/bg/news/2305700/ford-and-microsoft-among-usd1bn-green-bond-investors

[13] http://www.ft.com/cms/s/0/43e36770-4e05-11e3-8fa5-00144feabdc0.html

exchange-traded or mutual funds seeking to track an index. By being large and therefore taking up a large portion of a benchmark, many funds, passive or otherwise, will include them in their funds. It is therefore size, liquidity, currency and rating features which will ensure that green bonds are taken up by investors.

For mainstream investors, bonds that meet size and liquidity requirements are sufficient, but for SRI investors, attractiveness goes beyond this to other ESG factors (the method of incorporating these factors differs between portfolios). For SRI investors interested in green bonds, assurance of the environmental benefit of the bond is paramount.

In addition, unlike mainstream investors, some SRI investors have stated that they would prefer green bonds that finance new assets rather than existing assets. Evidence has shown that rhetoric differs from reality in some areas, as demand has not tended to discriminate between bonds for refinancing vs. bonds for new assets.

Refinancing is an essential part of the finance pipeline, especially as more than 90 % of projects are financed via bank lending. If banks are able to 'flip' this lending over to investors once construction risk has passed, they are able to lend more thus taking on the more risky stage of a project while leaving the long-term, stable returns to long-term investors.

Investors move this market forwards by creating demand. But demand can only be present if the conditions are right which is why they need large and liquid bonds that have comparable yield to similar products. This is where other stakeholders—banks, issuers and arrangers—come in.

6.1.1 Issuers

To grow the market, issuers need to:

1. Produce high-rated and liquid financial instruments that qualify for market index inclusion
2. Ensure projects/assets included in green bonds are consistent with international standards
3. Aggregate smaller projects/loans into larger bonds

Sufficient supply of product requires issuers with qualifying assets or projects in need of financing (or refinancing). And issuers' willingness to issue is based on their ability to (a) access a cheaper cost of capital, (b) access a more diversified pool of investors, (c) meet any regulatory targets (e.g. potential government renewable energy mandates for utilities) and (d) gain any reputational or other benefit.

In the current market, issuing a climate bond does not guarantee a lower cost of capital compared to regular bonds, but as the market grows, policy changes and technologies become proven, this could change. It is not likely that the difference in cost of capital will be significant unless the risks are different or there is involvement by government to lower the cost of capital (through either reducing risk for investors or preferencing green investment or see more on the options for government involvement below).

Risk could be lower in specific cases where technology is proven and there is a demonstrable increase in the ability for debt to be repaid. For example, if a mortgage is taken out to purchase a zero/low-carbon home or if a mortgage is drawn down on to increase energy efficiency, the householder's regular utility bills will decrease, thus increasing ability of the mortgage holder to make mortgage payments. Such a reduction in risk could come with a reduction in the cost of capital.

Similarly, in the developing world where bank interest is a significant part of project costs, there is scope for bond financing enabling the issuer to get a lower cost of capital—it is likely that this will also only happen with support from development banks (see more below).

6.1.2 Banks

To growth the market, banks should:

- Facilitate the development of 'aggregators' well placed to manage project risk and obtain debt funding via banking and capital markets. These aggregators would also manage the mismatch between the term, interest rate profile and currency of underlying project-issued debt and bond market demand.
- Consider the potential for more complex instruments to emerge, including hybrid products that combine the potential for equity upside to traditional fixed interest returns.
- Look at loan portfolio for loans to put into climate bonds.
- Search client book for potential issuers.

Banks can act either as arrangers or issuers.

As arrangers, lead managers, underwriter or 'bookrunners', banks advise clients issuing bonds and are in charge of 'filling the book' or finding the investors to buy the bonds at issuance.

As arrangers, investment banks can grow the market by advising clients with green assets or projects to issue labelled green bonds and to have the bond certified by a third party.

In January 2014, a coalition of thirteen investment banks, led by Citi, Bank of America Merrill Lynch, JP Morgan and Crédit Agricole, published the Green Bond Principles.[14] The principles outline good practice for issuing a green or climate

---

[14] http://www.climatebonds.net/2014/01/12-thirteen-major-banks-issue-green-bond-principles/

bond; they suggest process for designating, disclosing, managing and reporting on the proceeds of a green bond; and they outline the possible types of green bonds (use-of-proceed bond, use-of-proceed revenue bond, project bond, securitised bond) as well as the four core principles behind issuing a green bond:

1. That green bonds are about green assets, not the 'greenness' of companies that issue them.
2. Transparency is critical:

   (a) Declaration of the use of proceeds of the bond—i.e. what the bond will be used to finance
   (b) Transparency over the process for project evaluation—i.e. how the investment is eligible to be called green and whether this fits within any external green standards or definitions
   (c) Management of proceeds to ensure that proceeds are tracked by the issuer and are going to the areas stated in 1)
   (d) Reporting to investors or the public on how proceeds have been allocated and where they remain unallocated.

All of these principles can be 'certified' by an external party if the issuer decides to do this. The principles define a hierarchy of assurance in order of increasing rigour: (1) second-party consultation to provide a second opinion or review of the bond, (2) the use of publicly available reviews and audits and (3) a third-party certification of the bond by a credible party against a standard.

The principles are designed to provide issuers with guidance on the key components involved in launching a green bond, to aid investors by ensuring the availability of information necessary to evaluate the environmental impact of their green bond investments and to assist underwriters by moving the market towards standard disclosures which facilitate transactions.

The principles do not, however, define which assets or investment should and shouldn't be defined as 'green'. This they leave to expert groups, academics and NGOs.

6.2   Policymakers and Development Banks

To grow the market, policymakers should
Public sector finance institutions can play different roles in supporting a green bond market:

1. Direct lenders
2. Issuers of green bonds
3. Sponsors of warehouses/conduit entities
4. Credit enhancers

Governments have used various forms of 'capital steerage' throughout history to shift investment into areas of urgent policy priority. Urban infrastructure such as sewers, railways and highways has depended on active government steps to ensure necessary capital investment. Capital steerage has involved tools ranging from policy and regulation to credit enhancement, guarantees and tax credits. At times, it has involved special preferencing—in the 1990s, the German government tweaked regulation of the Pfandbrief market to promote bank lending to housing and public sector projects in newly integrated East Germany.

These innovations illustrate the scale at which investment can be *steered*, given the appropriate market conditions.

The use of bond finance for policy priority investments in the past has been enormously successful.

Government's role need not be to fully fund but to sort out economic and energy planning and then to reduce key risks—notably government-related policy risk—enough to deliver secure long-term investment returns.

By lending directly to green projects, a development institution or government can provide junior or mezzanine debt and enable green bond issuance from investors at a suitable investment grade to attract private capital.

By issuing green bonds, governments can provide initial market product pipelines and liquidity, engaging investors and educating them about the asset class. Development banks such as the World Bank, European Investment Bank and International Finance Corp have been instrumental in driving the market thus far. Individual governments could continue this by issuing sovereign asset-linked green bonds.

As sponsors of warehouses/conduit entities, governments can assist SMEs and smaller borrowers to tap bond markets by enabling aggregation and packaging of loans. This could require special purpose institutions supported by developed banks.

Governments and development banks can help to de-risk the initial market by providing credit enhancement. Such credit enhancement will reduce the risk for investors thus enabling a higher rating and lower cost of capital on the bond. Credit enhancement can take many forms including guarantees on all or part of the bond or by taking a subordinated debt position

6.3   Challenges

6.3.1   Difference Between Addressing ESG Issues in Equity and Debt

Climate and green bonds fit within a much wider picture of responsible investment and the movement towards addressing environmental, social and governance issues within the previously neglected fixed income asset class.

The merits and feasibility of doing this are the source of much discussion and debate, to which this chapter does not contribute except in one area about assets and companies.

Climate bonds should be seen primarily as a positive investment tool where investments are contributing to a low-carbon economy. Inherently, they should also have a low stranded asset risk or climate risk but the discussion around green bonds is not synonymous with the discussion around the integration of ESG issued into fixed income portfolios.

This is an important point to note because when conflated, these two approaches (seeking to integrate ESG into fixed income and seeking positive ESG fixed income opportunities) can lead to adverse outcomes. For example, ESG/SRI investors are, from their experience within equities, accustomed to evaluating whole companies on what they do and how they operate to define whether they are 'investable'—i.e. whether they have significantly low environmental social and governance risks internally and in their supply chain or whether they generate sufficient revenue from environmentally or socially positive products/business.

Green bonds, however, define whether the <u>asset</u> that the bond is financing is green and then tracks the financing flows to ensure that the money goes there. This means that a green bond could be issued by a company that is not necessarily viewed as 'green' from a while company perspective.

For example, an energy utility could be deemed 'un-investable' as an equity by an SRI investor due, for example, to a high percentage of coal-fired power electricity generation. By assessing the whole company rather than the debt alone, some investors may choose to avoid the green bonds issued by the company. However, these bonds are raising finance to grow a part of the business that investors should be promoting (e.g. renewable energy).

Similarly, banks may issue a green bond linked to renewable energy loans, but if the company as a whole is not sufficiently green to be invested in and the green bond may not be invested in, it will not lead the bank to increase its loans to renewable energy projects. However, if investors targeted these types of investments instead, it becomes easier for banks to get certain types of loans off their books, and they are therefore likely to make more of those types of loans.

Avoiding green bonds on the basis of whole company metrics could lead to an underinvestment in green bonds and in the low-carbon economy and the status quo remains—i.e. underinvestment in key infrastructure. This will not get capital flowing. Therefore, we need a new lens to approach fixed income.

It is still possible for SRI investors to apply an additional issuer screen to a green bond that could exclude green bonds issued by highly carbon-intensive companies like oil and gas companies which may be seen as too high risk. The application of any additional screens is up to the individual investor, but the important principle remains that if sufficient capital is to be shifted, assets should be evaluated rather than companies. Overcoming this perception that whole companies have to be green to be investable is a key challenge.

Using Wrong Metrics? Carbon Footprinting
Carbon footprinting of equity portfolios is a common technique used to measure the impact of equity portfolios. The carbon footprint of a portfolio is usually measured by calculating the weighted average of the direct

(continued)

emissions of each company within a portfolio. This is then measured over time to see how it changes. It sounds like a great technique but it comes with caveats.

Carbon footprints measure the direct impact of a particular company without taking account of what they do—so by default, an electricity utility would have a high-carbon footprint (it generates electricity) while a bank would have a very low one. This could distort investment towards banks (whose loan portfolios are often dominated by coal) rather than utilities who are building wind farms.

6.3.2 Greenwash

In all ESG investing spheres, there is always a possibility that green public relations take over and investments do not make a genuine contribution to environmental or social goals. Investors have experienced this in many instances, particularly as the responsible investment movement was starting and investors were not yet accustomed to separating genuine environmental, social or governance credibility from green PR or 'greenwash'. While investors are more in tune to this now, there is still scope for greenwash, particularly in fast-growing areas such as green bonds.

Investors, banks and other stakeholders are well aware of potential greenwashing, and in November, the World Bank hosted a Green Bond Symposium where they stated that the goal of the market is 'to mobilize finance for environmental challenges at scale'. Ensuring that the market maintains its credibility, a few things are required:

1. Certainty that the money raised by the issuer is going to the stated projects/assets.
2. Certainty that the stated assets/projects are actually 'green'—i.e. making a genuine contribution to mitigating an environmental challenge.

On the first point, this is less necessary for trusted issuers such as the World Bank and other multilateral development banks but very much more necessary in the case of corporations.

However, on the second point, the determination of which assets and projects are 'green' should be steered by academics and experts in these areas. It is vital therefore that academic institutions, NGOs and other stakeholders be involved (see Standards below).

6.3.3 Clashing Issues

The majority of social and environmental goals are aligned with each other so that addressing one goal addresses or at least does not harm to the other goal. But there are instances where pursuing a social aim may clash with an environmental one and vice versa. The prime example is in water investment. Many investors see all water investments as 'green' but this is not always the case. The provision of clean drinking water is a vital social goal and one which should be supported but one that can also cause immense environmental damage—often to the detriment of people and the river systems (making further abstraction necessary)—sometimes through the over-abstraction of river systems, through highly energy-intensive desalination plants or highly energy-intensive water treatment plants. Such areas may require collaboration between different standards and organisations. For example, the EDF bond issued in 2013 was a renewable energy bond (therefore 'green' by all climate criteria), but they commissioned an additional set of criteria to assess other social, environmental and governance issues for each project undertaken to minimise any social or other impacts.

6.4 Opportunities

6.4.1 Standards

If greenwash ruins the credibility of the green bond marketplace, it will take years to get this back and market growth severely hampered. To ensure that finance is truly addressing environmental challenges (and meets the US$1 trillion required), each bond should meet clear and transparent (publicly available) environmental impact criteria in order to be called 'green' or 'climate'. Such criteria should be defined by independent experts and academics rather than by issuers or investors. The benefit of having an authoritative standard eases decision-making and focuses attention on credible climate change solution opportunities. The easier it is to use, the faster the market will grow.

Standards should then be used by independent third parties to determine whether an issuer meets the criteria and that the finance flows are being adequately tracked to ensure funds are flowing to the stated areas.

Standards should define which assets are included in a low-carbon economy (and therefore can be labelled as green) and which require additional criteria.

For example, with energy efficiency investments, hurdle rates need to be applied to ensure investments meet the requirements of a low-carbon economy. This is especially important when dealing with long-term infrastructure investments such as buildings. New buildings or even building retrofits are long-term investments and often received no additional investment for decades after initial building or retrofitting. Such long-term investments need to be aligned with what is required of them if a low-carbon economy is to be achieved—i.e. because buildings are only replaced after several decades, new buildings today should be built to meet the emission targets of 2050 rather being only marginally more energy efficient than the current building stock. If only incremental improvements are made, then our progress on climate change will be incremental. It is, therefore, essential that standards include hurdle rates for emission performance.

The Climate Bonds Initiative is working with academics and experts to develop definition for investors and guidelines for bond issuers on what are priority investments for a rapid shift to a low-carbon and climate resilient economy. The project aims to provide a blueprint of investments that are priorities for the transition, for example, in energy, buildings, low-carbon transport, sustainable agriculture and water.

'Almost Green'

Over the past few years, many companies have made greening claims. However, some companies, especially larger ones, have significant parts of their portfolios in relatively unsustainable assets. For these entities, the idea of ring-fencing assets to address labelling expectations is problematic. Doing so would mean identifying that a portion of their assets are not green, belying the public relations claims they have made in the less-regulated past. Issuing company green bonds without any qualification about their assets, on the other hand, risks embarrassing examination when asset criteria are compared with those of other bond issuers in the market. Investors who manage their portfolios in line with green- or climate-related standards will require a reasonable verification mechanism.

The Climate Bonds Initiative proposes an international standard labelling scheme using a transparent 'transition' model for the labelling of issuance by companies that have both sustainable and non-sustainable assets in their portfolios. This could provide a framework that would allow some flexibility in the first years, diminishing to a stricter set of definitions.

This position will likely attract the criticism, but a key precept behind the climate bond idea is that it provides a path for carbon sector companies to take advantage of growing investor interest in climate change-focused investments. The issue is the asset being funded, not the project managers past or unrelated activities.

6.4.2 Green Bond Funds and ETFs

As interest in the green bond market grows, dedicated green bond funds will become more prevalent. Dedicated green bond funds include:

- Calvert green bond launched in 2013.
- Rathbones ethical bond fund covers green as well as social bonds.
- Nikko World Bank Green Bond Fund which includes only World Bank Green Bonds.

The main driver behind these funds will be investors interested in the green space or those with a specific mandate to invest a percentage of their fund in low-carbon investment opportunities. While green/ESG mandates are fairly common in equities, they are only recently gaining traction in the fixed income asset class, spurred on in part by the increase in investment grade opportunities available to investors.

ETFs

Exchange-traded funds are a security that tracks an index like an index fund, but it trades like a stock on an exchange so you can buy a 'share' of an ETF. As such, the price of an ETF fluctuates with supply and demand. ETFs can be created for green bonds if there is an index to base them on.

> **Conclusions and Key Takeaways**
> - US$1 trillion per annum is required to keep climate change within 2 degrees of warming but if structured correctly, this can be investment not cost.
> - Bonds have been underutilised in financing climate-related infrastructure but are essential to meet the US$1 trillion target because of both the size of the global bond market and the suitability of bonds to financing long-term infrastructure projects.
> - The creation of a thematic green bond market is key to shifting capital towards climate infrastructure.
> - All stakeholders including issuers, investors, governments and NGOs have a role to play in growing the green bond market.
> - Standards are essential to ensure that investments are making a genuine contribution to climate change mitigation and adaptation.

References

OECD. (2014). Institutional investors and long-term investment. Project Report. Available from: http://www.oecd.org/daf/fin/ private-pensions/OECD-LTI-project.pdf

UNEP-SEFI. (2007). Global trends in sustainable investment 2007. Available from: http://www.unep.org/ pdf/72_Glob_Sust_Energy_Inv_Report_(2007).pdf

Appendix A: Bond Types

Bond type	Issuer	Description	Asset class	Examples
Treasury-backed bonds (balance sheet of issuer) with proceeds linked to a pool of qualifying assets, goods and services	National government	A country could issue a green bond with the proceeds earmarked for a specific green programme or even for their contribution to an international initiative like the UN Green Climate Fund	Sovereign bond	–

(continued)

Local govern-ment/ municipality	Municipalities and regional govern-ments General Obligation bonds where proceeds are allocated to qualifying investments. These are essentially the same as sovereign bonds	Municipal bond	Three French provinces have issued 'sustainabil-ity' bonds The State of Mas-sachusetts in the USA issued a US$100 million green bond in June 2013, with proceeds earmarked for environmental projects
Development bank	As above	Sovereign bond, financial institution bond	World Bank and IFC Green Bonds; EIB Climate Bond
Commercial banks	A bank can issue a bond linked to a pool of qualifying loans: wind and solar energy, rail and green buildings This could be in the form of: – A corporate bond for government and institutional investors – A retail bond for individual customers of the bank For credit purposes, the bond is the same as a standard corpo-rate treasury-backed bond, except that proceeds are only used to finance qual-ifying green investments	Financial institution bond	An Australian bank has been certified under the climate bond standard to issue a US$500 million climate bonds, with pro-ceeds allocated to a pool of wind energy loans
Corporations	Companies with substantial green assets on their bal-ance sheets A power company can issue a bond linked to its renew-able energy assets A car company can issue a bond linked to its electric vehi-cle assets	Corporate bond	Air Liquide in France in 2012 issued a 600 mil-lion euros 'health' corporate bond, with proceeds allo-cated exclusively to the purchase of a portfolio of hospitals

(continued)

'Dual recourse' bonds (covered bonds): the investor gets both a treasury backing and recourse to the underlying pool of assets. If the issuer fails, the investor owns the asset pool	Commercial banks	The extra assurance of dual recourse allows banks to borrow at a lower rate than their usual bank credit rating, reducing their usual cost of funds Most covered bonds are issued by banks, operating under governing national legislation providing assurance for investors Asset pools are mostly made up of home mortgages, with loans for public sector buildings also included in Germany The Climate Bonds Initiative has proposed including renewable energy assets in cover pools and a tiered risk weighting structure that puts a lower risk-weighting on green mortgages, as there is emerging evidence that the repayment risk for more energy effi-cient homes is lower.	Covered bond	The established covered bond mar-kets are worth US$3 trillion. However, there are not yet any specific green covered bonds
	Local governments	Green assets could be refinanced with dual recourse bonds, providing credit transparency to what are often opaque assets	Covered bond	–
	Corporations	Utilities could issue structured covered bonds secured against renewable energy assets as a way to reduce their cost of capital	Covered bond	–
Cash-flow-backed debt securities	Local government	Revenue bonds: local governments, special purpose in-frastructure or	Municipal bond	Property-assessed clean energy bonds

(continued)

		transport entities, etc. In this case, the bond is backed purely by cash flows from the underlying asset. Revenues may be guaranteed by government, such as with minimum passenger revenues on a rail line		
Finance company	Companies seeking to refinance a mature (low-return, low-risk) portfolio of loans or assets so they can recycle funds into new lending or developments that have higher returns Consumer loans for solar rooftops, electric vehicles Aggregated property improvement loan bonds ESCOs issue bonds backed by energy performance contracts Leasing companies, e.g. leases for electric vehicles Insurers—cash flows from renewable energy insurance	Asset-backed securities Mortgage-backed securities	Two solar rooftop securitisations are being prepared by US banks Green mortgage-backed securities An ESCO bond is being developed in Mexico by the Inter-American Development Bank
Special project vehicles (SPVs)	Project development company or SPV In energy sectors, these are typically backed by cash flows guaranteed by a power purchase agreement with a blue-chip credit rating	Project bond	MidAmerican solar project bonds in the US market

Prepared for the Future? ESG Competences Are Key

Katharina Serafimova and Thomas Vellacott

Banks are only gradually starting to realise that environmental and social risks have much wider repercussions than simply the potential damage to their reputation. The conventional initiatives taken by banks in the area of corporate social responsibility (CSR) are woefully inadequate for tackling the global environmental challenges they currently face. It is not enough to take environmental and social risks into consideration when financing projects and developing individual 'green' investment products. Instead, a paradigm shift is required—in the interest of both the banks and their clients. To be properly prepared for the imminent changes such as disruptions resulting from the growing scarcity of resources or changing regulations and to be able to realistically assess potential risks and opportunities, banks must successfully incorporate environmental and social challenges into the decision processes of their core business activities.

Banks can play a pivotal role in promoting a more sustainable, low-carbon economy. For example, they can steer investments towards more sustainable business models by applying environmental and social criteria in their lending practices. Such conditions often take the form of policies covering particularly controversial sectors, such as palm oil, mining or hydropower.

Environmental and social risks are especially relevant for banks operating in emerging economies: in some countries, a poorly developed regulatory framework, often coupled with inconsistent implementation, presents a particular challenge. The pressure exerted by civil society, through groups such as NGOs, is also often less strong and therefore only plays a limited role as a driver for improving environmental and social standards. However, the high-growth emerging economies, along with the financing activities in these regions, are becoming an increasingly important source of revenue for banks. A systematic understanding of the environmental risks and opportunities in these countries is essential—not least

K. Serafimova • T. Vellacott (✉)
WWF, Hohlstrasse 110, Postfach, 8010 Zurich, Switzerland
e-mail: Thomas.Vellacott@wwf.ch

© Springer International Publishing Switzerland 2015
K. Wendt (ed.), *Responsible Investment Banking*, CSR, Sustainability, Ethics & Governance, DOI 10.1007/978-3-319-10311-2_40

601

because fragile ecosystems, such as the Amazon, are globally important for preserving biodiversity and meeting climate targets. Our prior experience in working with (European) banks shows that most of them have not yet acquired the necessary know-how to effectively manage environmental and social risks, especially where developing countries are concerned. Furthermore, implementing corporate environmental and social policies in everyday business operations far removed from company headquarters is a challenge, especially when facing direct competition from local financial providers with lower environmental standards. WWF therefore works with banks financing projects in Southeast Asia, for example, in an attempt to help them implement effective environmental standards—the aim is to improve the environmental standards of international banks operating in the region but also of midsized and upcoming Asian banks, which are increasingly competing with European and American banks for the financing of projects in critical areas such as palm oil.

1 Environment Mainly Seen as a Reputational Risk in Project Financing

Globally active banks in particular have taken significant steps in recent years to introduce robust processes designed to manage the downside reputational risks presented by environmental and social issues, especially in the area of project financing. Leading banks in this field have extended their groupwide risk management systems to include environmental and social aspects and have these externally verified through accreditation systems such as ISO 14001. A number of global banks are now starting to apply international standards such as the Equator Principles not just narrowly to project financing but to all their financing activities.

A study produced in 2012 by the WWF and KPMG[1] found that the global banks whose business activities give them greater direct exposure to environmental risks and who have been subject in the past to stronger pressure from NGOs than smaller institutions are now better equipped to handle environmental risks. In other words, the trend is for global banks to move from the ad hoc evaluation of environmental and social risks in individual cases towards putting into place screening processes and risk assessment tools at portfolio level. So far, however, hardly any of the (Swiss) banks examined systematically identify, assess, control and monitor environmental or social risks at inception and throughout the lifetime of their originated loans or investments.

---

[1] WWF, KPMG, "Environmental performance of Swiss banks: Shifting gears towards next generation banking.

2 Environment as a Niche Investment Theme

In the world of modern investment, the management of environmental themes is only gradually integrated into the mainstream decision-making process. However, the majority of banks currently offer 'green' investment products to interested customers. While banks mainly view environmental issues in their financing activities in terms of their downside (reputational) risks, the emphasis on the investment side is more on the potential opportunities and the ability to set themselves apart from the competition with green 'premium products'. Although sustainable investments have been offered by individual pioneering Swiss providers such as RobecoSAM and Bank Safra Sarasin for two decades now, their overall percentage market share is still only in the single digits. The active integration of environmental aspects into the mainstream investment process—from macroeconomic analysis to asset allocation and portfolio construction—is still at a very early stage. Even in the case of green investment products, our research has shown that consideration is only given to environmental themes primarily—or even exclusively—in the company analysis stage. Although leading asset managers assess the environmental risks and opportunities associated with individual stocks, little attention is paid to ecological issues in the other stages of the investment process, such as asset allocation or portfolio construction.

3 Environmental Expertise as a Business Driver

In a nutshell, many banks view environmental issues on the risk side mainly in terms of possible damage to their reputation, while the potential opportunities seem to be limited to individual niche offerings. This short-sighted attitude means banks are not very well prepared to adjust their business model to forthcoming changes, such as tightening energy and climate regulation or changing demand patterns.

In addition to minimising reputational risks, there are concrete economic reasons for banks to integrate environmental aspects into their mainstream business. For example, for a bank considering a loan to a company working in the pulp and paper industry, applying a credible environmental standard such as FSC along the entire supply chain for raw materials reduces the risk of defaults caused by shortages in the supply of raw material. Such shortages can occur when forests are simply clear cut instead of being managed sustainably. In a similar scenario, a study[2] published by the WWF in 2012 showed that palm oil producers who apply a better environmental standard (RSPO) enjoy advantages not only in their cost structures but subsequently in their profitability and competitiveness as well. The production of agricultural or 'soft' commodities has a strong impact on the environment: it can lead to soil erosion, the mutation or loss of ecosystems and with it the destruction of

---

[2] Levin, Joshua, Profitability and Sustainability in Palm Oil Production, WWF 2012.

biodiversity, as well as increased greenhouse gas emissions from farming. WWF has collected case studies from working with global companies along the value chains of 10 soft commodities and drawn up a list of criteria for banks and investors interested in responsible investment in agricultural commodities.[3]

Banks play a pivotal role in influencing the conduct of clients with unsustainable business models. Particularly in controversial industries such as palm oil production, there is evidence that a deeper understanding of the environmental and social risks that companies are exposed to can actually bolster the relationship between the bank and the client.

4   Are Banks Prepared for Climate Change?

A similar situation exists with regard to climate change. A lack of understanding of the risks resulting from climate change may result in direct negative financial consequences for banks and their clients. One example is European oil and gas companies, which are coming under increasing pressure from the introduction of tougher rules on CO_2 emissions. In 2013, HSBC[4] warned that this could trigger a domino effect in which weaker demand for oil and gas could force down prices and cut companies' market capitalisations by as much as 40–60 %. Oil and gas companies continue to invest massive sums into expanding their reserves of fossil fuels, on which much of their valuation depends, despite the fact that the vast majority of these reserves will never be allowed to be burnt, even allowing for conservative assumptions about future climate regulations. In addition to the threat to share prices that this entails, S&P also highlighted in that the ability of companies active in the oil sands industry to maintain dividend and capital spending levels would be significantly pressured by stricter regulations on climate change. According to S&P, this has repercussions for the credit rating of the companies in question.

The efforts to limit climate change to a level at which its consequences are still manageable require a fundamental shift in many parts of the real economy as regards production methods, technologies, fuel types and efficiency levels. Climate change therefore presents substantial risks for assets and investments, particularly as a result of regulatory uncertainties. Banks need to understand how exposed individual companies and entire industries are to the issue of climate change and how well they are able to adapt. In both their own and their clients' interest, banks should also ask themselves which of their current business activities and which proportion of their earnings could be jeopardised by stricter energy and climate

---

[3] WWF, "The 2050 Criteria: Guide to Responsible Investment in Agricultural, Forest, and Seafood Commodities", 2012: http://awsassets.panda.org/downloads/the_2050_critera_report.pdf

[4] Spedding, Paul et al: Oil and Carbon revisited—Value at risk from "unburnable" carbon, HSBC global research, 2013.

regulations, technological innovations or changing customer requirements. In addition, banks need to be able to assess what impact this would have on individual financial products as well as on the portfolio as a whole.

5 Compliance Rather than Leadership

WWF's experience of working with financial institutions worldwide shows that banks are lagging well behind companies in the real economy when it comes to proactively incorporating environmental issues into their business models as strategic factors. With the exception of specialised niche players, very few banks are willing to become pioneers in the field of sustainability and to set themselves apart from the competition by aiming for higher environmental standards. Instead, banks tend to show a herd mentality where on the one hand no bank wants to attract negative publicity through adverse environmental news, but on the other hand no bank is prepared to take a significant step forward and integrate environmental themes into their mainstream business. Some of the obstacles commonly cited include short-term pressure from shareholders, poorly directed incentive structures or unclear responsibilities. Many banks are struggling with a constant flow of new regulation and shorter-term risks in their balance sheets, while still attempting to ride out—or recover from—turbulence on the financial markets.

6 Environmental Framework for the Financial Services Industry?

Violating regulations can result in fines for banks or their clients, as well as sanctions—not to mention the potential harm to their reputation. This can lead to the bank losing its actual or perceived 'licence to operate'.

Over the past several years, the number of environmental regulations has multiplied. We have seen the introduction of carbon taxes, carbon-offsetting requirements, obligations to introduce energy management systems or incentives for renewable energies, to name but some of the instruments introduced. These regulations can have enormous financial consequences for the companies concerned and ultimately for their investors as well. An understanding of these interconnections is imperative for decision-making in financing and investment and allows the identification of future winners and losers.

Environmental issues have so far not played a prominent role in international financial market regulation, either as regards national financial market regulators or the Bank for International Settlements (BIS) or bodies such as the Financial Stability Board (FSB). More recently, however, regulation seems to have intensified in this area as well—especially in the emerging markets.

Example (1) China: Financial market regulation is used to impose strong
environmental and social risk controls. Credit volumes to overcapacity, high-
consumption industries are restricted and the China Banking Regulatory
Commission has issued the Green Credit Guidelines.

Example (2) Brazil: The Central Bank recently introduced a resolution on
mandatory environmental and social policies for all banks under its
jurisdiction.

Because banks' activities and decision-making processes are very much driven
by a 'compliance' approach, we can expect environmental aspects to become much
more important as soon as the regulator forces banks to disclose the environmental
impact of their business activities or to carry out 'environmental stress tests'. The
overall regulatory framework, combined with voluntary industry agreements, therefore acts as a crucial catalyst for change.

7 Not Just Risks: Opportunities of Historic Dimensions

It is frequently argued that banks can only respond passively to client needs and
therefore are not in a position to actively promote more sustainable financial
products. However, banks are able to actively create investment opportunities,
especially in the areas of investment banking and asset management. A number
of examples, such as green infrastructure funds or impact investment solutions,
highlight banks' ability to offer investment alternatives to provide financing precisely where it is urgently required from an environmental perspective. One of the
key questions is how to mainstream and make scalable investment products that are
appealing in terms of the real economy, society and the environment.

In a recently published article, Huwyler et al. showed that the financing requirement for protecting the most important ecosystems worldwide is roughly 20–30
times greater than currently available funding. To close this gap will require more
than just public spending: the necessary funds could be raised through the financial
system if just 1 % of the capital of key private investor groups were diverted into
this type of investment product. A joint study published in 2011 by WWF and
Credit Suisse[5] estimated that investments of at least USD 700–850 billion per year
are needed in order to limit global warming to 2 °C and for adaptation to its

---

[5] WWF, Credit Suisse, „Auf dem Weg zu einer kohlenstoffarmen Wirtschaft: Die Rolle der
Banken", 2011.

unavoidable consequences. Admittedly, this is a huge challenge, but one which the global economy can overcome. Furthermore, it not only presents risks for banks but also opportunities. As far as future performance is concerned, this could generate additional revenues in the region of USD 25–30 billion up to 2020.

The role that banks will play in financing the energy revolution, in the transition to a more sustainable economy and in the preservation of ecosystems depends on how well they understand not just the risks but also the opportunities in the environmental domain and manage to incorporate them at an early stage into their decision processes.

Conclusion and Outlook

To address the substantial environmental challenges and to be prepared to master the changes associated with them—driven by new regulations, shifting consumer demands and the direct impacts of the growing scarcity of natural resource and of climate change—there must be a systemic transformation that enables banks to tailor their business models to the emerging risks resulting, e.g., from changes in regulatory conditions or consumption patterns.

If banks want to avoid having to scramble to catch up with increasingly demanding environmental regulation, they cannot wait passively until the regulator introduces new requirements or stakeholders and clients exert greater pressure. A thorough understanding of environmental issues, as well as the systematic integration of environmental aspects into their core business, is in the banks' own interest but takes time to develop and needs to go far beyond mere reputational risk management or green products aimed at niche markets.

Stakeholder Engagement Model: Making Ecotourism Work in Peru's Protected Areas

Alicia De la Cruz Novey

Abstract During the past two decades, there has been a shift in protected area management approaches from top-down management models to more diverse governance approaches that involve various forms and degrees of participation from local populations. These new participatory approaches seek to reaffirm cultural values, maintain cultural landscapes, recognise the relationship between people and nature, improve government citizen relationships, create "partners" in conservation, and contribute to the alleviation of poverty by providing socio-economic benefits beyond protected area boundaries. The development of resource management plans through public participation has been identified as an important step to accomplish these objectives. In 2007, research to test a hybrid model of public participation focused on understanding the factors that make public participation processes and the implementation of their results effective from the point of view of the participants rather than the managers. The study evaluated participatory processes used to develop tourism plans for two Peruvian national parks (Huascaran National Park and Yanachaga-Chemillén National Park). The findings suggested that perceptions of "success" were influenced by different key factors depending on the identity of a participant. People who participated, but represented the government and nonprofits, viewed the process as "successful" if several specific criteria were met, whereas people who represented communities, businesses, and their own interests viewed the process as "successful" largely via other criteria. These differences suggest that future participatory processes should create strategies to address the factors that assist both kinds of participants to believe a process was successful and effective.

1 Introduction

During the past 25 years, protected area management approaches have gradually changed from expert-driven, top-down governance models striving for strict preservation of ecosystems to governance models promoting various forms and degrees of participation from local populations and interest groups, with the goal of

A. De la Cruz Novey (✉)
ENVIRON, 4350 North Fairfax Drive, Suite 300, Arlington, VA 22203, USA
e-mail: adelacruz@environcorp.com

© Springer International Publishing Switzerland 2015   609
K. Wendt (ed.), *Responsible Investment Banking*, CSR, Sustainability, Ethics & Governance, DOI 10.1007/978-3-319-10311-2_41

balancing conservation and sustainable development (CBD 1992; IUCN 2003; Prato 2010; Prato and Fagre 2005; Shultis and Way 2006). The goal of these new participatory approaches is to provide venues for fair and competent communication, recognise the relationship between people and nature, improve government–citizen relationships, create "partners" in conservation, and contribute to the alleviation of poverty by providing socio-economic benefits beyond protected area boundaries (Ezebilo and Mattsson 2010; Naughton-Treves et al. 2005; Prato and Fagre 2005; Scherl 2004).

1.1   Peru's Protected Areas and Ecotourism

Peru is the third largest country in South America and is considered a mega-diverse country having 84 of the 117 existing life zones on the planet. It has a population of 30 million of people. The majority of these people live in urban areas and a small percentage who are typically less economically advantaged live in rural areas (INEI 2013). Peru also has the largest indigenous population (13 million) in South America (CIA 2013) and its economy is based on the use and extraction of natural resources. Its primary economic activities include mining, fishing, agriculture, and tourism (MEF 2010).

From 2002 to 2012, Peru's tourism industry grew by 254 %, with the nature-based tourism subsector seeing the biggest growth (MINCETUR 2013). Nature-based tourism in Peru mainly occurs within protected areas (PAs), and Peru's National Service of Protected Areas (SERNANP) claimed that in 2012, approximately 71 % of international tourists visited at least one of the 77 PA administrated at the national level. In addition, this activity generates 51 % of the public funds for Peru's Protected Areas System (SINANPE) and represents 45 % of the national tourism revenues. As a specific example of the growing importance of tourism, SERNANP states that in 2007, entrance fees generated US$1.7 million for the SINANPE, and tourism revenues received by local communities surrounding Paracas National Reserve totalled around US$10 million (León et al. 2009).

Peru's protected areas face the challenge of simultaneously promoting the value of biodiversity conservation while also supporting sustainable development within surrounding communities. To address these challenges, Peru's protected areas have developed policies that strongly promote stakeholder engagement in the planning and management of resources in each protected area (INRENA 2002). The outcome of this participation should ideally be reflected in a protected area's master and natural resource-specific plans (e.g. tourism plans) and the implementation of those plans.

1.2 Peru's PAs Stakeholder Engagement Strategies

In 1997, after several failed attempts to initiate processes for public participation, the Peruvian government enacted the Protected Areas Law, the first law to promote public participation in the management and policymaking of protected areas (Solano 2005). In 2001, the government enacted the Regulation for the Protected Areas Law that further identified and defined different procedures for public participation, providing the first legally sanctioned ideas of how to conduct real participation processes for local communities with the goal of creating "partners" in conservation (INRENA 2002; Solano 2005). Based on this legal framework, Peruvian protected areas are required to form a Citizen Advisory Committee (CAC) made up of community and stakeholder representatives with the purpose to act as a communication bridge between the protected area and the groups the committee represents. The goal of these regulations is to promote community ownership and support of the plan and its implementation.

In 2007, the Peruvian government, with the collaboration of the World Bank and the Global Environmental Facility (GEF), developed a methodology to map the involvement of stakeholders in the management of the PA over time. While this methodology provided PA managers with the tools to identify which stakeholders were not well engaged and prioritise their resources to engage them, it did not focus on understanding the reasons—from a stakeholder's point of view—for this lack of involvement and which factors managers should consider changing or improving.

Earlier themes of the literature on stakeholder engagement were focused on planner's perspective evaluations of typologies on how to achieve desired outcomes (manipulative, consultation, or self-mobilisation) (Irvin and Stansbury 2004; Pretty 1997; Pyhala 2002) as well as the appropriate logistical methods for successful decision-making processes (e.g. citizens juries, workshops, focus groups, public hearings, or community planning). Later studies have been increasingly focused on understanding the characteristics of an effective engagement process (procedures and outcomes) from participants' subjective feelings and beliefs (Carnes et al. 1998; Walters et al. 2000; Webler and Tuler 2000, 2002; Webler et al. 2001; Tyler 2005).

Most of the studies on stakeholder engagement have been focused on the field of law, conflict resolution, human health, and natural resources (Renn et al. 1995; Roberts 2004; Rowe and Frewer 2004; Seaba 2006). Despite all of these studies, there have been few that have examined theories or models in the context of protected areas. The proposed model of stakeholder engagement discussed in this chapter sought to fill a gap in the literature focused on protected area management. It incorporated participants' subjective views of what makes for an effective process and what outcomes allow or prevent the successful implementation of management plans; it then examined the relationship between those perceptions and participants' collaborative actions that influence the implementation of managerial plans based on the final objectives identified in each plan (De la Cruz-Novey et al. 2012).

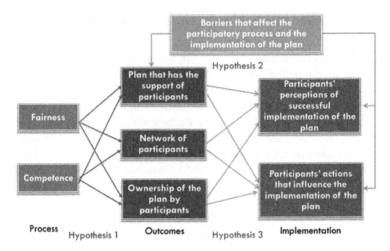

Fig. 1 Theoretical model of stakeholder engagement in PAs

1.3 Theoretical Model to Explain Participatory Outcomes

The proposed model aimed to understand what participants wanted from the process, how they perceived the participatory processes in which they were involved, and what could be improved. It used two leading theories of participation in natural resources, Procedural Justice theory (Lind and Tyler 1988) and Fairness and Competence theory (Webler and Tuler 2001), as well as previous studies about successful outcomes and evaluation of the successful implementation of plans. It is a hybrid model that combined and evaluated from the perspective of participants the factors that influence their perception of the outcomes (i.e. agreements, plans, decisions) of the process, the implementation of these outcomes, and their involvement in actions that influenced the implementation of the plan (Fig. 1).

1.3.1 Predictors of Effective Outcomes of the Process

As mentioned above, two leading theories of stakeholder engagement were used to create the first part of the model (sub-model 1):

1. Procedural Justice theory indicates the procedures used to arrive at decisions are significant determinants of satisfaction separate from the effect of the outcomes (Lawrence and Daniels 1997). People's feelings, attitudes, and behaviour are significantly affected by whether they feel they have been treated fairly and participants' perceptions of being involved in fair processes are the key to obtaining citizen's support of the decisions (Lind and Tyler 1988). It states that a fair process should allow the opportunity for all interested or affected parties to assume a legitimate role in the decision-making process.

2. Fairness and Competence theory acknowledges the importance of the fairness of the process but indicates that a fair process does not ensure the competence of the decisions (Webler and Tuler 2001). This theory indicates that public participatory processes should focus on the competence of the process to ensure and effective communication with the understanding that it develops an implicit commitment among participants to cooperate.

Both Procedural Justice and Fairness and Competence theories recognise the importance of the construct of fairness in participatory processes. However, their logic behind the need for a fair process is slightly different. While Procedural Justice theory focuses on the need of a fair procedure to ensure citizens' support of government decisions, Fairness and Competence theory focuses on the need for a fair procedure to ensure effective communication and collaboration, as well as raise commitments.

Predictors of the Successful Implementation of Outcomes

Stakeholder engagement processes in protected areas are often identified as a mandatory strategy to increase the support of stakeholders on specific plans, policies or projects (Carabias et al. 2003; Fernandez-Davila 2004; INRENA 2002; Prato and Fagre 2005) that usually have the objective to change the future of a specific situation (McCool and Guthrie 2001).

The second part of the model (sub-model 2) uses three constructs identified as important in the literature of stakeholder engagement to evaluate their influence on the stakeholders' perception of the successful implementation of the objectives identified during the process. The three constructs are ownership, support of the outcome, and networking. Ownership refers to the sense of responsibility towards the successful development and implementation of decisions reach through participation (McCool and Guthrie 2001; Solano 2005). Support of the outcome refers to participants' feelings of agreement with the final decisions or products (Lind and Tyler 1988; Webler and Tuler 2001). Finally, networking refers to the creation of improved relationships between participants that promote collaborative efforts to implement decisions (Waage 2003; Lachappelle et al. 2003).

In protected area management, it is particularly important to measure the future impact of the plans in the parks and the communities nearby. With the purpose of measuring the impact of the implementation of the outcome of a stakeholder engagement process, the model evaluates the relationship between the outcomes and their successful implementation from participants' perspectives. For this part, the model includes constructs related to the implementation of specific objectives identified on the plans.

Predictors of Stakeholders' Involvement in Actions That Influence
the Implementation of the Plan

On-the-ground protected area managers regularly deal with situations that threaten
conservation efforts and usually get involved in stakeholder engagement processes
with the purpose of changing the future of a specific situation (McCool and Guthrie
2001). These situations are often related to modifying or regulating an activity
performed by a group of stakeholders that might affect the conservation efforts of
the PA (e.g. noncontrolled tourism activities, grazing inside the protected area, etc.)
The third part of the model (sub-model 3) includes the analysis of the relation of the
outcomes of the process beyond the subjective support of the participants for the
managerial plans (Lubell 2002) and focuses on identifying whether the process
encouraged participants to take actions that contributed to the implementation of
the plans.

    In summary, the model considers that fair and competence procedures should
positively predict participants' perceptions of immediate outcomes such as support
of the plan, ownership, and improvement in their networking. These outcomes
would positively affect their perceptions of successful implementation and their
involvement in actions that influence these implementations.

2 Methods

The model was evaluated using a postpositivist research paradigm and a two-phase
sequential mixed methods strategy of inquiry with quantitative (survey research)
and qualitative (semi-structured interviews and archival data) methods. To provide
the most rigorous test of the model possible with two cases, it used contrasting
situations that reflect the main differences in Peru's protected areas tourism industry. These differences include the number of annual visitors, the degree to which the
tourism industry has developed, and the number of local vs. nonlocal tourism
operators. Additionally, the two parks—Huascaran National Park (HNP) and
Yanachaga National Park (YCHNP)—used different participatory processes to
develop their tourism plans.

    A small pilot test was run prior to the administration of the questionnaire to
ensure internal consistency. The questionnaire was developed by using open-ended
and close-ended questions based on the 07 constructs and 21 variables of the model.
An exploratory factor analysis was then used to reduce the variables into a small
number of factors, and a multiple regression test was run to identify the factors that
predict the effective processes, successful outcomes, and the implementation of
specific objectives.

3   Results

The response rate was more than 70 % of participants who were involved in the participatory processes in both parks. In analysing the questionnaires, respondents were pooled into two different groups (citizens and agency), based on their status either as a citizen or community representative whose livelihoods would be affected by the plan ($n = 47$) or as a park employee or NGO representative who was only indirectly affected by the plan ($n = 47$). Also, 44.3 % and 55.3 % of participants agreed to be interviewed in HNP and YCHNP, respectively.

After evaluating all the response and use factor analysis, 15 well-defined factors were identified and used to test the model and identify the factors that predict the effectiveness of the participatory processes through a multiple regression. This chapter focuses on the quantitative results of the evaluation of the model.

3.1   Predictors of Effective Outcomes of the Process

While citizens' perceptions of participating in a fair and competent process were found to moderately influence their perceptions of the development of effective outcomes—a sense of having a good plan, support of the plan, and networking—agency perceptions of having a competent process were found to strongly influence their perceptions of having a good plan.

For citizens, only six of 35 proposed paths were significant for the relationship between their perceptions and effective outcomes. And the strongest predictors were F1 ($\beta = 0.62$) on predicting the quality of the plan and F4 ($\beta = 61$) on predicting participants' livelihoods. For agency respondents, only five of the 35 proposed paths were significant. And the strongest predictor was F4 ($\beta = 0.66$) on predicting the quality of the plan, and the others were moderate to weak. Overall, the proposed model was moderately and weakly supported by the sub-models for both the citizens and agency groups (Table 1).

3.2   Predictors of the Successful Implementation of Outcomes

Because the number of YCHNP respondents from the citizen and agency groups who marked one of the Likert-type scale options (rather than the "I do not know" option) related to their perceptions of the successful implementation of the plan was too small, the model only uses the data from HNP to evaluate the predictors of successful implementation outcomes.

Citizens' perceptions of the successful implementation of specific objectives were predicted by the quality of the plan, networking of participants, and support of the plan, while for agency respondents, the quality of the plan was the main

Table 1 Stepwise regression (βs) for predictors of effective outcomes

	Citizens					Agency				
	F6_Commitment	F7_Good Plan	F8_Support of the Plan	F9_Livelihood	F10_Improve Relations	F6_Commitment	F7_Good Plan	F8_Support of the Plan	F9_Livelihood	F10_Improve Relations
F1_Decisions		0.62*							0.31*	0.35*
F2_Inclusiveness			0.34*					0.24*		
F3_Information										
F4_Competent Process				0.61*			0.66*			
F5_Competent Knowledge			0.28*		0.48*		0.23*			
F11_No_Barrier Politics										
F12_No_Barrier Procedures	0.41*									
Adjusted R^2	0.15	0.37	0.19	0.36	0.22	–	0.50	0.41	0.07	0.10
F	8.83	27.72	6.44	26.39	13.68	–	22.75	17.17	4.63	6.27
p	0.00	0.00	0.00	0.00	0.00		0.00	0.00	0.04	0.02

Note: – Indicates no statistically significant linear relationship between a predictor and the respective factor $p < 0.05$

*$p < .05$

Table 2 Stepwise regression (βs) for predictors for successful outcomes

	Citizens'			Agency		
	F13_Success Conservation	F14_Success Social	F15_Success Econo	F13_Success Conservation	F14_Success Social	F15_Success Econo
F6_Commitment						
F7_GoodPlan					**0.49**	**0.44**
F8_SupportofthePlan	**−0.35**		**−0.47**			
F9_Livelihood	**0.41**		**0.36**			
F10_Improve Relations						
F11_No_Barrier Politics						
F12_No_Barrier Procedures						
Adjusted R^2	0.23	0.07	0.29	–	0.19	0.16
F	5.68	3.47	7.41	–	5.08	4.66
p	0.001	0.07	<0.0005		0.04	0.04

Note 1: Boldface indicate variables that significantly predict the dependent variable $p < 0.05$

predictor of the successful implementation of objectives. Citizens' perceptions of successful implementation of the plan were then influenced by social networking, as well as the fairness and competence of the process (which were partially mediated by the quality of the plan and participants' support of the plan). Agency perceptions of implementation success were predicted by their perception of the quality of the plan, their networking, and the fairness of the process (Table 2).

For citizens, only four of the 21 proposed paths were statistically significant, for the relationship of participants' perceptions of support of the plan (F8) and participants' perceptions that the process helps them to improve their livelihood (F9) to the successful implementation of conservation and economic objectives, respectively. And the strongest predictors were F8 ($\beta = -0.47$) on predicting the success of economic objectives and F9 ($\beta = 0.41$) on predicting the successful implementation of conservation objectives related. For agency respondents, only two of the 21 proposed paths were significant, from the relationship of participants' perceptions of having a good plan (F7) to the successful implementation of social ($\beta = 0.49$) and economic ($\beta = 0.44$) objectives, respectively. Overall, the proposed model was weakly supported by sub-model 2 from citizens and agency groups (Table 2).

3.3   Predictors of Stakeholders' Involvement in Actions That Influence the Implementation of the Plan

Finally, participants' actions to help implement the plans were differently influenced in both groups; citizens' actions were positively predicted by the fairness of the process and negatively predicted by networking, while agency actions were negatively influenced by their networking.

This result did not concur with the literature on public participation that indicates that the improvement of relationships among participants may encourage participants to take action (Dietz and Stern 2008; Lachapelle and McCool 2005; McCool and Guthrie 2001). The results suggest that citizens' group respondents were more likely to not get involved in activities that helped implement the plan if they perceived that the process helped them to improve their livelihoods (F9) ($b = 1.43$, Wald Chi-square (1) $= 4.13$, p value $= 0.04$). On the other hand, respondents from the agency group were more likely to not get involved in activities if they perceived that the process helped them improve their relationships with other participants (F10) ($b = 0.69$, Wald Chi-square (1) $= 4.52$, p value $= 0.04$). Overall, both sub-models were moderately supported (Table 3).

The negative relationship might be related with the length of time that it took for the government to approve the plan and start its implementation after a participatory process that had been expected to improve the chaos of the tourism industry at HNP. This situation has been reported previously in the literature as "the frustration effect". It occurs when negative outcomes (the plan and its objectives are not

Table 3 Logistic regression results for predictors of participants' actions

Independent variable	Citizens					Agency				
	b	b (SE)	Wald statistic	p	Exp(b)	b	b (SE)	Wald statistic	p	Exp(b)
F6_Commitment	0.14	0.70	0.04	0.84	0.87	−0.70	0.52	1.78	0.18	2.01
F7_GoodPlan	0.23	0.70	0.11	0.74	0.80	0.59	0.44	1.86	0.17	0.55
F8_SupportthePlan	−0.26	0.67	0.15	0.70	1.29	−0.18	0.53	0.11	0.74	1.19
F9_Livelihood	1.43	0.71	4.13	0.04	0.24	1.04	0.55	3.58	0.06	0.35
F10_Improve Relations	−0.35	0.69	0.25	0.62	1.42	0.69	0.33	4.52	0.04	0.50
F11_No_Barrier Politics	−0.56	0.50	1.24	0.27	1.75	0.26	0.31	0.74	0.39	0.77
F12_No_Barrier Process	−0.54	0.59	0.83	0.36	1.71	0.57	0.39	2.12	0.15	0.57
Model Chi square	(7) = 15.43, p = 0.03					(7) = 20.31, p = 0.01				
Cox and Snell R^2	0.29					0.24				
Nagelkerke R^2	0.48					0.31				
Percent correctly classified	91.5 %					76.1 %				

approved) increase negative reactions (disappointment of participants) despite a process that had fair procedures (Lind and Tyler 1988).

3.4 Final Models of Stakeholder Engagement for Citizens and Agency Groups

The results indicate that the proposed model was partially supported and many proposed paths were not statistically significant. However, the linear regressions indicate that there are significant statistical differences in the factors that affect different perceptions of citizens and agency groups about the effectiveness of their engagement processes, their perceptions of the successful implementation of plans, and their involvement in actions that influenced the implementation of the plans, meaning that both groups have different expectations in regard to their roles and outcomes of their involvement in engagement processes.

As a result, two different models of stakeholder engagement in protected areas emerged, one from the citizens' perspective and the other from the perspective of the agency (Fig. 2). These findings concurred with the study by Tyler and Webler (2010), which demonstrated a correlation between people's perspectives on participatory processes and their institutional affiliation. However, it did not evaluate the predictor relationships among the factors of different affiliation.

The citizens' model of stakeholder engagement in protected areas indicates that their feeling and perception of being treated fairly (ideas were listened, participate during the discussions and decisions, and were recognised as informants) during the participatory process positively influence their perception of support and feeling of ownership of the plan that at the same time influences their perception that the plan was successfully implemented. It also indicates that citizens' perceptions that the process was competent in regard of information provided and its rules and regulations influence their support and ownership of the plan and their perception of improvement of their networking that in turn will influence participants'

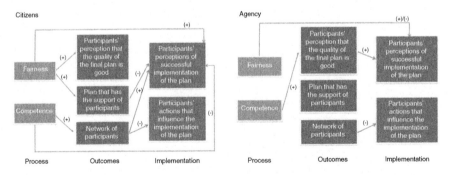

Fig. 2 Models of stakeholder engagement from the perceptions of citizens and agency groups

perceptions of the successful implementation of the plan and the likelihood for them surprisingly not to be involved in specific actions related to the implementation of the plan. Citizen representatives might feel frustrated that the objectives were not fully implemented after several years. And the weak intensity of this relationship might involve some of the objectives not being directly linked to occupations and livelihoods, feeling that the government should be in charge of implementing these objectives or that citizens' networking improved their livelihood by increasing their tourism activities outside the park (Fig. 2).

On the other hand, the agency's model of stakeholder engagement in protected areas indicates that their perception of being involved in a competent process influences their perception of the good quality of the plan. In turn, a plan perceived as being good quality will influence agency representatives' perspective of successful implementation (if the process was competent, the plan must be good and should be successfully implemented). Agency members usually get involved in actions as part of their job duties; it is surprising that the sole predictor of their involvement was the negative improvement of relationships with other participants and park staff. As with citizens, agency representatives might feel frustrated with the fact that the objectives were not fully implemented after several years (Fig. 2).

Conclusion

Even though it is important to have a strong framework of government rules, regulations and standards to plan for a successful stakeholder engagement process in protected areas, it is critical to understand differences in participants' expectations based on their role, participation, and outcomes during the engagement process to adequately design these processes.

The model confirms that the constructs of fairness and competence are also important for stakeholder engagement processes in protected area management as previously identified in other fields (i.e. law, conflict resolution, human health, and natural resources). Protected area planners should design fair and competent participatory processes, using different techniques to enhance the factors that are more important for citizens and agency groups. Also, protected area planners should ensure that all participants feel comfortable providing their perspectives and information about specific topics as well as encourage respondents' participation during the discussions, provide as much information as possible ahead of time, and allocate adequate time for meetings so that processes are considered as competent by their participants.

In addition, it is important to monitor the impact of management as well as peoples' perspectives (citizens and agency representatives) about their improvement on social, ecological, and economic factors. Planners should take special attention to identify objectives that can be implemented in the short term and put special care into the dissemination of the final tourism plans, as well as their implementation.

(continued)

Due to the importance of the quality of the plan for the perception of successful implementation for both groups, understanding how to make a plan perceived as high quality might have an effect on whether or not the plan is ultimately successful and also might influence the involvement of participants in future participatory processes. Future research, therefore, might do well to focus on aspects that lead to perceptions of plan quality.

Finally, replicating this study in other Peruvian protected areas that have also used participatory processes to develop tourism plans would add to our understanding of what works well in Peru and could help to better understand public participation processes more generally in protected areas.

Acknowledgments These results are the partial quantitative findings of a PhD dissertation at the University of Idaho, College of Natural Resources, Department of Conservation Social Sciences. The research was partially funded by OAS-Fulbright Program and the Foster Research Assistantship. The author acknowledges the help of Dr. Troy Hall as major professor as well as the dissertation committee during the research. In addition, this article acknowledges the comments and suggestions of the reviewers, which have improved the presentation.

References

Carabias, J., De la Maza, J., & Cadena, R. (2003). Capacity needs to manage protected areas: A global overview. In J. Carabias, J. De la Maza, & R. Cadena (Eds.), *Capacity needs to manage protected areas: Africa* (pp. 17–33). Arlington, VA: The Nature Conservancy.

Carnes, S. A., Schweitzer, M., Peelle, E. B., Wolfe, A. K., & Munro, J. F. (1998). Measuring the success of public participation on environmental restoration and waste management activities in the U.S. Department of Energy. *Technology in Society, 20*(4), 385–406.

Central Intelligence Agency. (2013). Peru. In *The world factbook*. Retrieved December 18, 2013, from http://cia.gov/library/publications/the-world-factbook

Convention on Biological Diversity (CBD). (1992). Earth Summit. Rio de Janeiro.

De la Cruz-Novey, A., Hall, T., Hollenhorst, S., & Camp, S. (2012). *The effectiveness of public participatory processes in two protected areas of Peru* (Doctoral Dissertation, University of Idaho: Conservation Social Sciences Department, 2012).

Dietz, T., & Stern, P. (2008). *Public participation in environmental assessment and decision making*. Washington, DC: National Academies Press.

Ezebilo, E., & Mattsson, L. (2010). Socio-economic benefits of protected areas as perceived by local people around Cross River National Park, Nigeria. *Forest Policy and Economics, 12*(3), 189–193.

Fernandez-Davila, P. (2004). The process of local ownership of the Tingo Maria National Park (Huanuco, Peru). In D. Hamú, E. Auchincloss, & W. Goldstein (Eds.), *Communicating protected areas* (pp. 175–181). Gland/Switzerland and Cambridge: IUCN.

INEI. (2013). Evolucion de la Pobreza Monetaria (2007–2012). Informe técnico

INRENA. (2002). Compendio de legislación de áreas naturales protegidas (1st ed.). Lima - Perú: Instituto Nacional de Recursos Naturales, Sociedad Peruana de Derecho Ambiental.

Irvin, R., & Stansbury, J. (2004). Citizen participation in decision making: Is it worth the effort? *Public Administration Review, 64*(1), 55–65.

IUCN. (2003). *The Durban Action Plan*. Vth IUCN World Parks Congress. Durban, South Africa, IUCN, Gland, Switzerland.

Lachapelle, P., & McCool, S. (2005). Exploring the concept of "ownership" in natural resource planning. *Society and Natural Resources, 18*, 279–285.

Lachapelle, P., McCool, S., & Patterson, M. (2003). Barriers to effective natural resource planning in a "messy" world. *Society and Natural Resources, 16*(6), 473–490.

Lawrence, R., & Daniels, S. (1997). Procedural justice and public involvement in natural resource decision making. *Society and Natural Resources, 10*(6), 577–590.

León, F., Rodríguez, A., Drumm, A., Murrugarra, F., Lindberg, K., & Gonzales, C. (2009). *Valoración económica del turismo en el sistema nacional de áreas naturales protegidas por el estado: Un estudio de caso en cuatro áreas naturales protegidas del Perú*. Lima: Ministerio del Ambiente.

Lind, A., & Tyler, T. (1988). *Social psychology of procedural justice*. New York: Plenum Press.

Lubell, M. (2002). Environmental activism as collective action. *Environment and Behavior, 34*(4), 431–454.

McCool, S. F., & Guthrie, K. (2001). Mapping the dimensions of successful public participation in messy natural resources management situations. *Society and Natural Resources, 14*(4), 309–323.

MEF. (2010). *Informe de seguimiento del marco macroeconómico multianual 2010–2012 revisado*. Lima: Ministerio de Economía y Finanzas.

MINCETUR. (2013). PENTUR. *Plan Estrategico Nacional de Turismo 2012–2021*. Lima, Peru.

Naughton-Treves, L., Holland, M. B., & Brandon, K. (2005). The role of protected areas in conserving biodiversity and sustaining local livelihoods. *Annual Review of Environment and Resources, 30*(1), 219–252.

Prato, T. (2010). Sustaining ecological integrity with respect to climate change: A fuzzy adaptive management approach. *Environmental Management, 45*(6), 1344–1351.

Prato, T., & Fagre, D. (2005). *National parks and protected areas: Approaches for balancing social, economic, and ecological values*. Ames, IA: Blackwell Pub Professional.

Pretty, J. (1997). The sustainable intensification of agriculture: Making the most of the land. *Natural Resources Forum, 21*(4), 247–256.

Pyhala, A. (2002). *Institutions, participation and protected area management in western Amazonia*. Paper presented at the Biennial Conference of IASCP. Victoria Falls, Zimbabwe, June 17–21, 2002.

Renn, O., Webler, T., & Wiedemann, P. (1995). *Fairness and competence in citizen participation: Evaluating models for environmental discourse* (Vol. 10). Netherlands: Kluwer Academic Publishers.

Roberts, N. (2004). Public deliberation in an age of direct citizen participation. *American Review of Public Administration, 34*(4), 315–353.

Rowe, G., & Frewer, L. (2004). Evaluating public-participation exercises: A research agenda. *Science, Technology, and Human Values, 29*(4), 512–556.

Scherl, L. M. (2004). *Can protected areas contribute to poverty reduction? Opportunities and limitations*. Gland: World Conservation Union.

Seaba, N. (2006). *Public participation: Rhetoric or reality? An analysis of planning and management in the Nanda Devi Biosphere Reserve*. Unpublished master thesis, University of Manitoba, Manitoba, Canada.

Shultis, J., & Way, P. (2006). Changing conceptions of protected areas and conservation: Linking conservation, ecological integrity and tourism management. *Journal of Sustainable Tourism, 14*(3), 223–237.

Solano, P. (2005). *La esperanza es verde*. Lima: Sociedad Peruana de Derecho Ambiental.

Tyler, T. (2005). *Procedural justice* (Vol. I). Aldershot, Hants: Ashgate Publishing Company.

Tyler, S., & Webler, T. (2010). How preferences for public participation are linked to perceptions of the context, preferences for outcomes, and individual characteristics. *Environmental Management, 46*(2), 254–267.

Waage, S. (2003). Collaborative salmon recovery planning: Examining decision making and implementation in northeastern Oregon. *Society and Natural Resources, 16*(4), 295.

Walters, L. C., Aydelotte, J., & Miller, J. (2000). Putting more public in policy analysis. *Public Administration Review, 60*(4), 349–359.

Webler, T., & Tuler, S. (2000). Fairness and competence in citizen participation: Theoretical reflections from a case study. *Administration and Society, 32*(5), 566–595.

Webler, T., & Tuler, S. (2001). Public participation in watershed management planning: Views on process from people in the field. *Human Ecology Review, 8*(2), 29–39.

Webler, T., & Tuler, S. (2002). Unlocking the puzzle of public participation. *Bulletin of Science, Technology and Society, 22*(3), 179–189.

Webler, T., Tuler, S., & Krueger, R. (2001). What is a good public participation process? Five perspectives from the public. *Environmental Management, 27*(3), 435–450.

Why Not? Sustainable Finance as a Question of Mindset: A Plea for a Confident Sustainable Business Strategy

Dustin Neuneyer

Abstract Sustainability in finance, including fundamental changes to business as usual and touching on alleged taboos, can and should be much more easily and effectively achievable than is generally accepted, but we shouldn't be frightened by this. Current economic development is widely considered to be unsustainable, which results in a number of challenges for financial institutions as a whole and specifically within any transaction. Pace and quality incorporating sustainability considerations into decision-making in finance in order to answer these challenges is not nearly sufficient. The situation has reached a kind of gridlock: despite the importance of the underlying facts and concepts and the urgency for adequate adjustments, there is an ongoing debate about exact definitions, the likelihood of certain developments and about who is responsible for what. The resulting uncertainty and specific obstacles are often perceived as or (mis)used as an argument for restraint or opposition; as a result there is a lot of awareness but only little and slow move towards sustainable finance. On the other hand, what is often not seen, or what is not want to be seen, the wide field of sustainable finance debate and considerations paves the way for a confident and decisive move to incorporate sustainability extensively into finance since it offers a number of modifications and alternatives to business as usual. This move is just possible and appropriate; it is more a question of financial institutions' self-conception and the underlying mindset. Determinedly navigating a way through the maze leads to innovation, development and mutual benefit for all parties involved. How to successfully break new ground and how to overcome the gridlock is exemplified in this article by looking at how sustainability management was developed and implemented at the corporate and investment bank WestLB between the years 2004 and 2012. From WestLB's approach, key elements of sustainable finance are deduced including an elaboration of the question of sustainable finance as a matter of mindset. The examples given include a far-reaching stakeholder dialogue, a first of its kind business strategy in coal-fired power generation, and another one in offshore oil drilling and production including in the Arctic.

D. Neuneyer (✉)
Consulting, Sustainability · Finance · Strategy & Implementation
e-mail: dn@neuneyer.com

© Springer International Publishing Switzerland 2015   625
K. Wendt (ed.), *Responsible Investment Banking*, CSR, Sustainability, Ethics &
Governance, DOI 10.1007/978-3-319-10311-2_42

1   The Ongoing Debate Over Sustainability and Tentative Actions

1.1   Sustainability Matters, Somehow: Two Perceptions

For many years now, there have been broad discussions on sustainability, definitions and content, across all disciplines and systems: discussions about the meaning of the word; what a certain definition means for a certain area of activity, a product and its production process or a service and the way it is provided; or what it means for patterns of behaviour and consumption. It is discussed from an aerial perspective as well as in detail.[1]

Both in science as well as in society, it is widely accepted that current economic development is unsustainable and that pace and quality incorporating sustainability considerations into decision-making is not nearly sufficient to answer the challenges.[2]

How can it be that there is broad and continuous debate that leads to theoretical knowledge, but relatively little consequence and only tentative action? It may well be that one reason is the debate itself. The issues of sustainable development are very complex; in some ways the debate seems to be endless and with no clear frontiers or focus. Such a broad discussion leads to two perceptions and effects, both of which are legitimate and reasonable:

1. On the one hand, it creates uncertainty and randomness about what it is all about and how to deal with it. This, combined with (alleged) responsibilities, may lead to gridlock where small things move slowly.
2. On the other hand, there is room for choice and the examples given below show that there are opportunities for innovation, progress and benefit if a focus is set and that much is possible even when it is generally believed that little is possible.

1.1.1   What Is at Stake?

By widening the focus, it's clear that all the elements under discussion belong to the same question: how people want to live with regard to their needs and desires, such as food, freedom, peace, but also economic prosperity, material welfare and convenience. It is about meeting these needs within the given boundaries of natural, human and economic resources.[3] Consequently, there are certainly constraints shaping the way we live, but there is also room for choice. Within these constraints, there are overarching and global issues such as human rights, climate change and

---

[1] cf. exemplary Meadows (1972) or Schneider and Schmidpeter (2012).

[2] Ibid.

[3] cf. The World Commission on Environment and Development's (the Brundtland Commission) 1987.

scarcity of natural resources and also a long list of more concrete issues such as specific labour conditions, extreme weather events, deforestation, fishing quotas and certain pandemic diseases.[4]

Each of these issues has a number of meanings, consequence and options for approach and action of their own, which create a high degree of uncertainty as to what sustainability then means. One thing is for sure, however: the subject isn't going away. It may be considered less important at times, displaced by, say, financial crisis, national fiscal problems and so on, but the fact remains, sustainability is still the overarching issue. It is not an issue exclusively relevant to the wealthy regions of today's world, or just to the place where a certain decision is made, nor only for the place of action and effect. Sustainability and the underlying issues are characterised by the interaction and interdependence of time and place.

There are clear indications and phenomena in everyday life, as well as in science and theory, that sustainability matters—somehow. Is it really that difficult to discover exactly how sustainability matters and what to do about it?

1.2   Implications of Sustainability for the Finance Sector

As a basic principle, the finance sector and banking do impact and are impacted by almost all sectors, products and services in society and the economy. Financial transactions implicate a certain state before and after any given item is financed.[5]

Investigating sustainable finance is, above all, a question of whether it does any harm or results in too high a cost if not profit for a financial institution and for society as a whole to ignore or to take into account and systematically incorporate the sustainability issues. With regard to the interdependency described above, these issues are inherent in the items financed and the corresponding transactions. What is ignored and what is incorporated into an economic decision frequently changes. Even the supposed core elements of capital theory and market evolve all the time.[6] And there is a peculiar simultaneity of rational and irrational elements, of tangible and intangible pieces, of figures and sentiments that shape perhaps less the theory, but certainly the reality of any given transaction.

There are many arguments for taking an active as well as a more passive approach when dealing with the evolving elements of economic activity. One can emphasise the all-too-many possible meanings of and implications and options for sustainable finance, as well as the luck of actually having such options. Over the

---

[4] cf. Manifold releases in politics, often science-based such as issued by the UN bodies, the EU commission, the G8, OECD etc.

[5] cf. in the context of sustainability, e.g. Kristof and Hennicke (2010).

[6] cf., e.g. Acceptance and critique of Capital Asset Pricing Model and Arbitrage Pricing Theory, e.g. Malevergne and Sornette (2006) or Camfferman and Zeff (2007).

past years, there has been progress in raising awareness about sustainability within finance and even introducing new elements for due diligence, etc.[7]

It has become a sort of consensus that in regard to returns as well as to societal duty, financial institutions further develop and implement sustainable finance. But, as described above, compared to the challenges, there has been far too little progress here, and globally, the challenges grow much faster than the responses to it. Either way, sooner or later, financial institutions will not be able to fully disregard that sustainability issues must be *substantially* imbedded into finance. Simple facts as well as public demand and, in perhaps the best cases, a financial institution's self-conception will shape the so-called new normal.

To give perhaps the most established example of global climate change and to propose a lowest denominator: even if climate change were to slow in the coming decades, there is much at stake, socially with respect to the environment as well as financial return. As long as we—and financial institutions in particular—cannot exclude the very material risks associated with it (even though there may be low probabilities attached to some of the most severe developments), it seems to be more prudent to take every precaution or opt for every available less risky alternative.[8]

1.3   Unable and Not Responsible?

There has been a lot of effort and much success in raising awareness and introducing sustainability consideration into finance. But compared to the size of the challenges and the urgent need for fundamental change (see above), the developments and innovations are small and slow. Many decision makers (not only) in the finance sector, including sustainability managers, see themselves as unable or not responsible for taking bigger steps.

Good examples of this are the intense debate on an adequate method for greenhouse gas accounting and reporting[9] or the view of the Equator Principles Association "not to act as a 'standard setter'."[10] There are many more examples with regard to almost every issue of sustainability, such as human rights, worst forms of child labour, controversial weapons and armaments, etc.

The complexity of the sustainability debate as a whole, of the specific issues and the consequences for the finance sector in particular, as well as limited and

---

[7] For example, the Equator Principles.

[8] cf. Onischka et al. (2007).

[9] cf. Financial Sector Guidance for Corporate Value Chain (Scope 3) Accounting and Reporting, http://www.ghgprotocol.org/.

[10] cf. Summary Response by Equator Principles Association to the Equator Principles Strategic Review Report. http://www.equator-principles.com/.

restricted duties and responsibilities are cited as reasons for hesitation, tentative action or restraint and opposition.

The following are early examples of sustainability management at WestLB that touched on fundamental principles of corporate and investment banking. Second is an analysis of the underlying preconditions, including the mindset, that made this possible. And, third, in the spirit of this publication, the focus is on the possibilities and choices to pragmatically deal with the issue of sustainability and its implications for decision and action in finance.

2 Touching on Alleged Taboos: Examples from WestLB

2.1 Organisational Setup and Approach Decided Upon

At its best, state and savings banks-owned WestLB was active as an international corporate and investment bank, with a significant market share in the energy sector, hard and soft commodities trading and project finance. With such a business model, a bunch of sustainability aspects, with regard to social and environmental impact related to the business activities, confronted WestLB. Nongovernmental organisations (NGOs) began to criticise its lax dealings with these issues. At a certain point, it became a public and political issue and the owners decided to introduce a new approach. Sustainability Management was founded at WestLB, as a central department, reporting directly to the board.

This department recruited in-house as well as externally to pool the expertise and experience that reflected the holistic and encompassing approach that was demanded and decided upon. From then on, the classic banking perspective was combined with that of an engineer, an emerging market as well as from a diverse stakeholder perspective. It is important to mention that as often happens, none of these perspectives was allowed to overrule the other and business proceeded with a balanced overlap between the three.

Therefore, lending criteria and processes had to be substantially modified. Obviously it was impossible to completely change the whole of WestLB's business, its products and services straight away, nor was this intention. Sustainability Management at WestLB took a decisive, step-by-step approach to substantially changing its business:

1. The bank instituted a stakeholder dialogue that was much more than a casual exchange of views. Twice a year, a firmly established group of people from inside the bank, from NGOs, from science and experts of specific topics gathered for a day to discuss and develop a systematic sustainability strategy for the whole bank. This was done in a moderated way and with agreed confidentiality. The sustainability strategy was then translated into a working programme formally approved by the board and publicly reported in the sustainability and in the annual reports.

2. The bank developed a general "Policy for Environmental and Social Issues" and several sector/theme policies following an analysis of what sustainability issues were most important with regard to the business of the bank and its impacts. Examples are the "Policy for Business Activities Related to Coal-Fired Power Generation" and the "Policy for Business Activities Related to Offshore Oil Drilling and Production", all defining minimum and exclusion criteria.[11]

3. The bank implemented and applied these policies and, at the same time, developed a strict approach with respect to sustainability on a deal-by-deal basis, in particular where the policies did not give clear guidance. In more and more credit decisions, reputational risk or product development processes, Sustainability Management was formally part of the due diligence, with the ability to set requirements, to escalate or to veto if necessary.

2.2 A Material Shift Away from Business as Usual

Probably the most important aspect of these elements of sustainable finance is the fact that each touched fundamental principles of banking and specific business and changed them. This stakeholder dialogue and the sector policies were the first of their kind. To have a confidential exchange with external stakeholders so firmly institutionalised and to commonly develop elements of the core business was new territory, as was formally and publically declaring that, henceforth, certain business would only be pursued under specific circumstances and defining the Artic as a no-go area.

There is a big difference in simply defining requirements, such as relative improvements of efficiency rates or more detailed social impact analyses, for example. In the case of coal-fired power generation, WestLB decided on a material shift away from business as usual. While for decades it was simply normal to finance this kind of activity, once the coal policy came into effect, it was only possible under very specific circumstances, with a significant number of cases where it was not possible at all[12]. General rule and exception were permuted.

Of course, there were good reasons for this. First, climate change and greenhouse gas emissions are at the very centre of every sustainability discussion since they are major global problems with severe environmental and social threat. Furthermore, because coal is the most carbon-intense energy source, a coal-fired power plant is a problem in itself, regardless of the efficiency rate, unless large-scale carbon capture and storage or usage work. In addition, there are high regulatory risks and little social acceptance (in many regions of the world), which result in economic uncertainty that eventually jeopardises the payback of high amount and long-tenure loan facilities. Finally, in the case of electricity generation, alternatives

---

[11] See http://www.linkedin.com/in/dustinneuneyer.

[12] For details of this policy, see http://www.linkedin.com/in/dustinneuneyer.

are available with proven and marketable technology. Another good but perhaps less rational reason was that WestLB had opted to contribute decisively to sustainable development as part of its self-conception.

Similarly, distinctly differentiated from business as usual and closely linked with this self-conception, i.e., as an act of free will (see Sect. 3.2), WestLB decided not to finance activities related to offshore oil drilling and production in the Arctic. Normally in finance, the definition of (topical or geographical) no-go areas is a no-go area in itself.

What was deemed impossible all of a sudden was possible.

2.3   Reactions and Benefits

WestLBs sustainability efforts paid off, even if there were still weak points. WestLB experienced this in regard to reactions to its sustainability management by NGOs and media, as well as by clients and owners.[13] The outcome as well as the reactions were positive. WestLB continued doing business, but differently. The clients and other stakeholders accepted and welcomed the new approach, and the owners benefited from being less prone to financial and nonfinancial risks. Deals, projects and enterprises changed where necessary and if possible, and when this was not the case, certain transactions were not pursued further. This way, the bank advanced its risk management and risk profile and instead of finding itself in a tight corner was a pioneer in generally shaping the changing environment all around.

In many cases, the externally highlighted concerns regarding risks or negative impacts of a certain (type of) transaction proved to be valid; if the overlap between economic, social and environmental aspects is not balanced, there is a higher risk of damage to each of these dimensions, not to mention the potential damage to the image of a financial institution or a financed enterprise.

3   A Possible Way: Analysis of Preconditions and Mindset for a Confident Sustainable Business Strategy

What made it possible to instigate such changes to business as usual, including touching on alleged taboos?

---

[13] For example, Carr 2012 or Herrmann (2012).

3.1 Essentials for Success

As described above, the wide field of the debate over sustainability and sustainable finance can be seen as a great opportunity to extensively incorporate sustainability. It offers many options, modifications and alternatives to business as usual. The following basic principles can be derived from the experience of sustainability management at WestLB. All of these were in place and existed at WestLB. They can be seen as a blueprint for a successful risk and business strategy on sustainable finance.

- **Capable protagonists**: Naturally, individuals play an important role. Be it agenda setting or standing up for a good cause and carrying it through: particularly in the case of innovation, it is crucial to have people that are capable, committed and intent on the issues they represent. Sustainability managers need also to be assertive as they are often confronted by different interests and resistance.
- **Education and capacity building**: Ideally, (a team of) sustainability managers in a financial institution combine(s) different education backgrounds and experience and expertise. This ensures that the different dimensions of sustainability (economic, social, environmental, etc.) are all taken into account, as well as various sectors and systems of society and economy that finance and sustainability relate to. For internal awareness raising, and in order to keep pace with new developments, continually alternating information, learning and training is essential.
- **Openness of attitude and action**: As a basic principle, even simply questioning what is established is good, since looking upwards helps raise standards, reduce risk and increase chances of success. Sustainability and sustainable finance mean new territory, innovation and change. Without being open minded, one cannot enter these fields and modify business as usual.
- **Analysis of relevance**: Relevance has several dimensions. First, there is the relevance from the point of view of sustainability: Is a certain topic actually linked to a significant issue of sustainable development?

  Second, is there a significant correlation between this topic and a given business, and will there be an impact?

  Third, is an assumed modification of a business relevant to the core business of an enterprise?[14]
- **Step by step**: To modify single pieces may lead to productive innovation. Trial and error means progress. With all the uncertainty and with all the reasons in favour of cautious change, obviously, in many areas and cases, the problem is not too little know-how, insufficient models or methods but a lack of implementation. While it might be appropriate radically to change business as usual, these fundamental shifts should not happen all at the same time. It is more practical to

---

[14] An example of a relevance analysis: Birnbaum et al. (2007).

begin gradually implementing sustainability where it has been identified as particularly relevant. In many cases, information, data and models are already available.[15]

- **Testing and learning**: Another crucial point is testing. Instead of endless debate and hesitation, just decide on a test, chose a relevant topic, an important part of the business, test it and learn from the outcome. Before drafting and publishing its sector policies, WestLB tested the underlying criteria for assessment either in a model or within single transactions.

- **Simplicity**: Keep it simple. Instead of trying to find the perfect method or data for every single item, focus instead on the pivotal things and make them doable and bankable. Too often, the endless sustainability debate is about the complexity of things. True, almost everything is complex. But should complexity paralyse us? It can be seen as a big contradiction that, with regard to sustainability, the world is restrained while, at the same time, there are many possibilities and opportunities, because the world is not predetermined; the question is how we want to deal with specific issues. Once it is analysed, what is relevant (see above) to the issues and changes usually should be quite simple.

- **Transparency**: Building coalitions and sharing the results of a test are, of course, a great help and are closely linked with testing and learning.[16] Transparency creates both a race to the top between different market participants and competitors as well as feedback loops for adjustment and improvement between market participants and stakeholders. Being transparent about banking can also be seen as a sort of taboo, but it is hardly ever necessary nor useful to be transparent about a particular transaction. WestLB gained reputation on sound risk management and on its innovative sustainable business strategy by being transparent on its related policies and approaches.

3.2 Sustainable Finance as a Matter of Mindset

The above-listed principles and elements lay the foundations for a mindset that enables decisive sustainable finance. But what constitutes a certain mindset is more complex and difficult to catch. It also includes intangible elements of a discourse and sentiments that sometimes, wrongly, are not considered real or material or relevant. In fact, the innovations described above taken by WestLB could only

---

[15] The discourse on sustainable development and sustainable finance produces an ongoing great number of analyses and methods to systematically change business as usual by incorporating relevant issues. A pragmatic and effective way for this is the decisive use of ESG key performance indicators, such as the ones developed by DVFA et al.: cf. http://www.dvfa.de/publikationen/standards/kpis-for-esg/. Also the decisive implementation of (minimum and/or exclusion) criteria for, e.g. lending is relatively easy to achieve but still rare with respect to relevance (cf. Sect. 3.1). And there are many more available, also complex data bases and criteria and methods.

[16] For example, Beckmann et al. (2007).

happen because there were also intangible elements such as confidence and conviction and a sense of ownership and responsibility that helped to systematically incorporate sustainability issues and to overcome inactivity, reserve and rejection. These correlations and their effect are examined in more detail below.

With a few exceptions, almost everything in society and the economy is up for decision most of the time. This means it is up to us to shape it the way we think reasonable. Time and again, we hear remarks such as

> "It would be good to have less pressure from the capital markets so that we do not have to invest all our resources in such an unsustainable way just to be able to present the best next quarterly report, but the economic system forces us to do so". Or,
> "We would like to take more responsibility, but liability law does not allow it".

Without being naïve, one can say neither the economic system nor the legal system is God given. We are deciding what these systems look like and what is perceived as a factual constraint and what is not. These wide playing fields and the indeterminacy are actually an advantage and offer the possibility of pragmatic solutions as well as a certain inherent spirit or even beauty. This spirit may simply be communicated by even worn-out interjections such as

> "Just do it", "Walk the talk", or even, "Yes we can" and "Another world is possible".

Another world *is* possible. And this spirit is appealing and optimistic since it creates a self-amplifying power. This power helps translate sustainability considerations and connects them to the economic system that can then easily be adjusted. Coming back to the economy (stupid), even the biggest romantic and completely emotional thing can attract money and generate return. Aren't the capital markets addicted to stories, dreams and creation? The political system and regulation on their part react to the economic system. Confidentially changing and shaping the way business is proceeded consequently create the opportunity to influence politics and regulation, be it on avoidable or unavoidable issues and challenges.[17]

The history of the development of society and the economy can be seen as a long list of major shifts in thought and action. To a wide extent, it is an irrational power, vision and our own volition that has brought us to where we are with progress. At the same time, there is automatically always a rational counterforce, and, through discourse and argument, a vision becomes translatable into sound concept and practice, a system of checks and balances.

A financial institution's self-conception can also be considered as part of the mindset. Banks do not operate in empty air space nor do they operate on the moon. They depend on and profit from a functioning societal, economic, political and legal environment, which also place demands on financial institutions. It is a give-and-take model where banks must fulfil a duty in their own interests.[18]

---

[17] cf. (social) systems theory by Niklas Luhmann.

[18] cf. O'Dwyer (2003).

The image of a financial institution, a product or a service is a relevant topic in this context. The phenomenon image and the worth it has in a market, for example, as a liable partner or as a quality brand, is more proof of the importance of intangible assets, difficult to pin down or to express in figures or even money, but unquestionably very material. A good reputation is worth much.

At the same time, and with regard to the challenges posed by unsustainable development mentioned above, this is less of a theoretical or idealistic approach but rather a pragmatic, compromising and interdisciplinary approach, which has proved that much is possible even when it is generally believed that little is possible.

Reducing it down to day-to-day business, it may be useful not to predict, wait for or negate the possibility of catastrophes and disaster, be they flooding or subprime crisis. Having a Plan B already prepared, tested and applied to certain areas of business seems sensible and just about possible.

3.2.1 A Bank That Does Not Lend

One thing is crucial to how a bank is perceived: what is financed and what is not. Some market participants boast that they finance renewable energy and argue that this is their contribution to sustainable development. Why is it so unpopular just not to finance something? It is probably because of both alleged taboos and the underlying mindset. With regard to risks and to a financial institution's self-conception, real change and a contribution to sustainable development have to mean not financing things that are clearly unsustainable. Again, doing this little by little in certain areas of the business, by excluding certain things and explaining why, can bring fundamental change without leading to the collapse of a system and its acting units. One thing is certain: there will always be something to finance. The example of WestLB and its approaches, for example, to coal, prove that it is very possible to advance this way.

3.2.2 A Pragmatic Dualism for Risk Reduction and Competitive Advantage

The dualism of elements of fundamental change on the one hand and the offer of solutions to adapt to existing problems of unsustainable economic activity on the other are the ways to avoid moral hazard. A good example of this, again, is climate change. It is fine to develop and sell weather derivatives, such as cat bonds, a promising market. These derivatives can be very useful to farmers. But the main point is, with regard to weather derivatives, it is possible to buy time to a certain extent for real change. It is short-term thinking to believe that weather derivatives alone will lead far, because end of the road solutions do not tackle problems at their root. An encompassing approach always has to deal with both dimensions of this dualism. And this goes hand in hand with market competition. It is about short-term flexibility and opportunism, on the one hand, and long-term preparation, on the other—a forward-looking business model as a competitive advantage.

Climate Change and Competitiveness

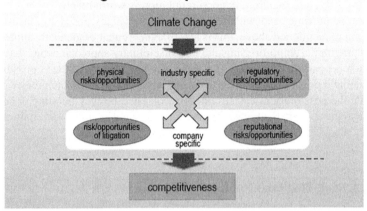

The chart illustrates the impacts and interdependency that a given sustainability issue (climate change in this case) can have on competiveness. As described earlier, it is assumed that these issues are inherent anyway to a particular transaction, enterprise, etc. Consequently, there are the options of being at the mercy of these impacts or co-shaping the effects. Certainly, innovation and progress are an investment. It is costly at first, and sometimes the outcome is unpredictable. But there is no way around it. The question is, how much investment, when and carried out by whom. Convincing arguments for making these investments are inherent to pure market logic.[19] It is a risk-reducing approach, the avoidance of too high risks. How much is at risk? If it is material or even fundamental, one has to draw a line somewhere. The existing economic system already offers many self-regulating elements that indicate the size of a risk, for example, in case a certain thing is not insurable, or if something is not asset backed, etc. Be it subprime crisis or the damage caused by extreme weather events, it is not always possible to bear these risks or the possible losses by trading, transferring and sharing them. A truly robust business has to investigate and to invest in its foundations and its conduct.

---

[19] cf. Neuneyer et al. (2005).

4 The Race to the Top: The Way Forward and Final Remarks

Never change a winning team. To a great extent, business for financial institutions is (still) running well, difficult to believe considering the market distortions since the subprime crisis since 2007. Be they subprime crisis or climate change, the challenges posed by unsustainable development seem to evoke a reflex pattern of behaviour: there is much effort to keep banking as it is and to stick to the paradigm of free markets and not to interlink with other aspects. But every closed system lacks something, and every boundary hinders something. Of course it would be unwise to change everything overnight. Or simply to open the doors and start a huge range of activities all at once. Anarchy would not get us very far. But the first and absolutely crucial thing is to allow ourselves free-thinking, to play around, to try and test and to put something into action against the hard-and-fast rules. Every rule has an exception and both are essential to long-term survival; sometimes it may be even appropriate to permute them.

The Equator Principles'[20] initiative is probably the most popular example of a set of sustainability standards that were agreed and established between an increasing number of members and market participants. This common approach was new territory and WestLB was among the small group of founding members. The Equator Principles have had a wide influence in raising awareness of sustainability considerations in financial institutions, and the members of the initiative benefited from being able to set a standard that quickly became a requirement of a significant share of the market participants. Today, on the other hand, with more than 70 member organisations, it has become increasingly difficult to agree on a standard that has significant relevance in respect of the growing need for development and substantial incorporation of sustainability aspects in finance. Agreement and balance between too many particular interests generally leads to the lowest common denominator.

In order to keep pace with the challenges sustainability considerations pose to finance, it is essential to tier and to move on in smaller groups and/or even as an individual financial institution. This way, it is possible that different initiatives and standards amplify and correct each other. Transparency and publicity help to keep discourse and progress going.[21]

The list of sustainability challenges, developments but also available criteria, data and methods is long: be it the development of approaches to calculate carbon financed or the development of social and environmental minimum and exclusion criteria for metals and mining activities in emerging markets or a policy on hydraulic fracturing. While navigating a way through the maze, a good test question is whether a given object or activity seeking finance accords with or contradicts a

---

[20] http://www.equator-principles.com/.

[21] Balch (2012).

(self-)defined goal. For example, in the case of fracking, it may be less a question of under which circumstances it could be financed and more a question of whether it is actually a contribution to the proclaimed transformation called "Energiewende" respectively to sustainable development.

It is also possible to tackle even more complex financial products and services than simply project or corporate finance where the proceeds of funds are fully known. It seems promising just to focus on the most relevant issues to ensure that the material issues are identified and then to choose and test enough robust but not necessarily perfect methods to finally apply and develop these further. With regard to the interaction of regulation and self-regulation,[22] it is also essential to lobby for and not against the evident issues of sustainable development and to co-shape an adjusted business as usual, a sustainable finance.

References

Balch, O. (2012, November 15). Sustainable finance: how far have the Equator Principles gone? *The Guardian.* http://www.guardian.co.uk/sustainable-business/sustainable-finance-equator-principles

Beckmann, K. M., Pricewaterhousecoopers, A. G., & Horst, D. (2007). Nachhaltigkeitsberichterstattung im Kontext aktueller Anforderungen an die Unternehmenspublizität. Rechnungslegung und Corporate Governance: Reporting, Steuerung und Überwachung der Unternehmen im Umbruch, S. 97.

Birnbaum, L., et al. (2007). *Kosten und Potenziale der Vermeidung von Treibhausgasemissionen in Deutschland, study on behalf of Bundesverband der Deutschen Industrie (BDI).* Berlin: McKinsey & Company.

Camfferman, K., & Zeff, S. A. (2007). *Financial reporting and global capital markets: A history of the international accounting standards committee, 1973–2000.* Oxford: Oxford University Press.

Carr, M. (2012, April 12). WestLB, Oil platform lender, Won't do arctic, antarctic business. *Bloomberg Businessweek.* http://www.businessweek.com/news/2012-04-27/westlb-oil-platform-lender-won-t-do-arctic-antarctic-business

ESG key performance indicators. DVFA et al. http://www.dvfa.de/publikationen/standards/kpis-for-esg/

Financial Sector Guidance for Corporate Value Chain (Scope 3) Accounting and Reporting. http://www.ghgprotocol.org/feature/financial-sector-guidance-corporate-value-chain-scope-3-accounting-and-reporting

Herrmann, G. (2012, April 20). Albtraum Arktis. Wegen Umweltgefahren warnen Experten vor eine Rohstoff-Euphorie im hohen Norden. Die WestLB schliesst solche Geschäfte aus. *Süddeutsche Zeitung,* 25.

Kristof, K., & Hennicke, P. (2010). Mögliche Kernstrategien für eine zukunftsfähige Ressourcenpolitik der Bundesregierung: Ökologische Modernisierung vorantreiben und Naturschranken ernst nehmen. *Ressourceneffizienz Papier, 7.* Jg.

Malevergne, Y., & Sornette, D. (2006). *Extreme financial risks.* Heidelberg: Springer.

Meadows, H. D. (1972). *Limits to growth.* New York: Universe Books.

---

[22] See Sarro (2012).

Neuneyer, D., et al. (2005). *Ökologische und soziale Nachhaltigkeit als Werttreiber. Corporate Governance, Unternehmensverantwortung und Berichterstattung.*

O'Dwyer, B. (2003). Conceptions of corporate social responsibility: The nature of managerial capture. *Accounting, Auditing and Accountability Journal, 16.* Jg., Nr. 4, S. 523–557.

Onischka, M., Neuneyer, D., & Kristof, K. (2007). *Financial markets – Ready for climate change.* Wuppertal: Ergebnisse einer Befragung von Finanzmarktexperten.

Sarro, D. (2012). Do lenders make effective regulators? An assessment of the equator principles on project finance. *German Law Journal, 13.* Jg., Nr. 12, S. 1522–1555.

Schneider, A., & Schmidpeter, R. (2012). Corporate social responsibility: Verantwortungsvolle Unternehmensführung in Theorie und Praxis.

Summary Response by Equator Principles Association to the Equator Principles Strategic Review Report. http://www.equator-principles.com

The Equator Principles. http://www.equator-principles.com/

The World Commission on Environment and Development's. (1987). (The Brundtland Commission) report Our Common Future. Oxford: Oxford University Press.

WestLB/Portigon AG Sustainability Management. http://www.portigon.com/sustainability

Managing Assets in a Complex Environment: An Innovative Approach to Sustainable Decision-Making

Barnim G. Jeschke

Abstract In a world of accelerating innovation cycles and expanding plurality of interests, corporate environments become increasingly complex. This is particularly true for asset management efforts, with their long-term implications and manifold impacts on investment prospects. This chapter explores the matter of business environment complexity and related challenges for sustainable decision-making. It discusses key aspects of the issue, categorises related approaches and derives criteria for complex decision support. Finally, the innovative approach of SUDEST ("Sustainable Decision Support Tool") is introduced. I developed SUDEST with Nils Mahnke, Professor of Applied Mathematics, as a pragmatic approach for corporate decision-makers. Part of this contribution is adopted from Jeschke and Mahnke (2013: 94–111).

1 Corporate Challenges

Investment activities demand a clear vision of the future. On the one hand, long-term business models need to be planned and appreciated with regard to their return and risk perspectives. On the other hand, active asset management calls for an anticipatory view on change and adjustment measures throughout the investment life cycle. A complex decision environment is likely to bring forth non-linear developments. Therefore, management needs to understand the underlying complexity—and to translate such information into future scenarios and proactive development. Compliance directives—such as the Global Reporting Initiative or the IFC Performance Standards—will help companies to avoid unethical business practice. However, they will not do the job of creating prudent business strategies. Hence, ethical corporate principles (e.g. Garriga and Domènec 2004) need to translate into commercial business analysis, striving for long-term legitimisation of a commercially sound business model.

B.G. Jeschke (✉)
Sustainable Management, FOM University of Applied Sciences, Munich, Germany
e-mail: barnim.jeschke@fom.de

© Springer International Publishing Switzerland 2015
K. Wendt (ed.), *Responsible Investment Banking*, CSR, Sustainability, Ethics & Governance, DOI 10.1007/978-3-319-10311-2_43

Investments are about rewarding returns in the light of estimated risk levels. Their vehicle is the facilitation of value-adding business models. The generation of such value demands innovation. Fertile ground for innovation is a dynamic environment. Such an environment calls for adequate tools of analysis—and ongoing learning efforts.

Resilience can be understood as the level of organisational stress tolerance towards external disturbance: The more anticipatory and flexible the investment strategy, the higher the ability to respond to unexpected occurrences and the lower the involved risk level. In nature, system's resilience is warranted by genetic diversity. With respect to human resources, it has been empirically proven that a higher level of diversity supports organisational resilience and performance—as it provides a wider range of possible reaction schemes (e.g. Hong and Page 2004). Sustainable investments are characterised by sound long-term commercial prospects, combined with a high level of resilience.

2 Grasping the Corporate Context

Decision-makers need to have a clear understanding of the underlying decision environment. Diffuse monitoring approaches will produce diffuse information. Contrary, an environment scanning approach that is too narrowly defined (e.g. only referring to directly interacting market players) is prone to miss the overall PESTEL picture.[1] Instead, implications of a complex environment need to be analysed systematically—and the explored system needs to be evaluated in the light of corporate interests.

2.1 Analysing Complexity

Systems theory provides a useful methodological basis for pinpointing complexity (e.g. Forrester 1977). Companies are viewed as open subsystems, interacting with its superordinate system (i.e. its corporate environment). The complexity of such superordinate system stands for the complexity of the relevant business context.

What factors constitute complexity and what are their implications for adequate analysis? The discussion on such characteristics (e.g. Sargut and McGarth 2011) boils down to four parameters characterising the design of a system: multiplicity, interdependency, diversity and dynamics:

- Multiplicity: How many elements describe the underlying system? Such system elements are either decision subjects (stakeholders) or decision objects (products that are subject to stakeholders' interaction).

---

[1] PESTEL refers to a company's macro environment with respect to political, economical, social, technological, ecological and legal matters.

- Interdependency: In how far are system elements intertwined in a bundle of interrelating cause/effect schemes? This parameter stands for the magnitude of system elements' interaction.
- Diversity: To what extent are system elements and the nature of their interrelations similar or dissimilar? Diversity can be operationalised by looking at the way relevant characteristics of the system elements deviate from the average.
- Dynamics: In how far are both, the set of relevant elements and their interrelations, subject to change over time? In how far—and to what magnitude—have stakeholders or relationship patterns changed within a given time period, and in how far can they be expected to do so in the future?

System complexity increases with increasing multiplicity, interdependency, diversity and dynamism of its constituting system elements. At the same time, each of the four complexity parameters claims its own specific management response: High multiplicity calls for a widened environmental scanning approach, typically reaching beyond directly interacting market partners. With a high degree of elements' interdependency, causal analysis will be required to grasp the "big picture". Otherwise, chances are that management focuses attention on symptoms, not causes. Highly diverse systems challenge corporate analysis to appreciate the particularities of the individual system elements. Flexibility and coordinative capacities are required to translate diversity into business implications. Finally, with increasing environmental dynamics, some continuous monitoring with early warning signals is required to continuously update on the business environment.

Dichotomising these parameters leads to a set of 16 types of system design, as illustrated in Fig. 1.

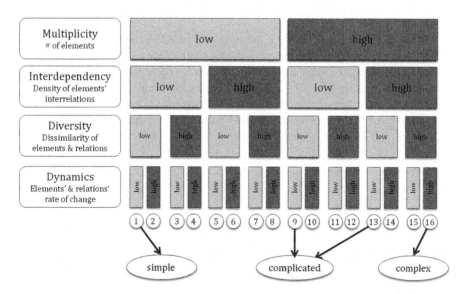

Fig. 1 Types of system design

Due to their limited degree of complexity, simple situations (1)—as they are quite common in our everyday life—can be interpreted with intuition. Complicated situations (9, 13), in contrast, will require support. Software programs, for instance, typically incorporate numerous variables (high multiplicity), either intensely inter-related or not (low/high interdependency). As a rather mechanistic tool, such pro-grams will appreciate all variables' effects with a binary code (low diversity), with the algorithmic functions remaining stable over time (low dynamics). Complex systems (16), in contrast, require a different rationale than a pure mechanistic one to account for environmental dynamics.

Take, for example, the German company Sanovita that produces natural calcite- and zeolite-based farming inputs. The company's business relates to three different types of system design, implying three different business models and management approaches:

- "Soil applications" are dedicated to the re-cultivation of degraded arable land by employing natural soil conditioners. The underlying system design is relatively simple: Treatment recipes are alike, no matter whether the project is situated in Costa Rica or Ghana. The set of relevant treatment parameters as well as their interrelations are limited (low multiplicity, low interdependency), their proper-ties are similar around the world (low diversity) and effectiveness schemes do not appear to change over time. Here, treatment recipes can be developed and standardised for global use.
- "Animal applications" refer to animal feed additives strengthening the animals' immune system. The respective system design is complicated: Industrial live-stock farming implies manifold aspects (high multiplicity). However, the system properties of this business model are comparable in their properties and stable over time (low diversity, low dynamics). Here, elaborated quantitative model-ling is required.
- "Plant applications" refer to the increase of crop yields and plant strengthening by employing foliar fertilisers and bio-stimulants. This matter is a complex one: Treatment recipes differ from crop to crop; moreover, climate and weather conditions require ongoing adjustment of the respective treatment approach, differing from region to region and from year to year. Here, sophisticated monitoring provides tailor-made and continuously updated solutions; further, agricultural engineers need to warrant flexible application approaches on the spot.

2.2 System Mapping

How can the context of a complex investment decision be described? As a first step, relevant stakeholders need to be identified and described. Stakeholders are interest groups whose aims are either in consent or dissent to corporate ones (Freeman 1984). Consequently, they are inclined to impact company's action, either positively (i.e. by consent) or negatively (i.e. by dissent), directly or indirectly and actually or potentially. This includes people, or groups of people, who are not currently interacting with the respective company (e.g. action groups) and, therefore, might be off the company's radar.

From the decision-maker's point of view, stakeholders' dispositions shall be described by the following aspects:

- Level of interest: Is the stakeholder's interest in consent or dissent to the interest of the decision-maker?
- Intensity of interest: How strong is the respective stakeholder interest as compared to the decision-maker's interest?
- Power: What is the impact potential of the respective stakeholder to enforce his interests towards the decision-maker—and other involved stakeholders?
- Aggressiveness: How ready is the respective stakeholder to exploit his power potential towards the decision-maker's interests?

In a given time period, stakeholders may either impact or may be impacted by other stakeholders. Translated into cybernetic terminology, they may act as independent or dependent system variable. Both impact flows, of course, may occur within the same time frame.

What are stakeholders'—and company's—interests all about? They are about resources, as "decision objects": Decision objects are measurable products which are relevant for the system and, therefore, subject to stakeholders' interests, impact and exchange. Such interests may either favour the increase or decrease of respective product quantities or adopt a neutral attitude. In line with Elkington's (1997) triple bottom line concept, such products may be of an economic, social or ecologic dimension:

- Product examples with economical connotation: profit, tax, liquidity, brand equity, customer churn rate, quantities of value chain-related materials and waste.
- Product examples with ecological connotation: soil, water and air quality (i.e. quantities of certain quality-relevant chemical ingredients), biodiversity, climate or energy.
- Product examples with social connotation: health and educational parameters, numbers and type of accidents, purchase power, income or even a "happiness index".
- Obviously, the listed product examples can be specified and operationalised at different levels of detail; water quality, for instance, may be measured by its underlying biological and chemical oxygen demand levels.

The distinction between decision subjects and objects is essential to approach reality. Reality is about exchanging products—but it is also about human dispositions. If corporate incident management, for instance, aims at cutting down on accidents at company's construction sites, both stakeholder and product levels are essential for comprehending the situation: products may refer to safety equipment, maintenance standards of involved machinery or the educational level of the workers. System understanding, however, will also need to include the dispositions of the stakeholders involved, e.g. with respect to attitudes towards safety measures. In essence, stakeholder decisions are not self-sufficient, but they are about increasing or decreasing certain system-relevant product quantities.

Products, in turn, impact other products (i.e. product quantities) as well as other stakeholder interests. Consequently, system mapping needs to identify a relevant set of system elements as well as possible cross-impacting relations amongst such elements. Underlying relationships may be of a linear, more likely though of a non-linear nature. Figure 2 describes a situation for a given time period. The situation is expressed by four sub-matrices:

(a)   The interaction amongst impacting and impacted stakeholders.
(b)   The interaction amongst impacting stakeholders and impacted products.
(c)   The interaction amongst impacting and impacted products.
(d)   The interaction amongst impacting products and impacted stakeholders.

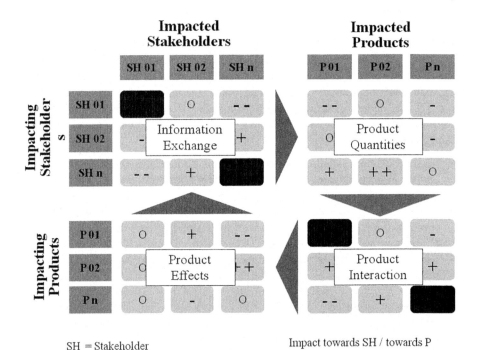

Fig. 2 SUDEST situation matrix

The causal chain for corporately impacted situations is initiated by the information exchange between impacting and impacted stakeholders. Such interaction will affect the existence and quantities of system-relevant products. Varying product quantities may lead to product interaction without any direct human stakeholder impact. The resulting changes of product quantities will, in turn, impact stakeholder interests.

Each matrix cell contains the functional relationship (here depicted as algebraic signs) between impacting and impacted force. The self-referencing diagonal cells are marked black as they will not be part of the cross-impact analysis (Lunz 2012). In case a situation would, for instance, not include any product interaction, the cell values of the "product interaction" sub-matrix would remain neutral, not affecting the ensuing steps of analysis.

For long-term investments, stakeholder mapping needs to forecast potential stakeholders along the investment life cycle—and to derive corresponding scenarios. Investors should not be taken by surprise because of "sudden opposition", as, for instance, it appears to be the case for quite a few infrastructure projects.

Early exchange of opinions—also and especially towards contrary stakeholder groups—will help to identify and influence business scenarios. Internet connectivity and emerging new media platforms tend to support anticipatory communication flows, including online surveys, chat rooms, focus groups and digital voting.

Current knowledge may allow the description of assumed relationships with elaborated quantitative algorithms. In other cases, only qualitative or unconfirmed data will be available to depict reality. And causal chain analysis should assist in exploring ulterior motives and basic concerns of the involved parties.

3 The Quest for Sustainable Decision-Making

About 10 years ago, I invested in a biofuel technology. Elsbett (developer of the first modern diesel engine injection system, the turbo charged "tdi") had developed a conversion kit to operate diesel engines with pure plant oils (not to be confused with esterified biodiesel; see Jeschke 2009). Due to rapidly increasing fossil fuel prices, this business model hyped, on the basis of an excise duty exemption on biofuels. However, this trend abruptly stalled with the upcoming discussion "food over feed, feed over fuel". What had happened? Elsbett had pursued a business perspective which was too limited. Within the analysed system boundaries, they had neglected the fact that arable land was "better" (i.e. more sustainably) used for food production rather than for biofuel crops. Moreover, while Elsbett cooperated with the Malaysian Palm Oil Board, cleared rain forests were converted into oil palm and soy plantations. At a superordinate system level, the pursued business model was causing more ecological damage than benefit. In a dynamic environment, Elsbett had ignored crucial system's knowledge jeopardising the whole venture. Sustainable management is about long-term business prospects. It is about stabilising the underlying system so that such system legitimises the corporate impact in the long run.

Decision-making is about selecting amongst alternative action paths. While discrete decisions aim at a defined set of alternatives, non-discrete decisions (such as the allocation of an advertising budget) need to consider a continuous range of decision scenarios. As information basis, decisions need to appreciate the business context. According to systems theory, such a context is described by the open system in which corporate business is embedded. This idea is derived from nature and, consequently, elaborated by natural sciences. While reflections on ecosystems emphasise interrelations of system elements in a given time period, reflections on biological evolution have added the aspect of dynamics by analysing the development of systems over time. Consequently, such deliberations have entered the world of social sciences by referring to bio-cybernetics (e.g. Wiener 1948; Ashby 1956; Cruse 1981) or, in Europe, by elaborating on its implications for business organisations (e.g. Ulrich 1968).

"Sustainable" management decisions shall refer to corporate action that supports the long-term equilibrium of the underlying system. Further, "absolute" sustainable management can be distinguished from "relative" sustainable management. Absolute sustainable management helps to stabilise a system in the long run with respect to specified system products, e.g. by introducing technologies that facilitate resource efficiencies. While relative sustainable business models destabilise a system, the destabilising impact is lower than that of the prior business conduct. In contrast, non-sustainable behaviour focuses only on selected system products, disregarding overall system stability and, therefore, perpetuity.

What does this mean for the corporate decision-maker? Decisions are about influencing the product quantities. Such impact may either support or hamper the perpetuity of the system itself—as defined within specified system boundaries. If corporate action stabilises the underlying system, such action will be viewed as "absolutely" sustainable. If corporate action still destabilises a system, but with less magnitude than before, such action can be viewed as "relatively" sustainable.

For an investor, the magnitude of risk management depends on the kind of investment and on the investor's role throughout the project life cycle. Figure 3 illustrates the contingencies of corporate risk management.

Technical commodity day trading would be an example for selective/discrete investment decisions, sporadically focusing on entry and exit signals. Would such commodities be subject to a real-life business model, e.g. by investing in sugar cane plantations, decision flows would become more continuous, e.g. responding to local weather conditions or suitable cultivation methods; in turn, risk management becomes more focused. Focused risk management also derives from selective but non-discrete situations, e.g. in case of periodical decisions at nonexecutive board meetings. However, whenever the decider attains a more prominent role (e.g. as the leading underwriter), he/she will exercise his influence throughout the project life cycle, pursuing a comprehensive risk management approach.

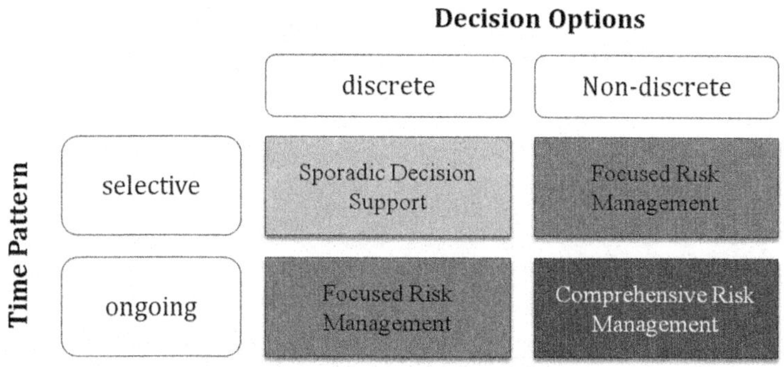

Decision Options

	discrete	Non-discrete
selective	Sporadic Decision Support	Focused Risk Management
ongoing	Focused Risk Management	Comprehensive Risk Management

Time Pattern

Fig. 3 Risk management contingencies

4 Approaches Supporting Sustainable Management

How can management approaches support corporate decision-making with respect to sustainable action that protects corporate legitimacy in the long run? How can they point out critical stakeholder, critical products, critical interrelations and the best way to transform such knowledge into sustainable, yet commercially viable sense?

According to their respective propositions, approaches can be categorised into descriptive, evaluative and prescriptive approaches:

- Descriptive approaches are dedicated to objectively describing past results of corporate decisions and actions. While such ex post analysis may serve as a valuable information basis for future planning, the implications of past findings cannot be readily extrapolated in a dynamic, non-linear environment.
- Evaluative approaches are normative but, again, refer to findings of the past. They do so by employing a retrospective view without direct reference to future decision-making. Therefore, their informational value may be useful—but limited with respect to future system scenarios.
- In contrast, prescriptive approaches focus on simulating future outcomes reflected by a given value system.

Figure 4 categorises sustainable management approaches by their propositions and their applicability. As for the latter, "specific" (i.e. with a particular

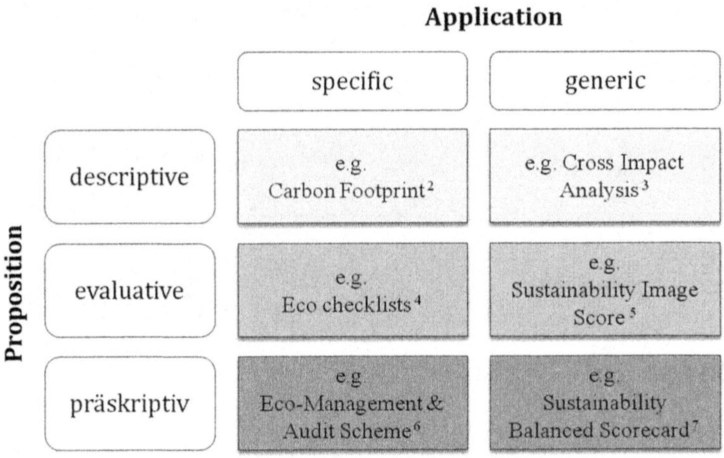

Application

	specific	generic
descriptive	e.g. Carbon Footprint[2]	e.g. Cross Impact Analysis[3]
evaluative	e.g. Eco checklists[4]	e.g. Sustainability Image Score[5]
präskriptiv	e.g. Eco-Management & Audit Scheme[6]	e.g. Sustainability Balanced Scorecard[7]

Proposition (left side label)

Fig. 4 Categorised approaches supporting sustainable management

application focus) and "generic" (i.e. generally applicable) approaches are distinguished.[2–7]

Descriptive approaches—such as the Carbon Footprint—may refer to specific system parameters (such as certain greenhouse gases or customer retention indicators) by objectively looking at the implications of previous corporate action. Generic approaches like the cross-impact analysis will be generally applicable in describing different system environments.

Evaluative approaches assess previous corporate behaviour based on a value system. Here, specific approaches such as checklist approaches or certifications refer to a clearly defined set of parameters. Other approaches, e.g. the Sustainability Image Score, are designed more flexibly in their scope of application.

In contrast, prescriptive approaches are dedicated to future corporate action and outcomes, either with regard to specific parameters—as with the EMAS approach—or in a more general way, as with the Sustainability Balanced Scorecard.

In principle, generic-prescriptive approaches are the most appropriate concept to support future decision-making. In particular, an approach that supports complex decision-making needs to respond to three challenges:

- A situation mapping, adequately reflecting and projecting the relevant corporate environment.
- An analysis approach able to describe multifold short- and long-term interrelating effects amongst the relevant system elements.

---

[2] Kranke (2010).

[3] Asan et al. (2004).

[4] Bihr and Deyhle (2000).

[5] Serviceplan Group (2014).

[6] EMAS (2010).

[7] Hahn and Wagner (2001).

- A monitoring routine tracking down changing patterns over time, fuelling an ever-learning organisation with relevant information on how to continuously adjust its decision-making approach.

5 SUDEST: An Innovative Decision Support Tool

As a generically applicable, prescriptive approach, SUDEST is based on a four step analysis: context analysis, scope of action, simulation of scenario outcomes and continuous learning.

5.1 SUDEST Context Analysis

The context analysis starts with the specification of the underlying system and its system boundaries. Complex decisions may refer to a single choice between two or more discrete alternatives without follow-up decisions to be considered for the future, e.g. the selection of a consumable object for purchase. More likely, however, complex decisions will require a consecutive string of decisions along an evolving situation. Corporate talent management, for instance, may start with job descriptions, recruitment procedures and employment contracts. The succeeding decision phases would then include trainee programs and feedback schemes. Further, career counselling, promotion planning and advanced training may guide a talent along the different steps of a corporate career path. To cut down on this overall picture will support failure in attaining corporate interests, e.g. by witnessing the migration of highly talented trainees due to the lack of adequate in-house career perspectives.

A consecutive decision complex is broken down chronologically into decision phases and subsumed decision moments. A decision moment is the most detailed level of system analysis, compiled as the SUDEST situation matrix (see Fig. 2), aggregating all changes from the preceding decision interval. Figure 5 illustrates the example of a production plant project.

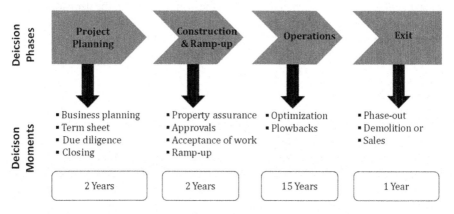

Fig. 5 Decision complex structuring (example: production plant)

From project planning to the final disinvestment, such project may last over 20 years. And initial decisions (e.g. on the business model design) will have long-term effects on the success of the project outcome (e.g. ongoing cost structures).

The overall process is described by four consecutive phases that shall be called "decision phases". A decision phase (e.g. the initial "project planning" phase) may subsume one or more system-relevant decisions that shall be called "decision moments" (e.g. the business planning). Each decision moment is governed by a set of simultaneous decisions made by stakeholders to influence other stakeholders at a specific point in time. In the example, the project planning phase typically refers to a stakeholder map which is limited to a small circle of parties. In contrast, the approvals within the decision phase "construction and ramp-up" will involve numerous stakeholders.

As earlier decisions (of preceding decision phases) impact later decisions (of succeeding decision phases), the initial project planning phase needs to anticipate the long-term implications for such a project. A less foresightful planning will most probably result in a less favourable starting position for the following construction phase.

A decision complex—understood as the sum of decision phases—can be a one-way street with defined starting point and end. Such straight-line decisions refer to a one-off stimulus of corporate decision-makers towards the system. In contrast, repetitive decision complexes are designed periodically, representing a repetitive constellation of preceding and succeeding decision phases.

Sciarelli and Tani (2013) review a wide array of stakeholder approaches, categorising them with respect to the decision-makers' stakeholder map and the way interrelations beyond the direct relations between stakeholder and enterprise are considered. Here, the category "Complete Network" approach considers both indirect relationships towards the enterprise but also amongst the stakeholders themselves: "This perspective will help managers get a holistic view of the environment and the actors operating in it as it will let them understand how the various stakeholders are related to each other" (Sciarelli and Tani 2013: 183). This approach is consistent with the contextual approach of SUDEST. The relevance of stakeholders is not governed by the directness of their ties to the decision-maker. Rather, it is a function of their overall system impact—and resulting repercussions for corporate interests.

5.1.1 Scope of Action

The scope of action stands for the range of conceivable decision alternatives. Such alternatives may either be clearly defined (e.g. alternative marketing approaches for customer retention management) or rather diffuse (e.g. "the best way of keeping existing customers happy"). Without specifiable action alternatives, of course, there is nothing to decide. Therefore, the corporate decider needs to respond to the following set of questions:

- At which point of the chronologically structured decision context is the corporate decider requested to take action (i.e. to impact the system)? Or, translated into SUDEST terminology: Which decision phase(s) and which specific decision moment(s) are subject to analysis?
- What kind of influence is the corporate decider inclined to exercise? Or, translated into SUDEST terminology: Which stakeholder or product relationships are subject to corporate management as an impacting stakeholder?
- What does such corporate action imply? Or, translated into SUDEST terminology: Which independent variables are impacting the consent/dissent profiles of the targeted stakeholder as well as the product quantities that are—directly or indirectly—impacted by stakeholder action?

5.1.2 Simulation of Scenario Outcomes

While the preceding SUDEST steps of analysis are dedicated to a standardised and systematised analysis, the model is now ready for the actual simulation. Possible simulation approaches are (a) the variation of initial values (i.e. corporate context assumptions), (b) the variation of corporate input at specific decision moments or (c) the variation of decision intervals (i.e. time between decision moments).

The simulation itself focuses on different decision outcomes for different time frames and decision scenarios. The product of chronologically ordered decision moment matrices—as the most detailed entities of analysis—results in the decision phase matrix. Further, the product of consecutive decision phase matrices results in the overall system matrix, representing the whole decision complex (see Fig. 6).

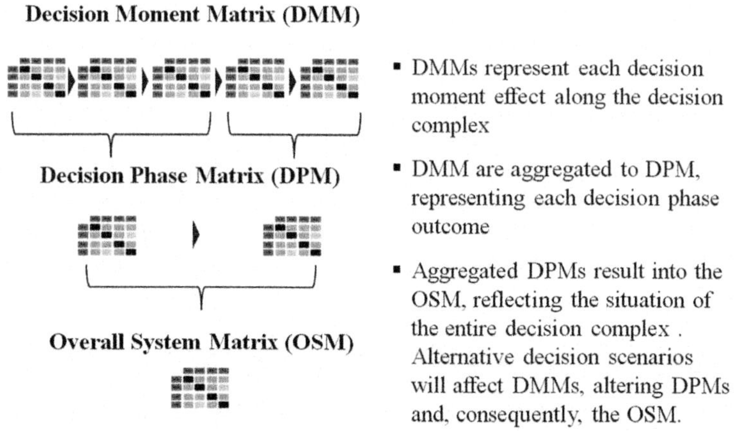

Decision Moment Matrix (DMM)

Decision Phase Matrix (DPM)

Overall System Matrix (OSM)

- DMMs represent each decision moment effect along the decision complex
- DMM are aggregated to DPM, representing each decision phase outcome
- Aggregated DPMs result into the OSM, reflecting the situation of the entire decision complex . Alternative decision scenarios will affect DMMs, altering DPMs and, consequently, the OSM.

Fig. 6 Modular design of SUDEST matrices

For the simulation of future scenarios, simulated results of a preceding decision phase will create the starting point for the directly succeeding phase, which is given by a set of stakeholder dispositions and product quantities. As each decision moment refers to all changes in the preceding decision interval and, therefore, to a complex decision situation, it will be described by individual decision moment-related matrices ("DMM").

Mathematically, the set of initial values of stakeholder dispositions and product quantities on which the decision moment matrices will act as functions of change are assorted in a row vector. For the starting point of the system analysis, this vector shall be called the initial vector. SUDEST data processing results in a matrix cascade of indicators, establishing a comprehensive information basis for the respective decision scenario. The emerging data set includes:

- Development of consent/dissent profiles of the involved stakeholders.
- Development of involved product quantities.
- Sensitivity of alternative action paths with respect to decision implications.
- Resilience levels for the derived scenarios plus resilience drivers and opponents with regard to their system impact.

In systems theory, the concept of resilience is typically used to describe system stability (e.g. Hamel and Välikangas 2003). In SUDEST terminology, resilience properties are explored by looking at the stability of system-relevant product quantities over time and under different impact scenarios. While resilience itself is not a normative concept, favourable resilience would be identified by looking at the desirability of the stabilised products.

Another useful mathematical figure is the nil potency. In case of periodic systems, when the decision phase matrices stay constant for each time period, the nil potency explores after how many periods a matrix product would become a nil matrix (absolute nil potency). In other words, after how many decision moments do relevant product quantities get reduced to zero? "Life expectancy" would be an example for the application of nil potency, relating to the previously mentioned case of "individual health" as the underlying system.

The aforementioned "key indicator" in the cascade is derived from the scalar product of the initial vector values with the final vector. Each change in the system leads to a change in the key indicator, as it represents a condensed comparison value of all changes. The relative importance of each decision moment (as laid down in each of the respective decision moment matrices) is expressed as a contribution to the key indicator. Thus, excluding a single decision phase matrix (DPM) in the calculation of the key indicator provides a measure of each DPM's impact.

Specifically, the resulting indicators provide information on the following aspects:

- At which decision moments do certain stakeholders become especially influential?
- Which interaction patterns have sensitive implications with regard to certain products, e.g. with respect to ongoing project costs or overall project profitability?

- Which trade-offs characterise the decision complex and what action alternatives can be derived?
- Which alternative action paths stabilise project resilience, thereby stabilising the amounts of relevant products?
- Looking at the overall, long-term picture, which action scenarios appear to be the most sustainable ones—and what are sustainability drivers and preventers?
- What are the commercial prospects of the derived scenarios?

5.1.3 Continuous Learning

Comprehending environmental dynamics requires continuous monitoring of relevant context drivers, i.e. of the system elements and its interrelationships. The employment of a decision support tool, therefore, asks for continuous organisational learning, both in psychological and administrative terms. Psychologically, new and unexpected information should not be coined as a disturbing nuisance but as an important stimulus for understanding system dynamics. Administratively, reporting systems and corporate planning need to incorporate the information requirements of such a tool. As a result, future scenarios (especially for repetitive decision complexes) can be anticipated with higher degrees of confidence, and corporate planning can make better use of the employed resources by incorporating system sensitivities.

Typically, situations will be described by qualitative information first, as in case of the discrete Likert scale used in Fig. 2. Increasing monitoring efforts are likely to bring out more elaborated data to analyse certain relationships. Take, as an example, the local sentiment towards an industrial settlement. Qualitative data may be used to broadly categorise various stakeholder groups (e.g. neighbours, municipality, ecological activist group) into supportive and nonsupportive parties. At a later stage, surveys may be able to provide a much more differentiated picture of consent and dissent profiles and relating motives.

Ongoing learning required a continuous comparison of planned effects and actual outcomes. Reviewing underlying assumptions will establish, increase and update system knowledge. As for SUDEST, new information can easily be incorporated into the modelling and simulation. Changing system maps are reflected in a modified matrix structure. Changing relationship patterns are appreciated by modified functions of the respective matrix cells. At the end, SUDEST application is about getting to know your system. This includes the issue of system boundaries: Do causal relationships reach beyond the current system definition so that the system perspective needs to be enlarged? SUDEST data should be part of the company's routine reporting activities. Highly sensitive, relevant information should be coined as key performance indicator (KPI).

6 Discussion

What value does SUDEST add to corporate decision-making? In terms of model output, SUDEST a) systematises and reflects complex situations for corporate decision-making, b) specifies and evaluates decision alternatives and c) operationalises sustainability effects of corporate action.

As a generic model, SUDEST is characterised by a wide range of application, especially for complex situations, e.g. approval procedures, infrastructure investments or change management projects. Other fields of application include value chain optimization, quality management approaches, corporate talent management or sales concepts.

However, decision support tools are no crystal balls; they support professional decision-making—but not professional data feed. According to the wisdom "garbage in-garbage out", corporate decision-makers need to be ready for the application. This presumes the willingness to reflect on a situation from different angles. Uncertainties or contradictory assessments should not discourage but invite to follow-ups.

In a discussion on innovative problem-solving approaches, Leclerc and Moldoveanu introduce five flexible solution "lenses", the so-called flexons (2013):

- The "networks flexon" refers to ". . . the decomposition of a situation into a series of linked problems of prediction (. . .) and optimisation (. . .) by presenting relationships among entities" (2013: 4–5).
- The "evolutionary flexon" suggests a test-and-learn approach, quickly filtering out suboptimal solutions within a setting of numerous variables.
- The "decision-agent flexon" reflects a problem by looking at it as "a series of competitive and cooperative interactions among agents" (2013: 6).
- The "system-dynamics flexon" develops a map of causal relationships along the evolving problem situation.
- Finally, the "information-processing flexon" is dedicated to a data generation approach that fills the blanks of a satisfactory decision basis most efficiently.

It seems as if SUDEST is suited to integrate such fragmented approaches into one consistent decision support tool.

References

Asan, U., Bozdag, C. E., & Polat, S. (2004). *A fuzzy approach to qualitative cross impact analysis.* Istanbul: Department of Industrial Engineering.

Ashby, W. R. (1956). *An introduction to cybernetics.* London: Chapman & Hall.

Bihr, D., & Deyhle, A. (2000). Early warning systems – Checklists. *Controllermagazin*, H4, Gaubing.

Cruse, H. (1981). Biological cybernetics – Introduction in the linear and non-linear system's theory. Verlag Chemie, Weinheim.

Elkington, J. (1997). *Cannibals with forks: The triple bottom line of 21st century business.* Oxford: Capstone

EMAS. (2010). EMAS Directives (EG) No. 1221/2009. European Parliament and Council. http://www.emas.de. February 5, 2014.

Forrester, J. W. (1977). *Industrial dynamics* (9th ed.). MIT Press, Cambridge

Freeman, R. E. (1984). *Strategic management. A stakeholder approach.* Boston: Pitman.

Garriga, E. D., & Domènec, M. (2004). Corporate social responsibility theories: Mapping the territory. *Journal of Business Ethics, 53*(1–2), 51–71.

Hahn, T., & Wagner, M. (2001). *Sustainability balanced scorecard: From theory to implementation.* Centre for Sustainable Management, Lueneburg.

Hamel, G., Välikangas, L (2003). The quest for resilience. *Harvard Business Review, 9*, Reprint R0309C, 1–13.

Hong, L., & Page, S. (2004). Groups of diverse problem solvers can outperform groups of high-ability problem solvers. *Proceedings of the National Academy of Sciences of the United States of America, 101*, 16385–16389.

Jeschke, B. G. (2009). Plant oil biofuel: Rationale, production and application. In: W. Soetaert, & E.J. Vandamme (Eds.), *Biofuels.* Chichester: Wiley.

Jeschke, B. G. & Mahnke, N. (2013, July–December). An innovative approach to sustainable decision-making in complex environments. *Business Systems Review, 2*(3), 94–111.

Kranke, A. (2010). How to compute the CO2 footprint. *VerkehrsRundschau, Issue, 51–52*, 36–38.

Leclerc, O., & Moldoveanu, M. (2013). Five routes to more innovative problem solving. *McKinsey Quarterly, 2013*, 1–11.

Lunz, J. (2012). *Incident-discrete systems* (2nd ed.). Wissenschaftsverlag, Munich.

Sargut, G., & McGarth, R. G. (2011). Learning to live with complexity. *Harvard Business Review, 9*, 1–10.

Sciarelli, M., & Tani, M. (2013). Network approach and stakeholder management. *Business Systems Review, 2(2)*, 175–190.

Serviceplan Group. (2014). *Sustainability Image Score 2013: Sustainability has arrived in the middle of society.* Serviceplan Gruppe. http://www.themenportal.de/wirtschaft/sustainability-image-score-2013-nachhaltigkeit-ist-in-der-mitte-der-gesellschaft-angekommen-82580. February 5, 2014.

Ulrich, H. (1968). *The enterprise as productive social system.* Haupt, Bern

Wiener, N. (1948). *Cybernetics.* MIT Press, New York.

Extra-Financial Performance Made Tangible: A Handprint Approach for Financial Institutions

Sebastian Philipps, Henrik Ohlsen, and Christina Raab

Abstract The financial industry has been engulfed in a crisis of confidence since 2007. This impacts strategic considerations in the industry and changes the immediate prospects of individual business areas and products. The authors of this chapter argue that financial institutions will face further potentially bigger challenges in the next 15 years. They propose a strategic tool to prepare for these challenges. The so-called handprint approach applies an expanded value concept. It reflects the economic, social and environmental added value generated by a financial institution. In contrast to exclusively risk-centred sustainability approaches, it opens up ways to make sustainability a driver of business development, proactive reputation management and capacity building. This chapter describes the handprint approach and relates it to major concepts such as integrated reporting. It further provides applied examples for how other industries start using the handprint approach and points out potential implications of this trend for the financial industry. Finally, it names specific starting points for using the handprint approach to increase the future viability of financial institutions.

1 Introduction

The financial industry has been engulfed in a crisis of confidence since 2007. As a consequence, banks and insurance companies find themselves confronted with a large number of regulation and supervision mechanisms, which are further

The authors would like to thank Katharina Beck for her helpful comments on this paper.

S. Philipps (✉)
Collaborating Centre on Sustainable Consumption and Production, Wuppertal, Germany
e-mail: sebastian.philipps@posteo.de

H. Ohlsen
Association for Environmental Management and Sustainability in Financial Institutions, Augsburg, Germany
e-mail: ohlsen@vfu.de

C. Raab
MADE-BY, Amsterdam, Netherlands
e-mail: christina.raab@gmail.com

© Springer International Publishing Switzerland 2015
K. Wendt (ed.), *Responsible Investment Banking*, CSR, Sustainability, Ethics & Governance, DOI 10.1007/978-3-319-10311-2_44

659

increasing in terms of quantity and intensity. This impacts strategic considerations in the industry and changes the immediate prospects of success of individual business sectors and products. The authors of this paper point out that the current pressure will appear light in view of the challenges and changes of the next 15 years. With the handprint concept, they recommend an approach on how financial institutions can prepare for a future where value creation is redefined. In such a future, mitigating negative social and environmental footprint will not be enough. Instead, companies will need to improve and report their social value added, i.e. their handprint. Recent initiatives in the manufacturing industry offer examples for translating this approach to financial institutions. And also within the financial industry, new developments prepare the methodological basis for such a transfer.[1]

With the integrated reporting approach (IIRC 2013), a framework for the integration of nonfinancial indicators into reporting and management concepts is being created that greatly fosters the implementation of the handprint approach. This process will, however, take time. The article therefore closes with specific recommendations for human resources development and management and suggests sector initiatives and proposals for an industry-wide, cross-sectoral cooperation. These approaches make it possible to apply the new handprint concept already now and pave the way for companies and organisations to actively invest in their future viability.

1.1 Global Megatrends Require a New Approach to Value Creation

In the future, global megatrends will require society and economy to expand their value creation concept to include areas in which policy has failed or is too slow. The management of challenges such as climate change, resource scarcity and demographic change at the individual and institutional level will be key, as they will determine economic success (UNEP 2013) in a globalised world lacking binding global governance structures.

Studies describe in detail how demographic change, resource depletion, climate change, migration, *big data* and radical geopolitical changes will transform lifestyles and needs at the consumer level. One example is the SPREAD 2050 project funded by the European Commission (Uyterlinde et al. 2012; Rijnhout and Lorek 2012). It describes potential scenarios from which fundamental changes in consumer needs can be derived. Megatrends such as sharing instead of owning (e.g. car sharing) or decentralisation of production using 3D printers challenge traditional business models. The crisis in the German energy sector is a good example of how even well-established systems have to rethink their revenue models and production infrastructure.

---

[1] Examples for this are activities in the area of *Financed Emissions* and/or *Avoided Emissions* (UNEP FI Investor Briefing 2013; 2° Investment Initiative 2013).

Many companies have therefore begun to concentrate more on coming changes and resulting opportunities. They commit themselves already today to the preservation of resources and urge policy-makers to support them more in this regard (Auer and Rakau 2011). In the absence of political regulations, they join organisations such as the World Business Council for Sustainable Development (WBCSD) and develop common strategies in collaboration with relevant stakeholders in. Our society, in turn, begins to hold companies increasingly accountable for the effects created by the use of their products, instead of looking at the impact of the production process only. The business environment for the chemical industry, for example, has changed considerably as a result of the European chemicals directive REACH. In the face of shifting consumer preferences, in particular, companies with direct consumer contact will have to take a broader view of their net value creation.

For companies in the financial industry, in their capacity as financing and capital market partners, and for insurers, it is particularly relevant to deal with megatrends and the prerequisites for a future-proof economy. The ability within financial institutions to assess the future viability of a investment strongly affects their own future viability. Nevertheless, the expansion of their added value concept is particularly challenging for financial services providers. More than any other service providers or even manufacturing companies, they need to pay attention to the fact that—bottom line— the financial value creation does not fall behind other identifiable value dimensions. What is therefore the significance of a changing corporate self-image that also defines corporate successes in nonfinancial or extra-financial terms?

1.2 Rate of Return, ESG Performance and Future Viability

In the context of a changing business environment, forward-looking strategies for the financial sector must look at more than just regulatory aspects. Forward-looking strategies need to address all aspects influencing the future remuneration of entrepreneurial performance. Monitoring, managing and communicating this combined financial *and* extra-financial added value will become a key success factor in an industry that reflects and manages values like no other and has the ability to support or distort them. Compliance and corporate due diligence remain the basis. In addition, however, formerly separate indicators such as *rate of return* and *ESG performance*[2] must be expanded and merged to a new value concept of future viability.

This future viability refers to both regulatory and reputational risks—including the loss of a *social license to operate*—but also to tangible business risks in the portfolios. Indirect portfolio risks usually outweigh direct ecological, social or technical risks for financial institutions. The reason for this immediacy is that

---

[2] ESG Performance stands for performance with regard to environment and social aspects and corporate governance.

megatrends, even though they may not affect the banks directly, have the potential to severely damage their investments and customers. This can result in increased defaults of individual loans but can also lead to a rapid loss in value of entire asset classes. The example of nuclear power in Germany after Fukushima shows how suddenly such risks can lead to losses of profit and write-downs.[3]

The case of nuclear power may be an extreme, and the debate about financed emissions and the related discussion on *stranded assets*, however, are good examples of less acute but potentially very substantial risks (Carbon Tracker Initiative and Grantham Research Institute 2013). The concept of stranded assets refers to assets that could drastically and quickly lose in value in the event of substantial political changes or slumps in demand with a climate reference. Especially long-term investors might be left stranded with such investments. The study of the 2° Investing Initiative (2013: 27), for example, explains that investments in industries such as fossil fuel provision, aerospace or automotive industry are exposed to considerable legal as well as political climate risks and could be noticeably affected by carbon markets. In spite of the fact that carbon markets are currently depressed and international governance processes not going anywhere, there is a risk that drastic measures may be taken in the future to make up for present failures—accompanied by social accusations and holding emitters politically liable.

But climate risks are only one of the examples of relationships between investment strategies and global megatrends in areas such as demographics, health, shortage of resources and technological development, which will significantly impact financial institutions. The future viability concept for the financial industry proposed here addresses these interactions and suggests a transfer of the value creation concept to the sector. Instead of minimising the damages caused by it, the financial industry could position itself as a financier of added social value and as a reliable partner in a volatile environment. It could also strengthen its own resilience against expected shocks.

2 How Value Creation Is Being Redefined in Practice

First, companies have already begun to redefine value creation. With the help of their stakeholders[4], they are busy expanding their concept of ESG performance and open up new options. Instead of limiting themselves to reducing negative effects of their activity, they are considering and supporting the creation of added social value—in analogy to reducing the negative footprint, this added value is referred to as handprint (see Fig. 1). This perspective opens up new ways for product development and communication as well as corporate strategy.

---

[3] After the nuclear power plant disaster in Fukushima, the German federal government switched off eight German nuclear power plants from the electricity market in one go; the plants had however already been written off (SZ 2012).

[4] The term "stakeholder" subsumes relevant external groups of stakeholders and influencers, e.g. from the political arena, civil society and research.

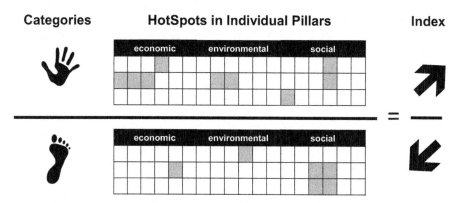

Fig. 1 The handprint concept uses an index to reflect an expanded added value. Source: Own illustration; symbols by shutterstock.com (2014)

The 2012 Sustainability Report of Henkel KGaA (Henkel 2012) reflects the approach of this novel handprint principle. The company has already tested the opportunity cost approach by Figge and Hahn (2004). It is now proceeding to assess its product improvements based on a combined index where hand- and footprint are put into relation to one another. Instead of concentrating on avoiding negative environmental and social effects—i.e. the footprint[5]—Henkel is improving its products from a perspective of added social value, i.e. by also looking at the positive handprint of its own corporate activity. The company can, for instance, provide more benefits to society by investing in further reducing the washing temperature on the consumer side than by investing in another tenth of a per cent in energy efficiency increase on the production side.

Henkel's handprint takes the previously applied *sustainable value* concept by Figge and Hahn (2004) to the next level. The latter reflects the number of units of gross national product generated by a company using its capital *and* resources, in comparison to a reference group. The handprint approach, on the other hand, is based on an expansion of the value creation concept. It also includes effects that are not mentioned in the company's direct environmental and social balance. Emissions generated when consumers use a product are a good example for this. But the concept is also suitable for including social aspects of entrepreneurial activity. Henkel, for example, does not only train hairdressers to efficiently use its products but concurrently provides opportunities for socially disadvantaged groups in emerging countries (SOS Children's Villages 2010).

In the future, policy-makers, consumers and civil society will have new instruments for accessing such information and comparable data and will be able to integrate it in their interactions with companies. Against this background, a broader handprint concept significantly helps companies to ensure their future viability, while it arguably is much more challenging than traditional product optimisation.

---

[5] "Footprint" has become an established indicator of negative external effects.

A company that addresses both footprint and handprint learns more about its customers, stakeholders and supply chain. Its sustainability management turns from an avoidance strategy to an added value strategy, thus enabling a different kind of internal cooperation in the company and with external stakeholders. Beyond new communication options, the company also expands its strategic choices.

The assessment of a combined hand- and footprint includes the identification of so-called hotspots. These hotspots highlight the major value drivers on the hand-print and the largest improvement potentials on the footprint side of the matrix (see Fig. 1). This enables focused responses and makes the broader added value iden-tification manageable and affordable. In many cases, civil society stakeholders also contribute significantly to specifying such hotspots. Hence, the company does not only gain access to a reflection of its commercial activities but also builds up long-term relationships with important groups of stakeholders.

The inclusion of a company's handprint in the development of products and business activities also adds to conventional market research. The knowledge of how their own products generate added social value can open the eyes of companies for new fields of business. It can provide them with a new perspective of their own innovative performance and portfolio. The insight that driving performance is more important for young urban groups of buyers than car ownership may, for example, have motivated car manufacturers to enter the car sharing market—even if this concept might in the long run lead to a reduction in absolute sales numbers. Following this line of argumentation, BMW's DriveNow programme would have resulted in successfully improving the company's handprint[6] and being one of the first manufacturer to open up a promising new field of business. Added value-oriented thinking can help companies to identify and seize such opportunities.

2.1 Innovations Raise New Expectations of the Financial Industry

A sole focus on immediate monetary value creation will negatively impact the financial industry's profitability. In the medium term, understanding and utilising new value creation concepts is of vital importance for financial institutions. Without developing competences in this respect, they will find it more difficult to continue fulfilling their basic functions. They might lose their predictive abilities and, hence, their power of interpretation; they might have difficulties to satisfy new requirements by equity owners, and they would not have a full understanding of their business clients' economic environment. Conversely, those financial institutions will profit that monitor and actively shape innovations in the areas of information management and controlling, both on the customer and on the investment side.

---

[6] For a definitive statement on the impact of the DriveNow programme, rebound effects would have to be taken into account.

The financial sector is the crystal ball of an economy. Dividend expectations can ruin careers, and future markets decide on power plant investments that will still impact the electricity market and world climate 40 years from now. This predictive function will become even more effective the more today's decisions are linked to future prosperity via fundamental factors such as climate change and shortage of resources. Actors in the economy and society are faced with the challenge to make decisions for the future, while knowledge about the effects of climate change and other trends continues to increase. Add to this the mass production of personal data described as *big data*. If the crystal ball of the financial markets now remains opaque with regard to exactly these future issues, while product markets, society and policy-makers are adjusting their value creation concept accordingly, analysts will lose influence. For individual financial institutions that fall behind this development, this may prove to be a strategic error in the medium term.

Successful producers have learned that they must adjust to new technological, political, societal and resource trends if they want to stay in the market. The same is true for companies in the financial sector, as their business involves assessing the performance of commercial enterprises and optimising capital flows accordingly. So far, however, the financial industry—more than any other industry—still measures performance based on financial parameters only. Due to the design of the financial system, other value dimensions than financial parameters can hardly be found in the language of the financial industry. Based on the same logic, credit institutions and investors prefer to issue capital to companies promising a fast return with a high risk-weighted dividend. Consistent with this approach, the current reporting and accounting standards are also almost exclusively geared towards the financial value dimension.

At the same time, new civil society stakeholders are using the availability of data to gain power of interpretation for areas that were previously not transparent, or examined by analysts only. The *Carbon Disclosure Project* organises the publication of emissions of large industrial companies and, in the meantime, has become well established. The transparency of pioneer companies increases the pressure on others companies to at least document and communicate their emissions. Furthermore, participating companies have begun to include emission management issues in their supplier selection and are therefore also passing on the responsibility along the value chain.

Emissions management has developed from a playing field of sustainability departments to a fixed reporting element. The *Asset Owner Disclosure Project* (AODP 2012) transfers this principle to institutional investors. It makes their climate risks transparent and addresses individual aspects such as transparency, investment and risk strategy. By doing so, AODP underlines the observation that, bottom line, actual climate risks and their effects on a business are borne by equity owners and not by the management. Hence, the indirect influence of megatrends such as climate change and shortage of resources widens the gap between equity owners as the principals and the management as their agents. Asset managers in particular and financial institutions in general are important mediators to bridge this gap. Initiatives such as AODP anticipate the basic trend of an increasing demand for this mediator function by investors in the future. Most players in the financial industry are currently not yet really prepared to offer such services.

Corporate customers will also exert increasing pressure on financial institutions the more the manufacturing industry changes towards a broader value creation concept. The social, economic and ecologic environment of the economy is busy changing. Companies are faced with greater influence from stakeholders and a new information architecture in which they interact with their stakeholders and customers. In this context, companies will increasingly expect their bank to develop a broader understanding of value creation and provide instruments for supporting corporate customers in implementing such a wider added value concept.

2.2   A Huge Opportunity for Financial Institutions

New value concepts provide huge opportunities for risk management as well as business and product development in financial institutions. On the one hand, they allow preparing for new framework conditions, and on the other hand, they offer the opportunity to introduce additional performance indicators. In times of big data, they enable companies to get more out of the available data volume.

According to the basic principles of portfolio management, an attempt to reach sustainability goals by exclusion lists would limit the success of sustainability portfolios. The reason is that negative lists reduce diversification options without offering additional indicators for risk reduction. With a comparable architecture, sustainable portfolios may therefore actually fall behind traditional portfolios in terms of financial return. Broader value creation concepts such as the handprint approach could counteract this. The systematic documentation of handprint indicators by companies will increase the amount of company information available to investors and lenders. This provides the latter with the opportunity to use this information for new and improved financial products. Instead of a passive distinction, the new handprint indicators allow to actively differentiate the considered investments. They do so by reflecting additional value drivers in companies and re-classifying known parameters, thereby making product innovations more tangible.

In addition to innovation opportunities, the handprint approach, in conjunction with approaches for integrated corporate reporting, offers great advantages for long-term risk management. On the example of implicit climate risks, the above-mentioned *stranded assets debate* pinpoints the importance of documenting implicit risks. If a financial institution is systematically looking at the handprint of its portfolio, it can use these analyses not only for identifying preferred investment options but also for a differentiated risk management of existing portfolios.

The strategic communications aspect of the handprint approach is of similar importance: it enables financial institutions to approach stakeholders as well as supervisory authorities backed by a solid information basis. Hence, handprint approaches can enable financial institutions to leave their defensive position behind and actively manage reputational risks. Here also, the subject of climate change provides a good example. While some banks such as Bank of America, Merrill Lynch, Rabobank or ASN Bank (2° Investing Initiative, 2013: 18) have started to actively address the emissions financed by them, other players shy away from such a step. Some are concerned that the availability of documented data might provide the ground for regulations and that transparent players might be publicly named and shamed. In the medium term, however, such players are taking high risks for their reputation, which are becoming more and more real in the context of projects such as the *Asset Owner Disclosure Project*. External stakeholders will increasingly come up with numbers on financed emissions which portfolio managers without a *financed emissions* model, for lack of own numbers, will be unable to either refute or provide an informed comment on. A communications strategy focusing on the added social value of a portfolio circumvents this problem. It creates an additional value for the respective financial institution, as it strengthens the confidence of policy-makers, society and customers in the core business. Ideally, this results in a positive underlying connotation, increased deposit and private customer business and a better brand value.

2.3 Realignment of the Industry Can Help Overcome Challenges

In the medium term, the adoption of the handprint concept by financial institutions would require integrated reporting, improved alignment of the reporting system with management systems and an adjustment of communications strategies. These three adjustments pose significant challenges for the financial industry. However, they are necessary adjustments, which need to happen even without implementing the handprint approach. The latter profits from these adjustments and makes it more worthwhile to overcome the obstacles connected with them.

The implementation of an expanded value concept represents fundamental challenges for financial institutions (Pictet Asset Management 2008). At first glance, the so far dominant quantification and monetarisation approaches render other types of valuation impossible, as they depend on currently not measurable and tradable extra-financial performance aspects. Sustainability reports and financial reports are regularly within the scope of responsibility of different departments of the reporting entity and not much linked (Haller and Fuhrmann 2012). The integrated reporting concept (IIRC 2013) provides a framework for overcoming these limitations. Companies such as Goldman Sachs and Deutsche Bank are among the supporters of the long-term goal to mainstreams such as integrated reporting (IIRC 2014).

According to Haller (2013), integrated reporting also suggests the use of jointly collected key performance indicators for management and compensation schemes. This requires new approaches in the areas of strategy and corporate management,

1. Conventional Mode of Separated Reporting

economic		environmental	social
Annual Report	+	Sustainability Report	

2. A First Step in the Direction of Integrated Reporting

	economic	environmental	social
✋	Economic Indicators	Explanation	Explanation
👣	–	Environmental and Social Footprint	

3. Integrated Reporting Using the Handprint Approach

	economic	environmental	social
✋	Which economic, environmental and social value added has the company created?		
👣	Which economic, environmental and social costs evolved from this value creation?		

Fig. 2 Development from traditional to integrated handprint reporting. Source: Own illustration; symbols from shutterstock.com (2014)

human resources development and software application. While their implementation constitutes a major burden, they may benefit other fields of corporate change, such as adjustment to Big Data or restructuring of business models in accordance with changing regulatory requirements. The prospect of implementing the handprint approach might make the introduction of integrated reporting even more worthwhile. In this context, the handprint approach constitutes a supplementation and expansion of integrated reporting concepts (see Fig. 2) that are already dealing with different value dimensions (IIRC 2013, p. 10).

The alignment of their communications strategy to an integrated assessment approach constitutes another barrier for many financial institutions. The reasons for this are of historical and structural nature. The great importance of confidentiality in financial transactions, complex processes and products as well as the high-profile financial market and compliance crises influences the communications culture and strategy. In this context, communication officers may regard the disclosure of additional information as an additional reputational risk. The fact that many financial institutions do not have an institutionalised dialogue with external stakeholders reinforces this view.

However, a reactive response to the interests of external stakeholders involves many dangers. Consumer goods and retail companies such as the REWE Group and Nestlé Deutschland abandon this approach in favour of proactive communications management in the form of advisory bodies and panels. The handprint approach and its expanded value definition provide an ideal and credible basis for such a use of sustainability communication for lowering reputational risks.

3 The Way Forward for Financial Institutions

The financial industry currently undergoes a period of reorientation. Many institutions are restructuring their operations due to European and national regulations in the wake of the crisis of the financial market. They are adjusting businesses models and looking at new development options. Regulatory requirements (for instance, BASEL III) set a narrow framework for this. In this context, the possibility to introduce a broader added value concept such as the handprint approach provides a huge potential on a strategic and communications level.

Social and political stakeholders as well as business partners critically observe the renewal phase of the financial industry, and even private customers are slowly turning into critical consumers. Their confidence in the industry is low. In this environment, financial institutions can use the handprint approach to regain trust by individual and joint initiatives, open up new options and work on their future viability. It will take time to develop an integrated reporting system that reflects both financial and extra-financial value creation, but short-term approaches are available. Examples are the introduction of new human resources development and management concepts, the expansion of industry initiatives by handprint approaches and cross-industry cooperation in the area of added value assessment.

3.1 Rethinking Human Resources Development and Management

Brains are the most important productivity factors in the financial industry. Well-trained and motivated employees continuously develop product innovations using the limits provided by the regulatory framework to the maximum. After the financial crisis revealed significant social risks stemming from some of these innovations, they are currently in the focus of new regulatory efforts. The handprint approach can considerably contribute to aligning product innovations with added social value. At the same time, it can offer benefits in the areas of strategy and credibility for the respective financial institution. Human resources development and management systems play a central role in this context.[7] Furthermore, a broader added value definition can mean additional motivation for employees.

The handprint concept supports the integration of sustainability in the core business. From this perspective, internal sustainability training can contribute to support innovations in the core business. So far, traditional sustainability training has frequently focused on minimising environmental and social damages, serving to enforce exclusion criteria within financial institutions. This approach counteracts the interests of those whose success depends on innovative performances within an

---

[7] Buch and Orbach (2003) provide a respective analysis for Germany.

as much as possible barrier-free playing field. Training sessions using the handprint principle to propagate a broader added value concept, however, provide more room for reconciling the interests of the various players within a company. They can have a motivating effect and promote innovation. In the context of such training, sustainability departments and human resources development cease to act as promoters of restrictions and rather become an internal source of ideas for new business models.

New training approaches alone can already have positive effects for a company. However, the simultaneous development of compensation schemes and management systems provides much further reaching levers for a reorientation of innovation in different fields of business. Extra-financial value creation must pay for employees to be enforced by them. New management systems are closely linked with the development of integrated reporting and the further development of key performance indicators and therefore profit from current trends in these areas. In the medium term, the assessment of the management of a company should also apply this broader framework of criteria.

3.2 Expanding Industry Initiatives

With the *United Nations Principles for Responsible Investment* (PRI; UNEP FI & UN Global Compact 2006) and the *Principles for Sustainable Insurance* (PSI), the financial industry has created important standards and frameworks for sustainable innovation. The implementation of these standards in financial services companies provides huge opportunities for implementing the handprint approach. It would in all likelihood prove to be profitable for the industry.

Both PRI and PSI suggest the development of new approaches for integrating sustainability in product development and analytical instruments. They support a reduction of negative environmental and social effects within the investment portfolios, recommend sustainability training and promise cooperation within the industry to overcome barriers. The implementation of these aspects can easily be supplemented by handprint concepts and integrated reporting principles. Their implementation can, in turn, profit from this addition, as portfolios will not just be reviewed for the potential damage they can cause but also for their benefits beyond a profitability aspect. New analysis instruments can pick up on methods that the real economy is already using and will continue to further develop. Specific industry initiatives such as initiatives for financed emissions may help to share implementation costs on a national or international level, promote standards and create comparability.

Altogether, the combination of a broader added value concept, integrated reporting and PRI and/or PSI would release additional dynamics within the industry. Change managers could bring strategies of financial institutions in line with PRI and PSI and demonstrate that integrating sustainability can create extra-financial as well as financial value for the industry.

3.3   Going Beyond Industry Limits

Cooperating with their target industries and external groups of stakeholders can significantly reduce the costs of changing to a new added value concept for the financial industry. Cooperation can also unleash substantial potentials in the field of standardised measuring methods. In the long term, a harmonisation across industries will also be vital for realising other ambitions such as integrated reporting.

Financial institutions profit tremendously from their deep insight in the industries they are working with. They need comparability of assets and of companies within industries. A broader value concept based on the handprint approach would provide new indicators for evaluating investment and lending decisions and help develop new sources of information. However, these advantages depend largely on the standardisation and harmonisation of new approaches within target industries and across industries. An uncoordinated development of methods for integrating social added value is likely to produce major coordination problems. The context of financing sustainability in small to medium-sized enterprises in Germany is an example for such a coordination problem (Philipps et al. 2012).

The implementation of new integrated reporting standards will take time and does so far not include handprint approaches. However, new networks on a national and European level provide the opportunity to start joint pilot projects on this subject, to determine mutual expectations and conduct joint cost-effectiveness analyses. The exchange between financial industry and real economy plays a key role in this process. First-mover companies will benefit from starting early learning curves. Pilot projects can build on traditional social value creation processes (Kuhndt and Philipps 2010) and expand them to value creation networks. Within these networks, customers, suppliers, financing partners and stakeholders can jointly develop solutions and advance innovations that create added social and environmental value. Such cooperation has the potential to distribute costs, strengthen the acceptance of the financial industry by society, maintain its innovative strength and thereby ensure its viability for the future.

References

2° Investing Initiative. (2013). *From financed emissions to long-term investing metrics*. State-of-the-art review of GHG Emissions Accounting for the Financial Sector.

Asset Owner Disclosure Project. (2012). *AODP global climate index: 2012 results*.

Auer, J., & Rakau, O. (2011). *Rohstoffboom birgt für deutsche Industrie nicht nur Risiko*. In Deutsche Bank Research. Aktuelle Themen, 522.

Busch, T., & Orbach., T. (2003). *Zukunftsfähiger Finanzsektor: Die Nachhaltigkeitsleistung von Banken und Versicherungen* (Wuppertal Papers No. 129).

Carbon Tracker Initiative, & Grantham Research Institute. (2013). *Unburnable carbon: wasted capital and stranded assets*.

Figge, F., & Hahn, T. (2004). Sustainable value added - ein neues Maß des Nachhaltigkeitsbeitrags von Unternehmen am Beispiel der Henkel KGaA. *Quarterly Journal of Economic Research, 73*, 126–141.

Haller, A. (2013). *Presentation for the trends and developments in sustainability reporting panel.* UNEP FI VFU Roundtable 2013.

Haller, A., & Fuhrmann, C. (2012). Die Entwicklung der Lageberichterstattung in Deutschland vor dem Hintergrund des Konzepts des "Integrated Reporting". *Zeitschrift für internationale und kapitalmarktorientierte Rechnungslegung: KoR 1/12* (2012), 17–25.

Henkel. (2012). *Sustainability report.* Retrieved February 2, 2014, from http://sustainabilityreport. henkel.com/report-2012.html

IIRC. (2013). *The International IR framework.* International Integrated Reporting Council.

IIRC. (2014). *Pilot programme investor network.* International Integrated Reporting Council. Retrieved February 2, 2014, from http://www.theiirc.org/companies-and-investors/pilot-programme-investor-network

Kuhndt, M., & Philipps, S. (2010). Nachhaltige Innovation durch strategische Allianzen in Wertschöpfungsketten. In T. Lemken, M. Helfert, M. Kuhndt, F. Lange, T. Merten, (Hg), *Strategische Allianzen für nachhaltige Entwicklung. Innovationen in Unternehmen durch Kooperationen mit NPOs.* Wuppertal.

Philipps, S., Pratt, N., Raab, C., & Wagner, T. (2012). *Nachhaltige Finanzierung in mittelständischen Unternehmen.* Erstellt im Auftrag der GIZ und des Deutschen Global Compact Netzwerks, Wuppertal.

Pictet Asset Management. (2008). *Das SRI-performance-paradox.* Messung und Reporting der extra-finanziellen Performance nachhaltiger Anlagen.

Rijnhout, L., & Lorek, S. (2012). *EU sustainable lifestyle roadmap and action plan 2050. Pathways for enabling social innovation and behaviour change.* EU SPREAD 2050, Wuppertal.

SOS Kinderdörfer. (2010). *Schwarzkopf Professional fördert Ausbildung.* Retrieved February 2, 2014, from http://www.sos-kinderdoerfer.de/informationen/freunde-und-partner/ unternehmen/ schwarzkopf-professional-shaping-futures-sos

SZ. (2012). *Sechs Monate AKW-Ausstieg. Wie Deutschland ohne Atomkraft-funktioniert.* Süddeutsche Zeitung. Retrieved February 2, 2014, from http://www.sueddeutsche.de/ wirtschaft/sechs-monate-akw-ausstieg-wie-deutschland-ohne-atomkraft-funktioniert-1.1275253

UNEP FI. (2013). *Principles for sustainable insurance.* Rio de Janeiro: UNEP FI.

UNEP. (2013). *GEO-5 for business: Impacts of a changing environment on the corporate sector.* UNEP

UNEP FI Investor Briefing. (2013). *Portfolio carbon measuring, disclosing and managing the carbon intensity of investments and investment portfolios.* UNEP FI Investor Briefing

UNEP FI & UN Global Compact. (2006). *Principles for responsible investment.* New York: UNEP FI & UN Global Compact.

Uyterlinde, M., Straver, K., Mont, O., Tigchelaar, C., & Breukers, S. (2012). *Future research agenda for sustainable lifestyles.* EU SPREAD 2050, Wuppertal.

Afterword

Damien Wynne

The Banking System Represents Society

The banking system represents society and the change that is happening in society at the moment, from the male more into the feminine. The male was more dominant before, and this is collapsing at the moment and is reflecting within the financial system. The male is more driven to success, to achieve, and to be more number one, thinking of only oneself, whereas the feminine is more about society and the collective and more about compassion. And this is what needs to come into the banking system to reflect more on society at the moment and to reflect more on the compassion and the relationship with nature, with the people, and with the children—everyone. The banking institution was the individual gaining finances, success, and power, but now it should be more about the collective and the environment and bring these aspects in. Then, there is going to be a huge change within the whole system, and the whole system will be transformed. The old paradigms are just being weeded out, and in the long run, they will not be supported. The same goes for the individuals who are not taking responsibility for their financial situations and blaming it onto the big brother, so to speak. So, the customer and the banking system both have to change, need to change to match what is happening in society and to match the transformation which is happening on this planet at the moment.

So, people need to take more responsibility for the way they are living their lives, the way they are dealing with their finances, and connect deeper with each other. The trust has been broken between both sides, and this trust needs to be built up again. This will only be built up through real, clear communication from both sides, sitting down at a table as individuals and in group meetings, sitting down with the town representatives, talking to the people directly, and seeing what their needs are,

D. Wynne (✉)
Creator and Director of Light Grids Working in Ireland, Hungary, Germany, USA,
Great Britain, Austria, Switzerland, Spain, Turkey, Greece

© Springer International Publishing Switzerland 2015
K. Wendt (ed.), *Responsible Investment Banking*, CSR, Sustainability, Ethics &
Governance, DOI 10.1007/978-3-319-10311-2

and if people are losing their homes, talk to these people. These are the people who have been feeding you for years, for generations, and now you have turned, and you are taking their homes away. This is not the way to grow a society on trust and compassion. This is creating destruction and fear in the field, and this needs to change. The whole system will collapse if it continues on like this.

The investment banking has been giving the money with the wrong intention behind, because the brokers were actually getting commission and focusing too much on their own commission rather than looking on the long-term success for themselves plus the customer.

It was too short term the way they were looking at it. So they need to really sit down, almost like a family that will live together on a long-term basis, and really tailor-make the loans and the investment for each company or business, which has been created. They have to weave the tapestry together in a more finally tuned way, which is flexible to change, flexible to increase or decrease, as matching the client and the changes within society. It is the rigidness which is creating the separation, which is destructive to both sides and is really harming both sides. It should be more flexible and more fluid, and there should be more communication and more trust between each other, to support each other.

The basis of investment banking has only been on the profit. That has been the male-driven goal, whereas this is only the top, but actually, you need to start at the bottom. So, the top has no foundation when you are only focusing on the profit margins. But you need to start off at the foundation, the grass roots. The grass roots is where you need to take care of "Where am I going to have my business, what is happening around the business?" You need to build up the community around the business and build up the environment around the business, and then you will have the profit at the top. But there is an imbalance here, which is not caring about the people within and around the company, the environmental impact of your business, and so on. This is the most important and the foundation for a long-term successful business.

As I said, the banking system at the moment is too male based and too profit based, and it is too much pressure on taking the cream off the top, which is starving the rest.

It is fundamentally important that you focus more on the long-term results and work from the grass roots up. Then, the people within your structure will feel more aware, more heart based, and warm in a friendly environment, and then the company will blossom, and the whole structure will grow into working, living, and being and will strive and create offspring. And this, for me, is the missing piece: to see and live and support the connection all the way from the outside of the business through the door all the way to the soul of the people working there and all the way to the top, to see the whole company as an organism working from the ground up supporting the collective and the company to grow together in a heart-based way. What we are often forgetting is that we all have been part of the system and we need to honour this part in us, which is in a major transition right now.

CPSIA information can be obtained at www.ICGtesting.com
Printed in the USA
LVOW04*0141080815

449368LV00006B/216/P